RUMINATION AND RELATED CONSTRUCTS

AF765214

RUMINATION AND RELATED CONSTRUCTS

CAUSES, CONSEQUENCES, AND TREATMENT OF THINKING TOO MUCH

ASHLEY BORDERS
The College of New Jersey, New Jersey, United States

ELSEVIER

ACADEMIC PRESS
An imprint of Elsevier

Academic Press is an imprint of Elsevier
125 London Wall, London EC2Y 5AS, United Kingdom
525 B Street, Suite 1650, San Diego, CA 92101, United States
50 Hampshire Street, 5th Floor, Cambridge, MA 02139, United States
The Boulevard, Langford Lane, Kidlington, Oxford OX5 1GB, United Kingdom

Copyright © 2020 Elsevier Inc. All rights reserved.

No part of this publication may be reproduced or transmitted in any form or by any means, electronic or mechanical, including photocopying, recording, or any information storage and retrieval system, without permission in writing from the publisher. Details on how to seek permission, further information about the Publisher's permissions policies and our arrangements with organizations such as the Copyright Clearance Center and the Copyright Licensing Agency, can be found at our website: www.elsevier.com/permissions.

This book and the individual contributions contained in it are protected under copyright by the Publisher (other than as may be noted herein).

Notices
Knowledge and best practice in this field are constantly changing. As new research and experience broaden our understanding, changes in research methods, professional practices, or medical treatment may become necessary.

Practitioners and researchers must always rely on their own experience and knowledge in evaluating and using any information, methods, compounds, or experiments described herein. In using such information or methods they should be mindful of their own safety and the safety of others, including parties for whom they have a professional responsibility.

To the fullest extent of the law, neither the Publisher nor the authors, contributors, or editors, assume any liability for any injury and/or damage to persons or property as a matter of products liability, negligence or otherwise, or from any use or operation of any methods, products, instructions, or ideas contained in the material herein.

British Library Cataloguing-in-Publication Data
A catalogue record for this book is available from the British Library

Library of Congress Cataloging-in-Publication Data
A catalog record for this book is available from the Library of Congress

ISBN: 978-0-12-812545-8

For Information on all Academic Press publications
visit our website at https://www.elsevier.com/books-and-journals

Publisher: Nikki Levy
Editorial Project Manager: Barbara Makinster
Production Project Manager:
Sujatha Thirugnana Sambandam
Cover Designer: Miles Hitchen

Typeset by MPS Limited, Chennai, India

ELSEVIER
Book Aid International
Working together to grow libraries in developing countries
www.elsevier.com • www.bookaid.org

Contents

Preface

As a life-long lover of Paul Simon's music, I still find it humorous that when I was 13, a friend commented that the song "Think Too Much" aptly described me. The basic gist of the song is reflected in the chorus, which is the line "maybe I think too much" repeated four times. To underscore the nature of this kind of repetitive thought, Simon wrote not one but two songs with the same title and chorus (both of which are on his album *Hearts and Bones*). The first of these two songs is light and happy, focusing on thinking about a girl he loved. But the second song is darker and sad, as he hopelessly tries to understand where the relationship went wrong and feels worn out from all his thinking.

This book is about the kind of thinking that Paul Simon describes—the kind of thinking that is repetitive, hard to stop, exhausting, and unproductive. It is something almost everyone does. Most people know what it is like to brood about how they cannot cope with work stress, rehash reasons why a relationship ended, focus on all the things that could go wrong on an upcoming presentation, and fixate on how they will respond to a perceived insult. This kind of repetitive thinking is called rumination and has been a focus of research by clinical, social, cognitive, and health psychologists since the early 1990s.

We know that the majority of people—both young and old—ruminate when they feel upset (Garnefski & Kraaij, 2006; Siewert, Kubiak, Jonas, & Weber, 2011; Siewert, Kubiak, Jonas, & Weber, 2013). Unfortunately, although it is a normative cognitive process, high levels of rumination contribute to a wide range of harmful mental and physical health outcomes, from depression and anxiety to eating disorders, substance abuse, aggressive behavior, and poor health. People also ruminate with others, with both positive and negative outcomes. Theories and evidence propose various reasons why people engage in this kind of thought process, despite its many negative consequences. Researchers have also explored cognitive and neural correlates of rumination. Finally, various kinds of interventions successfully decrease rumination. At a time when there are so many reasons to brood and worry, understanding what psychologists know about rumination may help people lead more productive lives while reducing unnecessary emotional distress. The most recent book summarizing the rumination field was published over 15 years ago and focused exclusively on rumination in the context of depression (Papageorgiou & Wells, 2004).

Thus, the field is in need of an updated and more comprehensive overview and integration of the hundreds of studies on rumination and related constructs.

This book comprises an exhaustive review of psychological research, theories, and treatments relating to rumination. As such, it should be a helpful scholarly resource for psychologists (both researchers and clinicians) and other social scientists. Second, it could serve as a textbook suitable for advanced undergraduate and graduate courses on rumination, coping, and/or emotion regulation. Given the paucity of books on this topic and how ubiquitous rumination is in people's lives, I also hope that this book is accessible to anyone who is curious about understanding the reasons why they engage in frequent rumination, what consequences it might have, and what they might do to stop this process (Interested readers can see Box 1 for brief explanations of important research terms and concepts). Although this is not a self-help book, Chapters 10–12 do provide references for treatment manuals and self-help books.

BOX 1

Research terms and concepts

For readers not as familiar with psychological research concepts and terms, I provide some brief definitions and explanations that may help in understanding the research language used throughout this book.

Constructs are the complex psychological concepts that researchers are interested in studying (e.g., rumination, anxiety, happiness, and avoidance). When researchers measure or manipulate a construct in a research study, it is called a *variable.*

Sometimes researchers are interested in understanding people's stable tendencies, or dispositions; these are called *traits.* Other times, researchers want to understand how people think and feel in the moment, or their current *state.* Many variables, like rumination, are studied at the trait (e.g., how are you generally?) and state (e.g., how are you right now?) level.

Psychological research employs several types of research designs:

- In *experimental studies,* researchers manipulate one or more independent variables (IV) and examine its/their effect on one or more dependent variables (DV). *Manipulation* means that researchers systematically vary the level (i.e., condition) of the IV (e.g., rumination or distraction conditions). Often, a variable that has been manipulated is said to be induced (e.g., induced rumination). Between-subject

continued

BOX 1 (*cont'd*)

experiments require that participants be randomly assigned to receive only one condition. The rationale of these experiments is that if the researchers can control for other variables that might influence the DV (including individual differences between people, via random assignment), any differences in the DV between conditions must be due to the effect of the IV. Because they can determine causal associations, experiments are often seen as the gold standard in research.

- In *nonexperimental (i.e., correlational and survey) studies,* participants generally complete several questionnaires (e.g., set of written questions), each measuring a construct of interest. Researchers then examine statistical associations between various constructs. Although nonexperimental research cannot determine causation, it can establish initial associations between constructs. Moreover, many constructs of interest in clinical psychology (e.g., psychological symptoms) cannot ethically be manipulated, leaving nonexperimental research the only option.
- Research studies can be *cross-sectional* (i.e., participants engage in the research only once) or *longitudinal* (i.e., participants engage in the research more than once). Whether experimental or nonexperimental, cross-sectional studies provide snapshots of a given point in time. Longitudinal studies allow researchers to examine naturally occurring change in individuals, or the effect of a manipulated variable, over time.
- *Experience sampling* studies are a particular kind of longitudinal study in which participants provide data frequently and repeatedly over a set period of time (e.g., every night for 2 weeks; several times a day for 1 week). This design allows researchers to determine the directionality of associations (e.g., is negative mood associated with increased rumination at the next assessment, and vice versa). It also allows for assessment of variables at the state level in contexts other than a lab setting.
- *Metaanalyses* are special types of literature reviews that combine statistical results (e.g., correlations and effect sizes) from many earlier studies and use these "data" to make statistically based conclusions about a body of research. Metaanalyses aggregate results from many individual studies, sometime even ones that have not been published, and can therefore identify important consistencies and/or inconsistencies in the literature, as well as determine average effect sizes of important associations.

continued

BOX 1 (*cont'd*)

Statistical terms:

- *Correlate* means that two variables are associated with each other in a linear manner, such that people who score high (or low) on one variable are likely to score high (or low) on the other variable. Just because two variables are correlated does not mean that one causes the other.
- The term *predict* is used in many ways in popular and even scientific writing. In this book, I use it to refer to associations for which there is some temporal precedence. In other words, if one variable (e.g., rumination) predicts another (e.g., anger), this means that rumination is not only associated with but comes before anger. This kind of conclusion is possible in longitudinal and/or experimental study designs.
- *Factor analysis* is a statistical procedure that discovers or confirms patterns of associations between items on one or more questionnaires. Based on the interrelationships between items, one or more factors (i.e., underlying variables) may emerge. For example, items on the angry rumination scale are interrelated in such a way that they suggest 4 separate but related factors (sometimes called subscales or facets) of angry rumination.
- *Moderation* occurs when one variable influences the strength of the association between two other variables. For example, stress moderates the association between rumination and depressive symptoms, such that rumination is only, or more strongly, associated with depressive symptoms for people high in stress. When one variable (e.g., stress) moderates the effect of another (e.g., rumination), they are said to *interact*.
- *Mediation* occurs when one variable statistically accounts for the association between two other variables. Conceptually, a mediational model asserts that one variable (e.g., rumination) causes the mediator (e.g., anger), which in turn causes another variable (e.g., aggression); in other words, the IV has an *indirect effect* on the DV via the mediator. Statistically, mediation is suggested when the association between two variables decreases when controlling for a potential mediator.

What is rumination?

Rumination has multiple definitions, reflecting the fact that it is often studied in the context of particular mental disorders. This book introduces the following forms of repetitive thinking: depressive rumination, brooding, reflective pondering, stress-reactive rumination, positive rumination, worry, anticipatory rumination, postevent rumination, trauma-focused rumination, intrusive rumination, deliberate rumination, angry rumination, desire thinking, eating-focused rumination, and corumination. As we will see in Chapters 1–6, each of these terms is narrowly defined.

General definitions of rumination also vary in scope. Martin and Tesser (1996) defined rumination as conscious, repetitive thoughts focused on a particular topic that occur in the absence of an environmental need for them. They suggested that rumination can be negative or positive (as when people reminisce, bask, or anticipate something positive). Similarly, Segerstrom, Stanton, Alden, and Shortridge (2003) defined repetitive thinking as thinking attentively, repetitively, or frequently about oneself and the world. They argued that positive forms of repetitive thinking may include emotional processing and benefit finding (see also Watkins, 2008). However, other general definitions focus on rumination about negative internal or external experiences. Brosschot, Gerin, and Thayer (2006) defined perseverative cognition as any type of cognition—conscious or unconscious—that is repetitive, prolonged in duration, and focuses on a particular stressor. Similarly, Ehring and Watkins (2008) defined repetitive negative thinking as a repetitive, passive and/or relatively uncontrollable thought process about negative content. All of these researchers have made notable contributions to the field. And even still, a consensus about the definition and even the name of this construct has not been reached.

My purpose is not to propose the correct definition. Instead, this book reviews the various literatures on rumination and related constructs. I use the phrase "rumination and related constructs" intentionally. Because I include research on more positive forms of repetitive thought (e.g., positive rumination and deliberate rumination), the phrases negative repetitive thought and perseverative cognition are not inclusive enough. At the same time, this book does not review literatures on mind wandering, daydreaming, defensive pessimism, or repetitive forms of problem-solving (e.g., rehearsal), which may also be forms of general repetitive thought (Watkins, 2008). In deciding which constructs to include in this book, I selected the types of repetitive thought that are clearly associated with clinical outcomes or constructs associated with clinical outcomes. I do not include forms of repetitive thought that are primarily associated with well-being or academic functioning. That said, there may be literatures not included here that we eventually learn are clinically relevant.

Structure of the book

I organize the literature on rumination and related constructs into three parts. In Section 1, six chapters describe the definitions, nature, and outcomes of rumination in its many forms, as well as disorder-specific theories. Chapter 1, Rumination and mood disorders, covers response styles theory and the extensive literature on rumination and depression, as well as the nascent research on rumination and bipolar disorder. Chapter 2, Rumination and anxiety-related disorders, reviews evidence and theories about how rumination, worry, and other related constructs are associated with a range of anxiety-related disorders. Chapter 3, Rumination, anger, and aggression, includes research and theory on rumination, anger, and aggression. Chapter 4, Rumination and dysregulated behaviors, covers several literatures all related to dysregulated behaviors, namely, substance abuse, disordered eating, self-harm and suicide, borderline personality, and psychosis. Chapter 5, Rumination and physical functioning, reviews the extensive research linking rumination with various physiological outcomes, such as cardiac, endocrine, and immune functioning, as well as sleep problems, pain, and health-related behaviors. Chapter 6, Consequences of expressed rumination, introduces readers to several literatures on the expression of rumination, both in writing and to other people, as well as its consequences. In each of these chapters, footnotes provide information to interested readers about questionnaires assessing specific forms of rumination.

In Section 2, three chapters describe causes and correlates of rumination. Chapter 7, Triggers of rumination, reviews control theory and research on emotional and stress-related triggers of rumination. Chapter 8, Beliefs, traits, and motivations underlying rumination, covers several individual difference variables that may influence whether people ruminate, such as beliefs about rumination, avoidance and suppression, neuroticism and related personality traits, and emotion regulation deficits and motives. Chapter 9, Rumination, cognition, and the brain, includes research on the cognitive and neural correlates of rumination.

In Section 3, three chapters describe treatments and related theories. Chapter 10, Cognitive behavioral therapies, covers rumination-based cognitive behavioral therapy, as well as evidence supporting various cognitive bias modification interventions. Chapter 11, Mindfulness-based therapies, reviews theory and basic research on the efficacy of mindfulness-related treatments for reducing rumination and related constructs. Chapter 12, Metacognitive therapy, introduces readers to the theory, treatment, and research supporting metacognitive therapy.

In the Afterword, I briefly reflect on two questions that I believe constitute important issues for the field to address. So that readers can ponder these questions themselves while reading the book, I pose them here: (1) Are differences between the various types of rumination meaningful? and (2) Why do people ruminate?

References

Brosschot, J. F., Gerin, W., & Thayer, J. F. (2006). The perseverative cognition hypothesis: A review of worry, prolonged stress-related physiological activation, and health. *Journal of Psychosomatic Research, 60*(2), 113–124. Available from https://doi.org/10.1016/j.jpsychores.2005.06.074.

Ehring, T., & Watkins, E. R. (2008). Repetitive negative thinking as a transdiagnostic process. *International Journal of Cognitive Therapy, 1*(3), 192–205. Available from https://doi.org/10.1521/ijct.2008.1.3.192.

Garnefski, N., & Kraaij, V. (2006). Relationships between cognitive emotion regulation strategies and depressive symptoms: A comparative study of five specific samples. *Personality and Individual Differences, 40*(8), 1659–1669. Available from https://doi.org/10.1016/j.paid.2005.12.009.

Martin, L., & Tesser, A. (1996). Some ruminative thoughts. In R. S. Wyer, Jr. (Ed.), *Ruminative thoughts, advances in social cognition* (Vol. IX, pp. 1–48). NJ: Lawrence Erlbaum Associates.

Moberly, N. J., & Watkins, E. R. (2008). Ruminative self-focus and negative affect. *Journal of Abnormal Psychology, 117*(2), 314–323. Available from https://doi.org/10.1037/0021-843X.117.2.314.

Papageorgiou, C., & Wells, A. (2004). *Depressive rumination*. England: John Wiley & Sons.

Segerstrom, S. C., Stanton, A. L., Alden, L. E., & Shortridge, B. E. (2003). A multidimensional structure for repetitive thought. *Journal of Personality and Social Psychology, 85*(5), 909–921. Available from https://doi.org/10.1037/0022-3514.85.5.909.

Siewert, K., Kubiak, T., Jonas, C., & Weber, H. (2011). Trait anger moderates the impact of anger-associated rumination on social well-being. *Personality and Individual Differences, 51*(6), 769–774. Available from https://doi.org/10.1016/j.paid.2011.06.030.

Siewert, K., Kubiak, T., Jonas, C., & Weber, H. (2013). The differential relations between perceived social support and rumination-associated goals. *Journal of Social and Clinical Psychology, 32*(10), 1075–1094. Available from https://doi.org/10.1521/jscp.2013.32.10.1075.

Takano, K., & Tanno, Y. (2011). Diurnal variation in rumination. *Emotion (Washington, DC), 11*(5), 1046–1058. Available from https://doi.org/10.1037/a0022757.

Watkins, E. R. (2008). Constructive and unconstructive repetitive thought. *Psychological Bulletin, 134*(2), 163–206. Available from https://doi.org/10.1037/0033-2909.134.2.163.

Acknowledgments

I started writing this book when my daughter was 3 months old, strapped to my chest and napping, while I bounced on a yoga ball and typed. Over the subsequent 3 and a half years, I received invaluable assistance and thank the following people: William Lai, Lara Heflin, Gretchen Boger, Jarret Crawford, Shaun Wiley, Candice Feiring, and Josephine Shih, for shoring me up when I needed it and making helpful suggestions about content and structure; Mitch Earleywine, for introducing me to numerous books about writing and modeling how to complete a book; Jeanine Vivona, for being an insightful, supportive, and fun writing buddy; Samuel Bucek, Caitlyn Flynn, Dara Kushnir, and Katie Napolitano, for assisting with the copious references in this book; my wonderful psychology colleagues at The College of New Jersey, for inspiring me by their own examples to be better at everything I do; and all of the students—past and present—in my research lab, for providing me with motivation and food for thought over weeks and months and years of discussions about rumination. This book would not have been possible without a year-long sabbatical, one of the amazing benefits I have received in my job as a professor. Finally, I thank my family—Evan, Julia, Andrea, Mike, Jodi, Gordon, Bo, and particularly Jen—for providing me with the gifts of encouragement, necessary distraction, and time during this process.

SECTION 1

Consequences of rumination

CHAPTER

1

Rumination and mood disorders

Overview

This chapter reviews the literature on depressive rumination, or repetitive thinking about the nature, causes, and consequences of depressive symptoms. After describing the development of this construct and the associated response styles theory, I review the empirical evidence linking depressive rumination to maintained or exacerbated sad mood and depressive symptoms. I then explore empirical evidence for the proposed mechanisms of depressive rumination: negative thinking, impaired problem-solving, behavioral avoidance, and poor social support. After an examination of the nascent field of rumination and bipolar disorder, I explore research on gender differences in depressive rumination. The chapter ends with a discussion of moderators of depressive rumination and a proposed theory that integrates the rumination literature with other known predictors of depression.

Ann was a client of mine for almost 2 years. She came to therapy a year after the death of her husband of 47 years. Now 69, she had never lived on her own and felt scared and adrift. She cried often, slept poorly, and had trouble finding the energy to do much of anything. She used to be a painter but seemed to have lost interest in what was once a great passion. Ann and her husband had no children, and she had not returned friends' calls for a while, so no one checked in on her regularly. Early in our getting to know each other, she shared that she had birthed a son before her marriage but had given him up for adoption. She now found herself constantly wondering about her son and regretting that hasty decision of her 19-year-old self. When Ann was 16 years old, her mother had been accidentally shot and killed by her father during one of their regular shouting matches. Soon after, Ann left her home in Missouri and moved to Los Angeles, trying to escape her grief by

Rumination and Related Constructs
DOI: https://doi.org/10.1016/B978-0-12-812545-8.00001-2

© 2020 Elsevier Inc. All rights reserved.

losing herself in the excitement of a Hollywood life. Now, however, she found herself reliving that horrible episode, longing for her mother, and feeling guilty for leaving behind her younger sister.

Cognitive theories propose that the content of people's thoughts contribute to depressive symptoms. For instance, Beck (1967) noted that depressed people have excessively negative views of themselves, others, and the future. These *negative beliefs* are usually not accurate but contribute to people feeling hopeless and helpless. Beck also proposed that everyone has deeply held and often unconscious core beliefs about themselves and the world. These core beliefs, or schemas, often originate in childhood and are shaped by important people and/or life events. Thus, her parents' frequent arguments about their children and her mother's sudden death may have contributed to Ann's core beliefs that she was defective and that support and love from others was fleeting and unreliable. Negative schemas like this make people more vulnerable to depression if and when they later encounter negative life events that activate relevant schemas. The activated schemas then serve as filters through which people perceive the world. For Ann, the death of her husband activated her negative schemas, which in turn colored the way she perceived events in her life. For instance, her observation that few friends called her triggered automatic thoughts that she was unlovable, rather than the more accurate conclusion that they might think she wanted to be left alone.

This cognitive theory of depression has been expanded over the years, and many other types of unhelpful thoughts have been identified, but the basic premise remains the same: the specific content of thoughts that arise in response to negative life events explains the onset and maintenance of depression. There is, however, a second group of cognitive models. These models focus less on the content of thought and more on the process of turning attention inward—a construct called *self-focused attention*.

Beginning in the early 1970s, researchers began conceptualizing self-focused attention as part of a self-evaluative process in which individuals compare their current and desired states (Duval & Wicklund, 1972). Immediately after a negative event, people automatically increase their self-focus and focus on the discrepancy between current and desired states, presumably in order to understand what went wrong and to try to feel better. This is a natural part of self-regulation, or coping (Carver & Scheier, 1998). In healthy functioning individuals, this self-focus should lead to better understanding and emotion modulation, and perhaps even to behavior change. With the passage of time, therefore, the need for self-focused attention decreases in non-depressed individuals. Another way to think of it is as a negative feedback loop: an undesired event triggers the mind to start paying attention more closely to one's feelings and thoughts. Ideally, this attention leads to successful regulation, which in turn shuts down the self-focused attention.

However, inward self-focus also elicits negative emotions, particularly when a negative discrepancy exists and when one fails to resolve such a discrepancy. When unresolvable discrepancies occur (e.g., the death of Anne's husband), the adaptive response might be to avoid further self-focus and move on to alternative goals (e.g., finding new friends). In some instances, however, individuals are unwilling or unable to move on and continue focusing their attention internally. This sustained self-focused attention intensifies negative affect and self-criticism, leading to depression (Pyszczynski & Greenberg, 1987). Once in a depressed mood, people may develop a depressive self-focusing style, in which their default mode is inward focus. These individuals now have a faulty negative feedback loop, in which self-focus is never turned off, even when the situation demands attention elsewhere (Ingram, 1990). In Anne's case, the self-focused attention triggered by the death of her husband contributed to her sustained depressed mood, which in turn elicited more self-focused attention. And now she focused not only on this one negative incident but other negative experiences in her past. She was stuck in a repetitive, internally-focused thought process—in essence, trapped in her own mind.

In sum, two fairly separate cognitive theories proposed that specific types of thought content *and* the degree to which people engage in an internal attentional process contribute to depression (Robinson & Alloy, 2003). Susan Nolen-Hoeksema proposed and spent years developing a theory that integrated these two cognitive approaches (Nolen-Hoeksema, 1991; Nolen-Hoeksema, Wisco, & Lyubomirsky, 2008). Her definition of depressive rumination combines negative thought content and sustained self-focus.

Response styles theory: definitions and measurement

Interestingly, the impetus for response styles theory (RST) was not merging two separate cognitive theories of depression, but rather explaining gender differences in the prevalence of depression. After reviewing and refuting other proposed explanations (e.g., genetics, hormones, and sex roles) for why women are diagnosed with depression twice as often as men, Nolen-Hoeksema (1987) argued that women and men have different ways of responding to, or coping with, depressed moods. Her basic hypothesis was that women are more likely to engage in a passive, ruminative response style—whereas men are more likely to engage in an active, distracting response style—when experiencing a sad mood. A ruminative response style amplifies and prolongs transient sad moods, making a longer depressive episode more likely. By contrast, engaging in distracting activities dampens and shortens depressed mood.

As evidence for gender differences in response styles, Nolen-Hoeksema (1987) presented college students with a list of things people do when depressed and asked them to rate how likely they would be to engage in each of the activities. Men scored significantly higher than women on "I avoid thinking of reasons why I'm depressed," "I do something physical," "I play a sport," and "I take drugs"—all activities that distract individuals from sad moods. Women, on the other hand, scored significantly higher on "I try to determine why I'm depressed," "I talk to other people about my feelings," and "I cry to relieve the tension"—responses that focus and maintain attention to sad mood.

Building on these results, Nolen-Hoeksema (1991) defined *depressive rumination* as passive and repetitive thoughts that focus one's attention on the symptoms, causes, and consequences of depression. She acknowledged that the content of depressive rumination may resemble the negative thoughts that Beck and other cognitive psychologists identified. However, the style, or *process*, of repetitive thinking makes this construct unique. Similar to rigid self-focused attention, rumination focuses individuals' attention on their emotional state and therefore inhibits actions or thoughts that might be more adaptive. Unlike theories of self-focused attention, however, Nolen-Hoeksema argued that depressive rumination does not have to be preceded by a negative life event—because sometimes depressed moods do not have a clear triggering cause. Instead, depressive rumination focuses attention on a negative emotional state. She also argued that self-focused attention was conceptualized as an automatic response, whereas depressive rumination is a purposeful coping effort.

In contrast to rumination, distraction involves purposefully turning attention away from depressive symptoms and their causes and consequences (Nolen-Hoeksema, 1991). Effective distractions are pleasant (or at least neutral), absorbing, and reinforcing activities such as going for a run, seeing a movie with friends, or concentrating on work (Nolen-Hoeksema et al., 2008). There are, of course, types of responses that may be distracting but also potentially harm oneself, such as abusing alcohol and drugs or driving recklessly. However, Nolen-Hoeksema focused on the potential of positive or neutral distractions to decrease depressed moods.

The basic hypothesis of RST is that ruminative responses to depressed mood amplify sad moods and lead to longer periods of depression. By contrast, distraction in response to depressed mood decreases sad moods. Nolen-Hoeksema also proposed several mechanisms of depressive rumination, which I cover later in this chapter.

In order to test her hypotheses, Nolen-Hoeksema developed a measure to assess tendencies for depressive rumination called the Ruminative Responses Scale (RRS: Nolen-Hoeksema & Morrow, 1991). This measure was originally one subscale of a larger measure called the Response Style Questionnaire, which also includes subscales measuring distraction, problem-solving, and dangerous activities. The 22-item RRS assesses rumination about depressed moods ("When you feel sad, down, or depressed, how often do you ...: think about how alone you feel, think 'Why do I always react this way?,'"). This measure has been used in hundreds of published studies and has been adapted for children (Abela, Brozina, & Haigh, 2002). However, the measure has been criticized for its overlap with symptoms of depression (Roberts, Gilboa, & Gotlib, 1998; Treynor, Gonzalez, & Nolen-Hoeksema, 2003). To address this problem, Nolen-Hoeksema and colleagues eliminated those items in the original measure that assess depressive symptoms (Treynor et al., 2003). The remaining 10 items load onto two factors: brooding reflects "a passive comparison of one's current situation with some unachieved standard," whereas reflective pondering assesses self-focused problem-solving efforts to understand and alleviate one's depressed mood (Treynor et al., 2003, p. 256).[1] As we will see, many studies have compared these two subscales.

There are several ways that the effects of depressive rumination have been studied. Cross-sectional studies examine whether measures of trait rumination correlate with depressive symptoms at that same time point. Prospective longitudinal studies assess whether rumination at an initial assessment predicts depressive symptoms at a later point in time. These types of nonexperimental designs address questions about the onset and duration of diagnosed depression, in addition to self-reported

1 Subsequent psychometric analyses of the revised RRS did not find evidence for a reflective pondering factor with depressed patients or a community sample (Griffith & Raes, 2015; Whitmer & Gotlib, 2011). Thus, the stability of this subscale is unclear. There is also a commonly used German version of the RSQ (Kühner, Huffziger, & Nolen-Hoeksema, 2007) that contains three subscales: symptom-focused rumination (similar to brooding), self-focused rumination (similar to reflective pondering), and distraction (items adapted from the original RSQ). Other measures of trait depressive rumination include the 13-item rumination on sadness scale (Conway, Csank, Holm, & Blake, 2000), the 22-item Sadness and Anger Rumination Inventory (Peled & Moretti, 2007), and the 6-item rumination subscale of the revised Leiden Index of Depression Sensitivity (Williams, Van der Does, Barnhofer, Crane, & Segal, 2008).

depressive symptoms. By contrast, experimental studies typically manipulate rumination and examine its causal effect on sad mood. These designs cannot provide insight into diagnosed depression or even many of the symptoms of depression, because these symptoms are not likely to change in response to any brief laboratory manipulation. Still, as we will see, experimental research has been able to test whether rumination increases sad mood.

Rumination and sad mood

Around the time she developed RST, Nolen-Hoeksema also developed a rumination manipulation that remains the gold standard in the larger rumination literature. In it, participants are asked to read and think about a series of 45 self-referential statements for 8 minutes (Lyubomirsky & Nolen-Hoeksema, 1993; Nolen-Hoeksema & Morrow, 1993). The statements are emotion-focused, symptom-focused, and self-focused but do not specify any particular emotion (e.g., "what your feelings might mean," "the kind of person you are," "the physical sensations in your body," and "why you react the way you do"). The control, or distraction condition involves thinking about statements that are externally focused and not related to symptoms or emotions (e.g., "a boat slowly crossing the Atlantic," "the expression on the face of the Mona Lisa," and "the layout of the local post-office"). Participants in both conditions are instructed to focus their attention intently on the prompts for 8 minutes (Nolen-Hoeksema & Morrow, 1993). In essence, this manipulation induces self-focused attention by directing participants' attention to how they are feeling, why, and what this means about them. This mirrors Nolen-Hoeksema's definition of depressive rumination as self-focused attention specifically about depressive symptoms. The only piece not included in the manipulation is a focus specifically on depression. In fact, statements in both conditions are equally neutral in terms of affective tone. This was done intentionally, in order to separate the effects of rumination and depression.

This manipulation has been used in various ways to show that induced rumination increases sad mood. In an early experiment, Nolen-Hoeksema included participants with high or low scores on a depression self-report scale (Nolen-Hoeksema & Morrow, 1993). They were randomly assigned to either the rumination or distraction manipulation. Dysphoric participants who ruminated showed an increase in their sad mood, whereas dysphoric participants in the distraction condition showed a significant decrease in their sad mood—to the level of sadness reported by nondysphoric participants. Neither rumination nor distraction affected sad mood in nondysphoric participants. These findings have been replicated in other similar studies (Lyubomirsky, Caldwell, & Nolen-Hoeksema, 1998; Lyubomirsky, Kasri, & Zehm, 2003; Lyubomirsky & Nolen-Hoeksema, 1993, 1995; Lyubomirsky, Tucker, Caldwell, & Berg, 1999; Watkins & Teasdale, 2001). When comparing participants diagnosed with major depressive disorder with nondepressed control participants, manipulated rumination also increases sad mood, relative to manipulated distraction (Donaldson & Lam, 2004; Lavender & Watkins, 2004; Park, Goodyer, & Teasdale, 2004). Alternatively, researchers have induced sad mood in participants *before* the rumination manipulation. In the first experiment using this procedure, participants read a sad story while listening to sad music (Barber's *Adagio for Strings*) in the background (Morrow & Nolen-Hoeksema, 1990). As expected, rumination while in a sad mood led to greater sad mood than did distraction. Subsequent versions of the same research design also find that manipulated rumination following a sad mood induction elicits more sad mood than does distraction (Ciesla & Roberts, 2007).

A research team in Germany developed a novel way of using the Nolen-Hoeksema rumination induction in daily life (e.g., Huffziger, Ebner-Priemer, Koudela, Reinhard, & Kuehner, 2012). Healthy undergraduates were given palm pilots for 2 days and were paged 10 times per day during a 12-hour window. At each page, participants were instructed to rate their momentary rumination and mood. On one of the 2 days (i.e., induction day), participants engaged in a 3-minute rumination induction after each of the 10 assessments, following by a second rating of momentary rumination and mood. On the noninduction day, participants simply provided 10 ratings following each page. The rumination induction involved reading and focusing on 10 rumination statements for a total of 3 minutes. At each time point the rumination induction immediately increased momentary rumination, negative mood, and agitation. Greater increases in state rumination were associated with larger increases in negative mood. Unlike in the laboratory experiments previously described, initial level of depressive symptoms did not moderate the effect of induced rumination.

Finally, researchers have studied the effect of naturally occurring rumination on sad mood. In two studies, some participants were given a delay period of 8 minutes after a sad mood induction, presumably during which high trait ruminators would spontaneously ruminate (Ciesla & Roberts, 2007; Conway et al., 2000). As expected, high trait ruminators who were given the opportunity to ruminate while in a sad mood reported more subsequent emotional distress. High ruminators who were not given the 8-minute delay did not report more distress than low trait ruminators in either condition (Conway et al., 2000). Researchers have also used experience sampling designs to study the longitudinal effect of rumination on sad mood. In a month-long study, the more that participants ruminated on a particular day in response to a depressed mood, the longer that mood lasted that day (Nolen-Hoeksema, Morrow, & Fredrickson, 1993). In addition, the amount of rumination on the first day of a moderately-severe depressed mood predicted how long that mood would last. Similarly, the more that participants were ruminating about their problems and feelings at any given time, the more sad they felt at the next page, roughly 90 minutes later (Moberly & Watkins, 2008).

In summary, across several different methodologies, naturally occurring and manipulated depressive rumination contribute to increased and prolonged sad moods. What the studies with manipulated rumination gain in internal validity, those with naturally occurring rumination gain in external validity. Taken together, the evidence is extremely convincing. I want to reiterate that the rumination manipulation actually induces self-focused attention to symptoms, causes, and consequences of individuals' current mood state. These manipulations only become *depressive* rumination when paired with a preexisting or induced sad mood. In the absence of such a sad mood, the rumination manipulations have no effect on sad mood. This makes sense, as rumination without something to ruminate about seems more like philosophical reflection.

Rumination and depression

Longitudinal research clearly indicates that rumination predicts worse depressive symptoms. In one study, college students enrolled in an introductory psychology course completed questionnaires assessing depressive rumination and depressive symptoms (Nolen-Hoeksema & Morrow, 1991). In a twist of fate, a 7.1 earthquake struck the area 2 weeks later. The quick-thinking researchers measured depressive rumination and depressive symptoms in these students 10 days and 7 weeks after the earthquake. Students who typically used more depressive rumination, as assessed before the earthquake, showed more severe depressive symptoms 10 days and 7 weeks after the earthquake, even after controlling for initial depressive symptoms. Similar results have been found with individuals who recently experienced the death of a family member or partner (Nolen-Hoeksema, McBride, & Larson, 1997; Nolen-Hoeksema, Parker, & Larson, 1994). Thus, depressive rumination relates to more severe depressive symptoms following a range of negative, stressful events. Since these initial studies, many other researchers have shown that rumination predicts the severity of depressive symptoms across a wide range of time frames, in people with and without initial diagnosed depression, and in children and adolescents as well as adults (for reviews, see Aldao, Nolen-Hoeksema & Schweizer, 2010; Nolen-Hoeksema et al., 2008; Papageorgiou & Wells, 2004; Rood, Roelofs, Bögels, Nolen-Hoeksema & Schouten, 2009). Of particular interest have been the unique effects of brooding versus reflective pondering. In many studies, brooding uniquely predicts depressive symptoms several months to 1 year later, in both adolescents and adults (Barnum, Woody, & Gibb, 2013; Burwell & Shirk, 2007; Hasegawa, Koda, Kondo, Hattori, & Kawaguchi, 2013; Padilla Paredes & Calvete Zumalde, 2015; Raes, Smets, Nelis & Schoofs, 2012; Treynor et al., 2003). By contrast, the effects of reflective pondering are mixed. Some studies found that it uniquely predicted increased depressive symptoms over time, controlling for brooding (Hasegawa et al., 2013; Padilla Paredes & Calvete Zumalde, 2015), whereas others found no such unique effect (Barnum et al., 2013; Pearson, Watkins, & Mullan, 2010; Raes et al., 2012). Moreover, in other studies reflective pondering uniquely predicted less depressive symptoms over time (Arditte & Joormann, 2011; Eisma et al., 2015; Treynor et al., 2003). These mixed results may be explained by moderators. For instance, reflective pondering interacted with age and gender to predict changes in depressive symptoms 1 year later (Verstraeten, Vasey, Raes, & Bijttebier, 2010). Specifically, for younger children, reflective pondering predicted increases in depressive symptoms; for somewhat older children, however, reflective pondering predicted decreased depressive symptoms. Moreover, reflective pondering predicted decreased depressive symptoms in general for boys but not for girls. Cross-sectional studies also found that reflective pondering predicted more depressive symptoms only for participants with poor coping skills (Brennan, Barnhofer, Crane, Duggan, & Williams, 2015; Marroquín, Fontes, Scilletta, & Miranda, 2010). Thus, reflective pondering may be adaptive for some people but not for others. Another possibility is that reflective pondering is indirectly associated with depressive symptoms via increased brooding. In fact, one study found that reflection predicted increased negative rumination over 3 weeks, but negative rumination did not predict subsequent reflection (Takano & Tanno, 2009). The implication is that reflective pondering may make people more likely to start brooding, perhaps if they experience negative events or affect. More research is needed to examine moderators and indirect effects of reflective pondering on depressive symptoms.

Depressive rumination is also related to diagnosed depression as well as the future onset of major depressive episodes. People with current diagnosed depression, as well as a past history of depression, report more depressive rumination tendencies than do people with no depression history (Nolen-Hoeksema, 2000). Depressive rumination also predicts the onset of a future depression diagnosis in adults

(Just & Alloy, 1997; Nolen-Hoeksema, 2000). Whether depressive rumination contributes to longer bouts of depression, however, is unclear. Several studies found that in adults who started out with a major depression diagnosis, depressive rumination did not predict diagnosed depression 6–18 months later (Just & Alloy, 1997; Lara, Klein, & Kasch, 2000; Nolen-Hoeksema, 2000). In clinical samples of patients being treated for major depression, depressive rumination by itself did not predict duration of depressive episodes. However, for patients at the end of their depression treatment, depressive rumination did predict reoccurrence of a depressive episode 3 months later (Kuehner & Weber, 1999). Moreover, undergraduate students who had more prolonged previous dysphoria reported more depressive rumination than those with brief previous dysphoria (Roberts et al., 1998). Thus, the evidence suggests that depressive rumination makes future new and recurrent depressive episodes more likely, but it may not relate to how long a depressive episode lasts. Nolen-Hoeksema suggests that rumination contributes to people crossing the threshold from sad mood to diagnosed depression, but that once depressed, other factors determine the duration of the episode (Nolen-Hoeksema et al., 2008).

A small literature examines the role of rumination in seasonal affective disorder, a variant of depression in which people experience depressive episodes starting in the fall or winter and ending in the spring. In this disorder the depression is usually characterized by fatigue, increased sleep, and increased appetite/weight, in addition to typical affective and cognitive symptoms. The dual vulnerability model proposes that seasonal affective disorder results from a physiological vulnerability to experience vegetative symptoms in response to seasonal changes in the physical environment, as well as a psychological vulnerability to develop affective and cognitive depressive symptoms in response to the vegetative symptoms (Enggasser & Young, 2007). In fact, trait depressive rumination measured in the summer or fall prospectively predicts severity of this kind of vegetative, "winter" depression (Rohan, Sigmon, & Dorhofer, 2003; Whitcomb-Smith et al., 2014). Moreover, this model suggests that rumination (i.e., a psychological vulnerability) combines—or interacts—with vegetative symptoms to predict affective and cognitive symptoms of seasonal depression. In support of this theory, depressive rumination prospectively predicts the severity of cognitive and affective depressive symptoms in individuals with a history of seasonal vegetative symptoms (Enggasser & Young, 2007). Moreover, in participants with clinical and subclinical symptoms of seasonal affective disorder, both trait and state rumination interact with daily or weekly vegetative symptoms to predict daily or weekly cognitive and affective symptoms (Whitcomb-Smith et al., 2014; Young, Reardon, & Azam, 2008).

Mechanisms of depressive rumination

The RST proposes several mechanisms of the effects of depressive rumination on depressive symptoms. Specifically, rumination is theorized to increase negative thinking, interfere with effective problem-solving, promote behavioral avoidance, and decrease social support (Nolen-Hoeksema, 1991; Nolen-Hoeksema et al., 2008). Evidence exists for all of these mechanisms.

Negative thinking

Nolen-Hoeksema proposed that rumination enhances the effects of depressed mood on thought content. In fact, research shows that depressive rumination is associated with several types of negative thinking. In an early experiment, college students read about several hypothetical problematic situations (e.g., being encouraged by friends to run for president of an organization but then losing the election) and were asked to report their thoughts and feelings about the situation, in order to reveal the types of interpretations they made (Lyubomirsky & Nolen-Hoeksema, 1995). Dysphoric participants in the rumination condition made more negative, pessimistic, and biased interpretations (e.g., minimizing successes and overgeneralizing from failures) than did dysphoric individuals in the distraction condition. Similarly, when participants spoke their thoughts aloud during the standard rumination versus distraction manipulation, the thoughts of dysphoric ruminators were more negative, self-critical, pessimistic, and reflected low perceived control (Lyubomirsky et al., 1999). By contrast, the thoughts of nondysphoric individuals who ruminated, as well as participants in the distraction condition, were more positive, optimistic, and less problem-focused. In correlational studies, depressive rumination is associated with tendencies for dysfunctional attitudes, pessimistic inferences, self-criticism, hopelessness, decreased self-confidence, self-esteem, and low perceived control (Abela, Brozina, & Haigh, 2002; Lam, Schuck, Smith, Farmer, & Checkley, 2003; Lo, Ho, & Hollon, 2008; Nolen-Hoeksema et al., 1994; Sarin, Abela, & Auerbach, 2005; Smith, Alloy, & Abramson, 2006; Weir & Jose, 2008). Several of these constructs—for example, pessimism, hopelessness, low self-esteem, and poor perceived control—mediate the effects of depressive rumination on depressive symptoms.

Depressive rumination is also associated with making more negative interpretations of ambiguous information. In one experiment, participants completed benign or negative word fragments at the end of brief scenarios like this: "While doing your calculus homework, you encounter a problem that you couldn't solve. The next day, you go to class and turn it in.

Later, you keep thinking about it and realize that, during class, everyone else seemed in_ec_re (*insecure*—benign interpretation)/co_fid_nt (*confident*—negative interpretation)" (Hertel, Maydon, Cottle, & Vrijsen, 2017). High trait ruminators who were induced to ruminate completed negative fragments more quickly than benign fragments, suggesting a negative interpretation bias. No differences emerged for low trait ruminators or participants in a distraction condition. Similarly, undergraduates high in trait depressive rumination showed a negative interpretation bias on a lexical decision task (Mor, Hertel, Ngo, Shachar, & Redak, 2013).

Rumination also makes dysphoric people more pessimistic about their futures. Dysphoric individuals in a rumination condition generated more negative future events that might happen to them in the coming weeks and years than did dysphoric individuals in a distraction condition (Lavender & Watkins, 2004). In a different study, dysphoric participants who ruminated generated as many happy events that might happen to them as did other participants; however, they were less hopeful that these events would actually happen to them (Lyubomirsky & Nolen-Hoeksema, 1995). Finally, dysphoric participants in a self-focus condition rated negative hypothetical events as more likely to happen to themselves and positive hypothetical events as more likely to happen to others, compared to dysphoric participants with an external focus (Pyszczynski & Greenberg, 1987).

Similarly, rumination and self-focused attention make dysphoric people more likely to remember negative events from their past. After a self-focus manipulation in which participants wrote a story with either first-person or third-person pronouns, dysphoric participants in the self-focused condition remembered more negative events that had happened to them recently than did dysphoric participants in the external-focus condition (Pyszczynski, Hamilton, Herring, & Greenberg, 1989). Similar results were found using Nolen-Hoeksema's depressive rumination manipulation (Lyubomirsky et al., 1998) and using a manipulation that contrasted ruminative with reflective thinking (McFarland & Buehler, 1998). These studies also found that dysphoric individuals in distraction conditions did not recall more negative memories than nondysphoric individuals, suggesting that distraction decreases negative memory bias.

Depressive rumination appears to increase retrieval of a particular type of memory called overgeneral memories. When depressed people are asked to recall specific personal memories, they are more likely to retrieve categorical summaries of repeated events (e.g., "I lost tennis matches") instead of individual events at a specific time and place (e.g., "I lost to my friend Juan at tennis last Sunday") (Williams et al., 2007). This memory bias is associated with the maintenance of depressive symptoms and suggests a poor prognosis. Researchers therefore have investigated whether ruminating while depressed is associated with overgeneral memories. In both dysphoric and clinically depressed individuals, rumination inductions lead to more overgeneral memories, whereas distraction inductions decrease overgeneral memories (Park et al., 2004; Watkins & Teasdale, 2001; Watkins, Teasdale, & Williams, 2000). Correlational results suggest that brooding in particular is associated with overgeneral memories, particularly in dysphoric individuals (Debeer, Hermans, & Raes, 2009; Raes et al., 2005; Romero, Vazquez, & Sanchez, 2014; but see Hamlat et al., 2015). The idea is that self-focused rumination, particularly when in a depressed mood, makes abstract self-representations more salient (e.g., "I am a failure"), which encourages elaboration of overgeneral memories (e.g., "I always lose in tennis").

Impaired problem-solving

Rumination also interferes with effective problem-solving. Psychologists often identify three stages of problem-solving: (1) definition or appraisal of the problem, (2) generation and selection of alternative solutions, and (3) implementation of the chosen solution(s) (e.g., D'Zurilla & Goldfried, 1971). Evidence suggests that depressive rumination impairs all three stages. In one study, following a rumination or distraction manipulation, participants were asked to list their three biggest current problems (e.g., with family, friends, work, school, and finances) and then provide appraisals of how severe each problem is and whether they could likely solve it (Lyubomirsky et al., 1999). Dysphoric participants who ruminated rated their problems as more severe and less solvable than did dysphoric participants in the distraction condition or nondysphoric participants. Thus, depressive rumination led to more negative and hopeless appraisals of perceived problems.

Several studies examined solutions participants generated to hypothetical interpersonal problems. Specifically, participants were presented with four problems common to undergraduate students: "(a) you realize that a friend is avoiding you, (b) your boyfriend/girlfriend tells you that he or she is very angry with you, (c) your professor writes to you that you may fail a class, and (d) you realize that a committee's suggestions will not work" (Lyubomirsky & Nolen-Hoeksema, 1995, p. 184). For each scenario, participants were provided with the beginning (e.g., "You notice that one of your friends seems to be avoiding you") and end ("The situation ends when he or she likes you again") of the story and asked to write what happens in the middle. Judges later rated participants' stories for problem-solving effectiveness. In both dysphoric and clinically depressed participants, induced rumination led to less effective solutions than did distraction (Lyubomirsky & Nolen-Hoeksema, 1995; Lyubomirsky et al., 1999). Dysphoric participants in the distraction condition generated as effective solutions as nondysphoric participants.

Finally, depressive rumination also decreases willingness to implement solutions. In some of the studies I just described, participants also rated how likely they were to use solutions they generated (Lyubomirsky et al., 1999). Interestingly, dysphoric participants who ruminated were less willing than dysphoric participants who distracted themselves to implement their own solutions. Similarly, rumination reduced dysphoric participants' willingness to engage in pleasant and distracting events in order to improve their mood (Lyubomirsky & Nolen-Hoeksema, 1993). Why might dysphoric individuals who ruminate be less willing to implement solutions? It could be that they simply do not have the motivation to make changes, a construct that is addressed in the next section. Alternatively, perhaps people believe that their solutions will not be effective. There is conflicting evidence about this possibility. In the two studies I just described, dysphoric participants who ruminated or distracted themselves reported equal confidence that their solutions would be effective (Lyubomirsky & Nolen-Hoeksema, 1993; Lyubomirsky et al., 1999). However, some correlational research suggests that rumination is associated with less confidence. In a pair of studies, students were asked to formulate complex and novel plans to revise the housing system or curriculum at their university (Ward, Lyubomirsky, Sousa, & Nolen-Hoeksema, 2003). Students with high depressive rumination tendencies reported less satisfaction and confidence in the plans they devised than did students low on depressive rumination. The researchers speculated that high ruminators might have a history of failed problem-solving and of past depression, both of which could contribute to decreased confidence about their solutions to problems. Given the link between depressive rumination and low self-confidence in general, it seems likely that in real-life situations, people who depressively ruminate are likely to question the quality of their solutions. This may particularly be the case for people who are already depressed or dysphoric. Clearly, more research is needed in this area.

Behavioral avoidance

Nolen-Hoeksema (1991) originally proposed that rumination interferes with the motivation to initiate instrumental—or constructive—behavior. A consequence of the negative thinking caused by rumination may be that people feel they lack the energy to take action. Clear evidence for this initial hypothesis is lacking. In a more recent reconceptualization of the RST, Nolen-Hoeksema proposed that depressive rumination promotes behavioral withdrawal (Nolen-Hoeksema et al., 2008). Specifically, depressive rumination might unconsciously function to convince people that they are facing a hopelessly uncontrollable situation and that any behavioral attempts to take action are pointless. This increased certainty in their helplessness gives people permission to withdraw and avoid trying to change a difficult situation. The reductions in distress that occur after withdrawing from aversive situations and "giving up" one's responsibility only serve to reinforce the rumination. However, the consequence of behavioral withdrawal is that people miss out on potentially enjoyable and meaningful experiences. In other words, people will develop a lack of positive reinforcement (e.g., hugs and friendship), an important proposed cause of depression in behavioral theory.

Substantial research evidence with both healthy and depressed participants links depressive rumination, particularly brooding, with self-reported behavioral avoidance or withdrawal (Brockmeyer et al., 2015; Cribb, Moulds, & Carter, 2006; Moulds, Kandris, Starr, & Wong, 2007; Ottenbreit, Dobson, & Quigley, 2014). Moreover, one cross-sectional study found that behavioral avoidance was associated with decreased positive reinforcement, and that this sequence of behavioral avoidance and lack of reinforcement explained the association between depressive rumination and depressive symptoms (Brockmeyer et al., 2015). Depressive rumination is also associated with behavioral disengagement from stressful situations (Hong, 2007). One longitudinal study found that grief-related rumination (assessed on average 18 months after the death of a loved one) predicted greater loss-related behavioral avoidance 6 months later, controlling for baseline depressive symptoms (Eisma et al., 2013). Thus, it seems clear that depressive rumination is associated with behavioral avoidance or withdrawal.

Poor social support

Nolen-Hoeksema also proposed that depressive rumination is counterproductive to relationships and likely results in decreased social support (Nolen-Hoeksema et al., 2008). In fact, depressive ruminators generally report less or worse perceived social support, as well as greater social isolation (Abela, Vanderbilt, & Rochon, 2004; Nolen-Hoeksema & Davis, 1999; Nolen-Hoeksema et al., 1994; Puterman, DeLongis, & Pomaki, 2010). In one study, depressive rumination predicted greater discontent with social support over the next 9 months, which in turn predicted depressive symptoms 9 months later (Flynn, Kecmanovic, & Alloy, 2010). Why might depressive rumination contribute to poor perceived social support? Empirical evidence suggests several possible reasons.

Interestingly, rumination is related to greater seeking out of social support. For instance, in individuals who recently lost a family member or close friend to terminal illness, depressive rumination is associated with more reaching out to others for support (Nolen-Hoeksema & Davis, 1999; but see Hong, 2007). Moreover, depressive rumination is associated with excessive reassurance seeking (Oppenheimer, Technow, Hankin, Young, & Abela, 2012; Weinstock & Whisman, 2007). Although seeking social support can certainly be adaptive, it may eventually strain social resources and/or generate interpersonal conflict, especially if not paired with active attempts to resolve distress. If this happens, the risk for depression actually increases (Joiner & Metalsky, 2001).

In addition, rumination predicts less adaptive relationship behaviors. In individuals with diagnosed depression, depressive rumination predicts poorer functioning in interpersonal relationships, such as problems with control, assertiveness, submission, and intimacy (Lam et al., 2003). Specifically, brooding is associated with a submissive interpersonal style, which is characterized by overly accommodating, nonassertive, and self-sacrificing interpersonal behaviors (Cheung, Gilbert, & Irons, 2004; Pearson, Watkins, Mullan, & Moberly, 2010). Submissiveness in fact mediates the association between brooding and depressive symptoms 6 months later (Pearson et al., 2010). Similarly, depressive rumination is related to greater unmitigated communion, which is defined as placing others' needs above one's own needs and feeling responsible for others' happiness (Nolen-Hoeksema & Jackson, 2001). The combination of seeking of social support with unhelpful relationship behaviors may contribute to poor perceived social support.

Finally, some evidence suggests that depressive rumination contributes to interpersonal stressors, characterized by conflict with another person. The stress generation hypothesis asserts that individuals who are depressed or vulnerable to becoming depressed play a role in generating stressful events in their lives, which in turn increases the likelihood and severity of depression (for a review, see Liu & Alloy, 2010). In line with this, depressive rumination predicted greater interpersonal stressors 9 months later in undergraduates (Flynn et al., 2010). This was only true for interpersonal problems that individuals contributed to themselves. Similarly, adolescents who reported more depressive rumination were more likely to experience physical and verbal aggression, social exclusion and rejection, and being the victim of gossip of rumors 7 months later (McLaughlin & Nolen-Hoeksema, 2012). Counterintuitively, this association was explained by increased communication with peers, perhaps indicating the combination of seeking out of social support but lacking adaptive interpersonal skills. As expected, exposure to peer victimization explained the association between depressive rumination and subsequent depressive symptoms. Several other studies also found that depressive rumination correlates with greater interpersonal stressors many months later in adolescents, although the associations were not robust when controlling for variables such as depressive symptoms and negative cognitive style (Calvete, Orue, & Hankin, 2015; Hamilton et al., 2013; Shapero, Hankin, & Barrocas, 2013).

Summary

In sum, there is generally strong support for RST's proposed mechanisms, although the emerging picture is more nuanced than originally suggested (see Fig. 1.1). Depressive rumination is associated with various types of negative thinking, such as self-criticism, hopelessness, poor self-esteem and self-confidence, low perceived control, negative interpretations of ambiguous information, pessimism about the future,

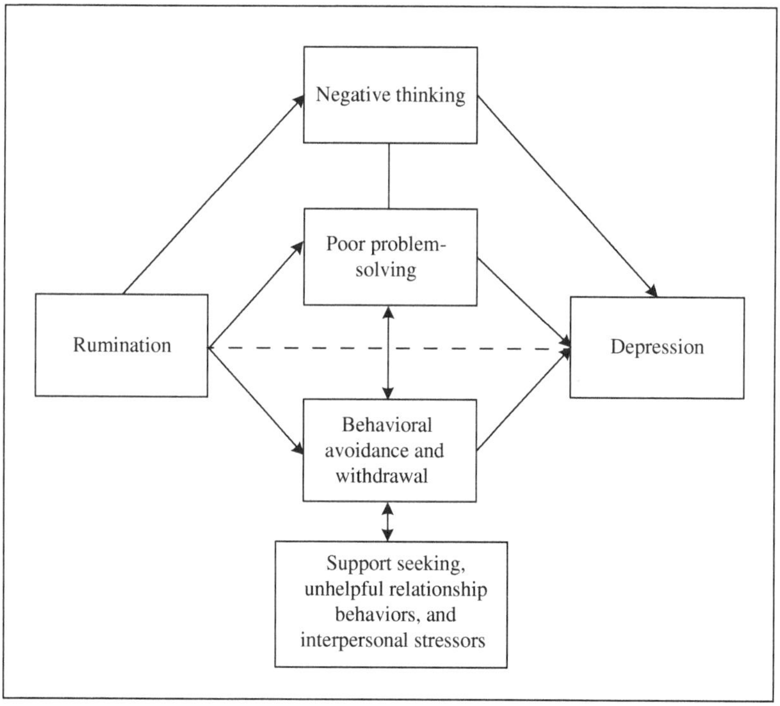

FIGURE 1.1 Mechanisms of the effect of rumination on depression. *Note*: All of the four mechanisms are interrelated (some of these associations are not shown here for simplicity). Source: *Adapted from Nolen-Hoeksema, S., Wisco, B., & Lyubomirsky, S. (2008). Rethinking rumination. Perspectives on Psychological Science* **3** *(5), 2008, 400–424. https://ezproxy.tcnj.edu:2083/10.1111/j.1745-6924.2008.00088.x.*

negative memory bias, and overgeneral memories. These types of negative thinking appear to mediate the association between depressive rumination and depressive symptoms. A handful of studies suggest that depressive rumination is associated with deficits in problem-solving, such as more negative appraisals of problems, less effective solutions, and decreased willingness to implement solutions. Whether this low willingness to implement solutions reflects less confidence in one's solutions needs further examination. Although RST's original proposed mechanism of low motivation for instrumental behavior has poor empirical support, data confirm the newer suggestion that rumination is associated with behavioral avoidance and withdrawal. Future research will need to examine whether this association reflects efforts to avoid responsibility for changing one's situation, as Nolen-Hoeksema suggests. Finally, the link between depressive rumination and poor perceived social support may reflect an interesting combination of greater seeking of social support paired with unhelpful relationship behaviors, perhaps contributing to greater interpersonal conflict and/or victimization.

Presumably these mechanisms are related to and influence each other, although rumination researchers have not focused on this point. For instance, negative thinking likely impairs problem-solving, which in turn may contribute to tendencies to avoid or withdraw from difficult situations. Similarly, social rejection or conflict may trigger various types of negative thinking as well as behavioral withdrawal. To better understand the detrimental effects of depressive rumination, researchers should explore the interplay of its various mechanisms.

Rumination and bipolar disorder

Researchers are starting to examine the role of depressive rumination in bipolar disorder (for a review, see Silveira & Kauer-Sant'Anna, 2015). Individuals with bipolar disorder report more depressive and general negative rumination than do nonclinical and general psychiatric participants (Green et al., 2011; Gruber, Eidelman, Johnson, Smith, & Harvey, 2011; Jones, Tai, Evershed, Knowles, & Bentall, 2006; Pavlickova, Turnbull, Myin-Germeys, & Bentall, 2014). A few studies found similar levels of rumination in patients with bipolar disorder compared to those with major depressive disorder (Kim, Yu, Lee, & Kim, 2011; Wolkenstein, Zwick, Hautzinger, Joormann, 2014). However, when only patients currently in a depressed mood are considered, those with bipolar disorder report greater rumination than those with major depression (Kim et al., 2011). Thus, bipolar depression may be associated with more rumination than is unipolar depression.

One important question is whether the association between rumination and bipolar disorder is driven by manic or depressive symptoms, or both. Depressive rumination is clearly associated with depressive symptoms in bipolar patients (Simon et al., 2006; Stange et al., 2015). In fact, although rumination is correlated with hypomanic traits in both undergraduate and bipolar samples, it is much more strongly associated with depressive symptoms (Bentall et al., 2011; Green et al., 2011; Knowles, Tai, Christensen, & Bentall, 2005). Moreover, other studies found that only current depressive—but not manic—symptoms are associated with depressive rumination (Johnson, McKenzie, & McMurrich, 2008; Pavlickova et al., 2013). In participants with bipolar disorder but not currently in a depressed or manic episode, depressive rumination is associated with a higher frequency of depressive episodes per year, but not manic episodes (Gruber et al., 2011; Thomas & Tai, 2007). Although the evidence is mixed, there is not robust evidence of a unique association between depressive rumination and greater manic symptoms. Instead, the greater tendencies for depressive rumination in people with bipolar disorder may be in large part related to the link between rumination and depressive symptoms.

Interestingly, recent work suggests that manic symptoms are associated with tendencies to ruminate about positive emotions. Viewed as a method of amplifying positive emotions, positive rumination involves recurrent thoughts about positive self-qualities, positive affective experience, and one's favorable life circumstances. In undergraduates, positive rumination is associated with more hypomanic traits and symptoms, even controlling for depressive symptoms (Feldman, Joormann, & Johnson, 2008). Similarly, people with a history of mania and/or current manic symptoms report more positive rumination than do healthy controls or individuals with major depression (Gruber et al., 2011; Johnson, et al., 2008; Shapero et al., 2015; Weinstock, Chou, Celis-deHoyos, Miller, & Gruber, 2018). Positive rumination is correlated with greater depressive rumination in these clinical and nonclinical samples. However, it had a unique effect on hypomanic symptoms in the one study that tested this (Feldman et al., 2008). Therefore, it seems plausible that rumination about negative emotions predicts worse depressive symptoms, whereas rumination about positive emotions predicts worse manic symptoms in individuals with bipolar disorder. Much more research needs to be done to better understand the role of rumination in bipolar disorder.

Gender differences in depressive rumination

Now I return to the question that originally inspired Nolen-Hoeksema to start the field of depressive rumination: does it explain gender differences in depression? In several early studies, Nolen-Hoeksema found that adult women report greater depressive rumination than men (Butler & Nolen-Hoeksema, 1994; Nolen-Hoeksema & Jackson, 2001; Nolen-Hoeksema, et al., 1993). Depressive rumination also accounts for the effect of gender on depressive symptoms (see also Nolen-Hoeksema, Larson, & Grayson, 1999).

Since these early studies, dozens more have tested for gender differences in depressive rumination—in children, adolescents, and adults. Recent metaanalyses combined the results from all of those studies to determine how strong the average effect of gender is on depressive rumination. Their results suggest that at all ages, females do report more depressive rumination than males (Johnson & Whisman, 2013; Rood, et al., 2009). However, the difference is a small-to-medium effect size. In addition, the gender difference seems to be weaker in children ($d = .14$) than in adolescents ($d = .36$) and adults ($d = .24$), and many individual studies found no gender differences in children's rumination. This is not surprising, as gender differences in depression only become consistently apparent starting in adolescence (Hankin et al., 1998). In fact, one study found that gender differences in rumination appear around the age of 12, and gender differences in depressive symptoms appear around the age of 13 (Jose & Brown, 2008). The association between rumination and depressive symptoms is also stronger and more robust in adolescents than in children (Rood, et al., 2009). Several researchers have hypothesized that coping responses may be less well developed in childhood (e.g., Abela et al., 2002). Furthermore, responses like rumination in particular may require metacognitive skills that are not typically established until adolescence.

In sum, there do appear to be meaningful gender differences in depressive rumination, at least in adolescents and adults. Moreover, these differences account for at least some of the fact that women are twice as likely to have depression as men. However, the gender differences in rumination do not appear to be overwhelmingly large, which suggests that other constructs also contribute to gender differences in depression. This leads us into other research suggesting that the depressive rumination does not act alone but rather in combination with other relevant constructs.

Moderators and integrated theory

As discussed at the beginning of the chapter, earlier cognitive theories of depression all incorporated the existence of negative events or stressors. Negative events can activate existing negative core beliefs, trigger inflexible self-focused attention, and/or provide opportunities for people with negative cognitive styles to make negative attributions and inferences. As such, all of these models are cognitive vulnerability–stress models of depression, in that they suggest that cognitively vulnerable individuals will be more likely to become and/or stay depressed when they encounter negative events. By contrast, RST was not originally conceptualized as a vulnerability–stress model. In fact, Nolen-Hoeksema (1991) argued that depressive rumination does not have to be preceded by a negative life event—merely a negative emotional state. This theory, however, overlooked an entire literature suggesting that the combination of maladaptive thinking and stressors predicts depression. Not surprisingly, some researchers have suggested ways of incorporating RST with cognitive vulnerability–stress models of depression.

Stressful life events

Rumination interacts with several indices of stress to predict depression. For instance, the association between perceived stress and depressive symptoms is stronger for people with tendencies for general and depressive rumination, particularly brooding (Kraaij et al., 2003; Morrison & O'Connor, 2008). Depressive rumination also amplifies the effects of chronic strain—assessed as lack of affirmation in close relationships, role burden, housework inequities, childcare inequities, and other parenting strains—on depressive symptoms 1 year later (Nolen-Hoeksema, et al., 1999). In studies assessing specific negative events, the association between life stressors and depressive symptoms over several weeks to 1 year is stronger for adolescents with greater rumination tendencies (Bastin, Mezulis, Ahles, Raes, & Bijttebier, 2015; Cox, Funasaki, Smith, & Mezulis, 2012; Kercher & Rapee, 2009; Stange, Hamilton, Abramson, & Alloy, 2014). Moreover, the frequency of negative life events only predicts the future onset of depressive episodes in adolescents high in depressive rumination (Abela & Hankin, 2011). One study found that rumination specifically about controllable or social events predicted depressive symptoms, whereas rumination about uncontrollable or nonsocial events did not (Nicolai, Laney, & Mezulis, 2013). Perhaps rumination about controllable events is characterized by greater self-reproach about how one might have behaved differently. Thus, certain types of stressors may be more likely to interact with rumination tendencies to predict depression.

One experiment tested the moderating effect of rumination on the stress–depression link. Experimenters first induced rumination by having some participants read descriptions of 30 positive and negative situations and spend a minute thinking about the causes, meanings, and implications of each situation (Watkins, Moberly, & Moulds, 2008). The other condition induced concrete thought hypothesized to be antithetical to rumination. Following the rumination induction, all participants tried to complete 30 anagrams that were very hard or unsolvable, after which they were told that their performance was indicative of future academic and career success and that they performed well below the average. This constituted a stress induction. Results indicated that participants who ruminated became more despondent after the stress induction, whereas participants in the control condition did not. Thus, rumination increased the effect of stress on helplessness.

In sum, many studies have found that rumination and stress in combination predict worse depressive symptoms. However, other similar studies failed to find such an interaction (Abela, Parkinson, Stolow, & Starrs, 2009; Jose & Brown, 2008; Padilla Paredes & Calvete Zumalde, 2015; Sarin et al., 2005; Weir & Jose, 2008). These mixed results suggest that there may be other constructs at play. Remember that rumination manipulations only elicit predicted outcomes when people start out in sad moods. Thus, stressful events may only interact with rumination to the extent that they are associated with negative moods. In fact, cognitive vulnerability–stress models of depression emphasize that the cognitive interpretation of negative events, rather than the events themselves, predict risk of depression. Accordingly, researchers have examined negative cognition as an additional moderator.

Negative thinking

Robinson and Alloy (2003) argued that whereas depressive rumination focuses attention on *existing* depressed moods, ruminating on negative cognitions about stressful life events might contribute to the *initiation* of depressed moods. Drawing on evidence that depression develops from a tendency for negative inferences (e.g., it is all my fault, things like this always happen to me) when a stressful life event occurs, they suggested that having a tendency to ruminate about those negative inferences increases the likelihood of depression. Thus, Alloy and colleagues (Alloy et al., 2000; Robinson & Alloy, 2003) defined *stress-reactive rumination* as the tendency to focus on negative inferences following stressful life events.[2] They found that the interaction between negative cognitive style and stress-reactive rumination predicted retrospective reports of major depressive episodes. Moreover, this interaction between negative thoughts and the tendency to ruminate about the negative thoughts

2 Robinson and Alloy (2003) created a 9-item measure of stress-reactive rumination that asks respondents how often they engage in this kind of thinking (e.g., "think about how the stressful event was all your fault" and "think about how things like this always happen to you") after a major negative event. A child version has also been created (Rood, Bögels, & Roelofs, 2010).

predicted the onset, duration, and frequency of future major depressive episodes (Robinson & Alloy, 2003).

It is worth noting that the measure of stress-reactive rumination shares almost 50% of its variance with the measure of depressive rumination. Not surprisingly, in the study just described, negative thoughts and depressive rumination interacted to predict the number and duration of future depressive episodes (Robinson & Alloy, 2003). Similarly, in individuals with high negative cognition, depressive rumination was associated with worse response to treatment for depression (Ciesla & Roberts, 2002). In a rare experiment testing this theory, participants were put into a sad mood and then underwent the typical rumination or distraction manipulations (Ciesla & Roberts, 2007). Self-esteem and dysfunctional attitudes more strongly predicted dysphoric mood at the end of the experiment for participants in the rumination condition. The same results were found when the researchers measured trait rumination and gave participants a delay period after the sad mood induction (presumably inducing naturally occurring rumination).

Thus, no matter what rumination measure is used, the evidence is fairly clear that rumination interacts with negative thinking to predict depressive symptoms, at least in adults. Some researchers argue that the crux of rumination is the process (vs content) of repetitive thinking, and that this repetitive thinking serves as a catalyst in the bidirectional association between negative thoughts and depression (Ciesla, Felton, & Roberts, 2011). In other words, the power of negative thinking to cause depression is increased by rumination, and likewise the degree to which depression elaborates and exacerbates negative thinking increases with rumination. In a rare study combining several moderators, these researchers found that individuals who had both negative cognitive style and high rumination tendencies showed an especially strong association between stressful life events and depressive symptoms.

Integration

Abramson and colleagues developed a model that integrates all of these factors (Hankin & Abramson, 2001; Hyde, Mezulis, & Abramson, 2008). They acknowledge the role of negative cognition, ruminative tendencies, and the occurrence of negative stressful events in the initiation and maintenance of depression. Their model starts with a causal chain in which negative events elicit negative affect, which in turn can lead to depressive symptoms (see Fig. 1.2). Cognitive vulnerabilities interact with negative events and/or resulting negative affect to increase the likelihood of experiencing eventual depression. Both negative cognitive styles (dysfunctional attitudes and negative attributions) *and* ruminative

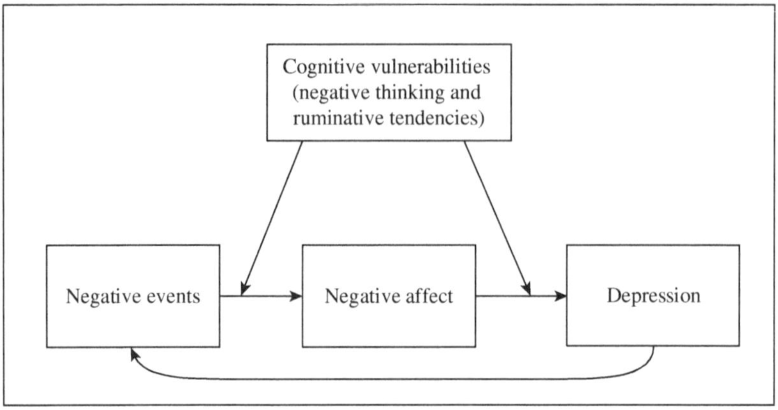

FIGURE 1.2 Integrated model highlighting the combination of rumination, stressful events, and negative thinking in predicting depression. Source: *Adapted from Hankin, B.L., & Abramson, L.Y. (2001). Development of gender differences in depression.* Psychological Bulletin, 127*(6), 773–796. Available from https://doi.org/10.1037/0033-2909.127.6.773.*

tendencies constitute cognitive vulnerabilities, and they may influence each other and operate in combination. Depressive symptoms—and rumination about them—can in turn generate new stressors, which maintain depression.

Taking it one step further, Abramson and colleagues suggest that this model can explain gender differences in depression. They point to evidence that females have not only greater cognitive vulnerability (e.g., more rumination and negative cognitive styles) but also experience more negative life events (particularly sexual abuse and harassment). Moreover, some studies found that rumination interacts with stressors to predict depressive symptoms only or more strongly in females (Hamlat et al., 2015; Hankin, 2009; Jose & Brown, 2008; Stange et al., 2014). Thus, the combination of rumination, negative cognitive style, and stressors together may better explain the gender difference in depression than rumination by itself.

Conclusion

In this chapter, I reviewed the research on rumination and mood disorders, primarily depression. The literature robustly shows that rumination maintains and exacerbates sad moods and depressive symptoms. The proposed mechanisms of depressive rumination have also received empirical support. Initial results suggesting that negative rumination contributes to bipolar depression, whereas positive rumination contributes to manic symptoms, are fascinating and deserve more attention in the field. Similarly, future research should continue to develop and test models that integrate rumination with other known predictors of depression.

The influence of Susan Nolen-Hoeksema is obvious throughout this entire chapter, as it will be in several subsequent chapters. Her conceptualization, measurement, and manipulation of depressive rumination, as well as the RST, remain seminal and relevant contributions to the rumination field. She tragically had an untimely death in 2013, at the age of 54, while still a preeminent and active scholar in this field that she helped create. She is greatly missed, and her many former graduate students continue to contribute meaningful research to the rumination field.

Because of the size of the literature reviewed in this chapter, as well as the strength of the research and findings, people might assume that rumination is unique to depression. As we will see in future chapters, this is not the case. Depressive rumination predicts several other clinical outcomes. Moreover, depressive rumination is just one type of rumination, with unique mechanisms. In fact, the gender differences that are so apparent in depressive rumination do not always emerge for other types of rumination. In addition, RST applies mainly to depression, not to all of the other outcomes this book covers. Several other important theories of rumination exist. Thus, the literature on depressive rumination is just one part of a much larger rumination field.

References

Abela, J., Brozina, K., & Haigh, E. (2002). An examination of the response styles theory of depression in third- and seventh-grade children: A short-term longitudinal study. *Journal of Abnormal Child Psychology, 30*(5), 515–527. Available from https://doi.org/1019873015594.

Abela, J. R. Z., & Hankin, B. L. (2011). Rumination as a vulnerability factor to depression during the transition from early to middle adolescence. *Journal of Abnormal Psychology, 120*(2), 259–271. Available from https://doi.org/10.1037/a0022796.

Abela, J. R. Z., Parkinson, C., Stolow, D., & Starrs, C. (2009). A test of the integration of the hopelessness and response styles theories of depression in middle adolescence. *Journal of Clinical Child & Adolescent Psychology, 38*(3), 354–364. Available from https://doi.org/10.1080/15374410902851630.

Abela, J. R. Z., Vanderbilt, E., & Rochon, A. (2004). A test of the integration of the response styles and social support theories of depression in third and seventh grade children. *Journal of Social and Clinical Psychology, 23*(5), 653–674. Available from https://doi.org/10.1521/jscp.23.5.653.50752.

Aldao, A., Nolen-Hoeksema, S., & Schweizer, S. (2010). Emotion-regulation strategies across psychopathology: A meta-analytic review. *Clinical Psychology Review, 30*(2), 217–237. Available from https://doi.org/10.1016/j.cpr.2009.11.004.

Alloy, L. B., Whitehouse, W. G., Lapkin, J. B., Abramson, L. Y., Hogan, M. E., Rose, D. T., ... Kim, R. S. (2000). The Temple-Wisconsin cognitive vulnerability to depression project.

Journal of Abnormal Psychology, *109*(3), 403–418. Available from https://doi.org/10.1037/0021-843X.109.3.403.

Arditte, K., & Joormann, J. (2011). Emotion regulation in depression: Reflection predicts recovery from a major depressive episode. *Cognitive Therapy and Research*, *35*(6), 536–543. Available from https://doi.org/10.1007/s10608-011-9389-4.

Barnum, S., Woody, M., & Gibb, B. (2013). Predicting changes in depressive symptoms from pregnancy to postpartum: The role of brooding rumination and negative inferential styles. *Cognitive Therapy and Research*, *37*(1), 71–77. Available from https://doi.org/10.1007/s10608-012-9456-5.

Bastin, M., Mezulis, A., Ahles, J., Raes, F., & Bijttebier, P. (2015). Moderating effects of brooding and co-rumination on the relationship between stress and depressive symptoms in early adolescence: A multi-wave study. *Journal of Abnormal Child Psychology*, *43*(4), 607–618. Available from https://doi.org/10.1007/s10802-014-9912-7.

Beck, A. T. (1967). *Depression: Causes and treatment*. Philadelphia, PA: University of Pennsylvania Press.

Bentall, R. P., Myin-Germeys, I., Smith, A., Knowles, R., Jones, S. H., Smith, T., & Tai, S. J. (2011). Hypomanic personality, stability of self-esteem and response styles to negative mood. *Clinical Psychology & Psychotherapy*, *18*(5), 397–410. Available from https://doi.org/10.1002/cpp.780.

Brennan, K., Barnhofer, T., Crane, C., Duggan, D., & Williams, J. M. G. (2015). Memory specificity and mindfulness jointly moderate the effect of reflective pondering on depressive symptoms in individuals with a history of recurrent depression. *Journal of Abnormal Psychology*, *124*(2), 246–255. Available from https://doi.org/10.1037/abn0000027.

Brockmeyer, T., Holtforth, M. G., Krieger, T., Altenstein, D., Doerig, N., Zimmermann, J., ... Bents, H. (2015). Preliminary evidence for a nexus between rumination, behavioural avoidance, motive satisfaction and depression. *Clinical Psychology & Psychotherapy*, *22*(3), 232–239. Available from https://doi.org/10.1002/cpp.1885.

Burwell, R. A., & Shirk, S. R. (2007). Subtypes of rumination in adolescence: Associations between brooding, reflection, depressive symptoms, and coping. *Journal of Clinical Child & Adolescent Psychology*, *36*(1), 56–65. Available from https://doi.org/10.1080/15374410709336568.

Butler, L. D., & Nolen-Hoeksema, S. (1994). Gender differences in responses to depressed mood in a college sample. *Sex Roles*, *30*(5–6), 331–346. Available from https://doi.org/10.1007/BF01420597.

Calvete, E., Orue, I., & Hankin, B. L. (2015). Cross-lagged associations among ruminative response style, stressors, and depressive symptoms in adolescents. *Journal of Social and Clinical Psychology*, *34*(3), 203–220. Available from https://doi.org/10.1521/jscp.2015.34.3.203.

Carver, C. S., & Scheier, M. F. (1998). *On the self-regulation of behavior* (1. publ. ed.). Cambridge [u.a.]: Cambridge Univ. Press.

Cheung, M. S.-, Gilbert, P., & Irons, C. (2004). An exploration of shame, social rank and rumination in relation to depression. *Personality and Individual Differences*, *36*(5), 1143–1153. Available from https://doi.org/10.1016/S0191-8869(03)00206-X.

Ciesla, J. A., Felton, J. W., & Roberts, J. E. (2011). Testing the cognitive catalyst model of depression: Does rumination amplify the impact of cognitive diatheses in response to stress? *Cognition & Emotion*, *25*(8), 1349–1357. Available from https://doi.org/10.1080/02699931.2010.543330.

Ciesla, J. A., & Roberts, J. E. (2002). Self-directed thought and response to treatment for depression: A preliminary investigation. *Journal of Cognitive Psychotherapy*, *16*(4), 435–453. Available from https://doi.org/10.1891/088983902780935650.

Ciesla, J. A., & Roberts, J. E. (2007). Rumination, negative cognition, and their interactive effects on depressed mood. *Emotion (Washington, D.C.)*, *7*(3), 555–565. Available from https://doi.org/10.1037/1528-3542.7.3.555.

Conway, M., Csank, P. A. R., Holm, S. L., & Blake, C. K. (2000). On assessing individual differences in rumination on sadness. *Journal of Personality Assessment*, *75*(3), 404–425. Available from https://doi.org/10.1207/S15327752JPA7503_04.

Cox, S., Funasaki, K., Smith, L., & Mezulis, A. (2012). A prospective study of brooding and reflection as moderators of the relationship between stress and depressive symptoms in adolescence. *Cognitive Therapy and Research*, *36*(4), 290–299. Available from https://doi.org/10.1007/s10608-011-9373-z.

Cribb, G., Moulds, M. L., & Carter, S. (2006). Rumination and experiential avoidance in depression. *Behaviour Change*, *23*(3), 165–176. Available from https://doi.org/10.1375/bech.23.3.165.

Debeer, E., Hermans, D., & Raes, F. (2009). Associations between components of rumination and autobiographical memory specificity as measured by a minimal instructions autobiographical memory test. *Memory*, *17*(8), 892–903. Available from https://doi.org/10.1080/09658210903376243.

Donaldson, C., & Lam, D. (2004). Rumination, mood and social problem-solving in major depression. *Psychological Medicine*, *34*(7), 1309–1318. Available from https://doi.org/10.1017/S0033291704001904.

Duval, S., & Wicklund, R. A. (1972). *A theory of objective self awareness*. Oxford, England: Academic Press.

D'Zurilla, T. J., & Goldfried, M. R. (1971). Problem solving and behavior modification. *Journal of Abnormal Psychology*, *78*(1), 107–126. Available from https://doi.org/10.1037/h0031360.

Eisma, M. C., Schut, H. A. W., Stroebe, M. S., Boelen, P. A., van den Bout, J., & Stroebe, E. (2015). Adaptive and maladaptive rumination after loss. A three-wave longitudinal study. *British Journal of Clinical Psychology*, *54*(2), 163–180. Available from https://doi.org/10.1111/bjc.12067.

Eisma, M. C., Stroebe, M., Schut, H. A. W., Stroebe, W., Boelen, P. A., & van den Bout, J. (2013). Avoidance processes mediate the relationship between rumination and symptoms of complicated grief and depression following loss. *Journal of Abnormal Psychology*, *122*(4), 961–970. Available from https://doi.org/10.1037/a0034051.

Enggasser, J., & Young, M. (2007). Cognitive vulnerability to depression in seasonal affective disorder: Predicting mood and cognitive symptoms in individuals with seasonal vegetative changes. *Cognitive Therapy and Research*, *31*(1), 3–21. Available from https://doi.org/10.1007/s10608-006-9076-z.

Feldman, G., Joormann, J., & Johnson, S. (2008). Responses to positive affect: A self-report measure of rumination and dampening. *Cognitive Therapy and Research*, *32*(4), 507–525. Available from https://doi.org/10.1007/s10608-006-9083-0.

Flynn, M., Kecmanovic, J., & Alloy, L. B. (2010). An examination of integrated cognitive-interpersonal vulnerability to depression: The role of rumination, perceived social support, and interpersonal stress generation. *Cognitive Therapy and Research*, *34*(5), 456–466. Available from https://doi.org/10.1007/s10608-010-9300-8.

Green, M. J., Lino, B. J., Hwang, E., Sparks, A., James, C., & Mitchell, P. B. (2011). Cognitive regulation of emotion in bipolar I disorder and unaffected biological relatives. *Acta Psychiatrica Scandinavica*, *124*(4), 307–316. Available from https://doi.org/10.1111/j.1600-0447.2011.01718.x.

Griffith, J. W., & Raes, F. (2015). Factor structure of the ruminative responses scale. *European Journal of Psychological Assessment*, *31*(4), 247–253. Available from https://doi.org/10.1027/1015-5759/a000231.

Gruber, J., Eidelman, P., Johnson, S. L., Smith, B., & Harvey, A. G. (2011). Hooked on a feeling: Rumination about positive and negative emotion in inter-episode bipolar disorder. *Journal of Abnormal Psychology, 120*(4), 956–961. Available from https://doi.org/10.1037/a0023667.

Hamilton, J., Stange, J., Shapero, B., Connolly, S., Abramson, L., & Alloy, L. (2013). Cognitive vulnerabilities as predictors of stress generation in early adolescence: Pathway to depressive symptoms. *Journal of Abnormal Child Psychology, 41*(7), 1027–1039. Available from https://doi.org/10.1007/s10802-013-9742-z.

Hamlat, E. J., Connolly, S. L., Hamilton, J. L., Stange, J. P., Abramson, L. Y., & Alloy, L. B. (2015). Rumination and overgeneral autobiographical memory in adolescents: An integration of cognitive vulnerabilities to depression. *Journal of Youth and Adolescence, 44*(4), 806–818. Available from https://doi.org/10.1007/s10964-014-0090-2.

Hankin, B. L. (2009). Development of sex differences in depressive and co-occurring anxious symptoms during adolescence: Descriptive trajectories and potential explanations in a multiwave prospective study. *Journal of Clinical Child & Adolescent Psychology, 38* (4), 460–472. Available from https://doi.org/10.1080/15374410902976288.

Hankin, B. L., & Abramson, L. Y. (2001). Development of gender differences in depression. *Psychological Bulletin, 127*(6), 773–796. Available from https://doi.org/10.1037/0033-2909.127.6.773.

Hankin, B. L., Abramson, L. Y., Moffitt, T. E., Silva, P. A., McGee, R., & Angell, K. E. (1998). Development of depression from preadolescence to young adulthood. *Journal of Abnormal Psychology, 107*(1), 128–140. Available from https://doi.org/10.1037/0021-843X.107.1.128.

Hasegawa, A., Koda, M., Kondo, T., Hattori, Y., & Kawaguchi, J. (2013). Longitudinal predictions of the brooding and reflection subscales of the Japanese ruminative responses scale for depression. *Psychological Reports, 113*(2), 566–585. Available from https://doi.org/10.2466/02.15.PR0.113x24z5.

Hertel, P. T., Maydon, A., Cottle, J., & Vrijsen, J. N. (2017). Cognitive bias modification: Retrieval practice to simulate and oppose ruminative memory biases. *Clinical Psychological Science, 5*(1), 122–130. Available from https://doi.org/10.1177/2167702616649366.

Hong, R. Y. (2007). Worry and rumination: Differential associations with anxious and depressive symptoms and coping behavior. *Behaviour Research and Therapy, 45*(2), 277–290. Available from https://doi.org/10.1016/j.brat.2006.03.006.

Huffziger, S., Ebner-Priemer, U., Koudela, S., Reinhard, I., & Kuehner, C. (2012). Induced rumination in everyday life: Advancing research approaches to study rumination. *Personality and Individual Differences, 53*(6), 790–795. Available from https://doi.org/10.1016/j.paid.2012.06.009.

Hyde, J. S., Mezulis, A. H., & Abramson, L. Y. (2008). The ABCs of depression. *Psychological Review, 115*(2), 291–313. Available from https://doi.org/10.1037/0033-295X.115.2.291.

Ingram, R. E. (1990). Self-focused attention in clinical disorders: Review and a conceptual model. *Psychological Bulletin, 107*(2), 156–176. Available from https://doi.org/10.1037//0033-2909.107.2.156.

Johnson, D. P., & Whisman, M. A. (2013). Gender differences in rumination: A meta-analysis. *Personality and Individual Differences, 55*(4), 367–374. Available from https://doi.org/10.1016/j.paid.2013.03.019.

Johnson, S., McKenzie, G., & McMurrich, S. (2008). Ruminative responses to negative and positive affect among students diagnosed with bipolar disorder and major depressive disorder. *Cognitive Therapy and Research, 32*(5), 702–713. Available from https://doi.org/10.1007/s10608-007-9158-6.

Joiner, T. E., & Metalsky, G. I. (2001). Excessive reassurance seeking: Delineating a risk factor involved in the development of depressive symptoms. *Psychological Science, 12*(5), 371–378. Available from https://doi.org/10.1111/1467-9280.00369.

Jones, S. H., Tai, S., Evershed, K., Knowles, R., & Bentall, R. (2006). Early detection of bipolar disorder: A pilot familial high-risk study of parents with bipolar disorder and their adolescent children. *Bipolar Disorders, 8*(4), 362–372. Available from https://doi.org/10.1111/j.1399-5618.2006.00329.x.

Jose, P., & Brown, I. (2008). When does the gender difference in rumination begin? gender and age differences in the use of rumination by adolescents. *Journal of Youth and Adolescence, 37*(2), 180–192. Available from https://doi.org/10.1007/s10964-006-9166-y.

Just, N., & Alloy, L. B. (1997). The response styles theory of depression. *Journal of Abnormal Psychology, 106*(2), 221–229. Available from https://doi.org/10.1037/0021-843X.106.2.221.

Kercher, A., & Rapee, R. M. (2009). A test of a cognitive diathesis-stress generation pathway in early adolescent depression. *Journal of Abnormal Child Psychology, 37*(6), 845–855. Available from https://doi.org/10.1007/s10802-009-9315-3.

Kim, S., Yu, B. H.; Lee, D. S., & Kim, J. (2011). Ruminative response in clinical patients with major depressive disorder, bipolar disorder, and anxiety disorders. *Journal of Affective Disorders, 136*(1), e81. Available from https://doi.org/10.1016/j.jad.2011.06.034.

Knowles, R., Tai, S., Christensen, I., & Bentall, R. (2005). Coping with depression and vulnerability to mania: A factor analytic study of the Nolen-Hoeksema (1991) response styles questionnaire. *The British Journal of Clinical Psychology, 44*(Pt 1), 99–112. Available from https://doi.org/10.1348/014466504X20062.

Kraaij, V., Garnefski, N., de Wilde, E., Dijkstra, A., Gebhardt, W., Maes, S., & ter Doest, L. (2003). Negative life events and depressive symptoms in late adolescence: Bonding and cognitive coping as vulnerability factors? *Journal of Youth and Adolescence, 32*(3), 185–193. Available from https://doi.org/1022543419747.

Kuehner, C., & Weber, I. (1999). Responses to depression in unipolar depressed patients: An investigation of Nolen-Hoeksema's response styles theory. *Psychological Medicine, 29*(6), 1323–1333. Available from https://doi.org/10.1017/S0033291799001282.

Kühner, C., Huffziger, S., & Nolen-Hoeksema, S. (2007). *Response styles questionnaire—Deutsche version (RSQ-D)*. Göttingen: Hogrefe.

Lam, D., Schuck, N., Smith, N., Farmer, A., & Checkley, S. (2003). Response style, interpersonal difficulties and social functioning in major depressive disorder. *Journal of Affective Disorders, 75*(3), 279–283. Available from https://doi.org/10.1016/S0165-0327(02)00058-7.

Lara, M. E., Klein, D. N., & Kasch, K. L. (2000). Psychosocial predictors of the short-term course and outcome of major depression. *Journal of Abnormal Psychology, 109*(4), 644–650. Available from https://doi.org/10.1037/0021-843X.109.4.644.

Lavender, A., & Watkins, E. (2004). Rumination and future thinking in depression. *British Journal of Clinical Psychology, 43*(2), 129–142. Available from https://doi.org/10.1348/014466504323088015.

Liu, R. T., & Alloy, L. B. (2010). Stress generation in depression: A systematic review of the empirical literature and recommendations for future study. *Clinical Psychology Review, 30*(5), 582–593. Available from https://doi.org/10.1016/j.cpr.2010.04.010.

Lo, C. S. L., Ho, S. M. Y., & Hollon, S. D. (2008). The effects of rumination and negative cognitive styles on depression: A mediation analysis. *Behaviour Research and Therapy, 46*(4), 487–495. Available from https://doi.org/10.1016/j.brat.2008.01.013.

Lyubomirsky, S., Caldwell, N. D., & Nolen-Hoeksema, S. (1998). Effects of ruminative and distracting responses to depressed mood on retrieval of autobiographical memories. *Journal of Personality and Social Psychology, 75*(1), 166–177. Available from https://doi.org/10.1037/0022-3514.75.1.166.

Lyubomirsky, S., Kasri, F., & Zehm, K. (2003). Dysphoric rumination impairs concentration on academic tasks. *Cognitive Therapy and Research, 27*(3), 309–330. Available from https://doi.org/1023918517378.

Lyubomirsky, S., & Nolen-Hoeksema, S. (1993). Self-perpetuating properties of dysphoric rumination. *Journal of Personality and Social Psychology, 65*(2), 339–349. Available from https://doi.org/10.1037/0022-3514.65.2.339.

Lyubomirsky, S., & Nolen-Hoeksema, S. (1995). Effects of self-focused rumination on negative thinking and interpersonal problem solving. *Journal of Personality and Social Psychology, 69*(1), 176–190. Available from https://doi.org/10.1037/0022-3514.69.1.176.

Lyubomirsky, S., Tucker, K. L., Caldwell, N. D., & Berg, K. (1999). Why ruminators are poor problem solvers. *Journal of Personality and Social Psychology, 77*(5), 1041–1060. Available from https://doi.org/10.1037/0022-3514.77.5.1041.

Marroquín, B. M., Fontes, M., Scilletta, A., & Miranda, R. (2010). Ruminative subtypes and coping responses: Active and passive pathways to depressive symptoms. *Cognition & Emotion, 24*(8), 1446–1455. Available from https://doi.org/10.1080/02699930903510212.

McFarland, C., & Buehler, R. (1998). The impact of negative affect on autobiographical memory. *Journal of Personality and Social Psychology, 75*(6), 1424–1440. Available from https://doi.org/10.1037/0022-3514.75.6.1424.

McLaughlin, K. A., & Nolen-Hoeksema, S. (2012). Interpersonal stress generation as a mechanism linking rumination to internalizing symptoms in early adolescents. *Journal of Clinical Child and Adolescent Psychology: The Official Journal for the Society of Clinical Child and Adolescent Psychology, American Psychological Association, Division 53, 41*(5), 584–597. Available from https://doi.org/10.1080/15374416.2012.704840.

Moberly, N. J., & Watkins, E. R. (2008). Ruminative self-focus and negative affect. *Journal of Abnormal Psychology, 117*(2), 314–323. Available from https://doi.org/10.1037/0021-843X.117.2.314.

Mor, N., Hertel, P., Ngo, T. A., Shachar, T., & Redak, S. (2013). Interpretation bias characterizes trait rumination. *Journal of Behavior Therapy and Experimental Psychiatry, 45*(1), 67–73. Available from https://doi.org/10.1016/j.jbtep.2013.08.002.

Morrison, R., & O'Connor, R. C. (2008). A systematic review of the relationship between rumination and suicidality. *Suicide & Life-Threatening Behavior, 38*(5), 523–538. Available from https://doi.org/10.1521/suli.2008.38.5.523.

Morrow, J., & Nolen-Hoeksema, S. (1990). Effects of responses to depression on the remediation of depressive affect. *Journal of Personality and Social Psychology, 58*(3), 519–527. Available from https://doi.org/10.1037/0022-3514.58.3.519.

Moulds, M. L., Kandris, E., Starr, S., & Wong, A. C. M. (2007). The relationship between rumination, avoidance and depression in a non-clinical sample. *Behaviour Research and Therapy, 45*(2), 251–261. Available from https://doi.org/10.1016/j.brat.2006.03.003.

Nicolai, K., Laney, T., & Mezulis, A. (2013). Different stressors, different strategies, different outcomes: How domain-specific stress responses differentially predict depressive symptoms among adolescents. *Journal of Youth and Adolescence, 42*(8), 1183–1193. Available from https://doi.org/10.1007/s10964-012-9866-4.

Nolen-Hoeksema, S. (1987). Sex differences in unipolar depression. *Psychological Bulletin, 101*(2), 259–282. Available from https://doi.org/10.1037/0033-2909.101.2.259.

Nolen-Hoeksema, S. (1991). Responses to depression and their effects on the duration of depressive episodes. *Journal of Abnormal Psychology, 100*(4), 569–582. Available from https://doi.org/10.1037/0021-843X.100.4.569.

Nolen-Hoeksema, S. (2000). The role of rumination in depressive disorders and mixed anxiety/depressive symptoms. *Journal of Abnormal Psychology, 109*(3), 504–511. Available from https://doi.org/10.1037/0021-843X.109.3.504.

Nolen-Hoeksema, S., & Davis, C. G. (1999). "Thanks for sharing that": Ruminators and their social support networks. *Journal of Personality and Social Psychology, 77*(4), 801–814. Available from https://doi.org/10.1037/0022-3514.77.4.801.

Nolen-Hoeksema., & Jackson, B. (2001). Mediators of the gender difference in rumination. *Psychology of Women Quarterly, 25*(1), 37–47. Available from https://doi.org/10.1111/1471-6402.00005.

Nolen-Hoeksema, S., Larson, J., & Grayson, C. (1999). Explaining the gender difference in depressive symptoms. *Journal of Personality and Social Psychology, 77*(5), 1061–1072. Available from https://doi.org/10.1037/0022-3514.77.5.1061.

Nolen-Hoeksema, S., McBride, A., & Larson, J. (1997). Rumination and psychological distress among bereaved partners. *Journal of Personality and Social Psychology, 72*(4), 855–862. Available from https://doi.org/10.1037/0022-3514.72.4.855.

Nolen-Hoeksema, S., & Morrow, J. (1991). A prospective study of depression and posttraumatic stress symptoms after a natural disaster. *Journal of Personality and Social Psychology, 61*(1), 115–121. Available from https://doi.org/10.1037/0022-3514.61.1.115.

Nolen-Hoeksema., & Morrow, J. (1993). Effects of rumination and distraction on naturally occurring depressed mood. *Cognition and Emotion, 7*(6), 561–570. Available from https://doi.org/10.1080/02699939308409206.

Nolen-Hoeksema, S., Morrow, J., & Fredrickson, B. L. (1993). Response styles and the duration of episodes of depressed mood. *Journal of Abnormal Psychology, 102*(1), 20–28. Available from https://doi.org/10.1037/0021-843X.102.1.20.

Nolen-Hoeksema, S., Parker, L. E., & Larson, J. (1994). Ruminative coping with depressed mood following loss. *Journal of Personality and Social Psychology, 67*(1), 92–104. Available from https://doi.org/10.1037/0022-3514.67.1.92.

Nolen-Hoeksema, S., Wisco B. and Lyubomirsky S., Rethinking rumination, Perspectives on Psychological Science 3(5), 400–424. Available from https://ezproxy.tcnj.edu:2083/10.1111/j.1745-6924.2008.00088.x

Oppenheimer, C. W., Technow, J., Hankin, B. L., Young, J. F., & Abela, J. R. Z. (2012). Rumination and excessive reassurance seeking: Investigation of the vulnerability model and specificity to depression. *International Journal of Cognitive Therapy, 5*(3), 254–267. Available from https://doi.org/10.1521/ijct.2012.5.3.254.

Ottenbreit, N. D., Dobson, K. S., & Quigley, L. (2014). An examination of avoidance in major depression in comparison to social anxiety disorder. *Behaviour Research and Therapy, 56*, 82–90. Available from https://doi.org/10.1016/j.brat.2014.03.005.

Padilla Paredes, P., & Calvete Zumalde, E. (2015). A test of the Vulnerability–Stress model with brooding and reflection to explain depressive symptoms in adolescence. *Journal of Youth and Adolescence, 44*(4), 860–869. Available from https://doi.org/10.1007/s10964-014-0148-1.

Papageorgiou, C., & Wells, A. (Eds.). (2004). *Depressive rumination: Nature, theory, and treatment*. John Wiley & Sons: West Sussex, England.

Park, R. J., Goodyer, I. M., & Teasdale, J. D. (2004). Effects of induced rumination and distraction on mood and overgeneral autobiographical memory in adolescent major depressive disorder and controls. *Journal of Child Psychology and Psychiatry, 45*(5), 996–1006. Available from https://doi.org/10.1111/j.1469-7610.2004.t01-1-00291.x.

Pavlickova, H., Turnbull, O. H., Myin-Germeys, I., & Bentall, R. P. (2014). The inter-relationship between mood, self-esteem and response styles in adolescent offspring of bipolar parents: An experience sampling study. *Psychiatry Research, 225*(3), 563–570. Available from https://doi.org/10.1016/j.psychres.2014.11.046.

Pavlickova, H., Varese, F., Smith, A., Myin-Germeys, I., Turnbull, O. H., Emsley, R., & Bentall, R. P. (2013). The dynamics of mood and coping in bipolar disorder: Longitudinal investigations of the inter-relationship between affect, self-esteem and response styles. *PLoS One, 8*(4), e62514. Available from https://doi.org/10.1371/journal.pone.0062514.

Pearson, K. A., Watkins, E. R., & Mullan, E. G. (2010). Submissive interpersonal style mediates the effect of brooding on future depressive symptoms. *Behaviour Research and Therapy, 48*(10), 966–973. Available from https://doi.org/10.1016/j.brat.2010.05.029.

Pearson, K. A., Watkins, E. R., Mullan, E. G., & Moberly, N. J. (2010). Psychosocial correlates of depressive rumination. *Behaviour Research and Therapy, 48*(8), 784–791. Available from https://doi.org/10.1016/j.brat.2010.05.007.

Peled, M., & Moretti, M. M. (2007). Rumination on anger and sadness in adolescence: Fueling of fury and deepening of despair. *Journal of Clinical Child & Adolescent Psychology, 36*(1), 66–75. Available from https://doi.org/10.1080/15374410709336569.

Puterman, E., DeLongis, A., & Pomaki, G. (2010). Protecting us from ourselves: Social support as a buffer of trait and state rumination. *Journal of Social and Clinical Psychology, 29*(7), 797–820. Available from https://doi.org/10.1521/jscp.2010.29.7.797.

Pyszczynski, T., & Greenberg, J. (1987). Self-regulatory perseveration and the depressive self-focusing style. *Psychological Bulletin, 102*(1), 122–138. Available from https://doi.org/10.1037/0033-2909.102.1.122.

Pyszczynski, T., Hamilton, J. C., Herring, F. H., & Greenberg, J. (1989). Depression, self-focused attention, and the negative memory bias. *Journal of Personality and Social Psychology, 57*(2), 351–357. Available from https://doi.org/10.1037//0022-3514.57.2.351.

Raes, F., Hermans, D., Williams, J. M. G., Demyttenaere, K., Sabbe, B., Pieters, G., & Eelen, P. (2005). Reduced specificity of autobiographical memory: A mediator between rumination and ineffective social problem-solving in major depression? *Journal of Affective Disorders, 87*(2), 331–335. Available from https://doi.org/10.1016/j.jad.2005.05.004.

Raes, F., Smets, J., Nelis, S., & Schoofs, H. (2012). Dampening of positive affect prospectively predicts depressive symptoms in non-clinical samples. *Cognition & Emotion, 26*(1), 75–82. Available from https://doi.org/10.1080/02699931.2011.555474.

Roberts, J., Gilboa, E., & Gotlib, I. (1998). Ruminative response style and vulnerability to episodes of dysphoria: Gender, neuroticism, and episode duration. *Cognitive Therapy and Research, 22*(4), 401–423. Available from https://doi.org/1018713313894.

Robinson, M., & Alloy, L. (2003). Negative cognitive styles and stress-reactive rumination interact to predict depression: A prospective study. *Cognitive Therapy and Research, 27*(3), 275–291. Available from https://doi.org/1023914416469.

Rohan, K. J., Sigmon, S. T., & Dorhofer, D. M. (2003). Cognitive-behavioral factors in seasonal affective disorder. *Journal of Consulting and Clinical Psychology, 71*(1), 22–30. Available from https://doi.org/10.1037/0022-006X.71.1.22.

Romero, N., Vazquez, C., & Sanchez, A. (2014). Rumination and specificity of autobiographical memory in dysphoria. *Memory (Hove, England), 22*(6), 646–654. Available from https://doi.org/10.1080/09658211.2013.811254.

Rood, L., Roelofs, J., Bögels, S. M., Nolen-Hoeksema, S., & Schouten, E. (2009). The influence of emotion-focused rumination and distraction on depressive symptoms in non-clinical youth: A meta-analytic review. *Clinical Psychology Review, 29*(7), 607–616. Available from https://doi.org/10.1016/j.cpr.2009.07.001.

Rood, L. R. J., Bögels, S., & Roelofs, J. (2010). Dimensions of negative thinking and the relations with symptoms of depression and anxiety in children and adolescents. *Cognitive Therapy and Research, 34*(4), 333–342. Available from https://doi.org/10.1007/s10608-009-9261-y.

Sarin, S., Abela, J., & Auerbach, R. (2005). The response styles theory of depression: A test of specificity and causal mediation. *Cognition & Emotion, 19*(5), 751–761. Available from https://doi.org/10.1080/02699930441000463.

Shapero, B. G., Hankin, B. L., & Barrocas, A. L. (2013). Stress generation and exposure in a multi-wave study of adolescents: Transactional processes and sex differences. *Journal of Social and Clinical Psychology, 32*(9), 989–1012. Available from https://doi.org/10.1521/jscp.2013.32.9.989.

Shapero, B. G., Stange, J. P., Goldstein, K. E., Black, C. L., Molz, A. R., Hamlat, E. J., ... Alloy, L. B. (2015). Cognitive styles in mood disorders: Discriminative ability of unipolar and bipolar cognitive profiles. *International Journal of Cognitive Therapy*, *8*(1), 35–60. Available from https://doi.org/10.1521/ijct.2015.8.1.35.

Silveira, M., & Kauer-Sant'Anna, M. (2015). Rumination in bipolar disorder: A systematic review. *Revista Brasileira De Psiquiatria (Sao Paulo, Brazil: 1999)*, *37*(3), 256–263. Available from https://doi.org/10.1590/1516-4446-2014-1556.

Simon, N. M., Pollack, M. H., Ostacher, M. J., Zalta, A. K., Chow, C. W., Fischmann, D., ... Otto, M. W. (2006). Understanding the link between anxiety symptoms and suicidal ideation and behaviors in outpatients with bipolar disorder. *Journal of Affective Disorders*, *97*(1), 91–99. Available from https://doi.org/10.1016/j.jad.2006.05.027.

Smith, J. M., Alloy, L. B., & Abramson, L. Y. (2006). Cognitive vulnerability to depression, rumination, hopelessness, and suicidal ideation: Multiple pathways to self-injurious thinking. *Suicide & Life-Threatening Behavior*, *36*(4), 443–454. Available from https://doi.org/10.1521/suli.2006.36.4.443.

Stange, J. P., Hamilton, J. L., Abramson, L. Y., & Alloy, L. B. (2014). A vulnerability-stress examination of response styles theory in adolescence: Stressors, sex differences, and symptom specificity. *Journal of Clinical Child & Adolescent Psychology*, *43*(5), 813–827. Available from https://doi.org/10.1080/15374416.2013.812037.

Stange, J. P., Hamilton, J. L., Burke, T. A., Kleiman, E. M., O'Garro-Moore, J. K., Seligman, N. D., ... Alloy, L. B. (2015). Negative cognitive styles synergistically predict suicidal ideation in bipolar spectrum disorders: A 3-year prospective study. *Psychiatry Research*, *226*(1), 162–168. Available from https://doi.org/10.1016/j.psychres.2014.12.042.

Takano, K., & Tanno, Y. (2009). Self-rumination, self-reflection, and depression: Self-rumination counteracts the adaptive effect of self-reflection. *Behaviour Research and Therapy*, *47*(3), 260–264. Available from https://doi.org/10.1016/j.brat.2008.12.008.

Thomas, K., & Tai, B. (2007). Response styles to depressed mood in bipolar affective disorder. *Journal of Affective Disorders*, *100*(1), 249–252. Available from https://doi.org/10.1016/j.jad.2006.10.017.

Thomsen., Jørgensen., Mehlsen., & Zachariae. (2004). The influence of rumination and defensiveness on negative affect in response to experimental stress. *Scandinavian Journal of Psychology*, *45*(3), 253–258. Available from https://doi.org/10.1111/j.1467-9450.2004.00402.x.

Treynor, W., Gonzalez, R., & Nolen-Hoeksema, S. (2003). Rumination reconsidered: A psychometric analysis. *Cognitive Therapy and Research*, *27*(3), 247–259. Available from https://doi.org/1023910315561.

Verstraeten, K., Vasey, M. W., Raes, F., & Bijttebier, P. (2010). Brooding and reflection as components of rumination in late childhood. *Personality and Individual Differences*, *48*(4), 367–372. Available from https://doi.org/10.1016/j.paid.2009.11.001.

Ward, A., Lyubomirsky, S., Sousa, L., & Nolen-Hoeksema, S. (2003). Can't quite commit: Rumination and uncertainty. *Personality and Social Psychology Bulletin*, *29*(1), 96–107. Available from https://doi.org/10.1177/0146167202238375.

Watkins, E., Moberly, N. J., & Moulds, M. L. (2008). Processing mode causally influences emotional reactivity. *Emotion (Washington, D.C.)*, *8*(3), 364–378. Available from https://doi.org/10.1037/1528-3542.8.3.364.

Watkins, E., & Teasdale, J. D. (2001). Rumination and overgeneral memory in depression. *Journal of Abnormal Psychology*, *110*(2), 353–357. Available from https://doi.org/10.1037/0021-843X.110.2.333.

Watkins., Teasdale., & Williams. (2000). Decentring and distraction reduce overgeneral autobiographical memory in depression. *Psychological Medicine*, *30*(4), 911–920. Available from https://doi.org/10.1017/S0033291799002263.

Weinstock, L., & Whisman, M. (2007). Rumination and excessive reassurance-seeking in depression: A Cognitive–Interpersonal integration. *Cognitive Therapy and Research, 31* (3), 333–342. Available from https://doi.org/10.1007/s10608-006-9004-2.

Weinstock, L. M., Chou, T., Celis-deHoyos, C., Miller, I. W., & Gruber, J. (2018). Reward and punishment sensitivity and emotion regulation processes differentiate bipolar and unipolar depression. *Cognitive Therapy and Research, 42*(6), 794–802. Available from https://doi.org/10.1007/s10608-018-9945-2.

Weir, K. F., & Jose, P. E. (2008). A comparison of the response styles theory and the hopelessness theory of depression in preadolescents. *The Journal of Early Adolescence, 28*(3), 356–374. Available from https://doi.org/10.1177/0272431608314662.

Whitcomb-Smith, S., Sigmon, S., Martinson, A., Young, M., Craner, J., & Boulard, N. (2014). The temporal development of mood, cognitive, and vegetative symptoms in recurrent SAD episodes: A test of the dual vulnerability hypothesis. *Cognitive Therapy and Research, 38*(1), 43–54. Available from https://doi.org/10.1007/s10608-013-9577-5.

Whitmer, A., & Gotlib, I. (2011). Brooding and reflection reconsidered: A factor analytic examination of rumination in currently depressed, formerly depressed, and never depressed individuals. *Cognitive Therapy and Research, 35*(2), 99–107. Available from https://doi.org/10.1007/s10608-011-9361-3.

Williams, J., Van der Does, A., Barnhofer, T., Crane, C., & Segal, Z. (2008). Cognitive reactivity, suicidal ideation and future fluency: Preliminary investigation of a differential activation theory of hopelessness/suicidality. *Cognitive Therapy and Research, 32*(1), 83–104. Available from https://doi.org/10.1007/s10608-006-9105-y.

Williams, J. M. G., Barnhofer, T., Crane, C., Hermans, D., Raes, F., Watkins, E., & Dalgleish, T. (2007). Autobiographical memory specificity and emotional disorder. *Psychological Bulletin, 133*(1), 122–148. Available from https://doi.org/10.1037/0033-2909.133.1.122.

Wolkenstein., Zwick., Hautzinger., & Joormann. (2014). Cognitive emotion regulation in euthymic bipolar disorder. *Journal of Affective Disorders, 160*, 92–97. Available from https://doi.org/10.1016/j.jad.2013.12.022.

Young, M., Reardon, A., & Azam, O. (2008). Rumination and vegetative symptoms: A test of the dual vulnerability model of seasonal depression. *Cognitive Therapy and Research, 32*(4), 567–576. Available from https://doi.org/10.1007/s10608-008-9184-z.

CHAPTER

2

Rumination and anxiety-related disorders

Overview

This chapter explores the literature linking rumination and worry with anxiety-related disorders. Starting with generalized anxiety disorder, I first address similarities and differences between worry and rumination before describing the avoidance theories of worry. The chapter then reviews theory and evidence for the roles of pre- and post-event rumination in social anxiety disorder, as well as trauma-focused rumination in posttraumatic stress disorder. I conclude by describing the nascent literature on rumination in both obsessive–compulsive disorder and illness anxiety disorder.

Given the frequent comorbidity between depression and anxiety disorders, it did not take long for researchers to question whether rumination might have similar effects on anxiety symptoms as it does on depressive symptoms. An early experiment used a procedure nearly identical to Nolen-Hoeksema's classic manipulation (Blagden & Craske, 1996). In it, undergraduates first went through an anxious mood induction and then read either self-focused rumination prompts (e.g., "I am afraid I will fail") or distraction prompts (e.g., "Harley-Davidson is a type of motorcycle") for 10 minutes. Although anxious mood decreased considerably following distraction, it remained stable following rumination, suggesting that rumination maintains preexisting anxiety. Similarly, some studies found that trait-depressive rumination was associated with greater anxious mood, both concurrently and prospectively

Rumination and Related Constructs
DOI: https://doi.org/10.1016/B978-0-12-812545-8.00002-4

© 2020 Elsevier Inc. All rights reserved.

(Nolen-Hoeksema, 2000; Nolen-Hoeksema & Morrow, 1991; Ward, Lyubomirsky, Sousa, & Nolen-Hoeksema, 2003).

Of course, the association between depressive rumination and anxious symptoms could merely reflect the overlap of depressive and anxious symptoms. In fact, some research found that when controlling for depressive symptoms, depressive rumination no longer predicted anxious symptoms (Hong, 2007; but see Nolen-Hoeksema, 2000). In an attempt to differentiate depressive and anxious rumination, some psychologists proposed that anxious rumination focuses on the perceived inability to cope with anxiety and consequences of failing to control anxiety, rather than on perceived causes and consequences of depressed mood (Rector, Antony, Laposa, Kocovski, & Swinson, 2008).

However, rather than being merely an offshoot of depressive rumination, the current field of anxiety-related rumination primarily reflects independent work by scholars of particular anxiety disorders. For instance, around the same time that Nolen-Hoeksema (1991) was developing her theory of depressive rumination, Tom Borkovec proposed a theory of worry and generalized anxiety disorder (GAD) that continues to be very influential in the rumination field (Borkovec, Alcaine, & Behar, 2004). Likewise, Clark and Wells (1995) developed a theory of social anxiety disorder that incorporated pre- and postevent rumination. As we will see in this chapter, the resulting field has yielded several constructs, all of which are related to but unique from depressive rumination (Siegle, Moore, & Thase, 2004). Although the research may seem a bit messy, it is at the same time appropriately complex and enriches our understanding of rumination in general.

Generalized anxiety disorder

People with GAD experience excessive and frequent worry about a range of everyday activities and events. Defined as repetitive and uncontrollable thoughts about perceived negative future life events, worry is characterized by anxious apprehension (Borkovec & Roemer, 1995). Most people know what it is like to occasionally worry about work or school, finances, relationships, health, and many other topics. By contrast, people with GAD worry all the time, even when there is nothing wrong. Because they cannot control their worrying, it tends to interfere with daily functioning. Reflective of gender differences in GAD, women report more worry than do men (Robichaud, Dugas, & Conway, 2003; Zlomke & Hahn, 2010).

Substantial evidence suggests that worry is associated with more negative emotions (for a review, see Newman & Llera, 2011). Self-report measures of trait worry[1] are associated with more state and trait anxiety and depressive symptoms, both concurrently and over time (e.g., Borkovec, Robinson, Pruzinsky, & DePree, 1983; Calmes & Roberts, 2007; Davey, Hampton, Farrell, & Davidson, 1992; Meyer et al., 1990; Segerstrom, Tsao, Alden, & Craske, 2000). Moreover, induced worry in the laboratory increases self-reported negative emotions. In a common experimental procedure, participants are asked to either relax (the control condition) or to worry intensely, in the way that they normally worry, about a topic of concern to them (e.g., Borkovec & Inz, 1990). Induced worry leads to greater negative affect and anxiety, particularly for individuals with GAD (Behar, Zuellig, & Borkovec, 2005; Hofmann et al., 2005; Llera & Newman, 2010; Stapinski, Abbott, & Rapee, 2010).

In addition, because worry itself is an unpleasant event, individuals start to worry about how much they are worrying. This metaworry intensifies both anxiety and worry and also leads to efforts to control worry and avoid situations that trigger worry (Wells, 2005). Moreover, metaworry predicts worse GAD symptoms in both old and young participants, even after controlling for trait anxiety and basic worry (Nuevo, Montorio, & Borkovec, 2004; Wells & Carter, 1999). In the following sections, I address the similarities and differences between worry and depressive rumination, as well as predominant theories about the functions of worry.

Worry and rumination

Researchers have long noticed the similarities between worry and rumination, in that both processes involve repetitive and uncontrollable negative thinking. In fact, worry is characterized by both anxious and depressed affect, leading some researchers to conclude that although worry focuses on uncertain future outcomes, it must also contain some depressive rumination about past events (Andrews & Borkovec, 1988).

1 Several measures assess worry. The 16-item Penn State Worry Questionnaire (Meyer, Miller, Metzger, & Borkovec, 1990) is the most widely-used measure of trait worry. Its items assess the excessiveness and uncontrollability of pathological worry (e.g., "I worry all the time," "My worries overwhelm me"). The 6-item worry subscale of the Thought Control Questionnaire (Wells & Davies, 1994) assesses whether people cope with intrusive, unwanted thoughts by worrying (e.g., "When I experience an unpleasant/unwanted thought, I dwell on other worries"). Other measures assess the content of worry. For instance, the 30-item Worry Domains Questionnaire (Tallis, Eysenck, & Mathews, 1992) assesses five domains of nonpathological worry: relationships, lack of confidence, aimless future, work incompetence, and financial concerns. In addition, the 22-item Anxious Thoughts Inventory (Wells, 1994) assesses worrying about social issues, health, and worry itself.

However, there is disagreement in the literature about just how much worry and depressive rumination overlap.

One way to examine similarities and differences between these constructs is to assess self-reported features of worry and depressive rumination. In these studies, participants rate their typical ruminative and worry-related thoughts on various dimensions, and researchers look for meaningful differences (Hoyer, Gloster, & Herzberg, 2009; Kircanski, Thompson, Sorenson, Sherdell, & Gotlib, 2015; McLaughlin, Borkovec, & Sibrava, 2007; Papageorgiou & Wells, 1999; Watkins, 2004; Watkins, Moulds, & Mackintosh, 2005). Common dimensions include frequency, duration, appraisal (e.g., controllability and how upsetting), nature of the thoughts (e.g., future- vs past-oriented, verbal- vs imagery-based), content of the thoughts (e.g., internal vs external, real vs hypothetical event, causes/meaning vs consequences vs solving), and associated emotions (e.g., sadness and fear). The most consistent difference, in both the clinical and nonclinical samples, is that depressive rumination is past-oriented, whereas worry is future-oriented. Worry is also more strongly associated with feelings of uncertainty and insecurity. One study found that worry was associated with dwelling on potential consequences of anxiety, whereas depressive rumination was associated with dwelling on causes and meanings of sadness (Watkins, 2004). Other than these differences, worry and rumination are both appraised as uncontrollable, automatic, difficult to dismiss, and internally oriented. Conflicting evidence exists about whether worrisome thoughts are more verbal (vs imagery based) than rumination, and whether rumination focuses more on a real problem than does worry. In sum, the few studies that directly compare worry versus rumination find that both the processes are repetitive, intrusive, and self-focused. The apparent differences seem to involve content. Rumination focuses on the past, perhaps in order to understand the causes and meaning of upsetting events. By contrast, worry focuses on the future, perhaps in an effort to anticipate consequences and decrease uncertainty. However, even these distinctions are likely fluid. For example, the content of worry often also includes dwelling on negative aspects of a past situation and thus may become more like rumination (Szabó & Lovibond, 2002). Another study found that rumination begins with a past focus but becomes more future-focused over time (McLaughlin et al., 2007). Thus, worry and rumination may in fact be generative of one another.

Factor analysis is another approach used to examine the overlap of worry and depressive rumination. Again, the results are mixed. Some studies find that depressive rumination and worry load onto separate factors (D'Hudson & Saling, 2010; Fresco, Frankel, Mennin, Turk, & Heimberg, 2002; Goring & Papageorgiou, 2008; Muris, Roelofs, Meesters, & Boomsma, 2004; Rood, Bögels, & Roelofs, 2010; Yang et al., 2014).

However, other studies find evidence for a general factor of negative repetitive thought (NRT). For instance, Segerstrom et al. (2000) showed that repetitive thinking explained the common variance in measures of both depressive rumination and worry. In line with the results summarized in the previous paragraph, these authors argued that although the content and motivation of depressive rumination and worry may differ, the basic thought process is the same. Specifically, they proposed that worry arises from unresolved safety goals, whereas rumination occurs in response to unresolved self-identity and understanding goals.

Researchers have also explored the unique contributions of worry and depressive rumination to relevant outcomes, with mixed findings. In adults and children, many studies show that depressive rumination (specifically brooding) and worry uniquely predict both depressive and anxious symptoms, with comparable effect sizes (Broeren, Muris, Bouwmeester, Heijden, & Abee, 2010; Fresco et al., 2002; Goring & Papageorgiou, 2008; Kircanski et al., 2015; McEvoy & Brans, 2013; Muris, Roelofs, Rassin, Franken, & Mayer, 2005; Rood et al., 2010; Segerstrom et al., 2000; Segerstrom, Stanton, Alden, & Shortridge, 2003; Verstraeten, Bijttebier, Vasey, & Raes, 2011; Watkins, 2004). Other studies, however, have found differences in outcomes (Calmes & Roberts, 2007; Ciesla, Reilly, Dickson, Emanuel, & Updegraff, 2012; D'Hudson & Saling, 2010). For instance, in some nonclinical samples, worry predicted depressive and anxious symptoms more strongly than did rumination (Hong, 2007; Hoyer et al., 2009; Muris et al., 2004; Olatunji, Naragon-Gainey, & Wolitzky-Taylor, 2013). In several clinical samples, by contrast, only worry uniquely predicted a GAD diagnosis and symptoms, whereas depressive rumination uniquely predicted a major depression diagnosis and symptoms (Hendriks et al., 2014; Yang et al., 2014; Yook, Kim, Suh, & Lee, 2010). In an experiment, undergraduate participants worried and ruminated intensely for 5 minutes each, in counterbalanced order (McLaughlin et al., 2007). Because of the within-subjects design, order effects could be examined. Although rumination increased anxiety, subsequent worry increased anxiety even more. Similarly, although worry increased depressed feelings, subsequent rumination increased them even more. Thus, the unique contributions of depressive rumination and worry to particular diagnoses remain unclear, with potential differences between clinical and nonclinical samples.

Ehring and Watkins (2008) argued that any results using common self-report measures of worry and depressive rumination may suffer methodologically due to confounds in the wording of items. For instance, all of the items in the Penn State Worry Questionnaire reference the word "worry." In addition, many of the items in the Ruminative Responses Scale reference depression, and the instructions for the measure direct respondents to answer about moments when they are sad. These methodological issues may explain why items from these measures load on different factors in some studies, and also why each measure is sometimes uniquely associated with its related symptoms.

A few studies attempted to reduce this methodological threat by excluding items from these questionnaires that are confounded by symptoms. One such study found that measures of depressive rumination and worry without symptom-specific items loaded onto a single factor of NRT in undergraduates (McEvoy, Mahoney, & Moulds, 2010). Taking it one step further, Topper, Molenaar, Emmelkamp, and Ehring (2014) found support for a bifactor model, in which measure-specific items loaded onto brooding and worry factors, and all the items also loaded onto a general NRT factor. Importantly, the brooding and worry factors were uncorrelated, suggesting that the NRT factor contained all of their shared variance. Moreover, only the NRT factor predicted increases in anxiety and depressive symptoms about a major exam. Finally, in a clinical sample of patients seeking treatment for mood and anxiety disorders, a bifactor model was again supported, in which the measure-specific items loaded onto brooding, reflective pondering, and worry factors and all the items also loaded onto a general NRT factor (McEvoy & Brans, 2013). This time, however, both NRT and brooding uniquely and strongly predicted anxiety and depressive symptoms (worry was a much weaker predictor). In all of these studies, worry loaded just a little more strongly on the NRT factor than did depressive rumination. Taken together, results suggest that general NRT may explain both anxiety and depressive symptoms in nonclinical populations. However, in clinical patients, brooding (i.e., asking why) may constitute an additional factor that contributes to mood and anxiety symptoms.

In sum, despite the mixed findings reviewed in this section, a fuzzy picture emerges. Specifically, depressive rumination and worry appear to share a common *process* of repetitive, uncontrollable, self-focused, and negative thinking. Worry may be a little more repetitive and depressive rumination a bit more negative, but any difference in process-related components is probably just a matter of degree. By contrast, depressive rumination and worry likely differ in meaningful ways by both *content* and *motivation*. Whereas depressive rumination involves attention to past losses or threats, worry focuses attention on future perceived threats. Relatedly, depressive rumination may reflect a desire to understand the causes of upsetting events and their meaning for one's identity, whereas worry may arise from a desire to identify, prevent, and/or solve perceived threats. Because of the evidence for a common process underlying both depressive rumination and worry, I review relevant literature on worry often throughout this book. As we will see, worry shares many similar outcomes. Moreover, the avoidance theories of worry that I review next have informed substantial research and theorizing about the functions of rumination.

Avoidance theories of worry

In the 1980s and 1990s, Borkovec and colleagues were some of the first researchers to study worry in participants with GAD. They made several interesting discoveries. First, worry was predominantly characterized by verbal/linguistic thought, rather than imagery (Borkovec & Inz, 1990). Second, speech-phobic participants who were induced to worry before imagining giving a speech showed very little cardiovascular reactivity (e.g., increased heart rate) to the task, compared to participants who relaxed before the imaginal task (Borkovec & Hu, 1990; Borkovec, Lyonfields, Wiser, & Deihl, 1993). Together with other findings that verbal articulation of a feared situation leads to less cardiovascular response than does imagery (Vrana, Cuthbert, & Lang, 1986), these results suggested that worry suppresses physiological reactivity to a feared stimulus. Finally, compared to participants without GAD, those with GAD were more likely to endorse that they use worry to distract themselves from more emotional and upsetting topics (Borkovec & Roemer, 1995).

Based on these findings, Borkovec developed the cognitive avoidance model of worry and GAD, which proposes that worry functions as an avoidance response to perceived future threats (Borkovec et al., 2004). This may happen in two ways. First, worry involves thinking of ways to prevent or avoid future feared events and cognitively prepare for the feared events (Borkovec & Roemer, 1995). In addition, the predominantly verbal quality of worry mutes emotional and physiological responses to fear-inducing images. Thus, worry is negatively reinforced because it reduces unpleasant emotional and somatic arousal. This restricted arousal likely prevents emotional processing of feared stimuli. In other words, worry serves the same function for someone with GAD as does avoiding bridges for an individual with a phobia of heights. Unfortunately, because it interferes with the emotional processing that is necessary for successful habituation and extinction, worry and subsequent anxiety are maintained. Later versions of this theory argued that people with GAD worry in order to avoid the experience of negative emotions in general, not just emotional processing of feared stimuli (Roemer, Salters, Raffa, & Orsillo, 2005).

As we will see throughout this book, the cognitive avoidance model of worry has informed theory and research in several areas of the rumination literature. However, some researchers question whether the early experiments actually support the idea that worry enables emotional avoidance. For instance, participants in the worry condition also reported more subjective fear following the imaginal task, which contrasts with the physiological results (Borkovec & Hu, 1990; Borkovec et al., 1993). Moreover, these studies compared arousal following the worry induction to arousal following the imaginal task (Borkovec et al., 1993; e.g., Borkovec & Hu, 1990). Baseline arousal and emotionality before the worry condition were not assessed. Given the findings reviewed above that worry itself increases negative affect, these initial experiments may only suggest that prior worry prevents a further increase in anxiety.

One research team has attempted to tease apart the immediate effects of worry versus the effects following a feared stimulus. In clever experiments, participants with and without GAD engaged in either worry, relaxation, or neutral inductions before watching emotion-inducing film clips (Llera & Newman, 2010, 2014). Self-reported emotion and physiological arousal were assessed at baseline, after the inductions, and after the films. *Immediately after inductions*, participants who worried reported greater increases in negative affect than did participants in the relaxation and neutral conditions. Participants with GAD who worried also had higher physiological activation, compared to relaxation. By contrast, *after the fear- and sadness-inducing films*, participants in the worry condition maintained or even decreased their levels of physiological arousal and negative affect, whereas participants in the relaxation condition became more emotionally and physiologically upset. Interestingly, participants in all three conditions showed similar changes in negative emotion from baseline to postfilm. It is just that people in the worry condition became upset earlier (e.g., after worrying), whereas other participants became upset only after watching the negative films. Taken together, these results support previous findings that worry increases arousal and negative emotion, particularly for people with GAD. They also dispute the theory that worry enables avoidance of negative emotions. Instead, worry appears to heighten negative emotionality such that no additional increases in negative emotionality occur in response to a fear stimulus.

These new results and reinterpretations of previous studies led to the contrast avoidance model of GAD (Newman & Llera, 2011), which asserts that worry increases negative emotionality in order to prevent sudden bursts of negative emotion should a distressing event occur (see Fig. 2.1). This model is based on the idea that a scary stimulus (e.g., seeing a mouse scurry across the kitchen floor) is perceived more negatively if it interrupts a positive emotional state. By contrast, that same scary stimulus may seem almost pleasant if someone is already feeling terrified (e.g., if the individual expects to see a dozen mice). The contrast avoidance model proposes, and empirical evidence confirms,

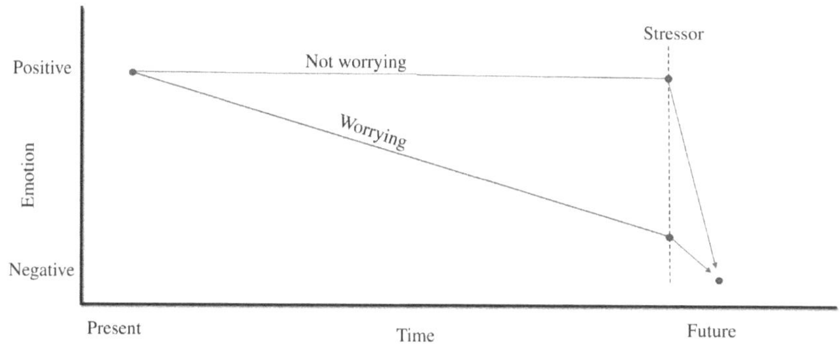

FIGURE 2.1 Graphical representation of the contrast avoidance theory of worry. Source: *Credit: Samuel Bucek. Reprinted by permission.*

that people with GAD find negative emotional contrasts (i.e., sudden shifts from positive to negative emotion) more upsetting than do nonanxious individuals (Llera & Newman, 2017). Because it increases negative emotion, worry in essence functions to prevent such a sharp emotional contrast. In other words, people with GAD use worry to create a chronically negative emotional state as a protective defense against future potential negative contrasts. It is as if they are emotionally bracing themselves for the worst possible outcome. Furthermore, worry may facilitate positive emotional contrasts, in which people feel a great sense of relief (e.g., decrease in negative emotion) if anticipated negative events do not occur. Both of these situations (preventing negative contrast and facilitating positive contrasts) lead to worry being reinforced. In fact, people with GAD reported that worry was more helpful than relaxation or neutral inductions in coping with emotional film clips (Llera & Newman, 2014).

This new model argues against the idea that worry enables the avoidance of negative emotions. However, the model does not contradict Borkovec's original contention that worry prevents emotional processing of feared events. According to behavioral theory (Foa & Kozak, 1986), emotional processing occurs when people experience the surge in anxious emotion and arousal following exposure to a feared stimulus. In preventing that emotional surge, worry also prevents habituation to the fears that are driving the worry and anxiety in the first place. In fact, Newman and Llera (2011) argue that although people with GAD do not avoid *experiencing* negative emotions, they do avoid *processing* negative emotions. Thus, even this revised model of worry suggests that worry functions primarily as a form of avoidance.

Social anxiety disorder

Social anxiety disorder is characterized by persistent fear of one or more social or performance situations in which someone is exposed to possible scrutiny and/or unfamiliar people. People with social anxiety fear that they will behave in ways that will be embarrassing, leading to criticism and social rejection. In a comprehensive cognitive model of social anxiety, Clark and Wells (1995) proposed that rumination both before *and* after feared social situations contributes to the maintenance of social anxiety. *Pre-event rumination,* also called *anticipatory processing,* involves thinking about a future social encounter. This likely involves thinking about past failures, imagining failure in the upcoming situation, and anticipating subsequent negative evaluation and social rejection. This kind of thinking increases anxiety before and during the encounter. Following the social event, individuals may engage in *post-event rumination,* often called *post-event processing,* especially if they did not receive unambiguous signs of social approval. This detailed review of the event is likely to be dominated by negative feelings and self-perceptions experienced during the event itself, contributing to the situation being remembered more negatively than it actually was. Post-event rumination also likely prompts memories of other past social failures, which may in turn maintain negative affect and negative self-perceptions.

Post-event rumination

A large literature has explored the nature and consequences of post-event rumination.[2] Many people, even those without social anxiety, engage in post-event rumination following distressing social situations (Fehm, Schneider, & Hoyer, 2007; Kocovski & Rector, 2007). However, people with social anxiety consistently report engaging in more post-event rumination than do people without social anxiety (for reviews,

2 The most commonly used questionnaire assessing this construct is the Post-Event Processing Questionnaire (Rachman et al., 2000). This 13-item measure assesses how much and how often people engage in post-event rumination following an anxiety-provoking social event (e.g., "Did your memories and thoughts about the event keep coming into your head even when you did not wish to think about it again?"). Other researchers have made tweaks to the items (McEvoy & Kingsep, 2006) or deleted some items (Kocovski & Rector, 2007). Another measure is the 24-item Thoughts Questionnaire (Abbott & Rapee, 2004), which assesses the frequency of negative and positive post-event thoughts during the week following a social interaction or performance. The measure includes 15 negative rumination items (e.g., "I looked stupid") and 9 positive rumination items (e.g., "My speech was good") and yields two separate subscales.

see Brozovich & Heimberg, 2008; Hofmann, 2007; Norton & Abbott, 2016; Penney & Abbott, 2014). Post-event rumination in socially anxious individuals often focuses on wanting to "turn back the clock," pondering how a situation may have gone better (called upward counterfactual, or "if only," thoughts) and wishing to avoid similar situations in the future (Kocovski, Endler, Rector, & Flett, 2005; Rachman et al., 2000). Socially anxious people also report that these kind of ruminative thoughts are intrusive and impair their ability to concentrate.

Laboratory studies have created mock social situations in order to elicit post-event rumination. For instance, participants were asked to give a 3-minute impromptu speech about a topic of their choice (Abbott & Rapee, 2004; Edwards, Rapee, & Franklin, 2003; Perini, Abbott, & Rapee, 2006; Rapee & Abbott, 2007). One week later, they reported how much they ruminated about the speech over the past week. In both clinical and nonclinical samples, participants higher in social anxiety reported more *negative* post-event rumination in the week following the speech. The same results were found when participants had to engage in 5–10 minutes conversations with a confederate, rather than give a speech (Dannahy & Stopa, 2007; Mellings & Alden, 2000). Interestingly, in all of these studies, socially anxious participants reported the same amount of *positive* post-event ruminative thoughts (e.g., "My speech was good") as did nonanxious participants. Thus, social anxiety appears to be characterized by an excessive amount of negative post-event processing.

Post-event rumination is, in turn, associated with more negative thoughts and feelings. Following a conversation with a stranger, post-event rumination was associated with more recall of negative self-related information in both socially anxious and nonanxious participants (Mellings & Alden, 2000). Post-event rumination also predicted remembering a speech more negatively 1 week later (Rapee & Abbott, 2007). In an experiment, participants gave an impromptu 3-minute speech and then went through a self-focused rumination or distraction manipulation (Wong & Moulds, 2009). Distraction led to decreased anxiety, whereas post-event rumination maintained anxiety in participants both high and low in social anxiety. In addition, in socially anxious participants only, induced rumination maintained negative beliefs about the self, whereas distraction decreased these beliefs. Similarly, socially anxious participants who ruminated about a hypothetical social event (e.g., first day on a new job) recalled autobiographical memories characterized by anxiety more than anxious participants who reflected or nonanxious individuals (Morgan & Banerjee, 2008).

Some researchers have explored moderators of these associations. For instance, a daily diary study found that social anxiety symptoms were associated with greater post-event rumination only following distressing social events that involved negative evaluation (Lundh & Sperling, 2002). In an interesting experiment, participants interacted with a participant of the opposite gender in a structured 45-minute conversation (Kashdan & Roberts, 2007). Some pairs asked each other increasingly personal questions (e.g., "What is your most treasured memory?") in order to encourage intimate personal disclosure. Other pairs asked general and nonpersonal questions, such as "If you could invent a new flavor of ice cream, what would it be?," in order to simulate small talk. The next day, participants reported on their negative affect and negative post-event rumination since the conversation. First, the general association between social anxiety and post-event rumination was only significant for participants high in depressive symptoms. Moreover, in individuals high in social anxiety who shared personal information, post-event rumination predicted increases in negative affect. By contrast, for anxious participants who engaged in small talk, rumination was associated with decreases in negative affect. The authors suggested that personal disclosure is especially threatening for people with social anxiety, because it opens the door for evaluation of intimate information. By contrast, rumination about unimportant interactions may have made people feel better. In sum, it appears that depressed mood and social contexts characterized by negative evaluation strengthen the associations between social anxiety, post-event rumination, and negative mood.

Pre-event rumination

There is less research on the role of pre-event, or anticipatory, rumination in social anxiety. However, the research that does exist supports the hypothesized importance of this construct.[3] Correlational studies find that socially anxious individuals engage in more pre-event rumination before social or performance situations than do nonanxious individuals (Hinrichsen & Clark, 2003; Laposa & Rector, 2016; Penney & Abbott, 2015; Vassilopoulos, 2004, 2008). Specifically, socially anxious individuals ruminate about past social failures, catastrophize about what might happen, rehearse what they will say, harp on negative

3 Trait anticipatory rumination can be assessed using the Anticipatory Social Behaviors Questionnaire (Hinrichsen & Clark, 2003). This 12-item questionnaire includes items that load onto avoidance (e.g., "I think about ways in which I could avoid having to face the situation") and preparation (e.g., "I go over in detail what might happen") factors. Researchers have also adapted the Post-Event Processing Questionnaire and Thoughts Questionnaire to assess rumination about an anticipated—rather than past—social situation (Laposa & Rector, 2016; Penney & Abbott, 2015).

distorted self-images from an observer perspective, plan how they will hide their anxiety, and ponder ways to escape or avoid the social encounter (Hinrichsen & Clark, 2003; Vassilopoulos, 2004, 2008). In addition, socially anxious people engage in more stagnant deliberation or repetitive dwelling on a stressful problem without coming up with anything productive (Vassilopoulos, 2008). Pre-event ruminative thoughts are perceived as intrusive and repetitive (Vassilopoulos, 2004).

Experimental research borrows methodology from the depression literature to manipulate pre-event rumination. For example, participants are generally told that they will engage in some kind of social interaction, like giving a speech or interacting with a researcher who will evaluate their social skills (Hinrichsen & Clark, 2003; Mills, Grant, Judah, & White, 2014; Vassilopoulos, 2005; Wong & Moulds, 2011). They are then asked to think about specific prompts in preparation for the interaction. Participants in the pre-event rumination condition think about things such as "your feelings about the speech," "how you are going to appear during the upcoming social situation," and "the worst thing that could happen." Participants in the distraction condition think about neutral and unrelated prompts (e.g., a boat slowly crossing the Atlantic) or engage in unrelated tasks (e.g., watching a film about insects). Irrespective of self-reported social anxiety symptoms, participants in the pre-event rumination condition exhibited increased self-reported and objectively measured anxious arousal, compared to the distraction condition. Pre-event rumination also predicted expectations of a worse performance, again regardless of level of social anxiety (Mills, Grant, Judah, & Lechner, 2014; Vassilopoulos, 2005). Socially anxious participants reported more negative self-images following pre-event rumination, compared to nonanxious participants (Brown & Stopa, 2006). Pre-event rumination was also indirectly associated with poorer speech performance via increased anxiety (but see Brown & Stopa, 2006; Wong & Moulds, 2011).

Some longitudinal research examined the associations between pre-event rumination, social anxiety, and post-event processing. One study found that pre-event rumination did not predict social anxiety symptoms 5 weeks later, but instead that social anxiety symptoms predicted future pre-event rumination (Mills, Grant, Lechner, & Judah, 2014). Furthermore, pre-event rumination was associated with more post-event rumination the week following a social encounter, which, in turn, predicted greater pre-event rumination before another encounter several weeks later (Laposa & Rector, 2016). Thus, pre-event rumination likely serves as a maintenance factor in social anxiety by increasing anxious arousal and post-event rumination following a feared social event, which, in turn, triggers negative thoughts and pre-event rumination before another event.

Summary

Unlike in the depression field, in which rumination generally only maintains or exacerbates depressed mood in participants who start out sad or depressed, the specificity of pre- and post-event rumination in social anxiety is less clear. Pre- and post-event rumination predict increased anxiety before and after stressful social experiences for most people, regardless of levels of social anxiety. However, socially anxious individuals engage in more pre- and post-event rumination than do nonanxious individuals. Moreover, in socially anxious individuals, post-event rumination is more negative and intrusive, and both types of rumination are more likely to elicit negative self-images and autobiographical memories. Thus, although repetitive thinking about feared social situations can make anyone more anxious, rumination in people with social anxiety disorder likely reinforces the negative beliefs that characterize social anxiety.

Posttraumatic stress disorder

PTSD involves four clusters of symptoms (e.g., reexperiencing, avoidance, heightened physiological arousal, and negative changes in thoughts and mood) that result from exposure to a traumatic event. Because not everyone who experiences trauma develops PTSD, researchers study factors that make people more vulnerable to the disorder. Several theories propose that various cognitive vulnerabilities become activated by traumatic events and influence how people understand, remember, and cope with these events (for a review, see Elwood, Hahn, Olatunji, & Williams, 2009). Of relevance, Anke Ehlers proposed that rumination specifically about trauma and reactions to trauma maintains PTSD symptoms (Ehlers & Clark, 2000; Ehlers & Steil, 1995).

Trauma-related rumination involves thinking about the causes and consequences of the trauma, why it happened, how it could have been prevented, and how justice may be achieved. The focus on counterfactuals (i.e., "what if" statements) occurs at the expense of focusing on the specific details of the trauma itself. As such, trauma-related rumination is conceptualized as a cognitive avoidance strategy, much like worry, in that individuals ruminate in an attempt to avoid processing specific traumatic memories or emotions. However, because it provides internal retrieval cues for trauma memories, trauma-related rumination may ironically lead to more intrusive memories and subsequent arousal and anxiety (Michael, Ehlers, Halligan, & Clark, 2005). In addition, rumination may maintain negative and distorted thoughts about the self and world, leading to secondary emotions such as sadness, shame, and guilt. Given the known links between rumination and anger (see Chapter 3: Rumination, anger, and aggression), trauma-related rumination may also in part explain why anger and aggression are so common in people with PTSD.

It might seem as if rumination is one type of reexperiencing symptom. However, Ehlers argued that *remembering* (i.e., reexperiencing) a traumatic event is different from *thinking* (i.e., ruminating) about it (Ehlers & Clark, 2000). Specifically, intrusive reexperiencing is a nonconscious process and likely reflects incomplete ways that the trauma memory was encoded. By contrast, trauma-related rumination is a conscious, cognitive attempt to control the perceived threat and posttraumatic symptoms. Some studies have used structured interviews to assess the phenomenology of rumination versus intrusive memories. In patients with diagnosed PTSD, intrusive memories tended to be brief sensory experiences, whereas rumination was primarily described as a verbal thought process that can last for hours (Speckens, Ehlers, Hackmann, Ruths, & Clark, 2007). Similarly, in male prisoners who were asked about a violent offense they committed, rumination was described as a chain of thoughts of changing content, as opposed to sensory intrusive memories that did not change much over time (Evans, Ehlers, Mezey, & Clark, 2007). These structured interviews also helped identify qualities of rumination that appear to be most maladaptive. For instance, rumination characterized by "what if" and "why" thinking predicted more severe posttraumatic stress symptoms (Michael, Halligan, Clark, & Ehlers, 2007). In addition, rumination that participants felt was more distressing, less productive, and more compulsive predicted worse symptoms (Evans et al., 2007; Michael et al., 2007).

Empirical studies testing the role of rumination in the maintenance of PTSD fall into two broad categories (Ehring, Kleim, & Ehlers, 2011; Elwood et al., 2009). Correlational studies allow for associations between rumination and PTSD to be explored across survivors of many kinds of trauma, ideally using longitudinal designs that allow for the prediction of future PTSD symptoms controlling for initial symptoms.[4] However, in addition to being unable to show causality, research with

4 Trauma-related rumination is most commonly measured using the Response to Intrusion Questionnaire (Clohessy & Ehlers, 1999; Ehring, Ehlers, & Glucksman, 2006). This measure assesses different types of responses to trauma and PTSD symptoms. The 8-item rumination subscale includes items such as "I think about why the event happened to me," "I think about how life would have been different if the event had not occurred," and "I think about what I could have done differently." The majority of correlational studies discussed here used this rumination subscale. Alternatively, some studies measure rumination with the intrusions subscale of the Impact of Events Scale—Revised (Weiss & Marmar, 1997). However, this measure assesses the symptom clusters of PTSD (the other subscales are avoidance and hyperarousal). As such, these studies operationalize trauma-related rumination as identical to the intrusive symptoms of PTSD. This runs counter to the research I described illustrating the differences between trauma-related rumination and the reexperiencing symptoms of PTSD. As such, I do not recommend this practice, and none of the studies I review use this measure for rumination.

trauma survivors relies on retrospective reports, which may be biased by current symptoms. By contrast, analog experimental studies with nontraumatized healthy populations expose participants to a distressing film or images depicting violence. Researchers then experimentally manipulate rumination before or after the stressor and examine resulting outcomes. Of course, whether reactions to these analog stressors are comparable to those of actual traumas is questionable. Information learned from these two types of research designs combine to create a fuller understanding of the role of rumination in PTSD.

Correlational studies clearly indicate that trauma-related rumination is associated with worse symptoms and greater likelihood of a PTSD diagnosis. This association has been found cross-sectionally in war veterans, people with cancer or HIV, emergency medical responders, bereaved individuals, women who recently had a stillbirth, and survivors of assault, natural disasters, and motor vehicle accidents (Blackburn & Owens, 2016; Borders, Rothman, & McAndrew, 2015; Chan, Ho, Tedeschi, & Leung, 2011; Clohessy & Ehlers, 1999; Ehring et al., 2006; Horsch, Jacobs, & McKenzie-McHarg, 2015; Michael et al., 2007; Nightingale, Sher, & Hansen, 2010; Normann, van Emmerik, & Morina, 2014; Taku, Calhoun, Cann, & Tedeschi, 2008; Turliuc, Măirean, & Turliuc, 2015; Zhou, Wu, Fu, & An, 2015). In an interesting twist, rumination was also related to PTSD severity in male offenders of serious violence (Evans et al., 2007). Longitudinal studies also indicate that trauma-related rumination predicts PTSD symptoms anywhere from 3 months to 3 years later in survivors of cancer, assault, natural disasters, and motor vehicle accidents (Ehlers, Mayou, & Bryant, 1998; Ehring, Ehlers, & Glucksman, 2008; Kleim, Ehlers, & Glucksman, 2007; Mayou, Ehlers, & Bryant, 2002; Salsman, Segerstrom, Brechting, Carlson, & Andrykowski, 2009; Zhou & Wu, 2015). Although most studies examine adults only, similar effects have been found with child survivors of accidents and assault (Ehlers, Mayou, & Bryant, 2003; Meiser-Stedman et al., 2014). A recent metaanalysis showed that the effect of rumination on PTSD symptoms is not moderated by type of trauma (Seligowski, Lee, Bardeen, & Orcutt, 2015).

One group of researchers has proposed that trauma-related rumination is not a unidimensional construct (Calhoun, Cann, Tedeschi, & McMillan, 2000; Taku, Cann, Tedeschi, & Calhoun, 2009). Instead, just like how depressive rumination can be separated into brooding and reflective pondering, trauma-related rumination can take two forms. Specifically, *intrusive* rumination involves uncontrolled and unwanted repetitive thoughts about the traumatic event, whereas *deliberate* rumination involves controlled and reflective repetitive thoughts focused on making sense of the event. Tedeschi and Calhoun (2004) further proposed that intrusive rumination following a trauma eventually transforms into deliberate rumination, with different outcomes. Initially, intrusive rumination about the trauma contributes to PTSD symptoms. Over time, however, people begin to intentionally spend time reflecting about changes that occurred because of the trauma, what they have learned, and how their life may be different going forward. This deliberate rumination contributes to posttraumatic growth, or positive changes that result from struggling with major life crises or traumatic events.

A small literature examines the effects of intrusive versus deliberate rumination.[5] In both cross-sectional and longitudinal studies, intrusive—but not deliberate—rumination uniquely predicted worse PTSD symptoms in students who had recently experienced a highly stressful or traumatic event, war veterans, leukemia patients undergoing chemotherapy, and child survivors of an earthquake (Blackburn & Owens, 2016; Cann et al., 2011; Danhauer et al., 2013; Taku et al., 2008; Triplett, Tedeschi, Cann, Calhoun, & Reeve, 2012; Wu, Zhou, Wu, & An, 2015; Zhou et al., 2015). Intrusive rumination soon after the trauma predicted recent intrusive rumination, suggesting that intrusive rumination starts soon after a trauma and continues, leading to PTSD symptoms. By contrast, deliberate rumination uniquely predicted posttraumatic growth (see also Allbaugh, Wright, & Folger, 2016; Cann, Calhoun, Tedeschi, & Solomon, 2010; Garcia, Cova, Rincon, Vazquez, & Paez, 2016; Groleau, Calhoun, Cann, & Tedeschi, 2013; Lindstrom, Cann, Calhoun, & Tedeschi, 2013). Furthermore, intrusive rumination robustly predicts increased deliberate rumination. In the only longitudinal study examining this association, adolescent survivors of an earthquake in China were assessed 6, 12, and 18 months after the earthquake (Zhou & Wu, 2015). Intrusive rumination at 6 months predicted intrusive rumination at 12 months, which predicted deliberate rumination at 12 months, which predicted posttraumatic growth at 18 months. Thus, evidence supports the hypothesis that intrusive rumination not only contributes to PTSD symptoms but also predicts greater deliberate rumination, which in turn contributes to personal growth following trauma.

Some studies examine whether *preexisting* rumination tendencies predict the onset of PTSD. Following the bombings at the Boston Marathon in 2013, a team of researchers realized that they had recently collected measures of trait rumination from a sample of adolescents living in the

5 The Event-Related Rumination Inventory (ERRI) assesses these two types of trauma-related rumination (Cann et al., 2011). With 10 items on each subscale, deliberate rumination correlates with reflection, whereas intrusive rumination correlates with negative rumination. The ERRI was based on the Rumination Inventory (Calhoun et al., 2000), a 7-item measure that assesses various aspects of intrusive and deliberate rumination. Although some researchers use this measure, the ERRI is preferable because of more rigorous psychometric testing.

Boston area. Within 2–4 weeks following the bombing, the researchers asked these same adolescents to complete measures of PTSD symptoms specifically related to the bombing (Jenness et al., 2016). Preexisting general rumination tendencies predicted worse PTSD symptoms after the bombing, even controlling for pretrauma internalizing symptoms. In another impressive study, researchers assessed almost 3000 participants initially and then 4 years later (Spinhoven, Penninx, Krempeniou, van Hemert, & Elzinga, 2015). Over that 4-year period, approximately 350 participants reported experiencing a trauma, of whom 14% had developed PTSD. In these 350 participants who experienced a trauma, trait rumination measured at baseline predicted the onset of a PTSD diagnosis 4 years later, controlling for demographic variables and psychiatric diagnoses at baseline. The effect of trait rumination was mediated in part by the cognitive appraisal that the traumatic event had a large impact on their lives.

Researchers are also starting to examine whether rumination is related to particular PTSD symptoms, given evidence that PTSD is best understood as a set of related but distinct symptoms clusters (Miller et al., 2010). Most research has focused on the reexperiencing cluster, and specifically intrusive memories. Trauma survivors report that rumination triggers intrusive memories and flashbacks (Birrer & Michael, 2011; Birrer, Michael, & Munsch, 2007; Evans et al., 2007; Michael et al., 2007). One week after watching a distressing film, rumination specifically about the film predicted more intrusive memories during the week and greater distress about the intrusions (Kubota, Nixon, & Chen, 2015; Laposa & Rector, 2012). Trauma-related rumination is associated with not only the frequency of intrusive memories but also with their vividness and perceptions that they are harmful (Clohessy & Ehlers, 1999; Ehlers et al., 1998; Schönfeld & Ehlers, 2006).

Experimental studies also examine the effect of induced rumination on intrusive memories, with mixed results. In two studies, after watching a distressing video of real-life footage from car crashes (e.g., injured people, dead bodies, and emergency personnel), participants in the rumination condition spent several minutes thinking about "why" and "what-if" prompts (e.g., "Why do people have to drive that recklessly?," "Would I ever be able to be the same person as before?,") (Ehring, Szeimies, & Schaffrick, 2009; Zetsche, Ehring, & Ehlers, 2009). Participants in the distraction condition were given unrelated recall tasks. In one of these studies, there was no effect of manipulated rumination on intrusive memories (Ehring, Szeimies, et al., 2009). In the other study, men—but not women—in the rumination condition reported more intrusive memories of the video than did men in the distraction condition (Zetsche et al., 2009). However, for both men and women and across all conditions, greater self-reported state rumination following the video predicted more intrusive memories. Another study selected participants with high rumination tendencies and had some of them ruminate about the distressing video for 5 minutes immediately following the video and then everyday for the next week (Ball & Brewin, 2012). Participants who ruminated reported more intrusive memories over the week. Similarly, participants provided a detailed narrative of a past negative event in their lives and then ruminated about the event (or distracted themselves) for 10 minutes (Ehring, Szeimies, et al., 2009). Induced rumination led to more frequent and distressing intrusive memories than did distraction. Thus, induced rumination may be most likely to lead to intrusive memories when it is about something that actually happened to them and for people who have preexisting rumination tendencies.

Finally, both longitudinal and experimental studies have examined the effect of trauma-related rumination on the cluster of PTSD symptoms that includes impaired memory and negative mood. Trauma-related rumination is associated with less specificity in the retrieval of autobiographical memories, a construct that is associated with the maintenance of both PTSD and depressive symptoms in trauma survivors (Kleim & Ehlers, 2008; Schönfeld & Ehlers, 2006). Moreover, induced rumination following a distressing video led to less recovery from negative affect, compared to distraction (Ehring, Fuchs, & Kläsener, 2009; Ehring, Szeimies, & Schaffrick, 2009; Zetsche et al., 2009). Induced rumination about real-world negative events (e.g., relationship breakup and death of a loved one) also maintained negative mood compared to distraction. When analyzing specific negative moods, the effects of induced rumination appeared for sad but not fearful moods. In a longitudinal study, trauma-related rumination predicted greater state anger 2 months later in assault survivors (Orth, Cahill, Foa, & Maercker, 2008). Thus, trauma-related rumination may generate increased sad and angry moods.

In sum, trauma-focused rumination predicts greater PTSD symptoms, particularly intrusive memories and negative moods, following a range of traumas. In addition to rumination following a trauma, preexisting tendencies for rumination also predict worse symptoms. Some evidence suggest that intrusive rumination about traumas, characterized by "what if" and "why" thinking, may over time predict greater deliberate rumination, which involves controlled and reflective efforts to make sense of the event and is associated with posttraumatic growth.

Obsessive–compulsive disorder

Obsessive–compulsive disorder (OCD) is marked by the presence of obsessions, compulsions, or both. Obsessions are defined as intrusive and unwanted thoughts, urges, or images that trigger intense anxiety and distress. Compulsions are repetitive behaviors (e.g., hand washing and checking) or mental acts (e.g., praying and counting) performed in an effort to prevent or reduce obsessions. The literature on rumination and OCD is in its infancy.

Only a few studies have examined the associations between rumination, worry, and OCD symptoms. In two samples of high school and college students, depressive rumination was associated with more severe OCD symptoms, even controlling for depressive symptoms (Wahl, Ertle, Bohne, Zurowski, & Kordon, 2011). When analyzing the measure by its subscales, brooding but not reflective pondering correlated with worse OCD symptoms after controlling for internalizing symptoms (Grisham & Williams, 2009). In a clinical sample of patients with OCD, depressive rumination and worry both correlated with OCD symptom severity, although the effect of worry was stronger (Dar & Iqbal, 2015). Similarly, patients with diagnosed OCD and GAD reported higher levels of worry and general rumination than nonclinical controls (Armstrong, Zald, & Olatunji, 2011).

Perhaps a more important question is whether rumination, worry, and obsessions constitute unique constructs. Like rumination, obsessions involve repetitive thoughts that are perceived to be out of one's control. In fact, in the 1970s and 1980s, researchers often called obsessions "obsessional rumination" (e.g., Rachman, 1971). Moreover, one of the most commonly used measures of obsessive–compulsive symptoms, the Padua Inventory—Revised (Van Oppen, Hoekstra, & Emmelkamp, 1995), has a subscale called rumination. Perhaps not surprisingly, the rumination subscale overlaps considerably with worry (Gönner, Ecker, & Leonhart, 2010), raising the question of whether and how obsessions differ from worry.

de Silva (2003) proposed that rumination in the context of OCD should refer to covert, or internal, compulsive behavior, usually triggered by an obsession. Specifically, obsessional rumination is the compulsive urge to think through, in a prolonged and effortful manner, some issues raised by an obsession. For instance, someone with OCD might have intrusive thoughts and images (i.e., obsessions) about her family dying; she might then ruminate about those thoughts for hours at a time. A case described in the literature is of a young man who had frequent obsessions about whether he was genetically flawed (De Silva & Rachman, 1992). "When this intrusion came, he would start his ruminative thinking, carefully but unproductively trying to think the matter through. This would include thoughts about his parents, grandparents and other relatives, the evidence for their sanity or otherwise, ideas about the heredity of mental illness, what kinds of tests could be done to find the answer to these questions, and so on. The thinking was quite time consuming and rather muddled. It never yielded any solution" (p. 36–37). These descriptions clearly differentiate obsessions and rumination, in a similar way as PTSD researchers distinguish between intrusive memories and rumination. In fact, some researchers created a revision of the Padua Inventory that included a rumination subscale assessing rumination as defined by de Silva (Gönner et al., 2010). In patients with OCD and anxious and depressed controls, this rumination subscale was associated with all OCD symptoms, but especially obsessions. Unfortunately, this particular revision has not been widely used by other researchers.

Researchers have also proposed that obsessions and worry differ in meaningful ways (Burns, Keortge, Formea, & Sternberger, 1996; Purdon & Clark, 1999). Specifically, obsessions are perceived as ego-dystonic, or contrary to one's belief system (e.g., harming others), whereas worry is usually about everyday, real-life concerns (e.g., finances, relationships, and work) and is therefore more ego-syntonic and acceptable. Worry is also proposed to occur as verbal thought, whereas obsessions can occur as thoughts, images, or impulses. Research with nonclinical samples in fact found that worries are more verbal (vs image based), ego-syntonic, and based in reality than are obsessions (Langlois, Freeston, & Ladouceur, 2000; Wells & Morrison, 1994). Based on these proposed differences between obsessions and worry, some researchers created yet another revision of the Padua Inventory (Burns et al., 1996). They rewrote or excluded items without specific content and assigned all items to one of five content subscales relevant to both obsessions and compulsions. This particular revision showed considerably less overlap with worry.

In sum, the limited existing literature suggests that both rumination and worry are associated with worse OCD symptoms, as assessed across several measures. Researchers have proposed theoretical differences between rumination, worry, and obsessions that could easily be tested using some of the same methodologies employed in GAD and PTSD studies. For instance, structured interviews could assess the phenomenology of obsessions versus rumination. Another task for future researchers is to theorize about the functions and consequences of rumination for people with OCD. If rumination is more like a compulsion than an obsession, then it might function as an attempt to cope with or avoid obsessional thoughts that are perceived as dangerous. Perhaps people believe that rumination will prevent an obsessional thought from coming true. As with all negative repetitive thinking, rumination about obsessions likely increases anxiety and other negative emotions. Moreover, the focus on understanding and preventing obsessional thoughts likely keeps the obsessions activated longer than they would be otherwise. Later in this book (Chapter 12, Metacognitive therapy),

I describe a metacognitive model of how rumination and worry contribute to OCD symptoms. This model needs much more empirical testing. Moreover, an avoidance model could also be developed that highlights the potential of rumination and/or worry to prevent emotional processing of upsetting obsessional thoughts.

Illness anxiety disorder

Health anxiety arises when harmless bodily sensations or symptoms are misinterpreted as a sign of a medical problem (Fergus, 2013). Severe health anxiety and accompanying preoccupation with health can contribute to significant distress and impairment, warranting a diagnosis of illness anxiety disorder (formerly hypochondriasis). As with OCD, theory and research on the roles of rumination and worry in health anxiety is in its infancy. Worry about health is conceptualized as a key component of severe health anxiety (Asmundson, Abramowitz, Richter, & Whedon, 2010). Specifically, individuals worry about the consequences of having a medical problem. Rumination about events or information related to perceived health threats is also theorized to contribute to health anxiety (Fink et al., 2004). Finally, unwanted intrusive thoughts about potential health threats and feared consequences of medical problems—similar to obsessions—are proposed to exacerbate health anxiety (Rachman, 2012).

Empirical evidence supports these theories. Measures of worry, brooding rumination, and unwanted intrusive thoughts were unique predictors of health anxiety in healthy adults (Fergus, 2013). In healthy adults and college students, rumination was associated with greater health anxiety (Görgen, Hiller, & Witthöft, 2014; Marcus, Hughes, & Arnau, 2008; Wolfradt, Oemler, Braun, & Klement, 2014). This association was mediated by negative affect. Limited work has included patients with diagnosed illness anxiety disorder. One qualitative study found that patients had tendencies to ruminate in response to illness-related intrusive images (Muse, McManus, Hackmann, Williams, & Williams, 2010). In a mixed-diagnosis treatment-seeking population, rumination was the symptom that best differentiated an illness anxiety diagnosis from other somatoform diagnoses or nonsomatoform diagnoses (Fink et al., 2004).

Two experiments examined the effect of rumination on illness-related memories. Undergraduates with varying levels of health anxiety engaged in rumination or mindfulness manipulations (Sansom-Daly, Bryant, Cohn, & Wakefield, 2014, 2016). In one study, participants were then asked to recall three self-defining memories that were strongly related to whom they are as people (Sansom-Daly et al., 2016).

Rumination led to more recall of illness-related memories than did mindfulness. In another experiment, participants were asked to recall specific memories or to imagine specific future events in response to positive, negative, or somatic-related cue words (Sansom-Daly et al., 2014). Participants in the rumination condition reported more specific illness-related memories but less specific illness-related future imaginings. These results suggest that repetitive thoughts about the past and future play different roles in health anxiety. Perhaps because illness-related memories play such a key role in individuals' current health anxiety, they are elaborated on in great detail. By contrast, repeated thoughts about potential future illnesses may be so threatening that they are only vaguely imagined—a manifestation of emotional avoidance that likely serves to maintain health anxiety.

Conclusion

In this chapter, I reviewed the mostly separate literatures on rumination and various anxiety-related disorders, specifically GAD, social anxiety disorder, PTSD, OCD, and illness anxiety disorder. Several points are worth highlighting because they broaden our scope from depressive rumination and become important themes in understanding the larger field. First, the avoidance theory of worry permeates much of the larger rumination literature. I explore potential avoidance functions of rumination in later chapters (see Chapter 8, Beliefs, traits, and motivations underlying rumination). Moreover, a cognitive behavioral therapy that specifically targets rumination assumes that avoidance underlies rumination (see Chapter 10: Cognitive behavioral therapies). Finally, several disorder-specific theories of rumination covered in this and subsequent chapters are informed by avoidance theory.

The construct of NRT is one that I will mention repeatedly throughout this book. Researchers have suggested that NRT encompasses both rumination and worry, as well as pre- and post-event rumination and trauma-focused rumination (e.g., Ehring & Watkins, 2008). I should note that obsessions and intrusive memories are generally not included as forms of NRT, for theoretical and empirical reasons discussed previously. In the next few chapters, I introduce other variants of rumination that do likely fall under the umbrella of NRT.

A final important point is that rumination may be adaptive in certain forms and for certain people (Watkins, 2008). For instance, deliberate rumination following trauma leads to increased posttraumatic growth. Moreover, one study found that in combat veterans without PTSD, greater daily negative rumination predicted *less* negative affect the next day (Kashdan et al., 2012). The authors speculated that over the course of a day, rumination may motivate well-functioning individuals to engage in mood repair, leading to less subsequent negative mood. Thus, perhaps over shorter time periods (e.g., a few hours) rumination maintains negative moods, whereas over longer time periods rumination fosters effective coping in individuals with healthy psychological functioning. Studies have not explicitly tested this hypothesis. In addition, some researchers speculate that worry in healthy individuals provides important motivation for adaptive behaviors. In fact, worry predicted better academic performance in first-year law students (Siddique, LaSalle-Ricci, Glass, Arnkoff, & Díaz, 2006) and workplace performance for individuals with higher reasoning skills (Perkins & Corr, 2005). These adaptive outcomes may occur because worry focuses more on future-oriented problem solving (Davey et al., 1992; Segerstrom et al., 2003), another speculation that has not been empirically tested. The idea that rumination can have adaptive outcomes was introduced briefly (see Chapter 1, Rumination and mood disorders) with findings that reflective pondering predicts less depressive symptoms for some people but not for others. Later chapters introduce other types of rumination that have positive outcomes (e.g., corumination, Chapter 6: Consequences of expressed rumination) and people for whom rumination may be helpful (e.g., individuals with low perceived risk of illness, Chapter 5: Rumination and physical functioning).

References

Abbott, M. J., & Rapee, R. M. (2004). Post-event rumination and negative self-appraisal in social phobia before and after treatment. *Journal of Abnormal Psychology, 113*(1), 136–144. Available from https://doi.org/10.1037/0021-843X.113.1.136.

Allbaugh, L. J., Wright, M. O., & Folger, S. F. (2016). The role of repetitive thought in determining posttraumatic growth and distress following interpersonal trauma. *Anxiety, Stress, & Coping, 29*(1), 21–37. Available from https://doi.org/10.1080/10615806.2015.1015422.

Andrews, V. H., & Borkovec, T. D. (1988). The differential effects of inductions of worry, somatic anxiety, and depression on emotional experience. *Journal of Behavior Therapy and Experimental Psychiatry, 19*(1), 21–26. Available from https://doi.org/10.1016/0005-7916(88)90006-7.

Armstrong, T., Zald, D. H., & Olatunji, B. O. (2011). Attentional control in OCD and GAD: Specificity and associations with core cognitive symptoms. *Behaviour Research and Therapy, 49*(11), 756–762. Available from https://doi.org/10.1016/j.brat.2011.08.003.

Asmundson, G., Abramowitz, J., Richter, A., & Whedon, M. (2010). Health anxiety: Current perspectives and future directions. *Current Psychiatry Reports, 12*(4), 306–312. Available from https://doi.org/10.1007/s11920-010-0123-9.

Ball, S. C., & Brewin, C. R. (2012). The effect of rumination on intrusive images and mood: An experimental investigation using the trauma film paradigm. *Journal of Experimental Psychopathology, 3*(2), 297–309. Available from https://doi.org/10.5127/jep.019511.

Behar, E., Zuellig, A. R., & Borkovec, T. D. (2005). Thought and imaginal activity during worry and trauma recall. *Behavior Therapy, 36*(2), 157–168. Available from https://doi.org/10.1016/S0005-7894(05)80064-4.

Birrer, E., & Michael, T. (2011). Rumination in PTSD as well as in traumatized and non-traumatized depressed patients: A cross-sectional clinical study. *Behavioural and Cognitive Psychotherapy, 39*(4), 381–397. Available from https://doi.org/10.1017/S1352465811000087.

Birrer, E., Michael, T., & Munsch, S. (2007). Intrusive images in PTSD and in traumatised and non-traumatised depressed patients: A cross-sectional clinical study. *Behaviour Research and Therapy, 45*(9), 2053–2065. Available from https://doi.org/10.1016/j.brat.2007.03.005.

Blackburn, L., & Owens, G. P. (2016). Rumination, resilience, and posttraumatic stress disorder symptom severity among veterans of iraq and afghanistan. *Journal of Aggression, Maltreatment & Trauma, 25*(2), 197–209. Available from https://doi.org/10.1080/10926771.2015.1107174.

Blagden, J. C., & Craske, M. G. (1996). Effects of active and passive rumination and distraction: A pilot replication with anxious mood. *Journal of Anxiety Disorders, 10*(4), 243–252. Available from https://doi.org/10.1016/0887-6185(96)00009-6.

Borders, A., Rothman, D. J., & McAndrew, L. M. (2015). Sleep problems may mediate associations between rumination and PTSD and depressive symptoms among OIF/OEF veterans. *Psychological Trauma: Theory, Research, Practice and Policy, 7*(1), 76–84. Available from https://doi.org/10.1037/a0036937.

Borkovec, T. D., Alcaine, O. M., & Behar, E. (2004). Avoidance theory of worry and generalized anxiety disorder. In R. Heimburg, C. L. Turk, & D. S. Mennin (Eds.), *Generalized anxiety disorder: Advances in research and practice* (pp. 77–108). New York: Guilford Press.

Borkovec, T. D., & Hu, S. (1990). The effect of worry on cardiovascular response to phobic imagery. *Behaviour Research and Therapy, 28*(1), 69–73. Available from https://doi.org/10.1016/0005-7967(90)90056-O.

Borkovec, T. D., & Inz, J. (1990). The nature of worry in generalized anxiety disorder: A predominance of thought activity. *Behaviour Research and Therapy, 28*(2), 153–158. Available from https://doi.org/10.1016/0005-7967(90)90027-G.

Borkovec, T. D., Lyonfields, J. D., Wiser, S. L., & Deihl, L. (1993). The role of worrisome thinking in the suppression of cardiovascular response to phobic imagery. *Behaviour Research and Therapy, 31*(3), 321–324. Available from https://doi.org/10.1016/0005-7967(93)90031-O.

Borkovec, T. D., Robinson, E., Pruzinsky, T., & DePree, J. A. (1983). Preliminary exploration of worry: Some characteristics and processes. *Behaviour Research and Therapy, 21*(1), 9–16. Available from https://doi.org/10.1016/0005-7967(83)90121-3.

Borkovec, T. D., & Roemer, L. (1995). Perceived functions of worry among generalized anxiety disorder subjects: Distraction from more emotionally distressing topics? *Journal of Behavior Therapy and Experimental Psychiatry, 26*(1), 25–30. Available from https://doi.org/10.1016/0005-7916(94)00064-S.

Broeren, S., Muris, P., Bouwmeester, S., Heijden, K., & Abee, A. (2010). The role of repetitive negative thoughts in the vulnerability for emotional problems in non-clinical children. *Journal of Child and Family Studies, 20*(2), 135–148. Available from https://doi.org/10.1007/s10826-010-9380-9.

Brown, M., & Stopa, L. (2006). Does anticipation help or hinder performance in a subsequent speech? *Behavioural and Cognitive Psychotherapy, 35*(2), 133–147. Available from https://doi.org/10.1017/S1352465806003481.

Brozovich, F., & Heimberg, R. G. (2008). An analysis of post-event processing in social anxiety disorder. *Clinical Psychology Review, 28*(6), 891–903. Available from https://doi.org/10.1016/j.cpr.2008.01.002.

Burns, G. L., Keortge, S. G., Formea, G. M., & Sternberger, L. G. (1996). Revision of the padua inventory of obsessive compulsive disorder symptoms: Distinctions between worry, obsessions, and compulsions. *Behaviour Research and Therapy, 34*(2), 163–173. Available from https://doi.org/10.1016/0005-7967(95)00035-6.

Calhoun, L., Cann, A., Tedeschi, R., & McMillan, J. (2000). A correlational test of the relationship between posttraumatic growth, religion, and cognitive processing. *Journal of Traumatic Stress, 13*(3), 521–527. Available from https://doi.org/10.1023/A:1007745627077.

Calmes, C., & Roberts, J. (2007). Repetitive thought and emotional distress: Rumination and worry as prospective predictors of depressive and anxious symptomatology. *Cognitive Therapy and Research, 31*(3), 343–356. Available from https://doi.org/10.1007/s10608-006-9026-9.

Cann, A., Calhoun, L. G., Tedeschi, R. G., & Solomon, D. T. (2010). Posttraumatic growth and depreciation as independent experiences and predictors of well-being. *Journal of Loss and Trauma, 15*(3), 151–166. Available from https://doi.org/10.1080/15325020903375826.

Cann, A., Calhoun, L. G., Tedeschi, R. G., Triplett, K. N., Vishnevsky, T., & Lindstrom, C. M. (2011). Assessing posttraumatic cognitive processes: The event related rumination inventory. *Anxiety, Stress & Coping, 24*(2), 137–156. Available from https://doi.org/10.1080/10615806.2010.529901.

Chan, M. W. C., Ho, S. M. Y., Tedeschi, R. G., & Leung, C. W. L. (2011). The valence of attentional bias and cancer-related rumination in posttraumatic stress and posttraumatic growth among women with breast cancer. *Psycho-Oncology, 20*(5), 544–552. Available from https://doi.org/10.1002/pon.1761.

Ciesla, J. A., Reilly, L. C., Dickson, K. S., Emanuel, A. S., & Updegraff, J. A. (2012). Dispositional mindfulness moderates the effects of stress among adolescents: Rumination as a mediator. *Journal of Clinical Child & Adolescent Psychology, 41*(6), 760–770. Available from https://doi.org/10.1080/15374416.2012.698724.

Clark, D. M., & Wells, A. (1995). A cognitive model of social phobia. In R. G. Heimberg, R. W. Liebowitz, D. A. Hope, & F. R. Schneier (Eds.), *Social phobia: Diagnosis, assessment, and treatment* (pp. 69–93). New York: The Guilford Press.

Clohessy, S., & Ehlers, A. (1999). PTSD symptoms, response to intrusive memories and coping in ambulance service workers. *The British Journal of Clinical Psychology, 38*(Pt (3)), 251–265. Available from https://doi.org/10.1348/014466599162836.

Danhauer, S., Russell, G., Tedeschi, R., Jesse, M., Vishnevsky, T., Daley, K., … Powell, B. (2013). A longitudinal investigation of posttraumatic growth in adult patients undergoing treatment for acute leukemia. *Journal of Clinical Psychology in Medical Settings, 20*(1), 13–24. Available from https://doi.org/10.1007/s10880-012-9304-5.

Dannahy, L., & Stopa, L. (2007). Post-event processing in social anxiety. *Behaviour Research and Therapy, 45*(6), 1207–1219. Available from https://doi.org/10.1016/j.brat.2006.08.017.

Dar, K. A., & Iqbal, N. (2015). Worry and rumination in generalized anxiety disorder and obsessive compulsive disorder. *The Journal of Psychology, 149*(8), 866–880. Available from https://doi.org/10.1080/00223980.2014.986430.

Davey, G. C. L., Hampton, J., Farrell, J., & Davidson, S. (1992). Some characteristics of worrying: Evidence for worrying and anxiety as separate constructs. *Personality and Individual Differences, 13*(2), 133–147. Available from https://doi.org/10.1016/0191-8869(92)90036-O.

de Silva, P. (2003). Obsessions, ruminations and covert compulsions. In R. G. Menzies, & P. de Silva (Eds.), *Obsessive-compulsive disorder: Theory, research and treatment* (pp. 195–208). Great Britain: Wiley. Retrieved from <http://ebooks.ciando.com/book/index.cfm/bok_id/493005>.

De Silva, P., & Rachman, S. (1992). *Obsessive-compulsive disorder*. Oxford: Oxford Univ. Press.

D'Hudson, G., & Saling, L. L. (2010). Worry and rumination in older adults: Differentiating the processes. *Aging & Mental Health, 14*(5), 524–534. Available from https://doi.org/10.1080/13607861003713141.

Edwards, S., Rapee, R., & Franklin, J. (2003). Postevent rumination and recall bias for a social performance event in high and low socially anxious individuals. *Cognitive Therapy and Research, 27*(6), 603–617. Available from https://doi.org/1026395526858.

Ehlers, A., & Clark, D. M. (2000). A cognitive model of posttraumatic stress disorder. *Behaviour Research and Therapy, 38*(4), 319–345. Available from https://doi.org/10.1016/S0005-7967(99)00123-0.

Ehlers, A., Mayou, R. A., & Bryant, B. (1998). Psychological predictors of chronic posttraumatic stress disorder after motor vehicle accidents. *Journal of Abnormal Psychology, 107*(3), 508–519. Available from https://doi.org/10.1037/0021-843X.107.3.508.

Ehlers, A., Mayou, R. A., & Bryant, B. (2003). Cognitive predictors of posttraumatic stress disorder in children: Results of a prospective longitudinal study. *Behaviour Research and Therapy, 41*(1), 1–10. Available from https://doi.org/10.1016/S0005-7967(01)00126-7.

Ehlers, A., & Steil, R. (1995). Maintenance of intrusive memories in posttraumatic stress disorder: A cognitive approach. *Behavioural and Cognitive Psychotherapy, 23*(3), 217–249. Available from https://doi.org/10.1017/S135246580001585X.

Ehring, T., Ehlers, A., & Glucksman, E. (2006). Contribution of cognitive factors to the prediction of post-traumatic stress disorder, phobia and depression after motor vehicle accidents. *Behaviour Research and Therapy, 44*(12), 1699–1716. Available from https://doi.org/10.1016/j.brat.2005.11.013.

Ehring, T., Ehlers, A., & Glucksman, E. (2008). Do cognitive models help in predicting the severity of posttraumatic stress disorder, phobia, and depression after motor vehicle accidents? A prospective longitudinal study. *Journal of Consulting and Clinical Psychology, 76*(2), 219–230. Available from https://doi.org/10.1037/0022-006X.76.2.219.

Ehring, T., Fuchs, N., & Kläsener, I. (2009). The effects of experimentally induced rumination versus distraction on analogue posttraumatic stress symptoms. *Behavior Therapy, 40*(4), 403–413. Available from https://doi.org/10.1016/j.beth.2008.10.001.

Ehring, T., Kleim, B., & Ehlers, A. (2011). Combining clinical studies and analogue experiments to investigate cognitive mechanisms in posttraumatic stress disorder. *International Journal of Cognitive Therapy, 4*(2), 165–177. Available from https://doi.org/10.1521/ijct.2011.4.2.165.

Ehring, T., Szeimies, A., & Schaffrick, C. (2009). An experimental analogue study into the role of abstract thinking in trauma-related rumination. *Behaviour Research and Therapy, 47*(4), 285–293. Available from https://doi.org/10.1016/j.brat.2008.12.011.

Ehring, T., & Watkins, E. R. (2008). Repetitive negative thinking as a transdiagnostic process. *International Journal of Cognitive Therapy, 1*(3), 192–205. Available from https://doi.org/10.1521/ijct.2008.1.3.192.

Elwood, L. S., Hahn, K. S., Olatunji, B. O., & Williams, N. L. (2009). Cognitive vulnerabilities to the development of PTSD: A review of four vulnerabilities and the proposal of an integrative vulnerability model. *Clinical Psychology Review, 29*(1), 87–100. Available from https://doi.org/10.1016/j.cpr.2008.10.002.

Evans, C., Ehlers, A., Mezey, G., & Clark, D. M. (2007). Intrusive memories and ruminations related to violent crime among young offenders: Phenomenological characteristics. *Journal of Traumatic Stress, 20*(2), 183–196. Available from https://doi.org/10.1002/jts.20204.

Fehm, L., Schneider, G., & Hoyer, J. (2007). Is post-event processing specific for social anxiety? *Journal of Behavior Therapy and Experimental Psychiatry, 38*(1), 11–22. Available from https://doi.org/10.1016/j.jbtep.2006.02.004.

Fergus, T. (2013). Repetitive thought and health anxiety: Tests of specificity. *Journal of Psychopathology and Behavioral Assessment, 35*(3), 366–374. Available from https://doi.org/10.1007/s10862-013-9340-y.

Fink, P., Ørnbøl, E., Toft, T., Sparle, K. C., Frostholm, L., & Olesen, F. (2004). A new, empirically established hypochondriasis diagnosis. *American Journal of Psychiatry, 161*(9), 1680–1691. Available from https://doi.org/10.1176/appi.ajp.161.9.1680.

Foa, E. B., & Kozak, M. J. (1986). Emotional processing of fear. *Psychological Bulletin, 99*(1), 20–35. Available from https://doi.org/10.1037/0033-2909.99.1.20.

Fresco, D., Frankel, A., Mennin, D., Turk, C., & Heimberg, R. (2002). Distinct and overlapping features of rumination and worry: The relationship of cognitive production to negative affective states. *Cognitive Therapy and Research, 26*(2), 179–188. Available from https://doi.org/1014517718949.

Garcia, F. E., Cova, F., Rincon, P., Vazquez, C., & Paez, D. (2016). Coping, rumination and posttraumatic growth in people affected by an earthquake/afrontamiento, rumiacion y crecimiento postraumatico en personas afectadas por un terremoto. *Psicothema, 28*(1), 59. Available from https://doi.org/10.7334/psicothema2015.100.

Gönner, S., Ecker, W., & Leonhart, R. (2010). The padua inventory: Do revisions need revision? *Assessment, 17*(1), 89–106. Available from https://doi.org/10.1177/1073191109342189.

Görgen, S., Hiller, W., & Witthöft, M. (2014). Health anxiety, cognitive coping, and emotion regulation: A latent variable approach. *International Journal of Behavioral Medicine, 21*(2), 364–374. Available from https://doi.org/10.1007/s12529-013-9297-y.

Goring, H., & Papageorgiou, C. (2008). Rumination and worry: Factor analysis of self-report measures in depressed participants. *Cognitive Therapy and Research, 32*(4), 554–566. Available from https://doi.org/10.1007/s10608-007-9146-x.

Grisham, J. R., & Williams, A. D. (2009). Cognitive control of obsessional thoughts. *Behaviour Research and Therapy, 47*(5), 395–402. Available from https://doi.org/10.1016/j.brat.2009.01.014.

Groleau, J. M., Calhoun, L. G., Cann, A., & Tedeschi, R. G. (2013). The role of centrality of events in posttraumatic distress and posttraumatic growth. *Psychological Trauma: Theory, Research, Practice, and Policy, 5*(5), 477–483. Available from https://doi.org/10.1037/a0028809.

Hendriks, S. M., Licht, C. M. M., Spijker, J., Beekman, A. T. F., Hardeveld, F., de Graaf, R., & Penninx, B. W. J. H. (2014). Disorder-specific cognitive profiles in major depressive disorder and generalized anxiety disorder. *BMC Psychiatry, 14*(1), 96. Available from https://doi.org/10.1186/1471-244X-14-96.

Hinrichsen, H., & Clark, D. M. (2003). Anticipatory processing in social anxiety: Two pilot studies. *Journal of Behavior Therapy and Experimental Psychiatry, 34*(3), 205–218. Available from https://doi.org/10.1016/S0005-7916(03)00050-8.

Hofmann, S. G. (2007). Cognitive factors that maintain social anxiety disorder: A comprehensive model and its treatment implications. *Cognitive Behaviour Therapy, 36*(4), 193–209. Available from https://doi.org/10.1080/16506070701421313.

Hofmann, S. G., Moscovitch, D. A., Litz, B. T., Kim, H., Davis, L. L., & Pizzagalli, D. A. (2005). The worried mind. *Emotion, 5*(4), 464–475. Available from https://doi.org/10.1037/1528-3542.5.4.464.

Hong, R. Y. (2007). Worry and rumination: Differential associations with anxious and depressive symptoms and coping behavior. *Behaviour Research and Therapy, 45*(2), 277–290. Available from https://doi.org/10.1016/j.brat.2006.03.006.

Horsch, A., Jacobs, I., & McKenzie-McHarg, K. (2015). Cognitive predictors and risk factors of PTSD following stillbirth: A short-term longitudinal study. *Journal of Traumatic Stress, 28*(2), 110–117. Available from https://doi.org/10.1002/jts.21997.

Hoyer, J., Gloster, A. T., & Herzberg, P. Y. (2009). Is worry different from rumination? Yes, it is more predictive of psychopathology. *Psycho-Social Medicine, 6*, Doc06. Retrieved from <https://www.ncbi.nlm.nih.gov/pubmed/19949448>.

Jenness, J. L., Jager-Hyman, S., Heleniak, C., Beck, A. T., Sheridan, M. A., & McLaughlin, K. A. (2016). Catastrophizing, rumination, and reappraisal prospectively predict adolescent PTSD symptom onset following a terrorist attack. *Depression and Anxiety, 33*(11), 1039–1047. Available from https://doi.org/10.1002/da.22548.

Kashdan, T. B., & Roberts, J. E. (2007). Social anxiety, depressive symptoms, and post-event rumination: Affective consequences and social contextual influences. *Journal of Anxiety Disorders, 21*(3), 284–301. Available from https://doi.org/10.1016/j.janxdis.2006.05.009.

Kashdan, T. B., Young, K. C., & McKnight, P. E. (2012). When is rumination an adaptive mood repair strategy? day-to-day rhythms of life in combat veterans with and without posttraumatic stress disorder. *Journal of Anxiety Disorders, 26*(7), 762–768. Available from https://doi.org/10.1016/j.janxdis.2012.07.004.

Kircanski, K., Thompson, R. J., Sorenson, J. E., Sherdell, L., & Gotlib, I. H. (2015). Rumination and worry in daily life. *Clinical Psychological Science, 3*(6), 926–939. Available from https://doi.org/10.1177/2167702614566603.

Kleim, B., & Ehlers, A. (2008). Reduced autobiographical memory specificity predicts depression and posttraumatic stress disorder after recent trauma. *Journal of Consulting and Clinical Psychology, 76*(2), 231–242. Available from https://doi.org/10.1037/0022-006X.76.2.231.

Kleim, B., Ehlers, A., & Glucksman, E. (2007). Early predictors of chronic post-traumatic stress disorder in assault survivors. *Psychological Medicine, 37*(10), 1457–1467. Available from https://doi.org/10.1017/S0033291707001006.

Kocovski, N. L., Endler, N. S., Rector, N. A., & Flett, G. L. (2005). Ruminative coping and post-event processing in social anxiety. *Behaviour Research and Therapy, 43*(8), 971–984. Available from https://doi.org/10.1016/j.brat.2004.06.015.

Kocovski, N. L., & Rector, N. A. (2007). Predictors of post-event rumination related to social anxiety. *Cognitive Behaviour Therapy, 36*(2), 112–122. Available from https://doi.org/10.1080/16506070701232090.

Kubota, R., Nixon, R. D. V., & Chen, J. (2015). Trauma-related rumination mediates the effect of naturally occurring depressive symptoms but not momentary low mood on trauma intrusions. *Australian Journal of Psychology, 67*(2), 75–86. Available from https://doi.org/10.1111/ajpy.12074.

Langlois, F., Freeston, M. H., & Ladouceur, R. (2000). Differences and similarities between obsessive intrusive thoughts and worry in a non-clinical population: Study 2. *Behaviour Research and Therapy, 38*(2), 175–189. Available from https://doi.org/10.1016/S0005-7967(99)00028-5.

Laposa, J. M., & Rector, N. A. (2012). The prediction of intrusions following an analogue traumatic event: Peritraumatic cognitive processes and anxiety-focused rumination versus rumination in response to intrusions. *Journal of Behavior Therapy and Experimental Psychiatry, 43*(3), 877–883. Available from https://doi.org/10.1016/j.jbtep.2011.12.007.

Laposa, J. M., & Rector, N. A. (2016). Can I really do this? An examination of anticipatory event processing in social anxiety disorder. *Journal of Cognitive Psychotherapy, 30*(2), 94–104. Available from https://doi.org/10.1891/0889-8391.30.2.94.

Lindstrom, C. M., Cann, A., Calhoun, L. G., & Tedeschi, R. G. (2013). The relationship of core belief challenge, rumination, disclosure, and sociocultural elements to posttraumatic growth. *Psychological Trauma: Theory, Research, Practice, and Policy, 5*(1), 50–55. Available from https://doi.org/10.1037/a0022030.

Llera, S. J., & Newman, M. G. (2010). Effects of worry on physiological and subjective reactivity to emotional stimuli in generalized anxiety disorder and nonanxious control participants. *Emotion, 10*(5), 640–650. Available from https://doi.org/10.1037/a0019351.

Llera, S. J., & Newman, M. G. (2014). Rethinking the role of worry in generalized anxiety disorder: Evidence supporting a model of emotional contrast avoidance. *Behavior Therapy, 45*(3), 283–299. Available from https://doi.org/10.1016/j.beth.2013.12.011.

Llera, S. J., & Newman, M. G. (2017). Development and validation of two measures of emotional contrast avoidance: The contrast avoidance questionnaires. *Journal of Anxiety Disorders, 49*, 114–127. Available from https://doi.org/10.1016/j.janxdis.2017.04.008.

Lundh, L., & Sperling, M. (2002). Social anxiety and the post-event processing of socially distressing events. *Cognitive Behaviour Therapy, 31*(3), 129–134. Available from https://doi.org/10.1080/165060702320338004.

Marcus, D. K., Hughes, K. T., & Arnau, R. C. (2008). Health anxiety, rumination, and negative affect: A mediational analysis. *Journal of Psychosomatic Research, 64*(5), 495–501. Available from https://doi.org/10.1016/j.jpsychores.2008.02.004.

Mayou, R. A., Ehlers, A., & Bryant, B. (2002). Posttraumatic stress disorder after motor vehicle accidents: 3-year follow-up of a prospective longitudinal study. *Behaviour Research and Therapy, 40*(6), 665–675. Available from https://doi.org/10.1016/S0005-7967(01)00069-9.

McEvoy, P., & Brans, S. (2013). Common versus unique variance across measures of worry and rumination: Predictive utility and mediational models for anxiety and depression. *Cognitive Therapy and Research, 37*(1), 183–196. Available from https://doi.org/10.1007/s10608-012-9448-5.

McEvoy, P. M., & Kingsep, P. (2006). The post-event processing questionnaire in a clinical sample with social phobia. *Behaviour Research and Therapy, 44*(11), 1689–1697. Available from https://doi.org/10.1016/j.brat.2005.12.005.

McEvoy, P. M., Mahoney, A. E. J., & Moulds, M. L. (2010). Are worry, rumination, and post-event processing one and the same? Development of the repetitive thinking questionnaire. *Journal of Anxiety Disorders, 24*(5), 509-519. Retrieved from <https://www.ncbi.nlm.nih.gov/pubmed/20409676>.

McLaughlin, K. A., Borkovec, T. D., & Sibrava, N. J. (2007). The effects of worry and rumination on affect states and cognitive activity. *Behavior Therapy, 38*(1), 23–38. Available from https://doi.org/10.1016/j.beth.2006.03.003.

Meiser-Stedman, R., Shepperd, A., Glucksman, E., Dalgleish, T., Yule, W., & Smith, P. (2014). Thought control strategies and rumination in youth with acute stress disorder and posttraumatic stress disorder following single-event trauma. *Journal of Child and Adolescent Psychopharmacology, 24*(1), 47–51. Available from https://doi.org/10.1089/cap.2013.0052.

Mellings, T. M. B., & Alden, L. E. (2000). Cognitive processes in social anxiety: The effects of self-focus, rumination and anticipatory processing. *Behaviour Research and Therapy, 38*(3), 243–257. Available from https://doi.org/10.1016/S0005-7967(99)00040-6.

Meyer, T. J., Miller, M. L., Metzger, R. L., & Borkovec, T. D. (1990). Development and validation of the penn state worry questionnaire. *Behaviour Research and Therapy, 28*(6), 487–495. Available from https://doi.org/10.1016/0005-7967(90)90135-6.

Michael, T., Ehlers, A., Halligan, S. L., & Clark, D. M. (2005). Unwanted memories of assault: What intrusion characteristics are associated with PTSD? *Behaviour Research and Therapy, 43*(5), 613–628. Available from https://doi.org/10.1016/j.brat.2004.04.006.

Michael, T., Halligan, S. L., Clark, D. M., & Ehlers, A. (2007). Rumination in posttraumatic stress disorder. *Depression and Anxiety, 24*(5), 307–317. Available from https://doi.org/10.1002/da.20228.

Miller, M. W., Wolf, E. J., Harrington, K. M., Brown, T. A., Kaloupek, D. G., & Keane, T. M. (2010). An evaluation of competing models for the structure of PTSD symptoms using external measures of comorbidity. *Journal of Traumatic Stress, 23*(5), 631–638. Available from https://doi.org/10.1002/jts.20559.

Mills, A. C., Grant, D. M., Judah, M. R., & Lechner, W. V. (2014). Consequences of anticipatory processing on cognitive symptoms of social anxiety. *Anxiety, Stress, and Coping, 27*(4), 394–409. Available from https://doi.org/10.1080/10615806.2013.866229.

Mills, A. C., Grant, D. M., Judah, M. R., & White, E. J. (2014). The influence of anticipatory processing on attentional biases in social anxiety. *Behavior Therapy, 45*(5), 720–729. Available from https://doi.org/10.1016/j.beth.2014.04.004.

Mills, A. C., Grant, D. M., Lechner, W. V., & Judah, M. R. (2014). Relationship between trait repetitive negative thinking styles and symptoms of psychopathology. *Personality and Individual Differences, 71*, 19–24. Available from https://doi.org/10.1016/j.paid.2014.07.022.

Morgan, J., & Banerjee, R. (2008). Post-event processing and autobiographical memory in social anxiety: The influence of negative feedback and rumination. *Journal of Anxiety Disorders, 22*(7), 1190–1204. Available from https://doi.org/10.1016/j.janxdis.2008.01.001.

Muris, P., Roelofs, J., Meesters, C., & Boomsma, P. (2004). Rumination and worry in non-clinical adolescents. *Cognitive Therapy and Research, 28*(4), 539–554. Available from https://doi.org/10.1023/B:COTR.0000045563.66060.3e.

Muris, P., Roelofs, J., Rassin, E., Franken, I., & Mayer, B. (2005). Mediating effects of rumination and worry on the links between neuroticism, anxiety and depression. *Personality and Individual Differences, 39*(6), 1105–1111. Available from https://doi.org/10.1016/j.paid.2005.04.005.

Muse, K., McManus, F., Hackmann, A., Williams, M., & Williams, M. (2010). Intrusive imagery in severe health anxiety: Prevalence, nature and links with memories and maintenance cycles. *Behaviour Research and Therapy, 48*(8), 792–798. Available from https://doi.org/10.1016/j.brat.2010.05.008.

Newman, M. G., & Llera, S. J. (2011). A novel theory of experiential avoidance in generalized anxiety disorder: A review and synthesis of research supporting a contrast avoidance model of worry. *Clinical Psychology Review, 31*(3), 371–382. Available from https://doi.org/10.1016/j.cpr.2011.01.008.

Nightingale, V. R., Sher, T. G., & Hansen, N. B. (2010). The impact of receiving an HIV diagnosis and cognitive processing on psychological distress and posttraumatic growth. *Journal of Traumatic Stress, 23*(4), 452–460. Available from https://doi.org/10.1002/jts.20554.

Nolen-Hoeksema, S. (1991). Responses to depression and their effects on the duration of depressive episodes. *Journal of Abnormal Psychology, 100*(4), 569–582. Available from https://doi.org/10.1037/0021-843X.100.4.569.

Nolen-Hoeksema, S. (2000). The role of rumination in depressive disorders and mixed anxiety/depressive symptoms. *Journal of Abnormal Psychology, 109*(3), 504–511. Available from https://doi.org/10.1037/0021-843X.109.3.504.

Nolen-Hoeksema, S., & Morrow, J. (1991). A prospective study of depression and posttraumatic stress symptoms after a natural disaster. *Journal of Personality and Social Psychology, 61*(1), 115–121. Available from https://doi.org/10.1037/0022-3514.61.1.115.

Normann, N., van Emmerik, A. P., & Morina, N. (2014). The efficacy of metacognitive therapy for anxiety and depression: A meta-analytic review. *Depression and Anxiety, 31*(5), 402–411. Available from https://doi.org/10.1002/da.22273.

Norton, A. R., & Abbott, M. J. (2016). Self-focused cognition in social anxiety: A review of the theoretical and empirical literature. *Behaviour Change, 33*(1), 44–64. Available from https://doi.org/10.1017/bec.2016.2.

Nuevo, R., Montorio, I., & Borkovec, T. D. (2004). A test of the role of metaworry in the prediction of worry severity in an elderly sample. *Journal of Behavior Therapy and Experimental Psychiatry, 35*(3), 209–218. Available from https://doi.org/10.1016/j.jbtep.2004.03.002.

Olatunji, B. O., Naragon-Gainey, K., & Wolitzky-Taylor, K. B. (2013). Specificity of rumination in anxiety and depression: A multimodal meta-analysis. *Clinical Psychology: Science and Practice, 20*(3), 225–257. Available from https://doi.org/10.1111/cpsp.12037.

Orth, U., Cahill, S. P., Foa, E. B., & Maercker, A. (2008). Anger and posttraumatic stress disorder symptoms in crime victims. *Journal of Consulting and Clinical Psychology, 76*(2), 208–218. Available from https://doi.org/10.1037/0022-006X.76.2.208.

Papageorgiou, C., & Wells, A. (1999). Process and meta-cognitive dimensions of depressive and anxious thoughts and relationships with emotional intensity. *Clinical Psychology & Psychotherapy,* 6(2), 156–162. https://doi.org/10.1002/(SICI)1099-0879(199905)6:2 < 156::AID-CPP196 > 3.0.CO;2-A.

Penney, E. S., & Abbott, M. J. (2014). Anticipatory and post-event rumination in social anxiety disorder: A review of the theoretical and empirical literature. *Behaviour Change, 31* (2), 79–101. Available from https://doi.org/10.1017/bec.2014.3.

Penney, E. S., & Abbott, M. J. (2015). The impact of perceived standards on state anxiety, appraisal processes, and negative pre- and post-event rumination in social anxiety disorder. *Cognitive Therapy and Research, 39*(2), 162–177. Available from https://doi.org/10.1007/s10608-014-9639-3.

Perini, S., Abbott, M., & Rapee, R. (2006). Perception of performance as a mediator in the relationship between social anxiety and negative post-event rumination. *Cognitive Therapy and Research, 30*(5), 645–659. Available from https://doi.org/10.1007/s10608-006-9023-z.

Perkins, A. M., & Corr, P. J. (2005). Can worriers be winners? The association between worrying and job performance. *Personality and Individual Differences, 38*(1), 25–31. Available from https://doi.org/10.1016/j.paid.2004.03.008.

Purdon, C., & Clark, D. A. (1999). Metacognition and obsessions. *Clinical Psychology & Psychotherapy,* 6(2), 102–110. <https://doi.org/10.1002/(SICI)1099-0879(199905)6:2 < 102::AID-CPP191 > 3.0.CO;2-5>.

Rachman, S. (1971). Obsessional ruminations. *Behavior Research & Therapy, 9,* 229–235. Available from https://doi.org/10.5127/jep.035713.

Rachman, S. (2012). Health anxiety disorders: A cognitive construal. *Behaviour Research and Therapy, 50*(7-8), 502–512. Available from https://doi.org/10.1016/j.brat.2012.05.001.

Rachman, S., Grüter-Andrew, J., & Shafran, R. (2000). Post-event processing in social anxiety. *Behaviour Research and Therapy, 38*(6), 611–617. Available from https://doi.org/10.1016/S0005-7967(99)00089-3.

Rapee, R. M., & Abbott, M. J. (2007). Modelling relationships between cognitive variables during and following public speaking in participants with social phobia. *Behaviour Research and Therapy, 45*(12), 2977–2989. Available from https://doi.org/10.1016/j.brat.2007.08.008.

Rector, N. A., Antony, M. M., Laposa, J. M., Kocovski, N. L., & Swinson, R. P. (2008). Assessing content domains of repetitive thought in the anxiety spectrum: Rumination and worry in nonclinical and clinically anxious samples. *International Journal of Cognitive Therapy, 1*(4), 352–377. Available from https://doi.org/10.1521/ijct.2008.1.4.352.

Robichaud, M., Dugas, M. J., & Conway, M. (2003). Gender differences in worry and associated cognitive-behavioral variables. *Journal of Anxiety Disorders, 17*(5), 501–516. Available from https://doi.org/10.1016/S0887-6185(02)00237-2.

Roemer, L., Salters, K., Raffa, S., & Orsillo, S. (2005). Fear and avoidance of internal experiences in GAD: Preliminary tests of a conceptual model. *Cognitive Therapy and Research, 29*(1), 71–88. Available from https://doi.org/10.1007/s10608-005-1650-2.

Rood, L. R. J., Bögels, S., & Roelofs, J. (2010). Dimensions of negative thinking and the relations with symptoms of depression and anxiety in children and adolescents. *Cognitive Therapy and Research, 34*(4), 333–342. Available from https://doi.org/10.1007/s10608-009-9261-y.

Salsman, J. M., Segerstrom, S. C., Brechting, E. H., Carlson, C. R., & Andrykowski, M. A. (2009). Posttraumatic growth and PTSD symptomatology among colorectal cancer survivors: A 3-month longitudinal examination of cognitive processing. *Psycho-Oncology, 18*(1), 30–41. Available from https://doi.org/10.1002/pon.1367.

Sansom-Daly, U. M., Bryant, R. A., Cohn, R. J., & Wakefield, C. E. (2014). Imagining the future in health anxiety: The impact of rumination on the specificity of illness-related memory and future thinking. *Anxiety, Stress, and Coping*, *27*(5), 587–600. Available from https://doi.org/10.1080/10615806.2014.880111.

Sansom-Daly, U. M., Bryant, R. A., Cohn, R. J., & Wakefield, C. E. (2016). Rumination and self-defining memories in the context of health concerns. *Memory*, *24*(7), 939–948. Available from https://doi.org/10.1080/09658211.2015.1059860.

Schönfeld, S., & Ehlers, A. (2006). Overgeneral memory extends to pictorial retrieval cues and correlates with cognitive features in posttraumatic stress disorder. *Emotion*, *6*(4), 611–621. Available from https://doi.org/10.1037/1528-3542.6.4.611.

Segerstrom, S., Tsao, J., Alden, L., & Craske, M. (2000). Worry and rumination: Repetitive thought as a concomitant and predictor of negative mood. *Cognitive Therapy and Research*, *24*(6), 671–688. Available from https://doi.org/1005587311498.

Segerstrom, S. C., Stanton, A. L., Alden, L. E., & Shortridge, B. E. (2003). A multidimensional structure for repetitive thought. *Journal of Personality and Social Psychology*, *85*(5), 909–921. Available from https://doi.org/10.1037/0022-3514.85.5.909.

Seligowski, A. V., Lee, D. J., Bardeen, J. R., & Orcutt, H. K. (2015). Emotion regulation and posttraumatic stress symptoms: A meta-analysis. *Cognitive Behaviour Therapy*, *44*(2), 87–102. Available from https://doi.org/10.1080/16506073.2014.980753.

Siddique, H., LaSalle-Ricci, V., Glass, C., Arnkoff, D., & Díaz, R. (2006). Worry, optimism, and expectations as predictors of anxiety and performance in the first year of law school. *Cognitive Therapy and Research*, *30*(5), 667–676. Available from https://doi.org/10.1007/s10608-006-9080-3.

Siegle, G., Moore, P., & Thase, M. (2004). Rumination: One construct, many features in healthy individuals, depressed individuals, and individuals with lupus. *Cognitive Therapy and Research*, *28*(5), 645–668. Available from https://doi.org/COTR.0000045570.62733.9f.

Speckens, A. E. M., Ehlers, A., Hackmann, A., Ruths, F. A., & Clark, D. M. (2007). Intrusive memories and rumination in patients with post-traumatic stress disorder: A phenomenological comparison. *Memory*, *15*(3), 249–257. Available from https://doi.org/10.1080/09658210701256449.

Spinhoven, P., Penninx, B. W., Krempeniou, A., van Hemert, A. M., & Elzinga, B. (2015). Trait rumination predicts onset of post-traumatic stress disorder through trauma-related cognitive appraisals: A 4-year longitudinal study. *Behaviour Research and Therapy*, *71*, 101–109. Available from https://doi.org/10.1016/j.brat.2015.06.004.

Stapinski, L. A., Abbott, M. J., & Rapee, R. M. (2010). Evaluating the cognitive avoidance model of generalised anxiety disorder: Impact of worry on threat appraisal, perceived control and anxious arousal. *Behaviour Research and Therapy*, *48*(10), 1032–1040. Available from https://doi.org/10.1016/j.brat.2010.07.005.

Szabó, M., & Lovibond, P. (2002). The cognitive content of naturally occurring worry episodes. *Cognitive Therapy and Research*, *26*(2), 167–177. Available from https://doi.org/10.1023/A:1014565602111.

Taku, K., Calhoun, L. G., Cann, A., & Tedeschi, R. G. (2008). The role of rumination in the coexistence of distress and posttraumatic growth among bereaved japanese university students. *Death Studies*, *32*(5), 428–444. Available from https://doi.org/10.1080/07481180801974745.

Taku, K., Cann, A., Tedeschi, R. G., & Calhoun, L. G. (2009). Intrusive versus deliberate rumination in posttraumatic growth across US and japanese samples. *Anxiety, Stress & Coping*, *22*(2), 129–136. Available from https://doi.org/10.1080/10615800802317841.

Tallis, F., Eysenck, M., & Mathews, A. (1992). A questionnaire for the measurement of nonpathological worry. *Personality and Individual Differences*, *13*(2), 161–168. Available from https://doi.org/10.1016/0191-8869(92)90038-Q.

Tedeschi, R. G., & Calhoun, L. G. (2004). Posttraumatic growth: Conceptual foundations and empirical evidence. *Psychological Inquiry*, *15*(1), 1–18. Retrieved from <https://www.jstor.org/stable/20447194>.

Topper, M., Molenaar, D., Emmelkamp, P., & Ehring, T. (2014). Are rumination and worry two sides of the same coin? A structural equation modelling approach. *Journal of Experimental Psychopathology*, *5*(3), 363–381. Available from https://doi.org/10.5127/jep.038813.

Triplett, K. N., Tedeschi, R. G., Cann, A., Calhoun, L. G., & Reeve, C. L. (2012). Posttraumatic growth, meaning in life, and life satisfaction in response to trauma. *Psychological Trauma: Theory, Research, Practice, and Policy*, *4*(4), 400–410. Available from https://doi.org/10.1037/a0024204.

Turliuc, M. N., Măirean, C., & Turliuc, M. D. (2015). Rumination and suppression as mediators of the relationship between dysfunctional beliefs and traumatic stress. *International Journal of Stress Management*, *22*(3), 306–322. Available from https://doi.org/10.1037/a0039272.

Van Oppen, P., Hoekstra, R. J., & Emmelkamp, P. M. G. (1995). The structure of obsessive-compulsive symptoms. *Behaviour Research and Therapy*, *33*(1), 15–23. Available from https://doi.org/10.1016/0005-7967(94)E0010-G.

Vassilopoulos, S. P. (2004). Anticipatory processing in social anxiety. *Behavioural and Cognitive Psychotherapy*, *32*(3), 303–311. Available from https://doi.org/10.1017/S1352465804001377.

Vassilopoulos, S. P. (2005). Anticipatory processing plays a role in maintaining social anxiety. *Anxiety, Stress & Coping*, *18*(4), 321–332. Available from https://doi.org/10.1080/10615800500258149.

Vassilopoulos, S. P. (2008). Social anxiety and ruminative self-focus. *Journal of Anxiety Disorders*, *22*(5), 860–867. Available from https://doi.org/10.1016/j.janxdis.2007.08.012.

Verstraeten, K., Bijttebier, P., Vasey, M. W., & Raes, F. (2011). Specificity of worry and rumination in the development of anxiety and depressive symptoms in children. *British Journal of Clinical Psychology*, *50*(4), 364–378. Available from https://doi.org/10.1348/014466510X532715.

Vrana, S. R., Cuthbert, B. N., & Lang, P. J. (1986). Fear imagery and text processing. *Psychophysiology*, *23*(3), 247–253. Available from https://doi.org/10.1111/j.1469-8986.1986.tb00626.x.

Wahl, K., Ertle, A., Bohne, A., Zurowski, B., & Kordon, A. (2011). Relations between a ruminative thinking style and obsessive-compulsive symptoms in non-clinical samples. *Anxiety, Stress & Coping*, *24*(2), 217–225. Available from https://doi.org/10.1080/10615806.2010.482985.

Ward, A., Lyubomirsky, S., Sousa, L., & Nolen-Hoeksema, S. (2003). Can't quite commit: Rumination and uncertainty. *Personality and Social Psychology Bulletin*, *29*(1), 96–107. Available from https://doi.org/10.1177/0146167202238375.

Watkins, E. (2004). Appraisals and strategies associated with rumination and worry. *Personality and Individual Differences*, *37*(4), 679–694. Available from https://doi.org/10.1016/j.paid.2003.10.002.

Watkins, E., Moulds, M., & Mackintosh, B. (2005). Comparisons between rumination and worry in a non-clinical population. *Behaviour Research and Therapy*, *43*(12), 1577–1585. Available from https://doi.org/10.1016/j.brat.2004.11.008.

Watkins, E. R. (2008). Constructive and unconstructive repetitive thought. *Psychological Bulletin*, *134*(2), 163–206. Available from https://doi.org/10.1037/0033-2909.134.2.163.

Weiss, D. S., & Marmar, C. R. (1997). The impact of event scale—Revised. In J. P. Wilson, & T. M. Keane (Eds.), *Assessing psychological trauma and PTSD* (pp. 399–411). New York: Guilford Press.

Wells, A. (1994). A multi-dimensional measure of worry: Development and preliminary validation of the anxious thoughts inventory. *Anxiety, Stress & Coping*, *6*(4), 289–299. Available from https://doi.org/10.1080/10615809408248803.

Wells, A. (2005). The metacognitive model of GAD: Assessment of meta-worry and relationship with DSM-IV generalized anxiety disorder. *Cognitive Therapy and Research, 29* (1), 107–121. Available from https://doi.org/10.1007/s10608-005-1652-0.

Wells, A., & Carter, K. (1999). Preliminary tests of a cognitive model of generalized anxiety disorder. *Behaviour Research and Therapy, 37*(6), 585–594. Available from https://doi.org/10.1016/S0005-7967(98)00156-9.

Wells, A., & Davies, M. I. (1994). The thought control questionnaire: A measure of individual differences in the control of unwanted thoughts. *Behaviour Research and Therapy, 32* (8), 871–878. Available from https://doi.org/10.1016/0005-7967(94)90168-6.

Wells, A., & Morrison, A. P. (1994). Qualitative dimensions of normal worry and normal obsessions: A comparative study. *Behaviour Research and Therapy, 32*(8), 867–870. Available from https://doi.org/10.1016/0005-7967(94)90167-8.

Wolfradt, U., Oemler, M., Braun, K., & Klement, A. (2014). Health anxiety and habitual rumination: The mediating effect of serenity. *Personality and Individual Differences, 71,* 130–134. Available from https://doi.org/10.1016/j.paid.2014.07.030.

Wong, Q. J. J., & Moulds, M. L. (2009). Impact of rumination versus distraction on anxiety and maladaptive self-beliefs in socially anxious individuals. *Behaviour Research and Therapy, 47*(10), 861–867. Available from https://doi.org/10.1016/j.brat.2009.06.014.

Wong, Q. J. J., & Moulds, M. L. (2011). Impact of anticipatory processing versus distraction on multiple indices of anxiety in socially anxious individuals. *Behaviour Research and Therapy, 49*(10), 700–706. Available from https://doi.org/10.1016/j.brat.2011.07.007.

Wu, X., Zhou, X., Wu, Y., & An, Y. (2015). The role of rumination in posttraumatic stress disorder and posttraumatic growth among adolescents after the wenchuan earthquake. *Frontiers in Psychology, 6,* 1335. Available from https://doi.org/10.3389/fpsyg.2015.01335.

Yang, M., Kim, B., Lee, E., Lee, D., Yu, B., Jeon, H. J., & Kim, J. (2014). Diagnostic utility of worry and rumination: A comparison between generalized anxiety disorder and major depressive disorder. *Psychiatry and Clinical Neurosciences, 68*(9), 712–720. Available from https://doi.org/10.1111/pcn.12193.

Yook, K., Kim, K., Suh, S. Y., & Lee, K. S. (2010). Intolerance of uncertainty, worry, and rumination in major depressive disorder and generalized anxiety disorder. *Journal of Anxiety Disorders, 24*(6), 623–628. Available from https://doi.org/10.1016/j.janxdis.2010.04.003.

Zetsche, U., Ehring, T., & Ehlers, A. (2009). The effects of rumination on mood and intrusive memories after exposure to traumatic material: An experimental study. *Journal of Behavior Therapy and Experimental Psychiatry, 40*(4), 499–514. Available from https://doi.org/10.1016/j.jbtep.2009.07.001.

Zhou, X., & Wu, X. (2015). The relationship between rumination, posttraumatic stress disorder, and posttraumatic growth among chinese adolescents after earthquake: A longitudinal study. *Journal of Affective Disorders, 193,* 242–248. Available from https://doi.org/10.1016/j.jad.2015.12.076.

Zhou, X., Wu, X., Fu, F., & An, Y. (2015). Core belief challenge and rumination as predictors of PTSD and PTG among adolescent survivors of the wenchuan earthquake. *Psychological Trauma: Theory, Research, Practice and Policy, 7*(4), 391–397. Available from https://doi.org/10.1037/tra0000031.

Zlomke, K. R., & Hahn, K. S. (2010). Cognitive emotion regulation strategies: Gender differences and associations to worry. *Personality and Individual Differences, 48*(4), 408–413. Available from https://doi.org/10.1016/j.paid.2009.11.007.

CHAPTER

3

Rumination, anger, and aggression

Overview

This chapter reviews the literature on angry rumination, or repetitive thinking about angering events. After describing the original development of the construct, I review the evidence linking rumination with anger. I then explore how rumination can be incorporated into relevant theories of aggression, as well as the sizable literature on rumination and various types of aggression. The chapter also addresses various mechanisms of angry rumination, such as increased desire for revenge and physiological activation, as well as decreased interest in forgiveness and moral prohibitions. After an examination of potential moderators of the effect of angry rumination, I conclude by reviewing an evolutionary hypothesis about possible societal functions—both negative and positive—of angry rumination.

Three-year-old Evan loves breath mints. As soon as his mother pulls into the driveway after work, he runs outside and asks, "Mommy, can I have a mint?" He knows that he is allowed one mint a day. So he is overwhelmed with anger and disappointment when one day his mother does not have a mint for him. He screams, stomps the floor, and repeatedly hits his weary mother before throwing himself on the driveway in tears. After a short time-out, lots of hugs, and the discovery of a caterpillar in the garden, little Evan is happily interacting with his mother. Now, fast-forward 7 years. Ten-year-old Evan is obsessed with baseball, and his 7-year-old sister Julia is also a budding athlete. One day, Julia accidentally spills her apple juice on Evan's brand new baseball mitt right before a game. Despite frantic attempts to clean the mitt, it is too

Rumination and Related Constructs
DOI: https://doi.org/10.1016/B978-0-12-812545-8.00003-6

© 2020 Elsevier Inc. All rights reserved.

sticky and wet to use. Evan furiously resigns himself to using his old mitt for the game. All he can think about is how angry he is at his sister for ruining his prized mitt. Two days later, Julia walks into her room to find her own new baseball mitt covered in whipped cream. She runs sobbing to her mom, while Evan watches, feeling both victorious and guilty.

Developmentally, most 3-year-olds will react automatically—and often aggressively—against someone who denies them a coveted treat. Luckily, anger fades from memory pretty quickly at this age, and closeness is soon restored. By contrast, most adults can probably relate to the impulse, if not the behavior, of 10-year-old Evan. Someone upsets us, and we wait until an opportune time to retaliate. Over the years, psychologists have offered various explanations for this kind of delayed aggression. According to behavioral theory, the only reason Evan was *not* aggressive in the moment is because he anticipated punishment for such behavior (Dollard, Miller, Doob, Mowrer, & Sears, 1939). However, this theory does not adequately explain why Evan retaliated 2 days later (for which he was most definitely punished). A somewhat better explanation of delayed aggression involves the transfer of physiological arousal (Zillmann, 1983). People become angry following a provocation, and the accompanying increased heart rate, respiration, and energy make subsequent aggression more likely. The problem with this explanation is that anger-related arousal does not last very long. Research in which participants watched a violent movie and then had opportunities to aggress at a later time suggests that arousal from the violent images dissipates within 15 minutes, if not less (Doob & Climie, 1972). Clearly, physiological arousal associated with anger cannot explain a 2-day lapse between provocation and retaliation. What, then?

In Italy in the 1980s, Gian Vittorio Caprara focused on rumination as an explanation. Specifically, Caprara (1986) wrote about dissipation and rumination being opposite ends of one continuum, corresponding to a decrease or increase, respectively, of aggression across a time lapse. He further proposed that this continuum described an enduring personality trait. Dissipators were people who got over angry feelings quickly and for whom the drive to seek revenge faded quickly. Ruminators, on the other hand, harbored and even enhanced feelings and the desire for revenge.

After creating a questionnaire to measure the trait of disposition–rumination, Caprara (1986) ran several experiments to test his hypotheses. He put his participants through a fairly common provocation–aggression research paradigm. In it, a participant was seated in a room with another supposed participant. They were instructed not to talk or communicate with each other directly but were allowed time to observe each other. The participant and confederate were then asked to report their impressions of each other by selecting from a list of adjectives, and then to exchange and read each other's adjective lists. One group of participants received a list of mostly negative adjectives from the confederate (the provocation condition) and the other received a list of mostly positive adjectives (the control condition). The participant was then seated at a console, and the confederate was taken to an adjoining room. In a task supposedly about extra sensory perception, the participant was asked to concentrate on the color of various cards and had the confederate guess the color. The participant informed the confederate whether the guess was correct by pressing a light switch (correct guess) or giving the confederate an electric shock (incorrect guess). The participant could choose among 24 levels of shocks, from mild to "rather strong." Of course, the confederate did not actually receive any shock but simply recorded the shock level selected by the participant. Over 30 trials, the confederate was wrong 21 times, meaning that the participant had 21 opportunities to choose the intensity of shocks. Not surprisingly, insulted participants (e.g., in the provocation condition) administered stronger shocks than noninsulted participants (Caprara, 1986; Caprara et al., 1987). Among those who were insulted, ruminators were more aggressive than dissipators.

Based on these results, Caprara argued for the importance of personality traits such as rumination in understanding aggression (Caprara & Pastorelli, 1989). Within 10 years, other researchers caught onto the potential of rumination to influence anger and aggression. Since then, the field of angry rumination has blossomed, yielding thought-provoking and timely information (for a review, see Denson, 2013). *Angry rumination* is defined as "unintentional and recurrent cognitive processes that emerge during and continue after an episode of anger experience" (Sukhodolsky, Golub, & Cromwell, 2001, p. 690). The emphasis is on the tendency for anger-related brooding, a cognitive activity that is different from the experience and expression of anger. Angry rumination involves recalling past anger experiences, attending to and reliving anger experiences, and pondering the causes and consequences of an anger experience, including thoughts of retaliation. A helpful example (adapted from Sukhodolsky et al., 2001), in the form of an inner monologue of someone who has just been stood up by a date, goes like this, "I cannot believe I got stood up by this #$%& – I am really mad (attention to anger experience)! This is just the kind of thing my ex used to do (memories of similar past experiences). I don't care if he is sick – I'm not returning his next call (cause and retaliation)."

In this chapter, I review evidence for the associations between rumination and anger, aggression, and related outcomes. I also explore potential moderators and mediators of these associations, as well as relevant theories about aggression and functions of angry rumination.

Along the way, we will touch on sports aggression, road rage, gang violence, and wars, as well as the more common occurrence of anger and aggression between two people.

Rumination and anger

We start with a familiar name from the depression literature. In an early set of experiments, Nolen-Hoeksema investigated the effect of rumination on angry mood (Rusting & Nolen-Hoeksema, 1998). After going through an angry mood induction, participants engaged in either rumination or distraction for 8 minutes—the same self-focused manipulation used in all of Nolen-Hoeksema's depression experiments. Participants then spent 5 minutes writing stories based on this prompt: "An older person is talking to a younger person." These stories were later rated for anger content. In all variants of this experiment, rumination increased anger, whereas distraction decreased or had no effect on preexisting anger. Even when participants were allowed to choose their response to anger, those who choose a ruminative imaginal task were angrier than those who chose a distraction imaginal task. This set of experiments provided the first evidence that rumination increased an existing angry mood.

Other researchers tested the same association using manipulations that were not borrowed from depression research. For many years, Walter Mischel and colleagues studied the difference between "hot" versus "cool" attentional focus (e.g., Metcalfe & Mischel, 1999). A "hot" focus involves directing attention to the arousing and emotional aspects of situations, whereas "cooling" strategies include distraction and cognitive reflections. Mischel hypothesized that the emotional, hot system makes effective self-regulation difficult and leads to reflexive responses. By contrast, the cool system facilitates emotional regulation and the control of impulsive tendencies. Although hot focus does not explicitly involve repetitive and uncontrollable thoughts, it clearly seems similar to rumination in its attention to upsetting events. In one experiment, participants were asked to recall an experience from their past that had made them feel intensely rejected, excluded, or abandoned (Ayduk, Mischel, & Downey, 2002). They then focused their attention on either their physiological and emotional reactions to the experience (e.g., "How did your heart beat? How did your face feel?"), or on the characteristics of the physical setting of the experience (e.g., "Where were you standing with respect to the people and the objects around you?"). As expected, participants in the hot-focus condition reported more anger and hostility on both self-report and implicit measures than in the cool-focus condition. Subsequent studies by these researchers also found that hot focus leads to greater anger, in both children and adults, concurrently and even 7 weeks later (Ayduk & Kross, 2008, 2010; Kross, Ayduk, & Mischel, 2005; Kross, Duckworth, Ayduk, Tsukayama, & Mischel, 2011).

Bushman (2002) created a memorable experimental manipulation to investigate the effect of ruminating while venting anger. The idea was that ruminating while expressing anger (e.g., hitting a punching bag) would lead to more anger than being distracted. Participants received negative feedback from a confederate, in the form of poor ratings of an essay they had just written arguing for their position on abortion. Participants then underwent rumination, distraction, or control manipulations. In the rumination condition, participants put on boxing gloves and were instructed to hit a punching bag as hard and as many times as they wanted *and* at the same time to think about the other student who criticized their work. Participants in the distraction condition focused their thoughts on becoming physically fit while they hit the punching bag. Finally, participants in the control condition sat quietly for 2 minutes. Bushman found that rumination while punching the bag led to more anger than did thinking about becoming fit or doing nothing. Unfortunately, the effect of rumination could not be separated from the effect of hitting a bag. Still, the instructions to think about someone who just criticized you seem to capture the essence of angry rumination.

In summary, rumination—manipulated in different ways and about different types of upsetting events—leads to more anger than does distraction. These experimental results are backed up by correlational studies showing that people with greater trait angry rumination[1] experience

1 The gold standard questionnaire of trait angry rumination is the 19-item anger rumination scale (ARS; Sukhodolsky et al., 2001), which assesses angry afterthoughts (e.g., "Whenever I experience anger, I keep thinking about it for a while"), thoughts of revenge (e.g., "When someone makes me angry I can't stop thinking about how to get back at that person"), angry memories (e.g., "I ponder about the injustices that have been done to me"), and understanding causes (e.g., "I think about the reasons people treat me badly"). The ARS has been adapted for use with children (Smith, Stephens, Repper, & Kistner, 2016). Caprara's (1986) 20-item measure of dissipation–rumination does not explicitly assess repetitive thinking, although many of the items inquire about what could be consequences of thinking repeatedly about insults (e.g., "Sometimes I can't sleep because of a wrong done to me," "If somebody harms me, I am not at peace until I can retaliate"). Other measures that assess angry rumination include the 13-item Rehearsal subscale of The Emotional Control Questionnaire (Roger & Najarian, 1989), the 10-item Angry Rumination subscale of The Displaced Aggression Questionnaire (Denson, Pedersen, & Miller, 2006), the 22-item Sadness and Anger Rumination Inventory (Peled & Moretti, 2007), the Intrusiveness subscale of the Impact of Event Scale (Horowitz, Wilner, & Alvarez, 1979; McCullough, Bono, & Root, 2007), and the 6-item Rumination about an Interpersonal Offense Scale (Wade, Vogel, Liao & Goldman, 2008).

more angry moods, express more anger, become more frustrated at losing sports matches, and have more hostile thoughts (Anestis, Anestis, Selby, & Joiner, 2009; Sukhodolsky et al., 2001). In an experience sampling study, momentary rumination predicted increased anger several hours later (Borders & Lu, 2017). Measures of both general rumination and angry rumination also correlate with increased vengefulness, or the tendency to seek revenge after suffering an interpersonal offense (Barber, Maltby, & Macaskill, 2005; McCullough, Bellah, Kilpatrick, & Johnson, 2001). One study even found that rumination is more strongly associated with events eliciting vengeful feelings than with anger-eliciting events (Elshout, Nelissen, & van Beest, 2015). As vengeance is a robust predictor of aggressive behavior (see McCullough et al., 2001), these results provide an excellent segue into the literature on rumination and aggression. I start by reviewing some of the major theories of aggression, to highlight the ways that both anger and rumination contribute to aggressive behavior.

Theories of aggression

Aggression is any form of behavior directed toward another individual that is intended to cause harm or injury (Anderson & Bushman, 2002). Researchers commonly make a distinction between hostile and instrumental aggression. *Hostile* aggression is an anger-driven, unplanned, retaliatory response to a perceived provocation that is ultimately intended to harm another person. This has also been called reactive, affective, "hot," and impulsive aggression. By contrast, *instrumental* (or proactive) aggression is premeditated, "cold-blooded" behavior having an ultimate goal other than harming the victim (i.e., to obtain money or justice). This distinction has been called into question in recent years by those who argue that hostile aggression can involve planning, just as instrumental aggression may involve some degree of impulsivity (Bushman & Anderson, 2001). Moreover, many acts of aggression have multiple goals. For example, robbery may involve an immediate goal to harm the person behind the cash register with the ultimate goal of making a financial profit (Anderson & Bushman, 2002). Although the distinction between hostile and instrumental aggression is flawed, the majority of aggression theories and research that I discuss concern hostile aggression.

The Cognitive Neoassociationistic Model (Berkowitz, 1990) proposes that many kinds of aversive events (e.g., interpersonal provocations, frustration, heat, pain, foul odors) produce negative affect. This negative affect automatically triggers thoughts, memories, physiological reactions, and behaviors that are associated with fight (i.e., aggressive) or flight (i.e., escape) tendencies. Both fight and flight reactions are automatically triggered, but the relative strength of each reaction depends on a variety of genetic, learned, and situational factors. This theory is based on the idea that mood-congruent information is organized together in long-term memory. Associative networks link together related memories, thoughts, feelings, and behavioral tendencies. Thus, the fight network links angry mood, hostile thoughts, angering memories, and various aggressive behaviors. Activation of any part of an associative network activates other components stored in that network. This theory can explain why a toddler spilling yogurt on one's new work pants could lead that parent to simultaneously feel angry, remember previous similar incidents, curse, and throw the toddler's unfinished yogurt into the trash.

However, Berkowitz also proposed that immediately after networks are automatically triggered, people have the opportunity to engage higher order cognitive processes; they might reflect on how they feel and consider consequences of acting on their feelings. These deliberate processes can either intensify or suppress activation of the network. Thus that same parent could, if she slept enough the previous night, catch herself before cursing and trashing the yogurt, take a deep breath, remind herself that she knows how to wash pants, pat the toddler's head, and head upstairs to change. Although this model did not explicitly incorporate rumination, Miller, Pedersen, Earleywine, and Pollock (2003) proposed that rumination about a provocation may maintain the activation of the aggressive network over time, making its components more accessible and subsequent aggressive behavior more likely. Therefore, if the parent instead spent the morning ruminating about how clumsy and thoughtless her child is, she would keep her aggression network activated and be more likely to lose patience with her child after school.

The General Aggression Model (GAM; Anderson & Bushman, 2002) integrates Berkowitz's network-based model with social learning approaches. The GAM proposes that individual differences (e.g., personality, learned beliefs, and values) interact with situational factors (e.g., frustration, provocation, pain, alcohol, and aggressive cues) to influence someone's internal state. This internal state is comprised of affect (anger), cognition (aggressive thoughts), and physiological arousal (elevated heart rate and blood pressure). These three aspects of one's internal state are interconnected—just like associative networks. Expanding on the network model, the GAM proposes that one's internal state is also influenced by and influences cognitive interpretations of situations. These interpretations are influenced by past learning, current resources, and future expectations. Returning to the yogurt incident, the parent might only become really angry at her child spilling yogurt if her past learning history had taught her to interpret accidents in a hostile way (i.e., hostile attribution), as indicative of the child trying to be hurtful or annoying. Also, if the parent is feeling distracted and stressed, she is less likely to look for alternative explanations (i.e., reappraisals), like remembering that the child is still awkward with a spoon. Finally, this interplay between internal state, predisposing personality traits, and cognitive attributions and reappraisals influences the likelihood of aggressive behavior. Unlike network models, in which aggression and anger are simultaneously triggered, the GAM asserts that past learning history, current cognitive resources, *and* an angry internal state influence whether individuals engage in aggression. Some of this learning history may include beliefs about when aggression is and is not acceptable, expected outcomes of aggression, and previous experience with aggression. Because of its emphasis on learning history and information processing, the GAM can explain both hostile and instrumental aggression.

There are several places for rumination in the GAM. First, tendencies for rumination may contribute to heightened anger, aggressive thoughts, and/or physiological arousal. This is the same idea as rumination maintaining an associative network. Rumination may also reinforce hostile attributions by encouraging selective attention to hostile stimuli, at the expense of attending to other, nonhostile cues (Wilkowski & Robinson, 2010). Ruminative selective attention of hostile stimuli will in turn exacerbate and prolong anger, making aggression more likely. This notion that rumination leads to a kind of myopia comes from the alcohol literature (Giancola, Josephs, Parrott, & Duke, 2010). The analogy is that, similar to the effect of being intoxicated, rumination narrows people's attention just to the angering event, so that they are less likely to notice other relevant information. Thus, if our parent is ruminating about her son's thoughtlessness, she might only remember that he had just whacked his little sister but not notice that he is sniffling and coughing from a nascent cold. In essence, rumination can impair higher order cognitive functioning, much like being drunk does.

Finally, a newer theoretical model organizes the many personality and situational factors that influence aggression. The I^3 (pronounced "I-cubed") theory emphasizes the role of poor self-control in understanding aggression (Finkel et al., 2012). Specifically, this theory proposes that aggression develops from a combination of instigating, impelling, and inhibiting factors. Instigation is exposure to provocations that create an urge to aggress. Impellance involves dispositional or situational factors that increase the urge to engage in aggressive behavior following an instigation. When both instigation and impellance are both high, aggression is likely. By contrast, inhibition involves dispositional or situational factors that override the urge to aggress. When inhibition is stronger than the urge to aggress, people behave nonaggressively. There are many sources of inhibition (e.g., reappraisal, beliefs about immorality of violence, good executive functioning, and desire for a relationship to last) and, on the flip side, disinhibition (e.g., fatigue, alcohol). Similarly, there are many possible impelling factors, such as tendencies for aggression and hostile attributions and rumination.

As we will see, researchers have drawn on all three of these theories to develop hypotheses about the link between rumination and aggressive behavior. I return to theoretical models later, when I discuss potential moderators and mechanisms of the effect of rumination on aggression.

Rumination and aggression

Early experiments showed that angry rumination leads to more hostile aggression. Collins and Bell (1997) randomly assigned low ruminators and high ruminators to provocation (e.g., negative feedback) or control conditions. Aggression was measured using the popular "Buss paradigm," in which participants competed with an "opponent" to score the most number of points. Participants could choose to increase their own number of points, deduct points from their opponent, or deliver a loud white noise to the opponent. The total number of noise blasts delivered to the opponent constituted the aggression measure. Results indicated that high ruminators who were provoked exhibited more aggression than low ruminators in the same condition. In fact, provocation did not affect the level of aggression displayed by the low ruminators; this group exhibited the same amount of aggression in both provocation and control conditions. Provocation only impacted the level of aggression for high ruminators. Similarly, in Bushman's (2002) experiment that I described earlier, after being insulted and punching a bag, participants engaged in a similar competitive task with the confederate. Participants who ruminated delivered longer and louder blasts of white noise than other participants.

Bushman also found that rumination could increase aggression 24 hours later. In this study (Bushman & Gibson, 2011), participants spent 20 minutes playing either violent or nonviolent video games (e.g., *Mortal Combat* or *Guitar Hero*). Participants in the rumination condition were then told, "In the next 24 hours, think about your play of the game, and try to identify ways your game play could improve when you play again" (p. 30). One day later, men who had played violent video games and been in the rumination condition blasted a partner with more white noise, compared to men who were not instructed to ruminate. Interestingly, there was no effect of violent video game or rumination for women. Because the experimenters did nothing to rig the video game or make participants fail, it is hard to argue that this study manipulated rumination specifically about a provocation. I prefer to interpret this study in the context of I^3 theory: exposure to violent video games and rumination can both be seen as impelling factors that, in combination, increase the likelihood of aggressive behavior.

All of these experiments measured the effect of rumination on hostile aggression in the laboratory, as measured by intensity of white noise blasts delivered to a stranger. It is fair to question how much these results apply to real life. Fortunately, studies have investigated different types and settings of aggressive behavior. For instance, both trait angry and depressive rumination are correlated with greater general tendencies for physical (e.g., hitting, shoving, and throwing something) and verbal (e.g., yelling, name-calling, and threatening) aggression, in both children and adults (Anestis et al., 2009; McLaughlin, Aldao, Wisco, & Hilt, 2014; Smith et al., 2016). Dispositional and manipulated angry rumination is also related to more aggressive driving (Denson et al., 2006; Suhr & Nesbit, 2013). In a rare study with high-risk adolescent males, angry rumination predicted aggressive behavior in the first month of incarceration at a juvenile justice facility (Smith et al., 2016). The effect of angry rumination has been shown in other cultures as well: Italian adolescents who ruminate are more likely to be aggressive and set fires (Del Bove, Caprara, Pastorelli, & Paciello, 2008), and athletes from the United Kingdom and Hong Kong who ruminate show greater sports-related aggression (Maxwell, Moores, & Chow, 2008). In a sorely underresearched area, adults higher in angry rumination engaged in more domestic abuse, or aggressive behaviors aimed at romantic partners (Denson et al., 2006; Sotelo & Babcock, 2013). Similarly, the brooding subscale of depressive rumination predicted physical aggression within intimate relationships among lesbian women (Lewis, Milletich, Derlega, & Padilla, 2014). In sum, both angry and depressive rumination are related to aggressive behavior against strangers, competitors, and loved ones.

Relational aggression encompasses methods of harming someone socially, such as spreading rumors, gossiping, excluding someone from a group, or anonymous insults on social media. This kind of aggression is more prevalent than overt (e.g., physical and verbal) aggression in children, adolescents, and adults, perhaps because it typically carries less serious consequences for offenders (Archer & Coyne, 2005). Despite biologically and socially based arguments that females likely engage in more relational aggression than males, the empirical data do not support that hypothesis (Card, Stucky, Sawalani, & Little, 2008). Instead, both females and males engage in similar amounts of relational aggression, which is strongly associated with depressive and anxious symptoms. Angry rumination is associated with greater relational aggression in children and undergraduates (García-Sancho, Salguero, & Fernández-Berrocal, 2016; Mathieson, Klimes-Dougan, & Crick, 2014; Smith et al., 2016). In young adults, trait depressive rumination also predicted relational aggression within romantic relationships (Goldstein, 2011). Experimental research is needed to determine the direction of association between rumination and relational aggression.

Whereas *direct* aggression is aimed at the source of an insult or provocation, *displaced* aggression targets an innocent person who is simply in the wrong place at the wrong time. There are three main reasons why people might engage in displaced aggression (Dollard et al., 1939). Sometimes retaliating directly against a provocateur simply is not feasible, as might occur if the other person left the situation, moved away, or died. Alternatively, direct retaliation may pose too much danger to the perpetrator, if for instance it is directed at a boss or really large, strong person. The initial provocation could also be an intangible entity, such as heat or a loud noise or something that smells terrible. In all of these situations, individuals may display displaced aggression toward anyone they come across in the course of their daily lives. In fascinating work, Edward Vasquez argued that gang members and affiliates are likely to engage in displaced aggression, in part because they may encounter provokers (e.g., police and violent family members) against whom they do not want or are unable to retaliate (Vasquez, Lickel, & Hennigan, 2009). He also suggested that gang members are more likely to engage in rumination due to norms of honor, reputation, and aggression reciprocity that may motivate them to think more about revenge. In a sample of adolescents from England, gang affiliation was in fact associated with greater tendencies for displaced aggression and angry rumination (Vasquez, Osman, & Wood, 2012). In addition, particularly in those adolescents who had gang associations, angry rumination related to more displaced aggression.

There is even more research on a construct called *triggered displaced* aggression. This is similar to displaced aggression, in that it targets someone other than the original provoker. But this time, the target of aggression provides some kind of trivial annoyance, or "trigger". I call this the kick-the-dog phenomenon. For instance, say I am angry about receiving some reviews that I perceive as unfair. It would not be a wise career move to retaliate against the actual reviewers. Instead, an hour later when my dog throws up yet again on our one white rug, I yell at him much more forcefully than he deserves, and more than I normally would when I am not already upset about something else. Research shows that even minor annoyances can trigger relatively high levels of aggression in previously provoked individuals, aggression that far surpasses what would be expected in normal, tit-for-tat interactions. Miller et al. (2003) argued that except in those instances when the initial provocation precedes the minor trigger by only a few minutes, triggered displaced aggression reflects the effect of angry rumination. In other words, this is the perfect application of the phenomenon Caprara initially wanted to understand: how hostile, retaliatory aggression can be delayed longer than angry arousal would realistically persist.

Several studies support the proposed role of rumination in triggered displaced aggression. Bushman, Bonacci, Pedersen, Vasquez, and Miller (2005) asked participants to complete several really difficult anagrams (e.g., NVTNIMEREON) while listening to distracting background music. Then, the experimenter got irritated with the participant for doing so poorly, saying in an exasperated voice that the data were not useable and that the participant should do them again, but that the experimenter did not want to waste his time so they should just move on. This lovely bit of acting constituted the provocation. Next came 25-minute rumination or distraction manipulations, which again were based on Nolen-Hoeksema's self-focused rumination manipulations. Finally, participants watched a video of an undergraduate research assistant posing trivia questions and were supposed to answer as many questions as possible. The experimenter said that the research assistant on the tape had applied for a coveted position as a paid researcher in a faculty member's lab and that the faculty member wanted participants to evaluate applicants. In one version of the tape, the research assistant read the trivia questions too quickly and mispronounced some names (e.g., Leonardo da Vinci was pronounced Leon Divinsky). In another version of the tape, the research assistant was composed and accurate. The fumbling research assistant was intended as the trigger—a minor annoyance that normally would not elicit a strong aggressive response. However, participants who ruminated for 25 minutes following the initial provocation were more upset by the fumbling research assistant and gave him more negative evaluations (the measure of aggression) than did participants in the distraction condition. Interestingly, rumination did not increase aggression in the absence of a trigger, which suggests that rumination did not increase mere displaced aggression.

Subsequent variants of this study paradigm replicated the main findings with different measures of aggression. For instance, participants who ruminated following a provocation also gave a mildly insulting partner more hot sauce to eat (while knowing that this person hated spicy food) than did participants in the distraction condition (Bushman et al., 2005). Rumination after watching a video of a robbery-related murder also led to longer prison sentences following the minor frustration of having to deal with a broken VCR player (Vasquez, Bartsch, Pedersen, & Miller, 2007). Even 8 hours after an initial provocation, participants who were asked to ruminate about a negative evaluation they received delivered more white noise blasts to a mildly annoying partner than did participants not asked to ruminate (Bushman et al., 2005). In all of these experiments on triggered displaced aggression, manipulated rumination only produced aggressive outcomes if it followed a provocation or angering event (Bushman, 2002; Bushman et al, 2005). Rumination by itself, without any precipitant angering experience, did not lead to increased aggression. Interestingly, rumination following more severe provocations led to more triggered displaced aggression than did rumination following moderate provocations (Vasquez et al., 2013). This suggests that rumination may be particularly associated with hostile, or retaliatory aggression.

What about the other type of aggression? Might not repeated thoughts about angering experiences also contribute to more calculated, "cold-blooded," instrumental aggression? White and colleagues have investigated this research question. In two of three studies with undergraduate students, angry rumination predicted greater instrumental aggression even after controlling for hostile aggression (Guerra & White, 2017; Turner & White, 2015; White & Turner, 2014). Instrumental aggression was most likely for men with low self-esteem who had high rumination tendencies (Turner & White, 2015). Of course, predicting instrumental aggression as self-reported by undergraduate students seems a far cry from understanding what drives armed robbers or mass murderers or even children who bully other kids. This is clearly an important gap that future research should address.

In sum, the research clearly indicates that angry rumination predicts increased aggression. This association emerges for laboratory-induced aggression and self-reported aggression of many types. Now, I turn to questions of *how* and *for whom*. Namely, what is it about angry rumination that contributes to aggressive behavior? Are there some people for whom the rumination–aggression link is stronger or weaker?

Mechanisms of the effect of rumination on aggression

The most basic explanation for rumination's effect on aggression is that it prolongs and exacerbates anger. I have already reviewed the literature linking rumination to anger, as well as the major theories of aggression, all of which suggest that angry moods can trigger aggression. Prolonged anger by itself, however, is not a satisfying explanation for the rumination–aggression link. We all get angry often, perhaps even several times a day, but most of us are not aggressive every time we feel anger. Therefore the more interesting question to explore is what features or consequences of rumination make people more likely to respond to anger with aggression. In the language of I^3 theory, how does rumination about an angering event overcome all of the inhibitory factors that keep most of us from acting aggressively most of the time? In an integrative review, Denson (2013) suggested several potential mechanisms that address this more nuanced question.

First, rumination allows people to mentally rehearse revenge and prevents forgiveness. I have already mentioned that rumination predicts increased vengeance, or the tendency to seek revenge after suffering an interpersonal offense. Vengeance can be seen as a flip side of forgiveness, which involves reduced motivation for revenge and increased motivation for relationship enhancement (McCullough et al., 2001). A sizable literature shows that angry and depressive rumination are associated with less forgiveness, both at the trait level and regarding particular offenses and individuals, cross-sectionally and over time (Burnette, Taylor, Worthington, & Forsyth, 2007; Fatfouta, 2015; Lucas, Young, Zhdanova, & Alexander, 2010; McCullough et al., 1998, 2007; Thompson et al., 2005). Interestingly, the thoughts of revenge subscale of the anger rumination scale are particularly related to less forgiveness (Barber et al., 2005). Similarly, angry rumination is particularly related to an increased motivation for revenge. Thus, rumination may lead to increased aggressive behavior when people are angry because it increases a desire for revenge, which inherently reduces the likelihood of forgiveness—an important inhibiting factor.

Rumination also leads to beliefs that aggression is legitimate. Caprara et al. (2013, 2014) studied a construct called moral disengagement, which encompasses justification of harming others (e.g., "It's OK to fly off the handle to protect my friends"), advantageous comparison (e.g., "Damaging property is no big deal when you consider that others are beating people up"), distortion of consequences (e.g., "teasing someone doesn't really hurt her"), euphemistic labeling (e.g., "Slapping someone is just a way of joking"), and attribution of blame (e.g., "People who get mistreated usually do things to deserve it"). These kinds of cognitive distortions presumably allow people to engage in self-serving behavior that they would not normally approve of. Caprara in fact found that rumination contributed to moral disengagement 2 years later, which in turn predicted engagement in aggressive behavior. Relatedly, when individuals were asked about the reasons why they engage in angry rumination, a common response was that it justifies any action they take in response to anger (Simpson & Papageorgiou, 2003). I should note that anger itself increases justification (Anderson & Bushman, 2002), so rumination's effect on anger may partially account for these results. Clearly, morals are a major source of inhibition when it comes to acting aggressively. If rumination can overcome or disengage people's morals and lets them justify harmful behavior, they will be more likely to engage in aggression.

Third, rumination appears to decrease self-control, a factor that contributes to aggressive behavior (Denson, DeWall, & Finkel, 2012). Support for this mechanism comes from several lines of research. Using the familiar procedure of negative feedback about difficult anagrams followed by 20 minutes of either a rumination or distraction manipulation, Denson, Pedersen, Friese, Hahm, and Roberts (2011) found that provoked participants who ruminated reported less self-control and provided more negative evaluations. Reduced self-control statistically mediated the association between rumination and aggression. Rumination is also related to the tendency to behave rashly in response to negative emotions, a construct called negative urgency that is considered one type of impulsive behavior (Peters, Eisenlohr-Moul, Upton, & Baer, 2013). People high in negative urgency tend to lose control of their behavior when experiencing sadness, fear, anger or other unpleasant emotions. In fact, negative urgency mediated the association between rumination and aggressive behavior (Kiselica & Borders, 2012). I discuss the extensive research linking rumination with cognitive indices of self-control (e.g., executive functioning) in a later chapter (see Chapter 9, Rumination, cognition, and the brain).

Finally, rumination may also prepare the body for physical action. This hypothesis is supported by research showing links between rumination and increased blood pressure and heart rate (Ottaviani et al., 2016). Rumination following a provocation is also associated with delayed cardiovascular recovery. I explore this literature in detail in Chapter 5, Rumination and physical functioning.

Taken together, the research on mechanisms suggests that rumination overcomes typical inhibitions against aggression by maintaining anger, increasing the desire for revenge, decreasing interest in forgiveness, and disengaging moral prohibitions. These cognitive factors may be accompanied by decreased self-control and increased physical activation. Thus, rumination appears to function at cognitive, physical, and behavioral levels to increase the likelihood of people acting aggressively in response to anger (see Fig. 3.1).

Moderators of the effect of rumination on aggression

I turn next to potential moderators of the association between rumination and aggressive behavior. Given the marked gender differences observed in depressive rumination, it makes sense that researchers have examined whether the experience and consequences of angry rumination also differ in women versus men. Other potential moderators include disinhibition and the type of rumination.

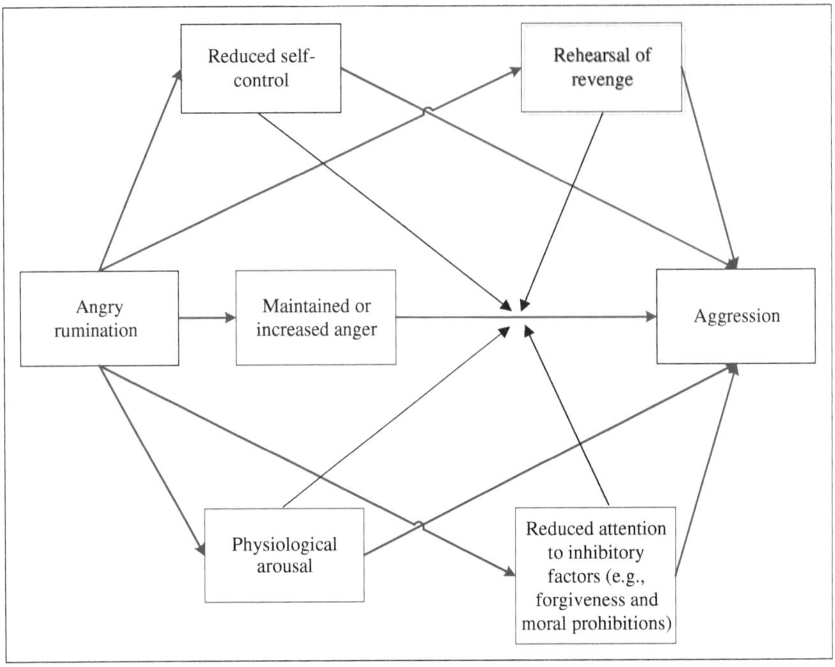

FIGURE 3.1 Proposed mechanisms of angry rumination.
Note: All of the mechanisms are also likely interrelated.

Gender

The first question is whether women and men experience different levels of angry rumination. Unlike with depressive rumination, the literature here is mixed and complex. The vast majority of research suggests that men and women self-report similar levels of angry rumination, across several different questionnaires (Barber et al., 2005; Burnette et al., 2007; Denson et al., 2006; Maxwell, 2004; McCullough et al., 2001; Peled & Moretti, 2010; Sukhodolsky et al., 2001). Conflicting results do exist, however, with a couple of studies finding higher angry rumination in males (Guerra & White, 2017; Maxwell, Sukhodolsky, Chow, & Wong, 2005) but another finding more angry rumination in females (Peled & Moretti, 2007).

Interestingly, some experiments examined whether there are gender differences in whether people *choose* to ruminate when angry. An early experiment had men and women either write or not write down their thoughts following a provocation (Frodi, 1978). Men who wrote their thoughts tended to focus on thoughts of anger and revenge and were subsequently more aggressive. By contrast, women who wrote their thoughts downplayed anger and in turn exhibited less subsequent aggression. In an attempt to replicate these results specifically with rumination, Rusting and Nolen-Hoeksema (1998) first put participants into angry or neutral moods and then asked them to choose to either ruminate or distract themselves for 5 minutes. Across two different mood manipulation procedures, women were more likely to distract themselves when angry and to ruminate when in a neutral mood. Men were equally likely to choose rumination or distraction, no matter their mood. Thus, two experiments suggest that women try to distract themselves from or avoid anger and aggression.

A more recent study operationalized the choice to ruminate following a provocation as selecting negative media stories (Knobloch-Westerwick & Alter, 2006). The underlying theory is that people choose their media consumption in a way that helps set a desired mood. Selecting happy news stories would function to dissipate angry moods, whereas selecting negative news stories would maintain angry moods, similar to the presumed functions of distraction versus rumination. Maintaining an angry mood was assumed to be necessary, or at least helpful, for later retaliation. In this experiment, after experiencing bogus negative feedback on a test performance, some participants were led to believe that they would evaluate the experimenter later in the study. All participants then browsed through an "experimental online news magazine," with headlines they could click on to read. Knowing that they would only have time to read some of the stories, participants had to select among 12 news reports—6 positive and 6 negative. In line with previous results, women who anticipated the opportunity to retaliate spent more time reading positive news stories, which resulted in less aggression. By contrast, men who anticipated the chance to retaliate spent more time reading negative news reports, which resulted in more negative evaluations.

In sum, even though the bulk of the evidence suggests that women and men report similar *tendencies* for angry rumination, men in laboratory settings choose to ruminate more than women do. When given a choice, by contrast, women prefer to not ruminate about angering events. This may reflect greater conflict in women about experiencing and expressing anger and aggression. One question these findings raise is whether women experience angry rumination as more uncomfortable or ego-dystonic than men. It also suggests that women are more likely to perceive angry rumination as uncontrollable, because if given the choice, they would prefer to engage in distraction. Future research will need to examine these and other questions about gender differences in the *experience* of angry rumination.

A separate question is whether the *effects* of rumination on anger and aggression vary for women versus men. Once again, the results are mixed. Most studies generally find no interaction between rumination and gender when predicting anger and aggression (Guerra & White, 2017; Peled & Moretti, 2007, 2010; Smith et al., 2016; Turner & White, 2015; Verona, 2005). However, conflicting results again exist, with one study finding that depressive rumination predicted future aggression only for boys but not girls (McLaughlin et al., 2014). Similarly, trait rumination predicted increased hostility in men but decreased hostility for women (Verona, 2005). By contrast, in a triggered displaced aggression experiment, although men generally were more aggressive than women, there were no gender differences in aggression in the rumination condition (Bushman et al., 2005). These results suggest that rumination may have erased gender differences in aggression by presumably having stronger effects for women. Thus, although the majority of studies do not generally find gender differences in the effect of angry rumination, mixed results exist. A better understanding of gender differences in women and men's *experience* of angry rumination may shed light on differences in the *effects* of angry rumination. In addition, the presence of mixed results suggests, as always, that other constructs may moderate the effect of gender.

Disinhibition

The potential moderating role of disinhibition comes from a few literatures. First, several studies suggest that alcohol consumption enhances the rumination–aggression link. Alcohol intoxication by itself is a robust contributor to aggression (Ito, Miller, & Pollock, 1996). An initial survey study found that rumination was more strongly associated with aggression in the past 6 months for individuals who drank heavily (Borders, Barnwell, & Earleywine, 2007). In a follow-up experiment, participants drank either an alcoholic beverage or a placebo drink made to look and smell like it had alcohol and then engaged in a competitive task with a confederate (Borders & Giancola, 2011). The association between measured angry rumination and aggressive behavior was much stronger in participants who were intoxicated than sober. In a similar experiment with heterosexual couples, participants were randomly assigned to drink an alcoholic or placebo beverage (Watkins, DiLillo, & Maldonado, 2015). Participants then identified an unresolved issue in their relationship that made them angry and were instructed to ruminate about or reappraise the issue for 2 minutes. Participants then played a competitive task with their partner. Once again, rumination interacted with alcohol consumption to predict stronger aggression. By contrast, Denson failed to find an interaction between manipulated rumination and alcohol consumption in two studies of triggered displaced aggression (Denson, Spanovic, & Miller, 2009; Denson, White, &

Warburton, 2009). Future research will need to examine why alcohol consumption appears to moderate the effect of rumination on direct but not triggered displaced aggression.

Additional evidence for the moderating effect of disinhibition comes from studies examining psychopathy. A risk factor for aggressive behaviors, psychopathy describes a group of traits including callousness, lack of empathy or remorse, irresponsibility, impulsivity, and antisocial behaviors. One experiment found that the effect of rumination about a provocation on triggered displaced aggression was stronger at higher levels of psychopathy (Denson, Spanovic, et al., 2009; Denson, White, et al., 2009). Similarly, a survey study found that the association between angry rumination and hostile aggression was much stronger for individuals high in the impulsive and antisocial traits of psychopathy (Guerra & White, 2017). Relatedly, the association between rumination and frequency of intimate partner violence in the last year was stronger for men high in trait impulsivity (Sotelo & Babcock, 2013). In sum, rumination may interact with tendencies for poor impulse control, a disregard for social norms, and ruthlessness, making aggression more likely.

Finally, some work has focused on angry rumination and autism. Individuals on the autism spectrum may become fixated on a particular stimulus and have a hard time disengaging from and inhibiting behavior related to that stimulus. They also have difficulty understanding other people's emotions and perspectives, a key component of empathy. Interestingly, one study found that having autism spectrum characteristics strengthened the associations between angry rumination and physical aggression (Pugliese, Fritz, & White, 2015).

Type of rumination

In earlier sections, I reviewed evidence that measures assessing both angry and depressive rumination predicted greater anger and aggression. One understandable question is whether angry rumination is more strongly associated with aggression than are other types of rumination. It makes intuitive sense that repetitive thinking specifically about being angry and past insults might be more strongly predictive of aggressive behavior. A few researchers have directly compared the effects of different types of rumination on aggression.

Maya Peled and Marlene Moretti (2007, 2010) conducted two survey studies in which they compared parallel self-report measures of angry and depressive rumination. In undergraduate students as well as adolescents with mental health or behavioral problems, angry rumination but not depressive rumination uniquely predicted greater anger, relational aggression, and physical and verbal aggression. Similarly, depressive rumination uniquely predicted depressive symptoms. Interestingly, depressive rumination predicted *less* physical and verbal aggression when controlling for angry rumination. This is in contrast to positive zero-order correlations they and others found between depressive rumination and aggression (e.g., Goldstein, 2011; Lewis et al., 2014; McLaughlin et al., 2014). However, controlling for angry rumination when examining the effect of depressive rumination basically takes out the ruminative process and leaves only depressive symptoms. In other words, depressive rumination correlated with *more* aggression, but depressive symptoms without rumination predicted *less* aggression. This suggests that the *process* of rumination—not the *content* of depressive thoughts—fuels the association of depressive rumination with aggression.

No experiments have yet contrasted the effects of rumination about an angering event versus rumination about a sad mood on subsequent aggression. This type of design would help answer the question at hand. However, Pedersen et al. (2011) compared two types of manipulated rumination following a provocation. *Provocation-focused* rumination involved participants writing for 20 minutes about what had occurred so far in the experiment (e.g., the provocation). By contrast, *self-focused* rumination involved Nolen-Hoeksema's classic rumination manipulation (i.e., writing about self-focused phrases like "what kind of person you are"). Interestingly, both provocation-focused and self-focused rumination led to more triggered displaced aggression than did distraction (see also Denson et al., 2006). However, the routes to aggression varied somewhat for each type of rumination. Specifically, provocation-focused rumination led to aggression because it increased angry affect. By contrast, self-focused rumination led to aggression via both angry affect and self-critical negative affect (e.g., regret and disgraced). Furthermore, only provocation-focused rumination led to increases in blood pressure. In sum, the *process* of ruminating following an angering event may be the driving factor in predicting aggression, largely because it maintains anger. At the same time, the *content* of rumination appears to differentially influence experienced emotions and physiological changes.

Conclusion

In this chapter, I reviewed the literature showing that rumination is associated with maintained or increased anger, as well as various types of aggressive behavior. Most of this literature assessed angry rumination, or ruminative thinking specifically about anger and angering events. Rumination fits nicely into major theories of aggression, as it both maintains anger and functions as an impelling factor that overcomes existing inhibitions against aggression. Specifically, the research reviewed on mediators and moderators can be integrated to suggest that the *process* of repetitive thinking facilitates vengeful aggression by reducing self-control, increasing physiological arousal, and narrowing people's attention on hostile stimuli at the expense of focusing on inhibitory information such as reasons for forgiveness and moral prohibitions against aggression. The effects of rumination on aggression may be particularly strong for people who are already less inhibited (e.g., intoxication and psychopathy). Future research should continue to explore gender differences in the experiences and effect of angry rumination.

Research also needs to further examine the similarities and differences between angry rumination and other types of rumination. They likely share a common process but differ in thought content. Naturally, rumination about anger is focused on another person or the angering event approximately 73% of the time; it is focused on oneself only 27% of the time (Siewert, Kubiak, Jonas, & Weber, 2011). In other words, angry rumination may not naturally be a self-focused thought process, in the way that depressive rumination is. Angry rumination is also likely both past- and future-focused, because it involves thoughts about past angering events as well as plans for future retaliation. Angry and depressive rumination share approximately 25% of their variance (e.g., Gilbert, Cheung, Irons, & McEwan, 2005), suggesting that they are related but unique constructs. Unfortunately, the angry rumination literature has remained almost entirely separate from the depressive and anxious rumination/worry literatures. One of my hopes with this chapter is to encourage researchers to begin including angry rumination as one type of negative repetitive thought. Doing so might help shed light on the important question of the relative roles of process versus content in repetitive thought.

Another interesting question that arises from some of the studies reviewed here is how long angry rumination and its effects last. For instance, some experiments tested the effect of manipulated angry rumination 8 and even 24 hours later (Bushman et al., 2005; Bushman & Gibson, 2011). However, studies of naturally occurring rumination found that the average duration of angry rumination episodes was approximately 30 minutes, with 80% ending within 1 hour (Siewert et al., 2011). If we can assume that people are not ruminating for 8 or 24 hours nonstop, then what predicts the observed delayed effect of angry rumination? Findings that angry rumination increases willingness to forgiveness and perceived legitimacy of aggression suggests that rumination may influence cognitive factors that last well beyond the rumination process ends. Future research should explore this possibility, not just with angry rumination but with other forms of negative repetitive thinking.

Finally, I want to review some fascinating propositions about the evolutionary function of angry rumination. Denson (2013) noted the functional value of anger as a motivating force behind aggression, which is at times necessary in order to obtain sufficient resources for survival. Because anger is a relatively short-lived emotion, aggression carried out in response to an immediate angering event could come at the risk of a costly confrontation. By contrast, angry rumination can persist over long periods of time. Thus, angry rumination might serve to maintain anger until a more opportune time, when aggression would most likely be effective and carry fewer risks. Anthropological research on blood revenge suggests that retribution can occur decades or even generations after the initial provocation. In order to maintain outrage over years, groups may engage in *collective* angry rumination, in which they retell the provocation and harp on the perceived injustice and means of retaliation.

One implication of this theory is that angry rumination, both individually and collectively in a group, might explain the existence of long-held national grievances that ultimately lead to wars (Denson, 2013). Many wars are examples of both vicarious retribution and displaced aggression, because members of one group fight against members of another group for an initial provocation that did not actually harm them and was not perpetrated by the specific individuals fighting the war (Lickel, Miller, Stenstrom, Denson, & Schmader, 2006). If individuals and/or groups are angrily ruminating over time about perceived provocations, this process may explain intergenerational hatred, out-group prejudice, and acts of revenge for harm that occurred decades ago.

At the same time, angry rumination may also motivate people to engage in constructive efforts to combat injustice. In several studies, my colleague and I tested whether angry rumination was associated with increased willingness to engage in collective action, or efforts such as signing petitions and attending rallies that aim to improve the position of one's group in society (Borders & Wiley, 2019). One of the primary predictors of collective action is anger about perceived injustice (van Zomeren, Postmes, & Spears, 2008). However, anger is not a satisfactory explanation for how perceived injustice translates into collective action. Anger can be fleeting, whereas collective action is a planned, long-term behavior. It requires not only that individuals feel angry in a moment, but also that they sustain anger over a period of time. Thus, a more complete understanding of collective action may require an emphasis on strategies that sustain anger about injustice. In survey studies with ethnic minorities, sexual minorities, and women, rumination specifically about perceived discrimination mediated the association between anger about discrimination and willingness to engage in collective action. A follow-up experiment induced anger by asking women to read an article about gender harassment and then manipulated rumination versus distraction. As expected, rumination maintained anger about gender harassment, whereas distraction decreased anger. Moreover, the rumination condition indirectly predicted greater collective action intentions via anger, even controlling for other known predictors of collection action. In sum, the consequences of rumination about angering events may not all be negative.

References

Anderson, C. A., & Bushman, B. J. (2002). Human aggression. *Annual Review of Psychology, 53*(1), 27–51. Available from https://doi.org/10.1146/annurev.psych.53.100901.135231.

Anestis, J. C., Anestis, M. D., Selby, E. A., & Joiner, T. E. (2009). Anger rumination across forms of aggression. *Personality and Individual Differences, 46*(2), 192–196. Available from https://doi.org/10.1016/j.paid.2008.09.026.

Archer, J., & Coyne, S. M. (2005). An integrated review of indirect, relational, and social aggression. *Personality and Social Psychology Review: An Official Journal of the Society for Personality and Social Psychology, Inc, 9*(3), 212–230. Available from https://doi.org/10.1207/s15327957pspr0903_2.

Ayduk, Ö., & Kross, E. (2008). Enhancing the pace of recovery: Self-distanced analysis of negative experiences reduces blood pressure reactivity. *Psychological Science, 19*(3), 229–231. Available from https://doi.org/10.1111/j.1467-9280.2008.02073.x.

Ayduk, Ö., & Kross, E. (2010). From a distance. *Journal of Personality and Social Psychology, 98*(5), 809–829. Available from https://doi.org/10.1037/a0019205.

Ayduk, O., Mischel, W., & Downey, G. (2002). Attentional mechanisms linking rejection to hostile reactivity: The role of "Hot" versus "Cool" focus. *Psychological Science, 13*(5), 443–448. Available from https://doi.org/10.1111/1467-9280.00478.

Barber, L., Maltby, J., & Macaskill, A. (2005). Angry memories and thoughts of revenge: The relationship between forgiveness and anger rumination. *Personality and Individual Differences, 39*(2), 253–262. Available from https://doi.org/10.1016/j.paid.2005.01.006.

Berkowitz, L. (1990). On the formation and regulation of anger and aggression. *American Psychologist, 45*(4), 494–503. Available from https://doi.org/10.1037/0003-066X.45.4.494.

Borders, A., Barnwell, S. S., & Earleywine, M. (2007). Alcohol-aggression expectancies and dispositional rumination moderate the effect of alcohol consumption on alcohol-related aggression and hostility. *Aggressive Behavior, 33*(4), 327–338. Available from https://doi.org/10.1002/ab.20187.

Borders, A., & Giancola, P. R. (2011). Trait and state hostile rumination facilitate alcohol-related aggression. *Journal of Studies on Alcohol and Drugs, 72*(4), 545–554. Available from https://doi.org/10.15288/jsad.2011.72.545.

Borders, A., & Lu, S. (2017). The bidirectional associations between state anger and rumination and the role of trait mindfulness. *Aggressive Behavior, 43*(4), 342–351. Available from https://doi.org/10.1002/ab.21693.

Borders, A., & Wiley, S. (2019). Rumination about discrimination mediates the unique association between anger and collective action intentions. *Group Processes & Intergroup Relations*. Available from https://doi.org/10.1177/1368430219875214.

Burnette, J. L., Taylor, K. W., Worthington, E. L., & Forsyth, D. R. (2007). Attachment and trait forgivingness: The mediating role of angry rumination. *Personality and Individual Differences*, *42*(8), 1585–1596. Available from https://doi.org/10.1016/j.paid.2006.10.033.

Bushman, B. J. (2002). Does venting anger feed or extinguish the flame? catharsis, rumination, distraction, anger, and aggressive responding. *Personality and Social Psychology Bulletin*, *28*(6), 724–731. Available from https://doi.org/10.1177/0146167202289002.

Bushman, B. J., & Anderson, C. A. (2001). Is it time to pull the plug on the hostile versus instrumental aggression dichotomy? *Psychological Review*, *108*(1), 273–279. Available from https://doi.org/10.1037/0033-295X.108.1.273.

Bushman, B. J., Bonacci, A. M., Pedersen, W. C., Vasquez, E. A., & Miller, N. (2005). Chewing on it can chew you up. *Journal of Personality and Social Psychology*, *88*(6), 969–983. Available from https://doi.org/10.1037/0022-3514.88.6.969.

Bushman, B. J., & Gibson, B. (2011). Violent video games cause an increase in aggression long after the game has been turned off. *Social Psychological & Personality Science*, *2*(1), 29–32. Available from https://doi.org/10.1177/1948550610379506.

Caprara, G. V. (1986). Indicators of aggression: The dissipation-rumination scale. *Personality and Individual Differences*, *7*(6), 763–769. Available from https://doi.org/10.1016/0191-8869(86)90074-7.

Caprara, G. V., Alessandri, G., Tisak, M. S., Paciello, M., Caprara, M. G., Gerbino, M., & Fontaine, R. G. (2013). Individual differences in personality conducive to engagement in aggression and violence. *European Journal of Personality*, *27*(3), 290–303. Available from https://doi.org/10.1002/per.1855.

Caprara, G. V., Gargaro, T., Pastorelli, C., Prezza, M., Renzi, P., & Zelli, A. (1987). Individual differences and measures of aggression in laboratory studies. *Personality and Individual Differences*, *8*(6), 885–893. Available from https://doi.org/10.1016/0191-8869(87)90140-1.

Caprara, G. V., & Pastorelli, C. (1989). Toward a reorientation of research on aggression. *European Journal of Personality*, *3*(2), 121–138. Available from https://doi.org/10.1002/per.2410030206.

Caprara, G. V., Tisak, M. S., Alessandri, G., Fontaine, R. G., Fida, R., & Paciello, M. (2014). The contribution of moral disengagement in mediating individual tendencies toward aggression and violence. *Developmental Psychology*, *50*(1), 71–85. Available from https://doi.org/10.1037/a0034488.

Card, N. A., Stucky, B. D., Sawalani, G. M., & Little, T. D. (2008). Direct and indirect aggression during childhood and adolescence: A meta-analytic review of gender differences, intercorrelations, and relations to maladjustment. *Child Development*, *79*(5), 1185–1229. Available from https://doi.org/10.1111/j.1467-8624.2008.01184.x.

Collins, K., & Bell, R. (1997). Personality and aggression: The dissipation-rumination scale. *Personality and Individual Differences*, *22*(5), 751–755. Available from https://doi.org/10.1016/S0191-8869(96)00248-6.

Del Bove, G., Caprara, G., Pastorelli, C., & Paciello, M. (2008). Juvenile firesetting in italy: Relationship to aggression, psychopathology, personality, self-efficacy, and school functioning. *European Child & Adolescent Psychiatry*, *17*(4), 235–244. Available from https://doi.org/10.1007/s00787-007-0664-6.

Denson, T. F. (2013). The multiple systems model of angry rumination. *Personality and Social Psychology Review*, *17*(2), 103–123. Available from https://doi.org/10.1177/1088868312467086.

Denson, T. F., DeWall, C. N., & Finkel, E. J. (2012). Self-control and aggression. *Current Directions in Psychological Science*, *21*(1), 20–25. Available from https://doi.org/10.1177/0963721411429451.

Denson, T. F., Pedersen, W. C., Friese, M., Hahm, A., & Roberts, L. (2011). Understanding impulsive aggression: Angry rumination and reduced self-control capacity are mechanisms underlying the provocation-aggression relationship. *Personality and Social Psychology Bulletin, 37*(6), 850–862. Available from https://doi.org/10.1177/0146167211401420.

Denson, T. F., Pedersen, W. C., & Miller, N. (2006). The displaced aggression questionnaire. *Journal of Personality and Social Psychology, 90*(6), 1032–1051. Available from https://doi.org/10.1037/0022-3514.90.6.1032.

Denson, T. F., Spanovic, M., & Miller, N. (2009). Cognitive appraisals and emotions predict cortisol and immune responses. *Psychological Bulletin, 135*(6), 823–853. Available from https://doi.org/10.1037/a0016909.

Denson, T. F., White, A. J., & Warburton, W. A. (2009). Trait displaced aggression and psychopathy differentially moderate the effects of acute alcohol intoxication and rumination on triggered displaced aggression. *Journal of Research in Personality, 43*(4), 673–681. Available from https://doi.org/10.1016/j.jrp.2009.04.003.

Dollard, J., Miller, N. E., Doob, L. W., Mowrer, O. H., & Sears, R. R. (1939). *Frustration and aggression*. New Haven, CT: Yale University Press.

Doob, A. N., & Climie, R. J. (1972). Delay of measurement and the effects of film violence. *Journal of Experimental Social Psychology, 8*(2), 136–142. Available from https://doi.org/10.1016/0022-1031(72)90031-5.

Elshout, M., Nelissen, R. M. A., & van Beest, I. (2015). Vengeance is self-focused: Comparing vengeful to anger-driven responses. *Cognition and Emotion, 29*(7), 1239–1255. Available from https://doi.org/10.1080/02699931.2014.976181.

Fatfouta, R. (2015). How forgiveness affects processing time: Mediation by rumination about the transgression. *Personality and Individual Differences, 82*, 90–95. Available from https://doi.org/10.1016/j.paid.2015.03.016.

Finkel, E. J., DeWall, C. N., Slotter, E. B., McNulty, J. K., Pond, R. S., Jr, & Atkins, D. C. (2012). Using I3 theory to clarify when dispositional aggressiveness predicts intimate partner violence perpetration. *Journal of Personality and Social Psychology, 102*(3), 533–549. Available from https://doi.org/10.1037/a0025651.

Frodi, A. (1978). Experiential and physiological responses associated with anger and aggression in women and men. *Journal of Research in Personality, 12*(3), 335–349. Available from https://doi.org/10.1016/0092-6566(78)90060-0.

García-Sancho, E., Salguero, J. M., & Fernández-Berrocal, P. (2016). Angry rumination as a mediator of the relationship between ability emotional intelligence and various types of aggression. *Personality and Individual Differences, 89*, 143–147. Available from https://doi.org/10.1016/j.paid.2015.10.007.

Giancola, P. R., Josephs, R. A., Parrott, D. J., & Duke, A. A. (2010). Alcohol myopia revisited: Clarifying aggression and other acts of disinhibition through a distorted lens. *Perspectives on Psychological Science, 5*(3), 265–278. Available from https://doi.org/10.1177/1745691610369467.

Gilbert, P., Cheung, M., Irons, C., & McEwan, K. (2005). An exploration into depression-focused and anger-focused rumination in relation to depression in a student population. *Behavioural and Cognitive Psychotherapy, 33*(3), 273–283. Available from https://doi.org/10.1017/S1352465804002048.

Goldstein, S. E. (2011). Relational aggression in young adults' friendships and romantic relationships. *Personal Relationships, 18*(4), 645–656. Available from https://doi.org/10.1111/j.1475-6811.2010.01329.x.

Guerra, R., & White, B. (2017). Psychopathy and functions of aggression in emerging adulthood: Moderation by anger rumination and gender. *Journal of Psychopathology and Behavioral Assessment, 39*(1), 35–45. Available from https://doi.org/10.1007/s10862-016-9563-9.

Horowitz, M., Wilner, N., & Alvarez, W. (1979). Impact of event scale: A measure of subjective stress. *Psychosomatic Medicine, 41*(3), 209–218. Available from https://doi.org/10.1097/00006842-197905000-00004.

Ito, T. A., Miller, N., & Pollock, V. E. (1996). Alcohol and aggression. *Psychological Bulletin, 120*(1), 60–82. Available from https://doi.org/10.1037/0033-2909.120.1.60.

Kiselica, A., & Borders, A. (2012). The role of impulsivity in the rumination-aggression association. In: *Paper presented at the Eastern Psychological Association.*

Knobloch-Westerwick, S., & Alter, S. (2006). Mood adjustment to social situations through mass media use: How men ruminate and women dissipate angry moods. *Human Communication Research, 32*(1), 58–73. Available from https://doi.org/10.1111/j.1468-2958.2006.00003.x.

Kross, E., Ayduk, O., & Mischel, W. (2005). When asking "Why" does not hurt distinguishing rumination from reflective processing of negative emotions. *Psychological Science, 16* (9), 709–715. Available from https://doi.org/10.1111/j.1467-9280.2005.01600.x.

Kross, E., Duckworth, A., Ayduk, O., Tsukayama, E., & Mischel, W. (2011). The effect of self-distancing on adaptive versus maladaptive self-reflection in children. *Emotion (Washington, D.C.), 11*(5), 1032–1039. Available from https://doi.org/10.1037/a0021787.

Lewis, R. J., Milletich, R. J., Derlega, V. J., & Padilla, M. A. (2014). Sexual minority stressors and psychological aggression in lesbian women's intimate relationships. *Psychology of Women Quarterly, 38*(4), 535–550. Available from https://doi.org/10.1177/0361684313517866.

Lickel, B., Miller, N., Stenstrom, D. M., Denson, T. F., & Schmader, T. (2006). Vicarious retribution: The role of collective blame in intergroup aggression. *Personality and Social Psychology Review: An Official Journal of the Society for Personality and Social Psychology, Inc, 10*(4), 372–390. Available from https://doi.org/10.1207/s15327957pspr1004_6.

Lucas, T., Young, J. D., Zhdanova, L., & Alexander, S. (2010). Self and other justice beliefs, impulsivity, rumination, and forgiveness: Justice beliefs can both prevent and promote forgiveness. *Personality and Individual Differences, 49*(8), 851–856. Available from https://doi.org/10.1016/j.paid.2010.07.014.

Mathieson, L. C., Klimes-Dougan, B., & Crick, N. R. (2014). Dwelling on it may make it worse: The links between relational victimization, relational aggression, rumination, and depressive symptoms in adolescents. *Development and Psychopathology, 26*(3), 735–747. Available from https://doi.org/10.1017/S0954579414000352.

Maxwell, J. P. (2004). Anger rumination: An antecedent of athlete aggression? *Psychology of Sport & Exercise, 5*(3), 279–289. Available from https://doi.org/10.1016/S1469-0292(03)00007-4.

Maxwell, J. P., Moores, E., & Chow, C. C. F. (2008). Anger rumination and self-reported aggression amongst British and Hong Kong Chinese athletes: A cross cultural comparison. *International Journal of Sport and Exercise Psychology, 5*(1), 9–27. Available from https://doi.org/10.1080/1612197X.2008.9671810.

Maxwell, J. P., Sukhodolsky, D. G., Chow, C. C. F., & Wong, C. F. C. (2005). Anger rumination in Hong Kong and Great Britain: Validation of the scale and a cross-cultural comparison. *Personality and Individual Differences, 39*(6), 1147–1157. Available from https://doi.org/10.1016/j.paid.2005.03.022.

McCullough, M. E., Bellah, C. G., Kilpatrick, S. D., & Johnson, J. L. (2001). Vengefulness: Relationships with forgiveness, rumination, well-being, and the big five. *Personality and Social Psychology Bulletin, 27*(5), 601–610. Available from https://doi.org/10.1177/0146167201275008.

McCullough, M. E., Bono, G., & Root, L. M. (2007). Rumination, emotion, and forgiveness. *Journal of Personality and Social Psychology, 92*(3), 490–505. Available from https://doi.org/10.1037/0022-3514.92.3.490.

McCullough, M. E., Rachal, K. C., Sandage, S. J., Worthington, E. L., Brown, S. W., & Hight, T. L. (1998). Interpersonal forgiving in close relationships. *Journal of Personality and Social Psychology, 75*(6), 1586–1603. Available from https://doi.org/10.1037/0022-3514.75.6.1586.

McLaughlin, K. A., Aldao, A., Wisco, B. E., & Hilt, L. M. (2014). Rumination as a transdiagnostic factor underlying transitions between internalizing symptoms and aggressive behavior in early adolescents. *Journal of Abnormal Psychology, 123*(1), 13–23. Available from https://doi.org/10.1037/a0035358.

Metcalfe, J., & Mischel, W. (1999). A hot/cool-system analysis of delay of gratification. *Psychological Review, 106*(1), 3–19. Available from https://doi.org/10.1037/0033-295X.106.1.3.

Miller, N., Pedersen, W. C., Earleywine, M., & Pollock, V. E. (2003). A theoretical model of triggered displaced aggression. *Personality and Social Psychology Review, 7*(1), 75–97. Available from https://doi.org/10.1207/S15327957PSPR0701_5.

Ottaviani, C., Thayer, J. F., Verkuil, B., Lonigro, A., Medea, B., Couyoumdjian, A., & Brosschot, J. F. (2016). Physiological concomitants of perseverative cognition: A systematic review and meta-analysis. *Psychological Bulletin, 142*(3), 231–259. Available from https://doi.org/10.1037/bul0000036.

Pedersen, W. C., Denson, T. F., Goss, R. J., Vasquez, E. A., Kelley, N. J., & Miller, N. (2011). The impact of rumination on aggressive thoughts, feelings, arousal, and behaviour. *The British Journal of Social Psychology, 50*(Pt 2), 281. Retrieved from <https://www.ncbi.nlm.nih.gov/pubmed/21545459>.

Peled, M., & Moretti, M. (2010). Ruminating on rumination: Are rumination on anger and sadness differentially related to aggression and depressed mood? *Journal of Psychopathology and Behavioral Assessment, 32*(1), 108–117. Available from https://doi.org/10.1007/s10862-009-9136-2.

Peled, M., & Moretti, M. M. (2007). Rumination on anger and sadness in adolescence: Fueling of fury and deepening of despair. *Journal of Clinical Child & Adolescent Psychology, 36*(1), 66–75. Available from https://doi.org/10.1080/15374410709336569.

Peters, J. R., Eisenlohr-Moul, T. A., Upton, B. T., & Baer, R. A. (2013). Nonjudgment as a moderator of the relationship between present-centered awareness and borderline features: Synergistic interactions in mindfulness assessment. *Personality and Individual Differences, 55*(1), 24–28. Available from https://doi.org/10.1016/j.paid.2013.01.021.

Pugliese, C. E., Fritz, M. S., & White, S. W. (2015). The role of anger rumination and autism spectrum disorder–linked perseveration in the experience of aggression in the general population. *Autism, 19*(6), 704–712. Available from https://doi.org/10.1177/1362361314548731.

Roger, D., & Najarian, B. (1989). The construction and validation of a new scale for measuring emotion control. *Personality and Individual Differences, 10*(8), 845–853. Available from https://doi.org/10.1016/0191-8869(89)90020-2.

Rusting, C. L., & Nolen-Hoeksema, S. (1998). Regulating responses to anger. *Journal of Personality and Social Psychology, 74*(3), 790–803. Available from https://doi.org/10.1037/0022-3514.74.3.790.

Siewert, K., Kubiak, T., Jonas, C., & Weber, H. (2011). Trait anger moderates the impact of anger-associated rumination on social well-being. *Personality and Individual Differences, 51*(6), 769–774. Available from https://doi.org/10.1016/j.paid.2011.06.030.

Simpson, C., & Papageorgiou, C. (2003). Metacognitive beliefs about rumination in anger. *Cognitive and Behavioral Practice, 10*(1), 91–94. Available from https://doi.org/10.1016/S1077-7229(03)80012-3.

Smith, S., Stephens, H., Repper, K., & Kistner, J. (2016). The relationship between anger rumination and aggression in typically developing children and high-risk adolescents. *Journal of Psychopathology and Behavioral Assessment, 38*(4), 515–527. Available from https://doi.org/10.1007/s10862-016-9542-1.

Sotelo, J., & Babcock, J. (2013). BIS/BAS variables as moderators of the rumination-intimate partner violence link. *Journal of Family Violence, 28*(3), 233–242. Available from https://doi.org/10.1007/s10896-013-9500-6.

Suhr, K. A., & Nesbit, S. M. (2013). Dwelling on 'Road rage': The effects of trait rumination on aggressive driving. *Transportation Research Part F: Psychology and Behaviour, 21*, 207–218. Available from https://doi.org/10.1016/j.trf.2013.10.001.

Sukhodolsky, D. G., Golub, A., & Cromwell, E. N. (2001). Development and validation of the anger rumination scale. *Personality and Individual Differences, 31*(5), 689–700. Available from https://doi.org/10.1016/S0191-8869(00)00171-9.

Thompson, L. Y., Snyder, C. R., Hoffman, L., Michael, S. T., Rasmussen, H. N., Billings, L. S., ... Roberts, D. E. (2005). Dispositional forgiveness of self, others, and situations. *Journal of Personality, 73*(2), 313–360. Available from https://doi.org/10.1111/j.1467-6494.2005.00311.x.

Turner, K. A., & White, B. A. (2015). Contingent on contingencies: Connections between anger rumination, self-esteem, and aggression. *Personality and Individual Differences, 82*, 199–202. Available from https://doi.org/10.1016/j.paid.2015.03.023.

van Zomeren, M., Postmes, T., & Spears, R. (2008). Toward an integrative social identity model of collective action. *Psychological Bulletin, 134*(4), 504–535. Available from https://doi.org/10.1037/0033-2909.134.4.504.

Vasquez, E. A., Bartsch, V. O., Pedersen, W. C., & Miller, N. (2007). The impact of aggressive priming, rumination, and frustration on prison sentencing. *Aggressive Behavior, 33*(6), 477–485. Available from https://doi.org/10.1002/ab.20203.

Vasquez, E. A., Lickel, L., & Hennigan, K. (2009). Gangs, displaced, and group-based aggression. *Aggression and Violent Behavior, 15*(2), 130–140. Available from https://doi.org/10.1016/j.avb.2009.08.001.

Vasquez, E. A., Osman, S., & Wood, J. L. (2012). Rumination and the displacement of aggression in united kingdom Gang-Affiliated youth. *Aggressive Behavior, 38*(1), 89–97. Available from https://doi.org/10.1002/ab.20419.

Vasquez, E. A., Pedersen, W. C., Bushman, B. J., Kelley, N. J., Demeestere, P., & Miller, N. (2013). Lashing out after stewing over public insults: The effects of public provocation, provocation intensity, and rumination on triggered displaced aggression. *Aggressive Behavior, 39*(1), 13–29. Available from https://doi.org/10.1002/ab.21453.

Verona, E. (2005). Moderating effects of rumination and gender on context-specific aggression. *Aggressive Behavior, 31*(5), 420–436. Available from https://doi.org/10.1002/ab.20096.

Wade, N. G., Vogel, D. L., Liao, K. Y., & Goldman, D. B. (2008). Measuring state-specific rumination. *Journal of Counseling Psychology, 55*(3), 419–426. Available from https://doi.org/10.1037/0022-0167.55.3.419.

Watkins, L. E., DiLillo, D., & Maldonado, R. C. (2015). The interactive effects of emotion regulation and alcohol intoxication on lab-based intimate partner aggression. *Psychology of Addictive Behaviors: Journal of the Society of Psychologists in Addictive Behaviors, 29*(3), 653–663. Available from https://doi.org/10.1037/adb0000074.

White, B. A., & Turner, K. A. (2014). Anger rumination and effortful control: Mediation effects on reactive but not proactive aggression. *Personality and Individual Differences, 56*, 186–189. Available from https://doi.org/10.1016/j.paid.2013.08.012.

Wilkowski, B. M., & Robinson, M. D. (2010). The anatomy of anger: An integrative cognitive model of trait anger and reactive aggression. *Journal of Personality, 78*(1), 9–38. Available from https://doi.org/10.1111/j.1467-6494.2009.00607.x.

Zillmann, D. (1983). In J. T. Cacioppo, & R. F. Petty (Eds.), *Transfer of excitation in emotional behavior*. New York: Guilford Press.

CHAPTER

4

Rumination and dysregulated behaviors

Overview

This chapter explores the literatures linking rumination with mental disorders and behaviors characterized by dysregulation and impulsivity. I first describe evidence showing that rumination predicts substance use and substance-related problems, as well as potential mechanisms of these associations. The chapter then reviews theory and empirical support for the role of rumination in borderline personality and eating disorders. After next addressing the effect of rumination on suicidality and self-harm, I conclude by describing recent literature on rumination and psychotic symptoms.

Hostile aggression can be conceptualized as a form of impulsive behavior. The clear associations between rumination and hostile aggression covered in the previous chapter raise the question of whether rumination is implicated in other behaviors and mental disorders characterized by impulsivity. The association between rumination and impulsivity has surprisingly not been studied in great detail. Trait rumination and general impulsivity show small correlations (Boschloo et al., 2013; Dvorak, Simons, & Wray, 2011; Lucas, Young, Zhdanova, & Alexander, 2010). However, researchers now agree that impulsivity encompasses several, sometimes unrelated, facets (Cross, Copping, & Campbell, 2011). Sensation seeking, or a need for novel and exciting experiences, is not typically associated with rumination (Boschloo et al., 2013; Valderrama, Miranda, & Jeglic, 2016). By contrast, a construct called negative urgency, or rash responding to strong negative emotions, is consistently related to greater rumination (Anestis, Anestis,

Rumination and Related Constructs
DOI: https://doi.org/10.1016/B978-0-12-812545-8.00004-8

© 2020 Elsevier Inc. All rights reserved.

Selby, & Joiner, 2009; Selby, Anestis, & Joiner, 2008; Valderrama et al., 2016; Wang & Borders, 2018). Thus, rumination may predict impulsive or dysregulated responses to negative emotional states. In this chapter, I review the evidence linking rumination with substance-related problems, borderline personality, eating disorders, self-harm/suicidality, and psychotic symptoms. Along the way, I introduce two influential theories about the role of rumination in dysregulated behaviors: escape theory and the emotional cascade model.

Substance-related outcomes

Psychologists study different substance-related outcomes. *Substance use* refers to the frequency and quantity of consumption. Researchers often assess how many days in a given reference period (e.g., past week) participants drank or used drugs and the usual amount of substances consumed on each of those days. In addition to typical substance use, many studies assess the frequency of binge use. For alcohol, binge drinking is generally defined as men having five or more drinks and women having four or more drinks in one sitting.

Substance use differs from *substance-related problems*, or harmful use patterns and negative consequences, which are codified in the DSM-5 as substance use disorder. Common harmful patterns include using more than intended, failed attempts to stop or reduce using, cravings so strong that it is hard to think of anything else, needing more of the substance over time to achieve the same effect, and withdrawal symptoms (e.g., shakiness, nausea, fatigue, sweating, and racing heart) when intoxication wears off. Common negative consequences include problems at school or work and with family and friends, engaging in dangerous activities (e.g., drunk driving and unsafe sex), and anxiety or depression. Because alcohol is a legal substance, the majority of the research focuses on alcohol-related outcomes.

Substance use and substance-related problems

The association between rumination and substance use is mixed in the literature. Several studies found a positive association. For instance, in both healthy drinkers and patients with alcohol use disorder, trait depressive and angry rumination were related to higher substance use (Caselli, Bortolai, Leoni, Rovetto, & Spada, 2008; Ciesla, Dickson, Anderson, & Neal, 2011). Similarly, daily rumination about a stressful event predicted more alcohol consumption that day (Aldridge-Gerry et al., 2011), and rumination about negative work experiences was associated with greater alcohol use and binge drinking after work (Frone, 2015). Baseline depressive rumination also predicted more alcohol use 3, 6, and 12 months following brief cognitive-behavioral therapy for alcohol-related problems (Caselli et al., 2010), suggesting that tendencies for depressive rumination make relapse more likely following treatment. On the other hand, several studies with high school and college students have failed to find an associations between rumination and alcohol, drug, and cigarette use (Adrian, McCarty, King, McCauley, & Stoep, 2014; Ciesla et al., 2011; Dvorak et al., 2011; Goldstein, 2006; Richmond, Spring, Kaplan Sommerfeld, & McChargue, 2001; Willem, Bijttebier, Claes, & Raes, 2011; Willem, Bijttebier, Claes, Vanhalst, & Raes, 2014). Moreover, other studies found that depressive rumination was associated with less substance use and binge drinking (Ciesla et al., 2011; Willem et al., 2011, 2014). Thus, the associations between rumination and substance use vary from positive to nonsignificant to negative.

The associations between worry and substance use outcomes are also not robust. For instance, worry predicted more binge drinking in response to unpleasant interpersonal and intrapersonal situations (Goldsmith, Tran, Smith, & Howe, 2009), as well as greater drug use (Shoal, Castaneda, & Giancola, 2005). By contrast, worry was associated with *less* weekly drinking in undergraduate men and women, as well as *less* binge drinking in women (Ciesla et al., 2011). Several studies also found nonsignificant associations between worry and cigarette use (Dijkstra & Brosschot, 2003; Swayampakala et al., 2012; Yong et al., 2014; but see Finney Rutten, Blake, Hesse, Augustson, & Evans, 2011). In fact, a recent metaanalysis concluded that worry was not generally associated with a greater risk of substance use (Clancy, Prestwich, Caperon, & O'Connor, 2016).

Rumination is more consistently associated with worse substance-related problems. In cross-sectional studies, individuals with diagnosed alcohol use disorder or greater substance-related problems report more trait depressive rumination (particularly the brooding subscale), general rumination, and worry (Boschloo et al., 2013; Caselli et al., 2008; Willem et al., 2011). In longitudinal investigations, trait depressive rumination predicted increases in alcohol-related problems 1 year later in female adolescents and adults, as well as the onset of substance use disorder 3 years later (Nolen-Hoeksema & Harrell, 2002; Nolen-Hoeksema, Stice, Wade, & Bohon, 2007). The same results were not found with men (Nolen-Hoeksema & Harrell, 2002). Thus, rumination appears to predict future substance-related problems for women, although whether this association exists for men is unclear.

These mixed results suggest that rumination may be associated with substance-related outcomes more for some people than for others.

One potential moderator is gender, as a couple of these studies found different results for females and males. Specifically, worry predicted less binge drinking in women (Ciesla et al., 2011), whereas depressive rumination predicted increased alcohol-related problems in women (Nolen-Hoeksema & Harrell, 2002). The fact that worry and rumination predicted different outcomes for women is difficult to interpret based on only two studies. However, one tentative conclusion is that repetitive thinking is more strongly predictive of substance-related outcomes in general for women than for men. This hypothesis aligns with findings that depression and other negative moods predict alcohol use more for women (Nolen-Hoeksema, 2004). Men's substance-related outcomes may reflect other predictors, such as positive expectancies and tendencies for avoidant coping.

A few studies have explicitly examined other moderators. For instance, depressive rumination predicted more failed attempts to quit smoking only for participants high in trait impulsivity (Dvorak et al., 2011). In another study, rumination predicted worse substance use and problems for adolescents under high stress, but less substance-related outcomes for adolescents under low stress (Skitch & Abela, 2008). Thus, high trait impulsivity and stress may strengthen the association between rumination and substance-related outcomes. Another possible moderator of the association between rumination and substance use is having a substance use disorder. Just as rumination predicts worse negative mood particularly for people who start out in negative moods (e.g., Watkins, 2008), rumination may also predict greater substance use for individuals who already have substance use problems. On the flip side, existing rumination tendencies may interact with substance use to predict worse substance-related problems. Future research will have to test these and other potential moderation hypotheses.

A final conclusion from this section is that rumination appears to be more predictive of substance-related problems than it is of substance use. Frequent rumination may reflect other mental health struggles, which are more likely to be associated with problematic use than with recreational or social substance use (Nolen-Hoeksema, 2004). Why might rumination contribute to worse substance-related problems? Researchers have examined two promising mechanisms.

Coping with negative affect

The escape theory asserts that dysregulated behaviors are an attempt to escape from negative feelings associated with aversive self-awareness.

For instance, Baumeister (1991) suggested that excessive alcohol use may be an attempt to escape from self-focused attention. Alcohol consumption likely prevents both sustained self-focused attention and the resulting increases in negative emotion, which serves to negatively reinforce alcohol use. Thus, ruminators may drink in order to escape their ruminative thoughts and/or to escape the negative emotions that are exacerbated by rumination. Motivational models of alcohol use refer to this particular motivation as *drinking to cope* (Cooper, 1994). In particular, the emotion regulation motivations of alcohol involve either enhancing positive emotions or reducing negative emotions. Enhancement motives are generally associated with sensation seeking and alcohol use, whereas drinking to cope with negative affect is associated with depressive symptoms, avoidance coping, and alcohol-related problems (Cooper, 1994; Cooper, Frone, Russell, & Mudar, 1995). Thus, rumination has been theorized to be related to drinking to cope.

Empirical findings support this theorized association. Depressive, anxious, and angry rumination are related to drinking to cope (Harwell, Cellucci, & Iwata, 2011; Nolen-Hoeksema & Harrell, 2002; Selby et al., 2008). Rumination may in fact be a stronger predictor of drinking to cope than it is of other substance-related outcomes. For instance, in a population-based study in Australia, depressive rumination was more strongly related to drinking to cope than to drinking-related problems, both concurrently and across 4 years (Tait, Brinker, Moller, & French, 2014). In lesbian women, rumination was also more strongly related to drinking to cope than to drinking-related problems (Lewis, Mason, Winstead, Gaskins, & Irons, 2016). In fact, the association between rumination and drinking-related problems was mediated by drinking to cope (but see Nolen-Hoeksema & Harrell, 2002). Similarly, the association between generalized anxiety disorder symptoms and binge drinking in response to unpleasant situations was sequentially mediated by expectations that alcohol would reduce worry, which in turn predicted using alcohol to cope with negative affect (Goldsmith et al., 2009). Thus, drinking to cope appears to be one mechanism of the link between rumination and alcohol-related outcomes.

Craving

Other researchers study the specific symptom of craving, or desire for particular substances. Stronger cravings are known to predict substance use as well as substance-related problems (Hartwell & Ray, 2018). Gabriele Caselli has focused on the association between a unique type of repetitive thinking and craving. According to the elaborated intrusion theory of desire, the intensity and duration of cravings are increased by a process of cognitive elaboration called *desire thinking* (Kavanagh, Andrade, & May, 2005). This voluntary and perseverative process involves verbal perseveration about the need to achieve the desired object (e.g., thinking about what one could do in order to drink, repeatedly thinking about the need to taste alcohol). It also involves mental imagery (e.g., imagining stopping the car to order a drink at the local bar, imagining the taste of an alcoholic beverage).[1] Clearly, the verbal perseveration component is similar to rumination and constitutes one form of repetitive thinking. Moreover, individuals diagnosed with alcohol or smoking use disorders reported that their desire thinking felt uncontrollable (Caselli & Spada, 2010), similar to how people report their experiences of rumination and worry (see Chapter 2: Rumination and anxiety-related disorders). Because they elaborate on a desired target, both desire thinking and rumination likely exacerbate and maintain craving.

In support of this theory, desire thinking and rumination are empirically associated with greater craving for alcohol. In a sample of treatment-seeking problem drinkers, desire thinking correlated with greater craving (Caselli & Spada, 2010). Similarly, individuals diagnosed with alcohol or smoking use disorders reported that desire thinking increased craving, and most participants said that the only way to interrupt desire thinking was to engage in the target behavior (Caselli & Spada, 2010). In an experiment, participants were asked to think about a specific activity (excluding alcohol or drugs) for which they usually felt a moderate or high level of desire—activities such as eating, sex, physical exercise, or use of the Internet (Caselli, Soliani, & Spada, 2013). They were then randomly assigned to engage in 8 minutes of distraction (e.g., "Think about the layout of your school campus"), generic and abstract thinking about the activity (e.g., "Think about why people like to do this activity"), or desire thinking (e.g., "Try to imagine yourself while doing the activity" or "Try to plan everything you could do to practice this activity as soon as possible"). Current craving significantly increased in the desire thinking condition but not in the other conditions. In another experiment, treatment-seeking problem drinkers as well as a nonclinical control group engaged in the classic Nolen-Hoeksema rumination or distraction manipulations (Caselli et al., 2013). As hypothesized, induced rumination increased current craving for alcohol in problem drinkers only, compared to distraction. The authors

1 The 20-item Desire Thinking Questionnaire (Caselli & Spada, 2011) assesses both verbal perseveration (e.g., "When I begin to think about drinking alcohol I find it difficult to stop") and imaginal prefiguration (e.g., "I anticipate the sensations I would feel when drinking alcohol").

speculated that rumination may increase desire thinking, which is more proximally associated with craving. Future research will have to test this hypothesis.

Desire thinking, particularly the verbal perseveration component, is also associated with substance use and problems. For instance, individuals meeting criteria for alcohol use disorder reported more desire thinking than did nontreatment-seeking social drinkers (Caselli, Ferla, Mezzaluna, Rovetto, & Spada, 2012). However, only verbal perseveration (not mental imagery) differentiated individuals with alcohol use disorder from problem drinkers who did not meet criteria for the disorder. Similarly, verbal perseveration was associated with more severe nicotine-related problems (Caselli, Nikcevic, Fiore, Mezzaluna, & Spada, 2012). Finally, in one study, the association between verbal perseveration and alcohol use disappeared when controlling for craving, which suggests that craving may mediate the link between desire thinking and alcohol use (Caselli & Spada, 2011).

Summary

In sum, rumination appears to be more robustly associated with substance-related problems than with substance use. The effects of rumination on substance-related outcomes may be stronger for women and for people high in trait impulsivity and stress. In support of the escape theory, rumination predicts a stronger motivation to drink in order to cope with negative emotions, which in turn predict worse alcohol-related outcomes. Finally, rumination and the related construct of desire thinking may increase craving for substances by keeping the desired substance salient, which in turn makes substance use and problems more likely.

Borderline personality

Borderline personality disorder (BPD) is characterized by chronic and severe affective instability, chaotic interpersonal relationships, an unstable sense of self, and various impulsive behaviors. Individuals with BPD often feel empty, anxious, and depressed; fear rejection or abandonment by others; and experience strong anger at others for perceived insults. Interpersonal relationships are marked by intensity and instability. This emotional and interpersonal roller coaster is associated with a range of risky behaviors, from those that harm the individual (e.g., self-harm, alcohol/drug use, and binge eating) to behaviors that harm others (e.g., aggression). Individuals who do not meet criteria for a formal diagnosis of BPD can still display levels of borderline features that are associated with dysfunction. Accordingly, researchers study either clinical populations with diagnosed BPD or nonclinical individuals with borderline features.

Perhaps not surprisingly, the field of rumination and BPD began with depression researchers. Major depression and BPD often occur together and contribute to worse outcomes than major depression by itself. Accordingly, researchers have examined whether this cognitive vulnerability might explain susceptibility to comorbid depression and BPD. One early study found that individuals with comorbid BPD and major depression reported more depressive rumination than did individuals with only major depression or only BPD (Abela, Payne, & Moussaly, 2003). Subsequent research found that individuals with diagnosed BPD reported more brooding than did healthy controls (Bayes, Parker, & McClure, 2016; Zaki, Coifman, Rafaeli, Berenson, & Downey, 2013). Depressive rumination was also associated with more severe BPD symptoms, even controlling for depressive symptoms (Selby, Anestis, Bender, & Joiner, 2009; Watkins, 2009). Finally, depressive rumination was most strongly related to BPD than any other personality disorder, even after controlling for current and past depression (Smith, Grandin, Alloy, & Abramson, 2006; Watkins, 2009). Therefore, initial evidence suggested a unique relationship between depressive rumination and BPD.

However, individuals with a BPD diagnosis or BPD features also exhibit other types of rumination (as reviewed in Baer, Peters, Eisenlohr-Moul, Geiger, & Sauer, 2012). In particular, angry rumination is associated with greater BPD symptoms (Peters & Geiger, 2016; Peters, Smart, & Baer, 2015; Selby et al., 2008; Zielinski, Borders, & Giancola, 2015). In adult male offenders, angry rumination was more strongly associated with borderline features than were brooding or general rumination (Gardner, Dodsworth, & Selby, 2014). In college students, angry rumination was associated with borderline features more strongly than was depressive rumination, even controlling for anxiety, depressive symptoms, and negative affect (Baer & Sauer, 2011). In addition, only angry rumination, but not depressive rumination, uniquely predicted borderline features after controlling for negative affect, negative cognitive content, and thought suppression (Geiger, Peters, Sauer-Zavala, & Baer, 2013).

Edward Selby developed the emotional cascade model to explain the process by which rumination contributes to behavioral dysregulation in individuals with BPD (Selby et al., 2008; Selby & Joiner, 2009). An emotional cascade occurs when people's tendencies to ruminate about negative experiences lead to increased negative emotion, which in turn triggers more rumination, which leads to even more negative emotion. In such a way, a progressively increasing, reciprocal cycle of negative emotion and rumination (i.e., an emotional cascade) occurs that contributes to a highly aversive psychological state. This process may help explain the intense negative emotions and difficulty returning to emotional baseline experienced by people with BPD, as well as why a seemingly trivial event can trigger intensely negative mood states. Following an emotional cascade, individuals are highly motivated to escape or decrease the aversive state. However, normally adaptive distraction or coping strategies (e.g., reappraisal, talking to a friend, going for a walk) may not be strong enough to stop the cycle. Instead, it may require strong physical sensations (e.g., pain from self-harm, bingeing, or getting in a fight; an adrenaline rush from engaging in impulsive behaviors; physiological effects of intoxication) to distract people's attention away from their aversive mental state. Dysregulated behaviors are therefore negatively reinforced. Of course, engagement in these types of behaviors may trigger self-reproach, shame, and other negative emotions, setting off another emotional cascade.

The emotional cascade model has been tested in several ways. First, a few experiments have examined the effect of induced rumination on general negative affect in individuals with BPD. In one study, participants were instructed to think about something upsetting and to spend 5 minutes focusing on feelings about the problem, considering what these feelings mean, and analyzing the events surrounding the problem that contribute to their feelings (Selby et al., 2009). Even controlling for depressive symptoms, participants diagnosed with BPD showed a significantly larger increase in negative mood following induced rumination, compared to those without such a diagnosis. Thus, individuals with BPD were more emotionally reactive to rumination. In a different experiment, participants with diagnosed BPD wrote about a personal event that made them angry for 10 minutes (Sauer & Baer, 2012). They then concentrated on either rumination prompts or on mindfulness prompts for 8 minutes. As expected, the rumination induction contributed to significantly higher anger than did the mindfulness induction.

Several studies have also examined rumination as a mechanism of the effect of BPD on dysregulated behaviors. For instance, a latent variable of repetitive thinking mediated the associations between borderline features and behavioral dysregulation, including self-injurious behaviors (Gardner et al., 2014; Selby et al., 2009). Similarly, depressive rumination mediated the association between BPD symptoms and binge eating and nonsuicidal self-injury (Selby, Franklin, Carson-Wong, & Rizvi, 2013). In patients with BPD, angry rumination mediated the association between a diagnosis of BPD (vs other personality disorders) and aggressive tendencies (Martino et al., 2015). Thus, various types of rumination contribute to both negative affect and dysregulated behaviors in individuals with BPD.

To more directly test whether cycles of rumination and negative emotion lead to dysregulated behaviors, Selby used experience sampling studies. In one study, they recruited individuals with self-reported problems with behavioral dysregulation (Selby, Joiner, & Thomas, 2013). After completing baseline measures, participants were paged five times a day for 2 weeks. At each page, they recorded their current emotions and rumination, as well as whether they had engaged in any dysregulated behaviors since the last page (e.g., self-harm, alcohol use, reckless driving, binge eating, and aggression). The results indicated that state rumination and negative emotion interacted to predict higher total levels of dysregulated behaviors, particularly for individuals with diagnosed BPD. Using similar methodology, more sophisticated analyses indicated that elevated rumination and negative emotion at one time point predicted exponentially greater levels of rumination, negative emotion, and impulsive behaviors in the future (Selby, Kranzler, Panza, & Fehling, 2016). In other words, an exponential, rather than linear, model fit the data. In addition, rumination and negative emotion interacted to predict elevations in later rumination, negative emotion, and impulsive behaviors. These results provide good evidence for the concept of emotional cascades, in which rumination and negative emotion create an ever worsening reciprocal cycle that contributes to increases in dysregulated behaviors.

In sum, individuals with borderline personality features or disorder engage in high levels of depressive and angry rumination. The emotional cascade model proposes that reciprocal cycles of rumination and negative emotion create an increasingly aversive psychological state that can only be shut off by the strong physical sensations and distraction associated with dysregulated behaviors. Empirical evidence confirms that rumination contributes to negative emotions and dysregulated behaviors in people with BPD, and that the interaction of momentary rumination and negative emotion predict greater dysregulated behaviors. As we will see in the following sections, researchers have applied the emotional cascade model to other types of dysregulated behaviors.

Disordered eating

There are currently three main eating disorders in the DSM-5: anorexia, bulimia, and binge eating disorder. An additional concern for psychologists is subclinical disordered eating behaviors, such as fasting, bingeing, self-induced vomiting, or using appetite suppressants or diuretics. Over half of college women engage in these types of disordered eating behaviors (Clemens, Thombs, Olds, & Gordon, 2008). For some individuals, these behaviors may progress to clinically significant eating disorders over time (Neumark-Sztainer, Wall, Larson, Eisenberg, & Loth, 2011). Body dissatisfaction is also a core risk and maintaining factor for anorexia and bulimia. Accordingly, researchers have examined the associations between rumination and both body dissatisfaction and subclinical disordered eating, as well as the effect of rumination on all three eating disorders.

Rumination is robustly associated with more body dissatisfaction. For instance, depressive rumination correlates with greater body dissatisfaction, shame, and self-surveillance (e.g., thinking about how one looks) in nonclinical adolescents and adult women (Grabe, Hyde, & Lindberg, 2007; Maraldo, Zhou, Dowling, & Vander Wal, 2016). Several experiments examined the effect of manipulated rumination on body dissatisfaction in women. In the typical experiment, body dissatisfaction was induced by showing participants magazine-type clothing ads of attractive, thin women and asking participants to answer questions comparing their bodies to the models' bodies (Wade, George, & Atkinson, 2009). Next, participants were instructed to either think repetitively about how the induction made them feel (i.e., rumination) or experience any thoughts and emotions without judging them (i.e., acceptance). In normal-weight women, overweight women, and women with diagnosed anorexia or bulimia, manipulated rumination contributed to increased body dissatisfaction, compared to acceptance (Etu & Gray, 2010; Naumann & Svaldi, 2016; Svaldi, Naumann, Trentowska, Lackner, & Tuschen-Caffier, 2013; Wade et al., 2009).

Rumination is also associated with subclinical disordered eating behaviors. Depressive and angry rumination are associated with general disordered eating in nonclinical samples of adults and early adolescents (e.g., Aldao & Nolen-Hoeksema, 2010; Hilt, Roberto, & Nolen-Hoeksema, 2013; Wang & Borders, 2018). A metaanalysis found an average correlation of 0.26 between rumination and disordered eating (Aldao, Nolen-Hoeksema, & Schweizer, 2010). As in the depression literature, the association appears to be stronger for brooding than for reflection (Rawal, Park, & Williams, 2010). Rumination specifically about eating-related concerns was also associated with greater disordered eating in undergraduate women (Bybee, Zigler, Berliner, & Merisca, 1996). Similarly, in a sample of healthy adolescents, habitual thinking about negative body image predicted worse eating disturbance (Verplanken & Velsvik, 2008). Thus, various types of rumination predict worse subclinical disordered eating behaviors.

Anorexia

Anorexia is characterized by restriction of food intake to such an extent that people are drastically and dangerously underweight. The weight loss is accompanied by an intense fear of gaining weight and disturbances in the way one's body weight or shape is experienced. Common behaviors seen in people with anorexia include frequent weight checks, body checking (e.g., looking in mirrors, measuring specific body parts), obsessively counting calories, development of food rituals (e.g., eating foods in a certain order, excessive chewing, rearranging food on a plate), and excuses to avoid meal times or situations involving food.

People with diagnosed anorexia or anorexia symptoms are likely to engage in rumination. For instance, individuals with anorexia report more worry, general rumination, and depressive rumination, compared to healthy controls (Naumann, Tuschen-Caffier, Voderholzer, Schäfer, & Svaldi, 2016; Oldershaw, Lavender, Sallis, Stahl, & Schmidt, 2015; Rawal et al., 2010; Sassaroli et al., 2005; Startup et al., 2013; Sternheim et al., 2012; Troop, Holbrey, & Treasure, 1998). People with anorexia also engage in more rumination specifically about weight, food, and body shape than do people without anorexia (Cowdrey & Park, 2011; Seidel et al., 2016).[2] In terms of specific anorexia symptoms, depressive and angry rumination predict more restricting behavior in nonclinical college samples (Harrell & Jackson, 2008; Wang & Borders, 2018). In women with anorexia, rumination also predicts greater severity of disordered eating symptoms concurrently and over time (Gilboa-Schechtman, Avnon, Zubery, & Jeczmien, 2006; Rawal et al., 2010; Startup et al., 2013). Finally, an experience sampling study found that eating-related rumination was more strongly associated with negative affect for women with anorexia than for healthy controls (Seidel et al., 2016). Thus, rumination both occurs more often and predicts worse outcomes for people with anorexia. Women with anorexia also hold more positive beliefs about the benefits of rumination, believing that rumination is helpful to gain insight, solve problems, and cope with difficult events (Rawal et al., 2010).

2 To capture rumination specifically about eating, weight, and shape, Cowdrey and Park (2011) modified items from Nolen-Hoeksema's measure of depressive rumination. The 9-item Ruminative Response Scale for Eating Disorders assesses both brooding (e.g., "Think 'why can't I handle my eating better'?", "Think 'why do I have such issues with my eating, weight, and/or shape'?") and reflection (e.g., "Write down what you think about your eating, weight and/or shape and analyze it"). Scores on this eating disorder-specific rumination measure were uniquely associated with more general disordered eating in healthy participants (Cowdrey & Park, 2011, 2012).

Researchers have started incorporating rumination into maintenance theories of anorexia. These theories hinge on the fact that despite their resistance to eating, people with anorexia obsessively think about food and eating rituals (Park, Dunn, & Barnard, 2011; Schmidt & Treasure, 2006). This appears to be a natural result of starvation, just as reexperiencing is a natural response to trauma. However, the more that people experience excessive thoughts about food and eating, the more vigilant they become about not giving in to the drive to eat. Ironically, then, a ruminative focus on food-related thoughts may actually help individuals ignore hunger and other cues from their bodies. Park et al. (2011) argue that rumination about food and eating dominates during restricting phases of anorexia, during which people often feel a sense of control and accomplishment. They are distanced from their emotional and bodily experiences, which, at that level of starvation, are bound to be unpleasant. This conceptualization of rumination invokes a verbal, detail-oriented form of repetitive thought, clearly drawing on the avoidance theory of worry. By contrast, when individuals with anorexia fail in their attempts to control their weight or eating, they may become overwhelmed by emotional and bodily sensations. This mental state is associated with feelings of worthlessness and being out-of-control and may trigger bingeing. Ending or avoiding this out-of-control emotional state only further reinforces the perceived benefits of restricting and rumination.

Some evidence exists for this complex model of anorexia. People with anorexia do display tendencies for perfectionism, cognitive rigidity, and an unwillingness to remain in contact with unpleasant internal experiences (Park et al., 2011; Schmidt & Treasure, 2006). Moreover, induced rumination while in a sad mood led to increased desire to abstain for women with diagnosed anorexia (Naumann, Tuschen-Caffier, Voderholzer, Caffier, & Svaldi, 2015). However, whether eating-related rumination is associated with avoidance of emotional and physiological pain remains to be tested.

Bulimia and binge eating disorder

Bulimia is characterized by a repeated pattern of binge eating followed by inappropriate compensatory behaviors in order to prevent weight gain. Although people use the term "binge" colloquially to refer to occasional overeating, a binge episode is defined as eating an amount of food in a discrete time period (e.g., 2 hours) that is larger than most people would eat in that time period *and* feeling out-of-control during the episode. Following a binge, people often feel overwhelming shame over losing control and anxiety about gaining weight, leading to various compensatory behaviors (e.g., purging, laxative use, and excessive exercise). As with anorexia, people's self-evaluation is unduly influenced by their body shape and weight. Unlike anorexia, people with bulimia are generally not underweight; in fact, they tend to be average or even a little overweight. Binge eating disorder is characterized by recurrent binge episodes without subsequent compensatory behaviors. People with binge eating disorder are more likely to be obese and experience obesity-related health problems (Kessler et al., 2013).

Rumination is consistently related to worse bulimic symptoms. In nonclinical samples, both depressive and angry rumination predict greater bulimic symptoms concurrently and increases in these symptoms over time (Holm-Denoma & Hankin, 2010; Nolen-Hoeksema et al., 2007; Selby et al., 2008). One study found that the association between rumination and bulimic symptoms was only significant for people low in self-control (Breithaupt, Rallis, Mehlenbeck, & Kleiman, 2016). In clinical samples, women with diagnosed bulimia report more rumination and worry, compared to noneating disordered women (Naumann, Tuschen-Caffier, Voderholzer, & Svaldi, 2016; Sassaroli et al., 2005; Sternheim et al., 2012; Troop et al., 1998). Rumination also predicts more severe eating disorder symptoms in women with bulimia (Gilboa-Schechtman et al., 2006). An experimental study found that in women with bulimia, induced rumination while in a sad mood increased their desire to binge, compared to distraction (Naumann et al., 2015).

By contrast, the association between rumination and binge eating is mixed. Some cross-sectional studies with undergraduates found that rumination predicted more binge eating in the past week or 3 months, as well as general binge eating behaviors and thoughts (Connolly, Rieger, & Caterson, 2007; Gordon, Holm-Denoma, Troop-Gordon, & Sand, 2012; Harrell & Jackson, 2008; Mason & Lewis, 2015; Wang & Borders, 2018). Longitudinally, depressive rumination predicted the onset of recurrent binge eating over 3 years in adolescent females (Nolen-Hoeksema et al., 2007). By contrast, in lesbian women without current compensatory behaviors, rumination was not associated with binge eating (Mason & Lewis, 2015). Rumination also was not associated with frequency of binge episodes in the past month in undergraduate women (Connolly et al., 2007; Kelly, Lydecker, & Mazzeo, 2012). Finally, in obese individuals with binge eating disorder, depressive rumination was associated with higher severity of eating disorder psychopathology but not with number of binge episodes (Wang, Lydecker, & Grilo, 2017).

Relatedly, researchers have examined the role of rumination in eating for emotional reasons, again with mixed results. In a community sample, depressive rumination predicted consumptive coping (i.e., eating, drinking, or using other substances when upset) 1 year later (Sarin &

Nolen-Hoeksema, 2010). By contrast, experimenters asked normal-weight and obese participants to reexperience an angering memory and a neutral memory for 7 minutes (Appelhans, Whited, Schneider, Oleski, & Pagoto, 2011). After each mood induction, they were presented with six different types of food, all of which they had previously indicated they liked, and instructed to sample each food and eat as much as they like. Trait depressive rumination did not predict change in food consumption when angry for either normal-weight or obese participants.

In sum, rumination seems robustly related to bulimic symptoms as a whole but less consistently related to binge eating or eating for emotional reasons. The mixed results may reflect the presence of moderators. One study found that effect of rumination on binge eating was stronger for participants with greater body dissatisfaction (Gordon et al., 2012). Moreover, in obese adolescents who were participating in a 6-week inpatient weight management program, momentary rumination interacted with stress to predict a stronger desire to eat (Kubiak, Vögele, Siering, Schiel, & Weber, 2008). Thus, the association between rumination and binge eating may be stronger for people under stress and those with negative views of their bodies.

Another possibility is that rumination only indirectly, rather than directly, predicts binge eating. A few studies have examined mechanisms of the effect of rumination on bulimic symptoms. In adolescent females, worse perceived competence in one's physical appearance explained the association between depressive rumination and bulimic symptoms (Holm-Denoma & Hankin, 2010). Rumination is also related to hunger sensitivity, or heightened distress to sensations of hunger, a construct that is in turn related to bulimia symptoms (Walker, Hadjistavropoulos, Gagnon, & MacNab, 2015). Finally, a latent variable of emotion-focused coping (including rumination, catastrophizing, and self-blame) indirectly predicted binge eating via negative affect (Mason & Lewis, 2015). Thus, rumination may indirectly predict binge eating via more negative thoughts and beliefs.

The escape theory has been applied to disordered eating, particularly to binge eating behavior. Specifically, people with eating disorders are more likely to have high and exaggerated internal standards not only for bodily thinness but also in other areas of their lives (Heatherton & Baumeister, 1991). These high standards tend to make the self look bad in comparison. Self-focused rumination about negative discrepancies (e.g., perceived inadequacies in weight, shape, and eating habits) in turn elicits negative emotions. In order to escape this unpleasant rumination and related unpleasant emotions, people may engage in a range of behaviors aimed at narrowing their attention to immediate, concrete, low-level thinking. Basically, the idea is to shut down repetitive, abstract thoughts such as "Am I good/thin enough?" by refocusing on more concrete sensations. In the case of binge eating, this can occur by attending to the physical sensations of eating (e.g., chewing, tasting). This focus on concrete and immediate behaviors also decreases attention to inhibitions that are normally in place, such as the abstract idea that eating too much junk food is unhealthy. The combination of reduced internal obstacles to overeating plus a motivated attention to the physical sensations of eating increases the likelihood of a binge eating episode. Furthermore, if it successfully shuts down ruminative thoughts and related emotions, it is negatively reinforced, making it more likely to be used again as an escape behavior. Gibson (2012) even suggests that bingeing and comfort eating function more to avoid negative rumination than negative affect. Thus, rumination is theorized to be a key contributor to the onset and maintenance of bulimia and binge eating disorder.

The emotional cascade model also applies to binge eating (Selby et al., 2008). According to this model, negative events trigger a cycle of negative mood and rumination, which amplify each other until the negative mood state becomes so powerful that engaging in an equally intense behavior (e.g., bingeing) is the only perceived way to distract oneself. One study examined the emotional cascades theory in undergraduates with a history of eating disorder behaviors (Arbuthnott, Lewis, & Bailey, 2015). The experimenters induced rumination three times by asking participants to spend 3 minutes analyzing and thinking about an upsetting event in their lives. Positive and negative emotions were assessed following each rumination induction. Participants with a history of eating disorder behaviors reported greater decreases in positive emotions after the initial rumination induction, compared to participants without such a history. By the third rumination induction, this difference in positive emotion had disappeared, suggesting that participants with eating disorders had stronger initial reactions to rumination. The effect of rumination on mood was explained in part by poor emotion regulation.

Summary

In sum, rumination shows robust associations with greater body dissatisfaction and subclinical disordered eating, as well as symptoms of anorexia and bulimia. The effect of rumination on binge eating is more mixed and may reflect an indirect association and/or the presence of moderators. The creation of a rumination measure specifically about eating concerns is a notable contribution to this literature and will hopefully be used more in the future. In addition, the compelling theories for rumination's role in both anorexia and bulimia should help guide future research.

Suicidality and self-harm

Although suicidality and self-harm are symptoms of depression, they are also common among individuals with eating disorders and BPD. In addition, suicidal and self-harm behaviors are predicted by impulsivity (Anestis, Soberay, Gutierrez, Hernández, & Joiner, 2014). Thus, I explore the effects of rumination on suicidality and self-harm separate from their association with a particular disorder.

Suicidality

Suicidality includes both suicidal ideation and actual suicide attempts. Suicidal ideation refers to thoughts of death. The severity of suicidal ideation can vary, from fleeting and unwanted thoughts to a preoccupation with death that may involve detailed planning. Approximately 70% of people with suicidal ideation do not go on to make suicide attempts, although suicidal ideation is certainly a risk factor for suicide attempts (Nock et al., 2008).

There is a sizeable literature on the associations between depressive rumination and suicidal ideation (for a review, see Morrison & O'Connor, 2008). In cross-sectional studies, depressive rumination is associated with more serious suicidal ideation (Miranda, Tsypes, Gallagher, & Rajappa, 2013; Tucker et al., 2013). Depressive rumination also predicts the presence and increases in suicidal ideation over time in adults and adolescents (Burke et al., 2016; Miranda & Nolen-Hoeksema, 2007; Smith et al., 2006). Several studies have examined the separate subscales of brooding and reflective pondering. Brooding is generally associated with more suicidal ideation, in both community and clinical samples, cross-sectionally and over time (Miranda & Nolen-Hoeksema, 2007; O'Connor, O'Connor, & Marshall, 2007; O'Connor & Noyce, 2008; Polanco-Roman, Gomez, Miranda, & Jeglic, 2016; Surrence, Miranda, Marroquín, & Chan, 2009; Tucker et al., 2013; but see Cole et al., 2015; Stange et al., 2015). By contrast, some studies found that more reflective pondering predicts worse suicidal ideation (Cheref, Lane, Polanco-Roman, Gadol, & Miranda, 2015; Miranda & Nolen-Hoeksema, 2007; Polanco-Roman et al., 2016), whereas others found no relationship between these constructs (O'Connor & Noyce, 2008; Stange et al., 2015).

There is less research on individuals who have made suicide attempts, and the results are mixed. In undergraduates and adult inpatients, some studies found that individuals with a history of a suicide attempts report more brooding compared to individuals without such a history (Grassia & Gibb, 2009; Polanco-Roman, Jurska, Quiñones, & Miranda, 2015; Surrence et al., 2009). Other studies failed to find an association between depressive rumination and suicide attempts (Batterham & Helen, 2012; Crane, Barnhofer, & Williams, 2007). Similarly, researchers have found positive, negative, and nonsignificant associations between reflective pondering and history of suicide attempts (Crane et al., 2007; Grassia & Gibb, 2009; Polanco-Roman et al., 2015; Surrence et al., 2009).

Researchers have examined the effects of various moderators on the association between rumination and suicidality. For instance, depressive rumination is associated with suicidal ideation more strongly for individuals high in self-criticism and low in hope and optimism (Stange et al., 2015; Tucker et al., 2013). Brooding is also more strongly associated with suicidal ideation for people reporting high levels of perceived stress (Cole et al., 2015). Similarly, reflective pondering predicts more suicidal ideation for people with higher depressive symptoms and only among individuals with a history of suicide attempts or self-injury (Cheref et al., 2015; Polanco-Roman et al., 2015; Surrence et al., 2009). Likewise, angry rumination predicts suicidal ideation only for people with high depressive symptoms (Selby, Anestis, & Joiner, 2007). In sum, consistent with findings reviewed in previous chapters, rumination appears to predict suicidality particularly for people who are already feeling depressed or stressed and have a previous history of suicidality.

Self-harm

Nonsuicidal self-injury (NSSI) involves direct, intentional harm to one's body tissue without suicidal intent. It includes skin cutting, carving, burning, scratching, hitting body parts, and interfering with wound healing (Adler & Adler, 2007). Although NSSI is a symptom in BPD, it may also occur in the context of other mental disorders, as well as in nonclinical populations. Accordingly, psychologists often study NSSI as a discrete outcome behavior. Research evidence suggests that one of the main functions of NSSI is affect regulation (Klonsky, 2007). When asked why they engage in NSSI, most individuals identify the desire to decrease or escape from negative affect. Moreover, acute negative affect usually precedes acts of NSSI and is decreased after NSSI. Accordingly, much research and treatment for NSSI has focused on deficits in emotion regulation, and rumination has not surprisingly been a popular strategy to investigate.

Evidence for the associations between trait rumination and NSSI is mixed. In cross-sectional studies, college and high school students with a history of lifetime NSSI report more general and depressive rumination than do those without such a history (Armey & Crowther, 2008; Borrill, Fox, Flynn, & Roger, 2009; Hoff & Muehlenkamp, 2009; Polanco-Roman et al., 2015; Voon, Hasking, & Martin, 2014). In adolescent girls, brooding rumination was associated with NSSI specifically for the purpose of avoiding negative feelings and avoiding aversive social encounters (Hilt, Cha, & Nolen-Hoeksema, 2008). However, longitudinal research has yielded mixed results. In some experience sampling studies with college students, trait general and depressive rumination predicted the presence and frequency of NSSI episodes over several weeks (Nicolai, Wielgus, & Mezulis, 2016; Selby et al., 2013). Similarly, trait general rumination predicted NSSI 2 months later in seventh and eighth graders (Bjärehed & Lundh, 2008). However, in two studies with high school students, trait rumination did not predict NSSI severity or first onset of NSSI over 3 years (Voon, Hasking, & Martin, 2014b, 2014c). Similarly, trait depressive rumination did not predict the longitudinal course of NSSI from grades 10 to 12 (Barrocas, Giletta, Hankin, Prinstein, & Abela, 2015). Thus, it appears that rumination tendencies predict NSSI behavior up to 2 months but not several years in the future.

Researchers have examined factors that strengthen the association between rumination and NSSI. Not surprisingly, rumination predicts more NSSI particularly for individuals experiencing high levels of negative affect and psychological distress (Nicolai et al., 2016; Selby et al., 2013; Voon, Hasking, & Martin, 2014a; but see Tanner, Hasking, & Martin, 2014). Similarly, this association is especially strong for individuals with a history of painful or traumatic experiences (Selby, Connell, & Joiner, 2010). Rumination may also interact with other emotion regulation deficits and with a history of previous NSSI. In participants with a history of NSSI, for example, trait brooding predicted higher frequency of NSSI only for individuals who had difficulty making distinctions between similarly valenced emotions (e.g., sadness vs anger), one important aspect of emotion regulation (Zaki et al., 2013). Relatedly, an experiment induced rumination three different times by asking participants to spend 3 minutes analyzing and thinking about an upsetting event (Arbuthnott et al., 2015). The first rumination induction led to an increase in initial negative emotion only in participants with a history of NSSI, but not in participants without such a history. This effect of induced rumination in participants with NSSI histories was explained by more negative baseline mood and greater emotion regulation difficulties. Thus, the association between rumination and NSSI may to be particularly strong for individuals with existing psychological distress, emotion regulation deficits, and histories of NSSI.

Psychosis

Finally, researchers have started to examine the effects of rumination and worry on hallucinations and delusions, the two hallmarks of psychosis. Hallucinations are perceptual experiences that occur in the absence of a corresponding external stimulation. Delusions are false or distorted beliefs that persist despite contrary evidence and opinions. Although hallucinations and delusions occur in many mental disorders, particularly schizophrenia, they are also reported by members of the general population.

Theory and evidence focus on the association between rumination and auditory hallucinations in particular. For instance, Morrison, Haddock, and Tarrier (1995) proposed that auditory hallucinations occur when intrusive thoughts are attributed to an external source. Other researchers theorized that rumination specifically about interactions with people who are associated with trauma or negative events may provide raw material for perceived auditory hallucinations (Fowler et al., 2006). In healthy undergraduate and graduate students, rumination tendencies are associated with greater hallucination-proneness (Allé, Berna, & Berntsen, 2018; Jones & Fernyhough, 2009). Moreover, this association is mediated by greater intrusiveness of unwanted thoughts. Other studies have also found correlations between intrusive thoughts and auditory hallucinations (Morrison, Wells, & Nothard, 2000). Patients with schizophrenia report more rumination and worry than nonclinical controls, and rumination is associated with more distress about hallucinations (Badcock, Paulik, & Maybery, 2010). Finally, an experience sampling study of young adults with psychosis showed that state rumination and worry predicted subsequent auditory hallucinations, as well as the level of distress associated with these experiences (Hartley, Haddock, Vasconcelos, Emsley, & Barrowclough, 2014).

Even more research has examined the effects of rumination and worry on delusions. In healthy adults, rumination tendencies are associated with greater delusion-proneness (Carse & Langdon, 2013). Most of the research on rumination and delusions has focused on paranoia, or false beliefs about persecution or victimization by others. Cognitive-behavioral models of paranoia have emphasized the role of rumination and worry in maintaining paranoid beliefs. Specifically, Freeman, Garety, Kuipers, Fowler, and Bebbington (2002) proposed that because rumination narrows attention on negative experiences, it may lead to greater consideration of threat-based information about others and intense perceptions of victimization, which in turn reinforce paranoid beliefs. In other words, rumination enhances the significance of paranoid ideation by turning attention to these thoughts and/or their associated emotions and meanings. Nonexperimental studies in fact found correlations between rumination or worry and paranoid beliefs (Hartley et al., 2014; Startup, Freeman, & Garety, 2007). Similarly, patients with paranoid delusions report more rumination and worry than nonclinical controls (Černis et al., 2016; Morrison, & Wells, 2007). Longitudinally, rumination and worry predict more paranoia, new occurrences of paranoia, and longer duration of existing paranoid episodes (Freeman et al., 2012; Startup et al., 2007; Vorontsova, Garety, & Freeman, 2013). In an experiment with nonclinical undergraduates, manipulated rumination following a paranoia induction maintained levels of paranoia, whereas distraction lowered them (Martinelli, Cavanagh, & Dudley, 2013). In another experiment, patients with paranoid delusions who went through a worry induction reported increased perceptual anomalies and feelings of unreality, compared to participants in a control condition (Freeman et al., 2013). Finally, interventions that target worry reduce delusions and distress from delusions in patients with paranoid delusions (Foster, Startup, Potts, & Freeman, 2009; Hepworth, Startup, & Freeman, 2011).

Conclusion

In this chapter, I reviewed the literatures on rumination and substance-related outcomes, borderline personality, disordered eating, suicidality and self-harm, and psychotic symptoms. Taken together with the extensive literature on rumination and aggression (see Chapter 3: Rumination, anger, and aggression), it seems clear that rumination is associated with mental disorders or behaviors characterized by dysregulation and impulsivity. As I have noted in previous chapters, these literatures are largely separate from each other, even though these behaviors commonly cooccur. One exception is a handful of studies showing that rumination is associated with greater engagement in risky behaviors, a construct that include aggressive behavior, self-injurious behaviors, alcohol/drug use, unsafe sex, and rule-breaking/illegal activities (Auerbach, Claro, Abela, Zhu, & Yao, 2010; Borders & Hennebry, 2015; Borders, McAndrew, Quigley, & Chandler, 2012). Future research might explore whether rumination can help explain some of comorbidity between various forms of dysregulation.

The escape theory and emotional cascade model have been influential in the rumination field, inspiring researchers who typically only studied the effects of rumination on depression to branch out to dysregulated behaviors. Whether dysregulated behaviors actually provide an escape from or alleviation of rumination and related negative emotion remains to be studied. Researchers could also examine why some ruminators turn to escapist, dysregulated behaviors and some do not (Nolen-Hoeksema, Wisco, & Lyubomirsky, 2008).

One other important question to explore is how rumination predicts disorders and behaviors on both the internalizing and externalizing spectrums. Despite the high comorbidity between depression and anxiety disorders on the one hand (i.e., internalizing symptoms), and eating disorders, substance use disorder, and BPD on the other (i.e., externalizing symptoms), the behaviors associated with these two classes of disorders seem meaningfully different. People with depression and/or anxiety disorders often appear withdrawn and inhibited, which seems the opposite from the impulsive and sometimes dramatic actions of people with externalizing syndromes. How can rumination contribute to all of these behaviors?

Reasons for the comorbidity between internalizing and externalizing symptoms might provide some understanding (Lilienfeld, 2003). One possibility is that internalizing symptoms cause the development of externalizing symptoms. For instance, depression might impair people's ability to be concerned about negative consequences for their actions and narrow their attention, leading to decreased inhibitions against and increased engagement in aggression. A second possibility is that externalizing problems contribute to internalizing symptoms, such as when uncontrolled drinking leads to anxiety about its possible or actual negative consequences. Similarly, aggressive behavior could lead to depression or anxiety via peer rejection (Keiley, Lofthouse, Bates, Dodge, & Pettit, 2003). For both of these possible explanations, rumination might play a role by exacerbating the initial problem and/or maintaining it longer than would have occurred otherwise, thereby increasing the likelihood of the resulting outcome. Finally, a third suggestion is that both internalizing and externalizing symptoms share common features that distinguish them from nonsymptomatic states (Weiss, Süsser, & Catron, 1998). These researchers in fact suggested that excessive self-focus might be a common feature. Another possible common feature may be negative emotionality, or neuroticism (Keiley et al., 2003), a construct that is related to rumination in many forms (see Chapter 8: Beliefs, traits, and motivations underlying rumination). Finally, low levels of serotonin functioning in the brain can explain both internalizing and externalizing symptoms (Carver, Johnson, & Joormann, 2009) and is associated with greater rumination (Schepers & Markus, 2015). Thus, rumination and related constructs have been proposed to be common features underlying both externalizing and internalizing symptoms.

References

Abela, J. R. Z., Payne, A. V. L., & Moussaly, N. (2003). Cognitive vulnerability to depression in individuals with borderline personality disorder. *Journal of Personality Disorders, 17*(4), 319–329. Available from https://doi.org/10.1521/pedi.17.4.319.23968.

Adler, P. A., & Adler, P. (2007). The demedicalization of self-injury. *Journal of Contemporary Ethnography, 36*(5), 537–570. Available from https://doi.org/10.1177/0891241607301968.

Adrian, M., McCarty, C., King, K., McCauley, E., & Stoep, A. V. (2014). The internalizing pathway to adolescent substance use disorders: Mediation by ruminative reflection and ruminative brooding. *Journal of Adolescence, 37*(7), 983–991. Available from https://doi.org/10.1016/j.adolescence.2014.07.010.

Aldao, A., & Nolen-Hoeksema, S. (2010). Specificity of cognitive emotion regulation strategies: A transdiagnostic examination. *Behaviour Research and Therapy, 48*(10), 974–983. Available from https://doi.org/10.1016/j.brat.2010.06.002.

Aldao, A., Nolen-Hoeksema, S., & Schweizer, S. (2010). Emotion-regulation strategies across psychopathology: A meta-analytic review. *Clinical Psychology Review, 30*(2), 217–237. Available from https://doi.org/10.1016/j.cpr.2009.11.004.

Aldridge-Gerry, A. A., Roesch, S. C., Villodas, F., McCabe, C., Leung, Q. K., & Da Costa, M. (2011). Daily stress and alcohol consumption: Modeling between-person and within-person ethnic variation in coping behavior. *Journal of Studies on Alcohol and Drugs, 72*(1), 125–134. Available from https://doi.org/10.15288/jsad.2011.72.125.

Allé, M. C., Berna, F., & Berntsen, D. (2018). Involuntary autobiographical memory and future thought predicting hallucination proneness. *Clinical Psychological Science, 6*(6), 891–898. Available from https://doi.org/10.1177/2167702618785618.

Anestis, J. C., Anestis, M. D., Selby, E. A., & Joiner, T. E. (2009). Anger rumination across forms of aggression. *Personality and Individual Differences, 46*(2), 192–196. Available from https://doi.org/10.1016/j.paid.2008.09.026.

Anestis, M. D., Soberay, K. A., Gutierrez, P. M., Hernández, T. D., & Joiner, T. E. (2014). Reconsidering the link between impulsivity and suicidal behavior. *Personality and Social Psychology Review, 18*(4), 366–386. Available from https://doi.org/10.1177/1088868314535988.

Appelhans, B. M., Whited, M. C., Schneider, K. L., Oleski, J., & Pagoto, S. L. (2011). Response style and vulnerability to anger-induced eating in obese adults. *Eating Behaviors, 12*(1), 9–14. Available from https://doi.org/10.1016/j.eatbeh.2010.08.009.

Arbuthnott, A. E., Lewis, S. P., & Bailey, H. N. (2015). Rumination and emotions in nonsuicidal self-injury and eating disorder behaviors: A preliminary test of the emotional cascade model. *Journal of Clinical Psychology, 71*(1), 62–71. Available from https://doi.org/10.1002/jclp.22115.

Armey, M. F., & Crowther, J. H. (2008). A comparison of linear versus non-linear models of aversive self-awareness, dissociation, and non-suicidal self-injury among young adults. *Journal of Consulting and Clinical Psychology, 76*(1), 9–14. Available from https://doi.org/10.1037/0022-006X.76.1.9.

Auerbach, R., Claro, A., Abela, J., Zhu, X., & Yao, S. (2010). Understanding risky behavior engagement amongst Chinese adolescents. *Cognitive Therapy and Research, 34*(2), 159–167. Available from https://doi.org/10.1007/s10608-009-9238-x.

Badcock, J. C., Paulik, G., & Maybery, M. T. (2010). The role of emotion regulation in auditory hallucinations. *Psychiatry Research, 185*(3), 303–308. Available from https://doi.org/10.1016/j.psychres.2010.07.011.

Baer, R. A., Peters, J. R., Eisenlohr-Moul, T. A., Geiger, P. J., & Sauer, S. E. (2012). Emotion-related cognitive processes in borderline personality disorder: A review of the empirical literature. *Clinical Psychology Review, 32*(5), 359–369. Available from https://doi.org/10.1016/j.cpr.2012.03.002.

Baer, R. A., & Sauer, S. E. (2011). Relationships between depressive rumination, anger rumination, and borderline personality features. *Personality Disorders, 2*(2), 142–150. Available from https://doi.org/10.1037/a0019478.

Barrocas, A. L., Giletta, M., Hankin, B. L., Prinstein, M. J., & Abela, J. R. Z. (2015). Nonsuicidal self-injury in adolescence: Longitudinal course, trajectories, and intrapersonal predictors. *Journal of Abnormal Child Psychology, 43*(2), 369–380. Available from https://doi.org/10.1007/s10802-014-9895-4.

Batterham, P. J., & Helen. (2012). Longitudinal risk profiling for suicidal thoughts and behaviours in a community cohort using decision trees. *Journal of Affective Disorders, 142*(1), 306–314. Available from https://doi.org/10.1016/j.jad.2012.05.021.

Baumeister, R. F. (1991). *Escaping the self: Alcoholism, spirituality, masochism, and other flights from the burden of selfhood*. New York, N.Y: Basic Books. Retrieved from <http://catalog.hathitrust.org/Record/002495156>.

Bayes, A., Parker, G., & McClure, G. (2016). Emotional dysregulation in those with bipolar disorder, borderline personality disorder and their comorbid expression. *Journal of Affective Disorders, 204*, 103–111. Available from https://doi.org/10.1016/j.jad.2016.06.027.

Bjärehed, J., & Lundh, L. (2008). Deliberate self-harm in 14-year-old adolescents: How frequent is it, and how is it associated with psychopathology, relationship variables, and styles of emotional regulation? *Cognitive Behaviour Therapy, 37*(1), 26–37. Available from https://doi.org/10.1080/16506070701778951.

Borders, A., & Hennebry, K. A. (2015). Angry rumination moderates the association between perceived ethnic discrimination and risky behaviors. *Personality and Individual Differences, 79*, 81–86. Available from https://doi.org/10.1016/j.paid.2015.01.047.

Borders, A., McAndrew, L. M., Quigley, K. S., & Chandler, H. K. (2012). Rumination moderates the associations between PTSD and depressive symptoms and risky behaviors in U.S. veterans. *Journal of Traumatic Stress, 25*(5), 583–586. Available from https://doi.org/10.1002/jts.21733.

Borrill, J., Fox, P., Flynn, M., & Roger, D. (2009). Students who self-harm: Coping style, rumination and alexithymia. *Counselling Psychology Quarterly, 22*(4), 361–372. Available from https://doi.org/10.1080/09515070903334607.

Boschloo, L., Vogelzangs, N., van den Brink, W., Smit, J. H., Beekman, A. T. F., & Penninx, B. W. J. H. (2013). The role of negative emotionality and impulsivity in depressive/anxiety disorders and alcohol dependence. *Psychological Medicine, 43*(6), 1241–1253. Available from https://doi.org/10.1017/S0033291712002152.

Breithaupt, L., Rallis, B., Mehlenbeck, R., & Kleiman, E. (2016). Rumination and self-control interact to predict bulimic symptomatology in college students. *Eating Behaviors, 22*, 1–4. Available from https://doi.org/10.1016/j.eatbeh.2016.03.011.

Burke, T., Connolly, S., Hamilton, J., Stange, J., Abramson, L., & Alloy, L. (2016). Cognitive risk and protective factors for suicidal ideation: A two year longitudinal study in adolescence. *Journal of Abnormal Child Psychology, 44*(6), 1145–1160. Available from https://doi.org/10.1007/s10802-015-0104-x.

Bybee, J., Zigler, E., Berliner, D., & Merisca, R. (1996). Guilt, guilt-evoking events, depression, and eating disorders. *Current Psychology, 15*(2), 113–127. Available from https://doi.org/10.1007/BF02686944.

Carse, T., & Langdon, R. (2013). Delusion proneness in nonclinical individuals and cognitive insight: The contributions of rumination and reflection. *The Journal of Nervous and Mental Disease, 201*(8), 659–664. Available from https://doi.org/10.1097/NMD.0b013e31829c4fe7.

Carver, C. S., Johnson, S. L., & Joormann, J. (2009). Two-mode models of self-regulation as a tool for conceptualizing effects of the serotonin system in normal behavior and diverse disorders. *Current Directions in Psychological Science, 18*(4), 195–199. Available from https://doi.org/10.1111/j.1467-8721.2009.01635.x.

Caselli, G., Bortolai, C., Leoni, M., Rovetto, F., & Spada, M. M. (2008). Rumination in problem drinkers. *Addiction Research & Theory, 16*(6), 564–571. Available from https://doi.org/10.1080/16066350802100822.

Caselli, G., Ferla, M., Mezzaluna, C., Rovetto, F., & Spada, M. M. (2012). Desire thinking across the continuum of drinking behaviour. *European Addiction Research, 18*(2), 64–69. Available from https://doi.org/10.1159/000333601.

Caselli, G., Ferretti, C., Leoni, M., Rebecchi, D., Rovetto, F., & Spada, M. M. (2010). Rumination as a predictor of drinking behaviour in alcohol abusers: A prospective study. *Addiction, 105*(6), 1041–1048. Available from https://doi.org/10.1111/j.1360-0443.2010.02912.x.

Caselli, G., Gemelli, A., Querci, S., Lugli, A. M., Canfora, F., Annovi, C., ... Watkins, E. R. (2013). The effect of rumination on craving across the continuum of drinking behaviour. *Addictive Behaviors, 38*(12), 2879–2883. Available from https://doi.org/10.1016/j.addbeh.2013.08.023.

Caselli, G., Nikcevic, A., Fiore, F., Mezzaluna, C., & Spada, M. M. (2012). Desire thinking across the continuum of nicotine dependence. *Addiction Research & Theory, 20*(5), 382–388. Available from https://doi.org/10.3109/16066359.2011.644842.

Caselli, G., Soliani, M., & Spada, M. M. (2013). The effect of desire thinking on craving: An experimental investigation. *Psychology of Addictive Behaviors: Journal of the Society of Psychologists in Addictive Behaviors, 27*(1), 301–306. Available from https://doi.org/10.1037/a0027981.

Caselli, G., & Spada, M. M. (2010). Metacognitions in desire thinking: A preliminary investigation. *Behavioural and Cognitive Psychotherapy, 38*(5), 629–637. Available from https://doi.org/10.1017/S1352465810000317.

Caselli, G., & Spada, M. M. (2011). The desire thinking questionnaire: Development and psychometric properties. *Addictive Behaviors, 36*(11), 1061–1067. Available from https://doi.org/10.1016/j.addbeh.2011.06.013.

Černis, E., Dunn, G., Startup, H., Kingdon, D., Wingham, G., Evans, N., ... Freeman, D. (2016). The perseverative thinking questionnaire in patients with persecutory delusions. *Behavioural and Cognitive Psychotherapy, 44*(4), 472–481. Available from https://doi.org/10.1017/S1352465815000533.

Cheref, S., Lane, R., Polanco-Roman, L., Gadol, E., & Miranda, R. (2015). Suicidal ideation among racial/ethnic minorities: Moderating effects of rumination and depressive symptoms. *Cultural Diversity & Ethnic Minority Psychology, 21*(1), 31–40. Available from https://doi.org/10.1037/a0037139.

Ciesla, J., Dickson, K., Anderson, N., & Neal, D. (2011). Negative repetitive thought and college drinking: Angry rumination, depressive rumination, co-rumination, and worry. *Cognitive Therapy and Research, 35*(2), 142–150. Available from https://doi.org/10.1007/s10608-011-9355-1.

Clancy, F., Prestwich, A., Caperon, L., & O'Connor, D. B. (2016). Perseverative cognition and health behaviors: A systematic review and meta-analysis. *Frontiers in Human Neuroscience, 10*, 534. Available from https://doi.org/10.3389/fnhum.2016.00534.

Clemens, H., Thombs, D., Olds, R. S., & Gordon, K. L. (2008). Normative beliefs as risk factors for involvement in unhealthy weight control behavior. *Journal of American College Health, 56*(6), 635–642. Available from https://doi.org/10.3200/JACH.56.6.635-642.

Cole, A. B., Wingate, L. R., Tucker, R. P., Rhoades-Kerswill, S., O'Keefe, V. M., & Hollingsworth, D. W. (2015). The differential impact of brooding and reflection on the relationship between perceived stress and suicide ideation. *Personality and Individual Differences, 83*, 170–173. Available from https://doi.org/10.1016/j.paid.2015.04.013.

Connolly, A., Rieger, E., & Caterson, I. (2007). Binge eating tendencies and anger coping: Investigating the confound of trait neuroticism in a non-clinical sample. *European Eating Disorders Review, 15*, 479–486. <https://doi.org/10.1002/erv.765>.

Cooper, M. L. (1994). Motivations for alcohol use among adolescents. *Psychological Assessment, 6*(2), 117–128. Available from https://doi.org/10.1037/1040-3590.6.2.117.

Cooper, M. L., Frone, M. R., Russell, M., & Mudar, P. (1995). Drinking to regulate positive and negative emotions. *Journal of Personality and Social Psychology, 69*(5), 990–1005. Available from https://doi.org/10.1037/0022-3514.69.5.990.

Cowdrey, F. A., & Park, R. J. (2011). Assessing rumination in eating disorders: Principal component analysis of a minimally modified ruminative response scale. *Eating Behaviors, 12*(4), 321–324. Available from https://doi.org/10.1016/j.eatbeh.2011.08.001.

Cowdrey, F. A., & Park, R. J. (2012). The role of experiential avoidance, rumination and mindfulness in eating disorders. *Eating Behaviors, 13*(2), 100–105. Available from https://doi.org/10.1016/j.eatbeh.2012.01.001.

Crane, C., Barnhofer, T., & Williams, J. M. G. (2007). Reflection, brooding, and suicidality: A preliminary study of different types of rumination in individuals with a history of major depression. *The British Journal of Clinical Psychology, 46*(Pt 4), 497–504. Available from https://doi.org/10.1348/014466507X230895.

Cross, C. P., Copping, L. T., & Campbell, A. (2011). Sex differences in impulsivity. *Psychological Bulletin, 137*(1), 97–130. Available from https://doi.org/10.1037/a0021591.

Dijkstra, A., & Brosschot, J. (2003). Worry about health in smoking behaviour change. *Behaviour Research and Therapy, 41*(9), 1081–1092. Available from https://doi.org/10.1016/S0005-7967(02)00244-9.

Dvorak, R., Simons, J., & Wray, T. (2011). Impulsivity moderates the association between depressive rumination and number of quit attempt failures by smokers. *Addiction Research & Theory, 19*(3), 283–288. Available from https://doi.org/10.3109/16066359.2010.512110.

Etu, S. F., & Gray, J. J. (2010). A preliminary investigation of the relationship between induced rumination and state body image dissatisfaction and anxiety. *Body Image, 7*(1), 82–85. Available from https://doi.org/10.1016/j.bodyim.2009.09.004.

Finney Rutten, L., Blake, K., Hesse, B., Augustson, E., & Evans, S. (2011). Illness representations of lung cancer, lung cancer worry, and perceptions of risk by smoking status. *Journal of Cancer Education, 26*(4), 747–753. Available from https://doi.org/10.1007/s13187-011-0247-6.

Foster, C., Startup, H., Potts, L., & Freeman, D. (2009). A randomised controlled trial of a worry intervention for individuals with persistent persecutory delusions. *Journal of Behavior Therapy and Experimental Psychiatry, 41*(1), 45–51. Available from https://doi.org/10.1016/j.jbtep.2009.09.001.

Fowler, D., Freeman, D., Steel, C., Hardy, A., Smith, B., Hackman, C., ... Bebbington, P. (2006). The catastrophic interaction hypothesis: How do stress, trauma, emotion and information processing abnormalities lead to psychosis? In A. P. Morrison, & W. Larkin (Eds.), *Trauma and psychosis: New directions for theory and therapy* (pp. 101–124). Florence: Routledge Ltd. Available from https://doi.org/10.4324/9780203966013 Retrieved from <https://www.taylorfrancis.com/books/9781135447458>.

Freeman, D., Garety, P. A., Kuipers, E., Fowler, D., & Bebbington, P. E. (2002). A cognitive model of persecutory delusions. *The British Journal of Clinical Psychology, 41*(Pt 4), 331–347. Available from https://doi.org/10.1348/014466502760387461.

Freeman, D., Stahl, D., McManus, S., Meltzer, H., Brugha, T., Wiles, N., & Bebbington, P. (2012). Insomnia, worry, anxiety and depression as predictors of the occurrence and persistence of paranoid thinking. *Social Psychiatry and Psychiatric Epidemiology, 47*(8), 1195–1203. Available from https://doi.org/10.1007/s00127-011-0433-1.

Freeman, D., Startup, H., Dunn, G., Černis, E., Wingham, G., Pugh, K., ... Kingdon, D. (2013). The interaction of affective with psychotic processes: A test of the effects of worrying on working memory, jumping to conclusions, and anomalies of experience in patients with persecutory delusions. *Journal of Psychiatric Research, 47*(12), 1837–1842. Available from https://doi.org/10.1016/j.jpsychires.2013.06.016.

Frone, M. R. (2015). Relations of negative and positive work experiences to employee alcohol use: Testing the intervening role of negative and positive work rumination. *Journal of Occupational Health Psychology, 20*(2), 148–160. Available from https://doi.org/10.1037/a0038375.

Gardner, K. J., Dodsworth, J., & Selby, E. A. (2014). Borderline personality traits, rumination, and self-injurious behavior: An empirical test of the emotional cascades model in adult male offenders. *Journal of Forensic Psychology Practice, 14*(5), 398–417. Available from https://doi.org/10.1080/15228932.2014.962379.

Geiger, P. J., Peters, J. R., Sauer-Zavala, S. E., & Baer, R. A. (2013). Relationships among maladaptive cognitive content, dysfunctional cognitive processes, and borderline personality features. *Journal of Personality Disorders, 27*(4), 457–464. Available from https://doi.org/10.1521/pedi_2013_27_097.

Gibson, E. (2012). The psychobiology of comfort eating: Implications for neuropharmacological interventions. *Behavioural Pharmacology, 23*(5 and 6), 442–460. Available from https://doi.org/10.1097/FBP.0b013e328357bd4e.

Gilboa-Schechtman, E., Avnon, L., Zubery, E., & Jeczmien, P. (2006). Emotional processing in eating disorders: Specific impairment or general distress related deficiency? *Depression and Anxiety, 23*(6), 331–339. Available from https://doi.org/10.1002/da.20163.

Goldsmith, A. A., Tran, G. Q., Smith, J. P., & Howe, S. R. (2009). Alcohol expectancies and drinking motives in college drinkers: Mediating effects on the relationship between generalized anxiety and heavy drinking in negative-affect situations. *Addictive Behaviors, 34*(6), 505–513. Available from https://doi.org/10.1016/j.addbeh.2009.01.003.

Goldstein, B. (2006). Why do women get depressed and men get drunk? An examination of attributional style and coping style in response to negative life events among Canadian young adults. *Sex Roles, 54*(1), 27–37. Available from https://doi.org/10.1007/s11199-006-8867-8.

Gordon, K. H., Holm-Denoma, J. M., Troop-Gordon, W., & Sand, E. (2012). Rumination and body dissatisfaction interact to predict concurrent binge eating. *Body Image, 9*(3), 352–357. Available from https://doi.org/10.1016/j.bodyim.2012.04.001.

Grabe, S., Hyde, J. S., & Lindberg, S. M. (2007). Body objectification and depression in adolescents: The role of gender, shame, and rumination. *Psychology of Women Quarterly, 31*(2), 164–175. Available from https://doi.org/10.1111/j.1471-6402.2007.00350.x.

Grassia, M., & Gibb, B. E. (2009). Rumination and lifetime history of suicide attempts. *International Journal of Cognitive Therapy, 2*(4), 400–406. Available from https://doi.org/10.1521/ijct.2009.2.4.400.

Harrell, Z., & Jackson, B. (2008). Thinking fat and feeling blue: Eating behaviors, ruminative coping, and depressive symptoms in college women. *Sex Roles, 58*(9), 658–665. Available from https://doi.org/10.1007/s11199-007-9388-9.

Hartley, S., Haddock, G., Vasconcelos, E. Sa. D., Emsley, R., & Barrowclough, C. (2014). An experience sampling study of worry and rumination in psychosis. *Psychological Medicine, 44*(8), 1605–1614. Available from https://doi.org/10.1017/S0033291713002080.

Hartwell, E. E., & Ray, L. A. (2018). Craving as a DSM-5 symptom of alcohol use disorder in non-treatment seekers. *Alcohol and Alcoholism, 53*(3), 235–240. Available from https://doi.org/10.1093/alcalc/agx088.

Harwell, B. D., Cellucci, T., & Iwata, A. L. (2011). Rumination, anxiety sensitivity, and negative reinforcement drinking. *Journal of Substance Use, 16*(1), 79–85. Available from https://doi.org/10.3109/14659891.2010.487556.

Heatherton, T. F., & Baumeister, R. F. (1991). Binge eating as escape from self-awareness. *Psychological Bulletin, 110*(1), 86–108. Available from https://doi.org/10.1037/0033-2909.110.1.86.

Hepworth, C., Startup, H., & Freeman, D. (2011). Developing treatments of persistent persecutory delusions: The impact of an emotional processing and metacognitive awareness intervention. *The Journal of Nervous and Mental Disease, 199*(9), 653–658. Available from https://doi.org/10.1097/NMD.0b013e318229cfa8.

Hilt, L., Roberto, C., & Nolen-Hoeksema, S. (2013). Rumination mediates the relationship between peer alienation and eating pathology in young adolescent girls. *Eating and Weight Disorders—Studies on Anorexia, Bulimia and Obesity, 18*(3), 263–267. Available from https://doi.org/10.1007/s40519-013-0042-y.

Hilt, L. M., Cha, C. B., & Nolen-Hoeksema, S. (2008). Nonsuicidal self-injury in young adolescent girls. *Journal of Consulting and Clinical Psychology, 76*(1), 63–71. Available from https://doi.org/10.1037/0022-006X.76.1.63.

Hoff, E. R., & Muehlenkamp, J. J. (2009). Nonsuicidal self-injury in college students: The role of perfectionism and rumination. *Suicide & Life-Threatening Behavior, 39*(6), 576–587. Available from https://doi.org/10.1521/suli.2009.39.6.576.

Holm-Denoma, J. M., & Hankin, B. L. (2010). Perceived physical appearance mediates the rumination and bulimic symptom link in adolescent girls. *Journal of Clinical Child & Adolescent Psychology, 39*(4), 537–544. Available from https://doi.org/10.1080/15374416.2010.486324.

Jones, S. R., & Fernyhough, C. (2009). Rumination, reflection, intrusive thoughts, and hallucination-proneness: Towards a new model. *Behaviour Research and Therapy, 47*(1), 54–59. Available from https://doi.org/10.1016/j.brat.2008.09.008.

Kavanagh, D. J., Andrade, J., & May, J. (2005). Imaginary relish and exquisite torture. *Psychological Review, 112*(2), 446–467. Available from https://doi.org/10.1037/0033-295X.112.2.446.

Keiley, M., Lofthouse, N., Bates, J., Dodge, K., & Pettit, G. (2003). Differential risks of covarying and pure components in mother and teacher reports of externalizing and internalizing behavior across ages 5 to 14. *Journal of Abnormal Child Psychology, 31*(3), 267–283. Available from https://doi.org/1023277413027.

Kelly, N. R., Lydecker, J. A., & Mazzeo, S. E. (2012). Positive cognitive coping strategies and binge eating in college women. *Eating Behaviors, 13*(3), 289–292. Available from https://doi.org/10.1016/j.eatbeh.2012.03.012.

Kessler, R. C., Berglund, P. A., Chiu, W. T., Deitz, A. C., Hudson, J. I., Shahly, V., ... Xavier, M. (2013). The prevalence and correlates of binge eating disorder in the world health organization world mental health surveys. *Biological Psychiatry, 73*(9), 904–914. Available from https://doi.org/10.1016/j.biopsych.2012.11.020.

Klonsky, E. D. (2007). The functions of deliberate self-injury: A review of the evidence. *Clinical Psychology Review, 27*(2), 226–239. Available from https://doi.org/10.1016/j.cpr.2006.08.002.

Kubiak, T., Vögele, C., Siering, M., Schiel, R., & Weber, H. (2008). Daily hassles and emotional eating in obese adolescents under restricted dietary conditions—The role of ruminative thinking. *Appetite, 51*(1), 206–209. Available from https://doi.org/10.1016/j.appet.2008.01.008.

Lewis, R. J., Mason, T. B., Winstead, B. A., Gaskins, M., & Irons, L. B. (2016). Pathways to hazardous drinking among racially and socioeconomically diverse lesbian women. *Psychology of Women Quarterly, 40*(4), 564–581. Available from https://doi.org/10.1177/0361684316662603.

Lilienfeld, S. (2003). Comorbidity between and within childhood externalizing and internalizing disorders: Reflections and directions. *Journal of Abnormal Child Psychology, 31* (3), 285–291. Available from https://doi.org/1023229529866.

Lucas, T., Young, J. D., Zhdanova, L., & Alexander, S. (2010). Self and other justice beliefs, impulsivity, rumination, and forgiveness: Justice beliefs can both prevent and promote forgiveness. *Personality and Individual Differences, 49*(8), 851–856. Available from https://doi.org/10.1016/j.paid.2010.07.014.

Maraldo, T. M., Zhou, W., Dowling, J., & Vander Wal, J. S. (2016). Replication and extension of the dual pathway model of disordered eating: The role of fear of negative evaluation, suggestibility, rumination, and self-compassion. *Eating Behaviors, 23*, 187–194. Available from https://doi.org/10.1016/j.eatbeh.2016.10.008.

Martinelli, C., Cavanagh, K., & Dudley, R. E. J. (2013). The impact of rumination on state paranoid ideation in a nonclinical sample. *Behavior Therapy*, *44*(3), 385–394. Available from https://doi.org/10.1016/j.beth.2013.02.002.

Martino, F., Caselli, G., Berardi, D., Fiore, F., Marino, E., Menchetti, M., ... Sassaroli, S. (2015). Anger rumination and aggressive behaviour in borderline personality disorder. *Personality and Mental Health*, *9*(4), 277–287. Available from https://doi.org/10.1002/pmh.1310.

Mason, T. B., & Lewis, R. J. (2015). Minority stress and binge eating among lesbian and bisexual women. *Journal of Homosexuality*, *62*(7), 971–992. Available from https://doi.org/10.1080/00918369.2015.1008285.

Miranda, R., & Nolen-Hoeksema, S. (2007). Brooding and reflection: Rumination predicts suicidal ideation at 1-year follow-up in a community sample. *Behaviour Research and Therapy*, *45*(12), 3088–3095. Available from https://doi.org/10.1016/j.brat.2007.07.015.

Miranda, R., Tsypes, A., Gallagher, M., & Rajappa, K. (2013). Rumination and hopelessness as mediators of the relation between perceived emotion dysregulation and suicidal ideation. *Cognitive Therapy and Research*, *37*(4), 786–795. Available from https://doi.org/10.1007/s10608-013-9524-5.

Morrison, A. P., Haddock, G., & Tarrier, N. (1995). Intrusive thoughts and auditory hallucinations: A cognitive approach. *Behavioural and Cognitive Psychotherapy*, *23*(3), 265–280. Available from https://doi.org/10.1017/S1352465800015873.

Morrison, A. P., & Wells, A. (2007). Relationships between worry, psychotic experiences and emotional distress in patients with schizophrenia spectrum diagnoses and comparisons with anxious and non-patient groups. *Behaviour Research and Therapy*, *45*(7), 1593–1600. Available from https://doi.org/10.1016/j.brat.2006.11.010.

Morrison, A. P., Wells, A., & Nothard, S. (2000). Cognitive factors in predisposition to auditory and visual hallucinations. *The British Journal of Clinical Psychology*, *39*(1), 67–78. Available from https://doi.org/10.1348/014466500163112. *(Pt 1)*.

Morrison, R., & O'Connor, R. C. (2008). A systematic review of the relationship between rumination and suicidality. *Suicide & Life-Threatening Behavior*, *38*(5), 523–538. Available from https://doi.org/10.1521/suli.2008.38.5.523.

Naumann, E., & Svaldi, J. (2016). Effects of emotional acceptance and rumination on media-induced body dissatisfaction in anorexia and bulimia nervosa. *Journal of Psychiatric Research*, *82*, 119–125. Retrieved from <http://www.dx.doi.org/10.15496/publikation-24190>.

Naumann, E., Tuschen-Caffier, B., Voderholzer, U., Caffier, D., & Svaldi, J. (2015). Rumination but not distraction increases eating-related symptoms in anorexia and bulimia nervosa. *Journal of Abnormal Psychology*, *124*(2), 412–420. Available from https://doi.org/10.1037/abn0000046.

Naumann, E., Tuschen-Caffier, B., Voderholzer, U., Schäfer, J., & Svaldi, J. (2016). Effects of emotional acceptance and rumination on media-induced body dissatisfaction in anorexia and bulimia nervosa. *Journal of Psychiatric Research*, *82*, 119–125. Available from https://doi.org/10.1016/j.jpsychires.2016.07.021.

Naumann, E., Tuschen-Caffier, B., Voderholzer, U., & Svaldi, J. (2016). Spontaneous emotion regulation in anorexia and bulimia nervosa. *Cognitive Therapy and Research*, *40*(3), 304–313. Available from https://doi.org/10.1007/s10608-015-9723-3.

Neumark-Sztainer, D., Wall, M., Larson, N. I., Eisenberg, M. E., & Loth, K. (2011). Dieting and disordered eating behaviors from adolescence to young adulthood: Findings from a 10-year longitudinal study. *Journal of the American Dietetic Association*, *111*(7), 1004–1011. Available from https://doi.org/10.1016/j.jada.2011.04.012.

Nicolai, K. A., Wielgus, M. D., & Mezulis, A. (2016). Identifying risk for self-harm: Rumination and negative affectivity in the prospective prediction of nonsuicidal self-injury. *Suicide & Life-Threatening Behavior*, *46*(2), 223–233. Available from https://doi.org/10.1111/sltb.12186.

Nock, M. K., Borges, G., Bromet, E. J., Alonso, J., Angermeyer, M., Beautrais, A., ... Williams, D. (2008). Cross-national prevalence and risk factors for suicidal ideation, plans and attempts. *The British Journal of Psychiatry, 192*(2), 98–105. Available from https://doi.org/10.1192/bjp.bp.107.040113.

Nolen-Hoeksema, S. (2004). Gender differences in risk factors and consequences for alcohol use and problems. *Clinical Psychology Review, 24*(8), 981–1010. Available from https://doi.org/10.1016/j.cpr.2004.08.003.

Nolen-Hoeksema, S., & Harrell, Z. A. (2002). Rumination, depression, and alcohol use: Tests of gender differences. *Journal of Cognitive Psychotherapy, 16*(4), 391–403. Available from https://doi.org/10.1891/088983902780935687.

Nolen-Hoeksema, S., Stice, E., Wade, E., & Bohon, C. (2007). Reciprocal relations between rumination and bulimic, substance abuse, and depressive symptoms in female adolescents. *Journal of Abnormal Psychology, 116*(1), 198–207. Available from https://doi.org/10.1037/0021-843X.116.1.198.

Nolen-Hoeksema., Wisco, B., & Lyubomirsky, S. (2008). *Rethinking rumination.* eScholarship, University of California.

O'Connor, D. B., O'Connor, R. C., & Marshall, R. (2007). Perfectionism and psychological distress: Evidence of the mediating effects of rumination. *European Journal of Personality, 21*(4), 429–452. Available from https://doi.org/10.1002/per.616.

O'Connor, R. C., & Noyce, R. (2008). Personality and cognitive processes: Self-criticism and different types of rumination as predictors of suicidal ideation. *Behaviour Research and Therapy, 46*(3), 392–401. Available from https://doi.org/10.1016/j.brat.2008.01.007.

Oldershaw, A., Lavender, T., Sallis, H., Stahl, D., & Schmidt, U. (2015). Emotion generation and regulation in anorexia nervosa: A systematic review and meta-analysis of self-report data. *Clinical Psychology Review, 39*, 83–95. Available from https://doi.org/10.1016/j.cpr.2015.04.005.

Park, R. J., Dunn, B. D., & Barnard, P. J. (2011). Schematic models and modes of mind in anorexia nervosa I: A novel process account. *International Journal of Cognitive Therapy, 4*(4), 415–437. Available from https://doi.org/10.1521/ijct.2011.4.4.415.

Peters, J. R., & Geiger, P. J. (2016). Borderline personality disorder and self-conscious affect: Too much shame but not enough guilt? *Personality Disorders, 7*(3), 303–308. Available from https://doi.org/10.1037/per0000176.

Peters, J. R., Smart, L. M., & Baer, R. A. (2015). Dysfunctional responses to emotion mediate the cross-sectional relationship between rejection sensitivity and borderline personality features. *Journal of Personality Disorders, 29*(2), 231–240. Available from https://doi.org/10.1521/pedi_2014_28_151.

Polanco-Roman, L., Gomez, J., Miranda, R., & Jeglic, E. (2016). Stress-related symptoms and suicidal ideation: The roles of rumination and depressive symptoms vary by gender. *Cognitive Therapy and Research, 40*(5), 606–616. Available from https://doi.org/10.1007/s10608-016-9782-0.

Polanco-Roman, L., Jurska, J., Quiñones, V., & Miranda, R. (2015). Brooding, reflection, and distraction: Relation to non-suicidal self-injury versus suicide attempts. *Archives of Suicide Research, 19*(3), 350–365. Available from https://doi.org/10.1080/13811118.2014.981623.

Rawal, A., Park, R. J., & Williams, M. G. (2010). Rumination, experiential avoidance, and dysfunctional thinking in eating disorders. *Behaviour Research and Therapy, 48*(9), 851–859. Available from https://doi.org/10.1016/j.brat.2010.05.009.

Richmond, M., Spring, B., Kaplan Sommerfeld, B., & McChargue, D. (2001). Rumination and cigarette smoking. *Journal of Consulting and Clinical Psychology, 69*(5), 836–840. Available from https://doi.org/10.1037/0022-006X.69.5.836.

Sarin, S., & Nolen-Hoeksema, S. (2010). The dangers of dwelling: An examination of the relationship between rumination and consumptive coping in survivors of childhood sexual abuse. *Cognition & Emotion, 24*(1), 71–85. Available from https://doi.org/10.1080/02699930802563668.

Sassaroli, S., Bertelli, S., Decoppi, M., Crosina, M., Milos, G., & Ruggiero, G. M. (2005). Worry and eating disorders: A psychopathological association. *Eating Behaviors, 6*(4), 301–307. Available from https://doi.org/10.1016/j.eatbeh.2005.05.001.

Sauer, S. E., & Baer, R. A. (2012). Ruminative and mindful self-focused attention in borderline personality disorder. *Personality Disorders, 3*(4), 433–441. Available from https://doi.org/10.1037/a0025465.

Schepers, R., & Markus, C. R. (2015). Gene x cognition interaction on stress-induced eating: Effect of rumination. *Psychoneuroendocrinology, 54*, 41–53. Retrieved from <https://www.narcis.nl/publication/RecordID/oai:cris.maastrichtuniversity.nl:publications%2F0e23ecae-df2e-47aa-9a5b-28cc46053cf2>.

Schmidt, U., & Treasure, J. (2006). Anorexia nervosa: Valued and visible. A cognitive-interpersonal maintenance model and its implications for research and practice. *The British Journal of Clinical Psychology, 45*(Pt 3), 343–366. Available from https://doi.org/10.1348/014466505X53902.

Seidel, M., Petermann, J., Diestel, S., Ritschel, F., Boehm, I., King, J., ... Ehrlich, S. (2016). A naturalistic examination of negative affect and disorder-related rumination in anorexia nervosa. *European Child & Adolescent Psychiatry, 25*(11), 1207–1216. Available from https://doi.org/10.1007/s00787-016-0844-3.

Selby, E. A., Anestis, M. D., Bender, T. W., & Joiner, T. E. (2009). An exploration of the emotional cascade model in borderline personality disorder. *Journal of Abnormal Psychology, 118*(2), 375–387. Available from https://doi.org/10.1037/a0015711.

Selby, E. A., Anestis, M. D., & Joiner, T. E. (2007). Daydreaming about death. *Behavior Modification, 31*(6), 867–879. Available from https://doi.org/10.1177/0145445507300874.

Selby, E. A., Anestis, M. D., & Joiner, T. E. (2008). Understanding the relationship between emotional and behavioral dysregulation: Emotional cascades. *Behaviour Research and Therapy, 46*(5), 593–611. Available from https://doi.org/10.1016/j.brat.2008.02.002.

Selby, E. A., Connell, L. D., & Joiner, T. E. (2010). The pernicious blend of rumination and fearlessness in non-suicidal self-injury. *Cognitive Therapy and Research, 34*(5), 421–428. Available from https://doi.org/10.1007/s10608-009-9260-z.

Selby, E. A., Franklin, J., Carson-Wong, A., & Rizvi, S. L. (2013). Emotional cascades and self-injury: Investigating instability of rumination and negative emotion. *Journal of Clinical Psychology, 69*(12), 1213–1227. Available from https://doi.org/10.1002/jclp.21966.

Selby, E. A., Joiner, J., & Thomas, E. (2013). Emotional cascades as prospective predictors of dysregulated behaviors in borderline personality disorder. *Personality Disorders, 4*(2), 168–174. Available from https://doi.org/10.1037/a0029933.

Selby, E. A., & Joiner, T. E. (2009). Cascades of emotion. *Review of General Psychology, 13*(3), 219–229. Available from https://doi.org/10.1037/a0015687.

Selby, E. A., Kranzler, A., Panza, E., & Fehling, K. B. (2016). Bidirectional-compounding effects of rumination and negative emotion in predicting impulsive behavior: Implications for emotional cascades. *Journal of Personality, 84*(2), 139–153. Available from https://doi.org/10.1111/jopy.12147.

Shoal, G. D., Castaneda, J. O., & Giancola, P. R. (2005). Worry moderates the relation between negative affectivity and affect-related substance use in adolescent males: A prospective study of maladaptive emotional self-regulation. *Personality and Individual Differences, 38*(2), 475–485. Available from https://doi.org/10.1016/j.paid.2004.05.005.

Skitch, S., & Abela, J. (2008). Rumination in response to stress as a common vulnerability factor to depression and substance misuse in adolescence. *Journal of Abnormal Child Psychology*, *36*(7), 1029–1045. Available from https://doi.org/10.1007/s10802-008-9233-9.

Smith, J., Grandin, L., Alloy, L., & Abramson, L. (2006). Cognitive vulnerability to depression and axis II personality dysfunction. *Cognitive Therapy and Research*, *30*(5), 609–621. Available from https://doi.org/10.1007/s10608-006-9038-5.

Stange, J. P., Hamilton, J. L., Burke, T. A., Kleiman, E. M., O'Garro-Moore, J. K., Seligman, N. D., ... Alloy, L. B. (2015). Negative cognitive styles synergistically predict suicidal ideation in bipolar spectrum disorders: A 3-year prospective study. *Psychiatry Research*, *226*(1), 162–168. Available from https://doi.org/10.1016/j.psychres.2014.12.042.

Startup, H., Freeman, D., & Garety, P. A. (2007). Persecutory delusions and catastrophic worry in psychosis: Developing the understanding of delusion distress and persistence. *Behaviour Research and Therapy*, *45*(3), 523–537. Available from https://doi.org/10.1016/j.brat.2006.04.006.

Startup, H., Lavender, A., Oldershaw, A., Stott, R., Tchanturia, K., Treasure, J., & Schmidt, U. (2013). Worry and rumination in anorexia nervosa. *Behavioural and Cognitive Psychotherapy*, *41*(3), 301–316. Available from https://doi.org/10.1017/S1352465812000847.

Sternheim, L., Startup, H., Saeidi, S., Morgan, J., Hugo, P., Russell, A., & Schmidt, U. (2012). Understanding catastrophic worry in eating disorders: Process and content characteristics. *Journal of Behavior Therapy and Experimental Psychiatry*, *43*(4), 1095–1103. Available from https://doi.org/10.1016/j.jbtep.2012.05.006.

Surrence, K., Miranda, R., Marroquín, B. M., & Chan, S. (2009). Brooding and reflective rumination among suicide attempters: Cognitive vulnerability to suicidal ideation. *Behaviour Research and Therapy*, *47*(9), 803–808. Available from https://doi.org/10.1016/j.brat.2009.06.001.

Svaldi, J., Naumann, E., Trentowska, M., Lackner, H. K., & Tuschen-Caffier, B. (2013). Emotion regulation and its influence on body-related distress in overweight women. *Journal of Experimental Psychopathology*, *4*(5). Available from https://doi.org/10.5127/jep.028712, jep. 028712.

Swayampakala, K., Thrasher, J., Carpenter, M. J., Shigematsu, L. M. R., Cupertio, A., & Berg, C. J. (2012). Level of cigarette consumption and quit behavior in a population of low-intensity smokers—Longitudinal results from the international tobacco control (ITC) survey in Mexico. *Addictive Behaviors*, *38*(4), 1958–1965. Available from https://doi.org/10.1016/j.addbeh.2012.12.007.

Tait, R. J., Brinker, J., Moller, C. I., & French, D. J. (2014). Rumination, substance use, and self-harm in a representative Australian adult sample. *Journal of Clinical Psychology*, *70*(3), 283–293. Available from https://doi.org/10.1002/jclp.22025.

Tanner, A., Hasking, P., & Martin, G. (2014). Effects of rumination and optimism on the relationship between psychological distress and non-suicidal self-injury. *Prevention Science*, *15*(6), 860–868. Available from https://doi.org/10.1007/s11121-013-0444-0.

Troop, N. A., Holbrey, A., & Treasure, J. L. (1998). Stress, coping, and crisis support in eating disorders. *The International Journal of Eating Disorders*, *24*(2), 157–166. Available from https://doi.org/AID-EAT5 > 3.0.CO;2-D.

Tucker, R. P., Wingate, L. R., O'Keefe, V. M., Mills, A. C., Rasmussen, K., Davidson, C. L., & Grant, D. M. (2013). Rumination and suicidal ideation: The moderating roles of hope and optimism. *Personality and Individual Differences*, *55*(5), 606–611. Available from https://doi.org/10.1016/j.paid.2013.05.013.

Valderrama., Miranda., & Jeglic. (2016). Ruminative subtypes and impulsivity in risk for suicidal behavior. *Psychiatry Research*, *236*, 15–21. Available from https://doi.org/10.1016/j.psychres.2016.01.008.

Verplanken, B., & Velsvik, R. (2008). Habitual negative body image thinking as psychological risk factor in adolescents. *Body Image, 5*(2), 133–140. Available from https://doi.org/10.1016/j.bodyim.2007.11.001.

Voon, D., Hasking, P., & Martin, G. (2014a). Change in emotion regulation strategy use and its impact on adolescent nonsuicidal self-injury: A three-year longitudinal analysis using latent growth modeling. *Journal of Abnormal Psychology, 123*(3), 487–498. Available from https://doi.org/10.1037/a0037024.

Voon, D., Hasking, P., & Martin, G. (2014b). The roles of emotion regulation and ruminative thoughts in non-suicidal self-injury. *British Journal of Clinical Psychology, 53*(1), 95–113. Available from https://doi.org/10.1111/bjc.12030.

Voon, D., Hasking, P., & Martin, G. (2014c). Emotion regulation in first episode adolescent non-suicidal self-injury: What difference does a year make? *Journal of Adolescence, 37*(7), 1077–1087. Available from https://doi.org/10.1016/j.adolescence.2014.07.020.

Vorontsova, N., Garety, P., & Freeman, D. (2013). Cognitive factors maintaining persecutory delusions in psychosis: The contribution of depression. *Journal of Abnormal Psychology, 122*(4), 1121–1131. Available from https://doi.org/10.1037/a0034952.

Wade, T., George, W. M., & Atkinson, M. (2009). A randomized controlled trial of brief interventions for body dissatisfaction. *Journal of Consulting and Clinical Psychology, 77*(5), 845–854. Available from https://doi.org/10.1037/a0016879.

Walker, K. L., Hadjistavropoulos, T., Gagnon, M. M., & MacNab, Y. C. (2015). Development and validation of the hunger sensitivity scale (HSS) among university students. *Canadian Journal of Behavioural Science/Revue Canadienne Des Sciences Du Comportement, 47*(1), 1–11. Available from https://doi.org/10.1037/a0035764.

Wang, S. B., & Borders, A. (2018). The unique effects of angry and depressive rumination on eating-disorder psychopathology and the mediating role of impulsivity. *Eating Behaviors, 29*, 41–47. Available from https://doi.org/10.1016/j.eatbeh.2018.02.004.

Wang, S. B., Lydecker, J. A., & Grilo, C. M. (2017). Rumination in patients with binge-eating disorder and obesity: Associations with eating-disorder psychopathology and weight-bias internalization. *European Eating Disorders Review, 25*(2), 98–103. Available from https://doi.org/10.1002/erv.2499.

Watkins, E. R. (2008). Constructive and unconstructive repetitive thought. *Psychological Bulletin, 134*(2), 163–206. Available from https://doi.org/10.1037/0033-2909.134.2.163.

Watkins, E. R. (2009). Depressive rumination and co-morbidity: Evidence for brooding as a transdiagnostic process. *Journal of Rational-Emotive and Cognitive-Behavior Therapy: RET, 27*(3), 160–175. Available from https://doi.org/10.1007/s10942-009-0098-9.

Weiss, B., Süsser, K., & Catron, T. (1998). Common and specific features of childhood psychopathology. *Journal of Abnormal Psychology, 107*(1), 118–127. Available from https://doi.org/10.1037/0021-843X.107.1.118.

Willem, L., Bijttebier, P., Claes, L., & Raes, F. (2011). Rumination subtypes in relation to problematic substance use in adolescence. *Personality and Individual Differences, 50*(5), 695–699. Available from https://doi.org/10.1016/j.paid.2010.12.020.

Willem, L., Bijttebier, P., Claes, L., Vanhalst, J., & Raes, F. (2014). The cross-temporal associations between rumination subtypes and substance use in adolescence: Exploring the moderating role of gender. *Journal of Psychopathology and Behavioral Assessment, 36*(1), 143–154. Available from https://doi.org/10.1007/s10862-013-9373-2.

Yong, H. H., Borland, R., Thrasher, J. F., Thompson, M. E., Nagelhout, G. E., Fong, G. T., ... Cummings, K. M. (2014). Mediational pathways of the impact of cigarette warning labels on quit attempts. *Health Psychology, 33*(11), 1410–1420. Available from https://doi.org/10.1037/hea0000056.

Zaki, L. F., Coifman, K. G., Rafaeli, E., Berenson, K. R., & Downey, G. (2013). Emotion differentiation as a protective factor against nonsuicidal self-injury in borderline personality disorder. *Behavior Therapy, 44*(3), 529–540. Available from https://doi.org/10.1016/j.beth.2013.04.008.

Zielinski, M. J., Borders, A., & Giancola, P. R. (2015). Does hostile rumination mediate the associations between reported child abuse, parenting characteristics and borderline features in adulthood? *Personality and Mental Health, 9*(4), 288–297. Available from https://doi.org/10.1002/pmh.1306.

CHAPTER

5

Rumination and physical functioning

Overview

This chapter reviews the literature linking rumination and other types of repetitive thinking with physiological outcomes. After describing two bodily systems implicated in stress responses, I explain the perseverative cognitive hypothesis, the predominant theory describing the role of rumination in physiological functioning. I then review empirical evidence implicating rumination and other types of repetitive thinking in cardiovascular, endocrine, and immune functioning. This chapter also considers research literature on the effects of rumination and worry on sleep problems, pain, and health-related behaviors.

Once a year, I travel with my family across the country to visit my parents. For me, it is going back to my childhood home. People who do this are likely familiar with the accompanying mixed emotions and flood of memories. In addition, there are the 3-hour time change, nonchild-proofed homes, and extensive family dynamics to navigate. Not surprisingly, I often spend days and nights leading up to and during the trip worrying about how things will go and ruminating about past memories or recent interactions. During this period, I tend to feel both wound up and exhausted. I am physiologically aroused, sleep and eat poorly, and am more prone to throwing out my back. This connection between stressful events and impaired physical health has long been understood. Scientists have identified systems in our bodies that are "turned on" when we perceive stressors. Although short-term activation of these systems is necessary for survival, we now know that

Rumination and Related Constructs
DOI: https://doi.org/10.1016/B978-0-12-812545-8.00005-X

© 2020 Elsevier Inc. All rights reserved.

sustained activation puts damaging strain on the body. Two physiological systems in particular are implicated in responses to stress.

The autonomic nervous system (ANS) modulates, or controls, bodily processes over which we generally do not have volitional control (e.g., heart rate, blood pressure, respiration rate, and digestion). The ANS provides the body's most immediate response to stress, via its two major branches. First, the sympathetic nervous system prepares organisms to fight or flee by energizing the body. Specifically, it increases heart rate, blood pressure, and muscle strength, relaxes airways in the lungs, triggers the body to release stored energy, and slows down unnecessary processes such as digestion and immune functioning. Some of the changes can occur in seconds, before people even become consciously aware of a threat. Counteracting this sympathetic arousal is the parasympathetic nervous system, which restores the body to baseline. It does this by slowing down heart rate, decreasing blood pressure, constricting airways, and stimulating digestion so that energy reserves are restored. The parasympathetic nervous system is necessary for survival, because organisms do not thrive in a chronic state of fight or flight. In fact, sympathetic excitement typically wanes quickly, because the slowing effects of parasympathetic activity occur in mere milliseconds.

Ideally, the sympathetic and parasympathetic nervous systems are in a dynamic balance, allowing individuals to respond flexibly to changing external situations. In "normal" situations (i.e., assuming people are not under constant threat or danger), the parasympathetic system should be dominant, maintaining a healthy heart rate and blood pressure. When acute stressors are encountered, sympathetic activation energizes people to deal with the danger, and the parasympathetic system calms them down once they are safe. This flexible give and take occurs because several internal organs, such as the heart, have inputs from both systems. By contrast, autonomic imbalance occurs when one system—generally the sympathetic—is too powerful (Thayer & Brosschot, 2005). Prolonged sympathetic excitation reflects a failure of parasympathetic control, or insufficient parasympathetic activity. Chronic sympathetic hyperactivation is associated with hypertension and increased risk of cardiovascular disease (Thayer & Lane, 2007), as well as depression and anxiety disorders, which are themselves risk factors for diseases (Beauchaine & Thayer, 2015).

The bodily changes that occur during sympathetic excitation are strengthened and maintained by a slower, neural-endocrine circuit called the hypothalamic–pituitary–adrenal (HPA) axis. Put simply, if the brain detects continued danger, the hypothalamus alerts the pituitary gland (both of which are in the brain), which in turn alerts the adrenal glands (on the kidneys) to release adrenaline and cortisol into the blood stream. Adrenaline makes the heart beat faster and opens up airways. Cortisol triggers the release of glucose that is stored in the body. The release of cortisol is incredibly adaptive in the short term, as it allows the body to respond as long as needed to a perceived and acute threat. Chronically elevated cortisol, however, is associated with cardiovascular disease and a suppressed immune system (Dickerson & Kemeny, 2004). Fortunately, the HPA axis has its own built-in turn-off switch in the brain: the hippocampus is very sensitive to cortisol levels in the blood and typically inhibits the HPA axis when it detects elevated cortisol. Unfortunately, prolonged exposure to cortisol from repeated or extended stress can damage the hippocampus, leading to dysregulation of the HPA axis and chronically high levels of resting cortisol.

In sum, although sympathetic and HPA arousal in the short term is evolutionarily adaptive, chronic excitation of these systems is unhealthy. Moreover, research clearly indicates that discrete stressors produce prolonged physiological activation (for a review, see Pieper & Brosschot, 2005). A research team led by Jos Brosschot spent many years trying to better understand psychosocial factors contributing to sustained physiological activation, and the construct they zeroed in on is repetitive thought.

The *perseverative cognition hypothesis* defines perseverative cognition as any type of cognition that is repetitive and focused on a particular stressor (Brosschot et al., 2006). Types of perseverative cognition include rumination, worry, cognitive intrusions, and anticipatory and post-event processing. This model argues that perseverative cognition converts the immediate physiological consequences of stressors into prolonged physiological activation, which increases the risk of chronic disease. As such, perseverative cognition is conceptualized as a mediator, or "the final pathway" by which a stressor influences bodily functioning (see Fig. 5.1). Brosschot also proposes that perseverative cognition occurs when stressors are appraised as being uncontrollable and threatening. If people believe that they can effectively cope with and/or control a stressor, then there is no need for rumination or worry. However, helplessness, hopelessness, and/or low self-efficacy in the ability to cope with a stressful situation lead not only to acute stress responses but also prolonged and ineffective efforts at mental problem-solving, or perseverative cognition. Unlike acute stressors, which may trigger extreme increases in physiological activation, perseverative cognition produces more moderate but longer lasting activation of the cardiovascular, HPA, and immune systems. In fact, acute stress responses (e.g., peaks in physiological activation) do not automatically lead to prolonged stress responses. Instead, prolonged stress responses result from prolonged cognitive representations of stressors, as happens in perseverative cognition.

The perseverative cognition hypothesis has influenced a wealth of research examining the effects of rumination and worry on physical

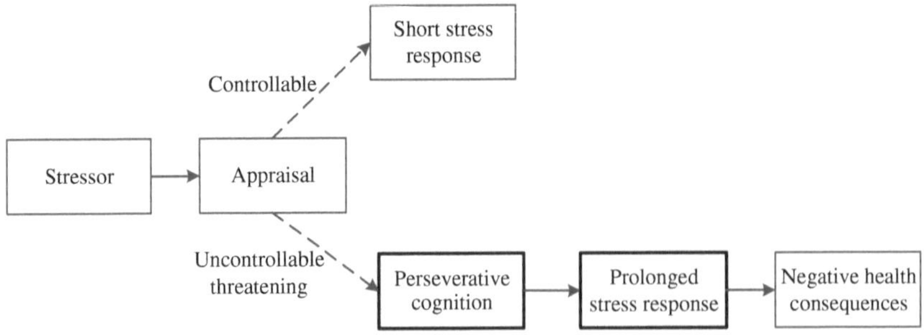

FIGURE 5.1 The perseverative cognition hypothesis. Source: *Adapted from Brosschot, J. F., Gerin, W., & Thayer, J. F. (2006). The perseverative cognition hypothesis: A review of worry, prolonged stress-related physiological activation, and health.* Journal of Psychosomatic Research, *60(2), 113–124. Available from https://doi.org/10.1016/j.jpsychores.2005.06.074.*

functioning. In this chapter, I first review the evidence linking rumination and other types of perseverative cognition to cardiovascular, endocrine, and immune functioning, three indicators of sympathetic arousal. I then turn to rumination's links with other indicators of physical functioning, specifically sleep problems, pain, and health behaviors.

Cardiovascular functioning

A large literature focuses on associations between rumination and cardiovascular functioning. Two common indicators of cardiovascular functioning include blood pressure and heart rate (i.e., beats per minute). In addition to heart rate, researchers have increasingly focused on a construct called heart rate variability (HRV), or the variation in heart rate from beat to beat. Recall that the heart is enervated by both the sympathetic and parasympathetic nervous systems. Increases in sympathetic activation lead to relative increases in heart rate, causing the intervals between heart beats to become shorter. On the flip side, increases in parasympathetic activation lead to relative decreases in heart rate and longer intervals between heart beats. Because parasympathetic effects are much faster than sympathetic effects, parasympathetic influences are the primary source of change in beat-to-beat variation of the heart. Thus, HRV is primarily understood as a measure of parasympathetic activity, with low HRV indicating low parasympathetic control of the heart. Deficits in parasympathetic activity leave individuals chronically aroused. A recent metaanalysis of 60 empirical studies found that perseverative cognition is associated with all three cardiovascular indicators: higher blood pressure and heart rate and lower HRV

(Ottaviani, Thayer, et al., 2016). To help make sense of this literature, I discuss different ways that cardiovascular functioning is measured.

Resting and ambulatory assessment

The easiest way to assess cardiovascular functioning is to obtain blood pressure and/or heart rate recordings while people are sitting down (i.e., at rest), similar to what occurs in a regular doctor visit. In fact, higher trait depressive rumination and worry are associated with lower resting HRV (Thayer, Friedman, & Borkovec, 1996; Williams et al., 2015). Unfortunately, single recordings in a laboratory setting may be influenced by nervousness. A better way to examine the effect of rumination on cardiovascular functioning is to assess the indicators over a 24-hour period while people are going about their regular lives. To do this, participants wear ambulatory blood pressure cuffs and/or electrocardiogram, and recordings are taken at regular intervals throughout the day and even overnight.

Perseverative cognition, particularly when measured at the state level, is generally associated with higher ambulatory heart rate and lower ambulatory HRV. In one study, every waking hour for four consecutive days, teachers reported whether they had engaged in perseverative thinking and/or experienced a stressful event in the past hour (Pieper, Brosschot, van der Leeden, & Thayer, 2007). At each time point, more state perseverative thinking and stressful events were both uniquely associated with higher heart rate and lower HRV. Interestingly, only perseverative thinking uniquely predicted changes in heart rate and HRV 2 hours later, whereas the effect of stressful events did not last more than an hour (Pieper, Brosschot, van der Leeden, & Thayer, 2010). In similar studies lasting only 1 day, state perseverative thinking was associated with lower ambulatory HRV (Ottaviani, Medea, Lonigro, Tarvainen, & Couyoumdjian, 2015; Ottaviani, Shahabi, et al., 2015; Ottaviani, Shapiro, & Fitzgerald, 2011). Interestingly, some researchers found that the *duration* of state worry, rather than the *frequency* of worry, predicted higher heart rate and lower HRV (Brosschot, Van Dijk, & Thayer, 2007). Results with trait measures are more mixed, with some studies finding that trait perseverative cognition is associated with higher heart rate and lower HRV (Brosschot et al., 2007; Ottaviani, Shahabi, et al., 2015), but other studies failing to find such an effect (Gerteis & Schwerdtfeger, 2016; Johnson, Key, Routledge, Gerin, & Campbell, 2014).

Ambulatory assessment also allows researchers to take into account normal variations that occur throughout the day. Blood pressure and heart rate typically decrease, and HRV increases, from midday to midnight, reflecting the prevalence of sympathetic activity during waking hours and parasympathetic activity during rest/sleep. In one study with healthy undergraduates, these typical changes from morning to evening (e.g., decreased heart rate and increased HRV) only emerged for participants with low levels of state rumination (Takano, Ueno, & Tanno, 2014). For participants with high levels of state rumination, HRV and heart rate changed little throughout the day. Similarly, higher trait rumination in undergraduate women was associated with less of the typical dip in blood pressure during nighttime sleep (Johnson et al., 2014). Thus, rumination may prevent the typical daily declines in autonomic arousal that contribute to healthy rest/sleep cycles.

Some studies examined moderators of the effect of rumination on ambulatory cardiac functioning. For instance, in men with high blood pressure, trait angry rumination predicted higher ambulatory blood pressure only for participants who also had tendencies to avoid anger (Hogan & Linden, 2004). Another study with healthy adults found that state rumination was associated with lower HRV and higher heart rate only when participants were involved in unsupportive social interactions (Gerteis & Schwerdtfeger, 2016). Thus, as we have seen before, the effect of rumination is most prominent when people are under stress and/or use other maladaptive coping strategies.

Reactivity

Cardiovascular *reactivity* involves changes (e.g., increased blood pressure and heart rate and decreased HRV) that occur in reaction to acute stressors. These changes are often part of a natural and adaptive response that prepares the body for immediate action. However, when individuals respond in a manner that is exaggerated given the demands of the situation, a cascade of physiological events may occur that result in tissue damage, system deregulation, and disease (Lovallo, 2010). In fact, exaggerated cardiovascular reactivity has been implicated in the development of hypertension, diabetes, and cardiovascular disease (Chida & Steptoe, 2010). In research assessing cardiovascular reactivity, heart rate and blood pressure are measured before, during, and sometimes immediately after a stressful task.

The effects of various types of rumination on cardiovascular reactivity are unclear. For instance, in women and children who imagined hypothetical sad scenarios, higher trait depressive rumination was associated with larger reductions in HRV (Borelli, Hilt, West, Weekes, & Gonzalez, 2014; Woody, Burkhouse, Birk, & Gibb, 2015). By contrast, an experiment in which dysphoric and nondysphoric participants underwent the classic rumination or distraction manipulations failed to find effects of depressive rumination on blood pressure or heart rate (Vickers & Vogeltanz-Holm, 2003). Similarly with trauma-related rumination, studies have found both positive and nonsignificant effects of manipulated rumination about distressing events on heart rate (Ehring, Fuchs, & Kläsener, 2009; Ehring, Szeimies, & Schaffrick, 2009). In regards to angry rumination, a recent metaanalysis found that *induced* angry rumination has large and significant effects on cardiovascular reactivity—particularly blood pressure—and that these effects are larger than those for induced depressive rumination (Busch, Pössel, & Valentine, 2017). The effects of *trait* angry rumination, however, are mixed. In patients with cardiovascular disease who recalled an angry memory, trait angry rumination predicted an increase in endothelin, a peptide in the body that constricts blood vessels and contributes to high blood pressure and heart disease (Fernandez et al., 2010). By contrast, trait angry rumination was not associated with changes in blood pressure after being insulted or watching violent film clips (Bushman & Geen, 1990; Caprara et al., 1987). In sum, the literature linking different types of rumination with cardiovascular reactivity is mixed.

A sizeable literature examines the effects of worry on cardiovascular reactivity. Some studies found that HRV decreased significantly—for participants with and without generalized anxiety disorder (GAD)—following worry inductions about a personal concern, compared to baseline (Meeten et al., 2016; Ottaviani, Watson, et al., 2016). However, other research found that induced worry, compared to relaxation or distraction, led to lower HRV only in high trait worriers or in participants diagnosed with GAD (Llera & Newman, 2010; Ottaviani et al., 2014). In one experiment, healthy undergraduates were asked to talk about a stressful personal event that occurred in the past or will occur in the future, after which they engaged in a 20-minute tracking task in which they had to keep the cursor in a slowly moving circle (Ottaviani, Shapiro, & Couyoumdjian, 2013). At intermittent intervals during this easy tracking task, participants reported whether they were focused on the task, distracted by external stimuli, ruminating/worrying, or engaged in mind-wandering. Perseverative thought (i.e., rumination and worrying) was associated with the highest HR and lowest HRV, compared to being focused on the task and mind-wandering. Importantly, the effect of perseverative cognition on HR was especially strong for high trait worriers. Thus, the worry literature suggests that perseverative thinking about a stressor may increase cardiovascular reactivity only or particularly for individuals who already have tendencies for perseverative cognition.

One possibility is that worry predicts cardiovascular reactivity more so than does rumination. In fact, a metaanalysis found that induced worry yields greater heart rate reactivity than did induced rumination

(Ottaviani, Thayer, et al., 2016). In an experiment directly comparing the effects of worry and rumination, adult participants with depression or GAD watched several emotion-eliciting film clips, after which they rated their current worry and rumination (Aldao, Mennin, & McLaughlin, 2013). State worry predicted less HRV during fearful and happy (but not sad) film clips, whereas rumination was not associated with HRV during any of the videos. The authors suggest that worry may be more strongly associated with cardiovascular reactivity because it is characterized more by perceived threat than is rumination.

Recovery

Researchers also study how long it takes for blood pressure and heart rate to return to normal after a stressor, a construct called cardiovascular *recovery*. Here, what matters is not how high the reactivity peak is above baseline but for how long the levels are elevated above normal. Although people who have exaggerated reactivity levels are also likely to take longer to return to baseline, evidence suggests that these constructs have unique effects on cardiovascular health (e.g., Stewart & France, 2001). In fact, delayed recovery predicts cardiovascular health outcomes several years later (for a review, see Larsen & Christenfeld, 2011). The perseverative cognition hypothesis argues that rumination and worry primarily have their effect on recovery, rather than reactivity, and that the total amount of time people experience heightened autonomic activation is the primary predictor of disease states. Cardiovascular recovery is usually assessed by measuring heart rate and blood pressure during a resting recovery period following a stressor.

Rumination is associated with delayed cardiovascular recovery. In some experiments (Glynn, Christenfeld, & Gerin, 2002; Radstaak, Geurts, Brosschot, Cillessen, & Kompier, 2011), participants either engaged in a stressful activity while being interrupted, insulted, or threatened (i.e., the emotionally upsetting task) or walked in place (i.e., the nonemotional task). Several minutes later, participants were asked to ruminate about the task for 3 minutes. Participants who ruminated about the emotionally upsetting task exhibited increased blood pressure both during the rumination induction and during a 5-minute recovery period. Thus, rumination contributed to both higher reactivity and delayed recovery. Furthermore, greater measured rumination about the task was associated with delayed blood pressure recovery. Some studies examined the effect of repeated rumination. For instance, when participants ruminated about an angering event three times over a 10-minute period, sympathetic activation increased with each successive repetition, both during rumination (i.e., reactivity) and during the delay period (i.e., recovery) (Ray, Wilhelm, & Gross, 2008). Even participants who waited an entire week to ruminate exhibited similar levels of elevated blood pressure as participants who ruminated only 30 minutes after the emotionally upsetting task (Glynn, Christenfeld, & Gerin, 2007). In showing that rumination separated from the actual stressor leads to higher reactivity and delayed recovery, these studies provide empirical support for the perseverative cognition hypothesis.

Researchers have also explored potential moderators of the effect of rumination on cardiovascular recovery. First, distraction appears to moderate the effect of rumination. In one experiment, participants described angering situations, after which they sat quietly for 10–12 minutes, either with nothing to look at or with distracting cards and magazines to read (Gerin, Davidson, Christenfeld, Goyal, & Schwartz, 2006). In participants with no distraction, trait angry rumination was associated with delayed blood pressure recovery. In participants who were distracted, by contrast, there was no effect of trait angry rumination on cardiovascular recovery (see also Ottaviani et al., 2011). Second, in line with past research, the effects of rumination about an angering event on cardiovascular recovery were stronger for participants with higher internalizing symptoms and worse coping tendencies (Ottaviani, Shapiro, Davydov, Goldstein, & Mills, 2009).

Summary

In sum, rumination and worry, especially when measured at the state level, are associated with greater resting and ambulatory cardiovascular activation. Rumination and worry also seem to predict exaggerated cardiovascular reactivity to stressors, particularly for people with strong tendencies for perseverative cognition. Finally, repetitive thinking predicts delayed cardiovascular recovery (e.g., continued arousal) following a stressor, especially for people with poor coping skills and greater existing psychological distress.

Endocrine functioning

Bodily levels of cortisol constitute a fairly good indicator of HPA activation. If rumination contributes to physiological activation and stress, then it should be associated with elevated cortisol levels. Researchers typically measure cortisol by taking saliva samples, accomplished by a quick swab of the tongue. As with cardiovascular functioning, there are different contexts in which cortisol levels are studied. Sometimes researchers assess resting cortisol levels at various times of day.

However, because cortisol increases in response to perceived stress, most researchers study the cortisol stress response by measuring or manipulating particular stressors and associated rumination and examining resulting changes in cortisol concentrations.

Resting cortisol

Resting cortisol has predictable fluctuations throughout the day. Most people experience a notable increase in cortisol within the first 30–45 minutes after waking in the morning. This increase is referred to as the cortisol awakening response (CAR). Cortisol levels then decline throughout the day, with the lowest levels typically occurring around midnight. Although these patterns of cortisol activity are fairly stable across days, there are individual differences—both between and within persons—that can be accounted for by psychosocial processes such as repetitive thinking.

The literature on the association between *trait* perseverative cognition and morning cortisol is mixed. For instance, healthy adults with greater trait worry had higher morning cortisol levels and/or a larger CAR (Schlotz, Hellhammer, Schulz, & Stone, 2004; Wüst, Federenko, Hellhammer, & Kirschbaum, 2000). By contrast, studies have found no associations or even negative associations between trait rumination and morning cortisol levels (Backhaus, Junghanns, & Hohagen, 2004; Kuehner, Holzhauer, & Huffziger, 2007; Rydstedt, Cropley, Devereux, & Michalianou, 2009; Zoccola, Dickerson, & Yim, 2011). In research examining moderators of these associations, trait negative rumination predicted a higher CAR only for women low in trait mindfulness (Daubenmier, Hayden, Chang, & Epel, 2014). In addition, trait rumination only predicted elevated morning cortisol levels for participants reporting high stress about their role at work (Rydstedt, Cropley, & Devereux, 2011). Thus, trait rumination may only predict higher morning cortisol levels in individuals with greater stress levels and worse coping skills. In addition, trait worry may be more predictive of morning cortisol than is trait rumination.

State or manipulated rumination is more clearly associated with higher morning cortisol levels. For instance, healthy undergraduates who engaged in state rumination and/or worry during the previous day had higher cortisol levels the hour after waking the next day, as well as a greater increase in cortisol the first 30 minutes after waking (Zoccola et al., 2011). In an experiment, healthy adults were randomly assigned to write about the most traumatic experience of their lives, the happiest experience of their lives, or their activities the previous day (O'Connor, Walker, Hendrickx, Talbot, & Schaefer, 2012). In all three conditions, participants visited the laboratory to write for 20 minutes on three successive days. At the end of the third day, participants reported how much they had thought about their topic since the beginning of the study and over their lives—an index of rumination. Results indicated that participants in the stressful writing condition who thought more about the stressful event exhibited a larger CAR 4 weeks later.

A few studies have measured cortisol at other times of day. For instance, rumination about a recent perceived transgression predicted higher daytime cortisol levels, measured in five biweekly laboratory visits between 10:00 a.m. and 4:00 p.m. (McCullough, Orsulak, Brandon, & Akers, 2007). In remitted depressed patients and healthy controls, daily depressive rumination was associated with higher daily cortisol levels (Huffziger et al., 2013). Finally, some researchers found that trait rumination predicts higher evening cortisol levels (Cropley, Rydstedt, Devereux, & Middleton, 2015; Rydstedt et al., 2009).

Cortisol stress response

Several studies examined the association between rumination and cortisol changes in response to stressors. As discussed previously, cortisol releases stored energy and modulates other systems (e.g., decreases immune functioning) so that the body can most effectively respond to short-term demands of a perceived threat. The cortisol system is theorized to be particularly responsive to threats to social standing, because lowered social status can have implications for survival and one's ability to effect change (Dickerson & Kemeny, 2004). In support of this theory, stressor tasks that are uncontrollable and characterized by negative social evaluations elicit the strongest cortisol stress response. Accordingly, the majority of studies examining the effect of rumination on the cortisol stress response have used social-evaluative stressors.

The most common social-evaluative stressor manipulation is called the Trier social stress test (TSST; Kirschbaum, Pirke, & Hellhammer, 1993). In this procedure, participants are instructed to give a 5-minute speech in which they explain why they would be an ideal candidate for a hypothetical job. They are led to believe that they will give the speech to two members of a selection committee, and also that the speech will be video-recorded and evaluated later. Participants are given several minutes to prepare, after which they deliver their speech to two individuals and answer several follow-up questions. Cortisol is generally assessed before and immediately after the speech task, as well as several times over the next 30–60 minute rest period. The levels of circulating cortisol in the blood typically peak (i.e., reactivity) 20–40 minutes after the onset of the TSST and then decrease to baseline (i.e., recovery) by 60 minutes after the TSST (Dickerson & Kemeny, 2004). As with cardiovascular functioning, an exaggerated cortisol stress response is characterized by heightened reactivity and prolonged recovery.

As with morning cortisol, the effect of *trait* rumination on the cortical stress response following the TSST is unclear. Several studies using healthy individuals found that trait depressive rumination was not associated with cortisol reactivity or recovery (Hilt, Aldao, & Fischer, 2015; Shapero, McClung, Bangasser, Abramson, & Alloy, 2017; Stewart, Mazurka, Bond, Wynne-Edwards, & Harkness, 2013). Interestingly, trait depressive rumination predicted less cortisol recovery following the TSST only in depressed adolescents (Stewart et al., 2013). By contrast, trait angry rumination was generally associated with greater cortisol reactivity and slower recovery (McCullough et al., 2007; Zoccola & Dickerson, 2015; Zoccola, Quas, & Yim, 2010). Thus, the effect of trait rumination on the cortisol stress response may depend on the type of rumination being measured. Specifically, angry rumination appears to predict higher cortisol levels, whereas depressive rumination may only affect recovery for already depressed individuals.

The effect of *state* or *manipulated* rumination on the cortisol stress response is more robust (Denson, Spanovic, & Miller, 2009). In general, state depressive rumination predicts higher cortisol reactivity and less recovery following the TSST (Hilt et al., 2015; Zoccola, Dickerson, & Zaldivar, 2008). In one experiment, cortisol levels declined more slowly for participants in a rumination condition and remained higher than for participants in a distraction condition, even 1 hour after the TSST (Zoccola, Rabideau, Figueroa, & Woody, 2014). Similarly, manipulated angry rumination following an insult maintained elevated cortisol levels throughout the experiment (Denson et al., 2009). One study examined whether state rumination about upsetting or angering events prevented habituation to repeated exposures to the TSST (Gianferante et al., 2014). Participants completed the TSST on 2 consecutive days, and as predicted by habituation, cortisol increases were less on the second day than on the first day. However, higher state rumination on the first day predicted greater cortisol responses on both the first and second day, suggesting that rumination is associated with a sustained cortisol response. Finally, several studies found that the effect of manipulated rumination on the cortisol stress response occurs only for individuals who are depressed or high in trait rumination (Kuehner, Huffziger, & Liebsch, 2009; LeMoult & Joormann, 2014; Shull et al., 2016). Thus, as we have seen elsewhere, the effect of manipulated rumination may be particularly strong in individuals who are already depressed and frequently ruminate.

Summary

A recent metaanalysis found that the overall association between rumination and cortisol functioning is robust, particularly in higher quality studies (Ottaviani, Thayer, et al., 2016). However, the presence of mixed results suggests the role of moderators. First, state and manipulated rumination are more consistently associated with higher cortisol levels than are measures of trait rumination (for a review, see Zoccola & Dickerson, 2012). Moreover, rumination about upsetting or angering events is consistently associated with higher cortisol levels, whereas the effects of depressive rumination have been mixed. These latter findings may reflect natural differences in cortisol functioning in depressed participants. For instance, individuals with diagnosed depression have lower resting cortisol levels in the morning and higher levels in the afternoon than do nondepressed individuals (Burke, Davis, Otte, & Mohr, 2005). Depressed individuals also show blunted cortisol reactivity and impaired recovery, compared to nondepressed individuals. These differences may contribute to significant variation between studies in the effect of depressive rumination on cortisol reactivity. The literature also points to additional moderators. Specifically, state rumination appears to predict elevated cortisol activity particularly for individuals who are already stressed, depressed, and/or typically use poor coping strategies (e.g., trait rumination).

Immune functioning

Rumination may also impact markers of immune system functioning. One way researchers have studied this is by measuring levels of lymphocytes, one type of white blood cell (Segerstrom & Miller, 2004). There are three major types of lymphocytes: thymus (T) and bone-marrow (B) cells detect foreign antigens and generate protective responses, such as antibodies, whereas natural killer (NK) cells identify and destroy cells with viruses or malignancies. Acute stressors are associated with an increase in NK cells and decreases in T and B cells, all of which are evolutionarily adaptive responses to fight-or-flight situations (Segerstrom & Miller, 2004). By contrast, chronic stress is associated with decreases in all immune markers, in part because cortisol suppresses immune functioning.

The majority of studies have examined the effect of perseverative cognition on lymphocyte and/or antibody levels in distressed individuals. For instance, worry is associated with lower T cell counts in women with HIV (Rehm & Konkle-Parker, 2017). Similarly, a metaanalysis of acute laboratory social stressors and mood inductions concluded that rumination is associated with suppressed T cell reactivity (Denson et al., 2009). In older adults caregiving for a spouse with dementia, more negative repetitive thought predicts fewer antibodies following vaccination, suggesting less B cell activation (Segerstrom, Schipper, & Greenberg, 2008). Rumination and worry are also associated with less NK cell activity, in both bereaved caregivers and animal-phobic individuals exposed to their feared animal (Esterling, Kiecolt-Glaser, Bodnar, & Glaser, 1994; Segerstrom, Glover, Craske, & Fahey, 1999). Similarly, higher trait worry was associated with lower numbers of NK cells soon after an earthquake, and the effect increased over a few months (Segerstrom, Solomon, Kemeny, & Fahey, 1998). In sum, greater rumination and worry predict suppressed immune functioning for people experiencing acute (e.g., laboratory manipulations) or chronic (e.g., caregiving, HIV) stressors.

The effect of rumination on lymphocyte functioning in nondistressed individuals, however, is less clear. In one study with healthy older adults, trait rumination was associated with higher total lymphocyte count and number of B cells (Thomsen, Jorgensen, Melsen, & Zachariae, 2004). In other research with healthy children, greater worry predicted higher levels of antibodies concurrently but lower levels of these antibodies 3 years later (Ma, Serbin, & Stack, 2018). These results suggest that perseverative cognition increases immediate immune responses in healthy individuals, perhaps because it constitutes a moderate stressor. Over time, however, chronic rumination or worry may function to suppress immune functioning.

Immune functioning is also reflected in inflammatory responses such as fevers and swelling. Although short-term inflammation promotes healing of injuries or illnesses, excessive and chronic inflammation can lead to tissue damage. Inflammatory responses are promoted by proinflammatory cytokines, which generally increase in response to stress (Segerstrom & Miller, 2004). A few researchers have examined the association between repetitive thinking and inflammatory markers. Trait rumination is generally not correlated with proinflammatory cytokine levels (Newton et al., 2017; Segerstrom et al., 2008). One experiment asked participants to engage in the TSST and then randomly assigned participants to rumination or distraction conditions (Zoccola et al., 2014). Induced rumination led to higher and sustained levels of C-reactive protein, an indication of inflammation, even 1 hour later. However, both conditions led to increases in proinflammatory cytokines. In a similar study, participants were randomly assigned to a distraction condition or a rest condition designed to maximize the opportunity for naturally-occurring rumination for 40 minutes following the TSST (Newton et al., 2017). There was no effect of condition on inflammatory cytokines and no correlation between state rumination and cytokine reactivity. Thus, the majority of existing evidence does not support an association between rumination and proinflammatory cytokine reactivity. However, inflammatory responses appear to peak 2 days after a stressor (Pepys & Hirschfield, 2003). Future research might include longer follow-up assessments of proinflammatory cytokines.

Sleep problems

Physiological dearousal (e.g., increased HRV, decreased heart rate) is believed to facilitate good sleep, and inhibition of this normal process may contribute to sleep problems (Espie, 2002). Not surprisingly, sleep theorists suggest that perseverative cognition and accompanying hyperarousal contribute to sleep problems. For example, Allison Harvey's (2002) model of insomnia proposes that excessive repetitive thought before bed triggers autonomic arousal and emotional distress. These repetitive thoughts often revolve around concerns about not getting enough sleep and whether it will be possible to function adequately during the day while suffering from fatigue, disturbed mood, or poor concentration. The heightened arousal and distress resulting from these thoughts contribute to perceptions of inadequate sleep, as well as actual sleep deficits.

In support of this theory, rumination is associated with a range of sleep problems in healthy individuals. In one study, trait rumination predicted greater presleep intrusive thoughts the night after an examination (Guastella & Moulds, 2007). High-trait ruminators who went through a rumination induction also reported more disrupted sleep the night after a midterm exam than did low-trait ruminators. In addition, greater trait and state rumination predicted a longer time to fall asleep (i.e., sleep onset latency) the night after a laboratory stressor (Zoccola, Dickerson, & Lam, 2009). Moreover, cross-sectional survey studies with healthy participants have consistently found that higher trait rumination correlates with worse self-reported sleep quality, a global construct that includes amount of sleep, sleep onset latency, number of awakenings during the night, sources of impaired sleep (e.g., snoring, breathing problems), difficulty staying awake during the day, and subjective judgments of sleep quality (Borders, Rothman, & McAndrew, 2015; Slavish & Graham-Engeland, 2015; Thomsen, Yung Mehlsen, Christensen, & Zachariae, 2003). In experience sampling studies, negative repetitive thought during the day and in the evening predict less total sleep time, longer time to fall asleep, worse sleep quality at night, and daytime tiredness (Ottaviani, Shahabi, et al., 2015; Pillai, Steenburg, Ciesla, Roth, & Drake, 2014; Takano et al., 2014).

Similar associations have been found with clinical samples. For instance, patients with insomnia ruminate more about sleep problems than do healthy controls (Backhaus et al., 2004). In fact, the presleep cognitive activity of people with insomnia differs from that of good sleepers by being more focused on worries about not sleeping, and this cognitive activity lasts longer, feels out of control, and causes difficulty falling asleep (Harvey, 2000; Wicklow & Espie, 2000). In participants with diagnosed insomnia, depressive rumination predicted prospective self-reports of sleep quality and sleep efficiency (i.e., percentage of time in bed spent sleeping), even controlling for depressive and anxious symptoms (Carney, Harris, Moss, & Edinger, 2010). In adults with insomnia, rumination was associated with increased beta activity (i.e., active brain waves) during sleep, suggesting that repetitive thought during the day contributes to hyperarousal during sleep (Hall et al., 2000).

Pain

The perception and experience of pain are influenced by many psychological factors. Specifically, psychologists hypothesize that people who engage in repetitive thought about pain will experience higher levels of subjective pain and greater pain-related disability (Aldrich, Eccleston, & Crombez, 2000; Sullivan et al., 2001). This may occur because of increased emotional distress, exaggerated perception that the pain is threatening, and increased attentional focus on pain. Researchers have defined pain-related rumination and worry as separate constructs.[1] Pain-related rumination involves thinking over and over about wanting existing pain to go away and how much the pain hurts (Sullivan et al., 1995). Pain-related worry revolves around uncertainties and potential negative consequences of future pain (Lefebvre et al., 2017). Not surprisingly, pain-related rumination and worry are highly correlated (Lefebvre et al., 2017).

Some of the literature on repetitive thought about pain has focused on chronic pain patients. In a qualitative study, chronic pain patients' repetitive thoughts about their pain focused primarily on uncertainty (e.g., "Is this new?" and "Why has the pain become worse?"), negative

1 Rumination about pain is commonly measured using the rumination subscale of the Pain Catastrophizing Scale (PCS; Sullivan, Bishop, & Pivik, 1995). Its other subscales are magnification and helplessness. Because the helplessness subscale has an item assessing pain-related worry and correlates strongly with the rumination subscale, some authors argue that the entire PCS assesses repetitive thinking about pain (Aldrich et al., 2000). The Worry About Pain Questionnaire (Lefebvre et al., 2017) has two subscales: worry about the impact of pain, and worry about the ability to manage pain.

consequences (e.g., "I can't do the ironing"), and the degree of pain (e.g., "This pain just keeps hurting") (Eccleston, Crombez, Aldrich, & Stannard, 2001). Compared to non-pain-related repetitive thoughts, pain-related repetitive thoughts were more intrusive, distressing, and difficult to dismiss. In patients with chronic pain, rumination and worry about pain correlate with greater pain intensity (Buenaver et al., 2012; Craner, Gilliam, & Sperry, 2016; Lefebvre et al., 2017; Sullivan, Lynch, & Clark, 2005; Sullivan, Sullivan, & Adams, 2002). Rumination about pain is also associated with more difficulties functioning in various areas of daily living (e.g., work, home, social, and self-care) and poorer quality of life (Craner et al., 2016; Sullivan et al., 2005). One study found that rumination predicted pain-related disability only in individuals who had chronic pain for 2 or more years, but not less (Sullivan et al., 2002). Thus, the evidence suggests that repetitive thinking about pain predicts greater pain and pain-related disability in individuals with chronic pain, particularly for people who have been suffering for several years.

Repetitive thought about pain has also been studied in individuals without chronic pain. In survey studies with healthy adolescents and young adults, rumination and worry about pain correlate with higher self-reported pain in the preceding month (Lefebvre et al., 2017; Tremblay & Sullivan, 2010). Most of the research with healthy participants, however, has assessed subjective ratings of pain in response to various stimuli. For instance, rumination about pain was associated with greater self-reported pain during a dental cleaning (Sullivan & Neish, 1998) or 4 minutes of flexing a bicep (Gilliam et al., 2010). Several other studies assessed pain ratings in response to a cold pressor task. In this procedure, participants submerge an arm in cold water (kept just above freezing, between 35°F and 40°F) and provide pain ratings during or immediately after submerging their arm. In undergraduates, trait rumination and worry about pain were associated with higher pain ratings after 1 minute of the cold pressor task (Lefebvre et al., 2017; Sullivan, Tripp, Rodgers, & Stanish, 2000). In an experiment, induced rumination about the cold pressor task (vs distraction) led to higher pain perception and greater distress at the end of the task (Brookes, Sharpe, & Dear, 2017). In sum, the bulk of evidence with healthy adults suggests that repetitive thought about pain is associated with more intense pain perceptions.

Understanding the mechanisms by which repetitive thought is associated with increased pain perception is important. As we know, rumination increases emotional distress and negative thinking, both of which may contribute to more intense perceived pain (Aldrich et al., 2000; Sullivan et al., 2001). In support of this hypothesis, several studies found that the significant association between rumination and pain-related outcomes disappears when helplessness is included as a predictor (Craner et al., 2016; Sullivan et al., 2005; Tremblay & Sullivan, 2010). This suggests that a feeling of helplessness may mediate the effect of rumination about pain. One study found that the rumination-pain link was mediated by poor sleep quality (Buenaver et al., 2012). Trait pain–related rumination was also associated with greater expectations that pain cues would lead to pain, even though evidence refuted these expectations (Van Damme, Crombez, & Eccleston, 2002, 2004). In other words, repetitive thought about pain might maintain incorrect beliefs about the causes of pain. Thus, initial evidence supports the hypothesis that rumination about pain increases pain perception because it increases emotional distress and negative thinking.

Theoretical models also propose that one mechanism of the effect of perseverative cognition on pain-related outcomes is increased attention to pain (Aldrich et al., 2000; Sullivan, Michael, et al., 2001). Researchers of attentional biases to pain differentiate *initial orientation* from *sustained attention* to pain-related stimuli. Initial orientation indicates vigilance to pain-related cues, whereas sustained attention suggests difficulty disengaging from pain. These studies typically show participants pain-related and neutral stimuli (e.g., words, images) and record how long it takes participants to respond to each stimulus. Initial orientation to pain is implied when participants attend more quickly to pain-related than to neutral cues. Sustained attention to pain is implied when participants respond more slowly to a neutral cue after viewing a pain cue, suggesting that their attention is still on the pain-related cue.

The association between rumination and initial orientation to pain is mixed. Two studies found that pain-related rumination was associated with less initial orientation to pain-related (vs neutral) faces (Vervoort et al., 2011; Vervoort, Trost, Prkachin, & Mueller, 2013). By contrast, neither trait nor manipulated rumination was associated with initial attention to pain-related words (Martin & Chapman, 2009; Van Damme et al., 2002, 2004). These divergent results could be due to differences in the pain cues. Pictures of people in pain may be interpreted as more threatening than words indicating pain, and higher threat is hypothesized to lead to greater initial orientation (Todd et al., 2015). It is interesting, then, that for ruminators, more threatening pain cues are associated with less initial orientation. It may be that the distress triggered by rumination makes people want to initially avoid pain-related cues. In fact, trait negative rumination is associated with less acceptance of chronic pain (McCracken, Barker, & Chilcot, 2014). Future research should examine whether rumination predicts initial avoidance particularly for pain-related cues that are more threatening.

By contrast, rumination is generally associated with greater sustained attention to pain-related cues. Trait pain–related rumination predicts greater difficulty disengaging attention from pain-related words

(Van Damme et al., 2002, 2004). Similarly, high ruminators who reported more pain in the past 3 months demonstrated longer gaze duration to both pain-related and neutral faces (Vervoort et al., 2013). These results may reflect an implicit bias in ruminators who are experiencing pain to interpret even neutral stimuli as threatening. In addition, ruminating about pain may make it difficult for people to turn away from pain-related cues once they are focused on them. Evidence suggests that difficulty disengaging from pain may be a better predictor of chronic pain that is initial orienting (Schoth, Nunes, & Liossi, 2012). Thus, the rumination-pain link may be best explained by increased difficulty disengaging from pain-related cues.

Health behaviors

Some researchers have proposed an extension of the perseverative cognition hypothesis that includes indirect pathways from repetitive thought to physical disease via health behaviors (Clancy, Prestwich, Caperon, & O'Connor, 2016). This revised model draws on the larger stress literature, which finds that stressors influence physical health indirectly through both health risk behaviors (e.g., substance use, food choice) and health promoting behaviors (e.g., physical activity, smoking cessation, treatment-related behaviors). Thus, the authors speculate that perseverative cognition about a stressor may negatively impact health behaviors, which in turn contribute to poor physical health (see Fig. 5.2). The association between rumination and substance use is covered in a previous chapter (Chapter 4, Rumination and dysregulated behaviors), but I address other types of health behaviors here.

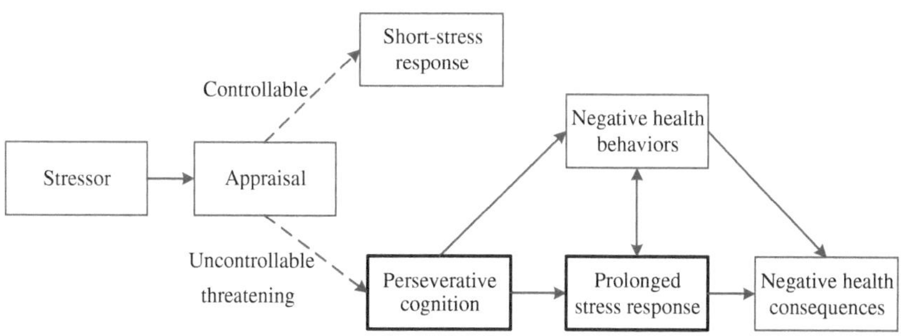

FIGURE 5.2 The modified perseverative cognition hypothesis, including the mediating role of negative health behaviors. Source: *Adapted from Clancy, F., Prestwich, A., Caperon, L., & O'Connor, D. B. (2016). Perseverative cognition and health behaviors: A systematic review and meta-analysis.* Frontiers in Human Neuroscience, 10, *534. Available from https://doi.org/10.3389/fnhum.2016.00534.*

Evidence for the association between repetitive thought and food choice is mixed. Adults who reported negative work-related rumination were more likely to eat unhealthy foods after work (Cropley, Michalianou, Pravettoni, & Millward, 2012). Similarly, data from the National Cancer Institute's Food Attitudes and Behavior Survey showed that health worry was related to nutrition-inhibiting behaviors, such as eating more meals in front of a TV and being less likely to restrict sugary or sweet foods (Ferrer, Bergman, & Klein, 2013). By contrast, two studies failed to find associations between rumination or worry and the likelihood of eating unhealthy foods (Bowen, Alfano, McGregor, & Andersen, 2004; Cropley et al., 2012). Still more conflicting, health worry was associated with more fruit and vegetable consumption (Ferrer, Bergman, et al., 2013). Thus, repetitive thought is related to both more and less healthy food choices. These mixed results may be explained by moderators. In one study, worry about cancer predicted an increased likelihood of meeting the recommendation of five fruits/vegetables a day, but only in individuals who perceived that they had low risk of developing cancer in the future (Ferrer, Portnoy, & Klein, 2013). By contrast, individuals who perceived high risk of *and* worried about cancer were less likely to eat fruits and vegetables.

The link between repetitive thought and physical exercise is also unclear. On the one hand, female undergraduates who had higher trait worry about cancer were more likely to meet the National Cancer Institute's recommendation of 4 hours of physical activity per week (Bernat, Anderson, Parrish-Sprowl, & Sparks, 2015). In older adults, by contrast, general health worry was associated with less physical exercise (Li, Cardinal, & Vuchinich, 2009). In still another study, breast cancer worry in women was not associated with regular physical exercise (Bowen et al., 2004). As with food choice, perceived risk may moderate this association. For instance, worry about cancer was associated with a higher likelihood of exercising in the past month, but only in individuals who also perceived that they had low risk of actually developing cancer in the future (Ferrer, Portnoy, et al., 2013). Individuals who perceived high risk *and* worried were less likely to exercise in the past month. In sum, repetitive thinking may negatively impact food choice and physical exercise for people who experience distress about their health.

Another commonly studied health behavior is intention and attempts to stop smoking. Some studies found that health-related worry predicted greater intention to quit and likelihood of a quit attempt, both retrospectively and prospectively (Swayampakala et al., 2012; Yong et al., 2014). By contrast, other research showed that worry and depressive rumination were not uniquely related to future intentions or having a past quit attempt (Dvorak, Simons, & Wray, 2011; Finney Rutten, Blake, Hesse, Augustson, & Evans, 2011). In an examination of a potential moderator, worry predicted increased likelihood of attempting to quit 8 months later only among smokers with high self-efficacy (Dijkstra & Brosschot, 2003). Another study found that smoking-related worry predicted higher intentions to quit in adult smokers, particularly for participants with low perceived risk (Klein, Zajac, & Monin, 2009). By contrast, worry predicted less intention to quit for adults with high perceived risk.

Of course, an attempt to quit smoking can indicate desire to stop smoking or failures at self-control. What about successful smoking cessation? In adult smokers, health-related worry did not directly predict successful quitting 14 months later (Swayampakala et al., 2012). In fact, among ex-smokers with low self-efficacy, worry was associated with an increased risk of relapse in the past 8 months (Dijkstra & Brosschot, 2003). Similarly, depressive rumination predicted a greater lifetime number of failed quit attempts, particularly for smokers high in trait impulsivity (Dvorak et al., 2011). Thus, although repetitive thought may predict increased intentions and attempts to quit, particularly for people with higher self-efficacy and low perceived smoking-related risk, there is no evidence that it predicts successful smoking cessation.

Many studies suggest that repetitive thought predicts increased engagement in prevention-related behaviors in healthy individuals. For instance, health-related worry predicts higher likelihood of obtaining the flu shot, greater use of sunscreen, and stronger intentions to floss (Chapman & Coups, 2006; Kiviniemi & Ellis, 2014; Schmiege, Bryan, & Klein, 2009). In elderly healthy adults, stress-related rumination is associated with having more telephone consultations with health-care providers with one year later (Thomsen et al., 2004). Finally, a substantial literature has shown that worry about breast cancer is generally associated with higher likelihood of mammography screening, although the average effect is small (for a review, see Hay, McCaul, & Magnan, 2006).

By contrast, rumination may also predict low compliance and delay in treatment-seeking for people who are already ill. For example, in cancer patients, greater trait rumination was associated with less physician-rated compliance with treatment (Aymanns, Filipp, & Klauer, 1995). In female breast cancer survivors, higher trait depressive rumination was associated with delays of over 1 month in seeking treatment (Lyubomirsky, Kasri, Chang, & Chung, 2006). These authors found the same pattern of results when they asked healthy women to imagine finding a lump in their breast and report their likelihood of calling the doctor immediately. The authors explained these results by noting that depressive rumination is associated with negative thinking, helplessness, and impaired problem-solving, concentration, and motivation. These cognitive and motivational deficits, in combination with emotional distress, may impede individuals' help-seeking behaviors.

In sum, the literatures on food choice, physical activity, smoking cessation, and treatment behaviors all suggest that perseverative cognition is associated with both better and worse health behaviors. How can we make sense of these divergent results? Several possibilities exist. First, some studies found perceived risk to moderate the effect of repetitive thought (Ferrer, Portnoy, et al., 2013; Ferrer, Bergman, et al., 2013; Klein et al., 2009). Specifically, for people who perceive themselves at high risk, repetitive thought is associated with more unhealthy food choices, less exercise, and less intention to quit smoking. By contrast, repetitive thought in people who perceive their risk to be low reported better eating, more physical activity, and more intention to quit smoking. Similarly, repetitive thought predicts prevention-related behaviors in healthy individuals but low treatment compliance in people with existing illnesses. Perhaps rumination when people are at risk of or actually have an illness exacerbates negative emotions to such an extent that they have difficulty making healthy choices for themselves. They may become paralyzed with fear and/or exhibit poor self-control in the face of such distress. By contrast, repetitive thought at moderate or lower levels of perceived risk may provide motivation for people to engage in healthy behaviors without impairing self-control.

Alternatively, or in addition, the association between repetitive thought and health behaviors may not be linear. Some research has found support for an inverted-u-shaped relationship (Andersen, Smith, Meischke, Bowen, & Urban, 2003). For instance, moderate levels of breast cancer worry predicted high likelihood of engaging in regular breast self-exams (Bowen et al., 2004). However, women with low and high levels of worry were less likely to engage in this health behavior. Whereas women with low worry may not perceive the importance of screening, extreme worry may be so debilitating that it interferes with women's ability to conduct screening and/or results in denial/avoidance.

Some of the divergent results in this field may also be due to inconsistent measurement of repetitive thought. In the health psychology literature, health-related worry is generally operationalized as an emotional response to a perceived threat (e.g., Schmiege et al., 2009). This conceptualization of worry lacks the emphasis on repetitive thought. As such, some measures of health-related worry may assess anxiety and fear more so than the process of perseverative cognition. The interactions found between health worry and perceived risk may therefore suggest that perceived risk contributes to healthy behaviors when people are not overcome by fear and anxiety—an interesting conclusion, but not one that sheds much light on repetitive thought. Interestingly, a recent metaanalysis of 19 studies concluded that rumination, but not health-related worry, was directly associated with more risky health behaviors (Clancy et al., 2016). Thus, future research should better differentiate the effects of emotional distress from the ruminative process, and perhaps different types of perseverative cognition, on health behaviors.

Conclusion

In this chapter, I reviewed the perseverative cognition hypothesis (Brosschot et al., 2006) and several literatures showing associations between rumination or worry and various indices of physical functioning. Brosschot asserted that repetitive thinking converts the immediate physiological consequences of stressors into prolonged physiological activation. Accordingly, researchers have examined the effects of rumination and worry on cardiovascular, cortisol, and immune functioning—three common indicators of stress-induced autonomic arousal. The findings paint a somewhat more complex picture than the model proposes. Specifically, repetitive thinking—particularly when assessed at the state level—robustly predicts more autonomic activation, as well as greater reactivity to and delayed recovery from stressors, for people who are already experiencing emotional distress, life stress, physical illness, and poor coping (e.g., rumination tendencies). Similar results emerged with health behaviors: repetitive thinking predicts more risky health behaviors primarily for people who perceive themselves at greater risk or who are already sick.

It is worth noting that this pattern of results mirrors those in previous chapters, in that rumination contributes to negative clinical outcomes like depression particularly for people who are already distressed or have poor coping skills. Moreover, these results align with the hypothesis that repetitive thinking exacerbates the physiological effects of stressors. The data, however, suggest more of a moderation than a mediational model. In fact, repetitive thinking about health when people are not exceedingly distressed may contribute to better health behaviors. Other moderators suggested by the findings reviewed here include the type of repetitive thinking (e.g., depressive vs angry rumination vs worry) and whether repetitive thinking is measured at the state or trait level. In order to revise the theory, researchers should continue exploring these and other moderators of the association between perseverative cognition and physical functioning.

Interestingly, repetitive thinking is more consistently associated with sleep problems and perceived pain than with health behaviors or physiological indicators or sympathetic arousal. These effects may reflect exacerbated negative emotions and thoughts (i.e., cognitive arousal), rather than increased physiological arousal. Alternatively, the more consistent findings may reflect the fact that sleep problems and pain are most often self-reported, whereas physiological arousal is assessed using objective measures. Future research should examine both mechanisms and moderators of the effect of repetitive thinking on sleep problems and pain, as well as attempt to measure these outcomes both subjectively and objectively.

Finally, the perseverative cognition hypothesis argues that prolonged physiological activation resulting from repetitive thinking contributes to long-term health consequences. Perseverative cognition is associated with the general perception of poor health and self-reported somatic complaints, both in healthy individuals and in patients with cancer (Brosschot & van der Doef, 2006; Jellesma, Verkuil, & Brosschot, 2009; Segerstrom, Stanton, Alden, & Shortridge, 2003; Slavish & Graham-Engeland, 2015; Thomsen et al., 2004; Verkuil, Brosschot, & Thayer, 2007; Versluis, Verkuil, & Brosschot, 2016). However, very few studies have examined the effects of repetitive thinking on objective measures of illness or disease. In a longitudinal study of older, healthy Veterans, men reporting worry were twice as likely to have had a heart attack 20 years later and one-and-a-half times as likely to have coronary heart disease (Kubzansky et al., 1997). By contrast, in patients awaiting angiography, trait angry rumination was associated with greater self-reported cardiac symptoms but not with an objective measure of disease severity (Closa León, Nouwen, Sheffield, Jaumdally, & Lip, 2010). Similarly, in college students with colds, rumination was associated with more severe self-reported cold symptoms over a 7-day period, but it was not associated with the probability of experiencing a fever (Devoulyte & Sullivan, 2003). Of course, the association between repetitive thinking and objective diseases states may be indirect, via any of the constructs covered in this chapter. Much more research is needed on whether rumination and worry directly and/or indirectly predict long-term health consequences and objective disease states.

References

Aldao, A., Mennin, D., & McLaughlin, K. (2013). Differentiating worry and rumination: Evidence from heart rate variability during spontaneous regulation. *Cognitive Therapy and Research*, *37*(3), 613–619. Available from https://doi.org/10.1007/s10608-012-9485-0.

Aldrich, S., Eccleston, C., & Crombez, G. (2000). Worrying about chronic pain: Vigilance to threat and misdirected problem solving. *Behaviour Research and Therapy*, *38*(5), 457–470. Available from https://doi.org/10.1016/S0005-7967(99)00062-5.

Andersen, M. R., Smith, R., Meischke, H., Bowen, D., & Urban, N. (2003). Breast cancer worry and mammography use by women with and without a family history in a population-based sample. *Cancer Epidemiology Biomarkers & Prevention*, *12*(4), 314. Retrieved from <http://cebp.aacrjournals.org/content/12/4/314.abstract>.

Aymanns, P., Filipp, S. H., & Klauer, T. (1995). Family support and coping with cancer: Some determinants and adaptive correlates. *The British Journal of Social Psychology*, *34*(Pt 1), 107–124. Available from https://doi.org/10.1111/j.2044-8309.1995.tb01051.x.

Backhaus, J., Junghanns, K., & Hohagen, F. (2004). Sleep disturbances are correlated with decreased morning awakening salivary cortisol. *Psychoneuroendocrinology, 29*(9), 1184–1191. Available from https://doi.org/10.1016/j.psyneuen.2004.01.010.

Beauchaine, T. P., & Thayer, J. F. (2015). Heart rate variability as a transdiagnostic biomarker of psychopathology. *International Journal of Psychophysiology, 98*(2), 338–350. Available from https://doi.org/10.1016/j.ijpsycho.2015.08.004.

Bernat, J. K., Anderson, L. B., Parrish-Sprowl, J., & Sparks, G. G. (2015). Exploring the association between dispositional cancer worry, perceived risk, and physical activity among college women. *Journal of American College Health, 63*(3), 216–220. Available from https://doi.org/10.1080/07448481.2014.983927.

Borders, A., Rothman, D. J., & McAndrew, L. M. (2015). Sleep problems may mediate associations between rumination and PTSD and depressive symptoms among OIF/OEF veterans. *Psychological Trauma: Theory, Research, Practice and Policy, 7*(1), 76–84. Available from https://doi.org/10.1037/a0036937.

Borelli, J. L., Hilt, L. M., West, J. L., Weekes, N. Y., & Gonzalez, M. C. (2014). School-aged children's depressive rumination is associated with their reactivity to sadness but not fear. *Journal of Clinical Child & Adolescent Psychology, 43*(5), 799–812. Available from https://doi.org/10.1080/15374416.2013.814542.

Bowen, D. J., Alfano, C. M., McGregor, B. A., & Andersen, M. R. (2004). The relationship between perceived risk, affect, and health behaviors. *Cancer Detection and Prevention, 28*(6), 409–417. Available from https://doi.org/10.1016/j.cdp.2004.08.008.

Brookes, M. L., Sharpe, L., & Dear, B. F. (2017). Rumination induces a pattern of attention characterized by increased vigilance followed by avoidance of affective pain words. *European Journal of Pain, 21*(7), 1197–1208. Available from https://doi.org/10.1002/ejp.1020.

Brosschot, J. F., Gerin, W., & Thayer, J. F. (2006). The perseverative cognition hypothesis: A review of worry, prolonged stress-related physiological activation, and health. *Journal of Psychosomatic Research, 60*(2), 113–124. Available from https://doi.org/10.1016/j.jpsychores.2005.06.074.

Brosschot, J. F., & van der Doef, M. (2006). Daily worrying and somatic health complaints: Testing the effectiveness of a simple worry reduction intervention. *Psychology & Health, 21*(1), 19–31. Available from https://doi.org/10.1080/14768320500105346.

Brosschot, J. F., Van Dijk, E., & Thayer, J. F. (2007). Daily worry is related to low heart rate variability during waking and the subsequent nocturnal sleep period. *International Journal of Psychophysiology, 63*(1), 39–47. Available from https://doi.org/10.1016/j.ijpsycho.2006.07.016.

Buenaver, L. F., Quartana, P. J., Grace, E. G., Sarlani, E., Simango, M., Edwards, R. R., ... Smith, M. T. (2012). Evidence for indirect effects of pain catastrophizing on clinical pain among myofascial temporomandibular disorder participants: The mediating role of sleep disturbance. *Pain, 153*(6), 1159–1166. Available from https://doi.org/10.1016/j.pain.2012.01.023.

Burke, H. M., Davis, M. C., Otte, C., & Mohr, D. C. (2005). Depression and cortisol responses to psychological stress: A meta-analysis. *Psychoneuroendocrinology, 30*(9), 846–856. Available from https://doi.org/10.1016/j.psyneuen.2005.02.010.

Busch, L. Y., Pössel, P., & Valentine, J. C. (2017). Meta-analyses of cardiovascular reactivity to rumination: A possible mechanism linking depression and hostility to cardiovascular disease. *Psychological Bulletin, 143*(12), 1378–1394. Available from https://doi.org/10.1037/bul0000119.

Bushman, B. J., & Geen, R. G. (1990). Role of cognitive-emotional mediators and individual differences in the effects of media violence on aggression. *Journal of Personality and Social Psychology, 58*(1), 156–163. Available from https://doi.org/10.1037/0022-3514.58.1.156.

Caprara, G. V., Gargaro, T., Pastorelli, C., Prezza, M., Renzi, P., & Zelli, A. (1987). Individual differences and measures of aggression in laboratory studies. *Personality and Individual Differences*, *8*(6), 885–893. Available from https://doi.org/10.1016/0191-8869(87)90140-1.

Carney, C. E., Harris, A. L., Moss, T. G., & Edinger, J. D. (2010). Distinguishing rumination from worry in clinical insomnia. *Behaviour Research and Therapy*, *48*(6), 540–546. Available from https://doi.org/10.1016/j.brat.2010.03.004.

Chapman, G. B., & Coups, E. J. (2006). Emotions and preventive health behavior. *Health Psychology*, *25*(1), 82–90. Available from https://doi.org/10.1037/0278-6133.25.1.82.

Chida, Y., & Steptoe, A. (2010). Greater cardiovascular responses to laboratory mental stress are associated with poor subsequent cardiovascular risk status: A meta-analysis of prospective evidence. *Hypertension*, *55*(4), 1026–1032. Available from https://doi.org/10.1161/HYPERTENSIONAHA.109.146621.

Clancy, F., Prestwich, A., Caperon, L., & O'Connor, D. B. (2016). Perseverative cognition and health behaviors: A systematic review and meta-analysis. *Frontiers in Human Neuroscience*, *10*, 534. Available from https://doi.org/10.3389/fnhum.2016.00534.

Closa León, T., Nouwen, A., Sheffield, D., Jaumdally, R., & Lip, G. Y. H. (2010). Anger rumination, social support, and cardiac symptoms in patients undergoing angiography. *British Journal of Health Psychology*, *15*(Pt 4), 841–857. Available from https://doi.org/10.1348/135910710X491360

Craner, J., Gilliam, W., & Sperry, J. (2016). Rumination, magnification, and helplessness: How do different aspects of pain catastrophizing relate to pain severity and functioning? *The Clinical Journal of Pain*, *32*(12), 1028–1035. Available from https://doi.org/10.1097/AJP.0000000000000355.

Cropley, M., Michalianou, G., Pravettoni, G., & Millward, L. J. (2012). The relation of post-work ruminative thinking with eating behaviour. *Stress and Health*, *28*(1), 23–30. Available from https://doi.org/10.1002/smi.1397.

Cropley, M., Rydstedt, L. W., Devereux, J. J., & Middleton, B. (2015). The relationship between work-related rumination and evening and morning salivary cortisol secretion. *Stress and Health*, *31*(2), 150–157. Available from https://doi.org/10.1002/smi.2538.

Daubenmier, J., Hayden, D., Chang, V., & Epel, E. (2014). It's not what you think, it's how you relate to it: Dispositional mindfulness moderates the relationship between psychological distress and the cortisol awakening response. *Psychoneuroendocrinology*, *48*, 11–18.

Denson, T. F., Spanovic, M., & Miller, N. (2009). Cognitive appraisals and emotions predict cortisol and immune responses. *Psychological Bulletin*, *135*(6), 823–853. Available from https://doi.org/10.1037/a0016909.

Devoulyte, K., & Sullivan, M. (2003). Pain catastrophizing and symptom severity during upper respiratory tract illness. *The Clinical Journal of Pain*, *19*(2), 125–133. Available from https://doi.org/10.1097/00002508-200303000-00008.

Dickerson, S. S., & Kemeny, M. E. (2004). Acute stressors and cortisol responses. *Psychological Bulletin*, *130*(3), 355–391. Available from https://doi.org/10.1037/0033-2909.130.3.355.

Dijkstra, A., & Brosschot, J. (2003). Worry about health in smoking behaviour change. *Behaviour Research and Therapy*, *41*(9), 1081–1092. Available from https://doi.org/10.1016/S0005-7967(02)00244-9.

Dvorak, R., Simons, J., & Wray, T. (2011). Impulsivity moderates the association between depressive rumination and number of quit attempt failures by smokers. *Addiction Research & Theory*, *19*(3), 283–288. Available from https://doi.org/10.3109/16066359.2010.512110.

Eccleston, C., Crombez, G., Aldrich, S., & Stannard, C. (2001). Worry and chronic pain patients: A description and analysis of individual differences. *European Journal of Pain*, *5*(3), 309–318. Available from https://doi.org/10.1053/eujp.2001.0252.

Ehring, T., Fuchs, N., & Kläsener, I. (2009). The effects of experimentally induced rumination versus distraction on analogue posttraumatic stress symptoms. *Behavior Therapy, 40* (4), 403–413. Available from https://doi.org/10.1016/j.beth.2008.10.001.

Ehring, T., Szeimies, A., & Schaffrick, C. (2009). An experimental analogue study into the role of abstract thinking in trauma-related rumination. *Behaviour Research and Therapy, 47*(4), 285–293. Available from https://doi.org/10.1016/j.brat.2008.12.011.

Espie, C. A. (2002). Insomnia: Conceptual issues in the development, persistence, and treatment of sleep disorder in adults. *Annual Review of Psychology, 53*(1), 215–243. Available from https://doi.org/10.1146/annurev.psych.53.100901.135243.

Esterling, B. A., Kiecolt-Glaser, J. K., Bodnar, J. C., & Glaser, R. (1994). Chronic stress, social support, and persistent alterations in the natural killer cell response to cytokines in older adults. *Health Psychology, 13*(4), 291–298. Available from https://doi.org/10.1037/0278-6133.13.4.291.

Fernandez, A. B., Soufer, R., Collins, D., Soufer, A., Ranjbaran, H., & Burg, M. M. (2010). Tendency to angry rumination predicts stress-provoked endothelin-1 increase in patients with coronary artery disease. *Psychosomatic Medicine, 72*(4), 348–353. Available from https://doi.org/10.1097/PSY.0b013e3181d71982.

Ferrer, R. A., Bergman, H. E., & Klein, W. M. P. (2013). Worry as a predictor of nutrition behaviors. *Health Education & Behavior, 40*(1), 88–96. Available from https://doi.org/10.1177/1090198112439410.

Ferrer, R. A., Portnoy, D. B., & Klein, W. M. P. (2013). Worry and risk perceptions as independent and interacting predictors of health protective behaviors. *Journal of Health Communication, 18*(4), 397–409. Available from https://doi.org/10.1080/10810730.2012.727954.

Finney Rutten, L., Blake, K., Hesse, B., Augustson, E., & Evans, S. (2011). Illness representations of lung cancer, lung cancer worry, and perceptions of risk by smoking status. *Journal of Cancer Education, 26*(4), 747–753. Available from https://doi.org/10.1007/s13187-011-0247-6.

Gerin, W., Davidson, K. W., Christenfeld, N. J. S., Goyal, T., & Schwartz, J. E. (2006). The role of angry rumination and distraction in blood pressure recovery from emotional arousal. *Psychosomatic Medicine, 68*(1), 64–72. Available from https://doi.org/10.1097/01.psy.0000195747.12404.aa.

Gerteis, A. K. S., & Schwerdtfeger, A. R. (2016). When rumination counts: Perceived social support and heart rate variability in daily life. *Psychophysiology, 53*(7), 1034–1043. Available from https://doi.org/10.1111/psyp.12652.

Gianferante, D., Thoma, M. V., Hanlin, L., Chen, X., Breines, J. G., Zoccola, P. M., & Rohleder, N. (2014). Post-stress rumination predicts HPA axis responses to repeated acute stress. *Psychoneuroendocrinology, 49*, 244–252. Available from https://doi.org/10.1016/j.psyneuen.2014.07.021.

Gilliam, W., Burns, J. W., Quartana, P., Matsuura, J., Nappi, C., & Wolff, B. (2010). Interactive effects of catastrophizing and suppression on responses to acute pain: A test of an appraisal × emotion regulation model. *Journal of Behavioral Medicine, 33*(3), 191. Available from https://doi.org/10.1007/s10865-009-9245-0.

Glynn, L. M., Christenfeld, N., & Gerin, W. (2002). The role of rumination in recovery from reactivity: Cardiovascular consequences of emotional states. *Psychosomatic Medicine, 64*(5), 714–726. Available from https://doi.org/10.1097/00006842-200209000-00004.

Glynn, L. M., Christenfeld, N., & Gerin, W. (2007). Recreating cardiovascular responses with rumination: The effects of a delay between harassment and its recall. *International Journal of Psychophysiology, 66*(2), 135–140. Available from https://doi.org/10.1016/j.ijpsycho.2007.03.018.

Guastella, A. J., & Moulds, M. L. (2007). The impact of rumination on sleep quality following a stressful life event. *Personality and Individual Differences, 42*(6), 1151–1162. Available from https://doi.org/10.1016/j.paid.2006.04.028.

Hall, M., Buysse, D. J., Nowell, P. D., Nofzinger, E. A., Houck, P., Reynolds, C. F., & Kupfer, D. J. (2000). Symptoms of stress and depression as correlates of sleep in primary insomnia. *Psychosomatic Medicine*, *62*(2), 227–230. Available from https://doi.org/10.1097/00006842-200003000-00014

Harvey, A. G. (2000). Pre-sleep cognitive activity: A comparison of sleep-onset insomniacs and good sleepers. *The British Journal of Clinical Psychology*, *39*(3), 275–286. Available from https://doi.org/10.1348/014466500163284.

Harvey, A. G. (2002). A cognitive model of insomnia. *Behaviour Research and Therapy*, *40*(8), 869–893. Available from https://doi.org/10.1016/S0005-7967(01)00061-4.

Hay, J. L., McCaul, K. D., & Magnan, R. E. (2006). Does worry about breast cancer predict screening behaviors? A meta-analysis of the prospective evidence. *Preventive Medicine*, *42*(6), 401–408. Available from https://doi.org/10.1016/j.ypmed.2006.03.002.

Hilt, L. M., Aldao, A., & Fischer, K. (2015). Rumination and multi-modal emotional reactivity. *Cognition and Emotion*, *29*(8), 1486–1495. Available from https://doi.org/10.1080/02699931.2014.989816.

Hogan, B. E., & Linden, W. (2004). Anger response styles and blood pressure: At least don't ruminate about it. *Annals of Behavioral Medicine: A Publication of the Society of Behavioral Medicine*, *27*(1), 38. Available from https://doi.org/10.1207/s15324796abm2701_6.

Huffziger, S., Ebner-Priemer, U., Zamoscik, V., Reinhard, I., Kirsch, P., & Kuehner, C. (2013). Effects of mood and rumination on cortisol levels in daily life: An ambulatory assessment study in remitted depressed patients and healthy controls. *Psychoneuroendocrinology*, *38*(10), 2258–2267. Available from https://doi.org/10.1016/j.psyneuen.2013.04.014.

Jellesma, F. C., Verkuil, B., & Brosschot, J. F. (2009). Postponing worrisome thoughts in children: The effects of a postponement intervention on perseverative thoughts, emotions and somatic complaints. *Social Science & Medicine*, *69*(2), 278–284. Available from https://doi.org/10.1016/j.socscimed.2009.04.031.

Johnson, J., Key, B., Routledge, F., Gerin, W., & Campbell, T. (2014). High trait rumination is associated with blunted nighttime diastolic blood pressure dipping. *Annals of Behavioral Medicine*, *48*(3), 384–391. Available from https://doi.org/10.1007/s12160-014-9617-8.

Kirschbaum, C., Pirke, K., & Hellhammer, D. H. (1993). The 'Trier social stress test' – A tool for investigating psychobiological stress responses in a laboratory setting. *Neuropsychobiology*, *28*(1-2), 76–81. Available from https://doi.org/10.1159/000119004.

Kiviniemi, M., & Ellis, E. (2014). Worry about skin cancer mediates the relation of perceived cancer risk and sunscreen use. *Journal of Behavioral Medicine*, *37*(6), 1069–1074. Available from https://doi.org/10.1007/s10865-013-9538-1.

Klein, W., Zajac, L., & Monin, M. (2009). Worry as a moderator of the association between risk perceptions and quitting intentions in young adult and adult smokers. *Annals of Behavioral Medicine*, *38*(3), 256–261. Available from https://doi.org/10.1007/s12160-009-9143-2.

Kubzansky, L. D., Kawachi, I., Spiro, A., Weiss, S. T., Vokonas, P. S., & Sparrow, D. (1997). Is worrying bad for your heart?: A prospective study of worry and coronary heart disease in the normative aging study. *Circulation*, *95*(4), 818–824. Available from https://doi.org/10.1161/01.CIR.95.4.818

Kuehner, C., Holzhauer, S., & Huffziger, S. (2007). Decreased cortisol response to awakening is associated with cognitive vulnerability to depression in a nonclinical sample of young adults. *Psychoneuroendocrinology*, *32*(2), 199–209. Available from https://doi.org/10.1016/j.psyneuen.2006.12.007.

Kuehner, C., Huffziger, S., & Liebsch, K. (2009). Rumination, distraction and mindful self-focus: Effects on mood, dysfunctional attitudes and cortisol stress response. *Psychological Medicine*, *39*(2), 219–228. Available from https://doi.org/10.1017/S0033291708003553.

Larsen, B. A., & Christenfeld, N. J. S. (2011). Cognitive distancing, cognitive restructuring, and cardiovascular recovery from stress. *Biological Psychology, 86*(2), 143–148. Available from https://doi.org/10.1016/j.biopsycho.2010.02.011.

Lefebvre, J. C., Jensen, M. P., Waters, S. J., Molton, I. R., Keefe, F. J., & Caldwell, D. S. (2017). The development and assessment of the worry about pain questionnaire. *European Journal of Pain, 21*(7), 1154–1164. Available from https://doi.org/10.1002/ejp.1015.

LeMoult, J., & Joormann, J. (2014). Depressive rumination alters cortisol decline in major depressive disorder. *Biological Psychology, 100*, 50–55. Available from https://doi.org/10.1016/j.biopsycho.2014.05.001.

Li, K., Cardinal, B. J., & Vuchinich, S. (2009). Health worry, physical activity participation, and walking difficulty among older adults: A mediation analysis. *Research Quarterly for Exercise and Sport, 80*(1), 12–21. Available from https://doi.org/10.1080/02701367.2009.10599525.

Llera, S. J., & Newman, M. G. (2010). Effects of worry on physiological and subjective reactivity to emotional stimuli in generalized anxiety disorder and nonanxious control participants. *Emotion (Washington, DC), 10*(5), 640–650. Available from https://doi.org/10.1037/a0019351.

Lovallo, W. (2010). Cardiovascular responses to stress and disease outcomes: A test of the reactivity hypothesis. *Hypertension, 55*(4), 842–843. Available from https://doi.org/10.1161/HYPERTENSIONAHA.110.149773.

Lyubomirsky, S., Kasri, F., Chang, O., & Chung, I. (2006). Ruminative response styles and delay of seeking diagnosis for breast cancer symptoms. *Journal of Social and Clinical Psychology, 25*(3), 276–304. Available from https://doi.org/10.1521/jscp.2006.25.3.276.

Ma, D., Serbin, L. A., & Stack, D. M. (2018). Children's anxiety symptoms and salivary immunoglobulin A: A mutual regulatory system? *Developmental Psychobiology, 60*(2), 202–215. Available from https://doi.org/10.1002/dev.21590.

Martin, M., & Chapman, S. C. E. (2009). Cognitive processing in putative functional gastrointestinal disorder: Rumination yields orientation to social threat not pain. *European Journal of Pain, 14*(2), 207–213. Available from https://doi.org/10.1016/j.ejpain.2009.04.008.

McCracken, L., Barker, E., & Chilcot, J. (2014). Decentering, rumination, cognitive defusion, and psychological flexibility in people with chronic pain. *Journal of Behavioral Medicine, 37*(6), 1215–1225. Available from https://doi.org/10.1007/s10865-014-9570-9.

McCullough, M. E., Orsulak, P., Brandon, A., & Akers, L. (2007). Rumination, fear, and cortisol. *Health Psychology, 26*(1), 126–132. Available from https://doi.org/10.1037/0278-6133.26.1.126.

Meeten, F., Davey, G. C. L., Makovac, E., Watson, D. R., Garfinkel, S. N., Critchley, H. D., & Ottaviani, C. (2016). Goal directed worry rules are associated with distinct patterns of amygdala functional connectivity and vagal modulation during perseverative cognition. *Frontiers in Human Neuroscience, 10*, 553. Available from https://doi.org/10.3389/fnhum.2016.00553.

Newton, T. L., Fernandez-Botran, R., Lyle, K. B., Szabo, Y. Z., Miller, J. J., & Warnecke, A. J. (2017). Salivary cytokine response in the aftermath of stress: An emotion regulation perspective. *Emotion (Washington, DC), 17*(6), 1007–1020. Available from https://doi.org/10.1037/emo0000156.

O'Connor, D. B., Walker, S., Hendrickx, H., Talbot, D., & Schaefer, A. (2012). Stress-related thinking predicts the cortisol awakening response and somatic symptoms in healthy adults. *Psychoneuroendocrinology, 38*(3), 438–446. Available from https://doi.org/10.1016/j.psyneuen.2012.07.004.

Ottaviani, C., Medea, B., Lonigro, A., Tarvainen, M., & Couyoumdjian, A. (2015). Cognitive rigidity is mirrored by autonomic inflexibility in daily life perseverative cognition. *Biological Psychology, 107*, 24–30. Available from https://doi.org/10.1016/j.biopsycho.2015.02.011.

Ottaviani, C., Shahabi, L., Tarvainen, M., Cook, I., Abrams, M., & Shapiro, D. (2014). Cognitive, behavioral, and autonomic correlates of mind wandering and perseverative cognition in major depression. *Frontiers in Neuroscience, 8*, 433. Retrieved from <https://www.ncbi.nlm.nih.gov/pubmed/25601824>.

Ottaviani, C., Shahabi, L., Tarvainen, M., Cook, I., Abrams, M., & Shapiro, D. (2015). Cognitive, behavioral, and autonomic correlates of mind wandering and perseverative cognition in major depression. *Frontiers in Neuroscience, 8*, 433. Available from https://doi.org/10.3389/fnins.2014.00433.

Ottaviani, C., Shapiro, D., & Couyoumdjian, A. (2013). Flexibility as the key for somatic health: From mind wandering to perseverative cognition. *Biological Psychology, 94*(1), 38–43. Available from https://doi.org/10.1016/j.biopsycho.2013.05.003.

Ottaviani, C., Shapiro, D., Davydov, D. M., Goldstein, I. B., & Mills, P. J. (2009). The autonomic phenotype of rumination. *International Journal of Psychophysiology, 72*(3), 267–275. Available from https://doi.org/10.1016/j.ijpsycho.2008.12.014.

Ottaviani, C., Shapiro, D., & Fitzgerald, L. (2011). Rumination in the laboratory: What happens when you go back to everyday life? *Psychophysiology, 48*(4), 453–461. Available from https://doi.org/10.1111/j.1469-8986.2010.01122.x.

Ottaviani, C., Thayer, J. F., Verkuil, B., Lonigro, A., Medea, B., Couyoumdjian, A., & Brosschot, J. F. (2016). Physiological concomitants of perseverative cognition: A systematic review and meta-analysis. *Psychological Bulletin, 142*(3), 231–259. Available from https://doi.org/10.1037/bul0000036.

Ottaviani, C., Watson, D. R., Meeten, F., Makovac, E., Garfinkel, S. N., & Critchley, H. D. (2016). Neurobiological substrates of cognitive rigidity and autonomic inflexibility in generalized anxiety disorder. *Biological Psychology, 119*, 31–41. Available from https://doi.org/10.1016/j.biopsycho.2016.06.009.

Pepys, M. B., & Hirschfield, G. M. (2003). C-reactive protein: A critical update. *Journal of Clinical Investigation, 111*(12), 1805–1812. Available from https://doi.org/10.1172/JCI200318921.

Pieper, S., & Brosschot, J. (2005). Prolonged stress-related cardiovascular activation: Is there any? *Annals of Behavioral Medicine, 30*(2), 91–103. Available from https://doi.org/10.1207/s15324796abm3002_1.

Pieper, S., Brosschot, J. F., van der Leeden, R., & Thayer, J. F. (2007). Cardiac effects of momentary assessed worry episodes and stressful events. *Psychosomatic Medicine, 69*(9), 901–909. Available from https://doi.org/10.1097/PSY.0b013e31815a9230.

Pieper, S., Brosschot, J. F., van der Leeden, R., & Thayer, J. F. (2010). Prolonged cardiac effects of momentary assessed stressful events and worry episodes. *Psychosomatic Medicine, 72*(6), 570–577. Available from https://doi.org/10.1097/PSY.0b013e3181dbc0e9.

Pillai, V., Steenburg, L. A., Ciesla, J. A., Roth, T., & Drake, C. L. (2014). A seven day actigraphy-based study of rumination and sleep disturbance among young adults with depressive symptoms. *Journal of Psychosomatic Research, 77*(1), 70–75. Available from https://doi.org/10.1016/j.jpsychores.2014.05.004.

Radstaak, M., Geurts, S. A. E., Brosschot, J. F., Cillessen, A. H. N., & Kompier, M. A. J. (2011). The role of affect and rumination in cardiovascular recovery from stress. *International Journal of Psychophysiology, 81*(3), 237–244. Available from https://doi.org/10.1016/j.ijpsycho.2011.06.017.

Ray, R. D., Wilhelm, F. H., & Gross, J. J. (2008). All in the mind's eye? anger rumination and reappraisal. *Journal of Personality and Social Psychology, 94*(1), 133–145. Available from https://doi.org/10.1037/0022-3514.94.1.133.

Rehm, K. E., & Konkle-Parker, D. (2017). Association of CD4 + T cell subpopulations and psychological stress measures in women living with HIV. *AIDS Care, 29*(9), 1107. Available from https://doi.org/10.1080/09540121.2017.1281880.

Rydstedt, L. W., Cropley, M., & Devereux, J. (2011). Long-term impact of role stress and cognitive rumination upon morning and evening saliva cortisol secretion. *Ergonomics, 54*(5), 430–435. Available from https://doi.org/10.1080/00140139.2011.558639.

Rydstedt, L. W., Cropley, M., Devereux, J. J., & Michalianou, G. (2009). The effects of gender, long-term need for recovery and trait inhibition-rumination on morning and evening saliva cortisol secretion. *Anxiety, Stress & Coping, 22*(4), 465–474. Available from https://doi.org/10.1080/10615800802596378.

Schlotz, W., Hellhammer, J., Schulz, P., & Stone, A. A. (2004). Perceived work overload and chronic worrying predict weekend–weekday differences in the cortisol awakening response. *Psychosomatic Medicine, 66*(2), 207–214. Available from https://doi.org/10.1097/01.psy.0000116715.78238.56.

Schmiege, S. J., Bryan, A., & Klein, W. M. P. (2009). Distinctions between worry and perceived risk in the context of the theory of planned behavior. *Journal of Applied Social Psychology, 39* (1), 95–119. Available from https://doi.org/10.1111/j.1559-1816.2008.00431.x.

Schoth, D. E., Nunes, V. D., & Liossi, C. (2012). Attentional bias towards pain-related information in chronic pain; a meta-analysis of visual-probe investigations. *Clinical Psychology Review, 32*(1), 13–25. Available from https://doi.org/10.1016/j.cpr.2011.09.004.

Segerstrom, S. C., Glover, D. A., Craske, M. G., & Fahey, J. L. (1999). Worry affects the immune response to phobic fear. *Brain, Behavior, and Immunity, 13*(2), 80–92. Available from https://doi.org/10.1006/brbi.1998.0544.

Segerstrom, S. C., & Miller, G. E. (2004). Psychological stress and the human immune system. *Psychological Bulletin, 130*(4), 601–630. Available from https://doi.org/10.1037/0033-2909.130.4.601.

Segerstrom, S. C., Schipper, L. J., & Greenberg, R. N. (2008). Caregiving, repetitive thought, and immune response to vaccination in older adults. *Brain, Behavior, and Immunity, 22* (5), 744–752. Available from https://doi.org/10.1016/j.bbi.2007.11.004.

Segerstrom, S. C., Stanton, A. L., Alden, L. E., & Shortridge, B. E. (2003). A multidimensional structure for repetitive thought. *Journal of Personality and Social Psychology, 85*(5), 909–921. Available from https://doi.org/10.1037/0022-3514.85.5.909.

Segerstrom, S., Solomon, G., Kemeny, M., & Fahey, J. (1998). Relationship of worry to immune sequelae of the northridge earthquake. *Journal of Behavioral Medicine, 21*(5), 433–450. Available from https://doi.org/1018732309353.

Shapero, B., McClung, G., Bangasser, D., Abramson, L., & Alloy, L. (2017). Interaction of biological stress recovery and cognitive vulnerability for depression in adolescence. *Journal of Youth and Adolescence, 46*(1), 91–103. Available from https://doi.org/10.1007/s10964-016-0451-0.

Shull, A., Mayer, S. E., McGinnis, E., Geiss, E., Vargas, I., & Lopez-Duran, N. L. (2016). Trait and state rumination interact to prolong cortisol activation to psychosocial stress in females. *Psychoneuroendocrinology, 74,* 324–332. Available from https://doi.org/10.1016/j.psyneuen.2016.09.004.

Slavish, D. C., & Graham-Engeland, J. E. (2015). Rumination mediates the relationships between depressed mood and both sleep quality and self-reported health in young adults. *Journal of Behavioral Medicine, 38*(2), 204–213. Available from https://doi.org/10.1007/s10865-014-9595-0.

Stewart, J., Mazurka, R., Bond, L., Wynne-Edwards, K., & Harkness, K. (2013). Rumination and impaired cortisol recovery following a social stressor in adolescent depression. *Journal of Abnormal Child Psychology, 41*(7), 1015–1026. Available from https://doi.org/10.1007/s10802-013-9740-1.

Stewart, J. C., & France, C. R. (2001). Cardiovascular recovery from stress predicts longitudinal changes in blood pressure. *Biological Psychology, 58*(2), 105–120. Available from https://doi.org/10.1016/S0301-0511(01)00105-3.

Sullivan, M., Thorn, B., Haythornthwaite, J., Keefe, F., Martin, M., Bradley, L., & Lefebvre, J. (2001). Theoretical perspectives on the relation between catastrophizing and pain. *The Clinical Journal of Pain, 17*(1), 52–64. Available from https://doi.org/10.1097/00002508-200103000-00008.

Sullivan, M. J., & Neish, N. R. (1998). Catastrophizing, anxiety and pain during dental hygiene treatment. *Community Dentistry and Oral Epidemiology, 26*(5), 344–349. Available from https://doi.org/10.1111/j.1600-0528.1998.tb01971.x.

Sullivan, M. J. L., Bishop, S. R., & Pivik, J. (1995). The pain catastrophizing scale. *Psychological Assessment, 7*(4), 524–532. Available from https://doi.org/10.1037/1040-3590.7.4.524.

Sullivan, M. J. L., Lynch, M. E., & Clark, A. J. (2005). Dimensions of catastrophic thinking associated with pain experience and disability in patients with neuropathic pain conditions. *Pain, 113*(3), 310–315. Available from https://doi.org/10.1016/j.pain.2004.11.003.

Sullivan, M. J. L., Sullivan, M. E., & Adams, H. M. (2002). Stage of chronicity and cognitive correlates of pain-related disability. *Cognitive Behaviour Therapy, 31*(3), 111–118. Available from https://doi.org/10.1080/165060702320337988.

Sullivan, M. J. L., Tripp, D. A., Rodgers, W. M., & Stanish, W. (2000). Catastrophizing and pain perception in sport participants. *Journal of Applied Sport Psychology, 12*(2), 151–167. Available from https://doi.org/10.1080/10413200008404220.

Swayampakala, K., Thrasher, J., Carpenter, M. J., Shigematsu, L. M. R., Cupertio, A., & Berg, C. J. (2012). Level of cigarette consumption and quit behavior in a population of low-intensity smokers—Longitudinal results from the international tobacco control (ITC) survey in mexico. *Addictive Behaviors, 38*(4), 1958–1965. Available from https://doi.org/10.1016/j.addbeh.2012.12.007.

Takano, K., Ueno, M., & Tanno, Y. (2014). Self-focused thinking predicts nighttime physiological de-arousal. *Biological Psychology, 97*, 9–14. Available from https://doi.org/10.1016/j.biopsycho.2014.01.001.

Thayer, J. F., & Brosschot, J. F. (2005). Psychosomatics and psychopathology: Looking up and down from the brain. *Psychoneuroendocrinology, 30*(10), 1050–1058. Available from https://doi.org/10.1016/j.psyneuen.2005.04.014.

Thayer, J. F., Friedman, B. H., & Borkovec, T. D. (1996). Autonomic characteristics of generalized anxiety disorder and worry. *Biological Psychiatry, 39*(4), 255–266. Available from https://doi.org/10.1016/0006-3223(95)00136-0.

Thayer, J. F., & Lane, R. D. (2007). The role of vagal function in the risk for cardiovascular disease and mortality. *Biological Psychology, 74*(2), 224–242. Available from https://doi.org/10.1016/j.biopsycho.2005.11.013.

Thomsen, D. K., Jorgensen, M. M., Melsen, M. Y., & Zachariae, R. (2004). The influence of rumination and defensiveness on negative affect in response to experimental stress. *Scandinavian Journal of Psychology, 45*(3), 253–258. Available from https://doi.org/10.1111/j.1467-9450.2004.00402.x.

Thomsen, D. K., Yung Mehlsen, M., Christensen, S., & Zachariae, R. (2003). Rumination—Relationship with negative mood and sleep quality. *Personality and Individual Differences, 34*(7), 1293–1301. Available from https://doi.org/10.1016/S0191-8869(02)00120-4.

Todd, J., Sharpe, L., Johnson, A., Nicholson Perry, K., Colagiuri, B., & Dear, B. F. (2015). Towards a new model of attentional biases in the development, maintenance, and management of pain. *Pain, 156*(9), 1589–1600. Available from https://doi.org/10.1097/j.pain.0000000000000214.

Tremblay, I., & Sullivan, M. J. L. (2010). Attachment and pain outcomes in adolescents: The mediating role of pain catastrophizing and anxiety. *Journal of Pain, 11*(2), 160–171. Available from https://doi.org/10.1016/j.jpain.2009.06.015.

Van Damme, S., Crombez, G., & Eccleston, C. (2002). Retarded disengagement from pain cues: The effects of pain catastrophizing and pain expectancy. *Pain, 100*(1), 111–118. Available from https://doi.org/10.1016/S0304-3959(02)00290-7.

Van Damme, S., Crombez, G., & Eccleston, C. (2004). Disengagement from pain: The role of catastrophic thinking about pain. *Pain, 107*(1), 70–76. Available from https://doi.org/10.1016/j.pain.2003.09.023.

Verkuil, B., Brosschot, J. F., & Thayer, J. F. (2007). A sensitive body or a sensitive mind? associations among somatic sensitization, cognitive sensitization, health worry, and subjective health complaints. *Journal of Psychosomatic Research, 63*(6), 673–681. Available from https://doi.org/10.1016/j.jpsychores.2007.08.010.

Versluis, A., Verkuil, B., & Brosschot, J. F. (2016). Reducing worry and subjective health complaints: A randomized trial of an internet-delivered worry postponement intervention. *British Journal of Health Psychology, 21*(2), 318–335. Available from https://doi.org/10.1111/bjhp.12170.

Vervoort, T., Caes, L., Crombez, G., Koster, E., Van Damme, S., Dewitte, M., & Goubert, L. (2011). Parental catastrophizing about children's pain and selective attention to varying levels of facial expression of pain in children: A dot-probe study. *Pain, 152*(8), 1751. Available from https://doi.org/10.1016/j.pain.2011.03.015.

Vervoort, T., Trost, Z., Prkachin, K. M., & Mueller, S. C. (2013). Attentional processing of other's facial display of pain: An eye tracking study. *Pain, 154*(6), 836. Available from https://doi.org/10.1016/j.pain.2013.02.017.

Vickers, K., & Vogeltanz-Holm, N. (2003). The effects of rumination and distraction tasks on psychophysiological responses and mood in dysphoric and nondysphoric individuals. *Cognitive Therapy and Research, 27*(3), 331–348. Available from https://doi.org/1023970501448.

Wicklow, A., & Espie, C. A. (2000). Intrusive thoughts and their relationship to actigraphic measurement of sleep: Towards a cognitive model of insomnia. *Behaviour Research and Therapy, 38*(7), 679–693. Available from https://doi.org/10.1016/S0005-7967(99)00136-9.

Williams, D. P., Cash, C., Rankin, C., Bernardi, A., Koenig, J., & Thayer, J. F. (2015). Resting heart rate variability predicts self-reported difficulties in emotion regulation: A focus on different facets of emotion regulation. *Frontiers in Psychology, 6*, 261. Available from https://doi.org/10.3389/fpsyg.2015.00261.

Woody, M. L., Burkhouse, K. L., Birk, S. L., & Gibb, B. E. (2015). Brooding rumination and cardiovascular reactivity to a laboratory-based interpersonal stressor. *Psychophysiology, 52*(5), 722–725. Available from https://doi.org/10.1111/psyp.12397.

Wüst, S., Federenko, I., Hellhammer, D. H., & Kirschbaum, C. (2000). Genetic factors, perceived chronic stress, and the free cortisol response to awakening. *Psychoneuroendocrinology, 25*(7), 707–720. Available from https://doi.org/10.1016/S0306-4530(00)00021-4.

Yong, H. H., Borland, R., Thrasher, J. F., Thompson, M. E., Nagelhout, G. E., Fong, G. T., ... Cummings, K. M. (2014). Mediational pathways of the impact of cigarette warning labels on quit attempts. *Health Psychology, 33*(11), 1410–1420. Available from https://doi.org/10.1037/hea0000056.

Zoccola, P. M., & Dickerson, S. S. (2012). Assessing the relationship between rumination and cortisol: A review. *Journal of Psychosomatic Research, 73*(1), 1–9. Available from https://doi.org/10.1016/j.jpsychores.2012.03.007.

Zoccola, P. M., & Dickerson, S. S. (2015). Extending the recovery window: Effects of trait rumination on subsequent evening cortisol following a laboratory performance stressor. *Psychoneuroendocrinology, 58*, 67–78. Available from https://doi.org/10.1016/j.psyneuen.2015.04.014.

Zoccola, P. M., Dickerson, S. S., & Lam, S. (2009). Rumination predicts longer sleep onset latency after an acute psychosocial stressor. *Psychosomatic Medicine, 71*(7), 771–775. Available from https://doi.org/10.1097/PSY.0b013e3181ae58e8.

Zoccola, P. M., Dickerson, S. S., & Yim, I. S. (2011). Trait and state perseverative cognition and the cortisol awakening response. *Psychoneuroendocrinology, 36*(4), 592–595. Available from https://doi.org/10.1016/j.psyneuen.2010.10.004.

Zoccola, P. M., Dickerson, S. S., & Zaldivar, F. P. (2008). Rumination and cortisol responses to laboratory stressors. *Psychosomatic Medicine, 70*(6), 661–667. Available from https://doi.org/10.1097/PSY.0b013e31817bbc77.

Zoccola, P. M., Rabideau, E. M., Figueroa, W. S., & Woody, A. (2014). Cardiovascular and affective consequences of ruminating on a performance stressor depend on mode of thought. *Stress and Health, 30*(3), 188–197. Available from https://doi.org/10.1002/smi.2588.

Zoccola, P. M., Quas, J. A., & Yim, I. S. (2010). Salivary cortisol responses to a psychosocial laboratory stressor and later verbal recall of the stressor: The role of trait and state rumination. *Stress, 13*(5), 435–443. Available from https://doi.org/10.3109/10253891003713765.

Further reading

Kökönyei, G., Józan, A., Morgan, A., Szemenyei, E., Urbán, R., Reinhardt, M., & Demetrovics, Z. (2015). Perseverative thoughts and subjective health complaints in adolescence: Mediating effects of perceived stress and negative affects. *Psychology & Health, 30*(8), 969–986. Available from https://doi.org/10.1080/08870446.2015.1007982.

Lyubomirsky, S., Sousa, L., & Dickerhoof, R. (2006). The costs and benefits of writing, talking, and thinking about life's triumphs and defeats. *Journal of Personality and Social Psychology, 90*(4), 692–708. Available from https://doi.org/10.1037/0022-3514.90.4.692.

Miers, A., Rieffe, C. J., Meerum Terwogt, M., Cowan, R., & Linden, W. (2007). The relation between anger coping strategies, anger mood and somatic complaints in children and adolescents. *Journal of Abnormal Child Psychology, 35*(4), 653–664. Available from https://doi.org/10.1007/s10802-007-9120-9.

Segerstrom, S. C., Roach, A. R., Evans, D. R., Schipper, L. J., & Darville, A. K. (2010). The structure and health correlates of trait repetitive thought in older adults. *Psychology and Aging, 25*(3), 505–515. Available from https://doi.org/10.1037/a0019456.

Verkuil, B., Brosschot, J. F., Meerman, E. E., & Thayer, J. F. (2012). Effects of momentary assessed stressful events and worry episodes on somatic health complaints. *Psychology & Health, 27*(2), 141–158. Available from https://doi.org/10.1080/08870441003653470.

CHAPTER

6

Consequences of expressed rumination

Overview

This chapter reviews several literatures examining the negative and positive consequences of expressed repetitive thought. After briefly describing expressive writing, or repeated writing about thoughts and feelings about upsetting events, I explore the intrapersonal and interpersonal effects of co-rumination, or repeated discussions of a personal problem with a close other. I then turn to the extensive literature on social sharing of emotion. Finally, I describe the newer construct of collective rumination, or repeatedly talking about a shared grievance with similar others. I conclude by exploring similarities and differences of these various constructs, as well as potential mechanisms of the effects of expressed rumination.

So far, I have referred to rumination, and all forms of repetitive thought, as a private, internal process. What happens, however, when people verbally express the content of their negative, ruminative thinking? This could occur either through writing, such as in a journal, or in conversation with one or more people. In recent years, researchers have started exploring rumination as an expressive process. Some literature focuses on expressing thoughts and feelings through writing; most focuses on sharing negative thoughts and feelings with other people. In this chapter, I review three well-established literatures and one nascent literature. I then attempt to integrate these disparate fields and consider some as-of-yet unanswered questions about the idea of expressed rumination.

Rumination and Related Constructs
DOI: https://doi.org/10.1016/B978-0-12-812545-8.00006-1

© 2020 Elsevier Inc. All rights reserved.

Expressive writing

Since the 1980s, social psychologist James Pennebaker has been studying what happens when people write intensively about their thoughts and feelings about upsetting events in their lives. In his initial experiment, healthy undergraduates were assigned to write about one or more traumatic event for 15 minutes on 4 consecutive days (Pennebaker & Beall, 1986). Participants were assigned to write about only the facts of the trauma, only their emotions, or a combination of facts and emotions. Across all 4 days, writing about emotions—especially when paired with writing about facts—was associated with higher blood pressure and more negative state mood, compared to writing about facts alone and to a control condition that wrote about trivial topics. However, 4 months later, participants who wrote about emotions reported decreases in health problems, compared to the fact-only and control groups. In addition, participants in the combination emotion-fact group had made fewer visits to the student health and counseling center than did participants in any other condition. Thus, immediate increases in negative affect and arousal were counteracted by longer term health benefits.

This initial study spawned a large literature on the consequences of expressive writing (for a review, see Frattaroli, 2006). In college students, this expressive writing procedure contributes to reduced absences from work, improved GPAs, and improved immune functioning. In adults, expressive writing yields a range of benefits, such as findings jobs faster, reduced distress in migraine sufferers, and fewer doctor visits in both breast cancer patients and incarcerated men. A metaanalysis of over 100 experimental studies found that expressive writing has significant beneficial effects on measures of psychological functioning, such as general distress, depression, anxiety, and anger (Frattaroli, 2006). The benefit of expressive writing is particularly strong for pessimists and people experiencing stress. Interestingly, expressive writing also shows a small but significant effect on improved social relationships.

Some research has directly tested the association between expressive writing and rumination, with mixed results. For instance, in depression-vulnerable college students with tendencies to suppress emotions, 3 days of expressive writing about upsetting events led to decreases in the brooding subscale of depressive rumination 6 months later, compared to writing about trivial events (Gortner, Rude, & Pennebaker, 2006). By contrast, in a healthy sample of college students, 3 days of expressive writing about upsetting events did not predict changes in depressive rumination 1 month later (Maestas & Rude, 2012). Similar mixed results emerge with intrusive thoughts. In one study, college students who engaged in three sessions of expressive writing about a negative life event experienced greater reductions in intrusive thoughts about that event 2 months later, compared to students who wrote about a positive event or trivial issues (Klein & Boals, 2001). However, other studies failed to find an effect of expressive writing on intrusive thoughts (Lepore, 1997; Lepore, Greenberg, Bruno, & Smyth, 2002; Stroebe, Stroebe, Schut, Zech, & van den Bout, 2002).

Other research suggests that expressive writing buffers the effects of intrusive thoughts and rumination. An early study found that intrusive thoughts about the graduate record exam were associated with increased depressive symptoms over the month leading up to the exam, but only for students who wrote about trivial topics (Lepore, 1997). For students who engaged in expressive writing about the exam, the association between intrusive thoughts and change in depressive symptoms disappeared. This suggests that even a single session of expressive writing buffered the effect of intrusive thoughts. Similarly, expressive writing about a recent break-up made the association between intrusive thoughts and poor physical health disappear (Lepore et al., 2002). More recently, college students high in trait brooding who engaged in 3 days of expressive writing about traumatic life events showed reduced depressive symptoms 2, 4, and even 6 months later (Sloan, Marx, Epstein, & Dobbs, 2008). By contrast, rumination was associated with increased depressive symptoms over time for participants who wrote about trivial issues.

In sum, although repeated writing about the emotions associated with upsetting events can trigger immediate distress, it has long-term benefits for both emotional and physical health. Moreover, expressive writing appears to buffer the negative emotional effects of private rumination. This is a curious and potentially important finding that I return to at the end of the chapter. First, I review related but separate literatures on rumination with others.

Co-rumination

In an effort to better understand why their closer friendships did not buffer girls from psychological distress, developmental psychologist Amanda Rose (2002) introduced the construct of *co-rumination*, which she defined as extensively discussing personal problems with a close other. Co-rumination is characterized by frequently discussing problems, rehashing the same problem over and over, encouraging each other to discuss problems, speculating about causes and consequences of problems, and focusing on negative feelings. Co-rumination need not involve discussion of a shared problem. Rather, it is commonly conceived as a close pair (e.g., two friends, parent and child, romantic partners) discussing each person's problems repeatedly and in a way that harps on negativity rather than constructive problem-solving. The majority of research has assessed co-rumination with same-sex best friends, although we will see that there are important limitations of this approach. Although originally hypothesized to occur in face-to-face conversations, co-rumination between friends also occurs via texting, talking on the phone, and social media outlets such as Facebook (Keshishian, Watkins, & Otto, 2016; Murdock, Gorman, & Robbins, 2015; Swearingen, Byrd-Craven, & Kennison, 2016).

Based on the individual rumination literature, Rose hypothesized that co-rumination would be associated with negative intrapersonal outcomes. However, based on developmental research that self-disclosure increases perceived friendship quality, she hypothesized that co-rumination would also be associated with better interpersonal outcomes. As such, she argued that co-rumination is a complex construct that has adjustment trade-offs. Support generally exists for both hypotheses, although the data paint a more nuanced picture than Rose originally hypothesized.

Intrapersonal outcomes

Co-rumination is generally associated with greater depressive and anxious symptoms, although the effects are small-to-medium and considerable heterogeneity exists (for a review, see Spendelow, Simonds, & Avery, 2017).[1] Co-rumination also strengthens the association between general stressors and depressive symptoms (Murdock et al., 2015; Starr, 2015; White & Shih, 2012). Some research suggests that individual rumination mediates the associations between co-rumination and internalizing symptoms (Rose, 2002; Stone & Gibb, 2015). In other words, co-rumination with a close friend may trigger individual rumination, which in turn exacerbates psychological distress. Co-rumination also makes existing

1 To assess co-rumination, most researchers use some version of the co-rumination questionnaire (Rose, 2002), which contains anywhere from 27 (i.e., the original measure) to 9 items (Hankin, Stone, & Ann Wright, 2010). The co-rumination and depressive rumination questionnaires are only modestly correlated, suggesting that co-rumination is a distinct construct (Calmes & Roberts, 2008). Although the original analysis suggested a unidimensional factor structure, a more recent psychometric analysis yielded three related factors: rehashing (i.e., discussing aspects and implications of a problem in detail), mulling (i.e., a desire to repeatedly discuss problems), and encouraging problem talk (Davidson et al., 2014). A coding system for co-rumination (see Rose, Schwartz-Mette, Glick, Smith, & Luebbe, 2014) has also been used by various studies to code recorded conversations for four aspects of co-rumination: rehashing, focusing on the negative, speculating, and encouraging problem talk.

problems more salient, which may explain greater emotional distress (Rose, Glick, Smith, Schwartz-Mette, & Borowski, 2017). In an analysis of separate components of co-rumination, only dwelling on the negative was associated with depressive symptoms after controlling for individual depressive rumination (Rose et al., 2014). Other co-rumination components (e.g., rehashing problems, speculating about causes and consequences) were not uniquely related to depressive symptoms.

Co-rumination is also associated with eating psychopathology in women. For instance, co-rumination with a same-sex friend about perceived body/weight problems predicts more binging and purging behavior, particularly when the friend is not accepting and understanding (Arroyo, Segrin, Harwood, & Bonito, 2017). Co-rumination is also associated with body image cognitive distortions and general eating psychopathology (Rudiger & Winstead, 2013). In addition, college women who coruminate with their mothers about weight concerns report more self-objectification, or seeing their bodies as objects to be evaluated (Arroyo & Andersen, 2016). No research has examined the effect of co-rumination on disordered eating behaviors in men.

The associations between co-rumination and externalizing problems are mixed. Co-rumination was associated with more adolescent aggressive behavior in some studies but not others (Criss et al., 2016; Tompkins, Hockett, Abraibesh, & Witt, 2011). Also in adolescents, co-rumination predicted fewer conduct problems concurrently and 5 months later, although this association disappeared when controlling for internalizing symptoms and initial conduct problems (Hankin et al., 2010; Shapero, Hankin, & Barrocas, 2013). In Italian adolescents, co-rumination with a friend predicted decreased likelihood of engaging in nonsuicidal self-injury 6 months later (Latina, Giannotta, & Rabaglietti, 2015). Finally, co-rumination was associated with more weekly drinking in female college students but less weekly drinking in men (Ciesla, Dickson, Anderson, & Neal, 2011). In sum, the existing literature has found both positive, negative, and nonsignificant effects of co-rumination on externalizing symptoms. Even the significant effects are generally small, explaining less than 4% of the variance. Thus, it seems fair to conclude that the effects of co-rumination on externalizing symptoms are small at best and/or potentially influenced by gender and other moderators yet to be identified.

A few studies examined co-rumination and physical functioning. For instance, greater co-rumination between friends was associated with worse self-reported physical health in women (Swearingen et al., 2016). In a cortisol study, undergraduate female friend dyads either talked together about one of their current problems (i.e., co-rumination condition) or about the design of a recreation center (i.e., control condition) (Byrd-Craven, Geary, Rose, & Ponzi, 2008). Participants in the control condition exhibited decreases in cortisol after the discussion, whereas participants in the co-rumination condition exhibited unchanged cortisol levels. Moreover, in the co-rumination condition only, greater coded co-rumination—particularly dwelling on negative affect—predicted stronger increases in cortisol. These results were replicated in a second identical study (Byrd-Craven, Granger, & Auer, 2010). Thus, the limited existing research suggests that co-rumination increases or maintains physiological indices of stress.

Given the heterogeneity of associations between co-rumination and some psychological outcomes, researchers have examined moderators of the effect of co-rumination. One potential moderator is the specific close other with whom people coruminate. In young adults, same-sex best friends are most likely to be considered one's "closest confidant" (Barstead, Bouchard, & Shih, 2013). In line with this finding, co-rumination with a same-sex best friend or closest confidant is more strongly associated with emotional distress than is co-rumination with a parent, roommate, or romantic partner (Barstead et al., 2013; Spendelow et al., 2017; Waller & Rose, 2010). Researchers speculate that co-rumination with a close friend may be more passive, repetitive, and negative than co-rumination in other relationships. Another possibility is that people may discuss more emotionally negative problems with close friends than they do with parents, roommates, or romantic partners.

Researchers have also examined relationship quality and the nature of responses during co-rumination. In one study, co-rumination with a roommate was only associated with greater depressive symptoms for college students reporting poor relationship quality with their roommate (Guassi Moreira, Miernicki, & Telzer, 2016). Co-ruminating in the context of a high-quality relationship may provide concern and empathy, whereas co-ruminating with someone who is not supportive may lead to greater emotional distress. In a rare experiment in this literature, young adults were asked to engage in a conversation with a friend and were randomly assigned to be either the talker or the listener (Afifi, Afifi, Merrill, Denes, & Davis, 2013). Talkers simply talked about a current problem, whereas the listeners were asked to provide either good support (e.g., provide validation and support, ask questions) or poor support (e.g., appear distracted or disinterested, respond with blame and criticism) to their friend. Not surprisingly, talkers who received good support reported less state anxiety and individual rumination. In fact, talkers' self-report of co-rumination following the interaction was associated with more state anxiety when they received poor support but was unrelated to anxiety when they received good support. Thus, co-rumination may only contribute to negative intrapersonal outcomes in the context of unsupportive conversations.

The nature of problems discussed in co-rumination may also influence outcomes. Just as individual rumination about social stressors predicts greater depressive symptoms, so too does co-rumination about social stressors (Nicolai, Laney, & Mezulis, 2013). By contrast, individual and co-rumination about nonsocial stressors is not associated with depressive symptoms. Other research corroborates these findings. For instance, co-rumination with a close friend predicts depressive symptoms only for college students low in romantic relationship satisfaction (Whitton & Kuryluk, 2012). Co-rumination is also associated with depressive and posttraumatic stress disorder (PTSD) symptoms only for adolescents with weaker peer attachment and higher levels of peer victimization (Dam, Roelofs, & Muris, 2014; Guarneri-White, Jensen-Campbell, & Knack, 2015). Although none of these studies assessed the content of participants' co-rumination, it seems possible that individuals who are experiencing various social stressors (e.g., bullying, unsatisfying romantic relationships, poor attachment) turn to their close ones to discuss these problems. Because these problems are often associated with negative emotions and thoughts, co-rumination about these problems may be more likely to contribute to psychological distress.

Finally, the effects of co-rumination may differ by gender. Many studies find that females engage in co-rumination more than males do (Calmes & Roberts, 2008; Haggard, Robert, & Rose, 2011; Rose, 2002; Spendelow et al., 2017; Tompkins et al., 2011). In fact, co-rumination explains the effect of gender on internalizing symptoms in children, adolescents, and young adults (Calmes & Roberts, 2008; Rose, 2002). Accordingly, some researchers have conceptualized co-rumination as an activity that is primarily relevant for women. However, there are several reasons to question this assumption. First, males are more likely than females to co-ruminate with opposite-sex friends (Barstead et al., 2013). Thus, studies that only assess co-rumination with same-sex close friends may not be assessing the type of co-rumination that males typically engage in. In fact, when co-rumination with "closest confidant" is assessed, no gender differences emerge (Barstead et al., 2013). Second, although gender does not moderate the main effects of co-rumination on internalizing symptoms (Spendelow et al., 2017), it does appear to moderate the interaction of co-rumination and stress. In one study, greater co-rumination predicted a stronger link between stress and depression only for girls (Bastin, Mezulis, Ahles, Raes, & Bijttebier, 2015). By contrast, *low* co-rumination predicted more stress-related depressive symptoms for boys. Similarly, low co-rumination about work-related issues predicted a stronger association between work stress and depressive symptoms for adult men (Haggard et al., 2011). A similar pattern emerged for work-to-family conflict, which is when work problems spill over into one's home life. Specifically, work stress predicted more work-to-family conflict for men—but not women—who were low in co-rumination.

Why might males *low* in co-rumination be more likely to have negative emotional reactions to stress? One possibility is that the content of co-rumination differs for males and females. Men and boys may talk more about how to solve problems, whereas women and girls talk about aspects of problems that cannot be changed or that they do not understand (Bastin et al., 2015; Haggard et al., 2011). In fact, co-rumination is associated with more problem-solving and emotion regulation in male adolescents but more emotional numbing in females (Lentz, Glenwick, & Kim, 2016). Thus, coruminating in response to serious stressors may alleviate emotional distress for men, whereas it exacerbates emotional distress for women. In line with this, work-related co-rumination predicts higher job satisfaction only in men experiencing high work stress (Haggard et al., 2011). In sum, co-rumination in males may look different than co-rumination in females—both in terms of one's chosen partner and the content of the conversation. Future research should explore these and other gender differences in the nature and effects of co-rumination on intrapersonal outcomes.

Interpersonal outcomes

Co-rumination is associated with some positive social outcomes. In Rose's (2002) initial study, co-rumination predicted higher self-reported friendship quality and closeness, in both children and adolescents. Interestingly, this association was stronger for boys than girls, possibly reflecting the proposed gender differences in the nature and content of co-rumination discussed above. In line with her hypothesizing, the effect of co-rumination on friendship quality was accounted for by self-disclosure. Subsequent studies with adolescents, young adults, and adults confirm that co-rumination—both self-reported and observed in actual conversations—is associated with greater self-reported friendship closeness and quality, as well as better perceived social support (Afifi et al., 2013; Boren, 2014; Haggard et al., 2011; Rose, Carlson, & Waller, 2007; Rose et al., 2014; Rudiger & Winstead, 2013; Smith & Rose, 2011). In an analysis of the separate components of co-rumination, rehashing problems, encouraging problem talk, and speculating on causes and consequences all predicted friendship closeness, but dwelling on the negative did not (Rose et al., 2014). Finally, co-rumination is also associated with better communication with friends, a more secure friendship style, less avoidant attachment, better social perspective-taking, and better self-perceived social competence (Criss et al., 2016; Smith & Rose, 2011; Starr & Davila, 2009). However, without longitudinal data, we cannot know whether co-rumination precedes or results from better social skills and secure attachments.

In contrast to these social benefits, co-rumination also has social costs. For instance, co-rumination is associated with having fewer friends (Tompkins et al., 2011). Co-rumination between mothers and adolescents is associated with more enmeshment, or unhealthy closeness and lack of appropriate boundaries, particularly when the co-rumination focuses on the mother's problems (Waller & Rose, 2010). Of course, the directionality could go the other way, such that people with fewer friends and enmeshed relationships engage in more co-rumination. Longitudinal research, however, also demonstrates some social costs of co-rumination. In one study, co-rumination predicted losing female friends over a 1-year period (Starr & Davila, 2009). Co-rumination also predicted increases in interpersonal stressors over 5 months (Hankin et al., 2010).

Thus although co-rumination may have short-term benefits for friendships, it may wear on relationships over time, leading to strain and even dissolution. One reason for this may be that co-rumination leads adolescents to take on a friend's distress and experience it as their own (Smith & Rose, 2011). In fact, co-rumination explained the contagion of depressive and anxious symptoms over 6 months in same-sex friendship pairs (Schwartz-Mette & Rose, 2012). Therefore, talking about problems in a repetitive, speculative, and negative way may negatively affect both friends. Once again, interesting gender differences may exist. One study found that co-rumination predicted greater peer stress 9 months later for depressed females but *less* peer stress for depressed males (Rose et al., 2017). This provides additional evidence that co-rumination for boys may differ in nature and outcomes from co-rumination for girls.

Summary

In sum, co-rumination does appear to have adjustment trade-offs. For women in particular, it contributes to or maintains psychological symptoms, especially if the content focuses on social stressors and listeners are not supportive. By contrast, co-rumination in men may actually protect them from negative psychological effects of stress. In order to better understand these discrepant results, researchers will have to examine whether the content and nature of rumination differs by gender. Interpersonally, co-rumination also has trade-offs, in which immediate increases in friendship closeness and quality may be offset over time by increased strain on relationships. Also worth noting is that co-rumination consists of several different facets that may have different effects on outcomes. Dwelling on negative emotions with another person may contribute to psychological distress, whereas the more cognitive and interactive aspects of co-rumination (e.g., rehashing problems, encouraging problem talk, and speculating about causes and consequences) may predict interpersonal outcomes. This brings up the important question of how similar co-rumination is to individual rumination, a question I address at the end of the chapter.

Social sharing of emotion

Informed by the expressive writing literature, social psychologist Bernard Rimé studied a construct called social sharing of emotion (Rimé, 2009; Rimé, Finkenauer, Luminet, Zech, & Philippot, 1998). The idea is that when people experience intense emotional experiences, they generally need to share those experiences repeatedly with other people. Early studies simply asked people to recall emotional episodes and answer questions about the extent of their sharing (Rimé, Mesquita, Boca, & Philippot, 1991). In subsequent work, researchers assessed social sharing after surviving or experiencing some major emotional experience (e.g., childbirth, a car accident, bereavement, and the Rwandan genocide) or following daily emotional events. Across many studies, social sharing was reported following approximately 90% of major emotional events and approximately 60% of daily emotional events (Rimé et al., 1998). Social sharing occurs for both positive and negative emotional experiences. The more emotional an event, the greater extent of social sharing, both immediately and over time (Curci & Rimé, 2012; Garcia, Cova, Rincon, Vazquez, & Paez, 2016; Luminet, Bouts, Delie, Manstead, & Rimé, 2000). The modal pattern is for people to share soon after the experience (e.g., the next day, the first week) and to share several times with several close confidants (e.g., parents, spouse/romantic partner, and best friend). Thus, social sharing appears to be a repetitive process, much like individual rumination. Social sharing generally decreases over time, although some people show continued social sharing even months after an emotional event (Curci & Rimé, 2012).

As Rose (2002) did with co-rumination, Rimé proposed that social sharing would have both intrapersonal and interpersonal outcomes. He also suggested that social sharing was paradoxical in nature (Rimé, Philippot, Boca, & Mesquita, 1992). On the one hand, reliving negative experiences can be emotionally upsetting; on the other hand, confiding in others may foster emotional recovery and interpersonal connection.

Intrapersonal outcomes

The association between social sharing and emotional experience is complex. During social sharing of negative events, people report experiencing mental images of the event, as well as related feelings and bodily sensations (Rimé et al., 1991). In other words, social sharing makes people reexperience the upsetting event in the moment. At the same time, people subjectively perceive social sharing to be helpful. In fact, 94% of people are willing to share another past emotional experience on the spot. Even 2 months after talking about an upsetting event, participants report perceived benefits of social sharing of emotion (Zech & Rimé, 2005). Specifically, they perceive that the sharing brought emotional relief, insight, and feeling understood by someone else. Thus, social sharing has both positive and negative perceived consequences. However, the most common outcomes of social sharing that researchers study are emotional relief and recovery. Emotional relief is indicated by a shorter duration or intensity of negative emotion immediately after social sharing, whereas emotional recovery is a decrease in emotional intensity and/or increase in well-being over time.

Social sharing does appear to be associated with immediate emotional relief, at least for some emotions. In one study, participants reported on discrete episodes of negative emotion every day for several days, as well as their social sharing of each episode (Brans, Van Mechelen, Rimé, & Verduyn, 2013). Social sharing of anger- and sadness-related episodes predicted a shorter duration of each negative emotion. However, a similar study found that social sharing was associated with an immediate decrease in the subjective intensity of anger but not sadness (Brans, Van Mechelen, Rimé, & Verduyn, 2014). In an experiment, undergraduate participants role-played being customer service representatives and handled calls from either friendly or annoyed/rude confederates (McCance, Nye, Wang, Jones, & Chiu, 2013). They then shared their experiences in groups of 2–6 people, all of whom had been assigned to the same call condition. Compared to a no discussion control condition, social sharing reduced anger immediately after the difficult calls. Thus, social sharing is associated with immediate emotional relief of anger, with less clear results for sadness.

The association between social sharing and emotional recovery is mixed. Correlational research has generally shown that social sharing is not associated with self-reported emotional recovery (Finkenauer & Rimé, 1998; Rimé et al., 1991, 1998). Another study found that after controlling for importance of an upsetting event and initial emotional intensity, social sharing was not associated with a decrease in emotional intensity 3 days after the event (Brans et al., 2013). In experiments that instructed participants to talk about emotional or factual aspects of an upsetting event for 20 minutes, social sharing was not associated with change in negative emotions 1 week and 2 months after the events (Zech & Rimé, 2005). By contrast, other studies have found significant—although conflicting—associations. In call-center service representatives, social sharing about negative work events predicted better well-being

3 months later but also greater emotional exhaustion (Baranik, Wang, Gong, & Shi, 2014). Social sharing following trauma predicted greater subsequent posttraumatic growth (Garcia et al., 2016; Páez, Basabe, Ubillos, & González-Castro, 2007; Rimé, Páez, Basabe, & Martínez, 2010). One study found that social sharing was associated with decreases in emotional intensity several days later for anger-related episodes but not for sadness-related episodes (Brans et al., 2014). By contrast, repeated social sharing about the same emotional experience over several months predicted less decrease in emotional intensity (Curci & Rimé, 2012). Thus, although much of the literature suggests that social sharing is unrelated to emotional recovery from upsetting events, the effect may depend on the specific negative emotion or outcome studied. Moreover, repeated sharing of the same event over several months may in fact maintain negative emotions.

The association between social sharing and individual rumination is also mixed. Social sharing correlates with greater individual rumination in some studies but not others (Baranik et al., 2014; Finkenauer & Rimé, 1998; Rimé et al., 1991, 1992, 2010). One study found that, controlling for the intensity of the emotional event, the more quickly that people share the event, the more they individually ruminate about it (Rimé et al., 1991). Of course, it could also be that the more people individually ruminate about an event, the sooner they engage in social sharing. In another study, people were *less* likely to individually ruminate about events they had shared with others than about events they had not shared (Finkenauer & Rimé, 1998). It may be that people make sense of the event during social sharing, so they do not need to ruminate as much privately. Alternatively, people might share events that they already understand better. Finally, social sharing indirectly predicted more deliberate rumination via greater problem-focused coping (Garcia et al., 2016). Perhaps social sharing contributes to more intentional repetitive thoughts to gain insight. Of course, without longitudinal or experimental studies, the directionality of these associations cannot be known.

What might explain the mixed effects of social sharing on emotional recovery and individual rumination? Some researchers argue that a distinction should be made between the quantity (i.e., frequency) versus quality of social sharing. Higher quality sharing involves disclosing emotional and personally meaningful information in a private, safe, and understanding context, evoking support and reassurance from listeners. Lower quality sharing involves disclosing superficial material in a more judgmental, less private, and tense context, evoking negative or inappropriate reactions from listeners. Two studies support this distinction and suggest that higher quality social sharing predicts better outcomes. In hospitalized patients awaiting cardiac bypass surgery, quantity of social sharing was initially associated with greater presurgical distress (Panagopoulou, Maes, Rimé, & Montgomery, 2006). However, this association disappeared when controlling for quality of social sharing. Instead, higher quality of social sharing was associated with less presurgical distress. Similarly, in HIV/AIDS outpatients, higher quality of social sharing was associated with better general mental and physical health (Cantisano, Rimé, & Teresa Munoz Sastre, 2015).

Rimé (2009) proposed a further distinction between two different modes of high-quality social sharing that differentially influence outcomes. The core difference between these modes is the type of listener response, which in turn leads to different outcomes for the speaker. Socio-affective social sharing elicits support, empathy, and consolation, whereas cognitive social sharing elicits reappraisal or other types of helpful cognitive restructuring. Rimé (2009) argued that socio-affective sharing will provide immediate emotional relief because it provides validation and connection. However, if people have not cognitively processed the event, this relief may be only temporary. Instead, social sharing will only provide true emotional recovery if it enables people to engage helpful cognitive processing of upsetting events. Interestingly, spontaneous social sharing tends to be primarily socio-affective in nature. In fact, people self-report that the majority of their social sharing elicits support, rather than suggestions for cognitive reappraisal (Brans et al., 2013). In studies on motives, people share negative events in attempts to attain emotional relief, social support, and advice (Delelis & Christophe, 2016; Duprez, Christophe, Rimé, Congard, & Antoine, 2015). Rimé (2009), therefore, suggested that because social sharing is naturally more supportive than cognitive, it might provide only temporary emotional relief but not longer term emotional recovery. Moreover, the temporary nature of the relief makes people need to share repeatedly.

A few studies have explicitly compared these two modes of social sharing. One experience sampling study found that socio-affective—but not cognitive—social sharing was uniquely associated with a shorter duration of negative emotion (Brans et al., 2013). However, there was no effect of sharing mode on emotional recovery. Of course, the directionality of associations cannot be determined; it could be that shorter emotional episodes are less likely to trigger socio-affective social sharing. In a pair of experiments, participants watched an upsetting film clip and then shared their emotions with a confederate who was either supportive (i.e., socio-affective condition) or provided a different perspective on the movie (i.e., cognitive condition) (Lepore, Fernandez-Berrocal, Ragan, & Ramos, 2004). In both studies, participants reported less emotional distress and fewer intrusive thoughts when reexposed to the video 2 days later if they had engaged in cognitive sharing.

In a similar experiment, emotional distress and social connection were assessed immediately after social sharing, as well as 2 days later (Nils & Rimé, 2012). Interestingly, socio-affective sharing led participants to experience stronger negative emotions but also to feel less lonely and closer to their listening partner. Cognitive sharing led participants to experience less strong negative emotions and had no effect on closeness or loneliness. Two days later, after being reexposed to the negative videos, there was no effect of socio-affective sharing on negative emotion, whereas cognitive sharing again led to less strong negative emotion. There were no longer any effects on interpersonal variables, although participants subjectively reported receiving more benefits from socio-affective sharing. In sum, these studies suggest that socio-affective social sharing contributes to immediate outcomes, specifically more intense but shorter negative emotions and increased connection with the listener. By contrast, cognitive social sharing likely promotes emotional recovery a few days later.

Interpersonal outcomes

Rimé (2009) also focused on the interpersonal and collective consequences of social sharing of emotion, for both speakers and listeners. The research in this section focuses not only on social sharing in response to individually meaningful events but also on social sharing about events that occurred to many people or an entire society. Collective disasters such as terrorist attacks provide a powerful trigger for social sharing. In fact, the social stage model for coping with collective disasters (Pennebaker & Harber, 1993) identifies three stages of emotional and interpersonal reactions to disasters and incorporates both individual rumination and social sharing of emotion. The *emergency phase* lasts 1–4 weeks after the disaster and is characterized by high levels of anxiety and depression, individual rumination, and expressions of solidarity, as well as intensive and frequent social sharing with others. The *inhibition phase,* occurring generally in the second month after the event, sees a significant decrease in the amount of social sharing but similar levels of individual rumination. The *adaptation phase,* starting approximately 6–8 weeks after the event, is characterized by a decrease in solidarity and individual rumination.

Empirical evidence supports the theory that social sharing occurs following collective disasters. In the first week after the 9/11 terrorist bombings in the United States, for instance, 98% of respondents across the country said they coped by talking with others, and those who had a stronger stress response engaged in more frequent sharing (Schuster et al., 2001). In a longitudinal study, French citizens were assessed

1 week, 1 month, and 2 months after the 2015 Charlie Hebdo terrorist bombings in Paris (Pelletier & Drozda-Senkowska, 2016). Social sharing was high 1 week following the attacks and decreased over the next 2 months. Researchers also assessed college students and their relatives 1, 3, and 8 weeks after the 2004 terrorist bombings in Madrid (Rimé et al., 2010). Both social sharing and individual rumination occurred at very high levels 1 week after the bombings and decreased markedly at 3 weeks and even more by 8 weeks. Interestingly, people engaged in more social sharing than individual rumination 1 week after the disaster, whereas individual rumination was more frequent than social sharing by week 8. Thus, theory and data suggest that social sharing and individual rumination may be different coping mechanisms with unique trajectories in the wake of collective disasters.

Rimé (2009) hypothesized that sharing upsetting experiences with another person increases perceptions of empathy, perceived similarities, closeness, and ultimately liking of each other. As Rose (2002) recognized, people who engage in intimate disclosure are generally more well-liked than people who do not disclose (Collins & Miller, 1994). In support of Rimé's hypothesis, socio-affective sharing in particular contributed to feelings of increased closeness and decreased loneliness in the speaker (Nils & Rimé, 2012). Similarly, social sharing 1 week after the Madrid bombing predicted greater perceived social support and less loneliness in the weeks following (Rimé et al., 2010). In an experiment testing group solidarity, participants watched a movie and then were assigned to talk with three other people about either the emotional aspects or the technical aspects of the movie (see Rimé, 2009). Talking about emotions led to greater feelings of connection within the group. Similarly, following the Charlie Hebdo bombing, people who engaged in more social sharing were more likely to participate in a solidarity demonstration, suggesting again that social sharing can promote a sense of group connection (Pelletier & Drozda-Senkowska, 2016).

A consequence of the listeners' emotional response to social sharing may be the need to engage in social sharing themselves, a construct called *secondary social sharing*. People who are told about an emotional experience by a close other experience moderately strong emotions themselves (Christophe & Rimé, 1997; Christophe, Delelis, Antoine, & Nandrino, 2008; Curci & Bellelli, 2004). This emotional contagion may trigger the need for their own social sharing. In fact, anywhere from 66% to 85% of participants report engaging in secondary social sharing. The content of secondary social sharing may consist of details about the event, describing the original teller's reactions, and expressing their own opinion and emotional reactions to the event (Christophe et al., 2008). The recipient of secondary social sharing is almost always an intimate, such as a romantic partner, friend, or family member.

Interestingly, people are likely to share even when they have been asked to keep information secret (Curci & Bellelli, 2004). People report engaging in secondary social sharing of intense negative events in order to receive emotional support and to compare their reactions and perceptions of the event with those of someone else (Christophe et al., 2008). In fact, the more intense emotions people feel after hearing about an emotional experience from someone else, the more people they tell. Secondary social sharing is also more likely to occur when people hear unusual stories that violate their own expectations, rather than when the stories themselves and original storyteller are emotional (Harber, Podolski, & Dyer, 2014). Thus, secondary social sharing likely reflects the emotion of the second person, although it may not be the same emotion as the original storyteller.

Going one step further, there is even evidence that the majority of people engage in *tertiary social sharing*, or sharing something that they heard second hand. An ingenious field study followed 33 students after their visit to a hospital morgue as part of a class (Harber & Cohen, 2005). The intensity of these students' emotional reactions to this experience predicted the number of people they told (i.e., primary sharing), the number of people their friends told (i.e., secondary sharing), and the number of people their friends' friends told (i.e., tertiary sharing). In fact, within 10 days, nearly 900 people had heard about this event.

Because of the perpetuation of social sharing, social sharing of collective events may have larger societal consequences. Specifically, social sharing of events that are relevant to a large group may facilitate collective memory, or widely held memories of community members about important events that shape collective identity (Hirst & Manier, 2008). Collective memories, or shared narratives, may begin within and between individuals but are often formalized in the world in texts, art, monuments, museums, holidays, and even street names. Theories of collective memory argue that frequent recollection and discussion of common past events build collective narratives (Hirst & Manier, 2008). Talking about events is a form of memory rehearsal and contributes to better remembering within the individual. Memory researchers have also repeatedly found that talking can spread a memory—whether true or false—from one person to another (Coman, Brown, Koppel, & Hirst, 2009). Furthermore, discussing a shared experience makes individual memories of the experience more similar. In sum, social sharing of emotion, even if engaged in to provide support, connection, and emotional relief, may contribute to a collective rendering of shared past events. Stronger collective memory is in turn associated with strong group identification (e.g., Bellehumeur, Laplante, Lagace, & Rodrigue, 2011).

Finally, social sharing of shared emotional events may also contribute to perceived emotional climate, or how individuals think the majority of people are currently feeling in society (Rimé, 2007). Emotional climates often result from collectively shared emotional events and can exist separate from people's individual emotions. They are like collective moods or atmospheres. Two hypotheses can be made. First, because social sharing can reactivate event-related feelings, social sharing of negative collective events might contribute to a more negative perceived emotional climate. On the other hand, because sharing of emotions leads to increased intimacy and cohesion, it might facilitate a positive emotional climate. Data on this association are mixed. In the wake of the Madrid bombings, greater social sharing 1 week after the bombings predicted more positive emotional climate 2 months later (Páez et al., 2007). By contrast, social sharing following the 2015 Paris attacks was not associated with perceived emotional climate (Pelletier & Drozda-Senkowska, 2016). More research is needed on the effect of social sharing on perceived emotional climate.

Summary

In sum, social sharing occurs for both personally upsetting events and collective disasters. Most social sharing naturally tends to be supportive in nature and contributes to immediate emotional relief and interpersonal closeness. However, only sharing that encourages cognitive reappraisal or restructuring may be likely to promote actual emotional recovery over time. Despite the interpersonal closeness and solidarity that social sharing can promote, it also leads to a contagion effect, which can in turn trigger secondary and even tertiary social sharing. For this reason, social sharing may contribute to collective memory and perceived emotional climate. Cross-sectional associations between social sharing and individual rumination are mixed, but longitudinal work suggests that they follow unique trajectories. The amount of time elapsed since the upsetting event may moderate the correlation between social sharing and individual rumination, a hypothesis that future research can test.

Collective rumination

One novel but related question is whether people ruminate in *groups of similar others* about shared problems, a construct called *collective rumination*. In his review of the angry rumination field, Denson (2013) made some propositions about collective angry rumination. He suggested that the retelling of injustices toward oneself or others in one's group may maintain anger across years and even generations. This process may explain incidents of war, blood revenge, and terrorism that are carried out decades after a perceived provocation. The social psychological literature does suggest that social interaction and small group dynamics play a role in collective action, or efforts to improve the position of one's group in society. However, researchers have thus far only theorized about the construct of collective rumination.

My colleagues and I conducted a series of studies to address this gap. Specifically, our goal was to measure rumination with similar others about a shared grievance and examine whether it is associated with both intrapersonal and interpersonal outcomes. In order to examine this research question, we created a collective rumination questionnaire based on Rose's (2002) co-rumination questionnaire (Borders, 2017; Pruzniak, Playter, & Borders, 2016). The measure assessed the extent to which individuals talk repeatedly with other in-group members about group-related perceived discrimination. We hypothesized that greater perceived discrimination would be associated with more collective rumination about discrimination, which would in turn be related to greater anger and collective action intentions. In samples of ethnic minorities, women, and sexual minorities, we found that more perceived discrimination was associated with more collective rumination about discrimination. We also found that collective rumination correlated with more anger about discrimination, individual rumination, identification with one's group, and intentions to engage in normative collective action against discrimination.

I then attempted to manipulate collective rumination in a laboratory setting. Specifically, undergraduate students read an article about the bad quality food served by the same company that serviced their college (Borders, 2018). After this induction of a shared grievance, participants were randomly assigned to either expressively write about the issue or to discuss the issue with other students who had also just read the article. Interestingly, participants who wrote reported increased anger, whereas those who engaged in collective rumination reported decreased anger. Participants in the collective rumination condition also reported less individual rumination but more belonging with other students and a more positive emotional climate, compared to participants in the expressive writing condition.

Thus, these initial studies yielded some contradictory information. On the one hand, collective rumination about perceived discrimination—measured on a trait-based questionnaire—was associated with more anger and individual rumination. On the other hand, collective rumination about a shared grievance—manipulated as a discussion with other students—predicted less anger and individual rumination, compared to manipulated individual rumination. It could be that collective rumination leads to immediate emotional relief but that in general, people who collectively ruminate tend to have greater anger and engage in more individual rumination. Of course, cross-sectional survey studies cannot determine whether the anger and individual rumination occurred before or after the collective rumination. In all of these studies, collective rumination was associated with greater perceived connection and identification with one's group, mirroring findings from the co-rumination and social sharing literatures.

Conclusion

This chapter reviewed several distinct literatures, all of which focus on the effects of repeated expressions of negative emotions and associated events. Unlike the previous chapters, which reviewed primarily negative consequences of private rumination, expressed rumination has both positive and negative consequences. In this conclusion section, I examine similarities and differences between the various types of expressed rumination, as well as potential mechanisms of its effects.

First, there are some striking similarities with interpersonal outcomes. Co-rumination, social sharing, and collective rumination all contribute to perceptions of increased closeness and connection with others. This may occur because sharing feelings with others increases congruent emotions between people, which can increase group identification and/or sense of belonging. Only the co-rumination literature has examined long-term social consequences of repeated expression, finding that it may take a toll on relationships over time. In the short term, however, this kind of expression elicits support and fosters feelings of closeness. These literatures also found that expression in the context of a supportive listener either led to positive psychological outcomes or no negative outcomes.

Co-rumination, expressive writing, and social sharing differ in their conceptualizations, operationalization, and effects on psychological functioning. Rose (2002) defined co-rumination as similar to individual rumination, in that it involves repetitive conversations about the causes and consequences of negative experiences. As is common in clinical psychology, co-rumination is conceptualized primarily as a stable individual difference, and as such it is more often measured as a general tendency rather than manipulated. It is assessed as an activity that people engage in almost every time they see each other, with strong encouragement from each other, and at the exclusion of doing other intended activities. Thus, co-rumination is defined to be repetitive, intrusive, and possibly unintentional. Moreover, the aspects of co-rumination that involve dwelling on negative emotions and speculating about causes and consequences mirror common definitions of individual rumination. Not surprisingly, co-rumination is consistently correlated with individual rumination (Rose, 2002; Rose et al., 2017; Starr, 2015). Similar to individual rumination, co-rumination generally predicts worse psychological functioning, although the effects are small and inconsistent across outcomes.

By contrast, social sharing and expressive writing are conceptualized as intentional coping responses to a negative life event. Accordingly, and reflecting social psychology methodology, the majority of studies on social sharing and expressive writing manipulate these constructs. There is little attention in these literatures to trait-like individual differences. Descriptive research does indicate that social sharing is naturally repetitive, in that people share upsetting events multiple times, with several different people. However, there is no assumption that social sharing or expressive writing reflects general tendencies for repetitive, intrusive, and possibly unintentional expression. This may explain why social sharing and expressive writing are not robustly correlated with individual rumination. Moreover, they demonstrate notably different outcomes than is typical for individual rumination, at least in the long term. Specifically, expressive writing predicts improved psychological and physical functioning, and social sharing contributes to posttraumatic growth and well-being and is generally unrelated to emotional recovery. In a rare experimental comparison, Lyubomirsky, Sousa, and Dickerhoof (2006) contrasted private rumination, expressive writing, and talking about problems. Specifically, college students wrote, talked into a tape recorder, or thought privately (i.e., ruminated) about their worst life experiences for 15 minutes on 3 consecutive days. Both writing and talking about a negative experience led to improved life satisfaction, mental health, and social functioning and fewer physical health symptoms 4 weeks later, compared to private rumination.

What is it about expressive writing and social sharing that contributes to better psychological functioning, and why is co-rumination related, albeit inconsistently, to worse psychological functioning? Fortunately, researchers have shed light on potential mechanisms of expressive writing and social sharing.

First, expression may allow people to gain insight and engage in cognitive reappraisal. Pennebaker (1993) found that participants who benefit the most from expressive writing use increasingly more insight (e.g., consider and know) and causation words (e.g., because, cause, and effect) over the course of their writing. People also report that expressive writing helps them make sense of an event, provides meaning, and makes them feel that they want to discuss it with others (Guastella & Dadds, 2006). Similarly, expressive writing about traumatic events leads to a decrease in negative appraisals of the event (e.g., uncontrollability, threat, and stressfulness), as well as decreased avoidance (Páez, Velasco, & González, 1999; Park & Blumberg, 2002). Interestingly, the content of expressive writing progresses over subsequent sessions, such that essays become less focused on the event and the past and less traumatic (Guastella & Dadds, 2006). Instead, people's writing becomes more insightful, positive, present- and future-oriented, and focused on finding benefit and reappraising the negative event. In-person interviews of men who had lost partners to HIV indicated that second interviews (e.g., 4 weeks, as opposed to 2 weeks, after the death) were less focused on death and on the past, more positive, and contained more insight words (Pennebaker, Mayne, & Francis, 1997). Thus, the increased insight and positivity seen in expressive writing was mirrored in verbal expressions to another individual.

Expression may also provide an opportunity for exposure and habituation. Repeatedly describing and confronting a negative experience may lead to a decrease of associated thoughts and feelings, either through extinction and/or by providing increased self-efficacy in one's ability to confront difficult experiences (Sloan & Marx, 2004). In support of this mechanism, more frequent (e.g., at least 3 sessions) and prolonged (e.g., more than 15 minutes) expressive writing is associated with better psychological outcomes (Frattaroli, 2006). Moreover, distress and level of emotionality during expressive writing decrease during each successive writing session (Guastella & Dadds, 2006). Three sessions of expressive writing about the same traumatic experience leads to better outcomes than writing about a different experience in each session (Sloan, Marx, & Epstein, 2005). These results suggest that it is the repetitive nature of expressive writing that leads to better psychological outcomes.

Verbal expression requires that people make their thoughts and feelings more concrete and organized, so that they can communicate effectively (Pennebaker & Beall, 1986). Unlike a stream of consciousness, which can lack precision and coherence, writing and talking require creating some kind of narrative. This process of providing structure and labels to upsetting events may promote emotional processing (Lyubomirsky et al., 2006). For instance, putting feelings into words decreases the subjective intensity of the emotions (Lieberman, Inagaki, Tabibnia, & Crockett, 2011). In addition, expressive writing that instructs participants to create a narrative of an upsetting event is associated with less functional impairment resulting from physical symptoms than is writing in a fragmented manner (Smyth, True, & Souto, 2001). Finally, support for this mechanism comes from extensive work on the benefits of concrete processing, such as improved social problem solving, reduced intrusive thoughts, less negative self-evaluation, and fewer psychological symptoms (see Chapter 10: Cognitive behavioral therapies).

Similarly, putting affective responses into words in order to share them forces individuals to label their emotions, an important component of emotion regulation that may foster adaptive coping (Zaki & Williams, 2013). If social sharing also involves naming and assessing the causes of one's emotional response, this appraisal process may further facilitate coping. Other researchers argue that expression allows people to observe themselves experiencing, expressing, and controlling their emotions (Lepore et al., 2002). This may provide people with increased sense of self-efficacy in coping with difficult emotions, which might contribute to less negative appraisals of future stressful events. In fact, one study found that co-rumination with a friend was associated with better self-regulation in response to both anger and sadness, even though it was also related to more depressive symptoms (Criss et al., 2016). The authors speculated that sharing problems with friends may provide a safe context for expressing negative emotions, leading to more effective self-management. Thus, expression may increase people's capacity for emotion regulation.

Finally, some authors have questioned whether expressive writing and social sharing are beneficial because they involve catharsis, or emotional release. The modern idea that catharsis is helpful dates to Freud, who proposed that repressed and unexpressed negative emotions build up and cause psychosomatic symptoms, the treatment for which requires the expression of negative emotions. This idea has permeated Western culture so much that many laypeople would agree that merely talking about problems dissolves their emotional impact (Scheff, 2007). However, existing research does not generally support the benefits of catharsis. For instance, venting anger actually increases, rather than decreasing, aggression (Lohr, Olatunji, Baumeister, & Bushman, 2007). In addition, therapeutic evidence about the emotional consequences of talking about traumatic events suggests that it can lead to emotional distress (Lilienfeld, 2007). Even based on the literature presented in this chapter, the evidence for catharsis is mixed. In the moment, expressive writing generally leads to more negative emotions, whereas social sharing contributes to immediate emotional relief for anger but not necessary sadness. Thus, there is not sufficient evidence to suggest that emotional release is a mechanism for the beneficial effects of expressive writing and social sharing.

In sum, expressive writing and social sharing may contribute to better psychological functioning because they engender insight and cognitive reappraisal, provide opportunities for exposure and habituation, require the creation of more concrete narratives, and foster improved emotion regulation. There is no evidence that these changes in thinking patterns over time occur with private rumination. Moreover, writing or talking with others about a discrete upsetting event may lead to benefits precisely because they constitute intentional and active efforts to cope. In fact, it is possible that expressive writing and social sharing change the nature and content of private rumination, such that it becomes like the deliberate rumination (i.e., controlled and reflective repetitive thoughts focused on making sense of an event) studied by PTSD researchers (see Chapter 2: Rumination and anxiety-related disorders). Thus, expressing ruminative thoughts through intentional writing or social sharing may gradually shift the nature and content of internal rumination, such that actually it becomes constructive. This seems like an important possibility for future research to examine.

How might these mechanisms apply to co-rumination? There is no reason to think that co-rumination does not offer opportunities for exposure, increased concreteness, and improved emotion regulation. At the same time, it is possible that co-rumination fosters getting stuck in continued negativity. Because co-rumination involves focusing on negative feelings and encouragement of problem-talk by the listener, it may prevent people from changing their thinking over time to become more insightful, positive, and focused on finding benefit. It is worth noting that the co-rumination questionnaire assesses both insight-oriented concepts (e.g., speculating about causes and the nature of the problem itself) and negative appraisals (Rose, 2002). Because the measure is scored as a unidimensional construct, however, researchers may be missing opposing effects of these two facets of co-rumination. In one study that separated these facets, cognitive speculation was unrelated to psychological distress, whereas focusing on the negative was positively associated with psychological distress (Rose et al., 2017). Future studies should examine these facets separately and explore whether the exact content of co-rumination changes with repeated conversations. If not, it suggests that there is something about co-rumination, versus social sharing, that keeps people stuck in unhelpful discussions. One possibility is that people who have strong tendencies to repeatedly discuss problems with others, particularly if they dwell on negative emotions, may be using co-rumination less as an intentional coping strategy and more as an uncontrolled reaction to intolerable emotions. Co-rumination might even function as a passive form of behavioral avoidance.

Finally, I want to note that these literatures address different types of potential moderators. The co-rumination literature has examined whether the specific person one shares with (e.g., friend, parent, and romantic partner) and the specific problem discussed (e.g., social vs nonsocial) influence outcomes. This literature also suggests that important gender differences may exist in the nature and content of expression. The social sharing literature has focused on the specific nature of the listener response, such as whether the response is more emotionally supportive or fosters cognitive reappraisal. Each literature might benefit from exploring some of these potential moderators. Clearly, more research is needed to better understand in what circumstances and for whom repeated expression of negative experiences is helpful versus maladaptive.

References

Afifi, T., Afifi, W., Merrill, A. F., Denes, A., & Davis, S. (2013). "You need to stop talking about this!": Verbal rumination and the costs of social support. *Human Communication Research, 39*(4), 395–421. Available from https://doi.org/10.1111/hcre.12012.

Arroyo, A., & Andersen, K. (2016). The relationship between mother-daughter self-objectification: Identifying direct, indirect, and conditional direct effects. *Sex Roles, 74*(5), 231–241. Available from https://doi.org/10.1007/s11199-015-0554-1.

Arroyo, A., Segrin, C., Harwood, J., & Bonito, J. A. (2017). Co-rumination of fat talk and weight control practices: An application of confirmation theory. *Health Communication, 32*(4), 438–450. Available from https://doi.org/10.1080/10410236.2016.1140263.

Baranik, L. E., Wang, M., Gong, Y., & Shi, J. (2014). Customer mistreatment, employee health, and job performance: Cognitive rumination and social sharing as mediating mechanisms. *Journal of Management, 43*(4), 1261–1282. Available from https://doi.org/10.1177/0149206314550995.

Barstead, M. G., Bouchard, L. C., & Shih, J. H. (2013). Understanding gender differences in co-rumination and confidant choice in young adults. *Journal of Social and Clinical Psychology, 32*(7), 791–808. Available from https://doi.org/10.1521/jscp.2013.32.7.791.

Bastin, M., Mezulis, A., Ahles, J., Raes, F., & Bijttebier, P. (2015). Moderating effects of brooding and co-rumination on the relationship between stress and depressive symptoms in early adolescence: A multi-wave study. *Journal of Abnormal Child Psychology, 43*(4), 607–618. Available from https://doi.org/10.1007/s10802-014-9912-7.

Bellehumeur, C. R., Laplante, J., Lagace, M., & Rodrigue, V. (2011). Ingroup contact, collective memory and social identity of catholic youth ministers: The importance of remembering past events. *Journal of Psychology and Christianity, 30*(3), 196. Retrieved from <https://search.proquest.com/docview/911809240>.

Borders, A. (2017, November). *Collective rumination in response to perceived ethnic minority discrimination*. Paper presented at the annual convention of the Association of Behavioral and Cognitive Therapies, San Diego, CA.

Borders, A. (2018, November). *Discussing shared grievances to reduce individual rumination and improve negative mood and closeness with others*. Paper presented at the annual convention of the Association of Behavioral and Cognitive Therapies, Washington, D.C.

Boren, J. P. (2014). The relationships between co-rumination, social support, stress, and burnout among working adults. *Management Communication Quarterly, 28*(1), 3–25. Available from https://doi.org/10.1177/0893318913509283.

Brans, K., Van Mechelen, I., Rimé, B., & Verduyn, P. (2013). The relation between social sharing and the duration of emotional experience. *Cognition and Emotion, 27*(6), 1023–1041. Available from https://doi.org/10.1080/02699931.2012.762758.

Brans, K., Van Mechelen, I., Rimé, B., & Verduyn, P. (2014). To share, or not to share? Examining the emotional consequences of social sharing in the case of anger and sadness. *Emotion (Washington, DC), 14*(6), 1062–1071. Available from https://doi.org/10.1037/a0037604.

Byrd-Craven, J., Geary, D. C., Rose, A. J., & Ponzi, D. (2008). Co-ruminating increases stress hormone levels in women. *Hormones and Behavior, 53*(3), 489–492. Available from https://doi.org/10.1016/j.yhbeh.2007.12.002.

Byrd-Craven, J., Granger, D. A., & Auer, B. J. (2010). Stress reactivity to co-rumination in young women's friendships: Cortisol, alpha-amylase, and negative affect focus. *Journal of Social and Personal Relationships*, *28*(4), 469–487. Available from https://doi.org/10.1177/0265407510382319.

Calmes, C., & Roberts, J. (2008). Rumination in interpersonal relationships: Does co-rumination explain gender differences in emotional distress and relationship satisfaction among college students? *Cognitive Therapy and Research*, *32*(4), 577–590. Available from https://doi.org/10.1007/s10608-008-9200-3.

Cantisano, N., Rimé, B., & Teresa Munoz Sastre, M. (2015). The importance of quality over in quantity in the social sharing of emotions (SSE) in people living with HIV/AIDS. *Psychology, Health & Medicine*, *20*(1), 103–113. Available from https://doi.org/10.1080/13548506.2014.901544.

Christophe, V., Delelis, G., Antoine, P., & Nandrino, J. (2008). Motives for secondary social sharing of emotions. *Psychological Reports*, *103*(1), 11–22. Available from https://doi.org/10.2466/PR0.103.5.11-22.

Christophe, V., & Rimé, B. (1997). Exposure to the social sharing of emotion: Emotional impact, listener responses and secondary social sharing. *European Journal of Social Psychology*, *27*(1), 37–54. Available from https://doi.org/AID-EJSP806 > 3.3.CO;2-T.

Ciesla, J., Dickson, K., Anderson, N., & Neal, D. (2011). Negative repetitive thought and college drinking: Angry rumination, depressive rumination, co-rumination, and worry. *Cognitive Therapy and Research*, *35*(2), 142–150. Available from https://doi.org/10.1007/s10608-011-9355-1.

Collins, N. L., & Miller, L. C. (1994). Self-disclosure and liking: A meta-analytic review. *Psychological Bulletin*, *116*(3), 457. Retrieved from <https://search.proquest.com/docview/1296934433>.

Coman, A., Brown, A. D., Koppel, J., & Hirst, W. (2009). Collective memory from a psychological perspective. *International Journal of Politics, Culture, and Society*, *22*(2), 125–141. Available from https://doi.org/10.1007/s10767-009-9057-9.

Criss, M. M., Houltberg, B. J., Cui, L., Bosler, C. D., Morris, A. S., & Silk, J. S. (2016). Direct and indirect links between peer factors and adolescent adjustment difficulties. *Journal of Applied Developmental Psychology*, *43*, 83–90. Available from https://doi.org/10.1016/j.appdev.2016.01.002.

Curci, A., & Bellelli, G. (2004). Cognitive and social consequences of exposure to emotional narratives: Two studies on secondary social sharing of emotions. *Cognition & Emotion*, *18*(7), 881–900. Available from https://doi.org/10.1080/02699930341000347.

Curci, A., & Rimé, B. (2012). The temporal evolution of social sharing of emotions and its consequences on emotional recovery: A longitudinal study. *Emotion (Washington, DC)*, *12*(6), 1404–1414. Available from https://doi.org/10.1037/a0028651.

Dam, A., Roelofs, J., & Muris, P. (2014). Correlates of co-rumination in non-clinical adolescents. *Journal of Child and Family Studies*, *23*(3), 521–526. Available from https://doi.org/10.1007/s10826-012-9711-0.

Davidson, C. L., Grant, D. M., Byrd-Craven, J., Mills, A. C., Judah, M. R., & Lechner, W. V. (2014). Psychometric properties of the co-rumination questionnaire. *Personality and Individual Differences*, *70*, 171–175. Available from https://doi.org/10.1016/j.paid.2014.07.002.

Delelis, G., & Christophe, V. (2016). Motives for the acceptance of the social sharing of positive and negative emotions and perceived motives of the narrator for sharing the emotional episode. *International Review of Social Psychology*, *29*(1), 99. Available from https://doi.org/10.5334/irsp.4.

Denson, T. F. (2013). The multiple systems model of angry rumination. *Personality and Social Psychology Review*, *17*(2), 103–123. Available from https://doi.org/10.1177/1088868312467086.

Duprez, C., Christophe, V., Rimé, B., Congard, A., & Antoine, P. (2015). Motives for the social sharing of an emotional experience. *Journal of Social and Personal Relationships, 32* (6), 757–787. Available from https://doi.org/10.1177/0265407514548393.

Finkenauer, C., & Rimé, B. (1998). Socially shared emotional experiences vs. emotional experiences kept secret: Differential characteristics and consequences. *Journal of Social and Clinical Psychology, 17*(3), 295–318. Available from https://doi.org/10.1521/jscp.1998.17.3.295.

Frattaroli, J. (2006). Experimental disclosure and its moderators. *Psychological Bulletin, 132* (6), 823–865. Available from https://doi.org/10.1037/0033-2909.132.6.823.

Garcia, F. E., Cova, F., Rincon, P., Vazquez, C., & Paez, D. (2016). Coping, rumination and posttraumatic growth in people affected by an earthquake/afrontamiento, rumiacion y crecimiento postraumatico en personas afectadas por un terremoto. *Psicothema, 28*(1), 59. Available from https://doi.org/10.7334/psicothema2015.100.

Gortner, E., Rude, S. S., & Pennebaker, J. W. (2006). Benefits of expressive writing in lowering rumination and depressive symptoms. *Behavior Therapy, 37*(3), 292–303. Available from https://doi.org/10.1016/j.beth.2006.01.004.

Guarneri-White, M. E., Jensen-Campbell, L. A., & Knack, J. M. (2015). Is co-ruminating with friends related to health problems in victimized adolescents? *Journal of Adolescence, 39*, 15–26. Available from https://doi.org/10.1016/j.adolescence.2014.11.004.

Guassi Moreira, J., Miernicki, M., & Telzer, E. (2016). Relationship quality buffers association between co-rumination and depressive symptoms among first year college students. *Journal of Youth and Adolescence, 45*(3), 484–493. Available from https://doi.org/10.1007/s10964-015-0396-8.

Guastella, A., & Dadds, M. (2006). Cognitive-behavioral models of emotional writing: A validation study. *Cognitive Therapy and Research, 30*(3), 397–414. Available from https://doi.org/10.1007/s10608-006-9045-6.

Haggard, D. L., Robert, C., & Rose, A. J. (2011). Co-rumination in the workplace. *Journal of Business and Psychology, 26*(1), 27–40. Retrieved from <http://www.econis.eu/PPNSET?PPN=657043923>.

Hankin, B. L., Stone, L., & Ann Wright, P. (2010). Co-rumination, interpersonal stress generation, and internalizing symptoms: Accumulating effects and transactional influences in a multiwave study of adolescents. *Development and Psychopathology, 22*(1), 217–235. Available from https://doi.org/10.1017/S0954579409990368.

Harber, K. D., & Cohen, D. J. (2005). The emotional broadcaster theory of social sharing. *Journal of Language and Social Psychology, 24*(4), 382–400. Available from https://doi.org/10.1177/0261927X05281426.

Harber, K. D., Podolski, P., & Dyer, L. (2014). Hearing stories that violate expectations leads to emotional broadcasting. *Journal of Language and Social Psychology, 33*(1), 5–28. Available from https://doi.org/10.1177/0261927X13502793.

Hirst, W., & Manier, D. (2008). Towards a psychology of collective memory. *Memory, 16*(3), 183–200. Available from https://doi.org/10.1080/09658210701811912.

Keshishian, A. C., Watkins, M. A., & Otto, M. W. (2016). Clicking away at co-rumination: Co-rumination correlates across different modalities of communication. *Cognitive Behaviour Therapy, 45*(6), 473–478. Available from https://doi.org/10.1080/16506073.2016.1201848.

Klein, K., & Boals, A. (2001). Expressive writing can increase working memory capacity. *Journal of Experimental Psychology: General, 130*(3), 520–533. Available from https://doi.org/10.1037/0096-3445.130.3.520.

Latina, D., Giannotta, F., & Rabaglietti, E. (2015). Do friends' co-rumination and communication with parents prevent depressed adolescents from self-harm? *Journal of Applied Developmental Psychology, 41*, 120–128. Available from https://doi.org/10.1016/j.appdev.2015.10.001.

Lentz, C. L., Glenwick, D. S., & Kim, S. (2016). The relationship of coping style and ethnicity/culture to co-rumination in adolescents. *Journal of Social and Clinical Psychology, 35* (2), 171–180. Available from https://doi.org/10.1521/jscp.2016.35.2.171.

Lepore, S. J. (1997). Expressive writing moderates the relation between intrusive thoughts and depressive symptoms. *Journal of Personality and Social Psychology, 73*(5), 1030–1037. Available from https://doi.org/10.1037/0022-3514.73.5.1030.

Lepore, S. J., Fernandez-Berrocal, P., Ragan, J., & Ramos, N. (2004). It's not that bad: Social challenges to emotional disclosure enhance adjustment to stress. *Anxiety, Stress & Coping, 17*(4), 341–361. Available from https://doi.org/10.1080/10615800412331318625.

Lepore, S. J., Greenberg, M. A., Bruno, M., & Smyth, J. M. (2002). *Expressive writing and health: Self-regulation of emotion-related experience, physiology, and behavior. The writing cure: How expressive writing promotes health and emotional well-being* (pp. 99–117). Washington, DC: American Psychological Association. Available from https://doi.org/10.1037/10451-005. Retrieved from <https://search.proquest.com/docview/614159593>.

Lieberman, M. D., Inagaki, T. K., Tabibnia, G., & Crockett, M. J. (2011). Subjective responses to emotional stimuli during labeling, reappraisal, and distraction. *Emotion (Washington, DC), 11*(3), 468–480. Available from https://doi.org/10.1037/a0023503.

Lilienfeld, S. O. (2007). Psychological treatments that cause harm. *Perspectives on Psychological Science, 2*(1), 53–70. Available from https://doi.org/10.1111/j.1745-6916.2007.00029.x.

Lohr, J. M., Olatunji, B. O., Baumeister, R. F., & Bushman, B. J. (2007). The psychology of anger venting and empirically supported alternatives that do no harm. *The Scientific Review of Mental Health Practice: Objective Investigations of Controversial and Unorthodox Claims in Clinical Psychology, Psychiatry, and Social Work, 5*(1), 53–64.

Luminet, O., Bouts, P., Delie, F., Manstead, A. S. R., & Rimé, B. (2000). Social sharing of emotion following exposure to a negatively valenced situation. *Cognition & Emotion, 14* (5), 661–688. Available from https://doi.org/10.1080/026999300501176666.

Lyubomirsky, S., Sousa, L., & Dickerhoof, R. (2006). The costs and benefits of writing, talking, and thinking about life's triumphs and defeats. *Journal of Personality and Social Psychology, 90*(4), 692–708. Available from https://doi.org/10.1037/0022-3514.90.4.692.

Maestas, K., & Rude, S. (2012). The benefits of expressive writing on autobiographical memory specificity: A randomized controlled trial. *Cognitive Therapy and Research, 36*(3), 234–246. Available from https://doi.org/10.1007/s10608-011-9358-y.

McCance, A. S., Nye, C. D., Wang, L., Jones, K. S., & Chiu, C. (2013). Alleviating the burden of emotional labor. *Journal of Management, 39*(2), 392–415. Available from https://doi.org/10.1177/0149206310383909.

Murdock, K. F., Gorman, S., & Robbins, M. (2015). Co-rumination via cellphone moderates the association of perceived interpersonal stress and psychosocial well-being in emerging adults. *Journal of Adolescence, 38*, 27–37. Available from https://doi.org/10.1016/j.adolescence.2014.10.010.

Nicolai, K., Laney, T., & Mezulis, A. (2013). Different stressors, different strategies, different outcomes: How domain-specific stress responses differentially predict depressive symptoms among adolescents. *Journal of Youth and Adolescence, 42*(8), 1183–1193. Available from https://doi.org/10.1007/s10964-012-9866-4.

Nils, F., & Rimé, B. (2012). Beyond the myth of venting: Social sharing modes determine the benefits of emotional disclosure. *European Journal of Social Psychology, 42*(6), 672–681. Available from https://doi.org/10.1002/ejsp.1880.

Páez, D., Basabe, N., Ubillos, S., & González-Castro, J. L. (2007). Social sharing, participation in demonstrations, emotional climate, and coping with collective violence after the March 11th Madrid bombings. *Journal of Social Issues, 63*(2), 323–337. Available from https://doi.org/10.1111/j.1540-4560.2007.00511.x.

Páez, D., Velasco, C., & González, J. L. (1999). Expressive writing and the role of alexythimia as a dispositional deficit in self-disclosure and psychological health. *Journal of Personality and Social Psychology, 77*(3), 630–641. Available from https://doi.org/10.1037/0022-3514.77.3.630.

Panagopoulou, E., Maes, S., Rimé, B., & Montgomery, A. (2006). Social sharing of emotion in anticipation of cardiac surgery. *Journal of Health Psychology, 11*(5), 809–820. Available from https://doi.org/10.1177/1359105306066644.

Park, C., & Blumberg, C. (2002). Disclosing trauma through writing: Testing the meaning-making hypothesis. *Cognitive Therapy and Research, 26*(5), 597–616. Available from https://doi.org/1020353109229.

Pelletier, P., & Drozda-Senkowska, E. (2016). The Charlie Hebdo terror attack in Paris: Follow-up of French citizens' terrorist threat perception and its aftermath [L'attaque terroriste de Charlie Hebdo à Paris: Evolution temporelle de la perception de la menace terroriste et de ses conséquences auprès des citoyens Français]. *International Review of Social Psychology, 29*(1), 85. Available from https://doi.org/10.5334/irsp.51.

Pennebaker, J. W. (1993). Putting stress into words: Health, linguistic, and therapeutic implications. *Behaviour Research and Therapy, 31*(6), 539–548. Available from https://doi.org/10.1016/0005-7967(93)90105-4.

Pennebaker, J. W., & Beall, S. K. (1986). Confronting a traumatic event: Toward an understanding of inhibition and disease. *Journal of Abnormal Psychology, 95*(3), 274–281. Available from https://doi.org/10.1037/0021-843X.95.3.274.

Pennebaker, J. W., & Harber, K. D. (1993). A social stage model of collective coping: The loma prieta earthquake and the Persian Gulf War. *Journal of Social Issues, 49*(4), 125–145. Available from https://doi.org/10.1111/j.1540-4560.1993.tb01184.x.

Pennebaker, J. W., Mayne, T. J., & Francis, M. E. (1997). Linguistic predictors of adaptive bereavement. *Journal of Personality and Social Psychology, 72*(4), 863–871. Available from https://doi.org/10.1037/0022-3514.72.4.863.

Pruzniak, O., Playter, C., & Borders, A. (2016, March). *An exploratory analysis of collective rumination in response to perceived discrimination.* Paper presented at the annual convention of the Eastern Psychological Association, New York, NY.

Rimé, B. (2007). The social sharing of emotion as an interface between individual and collective processes in the construction of emotional climates. *Journal of Social Issues, 63*(2), 307–322. Available from https://doi.org/10.1111/j.1540-4560.2007.00510.x.

Rimé, B. (2009). Emotion elicits the social sharing of emotion: Theory and empirical review. *Emotion Review, 1*(1), 60–85. Available from https://doi.org/10.1177/1754073908097189.

Rimé, B., Finkenauer, C., Luminet, O., Zech, E., & Philippot, P. (1998). Social sharing of emotion: New evidence and new questions. *European Review of Social Psychology, 9*(1), 145–189. Available from https://doi.org/10.1080/14792779843000072.

Rimé, B., Mesquita, B., Boca, S., & Philippot, P. (1991). Beyond the emotional event: Six studies on the social sharing of emotion. *Cognition and Emotion, 5*(5-6), 435–465. Available from https://doi.org/10.1080/02699939108411052.

Rimé, B., Páez, D., Basabe, N., & Martínez, F. (2010). Social sharing of emotion, post-traumatic growth, and emotional climate: Follow-up of Spanish citizen's response to the collective trauma of March 11th terrorist attacks in Madrid. *European Journal of Social Psychology, 40*(6), 1029–1045. Available from https://doi.org/10.1002/ejsp.700.

Rimé, B., Philippot, P., Boca, S., & Mesquita, B. (1992). Chapter 8: Long-lasting cognitive and social consequences of emotion: Social sharing and rumination. *European Review of Social Psychology, 3*, 225. Retrieved from <https://search.proquest.com/docview/1311997351>.

Rose, A. J. (2002). Co-rumination in the friendships of girls and boys. *Child Development, 73*(6), 1830–1843. Available from https://doi.org/10.1111/1467-8624.00509.

Rose, A. J., Carlson, W., & Waller, E. M. (2007). Prospective associations of co-rumination with friendship and emotional adjustment. *Developmental Psychology, 43*(4), 1019–1031. Available from https://doi.org/10.1037/0012-1649.43.4.1019.

Rose, A. J., Glick, G. C., Smith, R. L., Schwartz-Mette, R. A., & Borowski, S. K. (2017). Co-rumination exacerbates stress generation among adolescents with depressive symptoms. *Journal of Abnormal Child Psychology, 45*(5), 985–995. Available from https://doi.org/10.1007/s10802-016-0205-1.

Rose, A. J., Schwartz-Mette, R. A., Glick, G. C., Smith, R. L., & Luebbe, A. M. (2014). An observational study of co-rumination in adolescent friendships. *Developmental Psychology, 50*(9), 2199–2209. Available from https://doi.org/10.1037/a0037465.

Rudiger, J. A., & Winstead, B. A. (2013). Body talk and body-related co-rumination: Associations with body image, eating attitudes, and psychological adjustment. *Body Image, 10*(4), 462–471. Available from https://doi.org/10.1016/j.bodyim.2013.07.010.

Scheff, T. J. (2007). Catharsis and other heresies: A theory of emotion. *Journal of Social, Evolutionary, and Cultural Psychology, 1*(3), 98–113. Available from https://doi.org/10.1037/h0099826.

Schuster, M. A., Stein, B. D., Jaycox, L. H., Collins, R. L., Marshall, G. N., Elliott, M. N., ... Berry, S. H. (2001). A national survey of stress reactions after the September 11, 2001, terrorist attacks. *The New England Journal of Medicine, 345*(20), 1507–1512. Available from https://doi.org/10.1056/NEJM200111153452024.

Schwartz-Mette, R. A., & Rose, A. J. (2012). Co-rumination mediates contagion of internalizing symptoms within youths' friendships. *Developmental Psychology, 48*(5), 1355–1365. Available from https://doi.org/10.1037/a0027484.

Shapero, B. G., Hankin, B. L., & Barrocas, A. L. (2013). Stress generation and exposure in a multi-wave study of adolescents: Transactional processes and sex differences. *Journal of Social and Clinical Psychology, 32*(9), 989–1012. Available from https://doi.org/10.1521/jscp.2013.32.9.989.

Sloan, D. M., & Marx, B. P. (2004). Taking pen to hand: Evaluating theories underlying the written disclosure paradigm. *Clinical Psychology: Science and Practice, 11*(2), 121–137. Available from https://doi.org/10.1093/clipsy.bph062.

Sloan, D. M., Marx, B. P., & Epstein, E. M. (2005). Further examination of the exposure model underlying the efficacy of written emotional disclosure. *Journal of Consulting and Clinical Psychology, 73*(3), 549–554. Available from https://doi.org/10.1037/0022-006X.73.3.549.

Sloan, D. M., Marx, B. P., Epstein, E. M., & Dobbs, J. L. (2008). Expressive writing buffers against maladaptive rumination. *Emotion, 8*(2), 302–306. Available from https://doi.org/10.1037/1528-3542.8.2.302.

Smith, R. L., & Rose, A. J. (2011). The "cost of caring" in youths' friendships: Considering associations among social perspective taking, co-rumination, and empathetic distress. *Developmental Psychology, 47*(6), 1792. Retrieved from <https://www.ncbi.nlm.nih.gov/pubmed/21895362>.

Smyth, J., True, N., & Souto, J. (2001). Effects of writing about traumatic experiences: The necessity for narrative structuring. *Journal of Social and Clinical Psychology, 20*(2), 161–172. Available from https://doi.org/10.1521/jscp.20.2.161.22266.

Spendelow, J., Simonds, L. M., & Avery, R. E. (2017). *The relationship between co-rumination and internalizing problems: A systematic review and meta-analysis.* Retrieved from <http://epubs.surrey.ac.uk/811973/>.

Starr, L. R. (2015). When support seeking backfires: Co-rumination, excessive reassurance seeking, and depressed mood in the daily lives of young adults. *Journal of Social and Clinical Psychology, 34*(5), 436–457. Available from https://doi.org/10.1521/jscp.2015.34.5.436.

Starr, L. R., & Davila, J. (2009). Clarifying co-rumination: Associations with internalizing symptoms and romantic involvement among adolescent girls. *Journal of Adolescence, 32*(1), 19–37. Available from https://doi.org/10.1016/j.adolescence.2007.12.005.

Stone, L. B., & Gibb, B. E. (2015). Brief report: Preliminary evidence that co-rumination fosters adolescents' depression risk by increasing rumination. *Journal of Adolescence, 38*, 1–4. Available from https://doi.org/10.1016/j.adolescence.2014.10.008.

Stroebe, M., Stroebe, W., Schut, H., Zech, E., & van den Bout, J. (2002). Does disclosure of emotions facilitate recovery from bereavement? Evidence from two prospective studies. *Journal of Consulting and Clinical Psychology, 70*(1), 169–178. Available from https://doi.org/10.1037/0022-006X.70.1.169.

Swearingen, C., Byrd-Craven, J., & Kennison, S. M. (2016). *The relationship between co-rumination and health in young women: Evidence from Facebook communications*.

Tompkins, T. L., Hockett, A. R., Abraibesh, N., & Witt, J. L. (2011). A closer look at co-rumination: Gender, coping, peer functioning and internalizing/externalizing problems. *Journal of Adolescence, 34*(5), 801–811. Available from https://doi.org/10.1016/j.adolescence.2011.02.005.

Waller, E. M., & Rose, A. J. (2010). Adjustment trade-offs of co-rumination in mother–adolescent relationships. *Journal of Adolescence, 33*(3), 487–497. Available from https://doi.org/10.1016/j.adolescence.2009.06.002.

White, M. E., & Shih, J. H. (2012). A daily diary study of co-rumination, stressful life events, and depressed mood in late adolescents. *Journal of Clinical Child & Adolescent Psychology, 41*(5), 598–610. Available from https://doi.org/10.1080/15374416.2012.706518.

Whitton, S. W., & Kuryluk, A. D. (2012). *Intrapersonal moderators of the association between relationship satisfaction and depressive symptoms*. London, England: SAGE Publications. Available from https://doi.org/10.1177/0265407512467749.

Zaki, J., & Williams, W. C. (2013). Interpersonal emotion regulation. *Emotion, 13*(5), 803–810. Available from https://doi.org/10.1037/a0033839.

Zech, E., & Rimé, B. (2005). Is talking about an emotional experience helpful? Effects on emotional recovery and perceived benefits. *Clinical Psychology & Psychotherapy: An International Journal of Theory and Practice*. Available from https://doi.org/10.1002/cpp.460.

SECTION 2

Causes and correlates

CHAPTER

7

Triggers of rumination

Overview

This chapter explores reasons why people ruminate. After first describing the influential control theory of rumination, I explore how rumination can be conceptualized in terms of Lazarus and Folkman's (1984) coping theory. I then examine the empirical evidence showing that various negative emotions trigger rumination. The chapter then explores ways that stressful events trigger rumination, including characteristics of stressors that make rumination more likely, as well as research on three major types of triggers: interpersonal, childhood, and stigma-related stressors.

The assumption of the rumination literatures already reviewed is that people ruminate about something in particular. It might be a negative mood, mental health symptom, perceived physical ailment, interpersonal interaction, feared outcome, upsetting/traumatic event, or merely an unwanted state of being. In fact, it is difficult to understand someone ruminating without something to ruminate about. Perhaps because this assumption seems so obvious, there is much less research on the triggers of rumination than on its consequences. This chapter first describes two theories that propose what types of experiences likely trigger rumination. I then review the existing empirical literature on two main triggers: negative moods and stressors.

Control theory

Control theory proposes that rumination is triggered by perceived discrepancies in goal progress (Carver & Scheier, 1998; Martin & Tesser, 1996). As discussed in an earlier chapter (Chapter 1, Rumination and

DOI: https://doi.org/10.1016/B978-0-12-812545-8.00007-3

© 2020 Elsevier Inc. All rights reserved.

mood disorders), common theories of self-regulation argue that people frequently compare their current and desired states. If the comparison comes up lacking, they may turn their attention inward (i.e., self-focused attention), presumably in order to understand the discrepancy and figure out a way to solve it. Drawing on these theories, Martin and Tesser (1996) asserted that ruminative thoughts reflect people's mental attempts to reduce a perceived discrepancy. Rumination will recur until people have resolved the discrepancy, either by attaining their desired goal or by abandoning their desire for it. An important point of this theory is that rumination occurs in the absence of immediate environmental demands. Thus, a boy who has lost the affection of a girl he loves will find himself thinking about her and trying to understand what went wrong, even while taking a math test or playing a soccer match. This emphasis on unintentional shifts of attention away from current tasks suggests that rumination may not occur in predictable moments, such as immediately after a stressor.

In this theory, rumination can have constructive or unconstructive consequences. If rumination helps to resolve a perceived discrepancy, it may improve mood and other outcomes. For instance, the boy's rumination may involve crafting a plan to win the girl back and then mentally rehearsing his solution, which, if successful, will end the rumination. However, rumination becomes unconstructive if an individual does not make progress in resolving a discrepancy and refuses to abandon the desired goal. In this case, rumination only increases attention to the discrepancy, which in turn worsens mood and maintains the rumination. In our example, if the boy is unsuccessful at winning back his love, then continuing to keep her as the object of his desire will only lead to more wasted mental energy and will prevent his broken heart from mending.

Some evidence supports the idea that rumination occurs in response to unattained goal progress and wasted efforts at achieving a goal. Rumination occurs more when individuals report low levels of goal achievement for a goal that is personally important (Moberly & Watkins, 2010). For instance, in single women, higher commitment to the goal of finding a life partner is associated with greater rumination about being single (Gebhardt, Van Der Doef, Massey, Verhoeven, & Verkuil, 2010). In first-year college students, the less they are able to continue participating in activities that had been important to them before college (i.e., presumably indicating failed goal progress), the more they ruminate (Millar, Tesser, & Millar, 1988). One study asked participants to think about either an unresolved concern that had stressed them out during the past week or a concern that had previously bothered them but was now resolved (Roberts, Watkins, & Wills, 2013). As expected, thinking about an unresolved goal led to more state rumination than did thinking about a resolved goal, but only in participants high in trait rumination. In another study, trait and manipulated depressive rumination was associated with persisting longer in trying to solve unsolvable anagrams, suggesting that ruminators have difficulty disengaging from unsolvable problems (van Randenborgh et al., 2010).

Martin and Tesser (1996) believed that people are most likely to ruminate about goals that are central to their well-being. Thus, discrepancies that are especially threatening to people's sense of self, worldview, and well-being are more likely to trigger rumination. In support of this assumption, the more central a previous stressful life event is to participants' self-identity, the more rumination they report (Allbaugh, Wright, & Folger, 2016; Groleau, Calhoun, Cann, & Tedeschi, 2013). Similarly, greater challenge to core beliefs and worldviews following a trauma predict more rumination (Cann, Calhoun, Tedeschi, & Solomon, 2010; Cann et al., 2011; Danhauer et al., 2013; Lindstrom, Cann, Calhoun, & Tedeschi, 2013; Zhou, Wu, Fu, & An, 2015). In a diary study, negative events that were related to personal goals produced more rumination than did negative events not related to personal goals (Lavallee & Campbell, 1995). Rumination mediated the association between goal relevance and negative affect.

The control theory also emphasizes the hierarchical nature of goals. People pursue lower level goals in order to attain higher level goals. For instance, the high-level (i.e., abstract) goal of being happy is attained when people engage in specific (i.e., concrete) behaviors such as doing meaningful work, raising children, exercising, and talking with good friends. Because higher level goals are often perceived as more central to one's well-being, people are likely to ruminate about high-level, abstract goals (evidence for this assertion is reviewed in Chapter 10: Cognitive behavioral therapies). However, control theory further asserts that people may ruminate about a lower level goal if they perceive the goal as an indication of their inability to achieve a higher level goal. In some experiments, participants attempted to complete unsolvable verbal analogies that they were told assessed general intelligence and predicted future career success (Beckmann, 1994; Koole, Smeets, van Knippenberg, & Dijksterhuis, 1999). Thus, this was a manipulation of failure at a lower level goal that was linked to a higher order goal. This failure feedback led to higher rumination, compared to control groups that were distracted, received no failure feedback, or received information that the analogies did not really assess intelligence. In another experiment, medical students who failed a task supposedly indicating their competence in medical situations next took another "test" that either was related or unrelated to being a doctor (Brunstein & Gollwitzer, 1996). Interestingly, taking a second test that was *unrelated* to being a doctor led to more rumination. In other words, medical students ruminated when they were unable to progress toward an important goal (e.g., becoming a good doctor) by compensating for a related failure.

Some researchers have assessed individual differences in the tendency to *link* failure of lower level goals to the higher level goal of being happy. In one study, the more that participants linked lower level goals (e.g., a romantic relationship, financial security, and ideal weight) with happiness, the more they ruminated and felt unhappy (McIntosh & Martin, 1992). These effects emerged only for lower level goals that people desired but had not attained. Other research confirms that linkers are more likely to engage in rumination and worry (McIntosh, Gillanders, & Rodgers, 2010; McIntosh, Harlow, & Martin, 1995; Verkuil, Brosschot, Gebhardt, & Korrelboom, 2015). These results suggest that there is no necessary association between particular events and the occurrence of rumination. Rather, whether people ruminate in response to an experience (e.g., being late for an appointment) depends on the meaning they assign that experience. If being late for that particular appointment was a one-off occurrence and has no negative consequences, there is little chance of rumination. However, if being late threatens something of value (e.g., a job, relationship, view of one-self as timely, and responsible), it is likely to trigger rumination.

Coping theory

Control theory has some conceptual overlap with Lazarus and Folkman's (1984) theory of stress and coping. These researchers argued that events becomes stressors only when people appraise them as important and difficult to cope with. Specifically, primary appraisals are people's evaluations of an event as potentially threatening to their well-being. This is similar to control theory's emphasis on linking events with threats to higher level goals. The stress and coping theory, however, argues that people make a second appraisal about whether they have the ability to handle the situation. If people do not believe that they have adequate resources to cope with an important event, the event is likely to be perceived as stressful. Thus, the meaning assigned to a situation involves not only its relevance to one's well-being but also whether people believe they can handle it. Following appraisals of events as stressful, individuals engage in coping efforts, or behavioral and cognitive strategies aimed at managing stressors and associated emotions. In line with this theory, rumination constitutes an effort to cope with events that are perceived to be important and difficult to cope with. In control theory terminology, rumination occurs when people are trying to cope with (i.e., reduce) a discrepancy between perceived situational demands and personal resources.

Researchers are not in agreement about what type of coping strategy rumination represents. There are many proposed systems for categorizing coping strategies, which can cause confusion in the field. Lazarus and Folkman (1984) distinguished between problem-focused strategies, aimed at changing a negative situation, and emotion-focused strategies, aimed at managing emotional reactions. Another common distinction is between approach-oriented strategies, or active attempts to manage the situation or associated emotions, and avoidance-oriented strategies, or attempts to withdraw from the threatening situation and emotions (Billings & Moos, 1984). Although rumination seems initially like an emotion-focused strategy, people may hope that it helps them come up with a solution or response to a negative situation. Similarly, rumination has been explained as both an approach and avoidance strategy (e.g., Connor-Smith, Compas, Wadsworth, Harding Thomsen, & Saltzman, 2000). Some researchers argued that coping strategies should instead be categorized by type of action, rather than by function (e.g., problem- vs emotion-focused) or topology (e.g., approach vs avoidance) (Skinner, Edge, Altman, & Sherwood, 2003). Specifically, they proposed that rumination constitutes its own type of coping strategy, distinct from the strategies of problem solving, support seeking, escape, distraction, and cognitive reframing. Until researchers agree on a single system for categorizing coping strategies, this approach of treating rumination as a unique coping strategy perhaps makes the most sense.

Another point that researchers differ on is whether rumination—and coping in general—is best conceptualized as a mediator or moderator of the clinical effects of stressors. Lazarus and Folkman (1984) asserted that rumination is a mechanism between stressors and subsequent outcomes. In other words, stressors cause people to activate coping strategies such as rumination, which in turn influence psychological functioning. By contrast, a moderation model proposes that individuals who possess poor coping skills experience more difficulty when stressors occur in their lives (e.g., Cooper, Agocha, & Sheldon, 2000). Specifically, although stressors are difficult for most people, they are especially challenging for people who have tendencies to ruminate. Of course, the truth is probably that both models are correct: specific stressors are more likely to activate rumination for people who already have ruminative tendencies. As we will see later, few studies test both moderation and mediation.

Negative emotions

One of the basic assumptions about rumination is that it occurs in response to negative emotions. Many of the most common measures of rumination assume a triggering negative emotion, such as sadness, anxiety, or anger. In the response style theory, for example,

Nolen-Hoeksema (1991) proposed that depressive rumination focuses on a negative emotional state rather than a negative life event, because depressed moods do not necessarily have a clear external trigger. In terms of control theory, experiencing negative emotions may trigger a perceived discrepancy between how people currently feel and how they want to feel (Martin & Tesser, 1996). Control theory also argues that negative moods can make people more likely to perceive that they are failing in their goal progress. In addition, persistent negative moods may make people more likely to stop pursing desired goals, which leaves a perceived discrepancy unresolved (Watkins, 2008). Thus, negative moods may directly contribute to a perceived discrepancy, increase the perception of failure at goal progress, and prevent discrepancies from being resolved, all of which will lead to rumination.

Empirical evidence supports the theoretical argument that negative emotions trigger rumination. Some studies used experience sampling methodology to assess state rumination and general negative affect several times a day. Even controlling for trait rumination, negative affect predicted greater rumination at the next time point, on average 90 minutes later (Moberly & Watkins, 2008a,b; Moberly & Watkins, 2010). However, negative affect did not predict state rumination the next day (Kashdan, Young, & McKnight, 2012). Perhaps the direct effect of negative mood on rumination only lasts a certain amount of time (e.g., 90 minutes but not 24 hours). It is also possible that specific negative moods are more or less likely to elicit rumination.

Sad and anxious moods and symptoms predict greater subsequent rumination. For instance, depressive symptoms predict greater depressive rumination 6 months to 3 years later (Huffziger, Reinhard, & Kuehner, 2009; Nolen-Hoeksema, Stice, Wade, & Bohon, 2007). The effect of sad mood on rumination may be particularly robust for depressed and formerly depressed individuals (Huffziger et al., 2009; Ingram & Wisnicki, 1999). In the social anxiety literature, anxiety about an upcoming speech and fear of negative evaluation following social events predict greater anticipatory and post-event rumination, respectively (Fehm, Schneider, & Hoyer, 2007; Penney & Abbott, 2015). Depressive and anxious symptoms are also associated with greater angry rumination 5 years later (Izadpanah, Schumacher, & Barnow, 2017).

Less research has focused specifically on anger as a triggering emotion. In an experience-sampling study, college students reported on their state rumination and angry mood several times a day for a week (Borders & Lu, 2017). Controlling for trait anger and rumination, state anger did not uniquely predict changes in state rumination several hours later. Instead, anger only indirectly predicted subsequent rumination, via its effect on concurrent rumination. Again, perhaps anger by itself does not last 3–4 hours to directly influence subsequent rumination. In another study, participants described a situation in which they had felt either anger or revenge because of another person's behavior toward them (Elshout, Nelissen, & van Beest, 2015). Events characterized by vengefulness were associated with more rumination than were events characterized by anger. Future research might further explore the triggering effect of feelings of revenge on rumination.

Interestingly, the bulk of research linking emotions to subsequent rumination focuses on the self-conscious emotions, such as shame, guilt, regret, and jealousy. Unlike the more basic emotions of sadness, anxiety, and anger, the self-conscious emotions generally emerge following an evaluative process whereby people compare themselves to others or to a set of standards or goals. Most existing studies examine the unique effects of shame and guilt on rumination. Although both of these emotions occur when people have failed to meet perceived moral standards, important differences exist (e.g., Tangney, 1996). Shame emerges when people interpret an act or event as reflecting a global and enduring defect in themselves. The entire self is evaluated negatively. By contrast, guilt emerges when people judge a specific act or failure to act as wrong, but they stop short of making generalizations to their global self. People who feel guilty may feel bad about a specific behavior but not necessarily about themselves, and a corrective action can often decrease the emotion. Because shame, but not guilt, indicates a rejection of the whole self, it is theorized to more negatively influence psychological and social functioning. In fact, shame is associated with increased depression, anger, and aggression (Orth, Berking, & Burkhardt, 2006; Tilghman-Osborne, Cole, Felton, & Ciesla, 2008). By contrast, guilt is generally associated with greater perspective-taking, empathic concern, desire to make amends, forgiveness-seeking behaviors, and reduced anger and aggression (Joireman, 2004; Riek, Luna, & Schnabelrauch, 2014; Tangney, Wagner, Hill-Barlow, Marschall, & Gramzow, 1996). Thus, many researchers hypothesize that shame in particular triggers rumination.

Empirical evidence tentatively supports this hypothesis. Dispositional shame (i.e., shame proneness) is associated with greater depressive, angry, and general negative rumination, even controlling for guilt (Cheung, Gilbert, & Irons, 2004; Cohen, Wolf, Panter, & Insko, 2011; Gilbert, Cheung, Irons, & McEwan, 2005; Johnson & O'Brien, 2013; Joireman, 2004; Novin & Rieffe, 2015; Peters & Geiger, 2016; Peters, Geiger, Smart, & Baer, 2014). Furthermore, rumination mediates the effect of trait shame on depression, distress, and BPD features (Cohen et al., 2011; Joireman, 2004; Peters et al., 2014). The brooding subscale of depressive rumination also mediates the association between childhood memories of being shamed by others and depressive symptoms in adults (Matos, Pinto-Gouveia, & Costa, 2013). Drawing on these results, a measure of self-critical rumination assesses repetitive thoughts that criticize the self for perceived mistakes, failures, shortcomings, bad habits, or general inadequacy (Smart, Peters, & Baer, 2016). Several of the items reference feeling ashamed, and the measure is strongly associated with shame proneness. In sum, shame is related to several types of rumination, even controlling for the related construct of guilt. Experimental and/or longitudinal studies are needed to determine the directionality of this association.

The association between guilt and rumination is much less clear. Zero-order correlations between these constructs range from small and nonsignificant to positive and significant (Johnson & O'Brien, 2013; Joireman, 2004; Novin & Rieffe, 2015; Smart et al., 2016). When controlling for shame, moreover, guilt is either not uniquely associated with rumination (Orth et al., 2006) or is uniquely associated with *less* depressive and angry rumination (Cohen et al., 2011; Peters & Geiger, 2016). What might explain these mixed findings? Arguing that guilt is a multidimensional construct, some have researchers assessed two components of guilt: fear of impending punishment and need for reparation (Caprara, Manzi, & Perugini, 1992). Fear of punishment, but not need for reparation, is associated with greater rumination. The authors suggest that guilt may have maladaptive or functional outcomes based on whether it is fear-driven or empathy-driven. Thus, the divergent results with guilt and rumination could reflect guilt being a more multifaceted construct than is usually assessed.

Regret is an emotion closely related to guilt. Whereas guilt usually occurs following situations involving harm to someone else, regret is a broader reaction that reflects a wish that a situation had gone differently than it did (Zeelenberg & Breugelmans, 2008). Thus, people may have regrets about something they did to someone else or for a decision they made for their own life. Regrets, particularly when they are unresolved, elicit rumination. For instance, older adults and health care providers who had regrets and did not come to terms with their past actions ruminated about what they wished they had done differently (Courvoisier, Agoritsas, Perneger, Schmidt, & Cullati, 2011; Ingersoll-Dayton & Krause, 2005). Similarly, in young adults who had recently experienced a relationship break-up, general and relationship-specific regret were associated with more rumination about the relationship (Saffrey & Ehrenberg, 2007). In one study, women who had regrets about earlier decisions to follow traditional female roles ruminated more if they did not make career-relevant changes in midlife (Stewart & Vandewater, 1999). In fact, rumination at age 43 mediated the association between unresolved regret (i.e., regret with no career change) at age 37 and physical health at age 48. In another study, caregivers of terminally ill individuals were interviewed before and several times after the death of their loved ones (Torges, Stewart, & Nolen-Hoeksema, 2008). Individuals who had more unresolved regrets 6 months after the loss engaged in more depressive rumination both concurrently and 1 year later.

Very limited research has examined associations between jealousy and rumination. College students who experience jealousy about a current romantic relationship also report greater rumination about that relationship (Carson & Cupach, 2000; Elphinston, Feeney, Noller, Connor, & Fitzgerald, 2013). Similarly, in early adolescents, feelings of jealousy about their best friend correlates with more rumination about problems with friends (Lavallee & Parker, 2009). Unfortunately, all of these studies were cross-sectional, so the directionality between rumination and jealousy could not be determined.

In summary, the existing literature does suggest that various negative moods predict subsequent rumination. This has been shown with depressed and anxious moods, as well as shame, regret, and jealousy. The data are less clear about anger and guilt. The vast majority of the research in this field is longitudinal at best, and most of it is cross-sectional. There are almost no experimental studies confirming that negative emotions contribute to increased rumination. In addition, experience sampling data suggest that the effect of momentary emotions on rumination may be time-limited. This is not surprising, as emotions are fleeting experiences. The next section covers triggers that can be more long-lasting.

Stressors

A previous chapter (Chapter 1, Rumination and mood disorders) reviewed the substantial literature showing that depressive rumination predicts subsequent stressful events, and that the association between stressful events and depressive symptoms is stronger for individuals who are ruminators. Thus, rumination both predicts and interacts with stressors to predict more negative outcomes. But what about the other direction: do stressors trigger rumination? Stress and coping theories argue that events appraised as stressful will trigger rumination as a coping effort. Even within control theory, stressful events can be interpreted as creating a discrepancy between one's current situation and ideal situation. Furthermore, the very concepts of stress-reactive and trauma-related rumination assume that repetitive thinking occurs in response to stressful events or trauma. Fortunately, there is substantial evidence supporting these types of assumptions. I begin by discussing general stress and stressors, but most of the literature focuses on specific kinds of stressful events that trigger rumination.

People who experience more stress in general also report more rumination. Cross-sectional studies have found this association for perceived stress (i.e., global feelings of being stressed), number of major life events (e.g., break up, illness, new baby, and new job) or daily hassles (e.g., unexpected traffic, a printer jam, and time pressure at work), and chronic stress (Abela, Parkinson, Stolow, & Starrs, 2009; Bastin, Mezulis, Ahles, Raes, & Bijttebier, 2015; Cole et al., 2015; Hankin, 2009; Herts, McLaughlin, & Hatzenbuehler, 2012; Marks, Sobanski, & Hine, 2010; McIntosh et al., 2010; Nolen-Hoeksema, Parker, & Larson, 1994; Shapero, Hankin, & Barrocas, 2013; Zawadzki, 2015). In experience sampling studies, the presence and number of recent negative events are also associated with greater state rumination (Ciesla, Reilly, Dickson, Emanuel, & Updegraff, 2012; Moberly & Watkins, 2008b; Ruscio et al., 2015). Moreover, rumination mediates the association between negative events and subsequent negative mood. Similarly, longitudinal research has found that more life stressors in both adolescents and adults predicts increases in depressive rumination several months later (Michl, McLaughlin, Shepherd, & Nolen-Hoeksema, 2013).

One important source of stress that predicts rumination is mental health symptoms. Greater depressive symptoms, bulimia symptoms, and alcohol-related problems predict increases in depressive rumination 6–12 months later in adolescents (Nolen-Hoeksema, Larson, & Grayson, 1999; Nolen-Hoeksema et al., 2007; Willem, Bijttebier, Claes, Vanhalst, & Raes, 2014). As discussed in an earlier chapter (Chapter 2, Rumination and anxiety-related disorders), social anxiety symptoms predict future pre-event rumination. Furthermore, the intrusive symptoms (e.g., nightmares, flashbacks, and intrusive memories) of posttraumatic stress disorder predict greater current and subsequent rumination (Cann et al., 2011; Evans, Ehlers, Mezey, & Clark, 2007; Salsman, Segerstrom, Brechting, Carlson, & Andrykowski, 2009). Given the information presented in the previous several chapters, the association between rumination and mental health symptoms is clearly reciprocal.

A growing literature also examines rumination in response to work-related stress. The construct was initially conceptualized as difficulty "switching off" or unwinding from work, which generally manifests as thinking about work during leisure hours (Cropley, Michalianou, Pravettoni, & Millward, 2012). Sometimes lack of disengagement from work in off-hours may reflect finding work exciting and stimulating. Other times, however, difficulty in turning attention away from work reflects stressors, concerns, and unhappiness at work. Researchers have recently coined the phrase *negative work rumination* to refer to preoccupation with and repetitive thoughts focused on negative work experiences that may extend into nonwork hours (Frone, 2015). A greater number of hours worked is associated with more negative work rumination during nonwork hours (Cropley et al., 2012). In addition, many types of work-related stressors, such as time pressure, conflict with customers, emotionally unpleasant work, heavy workload, role conflict/ambiguity, perceived unfairness, and an imbalance between effort and reward contribute to negative work rumination (Berset, Elfering, Lüthy, Lüthi, &

Semmer, 2011; Fritz & Sonnentag, 2006; Frone, 2015; King & DeLongis, 2014; Long & Christian, 2015; Volmer, Binnewies, Sonnentag, & Niessen, 2012; Wang et al., 2013). Negative work rumination mediates the associations between many of these stressors and negative outcomes such as alcohol use, impaired sleep, and even more negative mood the next morning (Berset et al., 2011; Frone, 2015; Wang et al., 2013).

Importantly, researchers have examined various characteristics of stressors that are particularly likely to trigger rumination. One characteristic that predicts rumination is severity of the stressor. For instance, being physically closer to the epicenter of a large earthquake as well as greater combat exposure are associated with more rumination (Blackburn & Owens, 2016; Taku, Cann, Tedeschi, & Calhoun, 2015). Similarly, indices of assault severity (e.g., more assailants, use of a weapon, longer duration, and injury severity) are associated with more rumination 2 weeks after the assault (Kleim & Ehlers, 2008). In addition to these objective measures, self-rated subjective severity and stressfulness of stressors predict more rumination (Danhauer et al., 2013; Garrison, Kahn, Miller, & Sauer, 2014; Lindstrom et al., 2013; Taku, Kilmer, Cann, Tedeschi, & Calhoun, 2012; Taku et al., 2015; Wu, Zhou, Wu, & An, 2015).

Another commonly studied characteristic is whether stressors are controllable or uncontrollable. Control theory suggests that rumination is particularly likely when people are not making progress toward a goal, perhaps because it is out of their control, or when they have failed to move on from a goal that is unattainable. Similarly, Nolen-Hoeksema et al. (1999) theorized that individuals with low perceived control ruminate in an attempt to find ways to better control their environment and decrease distress. In support of this theory, they found that less mastery predicted more rumination over time. By contrast, perceived control over hypothetical peer rejection was not associated with rumination (Zimmer-Gembeck & Skinner, 2015). Moreover, other studies have found that only controllable interpersonal stressors (e.g., fights with friends or family members), but not uncontrollable interpersonal stressors (e.g., parental divorce), predict subsequent rumination (Calvete, Orue, & Hankin, 2015; Hamilton, Stange, Abramson, & Alloy, 2015). Perhaps people ruminate only about stressors they feel they can do something about, a notion that makes intuitive sense but has not been included in previous theories. Thus, the data are mixed about whether uncontrollability of stressors is more likely to trigger rumination.

A third characteristic of stressors is the degree of uncertainty associated with them. Uncertainty is an uncomfortable experience, often causing anxiety and distress (Bar-Anan, Wilson, & Gilbert, 2009). People may exert substantial cognitive energy into deliberating about and resolving perceived uncertainties. If a basic human goal is to reduce uncertainty, people may ruminate until they feel they have met or have given up on that goal. The association between uncertainty and rumination has been explored in several different literatures. For instance, greater uncertainty about the causes of events in one's life is associated with more rumination and worry, particularly in patients with major depression and generalized anxiety disorder (GAD) (Kircanski, Thompson, Sorenson, Sherdell, & Gotlib, 2015; Tobin, Loxton, & Neighbors, 2014). In palliative care patients and their caregivers, greater uncertainty about the future is associated with greater rumination (Galfin & Watkins, 2012). Similarly, in individuals who identify as sexual minorities, greater uncertainty about their sexual orientation predicts more rumination (Borders, Guillén, & Meyer, 2014). Rumination also arises while waiting for uncertain news, such as the outcome of a medical test, job interview, or test result (Sweeny & Cavanaugh, 2012). In students who had just taken the California bar exam, rumination and corresponding anxiety about the exam were high immediately after the test but hit their highest levels immediately before learning the test results (Sweeny & Andrews, 2014). One last literature linking uncertainty and rumination exists in the field of identity development. Marcia (1966) proposed two dimensions to explain how people approach and resolve identity issues: exploration (i.e., considering diverse identity options) and commitment (i.e., adopting one or more of these alternatives). Over the years, researchers identified a type of exploration called *ruminative exploration,* in which individuals continually obsess over and question their choices (Luyckx, Soenens, Goossens, Beckx, & Wouters, 2008). This ruminative exploration can prevent making a commitment and is associated with a range of negative mental health outcomes (Luyckx et al., 2008; Schwartz et al., 2011).

In sum, certain types of stressors, particularly events that are severe and associated with uncertainty, are most likely to adversely impact mental and physical health. Research is mixed on whether controllable versus uncontrollable stressors predict rumination. In the following sections, I review the literatures on three specific yet overlapping types of stressors: interpersonal stressors, childhood stressors, and stigma-related stressors.

Interpersonal stressors

Stressors involving social evaluation and rejection may be especially likely to trigger rumination. Feeling rejected can challenge individuals' inherent need for social acceptance, as well as their self-identity, setting the stage for a perceived discrepancy between their ideal and actual selves (Zoccola, Dickerson, & Lam, 2012). In addition, negative evaluations can elicit strong feelings of shame. For both of these reasons, negative social evaluation and rejection are hypothesized to trigger rumination. Empirical evidence supports this theory. For instance, daily perceptions of being rejected and criticized by others are associated with greater daily rumination in adults (Starr & Davila, 2012). Experiences of peer victimization, or bullying, also predict increased rumination several months later in adolescents (Barchia & Bussey, 2009; Herts et al., 2012; McLaughlin & Nolen-Hoeksema, 2012). In sexual minority women, lack of peer acceptance of sexuality was associated with greater rumination (Kaufman, Baams, & Dubas, 2017). In some experiments, healthy undergraduates gave a 5-minute speech either in front of an evaluative panel, alone in a room, or in the presence of an inattentive confederate (Zoccola, Dickerson, & Zaldivar, 2008). Compared to the nonevaluative conditions, the social evaluative condition elicited more state rumination immediately, 40 minutes after the speech, later that night, and 3–5 days later (Zoccola et al., 2008, 2012). These effects were mediated by increased shame-related cognition and emotion. Similarly, one experiment that manipulated rejection by having participants play a computer game of toss found that participants who only received the ball twice (out of 30 throws) reported more rumination than participants who received the ball one-third of the time (Zwolinski, 2012). Interestingly, even anticipation of hypothetical rejection triggers rumination. Rejection sensitivity is the tendency to anxiously anticipate, identify experiences as, and overreact to rejection. Cross-sectional and longitudinal studies have shown that rejection sensitivity predicts greater rumination (Orue, Padilla, & Calvete, 2014; Pearson, Watkins, Mullan, & Moberly, 2010; Pearson, Watkins, & Mullan, 2011; Peters et al., 2015; Zimmer-Gembeck, 2015). Thus, both actual and anticipated rejection and social evaluation are likely triggers of rumination.

Poor perceived social support may also contribute to rumination. In recently bereaved individuals, people with low social support ruminated more about the loss, which was in turn associated with more depressive symptoms and grief reactions (Nolen-Hoeksema et al., 1994; van der Houwen, Stroebe, Stroebe, Schut, & Bout, 2010). In addition, stepparents who reported low levels of support from family and friends engaged in more rumination, which in turn predicted greater depressive symptoms 2 years later (DeLongis & Holzman, 2005). Unfortunately, none of these studies assessed the association between social support and rumination at different time points. Thus, the direction of this association is unclear. Some research suggests that rumination predicts worse social support several months later (e.g., Flynn et al., 2010). Therefore, the relationship between poor social support and rumination is likely bidirectional (see Chapter 1: Rumination and mood disorders).

An emerging literature examines engagement in social networking as a potential trigger of rumination. Research is mixed on whether amount of time spent on social networking sites in general and Facebook in particular predicts more rumination (Locatelli, Kluwe, & Bryant, 2012; Tran & Joormann, 2015; but see Davila et al., 2012; Shaw, Timpano, Tran, & Joormann, 2015). Instead, the impact of social networking on well-being seems to depend on the quality of usage (e.g., Davila et al., 2012). For example, the more negative posts that students posted on Facebook, the more rumination they reported (Locatelli et al., 2012). Similarly, more negative and less positive interactions with others on social networking sites were associated with greater rumination (Davila et al., 2012). Furthermore, passive Facebook use (e.g., viewing others' statuses and updates), rather than interactive Facebook use (e.g., chatting with friends, writing on others' wall), was associated with greater rumination (Shaw et al., 2015). The more students made negative social comparisons while on Facebook, the more they ruminated 3 weeks later (Feinstein et al., 2013). In Chinese adolescents, self-reported addiction to social networking sites and mobile phones predicted greater rumination (Liu et al., 2017; Wang et al., 2018). Thus, various negative qualities of social networking appear to predict greater rumination.

Dissolution of and conflict within romantic relationships constitute major interpersonal stressors for many people. In fact, a relationship break-up was an early exemplar of a perceived discrepancy that might trigger rumination because people would be unwilling to let it go (Pyszczynski & Greenberg, 1987). Research does indeed indicate that depressive rumination is especially prominent following a romantic loss (Keller & Nesse, 2006). Among students who had experienced the end of a romantic relationship, those whose partners wanted to end the relationship ruminated more about the relationship than did participants who themselves wanted to end the relationship (Cupach, Spitzberg, Bolingbroke, & Tellitocci, 2011; Davis, Shaver, & Vernon, 2003; Perilloux & Buss, 2008). Greater emotional investment and believing that they were most responsible for maintaining the relationship also predicted more rumination following a break up (Collins & Clark, 1989; Davis et al., 2003). In addition to break-ups, partner behaviors may also be sources of stress. In cohabitating couples, one partner's social withdrawal was associated with greater rumination in the other partner (King & DeLongis, 2014). In people whose romantic partner had committed a relationship transgression (e.g., infidelity, dishonesty, and inconsiderate behavior), greater fear of losing their partner was associated with more rumination about the transgression and about their initial confrontation about the transgression (Roloff, Soule, & Carey, 2001). Building from this literature, researchers created a relational rumination measure that contains three subscales: rumination about a past break-up, rumination about finding a romantic partner, and rumination about current relationship uncertainty (Senkans, McEwan, Skues, & Ogloff, 2015). Interestingly, single participants reported more rumination on all subscales than did partnered participants. Thus, relationship break-ups, dealing with problematic partner behavior, and being single are all potential triggers of rumination.

Some authors theorize that rumination is an integral stage of serial arguments, or repeated conflicts over time about the same topic (Bevan, Finan, & Kaminsky, 2008). Serial arguments are common in long-term intimate relationships, such as between romantic partners or parents and children. Rumination is proposed to occur following episodes of serial arguments, both out of frustration and as an attempt at making sense of the unresolved conflict. In support of this theory, participants in a current romantic relationship who recalled a serial argument reported more rumination than did participants who recalled a nonserial argument (Bevan, Hefner, & Love, 2014). Moreover, higher perceived intensity and unresolvability of on-going serial arguments was associated with more rumination about the conflict (Carr, Schrodt, & Ledbetter, 2012). Interestingly, these researchers theorize that rumination functions to increase motivation to continue serial arguments (Bevan et al., 2008). In control theory terminology, relationship conflict constitutes a perceived discrepancy, and rumination about this discrepancy should continue until the conflict is resolved. Thus, rumination may serve to maintain negative emotions in order to foster continued conflict, with the aim of eventual resolution. In fact, rumination predicted an increased likelihood of an argument episode over several weeks (Carr et al., 2012).

Finally, rumination is likely following the death of a loved one. In fact, a research team has defined grief rumination as repetitive thoughts about the reasons for and meaning of a loss and general loss-related emotions (Eisma et al., 2014). They note that grief rumination likely differs from depressive rumination because bereaved individuals commonly experience a range of negative emotions (e.g., sadness, anxiety, and anger) and focus specifically on making sense of one particular event (e.g., loss of a loved one). Factor analyses of a measure to assess grief rumination yield five factors: rumination about the unfairness of the loss, the meaning and consequences of the loss, negative emotional reactions to the loss, social interactions related to the loss, and counterfactual thoughts about events leading up to the loss (Eisma et al., 2014). Grief rumination is uniquely associated with worse depressive symptoms and complicated grief, even controlling for depressive rumination (Eisma et al., 2014, 2015). Greater centrality of the loss to participants' self-identity is associated with more grief rumination (Boelen, 2012). Difficulty making sense of the loss and poorer social support also predict more rumination (Michael & Snyder, 2005; Nolen-Hoeksema et al., 1994; van der Houwen et al., 2010). I note that some researchers conceptualize grief rumination to be distinct from the concept of *grief work,* which has traditionally involved confronting the reality of the loss and actively processing related emotions (see Stroebe et al., 2007). Healthy grief work promotes effective problem-solving, engaging in instrumental behaviors, and making healthy action plans. Future research will need to empirically test this theorized distinction between maladaptive grief rumination and adaptive grief work.

Childhood stressors

Ruminative tendencies are more likely in adults who experienced childhood maltreatment. Nolen-Hoeksema (2004) suggested that a history of childhood abuse or neglect may predispose children to be more physiologically reactive to stress, which in turn could develop into a focus on negative emotions and subsequent rumination. In support of this theory, people who retrospectively report experiencing childhood physical, emotional, and/or sexual abuse and neglect have greater depressive and angry rumination tendencies (Raes & Hermans, 2008; Sarin & Nolen-Hoeksema, 2010; Spasojević & Alloy, 2002; Zielinski, Borders, & Giancola, 2015). Rumination also mediates the associations between childhood maltreatment and various clinical outcomes such as depressive symptoms, eating/drinking to feel better, and borderline personality features. In adult assault survivors, a history of child abuse was associated with greater rumination about the recent assault (Kleim & Ehlers, 2008). Thus, rumination might be a mechanism by which childhood trauma leads to symptoms of psychopathology in adulthood, even when the symptoms occur in response to recent events (Baer, Peters, Eisenlohr-Moul, Geiger, & Sauer, 2012).

Particular caregiver behaviors can also constitute important stressors for children that influence the later development of ruminative tendencies. In general, caregiving characterized by low care or warmth and high overprotection is associated with poor adjustment in children (Thomasgard & Metz, 1993). In adults, retrospective reports of parental overprotection and lower care are in fact associated with current tendencies for depressive and angry rumination and worry (Donnelly, Renk, & McKinney, 2013; Kertz & Woodruff-Borden, 2011; Mancini, D'Olimpio, Prunetti, Didonna, & Del Genio, 2000; Muris, Meesters, Merckelbach, & Hülsenbeck, 2000; Spasojević & Alloy, 2002; Williams, Harfmann, Ingram, Hagan, & Kramer, 2015; Zielinski et al., 2015). The association between parental rejection in childhood and ruminative tendencies in adulthood may be mediated by greater belief in maladaptive schemas such as emotional deprivation, alienation, shame, and insufficient self-control (Quirk, Wier, Martin, & Christian, 2015). Other research shows that use of corporal punishment, inconsistent parenting, family conflict, and less cohesion are associated with depressive rumination (Donnelly et al., 2013; Young, 2016). Some evidence also suggests that emotionally invalidating childhood environments (e.g., parents telling children they are overreacting) predict greater ruminative tendencies (Sauer-Zavala, Walsh, Eisenlohr-Moul, & Lykins, 2013; but see Cox, Mezulis, & Hyde, 2010). Finally, 11-year-old children whose mothers encouraged them to focus on their feelings (vs active problem-solving) following a stressful task reported more rumination at age 15 (Cox et al., 2010). In sum, children who feel little control over their environment, lack parental warmth or love, experience harsh or inconsistent parenting, and who do not learn active coping strategies may develop tendencies to ruminate in adolescence and adulthood.

Attachment styles are interaction patterns learned from caregivers that influence subsequent social development. Attachment theory proposes that young children's interactions with their primary caregivers influence how they see themselves and others, setting the stage for reactions and behaviors in later adult relationships (Bowlby, 1982). When caregivers are available, loving, and responsive to their children's needs, children develop a secure bond with their caregivers and learn to trust themselves and others. On the flip side, when caregivers do not provide protection or respond sensitively, children may experience distress and develop an insecure bond, or attachment, with their caregivers. Insecure attachments are often characterized on two dimensions: anxiety and avoidance. Attachment anxiety involves fear of being abandoned or rejected by an attachment figure, whereas attachment avoidance involves discomfort being emotionally close with and depending on others. Individuals' childhood attachments with their caregivers provide an internal model that is carried forward into adulthood, influencing how they experience and behave with friends and romantic partners.

When experiencing an attachment threat (e.g., relationship transgression), individuals with anxious attachment styles become preoccupied about whether they are cared for, exaggerate relationship difficulties, and catastrophize negative consequences of the transgression. All of these factors amplify negative emotions, which should contribute to heightened rumination. Empirical evidence supports this hypothesis, although primarily by measuring adult attachment rather than parent–child attachment. For instance, attachment anxiety in undergraduates and adults is associated with greater depressive rumination, pain rumination, grief rumination, and daily rumination about negative events (Burnette, Davis, Green, Worthington, & Bradfield, 2009; Caldwell & Shaver, 2012; Davis et al., 2003; Garrison et al., 2014; Lanciano, Curci, Kafetsios, Elia, & Zammuner, 2012; Saffrey & Ehrenberg, 2007; Tremblay & Sullivan, 2010; van der Houwen et al., 2010). In most of these studies, rumination mediated the links between attachment anxiety and various types of psychological distress. Some research has assessed attachment specifically in romantic relationships. For instance, adolescents who had insecure attachments with their current or former romantic partners engaged in more rumination about the relationship (Margolese, Markiewicz, & Doyle, 2005; Saffrey & Ehrenberg, 2007). In an interesting application, attachment anxiety predicted greater rumination about a secret that participants were keeping from their romantic partners, and this association was mediated by guilt about the secret (Merrill & Afifi, 2015). In some of the few studies assessing parent--child attachment, adolescents and college students with more insecure parental attachment reported more rumination and worry (Brown & Whiteside, 2007; Cabral, Matos, Beyers, & Soenens, 2012; Ruijten, Roelofs, & Rood, 2011). Finally, in children ages 9–12, attachment insecurity with their mothers was associated with more rumination, but only in children who had a genetic risk for dysregulated hypothalamic–pituitary–adrenal activity (Borelli et al., 2017). In sum, adult anxious attachment with romantic partners and with parents predicts greater rumination tendencies.

The literature is unclear about whether avoidant attachment also predicts rumination. When faced with an attachment threat, avoidantly attached people seek physical and psychological distance, downplay the relationship in their minds, and attempt to avoid or suppress their emotional distress. Thus, some researchers hypothesize a nonmeaningful or even negative association between avoidant attachment and rumination. In fact, some studies found close-to-zero associations between these constructs (Burnette et al., 2009; Caldwell & Shaver, 2012; Chung, 2014; Davis et al., 2003; Garrison et al., 2014). On the other hand, avoidantly attached people do not actually succeed at escaping distress and in fact are likely to be depressed and anxious (Lee & Hankin, 2009). Therefore, some researchers hypothesized and in fact found that avoidant attachment correlated with greater rumination (Bond & Borelli, 2017; Lanciano et al., 2012; Merrill & Afifi, 2015; Pearson et al., 2010; van der Houwen et al., 2010).

Interestingly, the inability to correctly perceive and manage emotions and greater depressive symptoms mediated the links between both anxious and avoidant attachment and rumination (Lanciano et al., 2012; Pearson et al., 2010). Thus, it may be that any type of insecure attachment depletes resources available for emotional processing, leading to greater negative affect and rumination. Unfortunately, because all of these studies on attachment and rumination are cross-sectional, and because most of them assess adult attachment, we do not know whether the quality of attachment experienced with primary caregivers at a young age is prospectively associated with rumination. Future research will need to confirm whether childhood insecure attachment actually constitutes a stressor that contributes to later ruminative tendencies.

Stigma-related stressors

An emerging literature explores the associations between stigma-related stressors and rumination in minority populations. Most of the research examines *perceived discrimination,* or the subjective experience of differential treatment of oneself and/or one's group by individuals and social institutions. Because it emphasizes appraisal, perceived discrimination is not limited to objective discriminatory occurrences but also includes more subtle experiences that outside observers might not identify as discrimination. Discrimination by individuals and institutions is a core stressor affecting minority populations, impairing both psychological and physical functioning (Herek, Gillis, & Cogan, 1999; Kessler, Mickelson, & Williams, 1999). In addition to perceptions of external discriminatory events, researchers also study negative beliefs about one's own group, or *internalized stigma.* Endorsing negative societal attitudes about one's self and group creates cognitive dissonance that understandably leads to increased psychological distress. Finally, stigmatized individuals may be perpetually on guard when interacting with majority group members, always vigilant for the possibility of possible prejudice or violence. This *stigma consciousness,* as it is called, constitutes another chronic stressor for minority group members (Meyer, 2003). In sum, because these minority stressors threaten individuals' sense of self, safety, and emotional well-being, researchers hypothesize that they may trigger ruminative thoughts.

This hypothesis has been studied in ethnic minority samples. In a daily diary study (Hatzenbuehler, Nolen-Hoeksema, & Dovidio, 2009), African-American adults reported more depressive rumination on days when they reported more instances of ethnic discrimination (e.g., treated with less courtesy and respect than other people, being called names or insulted, being threatened or harassed, and being avoided). In another study, African-American students at a historically Black university completed questionnaires approximately 6 months after George Zimmerman was prosecuted and acquitted in the fatal shooting of an African-American teenager, Trayvon Martin (Hacker et al., 2016). This shooting and subsequent trial was one of many highly publicized cases in the United States in which race potentially played a role in the killing of African Americans. Participants' prior experiences with ethnic discrimination were associated with more rumination over the past week about the Zimmerman trial, which in turn predicted more negative affect and less willingness to forgive Zimmerman. Similarly, in survey studies with ethnic minority adolescents and young adults, perceived ethnic discrimination is associated with greater depressive and angry rumination, which in turn predict worse clinical outcomes such as depressive symptoms and aggressive tendencies (Borders & Hennebry, 2015; Borders & Liang, 2011; Liang & Molenaar, 2016; Miranda, Tsypes, Gallagher, & Rajappa, 2013; Young, 2016). In one study, the effect of ethnicity-related stressors on angry rumination was mediated by greater beliefs that the world is unjust (Liang & Molenaar, 2016). Interestingly, another study found that angry rumination interacted with perceived discrimination, such that discrimination predicted greater externalizing behaviors only for individuals with high tendencies for angry rumination (Borders & Hennebry, 2015). Thus, it is possible that perceived ethnic discrimination both increases rumination and interacts with rumination to predict worse psychological functioning. Longitudinal and/or experimental studies are needed to determine the directionality of these associations. Moreover, no research has yet examined whether internalized racism or stigma consciousness are also associated with rumination.

Only minimal research has explored the link between stigma-related stressors and rumination in women. In one study with sexual minority women, perceived sexism in the past year as well as internalized sexism were associated with more depressive rumination (Szymanski, Dunn, & Ikizler, 2014). Similarly, in a college sample, women who endorsed more beliefs in traditional roles for women (e.g., women's needs for heterosexual intimacy and dependence on men's protection) reported more depressive rumination (Yoder & Lawrence, 2011). The authors speculated that depressive rumination is a feminine-stereotyped response to emotional distress. However, another possibility is that internalized sexism leads to psychological distress, which in turn contributes to greater rumination. Much more research is needed in this area.

Several studies have examined the association between sexual- and gender-minority stressors and rumination. For instance, among sexual minority (e.g., lesbian, gay, and bisexual) men and women, greater perceived discrimination is associated with more depressive rumination (Hatzenbuehler, Dovidio, Nolen-Hoeksema, & Phills, 2009; Lewis, Mason, Winstead, Gaskins, & Irons, 2016; Lewis, Milletich, Derlega, & Padilla, 2014; Lewis, Milletich, Mason, & Derlega, 2014; Szymanski et al., 2014), as well as rumination specifically about sexual-minority stressors (Galupo & Bauerband, 2016; Wang & Borders, 2017). Similarly, in sexual minority adolescents, perceived microaggressions, or subtle everyday comments such as someone saying "you know how gay people are ..." or "I don't mind gay people, they just shouldn't be so public," predict greater depressive rumination (Kaufman et al., 2017). Internalized homonegativity and stigma consciousness are also associated with greater rumination (Galupo & Bauerband, 2016;

Hatzenbuehler, Dovidio, et al., 2009; Hatzenbuehler, Nolen-Hoeksema, et al., 2009; Lewis et al., 2016; Lewis, Milletich, Derlega, et al., 2014; Lewis, Milletich, Mason, et al., 2014; Szymanski et al., 2014; Wang & Borders, 2017). These studies also found that rumination mediated the associations between sexual-minority stressors and psychological distress, aggressive behaviors, and alcohol-related outcomes. Mechanisms of the effect of stigma-related stressors on rumination include expectations for rejection and difficulties talking to family and friends about sexual identity issues (Lewis, Milletich, Derlega et al., 2014; Lewis, Milletich, Mason et al., 2014; Liao, Kashubeck-West, Weng, & Deitz, 2015). In the sexual minority literature, researchers also study concealment of sexual orientation, which despite being an attempt to avoid stigma can result in intrusive thoughts and psychological distress (Meyer, 2003). Interestingly, perceived need for concealment is associated with greater rumination about sexual-minority stigmas in men but not women (Lewis, Milletich, Derlega, et al., 2014; Lewis, Milletich, Mason, et al., 2014; Wang & Borders, 2017). These results imply that concealment may constitute more of a stressor for sexual minority men than women. In fact, one study found that perceived discrimination was correlated with concealment for sexual minority men but not women, suggesting that discrimination may fuel men's efforts to conceal their sexual orientation (Wang & Borders, 2017). Finally, in the only study to also include transgender participants, greater perceived gender-minority stigma and less gender identity acceptance were associated with more rumination about one's gender identity (Bauerband & Galupo, 2014).

A final question some researchers have asked is whether individuals of minority groups are more likely to engage in rumination. A single study found that sexual minority adolescents reported more tendencies for depressive rumination than did their heterosexual peers (Hatzenbuehler, McLaughlin, & Nolen-Hoeksema, 2008). Limited comparisons of ethnic groups have yield mixed results. For instance, some studies found that African-American and Asian-American individuals reported greater tendencies for depressive rumination than did Caucasian/European Americans (Chang, Tsai, & Sanna, 2010; Lewis et al., 2016). Other studies found no differences in depressive or angry rumination between ethnic minority and White participants (Borders & Liang, 2011; Mason & Lewis, 2016; Miranda et al., 2013). As reviewed in previous chapters, women generally report more tendencies for depressive rumination and worry than do men, although similar gender differences in angry rumination are not observed (see Chapter 1: Rumination and mood disorders, Chapter 2: Rumination and anxiety-related disorders, and Chapter 3: Rumination, anger, and aggression). It is difficult to know how to interpret demographic differences in a cognitive variable like rumination. Any robust differences might reflect the influence of socialization, biology, and/or stressors commonly experienced by members of various minority groups. In addition, differences between demographic groups may mask important differences within these groups. For instance, one study with lesbian women found that lower socioeconomic status was associated with more depressive rumination (Lewis et al., 2016). For these reasons, research examining specific stressors (like those reviewed in this chapter) or other contributing factors to rumination is likely more informative than investigating demographic differences.

Summary

In sum, many kinds of perceived stressors, particularly those that are severe and associated with uncertainty, induce rumination. Martin and Tesser (1996) theorized that rumination is especially likely in response to perceived threats to an individual's sense of self and well-being. The empirical literature supports this in many ways. Specifically, stressors involving inter- and intra-personal threats or losses—whether in childhood (e.g., maltreatment and insecure attachment) or adulthood (e.g., break-ups and work strain) and whether involving close others (e.g., parents, romantic partners, and peers) and/or societal institutions (e.g., perceived stigma and social networking sites)—trigger rumination. The few studies exploring mechanisms of these associations suggest that the self-conscious emotions, in particular (e.g., shame and regret), negative beliefs (e.g., unjust world belief and maladaptive schemas), and difficulty managing negative emotions may mediate the effect of stressors on increased rumination.

Conclusion

In this chapter, I reviewed reasons why people engage in rumination. Other than Nolen-Hoeksema's response styles theory (see Chapter 1: Rumination and mood disorders), control theory (Martin & Tesser, 1996) is arguably the most influential theory in the rumination field. It underpins much of the research reviewed in this book, including the empirical basis behind a promising treatment for rumination (see Chapter 10). The notion that rumination occurs in response to a perceived discrepancy between one's ideal and actual state is one that I return to repeatedly because it can describe so many particular situations. Although many researchers claim that rumination is a type of maladaptive coping strategy, better evidence for how rumination fits into common coping categories and compares with other coping strategies is needed.

As I reviewed here, researchers have primarily examined two types of triggers of rumination: negative emotions and stressors. A few points about this literature are worth highlighting. First, much of the research is cross-sectional and nonexperimental. Longitudinal and experimental studies are sorely needed to examine whether these triggers actually elicit rumination. In addition, researchers should explore whether these triggers contribute to state and/or trait rumination. Some experiences (e.g., a momentary negative mood and sudden stressor) are likely to trigger state rumination, whereas other experiences (e.g., childhood trauma, overprotective parenting, and exposure to pervasive discrimination) may influence both momentary levels of and trait-level tendencies for rumination. Measures of state and trait rumination are only moderately correlated, suggesting that the amount of rumination in any given moment only in part reflects general tendencies (Gianferante et al., 2014; Moberly & Watkins, 2008a; Zoccola et al., 2008).

Finally, I want to note that there is only one chapter in this book on the triggers of rumination, compared to six previous chapters on the consequences of rumination. This state of the literature may reflect psychologists' initial interest in studying rumination as a contributing factor to clinical problems such as depression, anxiety disorders, and aggressive behaviors. In addition, I believe the paucity of strong data on triggers of rumination reflects the assumption that rumination constitutes a stable tendency. However, research evidence demonstrates that any behavior results from a combination of trait-level and context-level factors (Fleeson, 2001). In statistical language, understanding within-person deviations from the mean provides important information that mean-level effects cannot provide. In other words, knowing that someone has tendencies for rumination is perhaps less interesting than understanding when or under what conditions that person actually ruminates. Some fascinating research assessed various qualities of rumination (e.g., valence, purpose, and duration) in several populations (e.g., law students, caregivers, and healthy individuals) five times over 7 months (Roach, Salt, & Segerstrom, 2010). Generalizability analyses indicated that participants' inconsistencies across time and situations consistently accounted for the most variance in rumination qualities. Taken together, therefore, evidence suggests that despite stable tendencies for rumination, individuals exhibit considerable variation in the amount and quality of rumination across contexts. For this reason, researchers should continue to examine triggers of rumination and strive to better incorporate context-level factors into models of rumination.

References

Abela, J. R. Z., Parkinson, C., Stolow, D., & Starrs, C. (2009). A test of the integration of the hopelessness and response styles theories of depression in middle adolescence. *Journal of Clinical Child & Adolescent Psychology, 38*(3), 354–364. Available from https://doi.org/10.1080/15374410902851630.

Allbaugh, L. J., Wright, M. O., & Folger, S. F. (2016). The role of repetitive thought in determining posttraumatic growth and distress following interpersonal trauma. *Anxiety, Stress, & Coping, 29*(1), 21–37. Available from https://doi.org/10.1080/10615806.2015.1015422.

Baer, R. A., Peters, J. R., Eisenlohr-Moul, T. A., Geiger, P. J., & Sauer, S. E. (2012). Emotion-related cognitive processes in borderline personality disorder: A review of the empirical literature. *Clinical Psychology Review, 32*(5), 359–369. Available from https://doi.org/10.1016/j.cpr.2012.03.002.

Bar-Anan, Y., Wilson, T. D., & Gilbert, D. T. (2009). The feeling of uncertainty intensifies affective reactions. *Emotion, 9*(1), 123–127. Available from https://doi.org/10.1037/a0014607.

Barchia, K., & Bussey, K. (2009). The psychological impact of peer victimization: Exploring social-cognitive mediators of depression. *Journal of Adolescence, 33*(5), 615–623. Available from https://doi.org/10.1016/j.adolescence.2009.12.002.

Bastin, M., Mezulis, A., Ahles, J., Raes, F., & Bijttebier, P. (2015). Moderating effects of brooding and co-rumination on the relationship between stress and depressive symptoms in early adolescence: A multi-wave study. *Journal of Abnormal Child Psychology, 43*(4), 607–618. Available from https://doi.org/10.1007/s10802-014-9912-7.

Bauerband, A. L., & Galupo, P. M. (2014). The gender identity reflection and rumination scale: Development and psychometric evaluation. *Journal of Counseling & Development, 92*(2), 219–231. Available from https://doi.org/10.1002/j.1556-6676.2014.00151.x.

Beckmann, J. (1994). Ruminative thought and the deactivation of an intention. *Motivation and Emotion, 18*(4), 317–334. Available from https://doi.org/10.1007/BF02856472.

Berset, M., Elfering, A., Lüthy, S., Lüthi, S., & Semmer, N. K. (2011). Work stressors and impaired sleep: Rumination as a mediator. *Stress and Health, 27*(2), e82. Available from https://doi.org/10.1002/smi.1337.

Bevan, J. L., Finan, A., & Kaminsky, A. (2008). Modeling serial arguments in close relationships: The serial argument process model. *Human Communication Research, 34*(4), 600–624. Available from https://doi.org/10.1111/j.1468-2958.2008.00334.x.

Bevan, J. L., Hefner, V., & Love, A. (2014). An exploration of topics, conflict styles, and rumination in romantic nonserial and serial arguments. *Southern Communication Journal, 79*(4), 347–360. Available from https://doi.org/10.1080/1041794X.2014.918645.

Billings, A. G., & Moos, R. H. (1984). Coping, stress, and social resources among adults with unipolar depression. *Journal of Personality and Social Psychology, 46*(4), 877–891. Available from https://doi.org/10.1037/0022-3514.46.4.877.

Blackburn, L., & Owens, G. P. (2016). Rumination, resilience, and posttraumatic stress disorder symptom severity among veterans of Iraq and Afghanistan. *Journal of Aggression, Maltreatment & Trauma, 25*(2), 197–209. Available from https://doi.org/10.1080/10926771.2015.1107174.

Boelen, P. (2012). Variables mediating the linkage between loss centrality and postloss psychopathology. *The Journal of Nervous and Mental Disease, 200*(9), 801–806. Available from https://doi.org/10.1097/NMD.0b013e318266ba02.

Bond, D. K., & Borelli, J. L. (2017). Maternal attachment insecurity and poorer proficiency savoring memories with their children. *Journal of Social and Personal Relationships, 34*(7), 1007–1030. Available from https://doi.org/10.1177/0265407516664995.

Borders, A., Guillén, L. A., & Meyer, I. H. (2014). Rumination, sexual orientation uncertainty, and psychological distress in sexual minority university students. *The Counseling Psychologist, 42*(4), 497–523. Available from https://doi.org/10.1177/0011000014527002.

Borders, A., & Hennebry, K. A. (2015). Angry rumination moderates the association between perceived ethnic discrimination and risky behaviors. *Personality and Individual Differences, 79*, 81–86. Available from https://doi.org/10.1016/j.paid.2015.01.047.

Borders, A., & Liang, C. T. H. (2011). Rumination partially mediates the associations between perceived ethnic discrimination, emotional distress, and aggression. *Cultural Diversity and Ethnic Minority Psychology, 17*(2), 125–133. Available from https://doi.org/10.1037/a0023357.

Borders, A., & Lu, S. (2017). The bidirectional associations between state anger and rumination and the role of trait mindfulness. *Aggressive Behavior, 43*(4), 342–351. Available from https://doi.org/10.1002/ab.21693.

Borelli, J. L., Smiley, P. A., Rasmussen, H. F., Gómez, A., Seaman, L. C., & Nurmi, E. L. (2017). Interactive effects of attachment and FKBP5 genotype on school-aged children's emotion regulation and depressive symptoms. *Behavioural Brain Research, 325*, 278–289. Available from https://doi.org/10.1016/j.bbr.2016.07.035.

Bowlby, J. (1982). Attachment and loss: Retrospect and prospect. *The American Journal of Orthopsychiatry, 52*(4), 664–678. Available from https://doi.org/10.1111/j.1939-0025.1982.tb01456.x.

Brown, A. M., & Whiteside, S. P. (2007). Relations among perceived parental rearing behaviors, attachment style, and worry in anxious children. *Journal of Anxiety Disorders, 22*(2), 263–272. Available from https://doi.org/10.1016/j.janxdis.2007.02.002.

Brunstein, J. C., & Gollwitzer, P. M. (1996). Effects of failure on subsequent performance. *Journal of Personality and Social Psychology, 70*(2), 395–407. Available from https://doi.org/10.1037/0022-3514.70.2.395.

Burnette, J. L., Davis, D. E., Green, J. D., Worthington, E. L., & Bradfield, E. (2009). Insecure attachment and depressive symptoms: The mediating role of rumination, empathy, and forgiveness. *Personality and Individual Differences, 46*(3), 276–280. Available from https://doi.org/10.1016/j.paid.2008.10.016.

Cabral, J., Matos, P. M., Beyers, W., & Soenens, B. (2012). Attachment, emotion regulation and coping in Portuguese emerging adults: A test of a mediation hypothesis. *The Spanish Journal of Psychology, 15*(3), 1000–1012. Available from https://doi.org/10.5209/rev_SJOP.2012.v15.n3.39391.

Caldwell, J. G., & Shaver, P. R. (2012). Exploring the cognitive-emotional pathways between adult attachment and ego-resiliency. *Individual Differences Research, 10*(3), 141–152.

Calvete, E., Orue, I., & Hankin, B. L. (2015). Cross-lagged associations among ruminative response style, stressors, and depressive symptoms in adolescents. *Journal of Social and Clinical Psychology, 34*(3), 203–220. Available from https://doi.org/10.1521/jscp.2015.34.3.203.

Cann, A., Calhoun, L. G., Tedeschi, R. G., & Solomon, D. T. (2010). Posttraumatic growth and depreciation as independent experiences and predictors of well-being. *Journal of Loss and Trauma, 15*(3), 151–166. Available from https://doi.org/10.1080/15325020903375826.

Cann, A., Calhoun, L. G., Tedeschi, R. G., Triplett, K. N., Vishnevsky, T., & Lindstrom, C. M. (2011). Assessing posttraumatic cognitive processes: The event related rumination inventory. *Anxiety, Stress & Coping, 24*(2), 137–156. Available from https://doi.org/10.1080/10615806.2010.529901.

Caprara, G. V., Manzi, J., & Perugini, M. (1992). Investigating guilt in relation to emotionality and aggression. *Personality and Individual Differences, 13*(5), 519–532. Available from https://doi.org/10.1016/0191-8869(92)90193-S.

Carr, K., Schrodt, P., & Ledbetter, A. M. (2012). Rumination, conflict intensity, and perceived resolvability as predictors of motivation and likelihood of continuing serial arguments. *Western Journal of Communication*, *76*(5), 480–502. Available from https://doi.org/10.1080/10570314.2012.689086.

Carson, C. L., & Cupach, W. R. (2000). Fueling the flames of the green-eyed monster: The role of ruminative thought in reaction to romantic jealousy. *Western Journal of Communication*, *64*(3), 308–329. Available from https://doi.org/10.1080/10570310009374678.

Carver, C. S., & Scheier, M. F. (1998). *On the self-regulation of behavior* (1. publ. ed.). Cambridge [u.a.]: Cambridge Univ. Press.

Chang, E. C., Tsai, W., & Sanna, L. J. (2010). Examining the relations between rumination and adjustment. *Asian American Journal of Psychology*, *1*(1), 46–56. Available from https://doi.org/10.1037/a0018821.

Cheung, M. S.-, Gilbert, P., & Irons, C. (2004). An exploration of shame, social rank and rumination in relation to depression. *Personality and Individual Differences*, *36*(5), 1143–1153. Available from https://doi.org/10.1016/S0191-8869(03)00206-X.

Chung, M. (2014). Pathways between attachment and marital satisfaction: The mediating roles of rumination, empathy, and forgiveness. *Personality and Individual Differences*, *70*, 246–251. Available from https://doi.org/10.1016/j.paid.2014.06.032.

Ciesla, J. A., Reilly, L. C., Dickson, K. S., Emanuel, A. S., & Updegraff, J. A. (2012). Dispositional mindfulness moderates the effects of stress among adolescents: Rumination as a mediator. *Journal of Clinical Child & Adolescent Psychology*, *41*(6), 760–770. Available from https://doi.org/10.1080/15374416.2012.698724.

Cohen, T. R., Wolf, S. T., Panter, A. T., & Insko, C. A. (2011). Introducing the GASP scale. *Journal of Personality and Social Psychology*, *100*(5), 947–966. Available from https://doi.org/10.1037/a0022641.

Cole, A. B., Wingate, L. R., Tucker, R. P., Rhoades-Kerswill, S., O'Keefe, V. M., & Hollingsworth, D. W. (2015). The differential impact of brooding and reflection on the relationship between perceived stress and suicide ideation. *Personality and Individual Differences*, *83*, 170–173. Available from https://doi.org/10.1016/j.paid.2015.04.013.

Collins, J. E., & Clark, L. F. (1989). Responsibility and rumination: The trouble with understanding the dissolution of a relationship. *Social Cognition*, *7*(2), 152–173. Available from https://doi.org/10.1521/soco.1989.7.2.152.

Connor-Smith, J. K., Compas, B. E., Wadsworth, M. E., Harding Thomsen, A., & Saltzman, H. (2000). Responses to stress in adolescence. *Journal of Consulting and Clinical Psychology*, *68*(6), 976–992. Available from https://doi.org/10.1037/0022-006X.68.6.976.

Cooper, M. L., Agocha, V. B., & Sheldon, M. S. (2000). A motivational perspective on risky behaviors: The role of personality and affect regulatory processes. *Journal of Personality*, *68*(6), 1059–1088. Available from https://doi.org/10.1111/1467-6494.00126.

Courvoisier, D. S., Agoritsas, T., Perneger, T. V., Schmidt, R. E., & Cullati, S. (2011). Regrets associated with providing healthcare: Qualitative study of experiences of hospital-based physicians and nurses. *PLoS One*, *6*(8), e23138. Available from https://doi.org/10.1371/journal.pone.0023138.

Cox, S. J., Mezulis, A. H., & Hyde, J. S. (2010). The influence of child gender role and maternal feedback to child stress on the emergence of the gender difference in depressive rumination in adolescence. *Developmental Psychology*, *46*(4), 842–852. Available from https://doi.org/10.1037/a0019813.

Cropley, M., Michalianou, G., Pravettoni, G., & Millward, L. J. (2012). The relation of post-work ruminative thinking with eating behaviour. *Stress and Health*, *28*(1), 23–30. Available from https://doi.org/10.1002/smi.1397.

Cupach, W. R., Spitzberg, B. H., Bolingbroke, C. M., & Tellitocci, B. S. (2011). Persistence of attempts to reconcile a terminated romantic relationship: A partial test of relational goal pursuit theory. *Communication Reports*, *24*(2), 99–115. Available from https://doi.org/10.1080/08934215.2011.613737.

Danhauer, S., Russell, G., Tedeschi, R., Jesse, M., Vishnevsky, T., Daley, K., ... Powell, B. (2013). A longitudinal investigation of posttraumatic growth in adult patients undergoing treatment for acute leukemia. *Journal of Clinical Psychology in Medical Settings, 20*(1), 13–24. Available from https://doi.org/10.1007/s10880-012-9304-5.

Davila, J., Hershenberg, R., Feinstein, B. A., Gorman, K., Bhatia, V., & Starr, L. R. (2012). Frequency and quality of social networking among young adults: Associations with depressive symptoms, rumination, and corumination. *Psychology of Popular Media Culture, 1*(2), 72–86. Available from https://doi.org/10.1037/a0027512.

Davis, D., Shaver, P. R., & Vernon, M. L. (2003). Physical, emotional, and behavioral reactions to breaking up: The roles of gender, age, emotional involvement, and attachment style. *Personality and Social Psychology Bulletin, 29*(7), 871–884. Available from https://doi.org/10.1177/0146167203029007006.

DeLongis, A., & Holtzman, S. (2005). Coping in context: The role of stress, social support, and personality in coping. *Journal of Personality, 73*(6), 1633–1656. Available from https://doi.org/10.1111/j.1467-6494.2005.00361.x.

Donnelly, R., Renk, K., & McKinney, C. (2013). Emerging adults' stress and health: The role of parent behaviors and cognitions. *Child Psychiatry & Human Development, 44*(1), 19–38. Available from https://doi.org/10.1007/s10578-012-0309-y.

Eisma, M. C., Schut, H. A. W., Stroebe, M. S., Boelen, P. A., van den Bout, J., & Stroebe, E. (2015). Adaptive and maladaptive rumination after loss. A three-wave longitudinal study. *British Journal of Clinical Psychology, 54*(2), 163–180. Available from https://doi.org/10.1111/bjc.12067.

Eisma, M. C., Stroebe, M. S., Schut, H. A. W., van den Bout, J., Boelen, P. A., & Stroebe, W. (2014). Development and psychometric evaluation of the Utrecht Grief Rumination Scale. *Journal of Psychopathology and Behavioral Assessment, 36*(1), 165–176. Available from https://doi.org/10.1007/s10862-013-9377-y.

Elphinston, R. A., Feeney, J. A., Noller, P., Connor, J. P., & Fitzgerald, J. (2013). Romantic jealousy and relationship satisfaction: The costs of rumination. *Western Journal of Communication, 77*(3), 293–304. Available from https://doi.org/10.1080/10570314.2013.770161.

Elshout, M., Nelissen, R. M. A., & van Beest, I. (2015). Vengeance is self-focused: Comparing vengeful to anger-driven responses. *Cognition and Emotion, 29*(7), 1239–1255. Available from https://doi.org/10.1080/02699931.2014.976181.

Evans, C., Ehlers, A., Mezey, G., & Clark, D. M. (2007). Intrusive memories and ruminations related to violent crime among young offenders: Phenomenological characteristics. *Journal of Traumatic Stress, 20*(2), 183–196. Available from https://doi.org/10.1002/jts.20204.

Fehm, L., Schneider, G., & Hoyer, J. (2007). Is post-event processing specific for social anxiety? *Journal of Behavior Therapy and Experimental Psychiatry, 38*(1), 11–22. Available from https://doi.org/10.1016/j.jbtep.2006.02.004.

Feinstein, B. A., Hershenberg, R., Bhatia, V., Latack, J. A., Meuwly, N., & Davila, J. (2013). Negative social comparison on Facebook and depressive symptoms. *Psychology of Popular Media Culture, 2*(3), 161–170. Available from https://doi.org/10.1037/a0033111.

Fleeson, W. (2001). Toward a structure- and process-integrated view of personality. *Journal of Personality and Social Psychology, 80*(6), 1011–1027. Available from https://doi.org/10.1037/0022-3514.80.6.1011.

Flynn, M., Kecmanovic, J., & Alloy, L. B. (2010). An examination of integrated cognitive-interpersonal vulnerability to depression: The role of rumination, perceived social support, and interpersonal stress generation. *Cognitive Therapy and Research, 34*(5), 456–466. Available from https://doi.org/10.1007/s10608-010-9300-8.

Fritz, C., & Sonnentag, S. (2006). Recovery, well-being, and performance-related outcomes. *Journal of Applied Psychology, 91*(4), 936–945. Available from https://doi.org/10.1037/0021-9010.91.4.936.

Frone, M. R. (2015). Relations of negative and positive work experiences to employee alcohol use: Testing the intervening role of negative and positive work rumination. *Journal of Occupational Health Psychology, 20*(2), 148–160. Available from https://doi.org/10.1037/a0038375.

Galfin, J. M., & Watkins, E. R. (2012). Construal level, rumination, and psychological distress in palliative care. *Psycho-Oncology, 21*(6), 680–683. Available from https://doi.org/10.1002/pon.1948.

Galupo, M. P., & Bauerband, L. A. (2016). Sexual orientation reflection and rumination scale: Development and psychometric evaluation. *Stigma and Health, 1*(1), 44–58. Available from https://doi.org/10.1037/sah0000017.

Garrison, A. M., Kahn, J. H., Miller, S. A., & Sauer, E. M. (2014). Emotional avoidance and rumination as mediators of the relation between adult attachment and emotional disclosure. *Personality and Individual Differences, 70*, 239–245. Available from https://doi.org/10.1016/j.paid.2014.07.006.

Gebhardt, W. A., Van Der Doef, M. P., Massey, E. K., Verhoeven, C. J. M., & Verkuil, B. (2010). Goal commitment to finding a partner and satisfaction with life among female singles. *Journal of Health Psychology, 15*(1), 122–130. Available from https://doi.org/10.1177/1359105309346212.

Gianferante, D., Thoma, M. V., Hanlin, L., Chen, X., Breines, J. G., Zoccola, P. M., & Rohleder, N. (2014). Post-stress rumination predicts HPA axis responses to repeated acute stress. *Psychoneuroendocrinology, 49*, 244–252. Available from https://doi.org/10.1016/j.psyneuen.2014.07.021.

Gilbert, P., Cheung, M., Irons, C., & McEwan, K. (2005). An exploration into depression-focused and anger-focused rumination in relation to depression in a student population. *Behavioural and Cognitive Psychotherapy, 33*(3), 273–283. Available from https://doi.org/10.1017/S1352465804002048.

Groleau, J. M., Calhoun, L. G., Cann, A., & Tedeschi, R. G. (2013). The role of centrality of events in posttraumatic distress and posttraumatic growth. *Psychological Trauma: Theory, Research, Practice, and Policy, 5*(5), 477–483. Available from https://doi.org/10.1037/a0028809.

Hacker, D. S., Haywood, J. E., Maduro, R. S., Mason, T. B., Derlega, V. J., Harrison, S. B., & Socha, T. J. (2016). Reactions of African American students to the George Zimmerman trial: Co-rumination and thought intrusions as mediators. *Journal of Loss and Trauma, 21*(6), 507–521. Available from https://doi.org/10.1080/15325024.2016.1157405.

Hamilton, J. L., Stange, J. P., Abramson, L. Y., & Alloy, L. B. (2015). Stress and the development of cognitive vulnerabilities to depression explain sex differences in depressive symptoms during adolescence. *Clinical Psychological Science, 3*(5), 702–714. Available from https://doi.org/10.1177/2167702614545479.

Hankin, B. L. (2009). Development of sex differences in depressive and co-occurring anxious symptoms during adolescence: Descriptive trajectories and potential explanations in a multiwave prospective study. *Journal of Clinical Child & Adolescent Psychology, 38*(4), 460–472. Available from https://doi.org/10.1080/15374410902976288.

Hatzenbuehler, M. L., Dovidio, J. F., Nolen-Hoeksema, S., & Phills, C. E. (2009). An implicit measure of anti-gay attitudes: Prospective associations with emotion regulation strategies and psychological distress. *Journal of Experimental Social Psychology, 45*(6), 1316–1320. Available from https://doi.org/10.1016/j.jesp.2009.08.005.

Hatzenbuehler, M. L., McLaughlin, K. A., & Nolen-Hoeksema, S. (2008). Emotion regulation and internalizing symptoms in a longitudinal study of sexual minority and heterosexual adolescents. *Journal of Child Psychology and Psychiatry, 49*(12), 1270–1278. Available from https://doi.org/10.1111/j.1469-7610.2008.01924.x.

Hatzenbuehler, M. L., Nolen-Hoeksema, S., & Dovidio, J. (2009). How does stigma "Get under the skin"? *Psychological Science, 20*(10), 1282–1289. Available from https://doi.org/10.1111/j.1467-9280.2009.02441.x.

Herek, G. M., Gillis, J. R., & Cogan, J. C. (1999). Psychological sequelae of hate-crime victimization among lesbian, gay, and bisexual adults. *Journal of Consulting and Clinical Psychology, 67*(6), 945–951. Available from https://doi.org/10.1037/0022-006X.67.6.945.

Herts, K., McLaughlin, K., & Hatzenbuehler, M. (2012). Emotion dysregulation as a mechanism linking stress exposure to adolescent aggressive behavior. *Journal of Abnormal Child Psychology, 40*(7), 1111–1122. Available from https://doi.org/10.1007/s10802-012-9629-4.

Huffziger, S., Reinhard, I., & Kuehner, C. (2009). A longitudinal study of rumination and distraction in formerly depressed inpatients and community controls. *Journal of Abnormal Psychology, 118*(4), 746–756. Available from https://doi.org/10.1037/a0016946.

Ingersoll-Dayton, B., & Krause, N. (2005). Self-forgiveness. *Research on Aging, 27*(3), 267–289. Available from https://doi.org/10.1177/0164027504274122.

Ingram, R., & Wisnicki, K. (1999). Situational specificity of self-focused attention in dysphoric states. *Cognitive Therapy and Research, 23*(6), 625–636. Available from https://doi.org/1018736808385.

Izadpanah, S., Schumacher, M., & Barnow, S. (2017). Anger rumination mediates the relationship between reinforcement sensitivity and psychopathology: Results of a 5-year longitudinal study. *Personality and Individual Differences, 110*, 49–54. Available from https://doi.org/10.1016/j.paid.2017.01.023.

Johnson, E. A., & O'Brien, K. A. (2013). Self-compassion soothes the savage EGO-threat system: Effects on negative affect, shame, rumination, and depressive symptoms. *Journal of Social and Clinical Psychology, 32*(9), 939–963. Available from https://doi.org/10.1521/jscp.2013.32.9.939.

Joireman, J. (2004). Empathy and the self-absorption paradox II: Self-rumination and self-reflection as mediators between shame, guilt, and empathy. *Self and Identity, 3*(3), 225–238. Available from https://doi.org/10.1080/13576500444000038.

Kashdan, T. B., Young, K. C., & McKnight, P. E. (2012). When is rumination an adaptive mood repair strategy? Day-to-day rhythms of life in combat veterans with and without posttraumatic stress disorder. *Journal of Anxiety Disorders, 26*(7), 762–768. Available from https://doi.org/10.1016/j.janxdis.2012.07.004.

Kaufman, T. M. L., Baams, L., & Dubas, J. S. (2017). Microaggressions and depressive symptoms in sexual minority youth: The roles of rumination and social support. *Psychology of Sexual Orientation and Gender Diversity, 4*(2), 184–192. Available from https://doi.org/10.1037/sgd0000219.

Keller, M. C., & Nesse, R. M. (2006). The evolutionary significance of depressive symptoms: Adverse situations lead to different depressive symptom patterns. *Journal of Personality and Social Psychology, 91*(2), 316–330. Available from https://doi.org/10.1037/0022-3514.91.2.316.

Kertz, S., & Woodruff-Borden, J. (2011). The developmental psychopathology of worry. *Clinical Child and Family Psychology Review, 14*(2), 174–197. Available from https://doi.org/10.1007/s10567-011-0086-3.

Kessler, R. C., Mickelson, K. D., & Williams, D. R. (1999). The prevalence, distribution, and mental health correlates of perceived discrimination in the united states. *Journal of Health and Social Behavior, 40*(3), 208–230. Available from https://doi.org/10.2307/2676349.

King, D. B., & DeLongis, A. (2014). When couples disconnect: Rumination and withdrawal as maladaptive responses to everyday stress. *Journal of Family Psychology: JFP: Journal of the Division of Family Psychology of the American Psychological Association (Division 43)*, *28*(4), 460–469. Available from https://doi.org/10.1037/a0037160.

Kircanski, K., Thompson, R. J., Sorenson, J. E., Sherdell, L., & Gotlib, I. H. (2015). Rumination and worry in daily life. *Clinical Psychological Science*, *3*(6), 926–939. Available from https://doi.org/10.1177/2167702614566603.

Kleim, B., & Ehlers, A. (2008). Reduced autobiographical memory specificity predicts depression and posttraumatic stress disorder after recent trauma. *Journal of Consulting and Clinical Psychology*, *76*(2), 231–242. Available from https://doi.org/10.1037/0022-006X.76.2.231.

Koole, S. L., Smeets, K., van Knippenberg, A., & Dijksterhuis, A. (1999). The cessation of rumination through self-affirmation. *Journal of Personality and Social Psychology*, *77*(1), 111–125. Available from https://doi.org/10.1037/0022-3514.77.1.111.

Lanciano, T., Curci, A., Kafetsios, K., Elia, L., & Zammuner, V. L. (2012). Attachment and dysfunctional rumination: The mediating role of emotional intelligence abilities. *Personality and Individual Differences*, *53*(6), 753–758. Available from https://doi.org/10.1016/j.paid.2012.05.027.

Lavallee, K. L., & Parker, J. G. (2009). The role of inflexible friendship beliefs, rumination, and low self-worth in early adolescents' friendship jealousy and adjustment. *Journal of Abnormal Child Psychology*, *37*(6), 873–885. Available from https://doi.org/10.1007/s10802-009-9317-1.

Lavallee, L. F., & Campbell, J. D. (1995). Impact of personal goals on self-regulation processes elicited by daily negative events. *Journal of Personality and Social Psychology*, *69*(2), 341–352. Available from https://doi.org/10.1037/0022-3514.69.2.341.

Lazarus, R. S., & Folkman, S. (1984). *Stress, appraisal, and coping*. New York: Springer.

Lee, A., & Hankin, B. L. (2009). Insecure attachment, dysfunctional attitudes, and low self-esteem predicting prospective symptoms of depression and anxiety during adolescence. *Journal of Clinical Child & Adolescent Psychology*, *38*(2), 219–231. Available from https://doi.org/10.1080/15374410802698396.

Lewis, R. J., Mason, T. B., Winstead, B. A., Gaskins, M., & Irons, L. B. (2016). Pathways to hazardous drinking among racially and socioeconomically diverse lesbian women. *Psychology of Women Quarterly*, *40*(4), 564–581. Available from https://doi.org/10.1177/0361684316662603.

Lewis, R. J., Milletich, R. J., Derlega, V. J., & Padilla, M. A. (2014). Sexual minority stressors and psychological aggression in lesbian women's intimate relationships. *Psychology of Women Quarterly*, *38*(4), 535–550. Available from https://doi.org/10.1177/0361684313517866.

Lewis, R. J., Milletich, R. J., Mason, T. B., & Derlega, V. J. (2014). Pathways connecting sexual minority stressors and psychological distress among lesbian women. *Journal of Gay & Lesbian Social Services*, *26*(2), 147–167. Available from https://doi.org/10.1080/10538720.2014.891452.

Liang, C. T. H., & Molenaar, C. M. (2016). Beliefs in an unjust world: Mediating Ethnicity-Related stressors and psychological functioning. *Journal of Clinical Psychology*, *72*(6), 552–562. Available from https://doi.org/10.1002/jclp.22271.

Liao, K. Y., Kashubeck-West, S., Weng, C., & Deitz, C. (2015). Testing a mediation framework for the link between perceived discrimination and psychological distress among sexual minority individuals. *Journal of Counseling Psychology*, *62*(2), 226–241. Available from https://doi.org/10.1037/cou0000064.

Lindstrom, C. M., Cann, A., Calhoun, L. G., & Tedeschi, R. G. (2013). The relationship of core belief challenge, rumination, disclosure, and sociocultural elements to posttraumatic growth. *Psychological Trauma: Theory, Research, Practice, and Policy*, *5*(1), 50–55. Available from https://doi.org/10.1037/a0022030.

Liu, Q., Zhou, Z., Yang, X., Kong, F., Niu, G., & Fan, C. (2017). Mobile phone addiction and sleep quality among Chinese adolescents: A moderated mediation model. *Computers in Human Behavior, 72,* 108–114. Available from https://doi.org/10.1016/j.chb.2017.02.042.

Locatelli, S. M., Kluwe, K., & Bryant, F. B. (2012). Facebook use and the tendency to ruminate among college students: Testing mediational hypotheses. *Journal of Educational Computing Research, 46*(4), 377–394. Available from https://doi.org/10.2190/EC.46.4.d.

Long, E. C., & Christian, M. S. (2015). Mindfulness buffers retaliatory responses to injustice: A regulatory approach. *The Journal of Applied Psychology, 100*(5), 1409–1422. Available from https://doi.org/10.1037/apl0000019.

Luyckx, K., Soenens, B., Goossens, L., Beckx, K., & Wouters, S. (2008). Identity exploration and commitment in late adolescence: Correlates of perfectionism and mediating mechanisms on the pathway to Well–Being. *Journal of Social and Clinical Psychology, 27*(4), 336–361. Available from https://doi.org/10.1521/jscp.2008.27.4.336.

Mancini, F., D'Olimpio, F., Prunetti, E., Didonna, F., & Del Genio, M. (2000). Parental bonding: Can obsessive symptoms and general distress be predicted by perceived rearing practices? *Clinical Psychology & Psychotherapy, 7*(3), 201–208. Available from https://doi.org/AID-CPP241>3.0.CO;2-K.

Marcia, J. E. (1966). Development and validation of ego-identity status. *Journal of Personality and Social Psychology, 3*(5), 551–558. Available from https://doi.org/10.1037/h0023281.

Margolese, S., Markiewicz, D., & Doyle, A. (2005). Attachment to parents, best friend, and romantic partner: Predicting different pathways to depression in adolescence. *Journal of Youth and Adolescence, 34*(6), 637–650. Available from https://doi.org/10.1007/s10964-005-8952-2.

Marks, A. D. G., Sobanski, D. J., & Hine, D. W. (2010). Do dispositional rumination and/or mindfulness moderate the relationship between life hassles and psychological dysfunction in adolescents? *Australian and New Zealand Journal of Psychiatry, 44*(9), 831–838. Available from https://doi.org/10.3109/00048674.2010.487478.

Martin, L. L., & Tesser, A. (1996). Some ruminative thoughts. *Advances in social cognition, 9,* 1–47.

Mason, T., & Lewis, R. (2016). Examining social support, rumination, and optimism in relation to binge eating among Caucasian and African–American college women. *Eating and Weight Disorders – Studies on Anorexia, Bulimia and Obesity, 22*(4), 693–698. Available from https://doi.org/10.1007/s40519-016-0300-x.

Matos, M., Pinto-Gouveia, J., & Costa, V. (2013). Understanding the importance of attachment in shame traumatic memory relation to depression: The impact of emotion regulation processes. *Clinical Psychology & Psychotherapy, 20*(2), 149–165. Available from https://doi.org/10.1002/cpp.786.

McIntosh, E., Gillanders, D., & Rodgers, S. (2010). Rumination, goal linking, daily hassles and life events in major depression. *Clinical Psychology & Psychotherapy, 17*(1), n/a. Available from https://doi.org/10.1002/cpp.611.

McIntosh, W. D., Harlow, T. F., & Martin, L. L. (1995). Linkers and nonlinkers: Goal beliefs as a moderator of the effects of everyday hassles on rumination, depression, and physical complaints. *Journal of Applied Social Psychology, 25*(14), 1231. Retrieved from <https://search.proquest.com/docview/1298121062>.

McIntosh, W. D., & Martin, L. L. (1992). The cybernetics of happiness: The relation of goal attainment, rumination, and affect. In M. S. Clark (Ed.), *Review of personality and social psychology, vol. 14. Emotion and social behavior* (pp. 222–246). Thousand Oaks, CA: Sage Publications, Inc.

McLaughlin, K. A., & Nolen-Hoeksema, S. (2012). Interpersonal stress generation as a mechanism linking rumination to internalizing symptoms in early adolescents. *Journal of Clinical Child and Adolescent Psychology: The Official Journal for the Society of Clinical Child and Adolescent Psychology, American Psychological Association, Division 53*, *41*(5), 584–597. Available from https://doi.org/10.1080/15374416.2012.704840.

Merrill, A. F., & Afifi, T. D. (2015). Attachment-related differences in secrecy and rumination in romantic relationships. *Personal Relationships*, *22*(2), 259–274. Available from https://doi.org/10.1111/pere.12078.

Meyer, I. H. (2003). Prejudice, social stress, and mental health in lesbian, gay, and bisexual populations. *Psychological Bulletin*, *129*(5), 674–697. Available from https://doi.org/10.1037/0033-2909.129.5.674.

Michael, S. T., & Snyder, C. R. (2005). Getting unstuck: The roles of hope, finding meaning, and rumination in the adjustment to bereavement among college students. *Death Studies*, *29*(5), 435–458. Available from https://doi.org/10.1080/07481180590932544.

Michl, L. C., McLaughlin, K. A., Shepherd, K., & Nolen-Hoeksema, S. (2013). Rumination as a mechanism linking stressful life events to symptoms of depression and anxiety. *Journal of Abnormal Psychology*, *122*(2), 339–352. Available from https://doi.org/10.1037/a0031994.

Millar, K. U., Tesser, A., & Millar, M. G. (1988). The effects of a threatening life event on behavior sequences and intrusive thought: A self-disruption explanation. *Cognitive Therapy and Research*, *12*(5), 441–457. Available from https://doi.org/10.1007/BF01173412.

Miranda, R., Tsypes, A., Gallagher, M., & Rajappa, K. (2013). Rumination and hopelessness as mediators of the relation between perceived emotion dysregulation and suicidal ideation. *Cognitive Therapy and Research*, *37*(4), 786–795. Available from https://doi.org/10.1007/s10608-013-9524-5.

Moberly, N. J., & Watkins, E. R. (2008a). Ruminative self-focus and negative affect. *Journal of Abnormal Psychology*, *117*(2), 314–323. Available from https://doi.org/10.1037/0021-843X.117.2.314.

Moberly, N. J., & Watkins, E. R. (2008b). Ruminative self-focus, negative life events, and negative affect. *Behaviour Research and Therapy*, *46*(9), 1034–1039. Available from https://doi.org/10.1016/j.brat.2008.06.004.

Moberly, N. J., & Watkins, E. R. (2010). Negative affect and ruminative self-focus during everyday goal pursuit. *Cognition & Emotion*, *24*(4), 729–739. Available from https://doi.org/10.1080/02699930802696849.

Muris, P., Meesters, C., Merckelbach, H., & Hülsenbeck, P. (2000). Worry in children is related to perceived parental rearing and attachment. *Behaviour Research and Therapy*, *38*(5), 487–497. Available from https://doi.org/10.1016/S0005-7967(99)00072-8.

Nolen-Hoeksema, S. (1991). Responses to depression and their effects on the duration of depressive episodes. *Journal of Abnormal Psychology*, *100*(4), 569–582. Available from https://doi.org/10.1037/0021-843X.100.4.569.

Nolen-Hoeksema, S. (2004). The response styles theory. In C. Papageorgiou, & A. Wells (Eds.), *Depressive rumination: Nature, theory, and treatment* (pp. 107–124). New York: Wiley.

Nolen-Hoeksema, S., Larson, J., & Grayson, C. (1999). Explaining the gender difference in depressive symptoms. *Journal of Personality and Social Psychology*, *77*(5), 1061–1072. Available from https://doi.org/10.1037/0022-3514.77.5.1061.

Nolen-Hoeksema, S., Parker, L. E., & Larson, J. (1994). Ruminative coping with depressed mood following loss. *Journal of Personality and Social Psychology*, *67*(1), 92–104. Available from https://doi.org/10.1037/0022-3514.67.1.92.

Nolen-Hoeksema, S., Stice, E., Wade, E., & Bohon, C. (2007). Reciprocal relations between rumination and bulimic, substance abuse, and depressive symptoms in female adolescents. *Journal of Abnormal Psychology, 116*(1), 198–207. Available from https://doi.org/10.1037/0021-843X.116.1.198.

Novin, S., & Rieffe, C. (2015). Validation of the brief shame and guilt questionnaire for children. *Personality and Individual Differences, 85*, 56–59. Available from https://doi.org/10.1016/j.paid.2015.04.028.

Orth, U., Berking, M., & Burkhardt, S. (2006). Self-conscious emotions and depression: Rumination explains why shame but not guilt is maladaptive. *Personality and Social Psychology Bulletin, 32*(12), 1608–1619. Available from https://doi.org/10.1177/0146167206292958.

Orue, I., Padilla, P., & Calvete, E. (2014). Brooding rumination as a mediator in the relation between early maladaptive schemas and symptoms of depression and social anxiety in adolescents. *Journal of Adolescence, 37*(8), 1281–1291. Available from https://doi.org/10.1016/j.adolescence.2014.09.004.

Pearson, K. A., Watkins, E. R., & Mullan, E. G. (2011). Rejection sensitivity prospectively predicts increased rumination. *Behaviour Research and Therapy, 49*(10), 597–605. Available from https://doi.org/10.1016/j.brat.2011.06.004.

Pearson, K. A., Watkins, E. R., Mullan, E. G., & Moberly, N. J. (2010). Psychosocial correlates of depressive rumination. *Behaviour Research and Therapy, 48*(8), 784–791. Available from https://doi.org/10.1016/j.brat.2010.05.007.

Penney, E. S., & Abbott, M. J. (2015). The impact of perceived standards on state anxiety, appraisal processes, and negative pre- and post-event rumination in social anxiety disorder. *Cognitive Therapy and Research, 39*(2), 162–177. Available from https://doi.org/10.1007/s10608-014-9639-3.

Perilloux, C., & Buss, D. M. (2008). Breaking up romantic relationships: Costs experienced and coping strategies deployed. *Evolutionary Psychology, 6*(1). Available from https://doi.org/10.1177/147470490800600119.

Peters, J. R., & Geiger, P. J. (2016). Borderline personality disorder and self-conscious affect: Too much shame but not enough guilt? *Personality Disorders, 7*(3), 303–308. Available from https://doi.org/10.1037/per0000176.

Peters, J. R., Geiger, P. J., Smart, L. M., & Baer, R. A. (2014). Shame and borderline personality features: The potential mediating role of anger and anger rumination. *Personality Disorders, 5*(1), 1–9. Available from https://doi.org/10.1037/per0000022.

Peters, J. R., Smart, L. M., Eisenlohr-Moul, T. A., Geiger, P. J., Smith, G. T., & Baer, R. A. (2015). Anger rumination as a mediator of the relationship between mindfulness and aggression: The utility of a multidimensional mindfulness model. *Journal of Clinical Psychology, 71*(9), 871–884. Available from https://doi.org/10.1002/jclp.22189.

Pyszczynski, T., & Greenberg, J. (1987). Self-regulatory perseveration and the depressive self-focusing style. *Psychological Bulletin, 102*(1), 122–138. Available from https://doi.org/10.1037/0033-2909.102.1.122.

Quirk, S., Wier, D., Martin, S., & Christian, A. (2015). The influence of parental rejection on the development of maladaptive schemas, rumination, and motivations for self-injury. *Journal of Psychopathology and Behavioral Assessment, 37*(2), 283–295. Available from https://doi.org/10.1007/s10862-014-9453-y.

Raes, F., & Hermans, D. (2008). On the mediating role of subtypes of rumination in the relationship between childhood emotional abuse and depressed mood: Brooding versus reflection. *Depression and Anxiety, 25*(12), 1067–1070. Available from https://doi.org/10.1002/da.20447.

Riek, B. M., Luna, L. M. R., & Schnabelrauch, C. A. (2014). Transgressors' guilt and shame. *Journal of Social and Personal Relationships, 31*(6), 751–772. Available from https://doi.org/10.1177/0265407513503595.

Roach, A., Salt, C., & Segerstrom, S. (2010). Generalizability of repetitive thought: Examining stability in thought content and process. *Cognitive Therapy and Research, 34*(2), 144–158. Available from https://doi.org/10.1007/s10608-009-9232-3.

Roberts, H., Watkins, E. R., & Wills, A. J. (2013). Cueing an unresolved personal goal causes persistent ruminative self-focus: An experimental evaluation of control theories of rumination. *Journal of Behavior Therapy and Experimental Psychiatry, 44*(4), 449–455. Available from https://doi.org/10.1016/j.jbtep.2013.05.004.

Roloff, M. E., Soule, K. P., & Carey, C. M. (2001). Reasons for remaining in a relationship and responses to relational transgressions. *Journal of Social and Personal Relationships, 18*(3), 362–385. Available from https://doi.org/10.1177/0265407501183004.

Ruijten, T., Roelofs, J., & Rood, L. (2011). The mediating role of rumination in the relation between quality of attachment relations and depressive symptoms in non-clinical adolescents. *Journal of Child and Family Studies, 20*(4), 452–459. Available from https://doi.org/10.1007/s10826-010-9412-5.

Ruscio, A. M., Gentes, E. L., Jones, J. D., Hallion, L. S., Coleman, E. S., & Swendsen, J. (2015). Rumination predicts heightened responding to stressful life events in major depressive disorder and generalized anxiety disorder. *Journal of Abnormal Psychology, 124*(1), 17–26. Available from https://doi.org/10.1037/abn0000025.

Saffrey, C., & Ehrenberg, M. (2007). When thinking hurts: Attachment, rumination, and postrelationship adjustment. *Personal Relationships, 14*(3), 351–368. Available from https://doi.org/10.1111/j.1475-6811.2007.00160.x.

Salsman, J. M., Segerstrom, S. C., Brechting, E. H., Carlson, C. R., & Andrykowski, M. A. (2009). Posttraumatic growth and PTSD symptomatology among colorectal cancer survivors: A 3-month longitudinal examination of cognitive processing. *Psycho-Oncology, 18*(1), 30–41. Available from https://doi.org/10.1002/pon.1367.

Sarin, S., & Nolen-Hoeksema, S. (2010). The dangers of dwelling: An examination of the relationship between rumination and consumptive coping in survivors of childhood sexual abuse. *Cognition & Emotion, 24*(1), 71–85. Available from https://doi.org/10.1080/02699930802563668.

Sauer-Zavala, S., Walsh, E., Eisenlohr-Moul, T., & Lykins, E. (2013). Comparing mindfulness-based intervention strategies: Differential effects of sitting meditation, body scan, and mindful yoga. *Mindfulness, 4*(4), 383–388. Available from https://doi.org/10.1007/s12671-012-0139-9.

Schwartz, S., Beyers, W., Luyckx, K., Soenens, B., Zamboanga, B., Forthun, L., ... Waterman, A. (2011). Examining the light and dark sides of emerging adults' identity: A study of identity status differences in positive and negative psychosocial functioning. *Journal of Youth and Adolescence, 40*(7), 839–859. Available from https://doi.org/10.1007/s10964-010-9606-6.

Senkans, S., McEwan, T. E., Skues, J., & Ogloff, J. R. P. (2015). Development of a relational rumination questionnaire. *Personality and Individual Differences, 90*, 27–35. Available from https://doi.org/10.1016/j.paid.2015.10.032.

Shapero, B. G., Hankin, B. L., & Barrocas, A. L. (2013). Stress generation and exposure in a multi-wave study of adolescents: Transactional processes and sex differences. *Journal of Social and Clinical Psychology, 32*(9), 989–1012. Available from https://doi.org/10.1521/jscp.2013.32.9.989.

Shaw, A. M., Timpano, K. R., Tran, T. B., & Joormann, J. (2015). Correlates of Facebook usage patterns: The relationship between passive Facebook use, social anxiety symptoms, and brooding. *Computers in Human Behavior, 48*, 575–580. Available from https://doi.org/10.1016/j.chb.2015.02.003.

Skinner, E. A., Edge, K., Altman, J., & Sherwood, H. (2003). Searching for the structure of coping. *Psychological Bulletin, 129*(2), 216–269. Available from https://doi.org/10.1037/0033-2909.129.2.216.

Smart, L. M., Peters, J. R., & Baer, R. A. (2016). *Development and validation of a measure of self-critical rumination*. Los Angeles, CA: SAGE Publications. Available from https://doi.org/10.1177/1073191115573300.

Spasojević, J., & Alloy, L. B. (2002). Who becomes a depressive ruminator? Developmental antecedents of ruminative response style. *Journal of Cognitive Psychotherapy, 16*(4), 405–419. Available from https://doi.org/10.1891/jcop.16.4.405.52529.

Starr, L., & Davila, J. (2012). Cognitive and interpersonal moderators of daily co-occurrence of anxious and depressed moods in generalized anxiety disorder. *Cognitive Therapy and Research, 36*(6), 655–669. Available from https://doi.org/10.1007/s10608-011-9434-3.

Stewart, A. J., & Vandewater, E. A. (1999). "If I had it to do over again . . .": Midlife review, midcourse corrections, and women's well-being in midlife. *Journal of Personality and Social Psychology, 76*(2), 270–283. Available from https://doi.org/10.1037/0022-3514.76.2.270.

Stroebe, M., Boelen, P. A., van, D. H., Stroebe, W., Salemink, E., & van, D. B. (2007). Ruminative coping as avoidance: A reinterpretation of its function in adjustment to bereavement. *European Archives of Psychiatry and Clinical Neuroscience, 257*(8), 462–472. Available from https://doi.org/10.1007/s00406-007-0746-y.

Sweeny, K., & Andrews, S. E. (2014). Mapping individual differences in the experience of a waiting period. *Journal of Personality and Social Psychology, 106*(6), 1015–1030. Available from https://doi.org/10.1037/a0036031.

Sweeny, K., & Cavanaugh, A. G. (2012). Waiting is the hardest part: A model of uncertainty navigation in the context of health news. *Health Psychology Review, 6*(2), 147–164. Available from https://doi.org/10.1080/17437199.2010.520112.

Szymanski, D. M., Dunn, T. L., & Ikizler, A. S. (2014). Multiple minority stressors and psychological distress among sexual minority women: The roles of rumination and maladaptive coping. *Psychology of Sexual Orientation and Gender Diversity, 1*(4), 412–421. Available from https://doi.org/10.1037/sgd0000066.

Taku, K., Cann, A., Tedeschi, R. G., & Calhoun, L. G. (2015). Core beliefs shaken by an earthquake correlate with posttraumatic growth. *Psychological Trauma: Theory, Research, Practice and Policy, 7*(6), 563–569. Available from https://doi.org/10.1037/tra0000054.

Taku, K., Kilmer, R. P., Cann, A., Tedeschi, R. G., & Calhoun, L. G. (2012). Exploring posttraumatic growth in Japanese youth. *Psychological Trauma: Theory, Research, Practice, and Policy, 4*(4), 411–419. Available from https://doi.org/10.1037/a0024363.

Tangney, J. P. (1996). Conceptual and methodological issues in the assessment of shame and guilt. *Behaviour Research and Therapy, 34*(9), 741–754. Available from https://doi.org/10.1016/0005-7967(96)00034-4.

Tangney, J. P., Wagner, P. E., Hill-Barlow, D., Marschall, D. E., & Gramzow, R. (1996). Relation of shame and guilt to constructive versus destructive responses to anger across the lifespan. *Journal of Personality and Social Psychology, 70*(4), 797–809. Available from https://doi.org/10.1037/0022-3514.70.4.797.

Thomasgard, M., & Metz, W. P. (1993). Parental overprotection revisited. *Child Psychiatry and Human Development, 24*(2), 67–80. Available from https://doi.org/10.1007/BF02367260.

Tilghman-Osborne, C., Cole, D. A., Felton, J. W., & Ciesla, J. A. (2008). Relation of guilt, shame, behavioral and characterological self-blame to depressive symptoms in adolescents over time. *Journal of Social and Clinical Psychology, 27*(8), 809–842. Available from https://doi.org/10.1521/jscp.2008.27.8.809.

Tobin, S. J., Loxton, N. J., & Neighbors, C. (2014). Coping with causal uncertainty through alcohol use. *Addictive Behaviors, 39*(3), 580–585. Available from https://doi.org/10.1016/j.addbeh.2013.11.009.

Torges, C. M., Stewart, A. J., & Nolen-Hoeksema, S. (2008). Regret resolution, aging, and adapting to loss. *Psychology and Aging*, *23*(1), 169–180. Available from https://doi.org/10.1037/0882-7974.23.1.169.

Tran, T. B., & Joormann, J. (2015). The role of Facebook use in mediating the relation between rumination and adjustment after a relationship breakup. *Computers in Human Behavior*, *49*, 56–61. Available from https://doi.org/10.1016/j.chb.2015.02.050.

Tremblay, I., & Sullivan, M. J. L. (2010). Attachment and pain outcomes in adolescents: The mediating role of pain catastrophizing and anxiety. *Journal of Pain*, *11*(2), 160–171. Available from https://doi.org/10.1016/j.jpain.2009.06.015.

van der Houwen, K., Stroebe, W., Stroebe, M., Schut, H., & Bout, J. V. D. (2010). Mediating processes in bereavement: The role of rumination, threatening grief interpretations, and deliberate grief avoidance. *Social Science & Medicine*, *71*(9), 1669–1676. Available from https://doi.org/10.1016/j.socscimed.2010.06.047.

van Randenborgh, A., Hüffmeier, J., LeMoult, J., & Joormann, J. (2010). Letting go of unmet goals: Does self-focused rumination impair goal disengagement? *Motivation and Emotion*, *34*(4), 325–332. Available from https://doi.org/10.1007/s11031-010-9190-9.

Verkuil, B., Brosschot, J. F., Gebhardt, W. A., & Korrelboom, C. W. (2015). Goal linking and everyday worries in clinical work stress: A daily diary study. *British Journal of Clinical Psychology*, *54*(4), 378–390. Available from https://doi.org/10.1111/bjc.12083.

Volmer, J., Binnewies, C., Sonnentag, S., & Niessen, C. (2012). Do social conflicts with customers at work encroach upon our private lives? A diary study. *Journal of Occupational Health Psychology*, *17*(3), 304–315. Available from https://doi.org/10.1037/a0028454.

Wang, M., Liu, S., Liao, H., Gong, Y., Kammeyer-Mueller, J., & Shi, J. (2013). Can't get it out of my mind: Employee rumination after customer mistreatment and negative mood in the next morning. *Journal of Applied Psychology*, *98*(6), 989–1004. Available from https://doi.org/10.1037/a0033656.

Wang, P., Wang, X., Wang, X., Wu, Y., Xie, X., Zhao, F., ... Lei, L. (2018). Social networking sites addiction and adolescent depression: A moderated mediation model of rumination and self-esteem. *Personality and Individual Differences*, *127*, 162–167. Available from https://doi.org/10.1016/j.paid.2018.02.008.

Wang, S., & Borders, A. (2017). Rumination mediates the associations between sexual minority stressors and disordered eating, particularly for men. *Eating and Weight Disorders - Studies on Anorexia, Bulimia and Obesity*, *22*(4), 699–706. Available from https://doi.org/10.1007/s40519-016-0350-0.

Watkins, E. R. (2008). Constructive and unconstructive repetitive thought. *Psychological Bulletin*, *134*(2), 163–206. Available from https://doi.org/10.1037/0033-2909.134.2.163.

Willem, L., Bijttebier, P., Claes, L., Vanhalst, J., & Raes, F. (2014). The cross-temporal associations between rumination subtypes and substance use in adolescence: Exploring the moderating role of gender. *Journal of Psychopathology and Behavioral Assessment*, *36*(1), 143–154. Available from https://doi.org/10.1007/s10862-013-9373-2.

Williams, C. L., Harfmann, E. J., Ingram, R. E., Hagan, K. E., & Kramer, N. M. (2015). Specificity of parental bonding and rumination in depressive and anxious emotional distress. *Personality and Individual Differences*, *79*, 157–161. Available from https://doi.org/10.1016/j.paid.2015.01.055.

Wu, X., Zhou, X., Wu, Y., & An, Y. (2015). The role of rumination in posttraumatic stress disorder and posttraumatic growth among adolescents after the Wenchuan earthquake. *Frontiers in Psychology*, *6*, 1335. Available from https://doi.org/10.3389/fpsyg.2015.01335.

Yoder, J., & Lawrence, C. (2011). Are gender differences in self-reported rumination explained by women's stereotyping? *Sex Roles*, *65*(1), 94–101. Available from https://doi.org/10.1007/s11199-010-9913-0.

Young, C. C. (2016). Familial factors, cognitive vulnerabilities, and stressful events related to depressive symptoms in Latino adolescents. *Hispanic Journal of Behavioral Sciences, 38* (3), 360–377. Available from https://doi.org/10.1177/0739986316644734.

Zawadzki, M. J. (2015). Rumination is independently associated with poor psychological health: Comparing emotion regulation strategies. *Psychology & Health, 30*(10), 1146–1163. Available from https://doi.org/10.1080/08870446.2015.1026904.

Zeelenberg, M., & Breugelmans, S. M. (2008). The role of interpersonal harm in distinguishing regret from guilt. *Emotion, 8*(5), 589–596. Available from https://doi.org/10.1037/a0012894.

Zhou, X., Wu, X., Fu, F., & An, Y. (2015). Core belief challenge and rumination as predictors of PTSD and PTG among adolescent survivors of the Wenchuan earthquake. *Psychological Trauma: Theory, Research, Practice and Policy, 7*(4), 391–397. Available from https://doi.org/10.1037/tra0000031.

Zielinski, M. J., Borders, A., & Giancola, P. R. (2015). Does hostile rumination mediate the associations between reported child abuse, parenting characteristics and borderline features in adulthood? *Personality and Mental Health, 9*(4), 288–297. Available from https://doi.org/10.1002/pmh.1306.

Zimmer-Gembeck, M. J. (2015). Emotional sensitivity before and after coping with rejection: A longitudinal study. *Journal of Applied Developmental Psychology, 41*, 28–37. Available from https://doi.org/10.1016/j.appdev.2015.05.001.

Zimmer-Gembeck, M. J., & Skinner, E. A. (2015). Adolescent vulnerability and the distress of rejection: Associations of adjustment problems and gender with control, emotions, and coping. *Journal of Adolescence, 45*, 149–159. Available from https://doi.org/10.1016/j.adolescence.2015.09.004.

Zoccola, P. M., Dickerson, S. S., & Lam, S. (2012). Eliciting and maintaining ruminative thought: The role of social-evaluative threat. *Emotion (Washington, D.C.), 12*(4), 673–677. Available from https://doi.org/10.1037/a0027349.

Zoccola, P. M., Dickerson, S. S., & Zaldivar, F. P. (2008). Rumination and cortisol responses to laboratory stressors. *Psychosomatic Medicine, 70*(6), 661–667. Available from https://doi.org/10.1097/PSY.0b013e31817bbc77.

Zwolinski, J. (2012). Psychological and neuroendocrine reactivity to ostracism. *Aggressive Behavior, 38*(2), n/a. Available from https://doi.org/10.1002/ab.21411.

CHAPTER

8

Beliefs, traits, and motivations underlying rumination

Overview

This chapter reviews several individual difference variables that may influence whether people ruminate. After describing the literature on metacognitive beliefs about rumination, I turn to theory and evidence suggesting that avoidance and suppression attempt fuel rumination. I then review associations between neuroticism and several related traits—emotional sensitivity, intolerance of uncertainty, perfectionism, and behavioral inhibition—and rumination. The chapter concludes with an examination of various ways that emotion regulation difficulties and motives might contribute to rumination.

As we have seen, negative emotions and stressors trigger rumination. Are these associations equally strong for all people? Surely there are individual differences in whether emotional and environmental stressors lead people to engage in rumination. This chapter covers several such individual differences. For instance, some people explicitly believe that rumination will be helpful. At the same time, people who attempt to avoid unpleasant thoughts and emotions engage in more rumination. Relatedly, people who are high in neuroticism and associated traits are more likely to ruminate. Finally, difficulties with various motives for emotion regulation have the potential to predict greater rumination. In this chapter, I cover each of these factors in turn.

Rumination and Related Constructs
DOI: https://doi.org/10.1016/B978-0-12-812545-8.00008-5

© 2020 Elsevier Inc. All rights reserved.

Beliefs about rumination

The use of rumination in response to negative emotions and experiences occurs in people who have beliefs about the potential benefits of these cognitive activities. Research in this area fits into a larger model emphasizing the importance of metacognitive beliefs about repetitive thinking (see Chapter 12: Metacognitive therapy). Metacognition refers to thoughts about cognitive processes. The model argues that people use rumination and worry because they have *positive* metacognitive beliefs about the usefulness of these processes. For instance, individuals may believe that rumination will help them cope with difficulties, or that worrying will help them be mentally prepared. Emotionally disordered or vulnerable individuals are more likely to have these kinds of positive metacognitive beliefs, which in turn contribute to chronic rumination and worry.

Substantial research supports the existence of positive metacognitive beliefs about rumination and worry. Most individuals with major depression or dysphoria report holding beliefs that rumination will help them cope with and understand depression, increase self-awareness, find meaning in life, solve problems, and prevent future mistakes (Lyubomirsky & Nolen-Hoeksema, 1995; Papageorgiou & Wells, 2001; Watkins & Baracaia, 2001). Similarly, in people with and without generalized anxiety disorder (GAD), common self-reported benefits of worry include increasing motivation, preparing for potential feared events, and preventing feared events and their emotional consequences from occurring (Borkovec & Roemer, 1995; Freeston, Rhéaume, Letarte, Dugas, & Ladouceur, 1994). Assault survivors with posttraumatic stress disorder report using rumination to try to get rid of intrusive memories (Michael, Halligan, Clark, & Ehlers, 2007). Moreover, common positive beliefs about angry rumination include preparing for similar future situations, gaining insight and understanding of the problem, and justifying a response to an angering event (Simpson & Papageorgiou, 2003). In general, people appear to have dual goals of searching for understanding and solving problems when they ruminate (Segerstrom, Roach, Evans, Schipper, & Darville, 2010; Segerstrom, Stanton, Alden, & Shortridge, 2003; Siewert, Kubiak, Jonas, & Weber, 2011; Siewert, Kubiak, Jonas, & Weber, 2013).

Positive metacognitive beliefs are generally associated with more repetitive thinking. People with or without depression who hold positive beliefs about rumination engage in more depressive rumination (Ophir & Mor, 2014; Papageorgiou & Wells, 2001; Watkins & Baracaia, 2001; Watkins & Moulds, 2005). In the social anxiety literature, positive beliefs about both anticipatory and post-event rumination are associated with more rumination (Wong & Moulds, 2010; Vassilopoulos, Brouzos, & Moberly, 2015). In a quasiexperiment, participants with high positive beliefs about rumination engaged in more stress-reactive rumination in response to a difficult anagram task, compared to participants with low positive beliefs (Moulds, Yap, Kerr, Williams, & Kandris, 2010). Finally, people who endorse higher positive beliefs about worry engage in more worry, although research is mixed about whether they are more likely to be diagnosed with GAD (Cartwright-Hatton & Wells, 1997; Davis & Valentiner, 2000; Esbjørn et al., 2015; Laugesen, Dugas, & Bukowski, 2003; Ruscio & Borkovec, 2004; Wells & Carter, 2001). Thus, positive beliefs are associated with more repetitive thinking, although they do not robustly distinguish clinical from nonclinical populations.

Positive metacognitive beliefs, however, are only half of the picture. People with positive beliefs also typically hold *negative* metacognitive beliefs about perseverative thought (Cartwright-Hatton & Wells, 1997; Davis & Valentiner, 2000; Papageorgiou & Wells, 2003). In depressed individuals, negative metacognitive beliefs often reflect the uncontrollability and harm of rumination (e.g., increased negative moods and thoughts, wasted time) and negative interpersonal and social consequences (e.g., withdrawal from people and activities) (Papageorgiou & Wells, 2001; Watkins & Baracaia, 2001). Similarly, people commonly believe that angry rumination can be harmful, most commonly by heightening angry mood and contributing to loss of temper and aggressive behavior (Simpson & Papageorgiou, 2003). Negative beliefs about worry include beliefs about the uncontrollability and danger of worry (e.g., inability to stop, become sick with worrying) and the need to control thoughts (e.g., poor control indicates weakness, responsibility if thoughts come true) (Cartwright-Hatton & Wells, 1997).

In addition to increasing negative affect, negative beliefs maintain the use of rumination and worry because people do not believe that they can effectively control these cognitive processes. Both depressed and nondepressed individuals who endorse more negative beliefs report more depressive rumination (Papageorgiou & Wells, 2001, 2003; Yilmaz, Gençöz, & Wells, 2015). Individuals with GAD also report more negative metacognitive beliefs about worry than do individuals with other anxiety disorders, worriers without GAD, and nonworried controls (Cartwright-Hatton & Wells, 1997; Davis & Valentiner, 2000; Esbjørn et al., 2015; Ruscio & Borkovec, 2004; Wells & Carter, 2001).

In sum, people hold both positive and negative metacognitive beliefs about rumination. Positive beliefs about the potential benefits of rumination and worry may predispose individuals to use these cognitive processes when faced with negative emotions or experiences. Negative metacognitive beliefs about the dangers and uncontrollability of rumination and worry then serve to maintain these cognitive processes, because people get stuck in a loop of ruminating and feeling concerned about their rumination, which only increases their subsequent rumination. I return to this metacognitive model in greater detail, as well as its accompanying treatment, in a later chapter (Chapter 12, Metacognitive therapy).

Avoidance

As discussed in the chapter about anxiety (Chapter 2, Rumination and anxiety-related disorders), many researchers believe that rumination serves avoidant functions. Demonstrating this empirically is not easy. One piece of the puzzle is research showing that people who have tendencies for avoidance of unpleasant emotions and thoughts in fact ruminate more than those who do not. Several different types of avoidance have been studied as potential predictors of rumination.

Experiential avoidance involves an unwillingness to experience and deliberate attempts to control or escape from unwanted emotions, thoughts, and physiological states (Hayes et al., 2004). Conceptually, it is the opposite construct of acceptance, or a willingness to experience all internal states, whether pleasant or unpleasant. Studies show associations between experiential avoidance and rumination. In depressed adults, for instance, self-reported attempts at experiential avoidance after watching sad film clips predicted greater state rumination (Liverant, Kamholz, Sloan, & Brown, 2011). In an implicit assessment of avoidance, bereaved adults were instructed to approach (e.g., pull a joystick closer to oneself, making a stimulus image larger on a computer screen) or avoid (e.g., push the joystick away, making the image smaller) in response to a stimulus feature (e.g., font color) that was unrelated to the content or valence of the stimulus (Eisma et al., 2015). One of the stimuli, unique for each participant, was a picture of a deceased loved one. Over several trials, faster reactions to pushing than pulling this loss-related image indicated an avoidance tendency. As expected, more implicit loss avoidance was associated with greater rumination about the loss. Similar associations between implicit avoidance and rumination or worry emerge when avoidance is assessed via using other methods (Eisma et al., 2014; Laguna, Ham, Hope, & Bell, 2004; Thomas, Raynor, & Ribott, 2015). Of course, none of these studies have determined the directionality of associations between experiential avoidance and rumination.

One aspect of experiential avoidance is cognitive avoidance, or the use of strategies to prevent oneself from having unpleasant thoughts. Common strategies include thinking about lots of smaller matters, distracting oneself with various activities, and avoiding objects that may trigger unpleasant thoughts. Cross-sectional studies show that tendencies for cognitive avoidance are associated with greater rumination and worry (Cribb, Moulds, & Carter, 2006; Krieger, Altenstein, Baettig, Doerig, & Holtforth, 2013; McEvoy, Mahoney, & Moulds, 2010; Moulds, Kandris, Starr, & Wong, 2007; Olatunji, Moretz, & Zlomke, 2010; Ottenbreit, Dobson, & Quigley, 2014; Sexton & Dugas, 2009). In a much-needed effort to determine directionality, healthy adolescents reported on their daily avoidance, depressive rumination, worry, and negative mood every day for 7 days (Dickson, Ciesla, & Reilly, 2011). Daily cognitive avoidance predicted increases in both depressive rumination and worry on the next day. Furthermore, rumination and worry mediated the effects of cognitive avoidance on negative moods.

How do attempts at avoidance lead to increased rumination? This seems like a paradoxical relationship, because rumination involves harping on an upsetting emotion, thought, or experience, which is the opposite of what people are trying to do with avoidance. One possible explanation is that avoidance prevents people from effectively resolving negative emotions or taking necessary action to address stressors (e.g., Gross & John, 2003). From a behavioral perspective, avoidance prevents the extinction of an acquired fear. Thus, avoidance may lead to increased rumination indirectly, via the maintenance of negative emotions and stressful situations.

Another convincing explanation lies in the field of thought suppression. Daniel Wegner has spent years studying the processes by which people try to not think about unpleasant images and thoughts. He has found that despite people's best efforts, suppressed thoughts are often difficult, if not impossible, to keep out of mind (e.g., Wegner, 1994). Here is a classic exercise that illustrates the difficulties of thought suppression:

> "First, spend a minute thinking very hard about a white bear ... think only of a white bear, imagining everything about it"... pause for 1 minute ... "Now, spend the next minute NOT thinking of a white bear ... think of anything else you want, but do not allow yourself to think of a white bear"... pause for 1 minute ...

Most people have a difficult time *not* thinking of a white bear during the second minute. In his ironic process theory, Wegner (1994) explained this phenomenon by proposing that thought suppression involves both an active attempt at distraction as well as an automatic and sometimes unconscious monitoring process that constantly searches for unwanted thoughts (Wenzlaff & Wegner, 2000). Ironically, this vigilant monitoring process keeps unwanted thoughts continually on one's mental backburner, which means they can be easily triggered (Wegner & Zanakos, 1994; Wenzlaff & Wegner, 2000). Thus, attempts at thought suppression ironically make the suppressed thoughts more accessible than they would be otherwise, resulting in increased intrusions of unwanted thoughts. Even more, individuals who try to suppress emotional thoughts become hypersensitive, so that the thoughts come to produce even greater emotional reactions than they did originally (Wegner & Zanakos, 1994). In essence, thought suppression creates a bond between suppressed thoughts and associated emotions (Wenzlaff, Wegner, & Klein, 1991). Any experience of the emotions may trigger the suppressed thought, and likewise, any experience of the suppressed thought can elicit the associated emotions.

Given this explanation of the process of thought suppression, particularly of emotion-laden content, it should not be surprising that researchers have proposed rumination to be one outcome of thought suppression (Gold & Wegner, 1995). Specifically, the more that people attempt to avoid disturbing thoughts, the more they will experience those very thoughts, and the more emotionally upsetting those thoughts will be. Empirical evidence supports this hypothesis. In cross-sectional studies, people high in trait thought suppression also report strong tendencies for rumination and worry (Erskine, Kvavilashvili, & Kornbrot, 2007; Gosselin et al., 2007; Jones & Fernyhough, 2009; Laugesen et al., 2003; Liverant et al., 2011; McEvoy et al., 2010; Szasz, 2009; Watkins & Moulds, 2009; Wenzlaff & Luxton, 2003). Longitudinal studies provide some evidence of the proposed directionality. For instance, individuals who were chronic thought suppressors and experienced high levels of stress reported more rumination 10 weeks later than did low suppressors or high suppressors who did not experience stress (Wenzlaff & Luxton, 2003). Relatedly, decreases in thought suppression following a brief intervention predicted less subsequent rumination (Nitzan-Assayag et al., 2017).

People in negative moods are particularly unsuccessful at suppressing unwanted thoughts. Usually, people suppress thoughts by thinking about other things. They switch from one distracter to another depending on whatever is on their minds, like an unfocused stream of consciousness (Wenzlaff et al., 1991). For instance, a typical individual's thought progression while trying to *not* think of a white bear may include thoughts about aspects of the room, recent memories, plans for upcoming events, and so forth. However, individuals' moods impact the kind of distracters they select. In a seminal study, depressed people used more negative distracter thoughts during suppression than did nondepressed individuals, whether they were suppressing positive or negative thoughts (Wenzlaff, Wegner, & Roper, 1988). They also experienced more intrusions of the negative thoughts during a subsequent expression period than did nondepressed participants, indicating a failure to suppress negative thoughts. Interestingly, depressed participants recognized that positive distracters would suppress negative thoughts better than negative distracters. However, even when presented with possible positive distracters, depressed individuals used more negative distracters to suppress negative thoughts than did nondepressed individuals. Thus, depressed people automatically selected negative distracter thoughts during suppression, even against their better judgment.[1] These findings suggest that people in negative moods are particularly likely to engage in rumination, because their efforts at thought suppression will work in the opposite way they would like. In fact, unsuccessful suppression attempts are more strongly associated with rumination tendencies then are successful suppression attempts (Andrews, Troop, Joseph, Hiskey, & Coyne, 2002; Dieler, Herrmann, & Fallgatter, 2014; Hertel & Gerstle, 2003; Ryckman & Lambert, 2015). Future research will have to determine whether this is particularly true for individuals in negative moods.

In sum, people with inclinations to avoid upsetting thoughts and emotions are more likely to ruminate. One reason for this seeming paradox is that efforts to suppress unpleasant thoughts tend to result in increased intrusions of the very same thoughts. Avoidance may also indirectly lead to increased rumination, via the maintenance of negative moods and stressors. Taken together with the previous section, rumination may be more likely following negative emotions and stressors for people who believe that it will be useful *and* who have avoidance tendencies. Interestingly, people who hold positive metacognitive beliefs about worry are more likely to exhibit tendencies for experiential avoidance and thought suppression (Laugesen et al., 2003; Ruiz & Odriozola-González, 2016). A common feature of these constructs is the assumption, explicit or not, that thoughts can and should be manipulated for a desired end goal (e.g., understanding or preparing for a situation, not having a particular thought or emotion anymore). It makes sense that this assumption makes people more likely to respond to negative emotions and stressful situations with rumination or worry.

Personality traits

Personality refers to characteristic patterns of thoughts, feelings, and/or behaviors that remain fairly stable across time and situations (Connor-Smith & Flachsbart, 2007). Probably the most well-known group of higher

1 A methodological implication of these results is that the typical distraction manipulation in depressive rumination studies (e.g., think about the layout of your school campus, think about a boat crossing the ocean) improves negative moods because it focuses participants' attention on mood-incongruent (e.g., positive or neutral) thoughts. Normally, however, dysphoric individuals may select mood-congruent (e.g., sad) distracter thoughts that unfortunately lead to even more cognitive intrusions. Thus, the distraction manipulations in studies with dysphoric participants may not represent typical distraction attempts in these individuals.

order personality traits are the big five: neuroticism, extraversion, agreeableness, conscientiousness, and openness to experience (McCrae et al., 2000). Of these traits, neuroticism is most robustly associated with rumination (Bagby & Parker, 2001; McEvoy & Mahoney 2013; Svansdottir et al., 2013; Trapnell & Campbell, 1999). In addition, several literatures explore the associations between several lower order personality traits, all of which are related to neuroticism, and rumination.

Neuroticism

Neuroticism involves the tendency to experience strong negative emotions and heightened reactivity to stressors. When conceptualized as a temperamental (e.g., biological) predisposition, neuroticism is often referred to as negative affectivity. People high in neuroticism experience frequent and intense anxiety, sadness, and hostility. They also have more negative reactions to major stressors and daily hassles (Suls & Martin, 2005). Not surprisingly, neuroticism constitutes a vulnerability for developing symptoms of depression and anxiety.

Psychologists have long speculated that the negative outcomes associated with neuroticism result in part from increased rumination and self-focused attention (Watson & Clark, 1984). Robust evidence supports this proposed association. Neuroticism and negative affectivity are associated with rumination and worry in healthy children, adolescents, and young adults, as well as in individuals with major depression (Broeren, Muris, Bouwmeester, Heijden, & Abee, 2011; Muris, Roelofs, Rassin, Franken, & Mayer, 2005; Nolan, Roberts, & Gotlib, 1998; Roberts, Gilboa, & Gotlib, 1998; Roelofs, Huibers, Peeters, Arntz, & van Os, 2008; Spinhoven, Drost, de Rooij, van Hemert, & Penninx, 2016; Trapnell & Campbell, 1999; van der Houwen, Stroebe, Stroebe, Schut, & van den Bout, 2010; Verstraeten, Bijttebier, Vasey, & Raes, 2011; Verstraeten, Vasey, Raes, & Bijttebier, 2009). Negative affectivity even predicts greater depressive rumination 2 years later (Mezulis, Simonson, McCauley, & Vander Stoep, 2011). Because temperamental differences are proposed to exist at an early age, some researchers have assessed negative affectivity in childhood. For instance, college students' retrospective reports of a childhood tendency for negative affectivity were associated with greater current angry rumination tendencies (Sauer-Zavala, Geiger, & Baer, 2013). In an impressive longitudinal study, mothers' reports of their child's negative affectivity at age 1 predicted their child's self-reported rumination at age 13 (Mezulis, Priess, & Hyde, 2011). In all of these studies, rumination mediated the associations between neuroticism or negative affectivity and various clinical symptoms.

Emotional sensitivity

Emotional sensitivity is the belief that negative emotions have harmful and undesirable consequences. For example, people may believe that negative emotions and emotional arousal will harm them physically, render them incapable of functioning socially or at work, indicate that they are "going crazy" or "having a breakdown," and make them do something harmful to themselves or someone else. Understandably, people who believe this tend to experience strong anxiety and fear in response to negative emotions. As such, emotional sensitivity is considered a primary manifestation of neuroticism (e.g., Norton & Mehta, 2007).

Cross-sectional evidence clearly suggests that people who fear negative emotions are more likely to engage in negative repetitive thinking. In both healthy individuals and mental health patients, fear of anxiety, sadness, and anger are associated with more depressive rumination, angry rumination, and worry (Giorgio et al., 2010; Hong & Cheung, 2015; Lee, Orsillo, Roemer, & Allen, 2010; Mennin, Heimberg, Turk, & Fresco, 2005; Olatunji et al., 2010; Robins, Keng, Ekblad, & Brantley, 2012; Roemer, Salters, Raffa, & Orsillo, 2005; Sexton & Dugas, 2009). Furthermore, rumination mediates the links between emotion sensitivity and clinical outcomes such as depression and aggression. Interestingly, even fear of positive emotions is associated with greater rumination.

Longitudinal and experimental examinations of these associations are rare. One longitudinal study found that fear of emotions predicted increases in worry 3 months later (Sugiura & Sugiura, 2015), although another suggested that worry was a stronger predictor of future anxiety sensitivity than the other way around (Dugas, Laugesen, & Bukowski, 2012). In an experiment, healthy undergraduates watched a psychology "prerecorded lecture" that informed them that high levels of anxiety are harmful (Buhr & Dugas, 2009). Compared to participants who learned that anxiety is normal and harmless, participants in the anxiety sensitivity condition worried more about giving an oral presentation.

Emotional sensitivity may be associated with rumination for several reasons. First, the strong secondary emotions in response to initial negative emotions may directly trigger rumination. In other words, emotional sensitivity should interact with the experience of initial negative emotions to predict greater rumination via greater secondary emotions. This hypothesis has not yet been tested. Second, people who fear negative emotions go to great lengths to avoid experiencing negative emotions. In fact, emotional sensitivity is associated with greater experiential and cognitive avoidance, as well as thought suppression (Lee et al., 2010; Mahaffey, Watson, Clark, & Kotov, 2016; Mansell & McEvoy, 2016; Olatunji et al., 2010; Roemer et al., 2005; Sexton & Dugas, 2009;

Wegner & Zanakos, 1994). Thus, fear of negative emotions may also indirectly increase rumination via avoidance and suppression attempts.

Intolerance of uncertainty

Another primary manifestation of neuroticism is intolerance of uncertainty (McEvoy & Mahoney, 2013; Norton & Mehta, 2007; van der Heiden et al., 2009). Whereas emotional sensitivity is the tendency to perceive negative emotions as threatening, intolerance of uncertainty is the tendency to perceive uncertainty or ambiguity as threatening. This personality trait involves both an active desire for predictability and cognitive and behavioral paralysis in response to uncertainty (Birrell, Meares, Wilkinson, & Freeston, 2011).

Intolerance of uncertainty was originally identified as a key contributor to GAD (Dugas, Marchand, & Ladouceur, 2005; Freeston et al., 1994). According to the Intolerance of Uncertainty Model, people with GAD experience uncertainty and ambiguity as upsetting and believe that worry will help them cope with or prevent these types of situations (Dugas et al., 2005). Thus, chronic worry is a natural consequence of intolerance of uncertainty. In support of this model, intolerance of uncertainty correlates with more worry and worry about worry, in both clinical and nonclinical samples (Buhr & Dugas, 2012; de Bruin, Muris, & Rassin, 2007; Dugas, Gosselin, & Ladouceur, 2001; Freeston et al., 1994; Yook, Kim, Suh, & Lee, 2010). Longitudinal studies and experiments likewise have found that changes in intolerance of uncertainty predict changes in worry (Dugas & Ladouceur, 2000; Dugas et al., 2012; Ladouceur, Gosselin, & Dugas, 2000). Thus, evidence is fairly clear that difficulty tolerating uncertainty and ambiguity contributes to pathological worry.

Similar results have been found with rumination. Specifically, intolerance of uncertainty correlates with more rumination in clinical and nonclinical participants (de Jong-Meyer, Beck, & Riede, 2009; McEvoy & Mahoney, 2013; Yook et al., 2010; for a metaanalysis, see Hong & Cheung, 2015). Furthermore, rumination mediates the relationships between intolerance of uncertainty and depressive and anxious symptoms (Liao & Wei, 2011; Yook et al., 2010). In one study, rumination emerged as a moderator among women, such that intolerance of uncertainty only predicted greater depressive symptoms for women with high levels of rumination (Liao & Wei, 2011). Thus, intolerance of uncertainty may both lead to increased rumination and interact with rumination to predict worse outcomes.

Given the unique contributions of emotional sensitivity and intolerance of uncertainty to repetitive thought, some researchers have proposed that rumination and worry arise as a result of conflicting cognitive–motivational states (see Buhr & Dugas, 2009). Specifically, intolerance of uncertainty contributes to an approach motivation, in order to attain a greater degree of certainty. By contrast, fear of emotions contributes to the desire to avoid negative arousal. These conflicting motivations create a dilemma for individuals: to stop engaging in approach behaviors may decrease certainty, but to continue approach will likely maintain or increase emotional distress (Koerner & Dugas, 2008). This internal dilemma likely triggers repetitive thoughts, perhaps in an attempt to resolve the conflict. In initial support of this theory, emotional sensitivity led to worry particularly for individual high in intolerance of uncertainty (Buhr & Dugas, 2009). It is possible that conflicting motivations may be perceived as a discrepancy, triggering rumination in an effort at self-regulation (Mennin & Fresco, 2015).

Perfectionism

Perfectionism is another lower order manifestation of neuroticism (e.g., Smith, Sherry, et al., 2016; Smith, Stephens, Repper, & Kistner, 2016) that is associated with rumination. Defined generally as the tendency to strive toward personal improvement and set high standards for oneself (Short & Mazmanian, 2013), perfectionism is conceptualized as a multidimensional phenomenon. Many of the specific facets of perfectionism that researchers study can be grouped into two higher order factors: perfectionistic concerns and perfectionistic striving (Bieling, Israeli, & Antony, 2004; Frost, Heimberg, Holt, Mattia, & Neubauer, 1993; Stoeber & Otto, 2006). Perfectionistic concerns include people's perception that significant others set high standards for them (e.g., socially prescribed perfectionism), concerns about mistakes they have made, and doubts about their ability (Frost, Marten, Lahart, & Rosenblate, 1990; Hewitt & Flett, 1991). Perfectionistic striving includes the tendencies to set high expectations and goals for oneself (e.g., self-oriented perfectionism, personal standards) and to value organization. In general, perfectionistic concerns predict greater depressive and anxious symptoms and exacerbate the negative outcomes of stress. The effects of perfectionistic striving are unclear, as it has been both a risk factor and protective factor against depression (e.g. Enns, Cox, & Clara, 2005; Smith, Sherry, et al., 2016; Smith, Stephens, et al., 2016). Perfectionistic striving is also associated with conscientiousness and more active coping (for a review, see Stoeber & Otto, 2006). Thus, there is a debate in the field about whether perfectionistic striving constitutes an adaptive form of perfectionism.

Perfectionistic concerns are robustly associated with rumination. In cross-sectional studies, socially prescribed perfectionism, concerns about mistakes, and doubts about one's ability correlate with more rumination and worry (Blankstein & Lumley, 2008; Brown & Kocovski, 2014; Di Schiena, Luminet, Philippot, & Douilliez, 2012; Egan, Hattaway, & Kane, 2014; Flett, Madorsky, Hewitt, & Heisel, 2002; Harris, Pepper, & Maack, 2008; Luyckx, Soenens, Goossens, Beckx, & Wouters, 2008; Nepon, Flett, Hewitt, & Molnar, 2011; O'Connor, O'Connor, & Marshall, 2007; Olson & Kwon, 2008; Santanello & Gardner, 2007; Short & Mazmanian, 2013; Stöber & Joormann, 2001). Moreover, rumination and worry mediate the associations between perfectionistic concerns and depressive, anxious, and somatic symptoms. A few longitudinal studies have shed light on the directionality of this association. One study asked undergraduates to complete a mistakes journal everyday for 5 days, in which they recorded any mistakes they made (Frost et al., 1997). Two weeks later, participants high in perfectionistic concern reported more rumination about the most important mistake than did participants low in perfectionistic concern. In academic employees, doubts about one's ability predicted more work-related rumination and worry during a subsequent vacation (Flaxman, Ménard, Bond, & Kinman, 2012). In socially anxious and healthy individuals, trait and state perfectionistic concerns predicted greater post-event rumination 1–2 days after an anxiety-inducing speech task (Brown & Kocovski, 2014; Cox & Chen, 2015).

The association between perfectionistic striving and rumination is less clear. On the one hand, self-oriented perfectionism correlates with greater rumination and worry (Flett, Coulter, Hewitt, & Nepon, 2011; Flett et al., 2002; Nepon et al., 2011; O'Connor et al., 2007; Olson & Kwon, 2008; Short & Mazmanian, 2013). On the other hand, personal standards and organization are not robustly associated with rumination, worry, or ruminative exploration in college students (Di Schiena et al., 2012; Harris et al., 2008; Luyckx et al., 2008; Santanello & Gardner, 2007; Stöber & Joormann, 2001). What might explain these mixed results? Some authors suggest that conflicting findings reflect shared variance between perfectionistic striving and perfectionistic concerns (Stoeber & Otto, 2006). In fact, controlling for socially prescribed perfectionism dramatically weakened the associations between self-oriented perfectionism and rumination (Blankstein & Lumley, 2008). The conflicting findings might also be due to differences between various measures of perfectionistic striving. Most items assessing self-oriented perfectionism are more extreme in their wording (e.g., "I demand nothing less than perfection of myself.") than are items assessing personal standards (e.g., "I expect higher performance in my daily tasks than most people."). More extreme wording is associated with more negative outcomes (Blasberg, Hewitt, Flett, Sherry, & Chen, 2016). Thus, the various measures of perfectionistic striving may not actually assess the same construct or have similar outcomes. Specifically, requiring perfectionism from oneself may trigger rumination, whereas aiming for excellence may not. Another possibility is that perfectionistic striving only leads to rumination when people's expectations and efforts for accomplishment are unsuccessful. Some evidence suggests that perfectionistic striving predicts depression only for people experiencing achievement-related stress (Békés et al., 2015). Future research should examine whether perfectionistic striving is more likely to predict rumination for people experiencing stressors that challenge their notions of success.

Reinforcement sensitivity

Gray's (1982) reinforcement sensitivity theory proposed the existence of neurobiologically based systems underpinning the personality traits of neuroticism and extraversion. More specifically, he argued that neuroticism primarily reflects sensitivity to punishment, whereas extraversion primarily reflects sensitivity to rewards. Although these motivational systems are necessary for survival, they can lead to psychological dysfunction (e.g., fear/anxiety and impulsivity, respectively) when any system is too dominant.

The current version of this theory proposes three separate biologically based systems that underpin people's behavioral tendencies (Corr & Perkins, 2006; Gray & McNaughton, 2003). The behavioral approach system (BAS) responds to rewards and the cessation of punishment. It activates emotions such as hope and happiness that encourage approach behaviors (Randles, Flett, Nash, McGregor, & Hewitt, 2010). Characterized by optimism, sensation seeking, and impulsivity, high BAS sensitivity predicts substance use and aggression (Bijttebier, Beck, Claes, & Vandereycken, 2009). The fight-flight-freeze system (FFFS) responds to immediate punishment or threats of harm. It activates emotions such as panic, fear, and rage that initiate escape, avoidance, and/or fight behaviors. High FFFS sensitivity is associated with phobias and panic disorder. Finally, the behavioral inhibition system (BIS) is responsible for resolving goal conflicts, such as between the BAS (approach) and FFFS (avoidance), or within each of these systems. When a conflict is detected (e.g., "Do I flee this dentist chair or endure the pain in order to have cleaner teeth?"; "Do we keep having sex or go calm our crying baby?"), the BIS elicits anxiety in order to inhibit ongoing behaviors, direct attention to the threat, and motivate a controlled assessment of the situation. Thus, whereas the BAS motivates hasty approach behaviors and the FFFS motivates active forms of avoidance, behavioral inhibition allows for cautious approach or passive avoidance of a perceived threat (Corr, 2013). The greater the perceived conflict and resulting anxiety, the more likely the BIS will inhibit BAS-mediated behavior and facilitate FFFS-mediated behavior. High BIS sensitivity is a risk factor for anxiety and depressive symptoms (Bijttebier et al., 2009; Degnan, Almas, & Fox, 2010). The revised theory and supporting evidence show that both FFFS and BIS are associated with neuroticism, whereas high BAS is associated with extraversion (Gray & McNaughton, 2003; Heym, Ferguson, & Lawrence, 2008).

Researchers propose that BIS sensitivity leads to rumination and worry because people become mentally stuck in a perceived conflict (Corr & Perkins, 2006). Unfortunately, the empirical research supporting this hypothesis is inconclusive. Because they can both trigger negative emotions and behavioral inhibition, BIS and FFFS in the original theory were not adequately differentiated. Accordingly, the original BIS subscale confounds BIS-related anxiety and FFFS-related fear. That said, BIS sensitivity is robustly associated with greater rumination and worry (Broeren et al., 2011; Denson, Pedersen, & Miller, 2006; Izadpanah, Schumacher, & Barnow, 2017; Keune, Bostanov, Kotchoubey, & Hautzinger, 2012; Leen-Feldner, Zvolensky, Feldner, & Lejuez, 2004; Li, Xu, & Chen, 2015; McGregor, Gailliot, Vasquez, & Nash, 2007; Randles et al., 2010). Unfortunately, we cannot know whether these associations are driven by BIS sensitivity or FFFS sensitivity, or both. In a rare study that separated these processes, both BIS and FFFS were associated with greater rumination (Randles et al., 2010).

Interestingly, some researchers also argue that BAS sensitivity predicts rumination. Specifically, people high in BAS sensitivity are likely to focus on future rewards, opening the door for frustration when their hopes are not met (Renn, Steinbauer, & Fenner, 2014). This discrepancy between desired and current states is proposed to contribute to rumination. However, the association between BAS sensitivity and rumination is mixed in the literature. For instance, general BAS sensitivity correlates with more general and depressive rumination (Li et al., 2015; Renn et al., 2014) but is not associated with angry rumination (Denson et al., 2006; Izadpanah et al., 2017). These mixed findings might reflect the multifaceted nature of BAS sensitivity, which is typically assessed via three subscales: drive (i.e., goal persistence), fun-seeking (i.e., pursuit of immediate rewards), and reward responsiveness (i.e., motivation for anticipated rewards). Studies that have examined these separate subscales find the most robust correlation between reward responsiveness and rumination (Keune et al., 2012; Li et al., 2015; Randles et al., 2010). The fact that reward responsiveness is also generally associated with greater BIS-related anxiety led some researchers to suggest that BAS-reward responsiveness and BIS share the feature of focusing on the future or past, respectively, for goal achievement, both of which may contribute to repetitive thinking (e.g., Heym et al., 2008).

In sum, evidence suggests that all three motivational systems, or at least facets of them, are associated with greater rumination. However, the majority of studies have not assessed BIS and FFFS separately. Moreover, researchers need to examine why BAS sensitivity is often associated with more rumination, when extraversion shows either nonsignificant or negative correlations with rumination (Bagby & Parker, 2001; McEvoy & Mahoney, 2013; Svansdottir et al., 2013; Trapnell & Campbell, 1999). In addition, some recent theorizing suggests that BAS, FFFS, and BIS sensitivities interact to predict outcomes (Corr, 2002). For instance, someone might have tendencies to withdraw and agonize over perceived conflicts (i.e., BIS) and also be motivated to attain rewards (i.e., BAS). However, the only study to test this with rumination found no such interactive effect (Izadpanah et al., 2017). Clearly, more theoretical and empirical work is needed to understand the effects of BAS, FFFS, and BIS sensitivities on rumination.

Summary

These various literatures demonstrate that neuroticism and several related predispositions—emotional sensitivity, intolerance of uncertainty, perfectionism, and behavioral inhibition sensitivity—are all associated with greater rumination. These traits are also associated with greater avoidance (Mahaffey et al., 2016; Mansell & McEvoy, 2016; Santanello & Gardner, 2007). In fact, researchers propose the concept of the neurotic cascade (Suls & Martin, 2005), in which individuals high in neuroticism react more strongly to life stressors (i.e., FFFS and BIS sensitivity) and appraise many experiences as threatening (i.e., emotional sensitivity, intolerance of uncertainty, and perfectionism), leading to simultaneous tendencies to focus on these experiences (i.e., rumination) and suppress negative thoughts (i.e., avoidance). As we know, these responses only result in the maintenance of negative mood. Interestingly, people high in trait neuroticism also report experiencing more negative life events, which provide triggers for this cascade. Thus, it may be that the stressors discussed in the previous chapter are not always independent of the personality traits covered here. In other words, people high in neuroticism and all of its manifestations are more likely to experience both actual stressors and perceived discrepancies, making frequent rumination a likely outcome.

Emotion regulation

Emotion regulation refers to the processes by which individuals influence which emotions they have and how they experience, express, and understand their emotions (Gross, 1998). Effective emotion regulation often involves being aware of and accepting emotions, differentiating between various emotions (i.e., clarity), maintaining self-control when experiencing negative emotions, and effectively using mood regulation strategies (Gratz & Roemer, 2004; Mennin, Holaway, Fresco, Moore, & Heimberg, 2007; Salovey, Mayer, Goldman, Turvey, & Palfai, 1995). Mood regulation strategies include activities that aim to repair negative moods or maintain positive moods, such as exercise, relaxation, thinking positively, listening to music, and talking with someone (Thayer, Newman, & McClain, 1994).

How might emotion regulation contribute to whether people engage in rumination? One possibility is that people use rumination when they lack more adaptive emotion regulation skills that can reduce negative emotion. Another possibility is that people use rumination when they believe that they must do everything possible to fix a negative mood. A third, more controversial possibility is that people use rumination when they want to maintain or increase a negative emotion.

Poor emotion regulation skills

People with weak emotion regulation abilities experience more intense negative emotions, have poor clarity about emotions, find negative emotions aversive, and do not effectively and appropriately manage their emotions. Several facets of poor emotion regulation are robustly associated with rumination.

Lack of acceptance and avoidance of negative emotions predict greater rumination. In line with the literature reviewed above on emotional sensitivity, the more that people judge themselves harshly for having negative emotions, the more they ruminate and worry (Liverant et al., 2011; Salters-Pedneault, Roemer, Tull, Rucker, & Mennin, 2006; Williams, Harfmann, Ingram, Hagan, & Kramer, 2015). In adults with diagnosed depression, following a sad mood induction, less acceptance of the emotional experience predicted greater state rumination (Liverant et al., 2011). A related construct is expressive suppression, or the inhibition of emotional expression (Gross, 1998). Similar to people who attempt to suppress thoughts, those who suppress their emotional expression in fact feel more negative emotions and fewer positive emotions (Gross & John, 2003). Not surprisingly, expressive suppression is also associated with more rumination (Boyes, Hasking, & Martin, 2016; Gross & John, 2003). In sum, findings from the emotion regulation literature parallel those discussed previously about the associations between emotional nonacceptance and rumination.

People who have low perceived competence at repairing negative moods and maintaining positive moods are also more likely to ruminate. In fact, robust evidence shows that low perceived mood regulation ability is associated with more rumination and worry (Lischetzke & Eid, 2003; Ramos, Fernandez-Berrocal, & Extremera, 2007; Salguero, Extremera, & Fernández-Berrocal, 2013; Salters-Pedneault et al., 2006; Williams et al., 2015). A related construct is negative problem orientation, or the tendency to doubt one's problem-solving ability and view problems as unsolvable. Across several studies, people with negative problem orientation report greater rumination and worry (González, Ibáñez, & Barrera, 2017; Laugesen et al., 2003; Robichaud & Dugas, 2005; Sugiura, 2007). Similarly, self-efficacy involves the belief that one has the ability to successfully attain desired outcomes and tackle challenges. People with less self-efficacy have more rumination tendencies (Di Giunta et al., 2017; Ebner, Schulte, Soucek, & Kauffeld, 2018; Takagishi, Sakata, & Kitamura, 2013). In sum, lack of confidence in one's ability to regulate emotions and solve challenges is associated with greater rumination.

Difficulty identifying one's emotions also triggers rumination, perhaps as an attempt to seek emotional clarity. Most studies have found that poor clarity is associated with more rumination and worry, although the effects are sometimes very small (Lischetzke & Eid, 2003; Salguero et al., 2013; Salovey et al., 1995; Salters-Pedneault et al., 2006; Vine, Aldao, & Nolen-Hoeksema, 2014; Williams et al., 2015). One research team found that low perceived competence at mood regulation mediated the link between low emotional clarity and rumination (Salguero et al., 2013). This suggests that confusion about emotions may lead people to believe that they cannot repair negative moods, which in turn triggers rumination.

Greater awareness of one's emotions should theoretically be related to rumination, because both involve attending to emotional states (Gross, 1998). However, the empirical literature on this association is mixed. Some studies have found that the tendency to pay attention to emotions is associated with more rumination (Lischetzke & Eid, 2003; Salguero et al., 2013; Salovey, Stroud, Woolery, & Epel, 2002; Swinkels & Giuliano, 1995), but others have found small and nonsignificant associations (Ramos et al., 2007; Salters-Pedneault et al., 2006; Williams et al., 2015). These conflicting results have several potential explanations. First, the effect of attention on emotions may depend on the nature of the emotions people are experiencing. Attention to neutral or positive moods may be a harmless activity that does not elicit repetitive thinking, whereas attention to negative moods may trigger rumination (Swinkels & Giuliano, 1995). Another possibility is that emotional awareness has positive or negative outcomes depending on whether people believe they can repair negative moods. One study found that emotional awareness predicted greater well-being for people high in perceived mood repair, whereas it predicted worse well-being for people low in perceived mood repair (Lischetzke & Eid, 2003). Thus, people who habitually attend to their emotions may ruminate only if they also believe that they do not have the skills to manage the emotions they are noticing. Finally, the effects of emotional awareness may be nonlinear, with a moderate amount of attention adaptively allowing people to track and respond to their moods, but too little attention indicating maladaptive avoidance and too much attention indicating an unhealthy level of self-focused attention and rumination.

Rules about fixing negative emotions

A separate research literature focuses on the perceived role of emotions and internal rules for responding to emotions. People generally interpret moods as providing information about whether a desired goal has been met (Martin & Davies, 1998). Positive moods often indicate that a goal has been attained. By contrast, people may interpret negative moods as indicating that they have not attained or made progress on a particular goal. This aligns with the idea of perceived goal discrepancy, such that a negative mood may indicate to people that a perceived discrepancy exists. Rather than a negative mood automatically triggering rumination, however, some researchers suggest that the effect of negative moods on behavior (e.g., rumination) depends on people's inherent stop rules (Meeten & Davey, 2011). Stop rules are explicit or implicit rules that people use to define the goals of a task. For instance, some people stop eating when their plates are objectively empty (i.e., *as many as can* rule), whereas others stop eating when they are subjectively full (*i.e., feel like continuing* rule). These stop rules can influence how people respond to positive and negative moods.

One seminal study instructed participants who were in either positive or negative moods to generate a list of birds (Martin, Ward, Achee, & Wyer, 1993). Half of the participants were told to stop listing birds when they no longer enjoyed doing so, whereas half were asked to stop when they thought they had generated enough. The authors expected that the same moods might have different effects on behavior (e.g., how long people worked at the task, how many birds they generated) depending on the stop rule. In fact, when participants were asked to stop listing birds when they no longer enjoyed it (*i.e., feel like continuing* rule), participants in negative moods stopped sooner than those in positive moods. By contrast, when participants were asked to stop when they thought they had generated enough (*i.e., as many as can* rule), those in negative moods worked longer than those in positive moods. Put another way, the combination of a negative mood with an *as many as can* stop rule led to the most task persistence. Researchers soon appreciated the potential implications for repetitive thinking. Specifically, the combination of negative mood with a tendency to employ an *as many as can* stop rule should lead to rumination and worry (Meeten & Davey, 2011).

Empirical evidence for this hypothesis first emerged in studies on worry. In this research, participants went through a catastrophizing interview, in which they were asked "what worries you most about [your main current worry]?", and then the question was asked again about their response to the first question, and so on, until participants could not think of any more answers. When instructed to engage in the interview using an *as many as can* rule, participants who were in negative moods generated more catastrophizing responses about their main worry than did participants who were in a happy mood (Meeten & Davey, 2011). By contrast, when instructed to use a *feel like continuing* rule, participants in negative moods generated fewer catastrophizing responses. Similar results were found when comparing high and low trait worriers instead of induced negative and positive mood (Startup & Davey, 2001). Specifically, the negative mood experienced by trait worriers in combination with an *as many as can* stop rule contributed to more catastrophizing about a current worry. Nonexperimental studies also show that people, both with and without GAD, who report adopting an *as many as can* stop rule about their worry report higher trait worry and generate more responses in a catastrophizing interview (Dash & Davey, 2011; Davey, Startup, MacDonald, Jenkins, & Patterson, 2005; Meeten et al., 2016; Turner, 2010). In sum, worry behavior appears to be elicited by negative moods paired with an *as many as can* stop rule.

Stop rules have also been explored as contributors to depressive rumination. In an adaptation of the catastrophizing interview, participants were asked "Why is it that [your main topic of recent depression] makes you feel depressed?", and so on until they stopped providing new reasons for being depressed (Watkins & Mason, 2002). When using an *as many as can* stop rule, participants in induced negative moods generated more responses than did participants in positive moods (Hawksley & Davey, 2010). Similarly, depressive ruminators generated more reasons for feeling depressed when using an *as many as can* rule than did nonruminators (Watkins & Mason, 2002). The same results were found when comparing participants with and without major depression (Chan, Davey, & Brewin, 2013). Furthermore, depressed participants were more likely to use an *as many as can* rule in response to negative moods in their everyday lives, and greater endorsement of this stop rule was associated with higher trait depressive rumination.

In sum, this literature suggests that people who believe that they should do as much as they can do fix negative moods are likely to ruminate or worry. This may occur because individuals who habitually use an *as many as can* stop rule apply this rule to their repetitive thinking, persisting until they believe they have fully solved the "problem" of rumination or worry. Unfortunately, an existing negative mood will provide feedback that they have not achieved their goal, so the rumination and worry continue.

Perceived need for a negative mood

Emotion regulation theories generally assume that people want to minimize negative emotions (e.g., Larsen, 2000). However, in some situations, it may be functional and even desirable to maintain a negative emotion. The mood-as-input model (Martin & Davies, 1998) proposes that people seek positive *outcomes*, not necessarily positive moods. Thus, if a negative mood leads to a positive outcome, then people may seek to maintain that negative mood. Similarly, the instrumental account of emotion regulation proposes that what people want to feel is a balance of both pleasure and utility (Tamir, 2009). Specifically, when immediate benefits (i.e., pleasure) outweigh long-term benefits (i.e., delayed pleasure derived from successful goal pursuit), people prefer pleasant emotions. However, when long-term benefits outweigh immediate benefits, people prefer useful emotions, even if they are unpleasant. Anyone who has put off hanging out with friends in order to spend hours or even days studying for a test is familiar with this balance. These theories suggest that people may ruminate because they have a reason for maintaining or increasing a negative mood. In the next section, I review some of the proposed reasons why people want to maintain or increase negative moods (see Tamir, 2016).

Performance motives

Emotions can help people optimize their performance in order to achieve desired goals. As an example, one strategy I often use to motivate myself to exercise is to think about how sad my children will be if I die young because of poor health. In other words, I sometimes stoke my health-related fears in order to get myself into running clothes and out the door. Empirical evidence for performance motives involves several specific emotions.

First, people prefer to experience sadness when they need to engage in careful, analytical thinking. A large literature suggests that sad mood promotes deliberative, analytical processing that enhances accuracy on complex tasks. For instance, although people make more negative judgments when they are sad or depressed, their judgments are often more accurate than those made by happy people (Strunk & Adler, 2009). In a series of experiments, individuals who were in sad mood and who expected to engage in a challenging cognitive task that required precision and analytical thinking were more likely to choose to listen to sad music than were individuals in a neutral mood (Cohen & Andrade, 2004). When asked why, participants indicated that they believed that a sad mood, with its accompanying focus and deep thinking, would help them perform the task better.

People may choose to experience fear if their goal is to avoid threats (Tamir, 2009). In one study, participants who expected to play videogames in which they had to avoid threatening monsters preferred to listen to fear-inducing music (Tamir & Ford, 2009). In fact, the more people expected the music to make them afraid, the more they wanted to listen to it. Similarly, people who implicitly indicated that fear is useful for avoiding threats were more likely to prefer fear-inducing stimuli before a threatening task (Tamir, Chiu, & Gross, 2007). These results suggest that people may not be consciously aware of their motives for increasing negative emotions but may nevertheless behave accordingly. Some people may also believe that anxiety contributes to better performance. In fact, anxiety can increase motivation for and mental effort at a task, leading to improved performance (Nieuwenhuys & Oudejans, 2012). In a test of this motive, participants high in neuroticism elected to experience anxiety before giving a speech (Tamir, 2005). Moreover, the choice to experience anxiety (vs happiness) predicted better performance on a difficult anagram task. Thus, neurotic people may prefer to feel anxiety when engaging in cognitively demanding tasks because they think it will improve their performance.

People connect feeling angry with succeeding in an anticipated conflict. In one study, participants were asked whether they preferred to recall certain events and listen to particular music selections before playing confrontational videogames (Tamir, Mitchell, & Gross, 2008). Although participants expected that the angering music and memories would be unpleasant, they were more likely to choose them (vs exciting music and memories) before playing confrontational videogames. Furthermore, participants who listened to angering music performed better in confrontational videogames (i.e., they killed more enemies). In a different study, participants were told that they would be playing the role of a landlord who had to negotiate with a tenant who had not paid rent (Tamir & Ford, 2012). Participants who were told that their goal was to get the money immediately (i.e., confrontation condition) preferred to watch anger-eliciting movie clips and recall angering memories, whereas participants whose goal was to maintain a long-term relationship (i.e., collaboration condition) preferred happiness-inducing activities. Angered participants were in fact more successful at getting their interaction partners to pay the requested money.

Social motives

Emotions may also help people achieve specific social goals. Specifically, people may prefer to feel particular emotions in order to get something they want from other people. For example, sadness can prompt helping behaviors from others, particularly when a person is trying to recruit help to cope with a loss. In one study, individuals imagined asking for help from a classmate about an upcoming paper they had not started (Hackenbracht & Tamir, 2010). Those who were told that a low grade would dramatically decrease their chance of obtaining a summer internship (i.e., loss condition) were more likely to prefer experiencing and expressing sadness while asking for help, compared to individuals who were told that a good grade would increase their chance of obtaining an internship (i.e., benefit condition). On the flip side, anger inspires people do something for and make more concessions to the angered individual (van Kleef, De Dreu, & Manstead, 2004). Interestingly, people also report increased respect for someone who is angry (Averill, 1983). In fact, in a series of studies, individuals supported a politician or job candidate more when the politician or candidate expressed anger, compared to sadness, and this effect occurred because they ascribed greater competence, status, and salary to the angered individual (Tiedens, 2001). Thus, whereas sadness can elicit helping behavior, anger can prompt respect and submissive behavior.

Emotions can also increase the feeling of social belonging. In one study, the more that Israeli students wanted to feel a part of Israeli society, the more they chose to experience sadness on a national day of mourning because they believed that feeling sad would increase their sense of belonging (Porat, Halperin, Mannheim, & Tamir, 2016). Furthermore, experimentally increasing participants' need to belong contributed to stronger preferences for feeling sad on this particular day. Sometimes social belonging requires matching emotions with another person. For instance, happy participants who expected to interact with a sad partner chose to read sad, versus happy or neutral, news stories prior to the interaction (Nelson, 1997). Similarly, participants who were primed with affiliation goals were more likely to match their emotions to the anticipated emotions of a future interaction partner (Huntsinger, Lun, Sinclair, & Clore, 2009). Thus, negative emotions can be instrumental in fostering social belongingness.

Emotions do not just occur at the individual level. Group-based emotions are experienced because of people's identification with a particular group. Group-based emotions, particularly if they are shared among group members, foster group solidarity (Mackie, Devos, & Smith, 2000; Páez, Rimé, Basabe, Wlodarczyk, & Zumeta, 2015). Group-based anger also predicts people's willingness to engage in political activism on behalf of one's group (van Zomeren, Postmes, & Spears, 2008). Thus, people may choose to feel group-based anger toward out-group members if the anger aligns with their group's goals. In a series of studies, Jewish Israelis who endorsed more right-wing ideology (e.g., preserving Israeli power, holding prejudicial attitudes) showed a greater preference for feeling anger toward Palestinians, even controlling for how angry they wanted to feel in general (Porat, Halperin, & Tamir, 2016). This ideologically motivated preference for anger in turn predicted greater anger in response to various political events and support for more aggressive policies.

Self-verification motives

Finally, people are often motivated to verify how they see themselves, and emotions can play a role in this process. For instance, people with lower self-esteem were less motivated to decrease sad feelings in part because these feelings were more familiar and because they did not believe they deserved to feel good (Wood, Heimpel, Manwell, & Whittington, 2009). Similarly, although they could have chosen to view happy stimuli, individuals with major depression elected to view sad images and listen to sad music more frequently than did nondepressed people (Millgram, Joormann, Huppert, & Tamir, 2015). Even when they were trained to use a strategy to decrease their emotional reactions to sad images, depressed people instead opted to use the strategy to *increase* their reactions to sad images. Thus, sad people intentionally chose to increase their sad moods. Similar results have been found with fear and anger, in that people higher in trait fear and anger wanted to experience fear and anger, respectively, because they were familiar with these emotions (Ford & Tamir, 2014; see also Tamir, 2005).

Summary

In sum, people may choose to maintain negative emotions with the longer term goals of improving performance, avoiding threats, increasing desired behavior from others, fostering social belonging with individuals and groups, and verifying their views of themselves. The instrumental model of emotion regulation (Tamir, 2009; Tamir, 2016) and most of this supporting literature does not include rumination as a relevant construct. However, it seems probable that rumination is an important mechanism by which people maintain and increase negative emotions that serve an instrumental purpose. Future research should examine whether these particular instrumental goals for negative emotions predict increased negative rumination.

Conclusion

In this chapter, I examined beliefs, personality traits, and motivations that make people more likely to ruminate. Specifically, individuals who ruminate are more likely to experience strong negative emotions in response to stressors (i.e., neuroticism), fear negative emotions and uncertainty, have concerns about the quality of their own performance (i.e., perfectionistic concerns), and experience anxiety in response to perceived threats or conflicts (i.e., BIS sensitivity). Ruminators also have difficulty identifying and understanding their emotions, believe that they are incapable of effectively managing their emotions, and interpret negative moods as indicating the need for continued efforts to "solve" the perceived problem (i.e., stop rules). Experiencing emotions as intense, unclear, and aversive and believing that emotions cannot effectively be modulated without great effort may understandably lead people to want to avoid unpleasant emotions, which only fuels more rumination. Finally, people may ruminate because they believe that these strategies will be helpful, either in coping with and preparing for perceived problems (i.e., metacognitive beliefs), or potentially in maintaining negative moods that will help them achieve desired goals. The material covered in this and the previous chapter raises several interesting possibilities and questions that I briefly address.

In the beginning of this chapter, I suggested that beliefs, traits, and motivations moderate the effect of triggers on the presence and frequency of rumination. However, a complementary possibility is that the triggers covered in the previous chapter may influence the constructs covered here, and vice versa, to lead to rumination. For instance, I mentioned above that people high in neuroticism experience more life stressors. As another example, child behavioral inhibition – a manifestation of neuroticism – may influence and be influenced by parenting behaviors (e.g., caring, overprotection, attachment), which in turn moderate the effect of behavioral inhibition on outcomes such as rumination (Degnan et al., 2010). Finally, although the majority of research tests for an interaction between negative mood and stop rules, it is also possible that negative moods elicit an *as many as can* stop rule, because people interpret the negative mood to indicate that their goal has not yet been met. In fact, a recent experiment found that endorsement of an *as many as can* stop rule for worry mediated the effect of induced negative mood on worry (Dash & Davey, 2011). Thus, the triggers and dispositional tendencies covered in these two chapters may play both mediational and moderational roles in predicting rumination. Much more research is needed to understand the interplay of multiple predictors of rumination.

One interesting question raised by examining predictors of rumination is whether rumination is intentional or unintentional. The field appears to be torn about this issue. On the one hand, evidence about positive beliefs about rumination implies that rumination occurs a response to conscious intentions. Similarly, Segerstrom's empirically based suggestion that repetitive thought varies along a purpose dimension (e.g., searching for understanding and new ideas vs solving problems and improving certainty) assumes intentionality (e.g., Segerstrom et al., 2003). Moreover, the potential role of motivations regarding desired emotions might suggest that rumination is an intentional attempt to achieve a desired cognitive or emotional state. On the other hand, control theory argued that rumination is an unintentional, automatic cognitive response to a perceived discrepancy (Martin & Tesser, 1996). Other researchers have classified rumination as an involuntary form of coping (Connor-Smith, Compas, Wadsworth, Harding Thomsen, & Saltzman, 2000). In their habit-goal framework of rumination, Watkins and Nolen-Hoeksema (2014) argued that habits are triggered by contextual cues, rather than goals and intentions. In fact, even when people might like, or intend, to stop a habitual behavior like rumination, it proves difficult because the habit is resistant to change. Empirically, people report that they ruminate and worry more than they intend to and that they fear that rumination and worry are uncontrollable (see also Chapter 2: Rumination and anxiety-related disorders). The fact that rumination is perceived to be uncontrollable suggests that the degree to which people ruminate is unintentional. Future research should more explicitly address this question of intentionality.

A related but different question is whether rumination occurs consciously or unconsciously. Certainly, any self-report measure of trait or state rumination assumes that it is a conscious experience that people can people reliably report. Similarly, rumination manipulations ask people to engage in conscious, intentional thoughts about particular topics. However, in talking with people anecdotally about rumination over the years, most of them share experiences of not always being fully conscious of their ruminating. The common story goes something like, "I suddenly realized that I had been ruminating about XXX for the past 20 minutes, and I only noticed it when I found myself tense or upset." Brosschot (2010) in fact theorized about the existence of unconscious perseverative cognition. He suggested that unconscious perseverative cognition is not necessarily inaccessible to awareness but is simply not attended to. Evidence from other psychology literatures increasingly suggests that complex mental processing can occur at an unconscious level. One account argued that people can pursue goals unconsciously, without having intention or monitoring their progress (Bargh & Morsella, 2008). These unconscious goals in turn generate unconscious behavioral impulses, which people may only become aware and make sense of after the fact. This account suggests that unconscious goals may trigger an unconscious impulse for rumination. In line with this, Nolen-Hoeksema et al. (2008) argued that depressive rumination and worry have both conscious and unconscious motives. Specifically, depressive rumination is consciously undertaken in order to understand why events, occurred, gain insight, and solve problems. Its unconscious motive is to avoid uncomfortable situations or feelings, as well as the need to take action to improve the situation. For worry, the conscious motive is to anticipate and prepare for threat, whereas the unconscious motive is to avoid negative emotions and uncomfortable images. Thus, perhaps rumination reflects both conscious and unconscious motives. A fascinating area for future research would be to examine whether the experience of and motives for rumination are conscious and/or unconscious, and whether this in turn influences outcomes.

References

Andrews, L., Troop, N., Joseph, S., Hiskey, S., & Coyne, I. (2002). Attempted versus successful avoidance: Associations with distress, symptoms, and strategies for mental control. *Personality and Individual Differences, 33*(6), 897–907. Available from https://doi.org/10.1016/S0191-8869(01)00200-8.

Averill, J. R. (1983). Studies on anger and aggression: Implications for theories of emotion. *American Psychologist, 38*(11), 1145–1160. Available from https://doi.org/10.1037/0003-066X.38.11.1145.

Bagby, R., & Parker, J. (2001). Relation of rumination and distraction with neuroticism and extraversion in a sample of patients with major depression. *Cognitive Therapy and Research, 25*(1), 91–102. Available from https://doi.org/1026430900363.

Bargh, J. A., & Morsella, E. (2008). The unconscious mind. *Perspectives on Psychological Science, 3*(1), 73–79. Available from https://doi.org/10.1111/j.1745-6916.2008.00064.x.

Békés, V., Dunkley, D. M., Taylor, G., Zuroff, D. C., Lewkowski, M., Elizabeth Foley, J., ... Westreich, R. (2015). Chronic stress and attenuated improvement in depression over 1 year: The moderating role of perfectionism. *Behavior Therapy, 46*(4), 478–492. Available from https://doi.org/10.1016/j.beth.2015.02.003.

Bieling, P. J., Israeli, A. L., & Antony, M. M. (2004). Is perfectionism good, bad, or both? Examining models of the perfectionism construct. *Personality and Individual Differences, 36*(6), 1373–1385. Available from https://doi.org/10.1016/S0191-8869(03)00235-6.

Bijttebier, P., Beck, I., Claes, L., & Vandereycken, W. (2009). Gray's reinforcement sensitivity theory as a framework for research on personality–psychopathology associations. *Clinical Psychology Review, 29*(5), 421–430. Available from https://doi.org/10.1016/j.cpr.2009.04.002.

Birrell, J., Meares, K., Wilkinson, A., & Freeston, M. (2011). Toward a definition of intolerance of uncertainty: A review of factor analytical studies of the intolerance of uncertainty scale. *Clinical Psychology Review, 31*(7), 1198–1208. Available from https://doi.org/10.1016/j.cpr.2011.07.009.

Blankstein, K., & Lumley, C. (2008). Multidimensional perfectionism and ruminative brooding in current dysphoria, anxiety, worry, and anger. *Journal of Rational-Emotive & Cognitive-Behavior Therapy, 26*(3), 168–193. Available from https://doi.org/10.1007/s10942-007-0068-z.

Blasberg, J. S., Hewitt, P. L., Flett, G. L., Sherry, S. B., & Chen, C. (2016). The importance of item wording. *Journal of Psychoeducational Assessment, 34*(7), 702–717. Available from https://doi.org/10.1177/0734282916653701.

Borkovec, T. D., & Roemer, L. (1995). Perceived functions of worry among generalized anxiety disorder subjects: Distraction from more emotionally distressing topics? *Journal of Behavior Therapy and Experimental Psychiatry, 26*(1), 25–30. Available from https://doi.org/10.1016/0005-7916(94)00064-S.

Boyes, M. E., Hasking, P. A., & Martin, G. (2016). Adverse life experience and psychological distress in adolescence: Moderating and mediating effects of emotion regulation and rumination. *Stress and Health, 32*(4), 402–410. Available from https://doi.org/10.1002/smi.2635.

Broeren, S., Muris, P., Bouwmeester, S., Heijden, K., & Abee, A. (2011). The role of repetitive negative thoughts in the vulnerability for emotional problems in non-clinical children. *Journal of Child and Family Studies, 20*(2), 135–148. Available from https://doi.org/10.1007/s10826-010-9380-9.

Brosschot, J. F. (2010). Markers of chronic stress: Prolonged physiological activation and (un)conscious perseverative cognition. *Neuroscience and Biobehavioral Reviews, 35*(1), 46–50. Available from https://doi.org/10.1016/j.neubiorev.2010.01.004.

Brosschot, J. F., Van Dijk, E., & Thayer, J. F. (2007). Daily worry is related to low heart rate variability during waking and the subsequent nocturnal sleep period. *International Journal of Psychophysiology, 63*(1), 39–47. Available from https://doi.org/10.1016/j.ijpsycho.2006.07.016.

Brown, J., & Kocovski, N. (2014). Perfectionism as a predictor of post-event rumination in a socially anxious sample. *Journal of Rational-Emotive & Cognitive-Behavior Therapy, 32*(2), 150–163. Available from https://doi.org/10.1007/s10942-013-0175-y.

Buhr, K., & Dugas, M. J. (2009). The role of fear of anxiety and intolerance of uncertainty in worry: An experimental manipulation. *Behaviour Research and Therapy, 47*(3), 215–223. Available from https://doi.org/10.1016/j.brat.2008.12.004.

Buhr, K., & Dugas, M. J. (2012). Fear of emotions, experiential avoidance, and intolerance of uncertainty in worry and generalized anxiety disorder. *International Journal of Cognitive Therapy, 5*(1), 1–17. Available from https://doi.org/10.1521/ijct.2012.5.1.1.

Cartwright-Hatton, S., & Wells, A. (1997). Beliefs about worry and intrusions: The meta-cognitions questionnaire and its correlates. *Journal of Anxiety Disorders, 11*(3), 279–296. Available from https://doi.org/10.1016/S0887-6185(97)00011-X.

Chan, J. C. S., Davey, G. C. L., & Brewin, C. R. (2013). Understanding depressive rumination from a mood-as-input perspective: Effects of stop-rule manipulation. *Behaviour Research and Therapy, 51*(6), 300–306. Available from https://doi.org/10.1016/j.brat.2013.02.007.

Cohen, J. B., & Andrade, E. B. (2004). Affective intuition and task-contingent affect regulation. *Journal of Consumer Research, 31*(2), 358–367. Available from https://doi.org/10.1086/422114.

Connor-Smith, J. K., Compas, B. E., Wadsworth, M. E., Harding Thomsen, A., & Saltzman, H. (2000). Responses to stress in adolescence. *Journal of Consulting and Clinical Psychology, 68*(6), 976–992. Available from https://doi.org/10.1037/0022-006X.68.6.976.

Connor-Smith, J. K., & Flachsbart, C. (2007). Relations between personality and coping. *Journal of Personality and Social Psychology, 93*(6), 1080–1107. Available from https://doi.org/10.1037/0022-3514.93.6.1080.

Corr, P. J. (2002). J. A. Gray's reinforcement sensitivity theory: Tests of the joint subsystems hypothesis of anxiety and impulsivity. *Personality and Individual Differences, 33*(4), 511–532. Available from https://doi.org/10.1016/S0191-8869(01)00170-2.

Corr, P. J. (2013). Approach and avoidance behaviour: Multiple systems and their interactions. *Emotion Review, 5*(3), 285–290. Available from https://doi.org/10.1177/1754073913477507.

Corr, P. J., & Perkins, A. M. (2006). The role of theory in the psychophysiology of personality: From Ivan Pavlov to Jeffrey Gray. *International Journal of Psychophysiology, 62*(3), 367–376. Available from https://doi.org/10.1016/j.ijpsycho.2006.01.005.

Cox, S. L., & Chen, J. (2015). Perfectionism: A contributor to social anxiety and its cognitive processes. *Australian Journal of Psychology, 67*(4), 231–240. Available from https://doi.org/10.1111/ajpy.12079.

Cribb, G., Moulds, M. L., & Carter, S. (2006). Rumination and experiential avoidance in depression. *Behaviour Change, 23*(3), 165–176. Available from https://doi.org/10.1375/bech.23.3.165.

Dash, S. R., & Davey, G. C. L. (2011). An experimental investigation of the role of negative mood in worry: The role of appraisals that facilitate systematic information processing. *Journal of Behavior Therapy and Experimental Psychiatry, 43*(2), 823–831. Available from https://doi.org/10.1016/j.jbtep.2011.12.002.

Davey, G., Startup, H., MacDonald, C., Jenkins, D., & Patterson, K. (2005). The use of "as many as can" versus "feel like continuing" stop rules during worrying. *Cognitive Therapy and Research, 29*(2), 155–169. Available from https://doi.org/10.1007/s10608-005-3162-5.

Davis, R. N., & Valentiner, D. P. (2000). Does meta-cognitive theory enhance our understanding of pathological worry and anxiety? *Personality and Individual Differences, 29*(3), 513–526. Available from https://doi.org/10.1016/S0191-8869(99)00211-1.

de Bruin, G. O., Muris, P., & Rassin, E. (2007). Are there specific meta-cognitions associated with vulnerability to symptoms of worry and obsessional thoughts? *Personality and Individual Differences, 42*(4), 689–699. Available from https://doi.org/10.1016/j.paid.2006.08.015.

de Jong-Meyer, R., Beck, B., & Riede, K. (2009). Relationships between rumination, worry, intolerance of uncertainty and metacognitive beliefs. *Personality and Individual Differences, 46*(4), 547–551. Available from https://doi.org/10.1016/j.paid.2008.12.010.

Degnan, K. A., Almas, A. N., & Fox, N. A. (2010). Temperament and the environment in the etiology of childhood anxiety. *Journal of Child Psychology and Psychiatry, 51*(4), 497–517. Available from https://doi.org/10.1111/j.1469-7610.2010.02228.x.

Denson, T. F., Pedersen, W. C., & Miller, N. (2006). The displaced aggression questionnaire. *Journal of Personality and Social Psychology, 90*(6), 1032–1051. Available from https://doi.org/10.1037/0022-3514.90.6.1032.

Dickson, K. S., Ciesla, J. A., & Reilly, L. C. (2011). Rumination, worry, cognitive avoidance, and behavioral avoidance: Examination of temporal effects. *Behavior Therapy, 43*(3), 629–640. Available from https://doi.org/10.1016/j.beth.2011.11.002.

Dieler, A. C., Herrmann, M. J., & Fallgatter, A. J. (2014). Voluntary suppression of thoughts is influenced by anxious and ruminative tendencies in healthy volunteers. *Memory (Hove, England), 22*(3), 184–193. Available from https://doi.org/10.1080/09658211.2013.774420.

Di Giunta, L., Iselin, A. R., Eisenberg, N., Pastorelli, C., Gerbino, M., Lansford, J. E., ... Thartori, E. (2017). Measurement invariance and convergent validity of anger and sadness self-regulation among youth from six cultural groups. *Assessment, 24*(4), 484–502. Available from https://doi.org/10.1177/1073191115615214.

Di Schiena, R., Luminet, O., Philippot, P., & Douilliez, C. (2012). Adaptive and maladaptive perfectionism in depression: Preliminary evidence on the role of adaptive and maladaptive rumination. *Personality and Individual Differences, 53*, 574–578. Retrieved from <http://hal.univ-lille3.fr/hal-00815526>.

Dugas, M., Gosselin, P., & Ladouceur, R. (2001). Intolerance of uncertainty and worry: Investigating specificity in a nonclinical sample. *Cognitive Therapy and Research, 25*(5), 551–558. Available from https://doi.org/1005553414688.

Dugas, M. J., & Ladouceur, R. (2000). Treatment of gad. *Behavior Modification*, *24*(5), 635–657. Available from https://doi.org/10.1177/0145445500245002.

Dugas, M. J., Laugesen, N., & Bukowski, W. M. (2012). Intolerance of uncertainty, fear of anxiety, and adolescent worry. *Journal of Abnormal Child Psychology*, *40*(6), 863–870. Available from https://doi.org/10.1007/s10802-012-9611-1.

Dugas, M. J., Marchand, A., & Ladouceur, R. (2005). Further validation of a cognitive-behavioral model of generalized anxiety disorder: Diagnostic and symptom specificity. *Journal of Anxiety Disorders*, *19*(3), 329–343. Available from https://doi.org/10.1016/j.janxdis.2004.02.002.

Ebner, K., Schulte, E., Soucek, R., & Kauffeld, S. (2018). Coaching as stress-management intervention: The mediating role of self-efficacy in a framework of self-management and coping. *International Journal of Stress Management*, *25*(3), 209–233. Available from https://doi.org/10.1037/str0000058.

Egan, S. J., Hattaway, M., & Kane, R. T. (2014). The relationship between perfectionism and rumination in post traumatic stress disorder. *Behavioural and Cognitive Psychotherapy*, *42*(2), 211–223. Available from https://doi.org/10.1017/S1352465812001129.

Eisma, M. C., Schut, H. A. W., Stroebe, M. S., Boelen, P. A., van den Bout, J., & Stroebe, E. (2015). Adaptive and maladaptive rumination after loss. A three-wave longitudinal study. *British Journal of Clinical Psychology*, *54*(2), 163–180. Available from https://doi.org/10.1111/bjc.12067.

Eisma, M. C., Stroebe, M. S., Schut, H. A. W., van den Bout, J., Boelen, P. A., & Stroebe, W. (2014). Development and psychometric evaluation of the Utrecht grief rumination scale. *Journal of Psychopathology and Behavioral Assessment*, *36*(1), 165–176. Available from https://doi.org/10.1007/s10862-013-9377-y.

Enns, M., Cox, B., & Clara, I. (2005). Perfectionism and neuroticism: A longitudinal study of specific vulnerability and diathesis-stress models. *Cognitive Therapy and Research*, *29*(4), 463–478. Available from https://doi.org/10.1007/s10608-005-2843-04.

Erskine, J. A. K., Kvavilashvili, L., & Kornbrot, D. E. (2007). The predictors of thought suppression in young and old adults: Effects of rumination, anxiety, and other variables. *Personality and Individual Differences*, *42*(6), 1047–1057. Available from https://doi.org/10.1016/j.paid.2006.09.016.

Esbjørn, B. H., Lønfeldt, N. N., Nielsen, S. K., Reinholdt-Dunne, M. L., Sømhovd, M. J., & Cartwright-Hatton, S. (2015). Meta-worry, worry, and anxiety in children and adolescents: Relationships and interactions. *Journal of Clinical Child & Adolescent Psychology*, *44*(1), 145–156. Available from https://doi.org/10.1080/15374416.2013.873980.

Flaxman, P. E., Ménard, J., Bond, F. W., & Kinman, G. (2012). Academics' experiences of a respite from work: Effects of self-critical perfectionism and perseverative cognition on postrespite well-being. *The Journal of Applied Psychology*, *97*(4), 854–865. Available from https://doi.org/10.1037/a0028055.

Flett, G., Madorsky, D., Hewitt, P., & Heisel, M. (2002). Perfectionism cognitions, rumination, and psychological distress. *Journal of Rational-Emotive and Cognitive-Behavior Therapy*, *20*(1), 33–47. Available from https://doi.org/1015128904007.

Flett, G. L., Coulter, L., Hewitt, P. L., & Nepon, T. (2011). Perfectionism, rumination, worry, and depressive symptoms in early adolescents. *Canadian Journal of School Psychology*, *26*(3), 159–176. Available from https://doi.org/10.1177/0829573511422039.

Ford, B. Q., & Tamir, M. (2014). Preferring familiar emotions: As you want (and like) it? *Cognition & Emotion*, *28*(2), 311–324. Available from https://doi.org/10.1080/02699931.2013.823381.

Freeston, M. H., Rhéaume, J., Letarte, H., Dugas, M. J., & Ladouceur, R. (1994). Why do people worry? *Personality and Individual Differences*, *17*(6), 791–802. Available from https://doi.org/10.1016/0191-8869(94)90048-5.

Frost, R., Trepanier, K., Brown, E., Heimberg, R., Juster, H., Makris, G., & Leung, A. (1997). Self-monitoring of mistakes among subjects high and low in perfectionistic concern over mistakes. *Cognitive Therapy and Research, 21*(2), 209–222. Available from https://doi.org/1021884713550.

Frost, R. O., Heimberg, R. G., Holt, C. S., Mattia, J. I., & Neubauer, A. L. (1993). A comparison of two measures of perfectionism. *Personality and Individual Differences, 14*(1), 119–126. Available from https://doi.org/10.1016/0191-8869(93)90181-2.

Frost, R. O., Marten, P., Lahart, C., & Rosenblate, R. (1990). The dimensions of perfectionism. *Cognitive Therapy and Research, 14*(5), 449–468. Available from https://doi.org/10.1007/BF01172967.

Giorgio, J. M., Sanflippo, J., Kleiman, E., Reilly, D., Bender, R. E., Wagner, C. A., ... Alloy, L. B. (2010). An experiential avoidance conceptualization of depressive rumination: Three tests of the model. *Behaviour Research and Therapy, 48*(10), 1021–1031. Available from https://doi.org/10.1016/j.brat.2010.07.004.

Gold, D. B., & Wegner, D. M. (1995). Origins of ruminative thought: Trauma, incompleteness, nondisclosure, and suppression. *Journal of Applied Social Psychology, 25*(14), 1245–1261. Available from https://doi.org/10.1111/j.1559-1816.1995.tb02617.x.

González, M., Ibáñez, I., & Barrera, A. (2017). Rumination, worry and negative problem orientation: Transdiagnostic processes of anxiety, eating behavior and mood disorders. *Acta Colombiana De Psicología, 20*(2), 42–52. Available from https://doi.org/10.14718/ACP.2017.20.2.3.

Gosselin, P., Langlois, F., Freeston, M. H., Ladouceur, R., Laberge, M., & Lemay, D. (2007). Cognitive variables related to worry among adolescents: Avoidance strategies and faulty beliefs about worry. *Behaviour Research and Therapy, 45*(2), 225–233. Available from https://doi.org/10.1016/j.brat.2006.03.001.

Gratz, K., & Roemer, L. (2004). Multidimensional assessment of emotion regulation and dysregulation: Development, factor structure, and initial validation of the difficulties in emotion regulation scale. *Journal of Psychopathology and Behavioral Assessment, 26*(1), 41–54. Available from https://doi.org/JOBA.0000007455.08539.94.

Gray, J. A. (1982). *The neuropsychology of anxiety*. Oxford [u.a.]: Clarendon Press [u.a.].

Gray, J. A., & McNaughton, N. (2003). *The neuropsychology of anxiety* (2nd ed.). Oxford [u.a.]: Oxford Univ. Press.

Gross, J. J. (1998). The emerging field of emotion regulation. *Review of General Psychology, 2*(3), 271–299. Available from https://doi.org/10.1037/1089-2680.2.3.271.

Gross, J. J., & John, O. P. (2003). Individual differences in two emotion regulation processes. *Journal of Personality and Social Psychology, 85*(2), 348–362. Available from https://doi.org/10.1037/0022-3514.85.2.348.

Hackenbracht, J., & Tamir, M. (2010). Preferences for sadness when eliciting help: Instrumental motives in sadness regulation. *Motivation and Emotion, 34*(3), 306–315. Available from https://doi.org/10.1007/s11031-010-9180-y.

Harris, P. W., Pepper, C. M., & Maack, D. J. (2008). The relationship between maladaptive perfectionism and depressive symptoms: The mediating role of rumination. *Personality and Individual Differences, 44*(1), 150–160. Available from https://doi.org/10.1016/j.paid.2007.07.011.

Hawksley, J., & Davey, G. C. L. (2010). Mood-as-input and depressive rumination. *Behaviour Research and Therapy, 48*(2), 134–140. Available from https://doi.org/10.1016/j.brat.2009.10.004.

Hayes, S., Strosahl, K., Wilson, K., Bissett, R., Pistorello, J., Toarmino, D., ... McCurry, S. (2004). Measuring experiential avoidance: A preliminary test of a working model. *The Psychological Record, 54*(4), 553–578. Available from https://doi.org/10.1007/BF03395492.

Hertel, P. T., & Gerstle, M. (2003). Depressive deficits in forgetting. *Psychological Science, 14*(6), 573–578. Available from https://doi.org/10.1046/j.0956-7976.2003.psci_1467.x.

Hewitt, P. L., & Flett, G. L. (1991). Perfectionism in the self and social contexts. *Journal of Personality and Social Psychology*, *60*(3), 456–470. Available from https://doi.org/10.1037/0022-3514.60.3.456.

Heym, N., Ferguson, E., & Lawrence, C. (2008). An evaluation of the relationship between gray's revised RST and Eysenck's PEN: Distinguishing BIS and FFFS in carver and white's BIS/BAS scales. *Personality and Individual Differences*, *45*(8), 709–715. Available from https://doi.org/10.1016/j.paid.2008.07.013.

Hong, R. Y., & Cheung, M. W.-L. (2015). The structure of cognitive vulnerabilities to depression and anxiety. *Clinical Psychological Science*, *3*(6), 892–912. Available from https://doi.org/10.1177/2167702614553789.

Huntsinger, J. R., Lun, J., Sinclair, S., & Clore, G. L. (2009). Contagion without contact: Anticipatory mood matching in response to affiliative motivation. *Personality and Social Psychology Bulletin*, *35*(7), 909–922. Available from https://doi.org/10.1177/0146167209335299.

Izadpanah, S., Schumacher, M., & Barnow, S. (2017). Anger rumination mediates the relationship between reinforcement sensitivity and psychopathology: Results of a 5-year longitudinal study. *Personality and Individual Differences*, *110*, 49–54. Available from https://doi.org/10.1016/j.paid.2017.01.023.

Jones, S. R., & Fernyhough, C. (2009). Rumination, reflection, intrusive thoughts, and hallucination-proneness: Towards a new model. *Behaviour Research and Therapy*, *47*(1), 54–59. Available from https://doi.org/10.1016/j.brat.2008.09.008.

Keune, P. M., Bostanov, V., Kotchoubey, B., & Hautzinger, M. (2012). Mindfulness versus rumination and behavioral inhibition: A perspective from research on frontal brain asymmetry. *Personality and Individual Differences*, *53*(3), 323–328. Available from https://doi.org/10.1016/j.paid.2012.03.034.

Koerner, N., & Dugas, M. J. (2008). *A cognitive model of generalized anxiety disorder: The role of intolerance of uncertainty. Worry and its psychological disorders* (pp. 201–216). Chichester, UK: John Wiley & Sons Ltd. Available from https://doi.org/10.1002/9780470713143.ch12. Retrieved from <https://onlinelibrary.wiley.com/doi/abs/10.1002/9780470713143.ch12>.

Krieger, T., Altenstein, D., Baettig, I., Doerig, N., & Holtforth, M. G. (2013). Self-compassion in depression: Associations with depressive symptoms, rumination, and avoidance in depressed outpatients. *Behavior Therapy*, *44*(3), 501–513. Available from https://doi.org/10.1016/j.beth.2013.04.004.

Ladouceur, R., Gosselin, P., & Dugas, M. J. (2000). Experimental manipulation of intolerance of uncertainty: A study of a theoretical model of worry. *Behaviour Research and Therapy*, *38*(9), 933–941. Available from https://doi.org/10.1016/S0005-7967(99)00133-3.

Laguna, L., Ham, L., Hope, D., & Bell, C. (2004). Chronic worry as avoidance of arousal. *Cognitive Therapy and Research*, *28*(2), 269–281. Available from https://doi.org/COTR.0000021545.79764.69.

Larsen, R. J. (2000). Toward a science of mood regulation. *Psychological Inquiry*, *11*(3), 129–141. Available from https://doi.org/10.1207/S15327965PLI1103_01.

Laugesen, N., Dugas, M., & Bukowski, W. (2003). Understanding adolescent worry: The application of a cognitive model. *Journal of Abnormal Child Psychology*, *31*(1), 55–64. Available from https://doi.org/1021721332181.

Lee, J. K., Orsillo, S. M., Roemer, L., & Allen, L. B. (2010). Distress and avoidance in generalized anxiety disorder: Exploring the relationships with intolerance of uncertainty and worry. *Cognitive Behaviour Therapy*, *39*(2), 126–136. Available from https://doi.org/10.1080/16506070902966918.

Leen-Feldner, E. W., Zvolensky, M. J., Feldner, M. T., & Lejuez, C. W. (2004). Behavioral inhibition: Relation to negative emotion regulation and reactivity. *Personality and Individual Differences*, *36*(6), 1235–1247. Available from https://doi.org/10.1016/S0191-8869(02)00113-7.

Li, Y., Xu, Y., & Chen, Z. (2015). Effects of the behavioral inhibition system (BIS), behavioral activation system (BAS), and emotion regulation on depression: A one-year follow-up study in Chinese adolescents. *Psychiatry Research, 230*(2), 287–293. Available from https://doi.org/10.1016/j.psychres.2015.09.007.

Liao, K. Y., & Wei, M. (2011). Intolerance of uncertainty, depression, and anxiety: The moderating and mediating roles of rumination. *Journal of Clinical Psychology, 67*(12), 1220–1239. Available from https://doi.org/10.1002/jclp.20846.

Lischetzke, T., & Eid, M. (2003). Is attention to feelings beneficial or detrimental to affective well-being? *Emotion, 3*(4), 361–377. Available from https://doi.org/10.1037/1528-3542.3.4.361.

Liverant, G., Kamholz, B., Sloan, D., & Brown, T. (2011). Rumination in clinical depression: A type of emotional suppression? *Cognitive Therapy and Research, 35*(3), 253–265. Available from https://doi.org/10.1007/s10608-010-9304-4.

Luyckx, K., Soenens, B., Goossens, L., Beckx, K., & Wouters, S. (2008). Identity exploration and commitment in late adolescence: Correlates of perfectionism and mediating mechanisms on the pathway to well-being. *Journal of Social and Clinical Psychology, 27*(4), 336–361. Available from https://doi.org/10.1521/jscp.2008.27.4.336.

Lyubomirsky, S., & Nolen-Hoeksema, S. (1995). Effects of self-focused rumination on negative thinking and interpersonal problem solving. *Journal of Personality and Social Psychology, 69*(1), 176–190. Available from https://doi.org/10.1037/0022-3514.69.1.176.

Mackie, D. M., Devos, T., & Smith, E. R. (2000). Intergroup emotions. *Journal of Personality and Social Psychology, 79*(4), 602–616. Available from https://doi.org/10.1037/0022-3514.79.4.602.

Mahaffey, B. L., Watson, D., Clark, L. A., & Kotov, R. (2016). Clinical and personality traits in emotional disorders: Evidence of a common framework. *Journal of Abnormal Psychology, 125*(6), 758–767. Available from https://doi.org/10.1037/abn0000187.

Mansell, W., & McEvoy, P. M. (2016). A test of the core process account of psychopathology in a heterogenous clinical sample of anxiety and depression. A case of the blind men and the elephant? *Journal of Anxiety Disorders, 46*, 4–10. Available from https://doi.org/10.1016/j.janxdis.2016.06.008.

Martin, L., & Davies, B. (1998). Beyond hedonism and associationism: A configural view of the role of affect in evaluation, processing, and self-regulation. *Motivation and Emotion, 22*(1), 33–51. Available from https://doi.org/1023092508471.

Martin, L., & Tesser, A. (1996). Some ruminative thoughts. In R. S. Wyer, Jr. (Ed.), *Ruminative thoughts, advances in social cognition* (Vol. IX, pp. 1–48). NJ: Lawrence Erlbaum Associates.

Martin, L. L., Ward, D. W., Achee, J. W., & Wyer, R. S. (1993). Mood as input. *Journal of Personality and Social Psychology, 64*(3), 317–326. Available from https://doi.org/10.1037/0022-3514.64.3.317.

McCrae, R. R., Costa, P. T., Ostendorf, F., Angleitner, A., Hřebíčková, M., Avia, M. D., ... Smith, P. B. (2000). Nature over nurture. *Journal of Personality and Social Psychology, 78*(1), 173–186. Available from https://doi.org/10.1037/0022-3514.78.1.173.

McEvoy, P. M., & Mahoney, A. E. J. (2013). Intolerance of uncertainty and negative metacognitive beliefs as transdiagnostic mediators of repetitive negative thinking in a clinical sample with anxiety disorders. *Journal of Anxiety Disorders, 27*(2), 216–224. Available from https://doi.org/10.1016/j.janxdis.2013.01.006.

McEvoy, P. M., Mahoney, A. E. J., & Moulds, M. L. (2010). Are worry, rumination, and post-event processing one and the same? Development of the repetitive thinking questionnaire. *Journal of Anxiety Disorders, 24*(5), 509. Retrieved from <https://www.ncbi.nlm.nih.gov/pubmed/20409676>.

McGregor, I., Gailliot, M. T., Vasquez, N., & Nash, K. A. (2007). Ideological and personal zeal reactions to threat among people with high self-esteem: Motivated promotion focus. *Personality and Social Psychology Bulletin, 33*(11), 1587–1599. Available from https://doi.org/10.1177/0146167207306280.

Meeten, F., Davey, G. C. L., Makovac, E., Watson, D. R., Garfinkel, S. N., Critchley, H. D., & Ottaviani, C. (2016). Goal directed worry rules are associated with distinct patterns of amygdala functional connectivity and vagal modulation during perseverative cognition. *Frontiers in Human Neuroscience, 10*, 553. Available from https://doi.org/10.3389/fnhum.2016.00553.

Meeten, F., & Davey, G. C. L. (2011). Mood as input and perseverative worrying following the induction of discrete negative moods. *Behavior Therapy, 43*(2), 393–406. Available from https://doi.org/10.1016/j.beth.2011.08.005.

Mennin, D. S., & Fresco, D. M. (2015). Advancing emotion regulation perspectives on psychopathology: The challenge of distress disorders. *Psychological Inquiry, 26*(1), 80–92. Available from https://doi.org/10.1080/1047840X.2015.969624.

Mennin, D. S., Heimberg, R. G., Turk, C. L., & Fresco, D. M. (2005). Preliminary evidence for an emotion dysregulation model of generalized anxiety disorder. *Behaviour Research and Therapy, 43*(10), 1281–1310. Available from https://doi.org/10.1016/j.brat.2004.08.008.

Mennin, D. S., Holaway, R. M., Fresco, D. M., Moore, M. T., & Heimberg, R. G. (2007). Delineating components of emotion and its dysregulation in anxiety and mood psychopathology. *Behavior Therapy, 38*(3), 284–302. Available from https://doi.org/10.1016/j.beth.2006.09.001.

Mezulis, A., Simonson, J., McCauley, E., & Vander Stoep, A. (2011). The association between temperament and depressive symptoms in adolescence: Brooding and reflection as potential mediators. *Cognition & Emotion, 25*(8), 1460–1470. Available from https://doi.org/10.1080/02699931.2010.543642.

Mezulis, A. H., Priess, H. A., & Hyde, J. S. (2011). Rumination mediates the relationship between infant temperament and adolescent depressive symptoms. *Depression Research and Treatment, 2011*, 487873. Retrieved from <https://www.ncbi.nlm.nih.gov/pubmed/21151502>.

Michael, T., Halligan, S. L., Clark, D. M., & Ehlers, A. (2007). Rumination in posttraumatic stress disorder. *Depression and Anxiety, 24*(5), 307–317. Available from https://doi.org/10.1002/da.20228.

Millgram, Y., Joormann, J., Huppert, J. D., & Tamir, M. (2015). Sad as a matter of choice? emotion-regulation goals in depression. *Psychological Science, 26*(8), 1216–1228. Available from https://doi.org/10.1177/0956797615583295.

Moulds, M. L., Kandris, E., Starr, S., & Wong, A. C. M. (2007). The relationship between rumination, avoidance and depression in a non-clinical sample. *Behaviour Research and Therapy, 45*(2), 251–261. Available from https://doi.org/10.1016/j.brat.2006.03.003.

Moulds, M. L., Yap, C. S. L., Kerr, E., Williams, A. D., & Kandris, E. (2010). Metacognitive beliefs increase vulnerability to rumination. *Applied Cognitive Psychology, 24*(3), 351–364. Available from https://doi.org/10.1002/acp.1681.

Muris, P., Roelofs, J., Rassin, E., Franken, I., & Mayer, B. (2005). Mediating effects of rumination and worry on the links between neuroticism, anxiety and depression. *Personality and Individual Differences, 39*(6), 1105–1111. Available from https://doi.org/10.1016/j.paid.2005.04.005.

Nelson, T. D. (1997). Mood regulation prior to social interaction: Mood maintenance versus neutralization. *The Journal of Social Psychology, 137*(4), 535–537. Available from https://doi.org/10.1080/00224549709595473.

Nepon, T., Flett, G. L., Hewitt, P. L., & Molnar, D. S. (2011). Perfectionism, negative social feedback, and interpersonal rumination in depression and social anxiety. *Canadian Journal of Behavioural Science/Revue Canadienne Des Sciences Du Comportement*, *43*(4), 297–308. Available from https://doi.org/10.1037/a0025032.

Nieuwenhuys, A., & Oudejans, R. R. D. (2012). Anxiety and perceptual-motor performance: Toward and integrated model of concepts, mechanisms, and processes. *Psychological Research*, *76*(6), 747–759. Available from https://doi.org/10.1007/s00426-011-0384-x.

Nitzan-Assayag, Y., Yuval, K., Tanay, G., Aderka, I., Vujanovic, A., Litz, B., & Bernstein, A. (2017). Reduced reactivity to and suppression of thoughts mediate the effects of mindfulness training on recovery outcomes following exposure to potentially traumatic stress. *Mindfulness*, *8*(4), 920–932. Available from https://doi.org/10.1007/s12671-016-0666-x.

Nolan, S., Roberts, J., & Gotlib, I. (1998). Neuroticism and ruminative response style as predictors of change in depressive symptomatology. *Cognitive Therapy and Research*, *22*(5), 445–455. Available from https://doi.org/1018769531641.

Nolen-Hoeksema., Wisco, B., & Lyubomirsky, S. (2008). *Rethinking rumination escholarship*. University of California.

Norton, P. J., & Mehta, P. D. (2007). Hierarchical model of vulnerabilities for emotional disorders. *Cognitive Behaviour Therapy*, *36*(4), 240–254. Available from https://doi.org/10.1080/16506070701628065.

O'Connor, D. B., O'Connor, R. C., & Marshall, R. (2007). Perfectionism and psychological distress: Evidence of the mediating effects of rumination. *European Journal of Personality*, *21*(4), 429–452. Available from https://doi.org/10.1002/per.616.

Olatunji, B. O., Moretz, M. W., & Zlomke, K. R. (2010). Linking cognitive avoidance and GAD symptoms: The mediating role of fear of emotion. *Behaviour Research and Therapy*, *48*(5), 435–441. Available from https://doi.org/10.1016/j.brat.2009.11.014.

Olson, M., & Kwon, P. (2008). Brooding perfectionism: Refining the roles of rumination and perfectionism in the etiology of depression. *Cognitive Therapy and Research*, *32*(6), 788–802. Available from https://doi.org/10.1007/s10608-007-9173-7.

Ophir, Y., & Mor, N. (2014). If I only knew why: The relationship between brooding, beliefs about rumination, and perceptions of treatments. *Behavior Therapy*, *45*(4), 553–563. Available from https://doi.org/10.1016/j.beth.2014.03.004.

Ottenbreit, N. D., Dobson, K. S., & Quigley, L. (2014). An examination of avoidance in major depression in comparison to social anxiety disorder. *Behaviour Research and Therapy*, *56*, 82–90. Available from https://doi.org/10.1016/j.brat.2014.03.005.

Páez, D., Rimé, B., Basabe, N., Wlodarczyk, A., & Zumeta, L. (2015). Psychosocial effects of perceived emotional synchrony in collective gatherings. *Journal of Personality and Social Psychology*, *108*(5), 711–729. Available from https://doi.org/10.1037/pspi0000014.

Papageorgiou, C., & Wells, A. (2001). Positive beliefs about depressive rumination: Development and preliminary validation of a self-report scale. *Behavior Therapy*, *32*(1), 13–26. Available from https://doi.org/10.1016/S0005-7894(01)80041-1.

Papageorgiou, C., & Wells, A. (2003). An empirical test of a clinical metacognitive model of rumination and depression. *Cognitive Therapy and Research*, *27*(3), 261–273. Available from https://doi.org/1023962332399.

Pieper, S., Brosschot, J. F., van der Leeden, R., & Thayer, J. F. (2010). Prolonged cardiac effects of momentary assessed stressful events and worry episodes. *Psychosomatic Medicine*, *72*(6), 570–577. Available from https://doi.org/10.1097/PSY.0b013e3181dbc0e9.

Porat, R., Halperin, E., Mannheim, I., & Tamir, M. (2016). Together we cry: Social motives and preferences for group-based sadness. *Cognition and Emotion*, *30*(1), 66–79. Available from https://doi.org/10.1080/02699931.2015.1039495.

Porat, R., Halperin, E., & Tamir, M. (2016). What we want is what we get: Group-based emotional preferences and conflict resolution. *Journal of Personality and Social Psychology, 110*(2), 167–190. Available from https://doi.org/10.1037/pspa0000043.

Ramos, N. S., Fernandez-Berrocal, P., & Extremera, N. (2007). Perceived emotional intelligence facilitates cognitive-emotional processes of adaptation to an acute stressor. *Cognition & Emotion, 21*(4), 758–772. Available from https://doi.org/10.1080/02699930600845846.

Randles, D., Flett, G. L., Nash, K. A., McGregor, I. D., & Hewitt, P. L. (2010). Dimensions of perfectionism, behavioral inhibition, and rumination. *Personality and Individual Differences, 49*(2), 83–87. Available from https://doi.org/10.1016/j.paid.2010.03.002.

Renn, R. W., Steinbauer, R., & Fenner, G. (2014). Employee behavioral activation and behavioral inhibition systems, manager ratings of employee job performance, and employee withdrawal. *Human Performance, 27*(4), 347–371. Available from https://doi.org/10.1080/08959285.2014.929694.

Roberts, J., Gilboa, E., & Gotlib, I. (1998). Ruminative response style and vulnerability to episodes of dysphoria: Gender, neuroticism, and episode duration. *Cognitive Therapy and Research, 22*(4), 401–423. Available from https://doi.org/1018713313894.

Robichaud, M., & Dugas, M. J. (2005). Negative problem orientation (part II): Construct validity and specificity to worry. *Behaviour Research and Therapy, 43*(3), 403–412. Available from https://doi.org/10.1016/j.brat.2004.02.008.

Robins, C. J., Keng, S., Ekblad, A. G., & Brantley, J. G. (2012). Effects of mindfulness-based stress reduction on emotional experience and expression: A randomized controlled trial. *Journal of Clinical Psychology, 68*(1), 117–131.

Roelofs, J., Huibers, M., Peeters, F., Arntz, A., & van Os, J. (2008). Rumination and worrying as possible mediators in the relation between neuroticism and symptoms of depression and anxiety in clinically depressed individuals. *Behaviour Research and Therapy, 46*(12), 1283–1289. Available from https://doi.org/10.1016/j.brat.2008.10.002.

Roemer, L., Salters, K., Raffa, S., & Orsillo, S. (2005). Fear and avoidance of internal experiences in GAD: Preliminary tests of a conceptual model. *Cognitive Therapy and Research, 29*(1), 71–88. Available from https://doi.org/10.1007/s10608-005-1650-2.

Ruiz, F. J., & Odriozola-González, P. (2016). A longitudinal comparison of metacognitive therapy and acceptance and commitment therapy models of anxiety disorders. *Anales De Psicología, 33*(1), 7. Available from https://doi.org/10.6018/analesps.32.3.227041.

Ruscio, A. M., & Borkovec, T. D. (2004). Experience and appraisal of worry among high worriers with and without generalized anxiety disorder. *Behaviour Research and Therapy, 42*(12), 1469–1482. Available from https://doi.org/10.1016/j.brat.2003.10.007.

Ryckman, N. A., & Lambert, A. J. (2015). Unsuccessful suppression is associated with increased neuroticism, intrusive thoughts, and rumination. *Personality and Individual Differences, 73*, 88–91. Available from https://doi.org/10.1016/j.paid.2014.09.029.

Salguero, J. M., Extremera, N., & Fernández-Berrocal, P. (2013). A meta-mood model of rumination and depression: Preliminary test in a non-clinical population. *Scandinavian Journal of Psychology, 54*(2), 166–172. Available from https://doi.org/10.1111/sjop.12026.

Salovey, P., Stroud, L. R., Woolery, A., & Epel, E. S. (2002). Perceived emotional intelligence, stress reactivity, and symptom reports: Further explorations using the trait meta-mood scale. *Psychology & Health, 17*(5), 611–627. Available from https://doi.org/10.1080/08870440290025812.

Salovey, P., Mayer, J. D., Goldman, S. L., Turvey, C., & Palfai, T. P. (1995). *Emotional attention, clarity, and repair: Exploring emotional intelligence using the trait meta-mood scale. Emotion, disclosure, & health* (pp. 125–154). Washington, DC: American Psychological Association. Available from https://doi.org/10.1037/10182-006. Retrieved from <https://search.proquest.com/docview/614156113>.

Salters-Pedneault, K., Roemer, L., Tull, M. T., Rucker, L., & Mennin, D. S. (2006). Evidence of broad deficits in emotion regulation associated with chronic worry and generalized anxiety disorder. *Cognitive Therapy and Research, 30*(4), 469–480. Available from https://doi.org/10.1007/s10608-006-9055-4.

Santanello, A., & Gardner, F. (2007). The role of experiential avoidance in the relationship between maladaptive perfectionism and worry. *Cognitive Therapy and Research, 31*(3), 319–332. Available from https://doi.org/10.1007/s10608-006-9000-6.

Sauer-Zavala, S. E., Geiger, P. J., & Baer, R. A. (2013). The effect of anger rumination in the relationship between borderline personality disorder symptoms and precursors. *Journal of Personality Disorders, 27*(4), 465–472. Available from https://doi.org/10.1521/pedi_2013_27_098.

Segerstrom, S. C., Roach, A. R., Evans, D. R., Schipper, L. J., & Darville, A. K. (2010). The structure and health correlates of trait repetitive thought in older adults. *Psychology and Aging, 25*(3), 505–515. Available from https://doi.org/10.1037/a0019456.

Segerstrom, S. C., Stanton, A. L., Alden, L. E., & Shortridge, B. E. (2003). A multidimensional structure for repetitive thought. *Journal of Personality and Social Psychology, 85*(5), 909–921. Available from https://doi.org/10.1037/0022-3514.85.5.909.

Sexton, K., & Dugas, M. (2009). An investigation of factors associated with cognitive avoidance in worry. *Cognitive Therapy and Research, 33*(2), 150–162. Available from https://doi.org/10.1007/s10608-007-9177-3.

Short, M. M., & Mazmanian, D. (2013). Perfectionism and negative repetitive thoughts: Examining a multiple mediator model in relation to mindfulness. *Personality and Individual Differences, 55*(6), 716–721. Available from https://doi.org/10.1016/j.paid.2013.05.026.

Siewert, K., Kubiak, T., Jonas, C., & Weber, H. (2011). Trait anger moderates the impact of anger-associated rumination on social well-being. *Personality and Individual Differences, 51*(6), 769–774. Available from https://doi.org/10.1016/j.paid.2011.06.030.

Siewert, K., Kubiak, T., Jonas, C., & Weber, H. (2013). The differential relations between perceived social support and rumination-associated goals. *Journal of Social and Clinical Psychology, 32*(10), 1075–1094. Available from https://doi.org/10.1521/jscp.2013.32.10.1075.

Simpson, C., & Papageorgiou, C. (2003). Metacognitive beliefs about rumination in anger. *Cognitive and Behavioral Practice, 10*(1), 91–94. Available from https://doi.org/10.1016/S1077-7229(03)80012-3.

Smith, M. M., Sherry, S. B., Rnic, K., Saklofske, D. H., Enns, M., & Gralnick, T. (2016). Are perfectionism dimensions vulnerability factors for depressive symptoms after controlling for neuroticism? A meta-analysis of 10 longitudinal studies. *European Journal of Personality, 30*(2), 201–212. Available from https://doi.org/10.1002/per.2053.

Smith, S., Stephens, H., Repper, K., & Kistner, J. (2016). The relationship between anger rumination and aggression in typically developing children and high-risk adolescents. *Journal of Psychopathology and Behavioral Assessment, 38*(4), 515–527. Available from https://doi.org/10.1007/s10862-016-9542-1.

Spinhoven, P., Drost, J., de Rooij, M., van Hemert, A., & Penninx, B. (2016). Is experiential avoidance a mediating, moderating, independent, overlapping, or proxy risk factor in the onset, relapse and maintenance of depressive disorders? *Cognitive Therapy and Research, 40*(2), 150–163. Available from https://doi.org/10.1007/s10608-015-9747-8.

Startup, H. M., & Davey, G. C. L. (2001). Mood as input and catastrophic worrying. *Journal of Abnormal Psychology, 110*(1), 83–96. Available from https://doi.org/10.1037/0021-843X.110.1.83.

Stöber, J., & Joormann, J. (2001). Worry, procrastination, and perfectionism: Differentiating amount of worry, pathological worry, anxiety, and depression. *Cognitive Therapy and Research, 25*(1), 49–60. Available from https://doi.org/1026474715384.

Stoeber, J., & Otto, K. (2006). Positive conceptions of perfectionism: Approaches, evidence, challenges. *Personality and Social Psychology Review: An Official Journal of the Society for Personality and Social Psychology, Inc, 10*(4), 295–319. Available from https://doi.org/10.1207/s15327957pspr1004_2.

Strunk, D. R., & Adler, A. D. (2009). Cognitive biases in three prediction tasks: A test of the cognitive model of depression. *Behaviour Research and Therapy, 47*(1), 34–40. Available from https://doi.org/10.1016/j.brat.2008.10.008.

Sugiura, Y. (2007). Responsibility to continue thinking and worrying: Evidence of incremental validity. *Behaviour Research and Therapy, 45*(7), 1619–1628. Available from https://doi.org/10.1016/j.brat.2006.08.001.

Sugiura, Y., & Sugiura, T. (2015). Emotional intensity reduces later generalized anxiety disorder symptoms when fear of anxiety and negative problem-solving appraisal are low. *Behaviour Research and Therapy, 71*, 27–33. Available from https://doi.org/10.1016/j.brat.2015.05.015.

Suls, J., & Martin, R. (2005). The daily life of the garden-variety neurotic: Reactivity, stressor exposure, mood spillover, and maladaptive coping. *Journal of Personality, 73*(6), 1485–1510. Available from https://doi.org/10.1111/j.1467-6494.2005.00356.x.

Svansdottir, E., van den Broek, K. C., Karlsson, H. D., Olason, D. T., Thorgilsson, H., & Denollet, J. (2013). The distressed (type D) and five-factor models of personality in young, healthy adults and their association with emotional inhibition and distress. *Personality and Individual Differences, 55*(2), 123–128. Available from https://doi.org/10.1016/j.paid.2013.02.008.

Swinkels, A., & Giuliano, T. A. (1995). The measurement and conceptualization of mood awareness: Monitoring and labeling one's mood states. *Personality and Social Psychology Bulletin, 21*(9), 934–949. Available from https://doi.org/10.1177/0146167295219008.

Szasz, P. L. (2009). Thought suppression, depressive rumination and depression: A mediation analysis. *Journal of Cognitive and Behavioral Psychotherapies, 9*(2), 199. Retrieved from <https://search.proquest.com/docview/201709533>.

Takagishi, Y., Sakata, M., & Kitamura, T. (2013). Influence of rumination and self-efficacy on depression in Japanese undergraduate nursing students. *Asian Journal of Social Psychology, 16*(3), 163–168. Available from https://doi.org/10.1111/ajsp.12000.

Tamir, M. (2005). Don't worry, be happy? Neuroticism, trait-consistent affect regulation, and performance. *Journal of Personality and Social Psychology, 89*(3), 449–461. Available from https://doi.org/10.1037/0022-3514.89.3.449.

Tamir, M. (2009). What do people want to feel and why? Pleasure and utility in emotion regulation. *Current Directions in Psychological Science, 18*(2), 101–105. Available from https://doi.org/10.1111/j.1467-8721.2009.01617.x.

Tamir, M. (2016). Why do people regulate their emotions? A taxonomy of motives in emotion regulation. *Personality and Social Psychology Review, 20*(3), 199–222. Available from https://doi.org/10.1177/1088868315586325.

Tamir, M., Chiu, C., & Gross, J. J. (2007). Business or pleasure? Utilitarian versus hedonic considerations in emotion regulation. *Emotion, 7*(3), 546–554. Available from https://doi.org/10.1037/1528-3542.7.3.546.

Tamir, M., & Ford, B. Q. (2009). Choosing to be afraid. *Emotion, 9*(4), 488–497. Available from https://doi.org/10.1037/a0015882.

Tamir, M., & Ford, B. Q. (2012). When feeling bad is expected to be good: Emotion regulation and outcome expectancies in social conflicts. *Emotion (Washington, D.C.), 12*(4), 807–816. Available from https://doi.org/10.1037/a0024443.

Tamir, M., Mitchell, C., & Gross, J. J. (2008). Hedonic and instrumental motives in anger regulation. *Psychological Science, 19*(4), 324–328. Available from https://doi.org/10.1111/j.1467-9280.2008.02088.x.

Thayer, R. E., Newman, J. R., & McClain, T. M. (1994). Self-regulation of mood. *Journal of Personality and Social Psychology, 67*(5), 910–925. Available from https://doi.org/10.1037/0022-3514.67.5.910.

Thomas, J., Raynor, M., & Ribott, D. (2015). Depressive rumination and experiential avoidance: A task based exploration. *Personality and Mental Health, 9*(1), 58–65. Available from https://doi.org/10.1002/pmh.1276.

Tiedens, L. Z. (2001). Anger and advancement versus sadness and subjugation. *Journal of Personality and Social Psychology, 80*(1), 86–94. Available from https://doi.org/10.1037/0022-3514.80.1.86.

Trapnell, P. D., & Campbell, J. D. (1999). Private self-consciousness and the five-factor model of personality. *Journal of Personality and Social Psychology, 76*(2), 284–304. Available from https://doi.org/10.1037/0022-3514.76.2.284.

Turner, L., & Wilson, C. (2010). Worry, mood and stop rules in young adolescents: Does the mood-as-input theory apply? *Journal of Experimental Psychopathology, 1*(1), jep.007810. Available from https://doi.org/10.5127/jep.007810.

van der Heiden, C., Melchior, K., Muris, P., Bouwmeester, S., Bos, A. E. R., & van der Molen, H. T. (2009). A hierarchical model for the relationships between general and specific vulnerability factors and symptom levels of generalized anxiety disorder. *Journal of Anxiety Disorders, 24*(2), 284–289. Available from https://doi.org/10.1016/j.janxdis.2009.12.005.

van der Houwen, K., Stroebe, W., Stroebe, M., Schut, H., & van den Bout, J. (2010). Mediating processes in bereavement: The role of rumination, threatening grief interpretations, and deliberate grief avoidance. *Social Science & Medicine, 71*(9), 1669–1676. Available from https://doi.org/10.1016/j.socscimed.2010.06.047.

van Kleef, G. A., De Dreu, C. K. W., & Manstead, A. S. R. (2004). The interpersonal effects of anger and happiness in negotiations. *Journal of Personality and Social Psychology, 86*(1), 57–76. Available from https://doi.org/10.1037/0022-3514.86.1.57.

van Zomeren, M., Postmes, T., & Spears, R. (2008). Toward an integrative social identity model of collective action. *Psychological Bulletin, 134*(4), 504–535. Available from https://doi.org/10.1037/0033-2909.134.4.504.

Vassilopoulos, S. P., Brouzos, A., & Moberly, N. J. (2015). The relationships between metacognition, anticipatory processing, and social anxiety. *Behaviour Change, 32*(2), 114–126. Available from https://doi.org/10.1017/bec.2015.4.

Verstraeten, K., Bijttebier, P., Vasey, M. W., & Raes, F. (2011). Specificity of worry and rumination in the development of anxiety and depressive symptoms in children. *British Journal of Clinical Psychology, 50*(4), 364–378. Available from https://doi.org/10.1348/014466510X532715.

Verstraeten, K., Vasey, M., Raes, F., & Bijttebier, P. (2009). Temperament and risk for depressive symptoms in adolescence: Mediation by rumination and moderation by effortful control. *Journal of Abnormal Child Psychology, 37*(3), 349–361. Available from https://doi.org/10.1007/s10802-008-9293-x.

Vine, V., Aldao, A., & Nolen-Hoeksema, S. (2014). Chasing clarity: Rumination as a strategy for making sense of emotions. *Journal of Experimental Psychopathology, 5*(3). Available from https://doi.org/10.5127/jep.038513, jep.038513.

Watkins, E., & Baracaia, S. (2001). Why do people ruminate in dysphoric moods? *Personality and Individual Differences, 30*(5), 723–734. Available from https://doi.org/10.1016/S0191-8869(00)00053-2.

Watkins, E., & Mason, A. (2002). Mood as input and rumination. *Personality and Individual Differences, 32*(4), 577–587. Available from https://doi.org/10.1016/S0191-8869(01)00058-7.

Watkins, E., & Moulds, M. (2005). Positive beliefs about rumination in depression—a replication and extension. *Personality and Individual Differences, 39*(1), 73–82. Available from https://doi.org/10.1016/j.paid.2004.12.006.

Watkins, E. R., & Moulds, M. L. (2009). Thought control strategies, thought suppression, and rumination in depression. *International Journal of Cognitive Therapy, 2*(3), 235–251. Available from https://doi.org/10.1521/ijct.2009.2.3.235.

Watkins, E. R., & Nolen-Hoeksema, S. (2014). A habit-goal framework of depressive rumination. *Journal of Abnormal Psychology, 123*(1), 24–34. Available from https://doi.org/10.1037/a0035540.

Watson, D., & Clark, L. A. (1984). Negative affectivity: The disposition to experience aversive emotional states. *Psychological Bulletin, 96*(3), 465. Retrieved from <https://search.proquest.com/docview/1296893125>.

Wegner, D. M. (1994). Ironic processes of mental control. *Psychological Review, 101*(1), 34–52. Available from https://doi.org/10.1037/0033-295X.101.1.34.

Wegner, D. M., & Zanakos, S. (1994). Chronic thought suppression. *Journal of Personality, 62*(4), 615–640. Available from https://doi.org/10.1111/j.1467-6494.1994.tb00311.x.

Wells, A., & Carter, K. (2001). Further tests of a cognitive model of generalized anxiety disorder: Metacognitions and worry in GAD, panic disorder, social phobia, depression, and nonpatients. *Behavior Therapy, 32*(1), 85–102. Available from https://doi.org/10.1016/S0005-7894(01)80045-9.

Wenzlaff, R., & Luxton, D. (2003). The role of thought suppression in depressive rumination. *Cognitive Therapy and Research, 27*(3), 293–308. Available from https://doi.org/1023966400540.

Wenzlaff, R. M., & Wegner, D. M. (2000). Thought suppression. *Annual Review of Psychology, 51*(1), 59–91. Available from https://doi.org/10.1146/annurev.psych.51.1.59.

Wenzlaff, R. M., Wegner, D. M., & Klein, S. B. (1991). The role of thought suppression in the bonding of thought and mood. *Journal of Personality and Social Psychology, 60*(4), 500–508. Available from https://doi.org/10.1037/0022-3514.60.4.500.

Wenzlaff, R. M., Wegner, D. M., & Roper, D. W. (1988). Depression and mental control. *Journal of Personality and Social Psychology, 55*(6), 882–892. Available from https://doi.org/10.1037/0022-3514.55.6.882.

Williams, C. L., Harfmann, E. J., Ingram, R. E., Hagan, K. E., & Kramer, N. M. (2015). Specificity of parental bonding and rumination in depressive and anxious emotional distress. *Personality and Individual Differences, 79*, 157–161. Available from https://doi.org/10.1016/j.paid.2015.01.055.

Wong, Q. J., & Moulds, M. L. (2010). Do socially anxious individuals hold positive metacognitive beliefs about rumination? *Behaviour Change, 27*(2), 69–83. Available from https://doi.org/10.1375/bech.27.2.69.

Wood, J. V., Heimpel, S. A., Manwell, L. A., & Whittington, E. J. (2009). This mood is familiar and I don't deserve to feel better anyway. *Journal of Personality and Social Psychology, 96*(2), 363–380. Available from https://doi.org/10.1037/a0012881.

Yilmaz, A. E., Gençöz, T., & Wells, A. (2015). Unique contributions of metacognition and cognition to depressive symptoms. *The Journal of General Psychology, 142*(1), 23–33. Available from https://doi.org/10.1080/00221309.2014.964658.

Yook, K., Kim, K., Suh, S. Y., & Lee, K. S. (2010). Intolerance of uncertainty, worry, and rumination in major depressive disorder and generalized anxiety disorder. *Journal of Anxiety Disorders, 24*(6), 623–628. Available from https://doi.org/10.1016/j.janxdis.2010.04.003.

CHAPTER

9

Rumination, cognition, and the brain

Overview

This chapter reviews the empirical literature on the cognitive and neural correlates of rumination. I first explore evidence linking rumination with various cognitive control processes, such as inhibition, updating, set shifting, and attention. I interpret the findings in light of theories on rumination and cognitive processes. The chapter then describes the research on rumination and the brain, specifically imaging studies of brain structures and networks. I focus on research and theories about three interrelated brain networks: the default mode network (DMN), salience network (SN), and central executive network (CEN).

All existing theories of rumination state that it is primarily a cognitive process. Accordingly, some researchers have explored whether cognitive deficits and biases in the processing of emotional information are associated with rumination. Other researchers are attempting to understand how rumination is associated with brain functioning, in order to gain a better understanding of the underlying mental state of rumination. The research presented in this chapter is exciting and also constitutes a departure from the primarily clinical research described in previous chapters. Accordingly, I provide basic descriptions of the various cognitive tests and brain structures covered in these literatures.

Rumination and Related Constructs
DOI: https://doi.org/10.1016/B978-0-12-812545-8.00009-7

© 2020 Elsevier Inc. All rights reserved.

Cognition

Cognitive control, also known as executing functioning, involves the ability to adjust and direct cognitive resources to complete goal-directed behaviors and optimize performance. It combines several interrelated lower order cognitive skills, such as (1) updating working memory, (2) set shifting, and (3) inhibition (Miyake et al., 2000). Cognitive control also typically encompasses several types of attention, including selective attention, attentional allocation, and attentional bias. In these sections, I define each construct and review the empirical literature exploring whether deficits in these cognitive control processes are associated with rumination.

Several theories of rumination and cognition propose that deficits in cognitive control contribute to the use of rumination, particularly when people are in a negative mood. For instance, Joormann (2010) proposed a model in which the combination of negative emotions or thoughts and deficits in inhibition lead to enhanced access of negative material and difficulties expelling negative material from working memory. These deficits in turn increase rumination and lead to difficulties using more adaptive strategies (e.g., reappraisal) for mood repair. The impaired disengagement hypothesis (Koster et al., 2011) draws on the control theory (see Chapter 7: Triggers of rumination) in understanding rumination as a normative process in response to stressful or negative life events. Typically, this self-focused, reflective, critical thinking solves the problem and/or becomes uncomfortable after a while, prompting people to shift their focus elsewhere. However, people who have impaired attentional control will have difficulty disengaging from their repetitive thoughts, resulting in chronic rumination. In other words, this hypothesis argues that impaired attentional control makes people unable to disengage from normative rumination. Of course, people who are depressed exhibit reduced attentional control, especially of self-relevant negative information, setting up a reciprocal cycle of poor attentional control leading to rumination, leading to worse depression and attentional control. Relatedly, Whiter and Gotlib (2013) proposed that negative moods contribute to a narrowed scope of attention, which limits the range of thoughts and actions that are activated and accessible, increasing the likelihood of repetitively focusing on the same negative thoughts over time. In sum, theories and evidence suggest that rumination is maintained by cognitive deficits in the context of negative moods.

Updating of working memory

Working memory refers to the ability to temporarily hold limited pieces of information in awareness while processing them. For example, imagine that I ask you *verbally* to "subtract 12 from 23, then multiply by 4."

In order to solve this mental arithmetic problem in your head, you need to hold three numbers in mind while you carry out the first operation, then add the resulting number to working memory while you carry out the second operation. Given the limited capacity of working memory, it needs to be frequently updated, such that unnecessary information is kept out and no-longer-relevant information is discarded. Negative moods are naturally associated with the activation of mood-congruent information in working memory (Siemer, 2005). People with difficulty controlling the content of working memory therefore allow more negative information to intrude and already-discarded negative information to return, which may contribute to rumination.

Data clearly indicate that people who ruminate have greater difficulties discarding negative thoughts and memories from working memory as they become irrelevant. There are several ways to measure updating. In one procedure, participants are shown two sets of words, after which they are asked to forget one of the two sets. Shortly afterward, they are presented with a single probe word and asked whether that word was from the set of words they were asked to remember or forget. The additional time it takes participants to identify a forgotten word compared a novel word is an index of difficulty with removal of irrelevant content. In both healthy adults and adults with diagnosed depression, tendencies for depressive rumination are associated with greater difficulty removing irrelevant information from working memory (Berman et al., 2011; Introzzi et al., 2016; Joormann & Gotlib, 2008; Zetsche et al., 2012). Importantly, this effect only emerges for negative, but not positive content (see also Joormann & D'Avanzato, 2010; Kaiser, Andrews-Hanna, Metcalf, & Dimidjian, 2015).

In addition to keeping irrelevant information out of working memory, people also need to be able to manipulate information that is currently held in working memory. For instance, in one procedure, participants first saw a single number in one, two, or three grids and were told to memorize these numbers (Meiran et al., 2011). They then saw instructions for a mathematical operation (e.g., " + 3") in one of the grids and had to update the appropriate number. They then saw a different operation—in either the same grid or a different grid—and so on. And at the end of the trial, participants reported the final resulting number(s) in each grid. In both healthy and clinical participants, trait brooding rumination was associated with worse performance on this test. In another procedure involving manipulation of words in working memory, trait rumination was associated with slower performance in depressed adults but not healthy controls (Joormann, Levens, & Gotlib, 2011).

Set shifting

Set shifting involves the ability to shift back and forth between multiple tasks or mental sets. Difficulty with set shifting is often referred to as perseveration or cognitive inflexibility. The association between rumination and set shifting has been examined in different ways. Many studies test set shifting using externally presented material. For instance, the Wisconsin Card Sorting Task asks participants to sort cards according to changing rules (Heaton, Chelune, Talley, Kay, & Curtis, 1993). To do well on the task, participants have to change their card-sorting behavior in response to feedback they are given that hints at the rules they should follow. In one study, undergraduates high in depressive rumination were more likely to continue using no-longer-correct rules, suggesting difficulty with set shifting (Davis & Nolen-Hoeksema, 2000). In a reversal learning task, participants learn via feedback to select one stimulus from a pair, and then halfway through the task the feedback reverses, such that the previously correct stimulus becomes incorrect. In healthy undergraduates, depressive and angry rumination were associated with slower reversal learning (Whitmer & Banich, 2012). Thus, ruminators had difficulty switching to new associations when they were no longer relevant. Similar results were found using other measurements of set shifting (Altamirano et al., 2010; De Lissnyder et al., 2010).

Set shifting can also be assessed using internally generated, rather than externally presented, information. In the internal switch task, participants see a series of angry or neutral faces and are instructed to keep a silent mental count of the number of faces in each emotion category. When a new face is presented, participants press the space bar as soon as they have updated their mental count for both categories. When a new face belongs to a different category than the previous face (i.e., a *switch* trial), participants are required to update a different category than the one they just updated. Therefore, the difference in reaction time between switch and nonswitch trials constitutes a measure of shifting ability. In addition to the emotional condition, in which they categorize faces as angry or neutral, participants also complete a nonemotional condition in which they categorize faces as male or female. In depressed, dysphoric, and healthy participants, depressive rumination is associated with higher reaction times—indicating greater difficulty with set shifting—in the emotional condition only (Beckwé, Deroost, Koster, De Lissnyder, & De Raedt, 2014; De Lissnyder, Koster, & De Raedt, 2012; De Lissnyder et al., 2012; Koster, De Lissnyder, & De Raedt, 2013). In one study assessing adults with remitted depression, poorer set-shifting predicted depressive rumination 1 year later, and rumination mediated the association between shifting and depressive symptoms (Demeyer, De Lissnyder, Koster, & De Raedt, 2012).

However, other studies failed to find an association between rumination and set shifting. For instance, in previously depressed and healthy adults, a different version of the Wisconsin Card Sorting Test was not associated with trait depressive rumination (Aker et al., 2014).

Similarly, in several cross-sectional studies with depressed and nondepressed adolescents and adults, trait rumination was not associated with various measures of set shifting (Connolly et al., 2013; Davis & Nolen-Hoeksema, 2000; Meiran et al., 2011; Piguet et al., 2016; Wagner, Alloy, & Abramson, 2015; Whitmer & Gotlib, 2012; Wilkinson & Goodyer, 2006). Moderators may explain these mixed findings. One study found that trait depressive rumination was associated with difficulties switching from self-generated thoughts to information provided by the environment, but only in individuals high in depressive symptoms (Rochat, Billieux, & Van der Linden, 2012). In a rare experiment, depressed and nondepressed adults engaged in the classic rumination and distraction manipulations before completing a set-shifting task (Whitmer & Gotlib, 2012). Induced rumination contributed to set shifting difficulties in depressed participants only, compared to distraction. Relatedly, in healthy undergraduates, poor set shifting only predicted depressive rumination 6–10 weeks later for individuals with high levels of current life stressors (De Lissnyder et al., 2011). Thus, as we have seen throughout this book, the association between rumination and deficits in set shifting may emerge only in individuals who are already depressed or stressed.

Inhibition

A substantial literature links rumination with impaired inhibition (for reviews, see Joormann, 2010; Koster, De Lissnyder, Derakshan, & De Raedt, 2011; Mor & Daches, 2015; Whitmer & Gotlib, 2013). The term broadly refers to ignoring, disengaging from, and resisting distraction from irrelevant information, as well as overriding automatic behavioral tendencies (Friedman & Miyake, 2004). Inhibition allows people to respond flexibly and appropriately and to adjust their behavior and emotional responses to changing situations (Joormann, 2010).

Friedman and Miyake (2004) identified three components of inhibition. (1) Resistance to proactive interference is the ability to inhibit internally generated information that was previously relevant but has since become irrelevant. This is sometimes referred to as cognitive inhibition, or suppression of irrelevant material, and is thought to involve verbal–linguistic interference. (2) Resistance to distractor interference is the ability to resist distracting information in the external environment that is not relevant to the task. It is thought to involve perceptual interference. Finally, (3) response inhibition refers to the ability to deliberately suppress dominant and/or automatic behavioral responses. This ability is thought to involve primarily motor interference. Interestingly, inhibition of distracting information and response inhibition are highly related, perhaps reflecting the fact that both abilities require maintaining a goal in the face of more dominant motor responses or distracting perceptual information in the environment (Friedman & Miyake, 2004). By contrast, inhibition of previously-relevant information is unrelated to distractor or response inhibition, suggesting that resistance to internally generated, linguistically based information is a unique ability.

Researchers have used various methods to test for associations between rumination and deficits in the inhibition of previously relevant information. One such assessment is the negative affective priming task. This procedure consists of several pairs of trials: a prime-trial and a test-trial (Joormann & Siemer, 2004). In each trial, participants see two adjectives: a distractor word that they are told to ignore and a target word that they rate as being positive or negative. In the negative priming condition, participants have to ignore an emotional distractor in the prime-trial and then respond to a word of the same valence in the following test-trial. The more that participants have inhibited the valence of the prime-trial distractor, the slower their response time will be for the target in the test-trial. In the control condition, the prime-trial distractor and test-trial targets have different valences. The association between rumination and inhibition on the negative priming task is inconsistent across several studies. In healthy undergraduates, trait depressive rumination was associated with poor inhibition on this task, even controlling for depressive symptoms (Joormann, 2006). High ruminators showed no difference in response time between negative priming and control conditions, indicating that there were unable to inhibit the valence of the initial distractor word. However, a later study failed to replicate this result (Zetsche & Joormann, 2011). In depressed adults, depressive rumination was associated with a negative priming effect, although this result was not found in previously depressed or healthy adults (Joormann & Gotlib, 2010). An alternative way to test negative priming is using pictures (e.g., happy and sad faces) instead of words. Although two studies failed to find a cross-sectional association between depressive rumination and negative priming using faces, one study found that poorer inhibition of sad faces predicted depressive rumination 6 months later (Goeleven, De Raedt, Baert, & Koster, 2006; Zetsche & Joormann, 2011). In sum, the associations between negative affective priming tasks and rumination are mixed in the literature. Some researchers contend that these particular tasks do not actually assess inhibition (e.g., Friedman & Miyake, 2004). Fortunately, other paradigms exist that assess inhibition of previously relevant material.

Backward inhibition procedures require participants to disengage from information that was previously relevant by asking them to switch attention to a new task. In one study, for instance, participants were presented with four faces, one of which varied from the other faces on one of three dimensions: emotion (e.g., happy vs angry), gender (e.g., male vs female), or color (e.g., dark vs light gray) (De Lissnyder et al., 2010). Shortly before seeing the four faces, participants saw a cue word indicating the dimension that they should use to identify the face that deviated from the other faces. In inhibitory sequences, the order of three successive trials went a–b–a (e.g., emotion, gender, and emotion), so that participants had to return to a recently discarded dimension. The additional time participants took for inhibitory sequences, compared to control sequences of c–b–a (e.g., color, gender, and emotion), was an index of inhibitory difficulties. High ruminators exhibited impaired inhibition of angry faces. Similarly, in a nonemotional version of this task using rectangles of varying dimensions, inhibition difficulties were associated with greater trait depressive rumination in healthy undergraduates (Whitmer & Banich, 2007). In sum, difficulty removing no-longer-relevant information when switching attention is associated with greater rumination.

Rumination is also related to difficulties inhibiting previously relevant information in long-term memory. Some studies have instructed participants to forget material they just learned. For instance, dysphoric and nondysphoric undergraduates were first asked to memorize pairs of words (Hertel & Gerstle, 2003). Each word pair consisted of a positive or negative adjective and a neutral noun (e.g., *cozy* vs *electric* chair). Next, participants were presented with adjectives and asked to either say the associated noun as quickly as possible or to avoid saying the associated noun. As the final test, participants were asked to recall the associated noun for all of the original adjectives, regardless of prior instructions. For both dysphoric and nondysphoric students, tendencies for rumination were associated with less forgetting of nouns from suppressed sets. This is likely because their efforts at suppression were less successful. In a similar experiment, participants high in depressive rumination again showed less forgetting of words they were supposed to forget, even controlling for depressive symptoms (Joormann & Tran, 2009). Whereas these two studies examined deficits in *intentional* forgetting of information, researchers also explored whether rumination is associated with *automatic* deficits in the ability to inhibit information in long-term memory (Whitmer & Banich, 2010). Participants first learned category-exemplar pairs (e.g., fruit-orange; fruit-strawberry) from different categories (e.g., fruit, metals). They then practiced retrieving some pairs but not others. Finally, participants were asked to recall of all the exemplars from each of the different categories. Typically, unpracticed exemplars that belong to categories that are practiced are less likely to be recalled than are exemplars from categories that are not practiced at all. Researchers believe that this occurs because when participants practice retrieving some exemplars in a category, related but unwanted information is automatically inhibited in order to facilitate retrieval of the desired information. However, undergraduates high in rumination showed greater recall of unpracticed exemplars from practiced categories. These results suggest that ruminators have trouble automatically inhibiting information in long-term memory.

In sum, difficulties inhibiting previously-relevant information appear to be associated with rumination, across all types of procedures other than negative affective priming tasks. These associations emerge in both depressed and healthy participants. I next review evidence on the associations between rumination and the two other components of inhibition: inhibition of distracting information and response inhibition.

Rumination is inconsistently associated with inhibition of distracting information. Unlike the previous paradigms, which assess interference from internal representations of previously rejected material, some tasks assess inference from simultaneously presented information. In the emotional version of the flanker test, for instance, participants see one target word in green and three distractor words in red. They are told to ignore the distractors and indicate as quickly as possible whether the target word is positive or negative. In *conflict* trials, the valence of the target is different from the valence of the distractor words; in *neutral* trials, all distractor words have a neutral valence. Slower response times for the conflict trials, compared to neutral trials, suggest that the irrelevant emotional words are interfering with the task. In healthy and depressed adults, one study found no association between trait depressive rumination and the ability to ignore emotional distractors (Zetsche, D'Avanzato, & Joormann, 2012). In a different study with healthy undergraduates, trait depressive rumination was actually associated with decreased interference on this task, suggesting better ability to ignore negative distracting information (Zetsche & Joormann, 2011). Other researchers tested the association between trait rumination and inhibition of self-relevant distractors (Daches, Mor, Winquist, & Gilboa-Schechtman, 2010). In this procedure, undergraduate participants wrote autobiographical memories related to each of eight words: four words about time and four about family. This initial procedure ensured that these eight words became self-relevant. Next, participants engaged in a speeded classification test in which they saw a word about either time or family and categorized it accurately. In some trials, only the eight self-relevant or eight non–self-relevant words were presented. Other trials included all 16 words, requiring participants to attend to one dimension while ignoring variation in self-relevance. Longer reaction times in these mixed trials compared to the nonmixed trials indicated interference. As expected, trait rumination was associated with greater interference by self-relevant information. In sum, although inhibition of negative distractors is not clearly associated with rumination, inhibition of self-relevant distractors may be impaired in ruminators.

The association between response inhibition and rumination has been assessed using the Stroop task, with mixed results. In this task, individuals view words of colors (e.g., red, blue, and green) that are printed in different color ink. In the original Stroop (1935) task, all of the words are printed in incongruent ink colors (e.g., "red" printed in green ink). Individuals are instructed to say aloud the ink color, rather than what the word says, as quickly as they can without making mistakes. This task primarily assesses response inhibition, as it requires people to override the stronger and more automatic impulse to read the word (Miyake et al., 2000). In two studies, there was no association between Stroop performance and trait depressive rumination in depressed, obsessive–compulsive, and healthy adults (Aker, Harmer, & Landrø, 2014; Meiran, Diamond, Toder, & Nemets, 2011). In a modification of the original Stroop task (Kane & Engle, 2003), incongruent trials are randomly intermixed with congruent trials (e.g., "red" printed in red ink). On this version, trait depressive rumination in undergraduates was associated with greater accuracy on incongruent trials and slower responding on congruent trials, all of which suggests that ruminators were less distracted and maintained the color-naming goal better than nonruminators (Altamirano, Miyake, & Whitmer, 2010). By contrast, dysphoric undergraduates induced to ruminate made more errors on the Stroop task than did nondysphoric participants induced to ruminate or participants in the distraction condition (Philippot & Brutoux, 2008). In sum, associations between trait rumination and response inhibition on the Stroop test are either nonsignificant or positive. However, one experiment found that induced rumination led to worse performance in dysphoric individuals.

Other procedures that assess response inhibition also exhibit inconsistent associations with rumination. In the antisaccade task, participants are instructed to look in the opposite direction from a visual cue that appears suddenly in their peripheral visual field (Miyake et al., 2000). Performance on these antisaccade trials is usually compared to prosaccade trials, in which participants are instructed to look toward the visual cue. One study found that trait ruminators exhibited slower response times than nonruminators on antisaccade trials, but not on prosaccade trials (De Lissnyder et al., 2011). This pattern of results suggests that ruminators had more difficulty inhibiting automatic responses to nonemotional material. In the emotional go/no-go task, participants view a rapid series of happy or sad faces presented briefly. In some trials, most of the faces are happy, and participants are instructed to press a button for each happy face. In other trials, most of the faces are sad, and participants press a button for each sad face. Thus, the test measures the ability to inhibit dominant responses to negative and positive information. In high trait ruminators, brooding rumination was associated with greater errors in the negative trials, suggesting greater difficulty inhibiting responses to negative information (Vanderhasselt, Kühn, & De Raedt, 2011). Finally, the stop-signal task instructs participants to respond to a stimulus presented briefly (Logan, Carr, & Dagenbach, 1994). However, if participants hear a *stop signal* (e.g., a beep) after the stimulus has been presented, they are supposed to withhold a response. Furthermore, the onset latency of the stop signal is variable, such that it increases if participants successfully withhold their response on the previous stop trial (i.e., making for a more difficult task) and decreases if participants fail the previous stop trial. Three studies with depressed, previously depressed, anxious, and healthy adults did not find an association between trait rumination and inhibition as measured by the stop-signal task (Aker et al., 2014; Introzzi, Andrés, Canet-Juric, Stelzer, & Richard's, 2016; Lau, Christensen, Lawley, Gemar, & Segal, 2007). By contrast, an unpublished study found that compared with induced distraction, induced rumination contributed to worse inhibition on this task in dysphoric—but not nondysphoric—participants (Whitmer & Gotlib, 2013).

In sum, the associations between rumination and inhibition of distracting information and response inhibition are mixed. Trait rumination may be related to difficulty inhibiting self-relevant distractors, although it is either unrelated or related to better inhibition of emotional distractors. Furthermore, trait rumination is related to worse response inhibition on some tasks (e.g., antisaccade and emotional go/no go) but unrelated on other tasks (e.g., Stroop and stop-signal). The two studies that manipulated rumination found a negative effect on inhibition of distracting information and response inhibition in dysphoric individuals only. Thus, the ability to inhibit distracting information and response inhibition is not robustly associated with general tendencies for rumination, although induced rumination in people who already exhibit depressive symptoms may impair these forms of inhibition.

Attention

Minimal research has examined the association between rumination and sustained attention, or the ability to remain consistently focused for a sustained period of time. In adults, sustained attention is often assessed by asking participants to watch single digits presented quickly and in random order for over 5 minutes and to press a key for every number except 3, for instance (Robertson et al., 1997). In one study, trait depressive rumination was marginally associated with more errors on this sustained attention task and was significantly associated with more task-irrelevant thoughts during the task (Murphy et al., 2013).

In children and adolescents, sustained attention can be measured by listening to a recording of beeps for several minutes and mentally counting the sounds. Depressive rumination was associated with worse sustained attention on this task only for adolescents high—but not low—in depressive symptoms (Wagner et al., 2015).

One study examined the association between rumination and the ability to allocate attention between two tasks, as happens when people are multitasking (Levens, Muhtadie, & Gotlib, 2009). In the procedure, depressed and nondepressed participants saw a set of three words, followed by a single word probe, and had to indicate whether the probe word was in the most recent word set. In some trials, the word probe was not in the recent word set but was in the two previous sets, creating the opportunity for interference. To make the task more difficult—and reflective of the multitasking that happens in regular life—participants also had to count the number of words in each word set that fit into various categories (e.g., things to save in case of a fire). Thus, this study's design assessed the ability to reroute—or allocate—attention between two simultaneous tasks and resolve cross-task interference. In depressed participants, brooding rumination was associated with poorer performance on trials that required both rerouting of attention and the resolution of cross-task interference. No such association emerged for nondepressed participants. The authors concluded that depressed individuals may have difficulty disengaging from ruminative thoughts because they have impairments in effectively allocating their attentional resources.

Researchers have also examined whether rumination is related to selective attention to negative information, a construct called attentional bias. One common method of measuring attentional bias is the dot probe task. In this task, two stimuli (e.g., words or images) are presented briefly in different locations on a computer screen. One of the stimuli is neutral in valence, and the other is emotional. Next, a dot (i.e., probe) appears in one of the two locations, and participants are instructed to respond to the probe as quickly as possible. Participants presumably respond faster to probes that appear in attended, rather than unattended, locations. If ruminators pay more attention to negative material, they should respond faster to probes that replace negative material. The evidence for this is mixed. In depressed and nondepressed adults, trait depressive rumination was associated with faster reaction times when the probe replaced negative words (Donaldson, Lam, & Mathews, 2007). In other healthy samples, however, attentional bias for negative images was not associated with trait or state rumination (Hilt & Pollak, 2013; Onie & Most, 2017). Moreover, induced rumination (vs distraction) did not contribute to an increase in attentional bias for negative words (Brookes, Sharpe, & Dear, 2017; Donaldson et al., 2007).

Other measures of attentional bias that do not rely on spatial attention also yielded mixed associations with trait depressive rumination (Alderman et al., 2015; Onie & Most, 2017).

What might explain these mixed results? Traditional attentional bias scores can confound attentional engagement and disengagement. For instance, an attentional bias for negative stimuli could indicate greater initial engagement (i.e., faster responding when the probe replaces an emotional stimulus) or difficulty disengaging (i.e., slower responding when the probe replaces a neutral stimulus). Researchers can untangle these effects by adding trials in which both stimuli are neutral. In this case, faster reaction times when the probe replaces an emotional stimulus, compared to a neutral stimulus in a neutral–neutral trial, indicate greater engagement with emotional material. Slower reactions times when the probe replaces a neutral stimulus in an emotional–neutral trial, compared to a neutral–neutral trial, indicate difficulty disengaging from emotional material. In one study, state rumination was associated with greater difficulty with disengaging—but not with engagement—in dysphoric undergraduates only (LeMoult, Arditte, D'Avanzato, & Joormann, 2013). In healthy undergraduates, by contrast, rumination was not related to difficulty with disengagement (see also Brookes et al., 2017). Thus, rumination may be related to problems with disengaging from emotional material—but not attentional engagement—for depressed but not healthy individuals.

Effortful control

Some self-report questionnaires attempt to measure these same constructs. The construct of effortful control (Rothbart, 1989) includes the ability to intentionally engage in both response inhibition and set shifting. It is conceptualized as a self-regulatory temperament trait. In cross-sectional research with children and adolescents, less effortful control is associated with greater worry and brooding rumination (Verstraeten, Bijttebier, Vasey, & Raes, 2011; Verstraeten, Vasey, Raes, & Bijttebier, 2009). By contrast, effortful control as self-reported at age 12 was not associated with depressive rumination at age 14 (Mezulis, Simonson, McCauley, & Vander Stoep, 2011). Interestingly, lower self-reported effortful control in youth ages 8–16 *indirectly* predicted an increase in depressive rumination 18 months later, via increased stress (Snyder & Hankin, 2016). In yet another example of the importance of interactions between predictors of rumination, a cross-sectional association between effortful control and trait rumination was stronger for adolescents high in neuroticism (Verstraeten et al., 2009). Similarly, a longitudinal study found that effortful control assessed in 4.5-year-old children was associated with higher trait rumination in adolescence only for participants who were high in negative affectivity (Hilt, Armstrong, & Essex, 2012). Thus, the effect of effortful control on rumination may be indirect (via increased stress) and/or moderated by stable personality traits (e.g., negative affectivity).

Summary

In sum, rumination is more consistently associated with some cognitive deficits than others. Specifically, regardless of whether people are depressed or not, difficulty in removing irrelevant negative information from working memory and inhibiting previously relevant information are associated with greater rumination. Thus, one cognitive mechanism underlying rumination may be trouble letting go of information that once occupied one's attention. Interestingly, difficulties inhibiting previously relevant information also predict greater thought suppression (Friedman & Miyake, 2004), a construct clearly related to rumination (see Chapter 8: Beliefs, traits, and motivations underlying rumination). These results suggest that inhibitory control influences the effectiveness of attempts to suppress thoughts. People with weaker ability to inhibit previously relevant material and remove it from working memory may have more rebounds of unwanted thoughts, which in turn contributes to the experience of rumination.

Several cognitive deficits and biases appear to be only or particularly associated with rumination for individuals who are depressed or high in negative affectivity. This is the case for difficulty manipulating information in working memory, disengaging from emotional material (a component of attentional bias), set shifting, attentional allocation, and sustained attention, as well as self-reported effortful control. These results align with theories described earlier that suggest that rumination is maintained by cognitive deficits in the context of negative moods.

Unfortunately, the majority of studies on rumination and cognition are nonexperimental, leaving open the question of directionality. Although several theories assume that cognitive deficits contribute to rumination, the other direction is also possible. In fact, resource-allocation theory proposes that the process of rumination depletes available cognitive resources for other task-relevant mental activities (Hertel, 2004; Watkins & Brown, 2002). The experiments showing that induced rumination contributes to worse response inhibition and set-shifting support this theory (Philippot & Brutoux, 2008; Whitmer & Gotlib, 2012). Other experiments have found that compared to induced distraction, induced rumination led to impaired concentration and more interfering thoughts while reading a passage in dysphoric participants only

(Lyubomirsky, Boehm, Kasri, & Zehm, 2011; Lyubomirsky, Kasri, & Zehm, 2003). Moreover, one longitudinal study showed that rumination contributed to worse sustained attention and set shifting 15 months later (Connolly et al., 2013). As with so many constructs, it seems most likely that rumination shares a bidirectional association with cognitive deficits. Future research will have to test this more explicitly.

Brain

Rumination involves sustained cognitive processing of emotional and self-focused material. As just reviewed, rumination is also associated with deficits in inhibition, attention, and other manifestations of executive control. Accordingly, researchers have used various methods to identify neurological manifestations of this type of processing.

Event-related potentials (ERPs) are changes observed in brain electrical activity in response to discrete events. In the emotion field, ERPs are commonly assessed in response to emotional stimuli such as negative images (for a review, see Hajcak, Weinberg, MacNamara, & Foti). Several specific ERP components have been identified, some occurring immediately (e.g., 300 ms) after a stimulus, and some occurring up to several seconds after a stimulus. One ERP component in particular—the late positive potential (LPP)—begins 300 ms after a stimulus and lasts for several seconds. As such, the LPP is believed to reflect sustained, elaborative processing of emotional content. Accordingly, some studies have examined the association between rumination and the LPP. In undergraduates, induced but not trait rumination was associated with heightened LPP in response to unpleasant images only (Lewis, Taubitz, Duke, Steuer, & Larson, 2015). In both depressed and nondepressed adolescent females, trait rumination was associated with larger LPP in response to losses than wins, even controlling for depressive symptoms (Webb et al., 2017). By contrast, trait rumination was not associated with a different ERP component that reflects immediate processing of losses and gains. Similarly, trait brooding rumination was associated with greater LPP—but was not associated with the immediate processing component—in response to failure (Whiteman & Mangels, 2016). These results provide brain-based evidence that rumination is associated with sustained, elaborative processing of negative emotional material.

The majority of research on rumination and the brain has focused on brain structures and networks. Specifically, researchers have investigated its association with structures and networks implicated in negative-emotional and self-referential processing, as well as inhibition and executive control. Most of this research relies on blood-oxygen-level dependent contrast imaging, which identifies the level of oxygen in the blood in various brain regions using functional magnetic resonance imaging (fMRI). The rationale for this method is that neuronal activity depends on oxygen being released by red blood cells. Therefore, the relative changes in oxygenated and deoxygenated blood indicate relative inactivity and activity, respectively, of various brain regions.

Although research linking rumination with individual brain regions has yielded interesting results, a newer approach to understanding brain–behavior connections has even greater promise. Researchers are increasingly able to identify large-scale brain networks that include various brain regions and the connections between them (Menon, 2011). Brain networks can be defined by *structural* connectivity, in which researchers identify the white matter connections between brain regions using MRIs or postmortem analyses. More commonly, researchers use fMRIs to assess *functional* connectivity, which is when several regions of the brain become active at the same time, leading to stronger than expected correlations between their activation levels. Brain networks link regions of the brain that may not be proximally related into systems that are implicated in distinct cognitive, emotional, and/or behavioral functions. In trying to understand connections between the brain and psychopathology, researchers investigate aberrant activity both *within* single brain networks and *between* multiple networks. In this section, I describe several brain networks that are relevant to rumination as well as the research on associations between rumination and functional connectivity within and between these networks.

Default mode network

The default mode network (DMN) has received substantial attention in the neuroscience of mental disorders (Broyd et al., 2009; Hamilton, Farmer, Fogelman, & Gotlib, 2015). The DMN is involved in self-referential processing, or the ability to reflect on oneself (Nordhoff et al., 2006; Schneider et al., 2008). The DMN is normally active when people are awake and restful. In fact, DMN activation is associated with greater heart rate variability, a robust measure of parasympathetic activity and an indication of restful bodily states (Thayer, Åhs, Fredrikson, Sollers, & Wager, 2012). Importantly, the DMN is implicated in activities such as mind wandering, day dreaming, and reminiscing—mental activities that people naturally engage in when they are not actively involved in attention-demanding or goal-directed tasks. These mental processes all involve a decoupling of conscious thought from immediate perception (Tops, Boksem, Quirin, Ijzerman, & Koole, 2014). Therefore, the DMN may be part of a system that controls cognition and behavior in familiar and predictable environments, working from existing internal models. In these relatively unchallenging and nondemanding situations, people have the luxury to turn their thoughts away from what is happening around them and instead let their thoughts drift to mental content that is irrelevant to their present circumstances.

The two main hubs of the DMN include (1) parts of the medial prefrontal cortex (mPFC) and adjacent anterior cingulate cortex (ACC) and (2) the posterior cingulate cortex (PCC) and adjacent precuneus (Hamilton et al., 2015). Specifically, the ventral (i.e., bottom) regions of the mPFC and the ACC determine whether various external and interoceptive stimuli are self-referential (Etkin, Egner, & Kalisch, 2010; Nordhoff et al., 2006). The PCC and precuneus are implicated in retrieving and integrating autobiographic information stored in long-term memory and taking the first-person perspective (Cavanna & Trimble, 2006). Working together, these regions of the DMN create and evaluate self-relevant mental representations, using autobiographical information stored in long-term memory (see Fig. 9.1). This kind of processing in which people elaborate on how internal representations are important for the self may begin in response to some external stimulus but can continue uncoupled from current perceptions (Smallwood et al., 2013).

Because of the DMN's involvement in self-referential processing, researchers have hypothesized that rumination may be associated with greater DMN activation. Indeed, rumination is generally associated with increased activity in individual structures in the DMN, at least in healthy individuals (Hamilton et al., 2015; Nejad, Fossati, & Lemogne, 2013). For instance, in healthy young adults, induced analytical rumination leads to greater activation of the PCC than does experiential self-focus (Burkhouse et al., 2017; Freton et al., 2014). In a rare study of angry rumination, induced rumination following a provocation led to increased activation in the mPFC and the ventral ACC (Denson, Pedersen, Ronquillo, & Nandy, 2009). Similarly, induced worry is associated with greater activation in and functional connectivity between

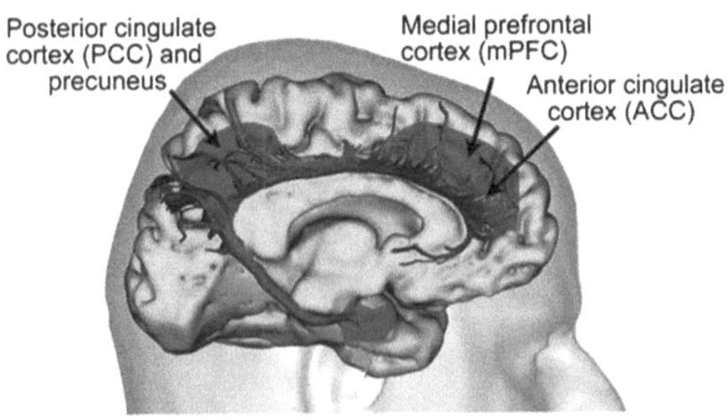

FIGURE 9.1 Brain regions of the Default Mode Network. Source: *Adapted from Sandrone and Catani (2013). ©2013 by Wolters Kluwer Health, Inc. Reprinted with permission.*

DMN regions (e.g., ACC, PCC, and precuneus) in individuals both with and without GAD (Andreescu, Sheu, Tudorascu, Walker, & Aizenstein, 2014; Hoehn-Saric, Schlund, & Wong, 2004; Ottaviani et al., 2016; Paulesu et al., 2010; Servaas, Riese, Ormel, & Aleman, 2014). In one study, healthy female participants viewed negative and neutral images and were instructed to increase or decrease their negative emotion in response to each image, or to just look at the image (Ray et al., 2005). Trait rumination was associated with greater activation in the ventral mPFC and ACC during trials in which participants both looked at negative images and increased negative emotion. Moreover, high ruminators showed significantly less activation in these areas when asked to decrease their negative emotion in response to negative images. This pattern of results suggests that ruminators may chronically recruit the DMN when interacting with negative stimuli, unless they are intentionally trying to think about a situation in less emotional terms.

Results in depressed individuals are more complex. Trait rumination is generally associated with greater activation of and functional connectivity within DMN regions in depressed and formerly depressed individuals (Farb, Anderson, Bloch, & Segal, 2011; Zhu et al., 2012). However, the effect of induced rumination is mixed. In some studies with currently and remitted depressed participants, induced rumination led to greater activation of the ventral mPFC, PCC, and precuneus (Burkhouse et al., 2017; Cooney, Joormann, Eugène, Dennis, & Gotlib, 2010). However, other studies failed to find effects of induced rumination on DMN region activation for depressed participants or high trait ruminators (Freton et al., 2014; Johnson, Nolen-Hoeksema, Mitchell, & Levin, 2009). Some researchers suggest that depressed individuals and trait ruminators may have chronically elevated DMN activation at baseline, so that rumination inductions do not necessarily lead to further increases in activation (e.g., Lemogne, Delaveau, Freton, Guionnet, & Fossati, 2012). In support of this hypothesis, compared to healthy controls, individuals with depression show less deactivation of DMN regions during cognitive and emotional tasks, compared to resting, suggesting that they have difficulty turning off their heightened resting-state self-focus even when asked to attend to external stimuli (e.g., Grimm et al., 2009, 2011).

Other researchers have focused on the role of the subgenual (i.e., bottom-most) ACC in depressive rumination. Activity in the subgenual ACC (also called the subgenual cingulate cortex) is associated with increased sadness, withdrawal, and depression (Hamani et al., 2011). In depressed adults, higher trait depressive rumination is associated with stronger activation of the subgenual ACC during self-referential processing of negative words (Siegle, Thase, & Carter, 2006). Depressed participants also exhibit more activation of the subgenual ACC during induced rumination than do healthy controls (Cooney et al., 2010). In fact, researchers speculate that increased connectivity between DMN regions and the subgenual ACC may constitute a neurological rendering of depressive rumination (Hamilton et al., 2015). Specifically, if self-referential processing (as mediated by the DMN) is combined with sad mood (as mediated by the subgenual ACC), depressive rumination emerges. The majority of evidence supports this hypothesis. In healthy participants, induced rumination leads to greater coactivation in the mPFC, PCC, and subgenual ACC, compared to both a resting state and induced mindfulness (Farb et al., 2007; Kross, Davidson, Weber, & Ochsner, 2009). Moreover, in depressed and nondepressed participants, higher trait depressive rumination is associated with greater resting-state connectivity between the PCC and the subgenual ACC (Berman et al., 2011).

Salience network

The salience network (SN) is involved in detecting, filtering, and determining the importance of external and interoceptive stimuli, including perceived conflict and discrepancies. Relatedly, the SN moderates physiological arousal via its association with the amygdala, which helps control the autonomic nervous system. As such, the SN is part of a system that guides behavior by identifying the most relevant—or subjectively salient—among the many internal and external stimuli that people encounter at any one time (Menon & Uddin, 2010).

Structurally, the SN includes the anterior (i.e., front) insula and adjacent inferior frontal gyrus (IFG), the dorsal (i.e., top) ACC, and the amygdala. The anterior insula is implicated in bottom-up detection of perceived discrepancies and coordinating various brain regions to facilitate access to necessary resources when a salient discrepancy is detected (Menon & Uddin, 2010). The dorsal ACC is involved in appraisal of emotional states and conflicts, as well as the use of top-down processing to respond to perceived emotional discrepancies (Etkin et al., 2010). Part of the ventrolateral PFC, the left IFG in particular is implicated in elaborative processing, specifically in reappraising the meaning of and assimilating new information into existing internal models (Tops et al., 2014). Finally, the amygdala is the alarm center of our brains, providing quick identification of potential threats (LeDoux, 1996). Once the alarm has been sounded, the amygdala alerts the hypothalamus, which triggers the sympathetic nervous system and HPA axis (see Chapter 5: Rumination and physical functioning). When everything is working properly, these structures work together to detect an external or internal event and determine that it requires autonomic and/or higher cognitive processing. However, the SN may erroneously judge the importance of particular internal or external events, triggering inappropriate autonomic or cognitive-behavioral responses. Accordingly, SN dysfunction may be a core feature of anxiety, depression, pain, and substance disorders (Menon, 2011).

Rumination is associated with greater anterior insula, dorsal ACC, and left IFG activation. In depressed adults, induced rumination leads to greater activation of the insula and dorsal ACC than does distraction (Cooney et al., 2010). Similarly, healthy participants exhibit greater activation of the anterior insula during induced worry, compared to a neutral control condition (Servaas et al., 2014). In healthy adults, trait depressive rumination is associated with greater anterior insula and left IFC activation during emotional tasks (Paul, Stanton, Greeson, Smoski, & Wang, 2013; Ray et al., 2005). In one study, greater daily rumination was associated with greater dorsal ACC and left IFG activation during rest than while doing speed tasks (Kühn et al., 2013). In healthy adults, induced rumination leads to greater activation in the left IFG, compared to both resting state, distraction, and induced mindfulness (Farb et al., 2007; Denson et al., 2009). In a study of healthy undergraduates, trait brooding rumination was associated with increased activity in the dorsal ACC while engaging in a task in which they had to inhibit a dominant response to sad faces, relative to inhibiting a dominant response to happy faces (Vanderhasselt et al., 2013). Interestingly, ruminators performed the task as well as nonruminators, but in doing so they recruited more ACC activation. This suggests that ruminators needed more mental resources to successfully inhibit a dominant response.

Substantial research also links rumination with heightened amygdala activation. For instance, in depressed and nondepressed adults, higher trait depressive rumination was associated with stronger amygdala activation while indicating whether negative words were relevant to them (Siegle et al., 2006). Similarly, trait depressive rumination was associated with greater amygdala activity during negative compared to positive emotional tasks (Siegle, Steinhauer, Thase, Stenger, & Carter, 2002), and this heightened amygdala activity for ruminators was sustained even after participants had moved on to a nonemotional task (Mandell, Siegle, Shutt, Feldmiller, & Thase, 2014). These results suggest that in ruminators, arousal from negative information persists even when that information is no longer relevant. Experimentally, compared to induced distraction, depressed participants exhibited greater amygdala activation during induced rumination than did nondepressed participants (Cooney et al., 2010). Finally, female participants viewed negative and neutral images and were instructed to increase or decrease their negative emotion in response to each image, or to just look at the image (Ray et al., 2005). When asked to increase their negative affect or simply look at negative pictures, participants higher in trait rumination exhibited greater amygdala activation.

Much less research has examined rumination and connectivity between SN brain regions. In a study with healthy females, more self-reported unwanted thoughts during rest were associated with greater resting-state functional connectivity between the left IFG and striatum, another structure belonging to the SN (Kühn, Vanderhasselt, De Raedt, & Gallinat, 2014). In an experiment, healthy undergraduates thought about an anger-inducing memory in an objective and positive way (i.e., reappraisal condition), while focusing on causes and consequences (i.e., analytical rumination condition), or while focusing on the emotional aspects of the event (i.e., angry rumination condition) (Fabiansson, Denson, Moulds, Grisham, & Schira, 2012). Interestingly, there were no differences in activation of specific brain regions by condition: all participants showed increased activation in the anterior insula, IFG, and amygdala. However, significant connectivity between the IFG and amygdala emerged only for participants in the two rumination conditions. The authors interpret these results to suggest that rumination may require greater efforts at cognitive control in an attempt to counteract increased emotional arousal. Alternatively, the increased connectivity might reflect greater abstract thinking by the frontal lobes (e.g., reflection on angry feelings, revenge planning, and making sense of past events) that is both fueled by and increases angry arousal and emotions.

Central executive network

The CEN maintains and manipulates information in working memory and is also responsible for decision-making and problem-solving in the pursuit of goal-directed behavior (Menon, 2011). Whereas the DMN shows activation during resting awake states, the CEN shows activation during cognitively and emotionally challenging activities. Its major nodes include the dorsolateral PFC and the lateral posterior parietal cortex. The lateral posterior parietal cortex integrates sensory and interoceptive information in order to facilitate sustained attention. The dorsolateral PFC manipulates material in working memory and weighs possible behavioral responses. In addition to involvement in practical decision-making, the CEN is also implicated in task-oriented (e.g., top-down) processing necessary for effective emotion-regulation. CEN hypoactivity is associated with depression and various cognitive disorders (Menon, 2011).

Because working memory deficits are associated with greater rumination, as reviewed previously, several researchers hypothesized that rumination would be associated with less CEN activation. However, the existing evidence is mixed and exclusively focuses on the dorsolateral

PFC. One the one hand, more self-reported unwanted thoughts during rest were associated with less resting-state activation in the dorsolateral PFC in healthy females (Kühn et al., 2014). Moreover, in healthy young adults, induced ruminative self-focus during rest led to less activation of the dorsolateral PFC than did experiential self-focus (Freton et al., 2014). By contrast, induced rumination was associated with greater activation in the dorsolateral PFC in depressed participants than in healthy controls, compared to induced distraction (Cooney et al., 2010). Similarly, induced worry led to increased activation in the dorsolateral PFC in both GAD participants and healthy controls (Paulesu et al., 2010; Servaas et al., 2014). In correlational studies, trait brooding rumination and worry were associated with more dorsolateral PFC activity during tasks requiring executive control (Forster, Nunez Elizalde, Castle, & Bishop, 2015; Vanderhasselt et al., 2011). These results could suggest that ruminators have to recruit more attentional resources in order to successfully disengage from negative material. Similarly, greater activation in depressed individuals might indicate a greater effort to regulate emotions during rumination. Thus, rumination may be associated with less dorsolateral PFC activation at rest for healthy individuals—a pattern that reflects the fact that the CEN is usually less active when the DMN is active (Hamilton et al., 2011). By contrast, rumination may be associated with more dorsolateral PFC activation during cognitively or emotionally demanding tasks, or for depressed individuals, because more executive resources are needed to overcome the effects of rumination. Clearly, more research is needed to test this and other hypotheses about the links between rumination and CEN activation. I should also note that no studies have examined associations between rumination and posterior parietal cortex activation or connectivity between regions of the CEN.

Interactions between networks

Two different models propose that rumination reflects nonoptimal connections between these brain networks, particularly the SN and DMN. The predictive and reactive control systems theory (Tops et al., 2014) proposes that because rumination involves elaboration of perceived discrepancies, it likely involves functional connectivity between the DMN and the SN—particularly the left IFG and anterior insula. The elaborative processing mediated by the SN should ideally facilitate adaptive coping to novel and problematic situations. However, when the SN is paired too closely with the DMN, the result may be elaborative processing of unresolvable and/or internal discrepancies, resulting in self-focused and unproductive ruminative processing. It is almost as if the SN hijacks the DMN, such that adaptive self-reflection—normally engaged in during safe situations and mediated by the DMN—becomes reactive and elaborative in response to perceived danger or internal discrepancies (Tops et al., 2014).

Evidence supports this hypothesis. For instance, depressive and anxious symptoms are associated with greater functional connectivity between the anterior insula and regions of the DMN (Dennis, Gotlib, Thompson, & Thomason, 2011; Horn et al., 2010). In adolescents with remitted depression, higher trait depressive rumination is associated with greater resting-state connectivity between the amygdala (representing the SN) and the PCC (representing the DMN) (Peters, Burkhouse, Feldhaus, Langenecker, & Jacobs, 2016). In one study with healthy adults, induced rumination led to greater functional connectivity between the anterior insula and the ventral mPFC (representing the DMN), compared to induced mindfulness (Farb et al., 2007). Interestingly, this connectivity was not apparent in adults who had participated in an 8-week mindfulness training. Instead, participants of the mindfulness training exhibited functional connectivity between the anterior insula and the dorsolateral PFC (representing the CEN), suggesting a better ability to regulate emotional arousal. Finally, in individuals with and without GAD, worry inductions lead to stronger connectivity between SN and DMN regions (Makovac et al., 2015; Simmons et al., 2013).

The triple network model (Menon, 2011) proposes that the SN—particularly the anterior insula—is crucial for determining the dynamic interplay between the CEN and the DMN (see Fig. 9.2). During stimulus-driven information processing, the CEN typically becomes activated and the DMN becomes deactivated. When the SN determines that some stimulus requires higher cognitive processing, it ideally activates the CEN and deactivates the DMN. However, connections between the SN and CEN and/or DMN may be too strong or too weak. The inflexible and maladaptive self-focus that characterizes rumination in particular may be associated with too much connectivity between the SN and DMN and a corresponding inability to switch to the CEN. This in turn likely undermines the capacity for effective cognitive functioning and emotion regulation.

In one study that examined this hypothesis, relative dominance of the DMN over the CEN was associated with greater trait brooding rumination, in depressed adults but not healthy controls (Hamilton et al., 2011). By contrast, trait reflective pondering was associated with relative dominance of the CEN over the DMN. These results may suggest that reflective pondering is more effortful than is passive brooding. Furthermore, depressed adults showed an increase in anterior insula (i.e., SN) activation at the onset of increased CEN activity, following a peak of DMN activity.

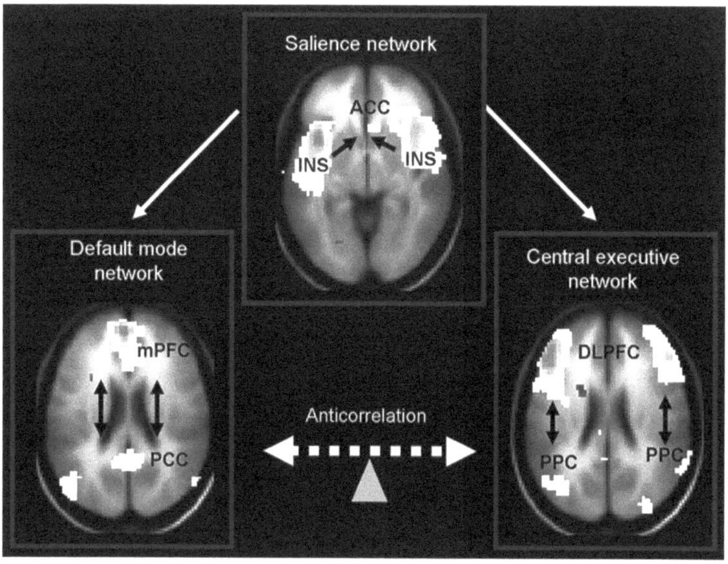

FIGURE 9.2 Interactions between the default mode, salience, and central executive networks. Source: *From Nekovarova, T., Fajnerova, I., Horacek, J., & Spaniel, F. (2014). Bridging disparate symptoms of schizophrenia: A triple network dysfunction theory. Frontiers in Behavioral Neuroscience, 8, 171. Available from https://doi.org/10.3389/fnbeh.2014.00171 (Nekovarova, Fajnerova, Horacek, & Spaniel, 2014).*

By contrast, healthy controls showed the opposite pattern of increased insula activity at the onset of increased DMN activity, following a peak of CEN activity. This second pattern of results suggests that in depressed individuals, self-referential thinking (i.e., rumination) is unpleasant or important enough to be "noticed" by the insula, leading to a switch in network activity. In healthy adults, by contrast, higher level thinking is more likely to be deemed salient by the insula, leading to a switch to a resting brain state.

Summary

In sum, rumination is associated with electrical brain activity suggestive of sustained processing of negative emotional material. This may reflect hyperactivation of and between the DMN and the SN, which together contribute to elaborative, self-referential processing of perceived threats and discrepancies. This kind of processing occurs at the expense of sustained attention, effective working memory, and deliberate decision-making, mediated by the CEN, that are necessary for adaptive emotion regulation.

Conclusion

In this chapter, I reviewed the literatures on the cognitive and neural correlates of rumination. Taken together, the evidence suggests that deficits in the ability to remove and inhibit previously relevant emotional and self-relevant material may underlie rumination in general. In addition, rumination also appears to be maintained by other cognitive deficits (e.g., set shifting, attentional bias, and sustained attention) in the context of negative emotion. These cognitive results complement the imaging findings that rumination is associated with hyperactivation in the DMN and SN at the expense of proper functioning of the CEN. Specifically, elaborative, self-referential processing takes over instead of effective cognitive control in the face of perceived challenges.

The concept that chronic or maladaptive rumination involves overly strong connections between the salience SN and DMN integrates other ideas discussed throughout this book. Self-regulation theorists have argued that self-focused, repetitive thinking is a natural and adaptive response to perceived discrepancies. Thus, self-focused thinking is not necessarily something that happens when people are at rest, but when they perceive a threat that needs a response. On the contrary, other types of repetitive thinking that are removed from immediate perception (e.g., mind-wandering, day dreaming, and reminiscing) tend to occur when people are at rest. Thus, unlike other forms of self-focused attention, rumination may involve self-focused thinking that occurs in a state of perceived stress, not at rest.

A major limitation of the literatures reviewed here is the correlational nature of most of the research. As such, we cannot know whether these cognitive and neural patterns contribute to rumination or constitute mechanisms by which rumination leads to the various emotional and behavioral consequences discussed in previous chapters. Nevertheless, this research is invaluable for finding more objective correlates of a construct that is primarily assessed using subjective, self-report measures. Continued research should yield novel and important insights about the causes, nature, and consequences of rumination. As reviewed in a later chapter (see Chapter 10, Cognitive behavioral therapies), researchers are also starting to adapt some cognitive paradigms described previously in order to decrease ruminative processing. Thus, a better understanding of cognitive and neural correlates of rumination can also contribute to effective treatments.

References

Aker, M., Harmer, C., & Landrø, N. I. (2014). More rumination and less effective emotion regulation in previously depressed women with preserved executive functions. *BMC Psychiatry, 14*(1), 334. Available from https://doi.org/10.1186/s12888-014-0334-4.

Alderman, B. L., Olson, R. L., Bates, M. E., Selby, E. A., Buckman, J. F., Brush, C. J., ... Shors, T. J. (2015). Rumination in major depressive disorder is associated with impaired neural activation during conflict monitoring. *Frontiers in Human Neuroscience, 9*, 269. Available from https://doi.org/10.3389/fnhum.2015.00269.

Altamirano, L. J., Miyake, A., & Whitmer, A. J. (2010). When mental inflexibility facilitates executive control: Beneficial side effects of ruminative tendencies on goal maintenance. *Psychological Science, 21*(10), 1377–1382. Available from https://doi.org/10.1177/0956797610381505.

Andreescu, C., Sheu, L. K., Tudorascu, D., Walker, S., & Aizenstein, H. (2014). The ages of anxiety—differences across the lifespan in the default mode network functional connectivity in generalized anxiety disorder. *International Journal of Geriatric Psychiatry, 29*(7), 704–712. Available from https://doi.org/10.1002/gps.4051.

Beckwé, M., Deroost, N., Koster, E., De Lissnyder, E., & De Raedt, R. (2014). Worrying and rumination are both associated with reduced cognitive control. *Psychological Research, 78*(5), 651–660. Available from https://doi.org/10.1007/s00426-013-0517-5.

Berman, M. G., Peltier, S., Nee, D. E., Kross, E., Deldin, P. J., & Jonides, J. (2011). Depression, rumination and the default network. *Social Cognitive and Affective Neuroscience, 6*(5), 548–555. Available from https://doi.org/10.1093/scan/nsq080.

Brookes, M. L., Sharpe, L., & Dear, B. F. (2017). Rumination induces a pattern of attention characterized by increased vigilance followed by avoidance of affective pain words. *European Journal of Pain, 21*(7), 1197–1208. Available from https://doi.org/10.1002/ejp.1020.

Broyd, S. J., Demanuele, C., Debener, S., Helps, S. K., James, C. J., & Sonuga-Barke, E. J. (2009). Default-mode brain dysfunction in mental disorders: A systematic review. *Neuroscience & Biobehavioral Reviews, 33*(3), 279–296.

Burkhouse, K., Jacobs, R., Peters, A., Ajilore, O., Watkins, E., & Langenecker, S. (2017). Neural correlates of rumination in adolescents with remitted major depressive disorder and healthy controls. *Cognitive, Affective, & Behavioral Neuroscience, 17*(2), 394–405. Available from https://doi.org/10.3758/s13415-016-0486-4.

Cavanna, A. E., & Trimble, M. R. (2006). The precuneus: A review of its functional anatomy and behavioural correlates. *Brain: A Journal of Neurology, 129*(Pt 3), 564–583. Available from https://doi.org/10.1093/brain/awl004.

Connolly, S. L., Wagner, C. A., Shapero, B. G., Pendergast, L. L., Abramson, L. Y., & Alloy, L. B. (2013). Rumination prospectively predicts executive functioning impairments in adolescents. *Journal of Behavior Therapy and Experimental Psychiatry, 45*(1), 46–56. Available from https://doi.org/10.1016/j.jbtep.2013.07.009.

Cooney, R., Joormann, J., Eugène, F., Dennis, E., & Gotlib, I. (2010). Neural correlates of rumination in depression. *Cognitive, Affective, & Behavioral Neuroscience, 10*(4), 470–478. Available from https://doi.org/10.3758/CABN.10.4.470.

Daches, S., Mor, N., Winquist, J., & Gilboa-Schechtman, E. (2010). Brooding and attentional control in processing self-encoded information: Evidence from a modified garner task. *Cognition & Emotion, 24*(5), 876–885. Available from https://doi.org/10.1080/02699930902954825.

Davis, R., & Nolen-Hoeksema, S. (2000). Cognitive inflexibility among ruminators and nonruminators. *Cognitive Therapy and Research, 24*(6), 699–711. Available from https://doi.org/1005591412406.

De Lissnyder, E., Derakshan, N., De Raedt, R., & Koster, E. H. W. (2011). Depressive symptoms and cognitive control in a mixed antisaccade task: Specific effects of depressive rumination. *Cognition & Emotion, 25*(5), 886–897. Available from https://doi.org/10.1080/02699931.2010.514711.

De Lissnyder, E., Koster, E., & De Raedt, R. (2012). Emotional interference in working memory is related to rumination. *Cognitive Therapy and Research, 36*(4), 348–357. Available from https://doi.org/10.1007/s10608-011-9352-4.

De Lissnyder, E., Koster, E. H., Derakshan, N., & De Raedt, R. (2010). The association between depressive symptoms and executive control impairments in response to emotional and non-emotional information. *Cognition and Emotion, 24*(2), 264–280.

De Lissnyder, E., Koster, E. H. W., Everaert, J., Schacht, R., Van den Abeele, D., & De Raedt, R. (2012). Internal cognitive control in clinical depression: General but no emotion-specific impairments. *Psychiatry Research, 199*(2), 124–130. Available from https://doi.org/10.1016/j.psychres.2012.04.019.

De Lissnyder, E., Koster, E. H. W., Goubert, L., Onraedt, T., Vanderhasselt, M.-A., & De Raedt, R. (2011). Cognitive control moderates the association between stress and rumination. *Journal of Behavior Therapy and Experimental Psychiatry, 43*(1), 519–525. Available from https://doi.org/10.1016/j.jbtep.2011.07.004.

Demeyer, I., De Lissnyder, E., Koster, E. H. W., & De Raedt, R. (2012). Rumination mediates the relationship between impaired cognitive control for emotional information and depressive symptoms: A prospective study in remitted depressed adults. *Behaviour Research and Therapy, 50*(5), 292–297. Available from https://doi.org/10.1016/j.brat.2012.02.012.

Dennis, E. L., Gotlib, I. H., Thompson, P. M., & Thomason, M. E. (2011). Anxiety modulates insula recruitment in resting-state functional magnetic resonance imaging in youth and adults. *Brain Connectivity, 1*(3), 245–254. Available from https://doi.org/10.1089/brain.2011.0030.

Denson, T. F., Pedersen, W. C., Ronquillo, J., & Nandy, A. S. (2009). The angry brain: Neural correlates of anger, angry rumination, and aggressive personality. *Journal of Cognitive Neuroscience, 21*(4), 734–744. Available from https://doi.org/10.1162/jocn.2009.21051.

Donaldson, C., Lam, D., & Mathews, A. (2007). Rumination and attention in major depression. *Behaviour Research and Therapy, 45*(11), 2664–2678. Available from https://doi.org/10.1016/j.brat.2007.07.002.

Eriksen, B. A., & Eriksen, C. W. (1974). Effects of noise letters upon the identification of a target letter in a nonsearch task. *Perception & Psychophysics, 16*(1), 143–149.

Etkin, A., Egner, T., & Kalisch, R. (2010). Emotional processing in anterior cingulate and medial prefrontal cortex. *Trends in Cognitive Sciences, 15*(2), 85–93. Available from https://doi.org/10.1016/j.tics.2010.11.004.

Fabiansson, E. C., Denson, T. F., Moulds, M. L., Grisham, J. R., & Schira, M. M. (2012). Don't look back in anger: Neural correlates of reappraisal, analytical rumination, and angry rumination during recall of an anger-inducing autobiographical memory. *NeuroImage, 59*(3), 2974–2981. Available from https://doi.org/10.1016/j.neuroimage.2011.09.078.

Farb, N. A. S., Anderson, A. K., Bloch, R. T., & Segal, Z. V. (2011). Mood-linked responses in medial prefrontal cortex predict relapse in patients with recurrent unipolar depression. *Biological Psychiatry, 70*(4), 366–372. Available from https://doi.org/10.1016/j.biopsych.2011.03.009.

Farb, N. A. S., Segal, Z. V., Mayberg, H., Bean, J., McKeon, D., Fatima, Z., & Anderson, A. K. (2007). Attending to the present: Mindfulness meditation reveals distinct neural modes of self-reference. *Social Cognitive and Affective Neuroscience, 2*(4), 313–322. Available from https://doi.org/10.1093/scan/nsm030.

Forster, S., Nunez Elizalde, A. O., Castle, E., & Bishop, S. J. (2015). Unraveling the anxious mind: Anxiety, worry, and frontal engagement in sustained attention versus off-task processing. *Cerebral Cortex (New York, NY: 1991)*, *25*(3), 609–618. Available from https://doi.org/10.1093/cercor/bht248.

Freton, M., Lemogne, C., Delaveau, P., Guionnet, S., Wright, E., Wiernik, E., ... Fossati, P. (2014). The dark side of self-focus: Brain activity during self-focus in low and high brooders. *Social Cognitive and Affective Neuroscience*, *9*(11), 1808–1813. Available from https://doi.org/10.1093/scan/nst178.

Friedman, N. P., & Miyake, A. (2004). The relations among inhibition and interference control functions. *Journal of Experimental Psychology: General*, *133*(1), 101–135. Available from https://doi.org/10.1037/0096-3445.133.1.101.

Goeleven, E., De Raedt, R., Baert, S., & Koster, E. H. W. (2006). Deficient inhibition of emotional information in depression. *Journal of Affective Disorders*, *93*(1–3), 149–157. Available from https://doi.org/10.1016/j.jad.2006.03.007.

Grimm, S., Boesiger, P., Beck, J., Schuepbach, D., Bermpohl, F., Walter, M., ... Northoff, G. (2009). Altered negative BOLD responses in the default-mode network during emotion processing in depressed subjects. *Neuropsychopharmacology*, *34*(4), 932–943. Available from https://doi.org/10.1038/npp.2008.81.

Grimm, S., Ernst, J., Boesiger, P., Schuepbach, D., Boeker, H., & Northoff, G. (2011). Reduced negative BOLD responses in the default-mode network and increased self-focus in depression. *World Journal of Biological Psychiatry*, *12*(8), 627–637. Available from https://doi.org/10.3109/15622975.2010.545145.

Hajcak, G., Weinberg, A., MacNamara, A., & Foti, D. *16 ERPs and the study of emotion.*

Hamani, C., Mayberg, H., Stone, S., Laxton, A., Haber, S., & Lozano, A. M. (2011). The subcallosal cingulate gyrus in the context of major depression. *Biological Psychiatry*, *69*(4), 301–308. Available from https://doi.org/10.1016/j.biopsych.2010.09.034.

Hamilton, J. P., Farmer, M., Fogelman, P., & Gotlib, I. H. (2015). Depressive rumination, the default-mode network, and the dark matter of clinical neuroscience. *Biological Psychiatry*, *78*(4), 224–230. Available from https://doi.org/10.1016/j.biopsych.2015.02.020.

Hamilton, J. P., Furman, D. J., Chang, C., Thomason, M. E., Dennis, E., & Gotlib, I. H. (2011). Default-mode and task-positive network activity in major depressive disorder: Implications for adaptive and maladaptive rumination. *Biological Psychiatry*, *70*(4), 327–333. Available from https://doi.org/10.1016/j.biopsych.2011.02.003.

Heaton, R. K., Chelune, G. J., Talley, J. L., Kay, G. C., & Curtis, G. (1993). *Wisconsin card sorting test manual: Revised and expanded.* Odessa, FL: Psychological Assessment Resources.

Hertel, P. (2004). *Memory for emotional and nonemotional events in depression. Memory and emotion* (pp. 186–216). New York: Oxford University Press. Available from https://doi.org/10.1093/acprof:oso/9780195158564.003.0006 Retrieved from <http://www.oxfordscholarship.com/view/10.1093/acprof:oso/9780195158564.001.0001/acprof-9780195158564-chapter-6>.

Hertel, P. T., & Gerstle, M. (2003). Depressive deficits in forgetting. *Psychological Science*, *14*(6), 573–578. Available from https://doi.org/10.1046/j.0956-7976.2003.psci_1467.x.

Hilt, L. M., Armstrong, J. M., & Essex, M. J. (2012). Early family context and development of adolescent ruminative style: Moderation by temperament. *Cognition & Emotion*, *26*(5), 916–926. Available from https://doi.org/10.1080/02699931.2011.621932.

Hilt, L. M., & Pollak, S. D. (2013). Characterizing the ruminative process in young adolescents. *Journal of Clinical Child and Adolescent Psychology: The Official Journal for the Society of Clinical Child and Adolescent Psychology, American Psychological Association, Division 53*, *42*(4), 519–530. Available from https://doi.org/10.1080/15374416.2013.764825.

Hoehn-Saric, R., Schlund, M. W., & Wong, S. H. Y. (2004). Effects of citalopram on worry and brain activation in patients with generalized anxiety disorder. *Psychiatry Research: Neuroimaging, 131*(1), 11–21. Available from https://doi.org/10.1016/j.pscychresns.2004.02.003.

Horn, D. I., Yu, C., Steiner, J., Buchmann, J., Kaufmann, J., Osoba, A., ... Walter, M. (2010). Glutamatergic and resting-state functional connectivity correlates of severity in major depression – the role of pregenual anterior cingulate cortex and anterior insula. *Frontiers in Systems Neuroscience,* 4. Available from https://doi.org/10.3389/fnsys.2010.00033.

Introzzi, I., Andrés, M. L., Canet-Juric, L., Stelzer, F., & Richard's, M. M. (2016). The relationship between the rumination style and perceptual, cognitive, and behavioral inhibition. *Psychology & Neuroscience, 9*(4), 444–456. Available from https://doi.org/10.1037/pne0000068.

Johnson, M. K., Nolen-Hoeksema, S., Mitchell, K. J., & Levin, Y. (2009). Medial cortex activity, self-reflection and depression. *Social Cognitive and Affective Neuroscience, 4*(4), 313–327. Available from https://doi.org/10.1093/scan/nsp022.

Joormann, J. (2006). Differential effects of rumination and dysphoria on the inhibition of irrelevant emotional material: Evidence from a negative priming task. *Cognitive Therapy and Research, 30*(2), 149–160. Available from https://doi.org/10.1007/s10608-006-9035-8.

Joormann, J. (2010). Cognitive inhibition and emotion regulation in depression. *Current Directions in Psychological Science, 19*(3), 161–166. Available from https://doi.org/10.1177/0963721410370293.

Joormann, J., & D'Avanzato, C. (2010). Emotion regulation in depression: Examining the role of cognitive processes. *Cognition & Emotion, 24*(6), 913–939. Available from https://doi.org/10.1080/02699931003784939.

Joormann, J., & Gotlib, I. H. (2008). Updating the contents of working memory in depression. *Journal of Abnormal Psychology, 117*(1), 182–192. Available from https://doi.org/10.1037/0021-843X.117.1.182.

Joormann, J., & Gotlib, I. H. (2010). Emotion regulation in depression: Relation to cognitive inhibition. *Cognition & Emotion, 24*(2), 281–298. Available from https://doi.org/10.1080/02699930903407948.

Joormann, J., Levens, S. M., & Gotlib, I. H. (2011). Sticky thoughts: Depression and rumination are associated with difficulties manipulating emotional material in working memory. *Psychological Science, 22*(8), 979–983. Available from https://doi.org/10.1177/0956797611415539.

Joormann, J., & Siemer, M. (2004). Memory accessibility, mood regulation, and dysphoria. *Journal of Abnormal Psychology, 113*(2), 179–188. Available from https://doi.org/10.1037/0021-843X.113.2.179.

Joormann, J., & Tran, T. B. (2009). Rumination and intentional forgetting of emotional material. *Cognition & Emotion, 23*(6), 1233–1246. Available from https://doi.org/10.1080/02699930802416735.

Kaiser, R., Andrews-Hanna, J., Metcalf, C., & Dimidjian, S. (2015). Dwell or decenter? Rumination and decentering predict working memory updating after interpersonal criticism. *Cognitive Therapy and Research, 39*(6), 744–753. Available from https://doi.org/10.1007/s10608-015-9697-1.

Kane, M. J., & Engle, R. W. (2003). Working-memory capacity and the control of attention. *Journal of Experimental Psychology: General, 132*(1), 47–70. Available from https://doi.org/10.1037/0096-3445.132.1.47.

Koster, E. H. W., De Lissnyder, E., & De Raedt, R. (2013). Rumination is characterized by valence-specific impairments in switching of attention. *Acta Psychologica, 144*(3), 563–570. Available from https://doi.org/10.1016/j.actpsy.2013.09.008.

Koster, E. H. W., De Lissnyder, E., Derakshan, N., & De Raedt, R. (2011). Understanding depressive rumination from a cognitive science perspective: The impaired disengagement hypothesis. *Clinical Psychology Review, 31*(1), 138–145. Available from https://doi.org/10.1016/j.cpr.2010.08.005.

Kross, E., Davidson, M., Weber, J., & Ochsner, K. (2009). Coping with emotions past: The neural bases of regulating affect associated with negative autobiographical memories. *Biological Psychiatry, 65*(5), 361–366. Available from https://doi.org/10.1016/j.biopsych.2008.10.019.

Kühn, S., Schmiedek, F., Brose, A., Schott, B. H., Lindenberger, U., & Lövden, M. (2013). The neural representation of intrusive thoughts. *Social Cognitive and Affective Neuroscience, 8*(6), 688–693. Available from https://doi.org/10.1093/scan/nss047.

Kühn, S., Vanderhasselt, M., De Raedt, R., & Gallinat, J. (2014). The neural basis of unwanted thoughts during resting state. *Social Cognitive and Affective Neuroscience, 9*(9), 1320–1324. Available from https://doi.org/10.1093/scan/nst117.

Lau, M. A., Christensen, B. K., Lawley, L. L., Gemar, M. S., & Segal, Z. V. (2007). Inhibitory deficits for negative information in persons with major depressive disorder. *Psychological Medicine, 37*(9), 1249–1259. Available from https://doi.org/10.1017/S0033291707000530.

LeDoux, J. E. (1996). *The emotional brain: The mysterious underpinnings of emotional life*. New York, NY [u.a.]: Simon & Schuster.

Lemogne, C., Delaveau, P., Freton, M., Guionnet, S., & Fossati, P. (2012). Medial prefrontal cortex and the self in major depression. *Journal of Affective Disorders, 136*(1–2), e11.

LeMoult, J., Arditte, K. A., D'Avanzato, C., & Joormann, J. (2013). State rumination: Associations with emotional stress reactivity and attention biases. *Journal of Experimental Psychopathology, 4*(5), 471. Available from https://doi.org/10.5127/jep.029112.

Levens, S. M., Muhtadie, L., & Gotlib, I. H. (2009). Rumination and impaired resource allocation in depression. *Journal of Abnormal Psychology, 118*(4), 757–766. Available from https://doi.org/10.1037/a0017206.

Lewis, K. L., Taubitz, L. E., Duke, M. W., Steuer, E. L., & Larson, C. L. (2015). State rumination enhances elaborative processing of negative material as evidenced by the late positive potential. *Emotion (Washington, DC), 15*(6), 687–693. Available from https://doi.org/10.1037/emo0000095.

Logan, G. D., Carr, T. H., & Dagenbach, D. (1994). *On the ability to inhibit thought and action: A users' guide to the stop signal paradigm. Inhibitory processes in attention, memory and language* (pp. 189–239). Academic Press. Retrieved from <https://www.narcis.nl/publication/RecordID/oai:dare.uva.nl:publications%2Fd72ffa14-a640-4cd8-9910-51634bf7ab36>.

Lyubomirsky, S., Boehm, J. K., Kasri, F., & Zehm, K. (2011). The cognitive and hedonic costs of dwelling on achievement-related negative experiences. *Emotion, 11*(5), 1152–1167. Available from https://doi.org/10.1037/a0025479.

Lyubomirsky, S., Kasri, F., & Zehm, K. (2003). Dysphoric rumination impairs concentration on academic tasks. *Cognitive Therapy and Research, 27*(3), 309–330. Available from https://doi.org/1023918517378.

Makovac, E., Meeten, F., Watson, D. R., Herman, A., Garfinkel, S. N., Critchley, H. D., & Ottaviani, C. (2015). Alterations in amygdala-prefrontal functional connectivity account for excessive worry and autonomic dysregulation in generalized anxiety disorder. *Biological Psychiatry, 80*(10), 786–795. Available from https://doi.org/10.1016/j.biopsych.2015.10.013.

Mandell, D., Siegle, G. J., Shutt, L., Feldmiller, J., & Thase, M. E. (2014). Neural substrates of trait ruminations in depression. *Journal of Abnormal Psychology, 123*(1), 35–48. Available from https://doi.org/10.1037/a0035834.

Meiran, N., Diamond, G. M., Toder, D., & Nemets, B. (2011). Cognitive rigidity in unipolar depression and obsessive compulsive disorder: Examination of task switching, Stroop, working memory updating and post-conflict adaptation. *Psychiatry Research, 185*(1), 149–156. Available from https://doi.org/10.1016/j.psychres.2010.04.044.

Menon, V. (2011). Large-scale brain networks and psychopathology: A unifying triple network model. *Trends in Cognitive Sciences, 15*(10), 483–506. Available from https://doi.org/10.1016/j.tics.2011.08.003.

Menon, V., & Uddin, L. Q. (2010). Saliency, switching, attention and control: A network model of insula function. *Brain Structure & Function, 214*(5–6), 655–667. Available from https://doi.org/10.1007/s00429-010-0262-0.

Mezulis, A., Simonson, J., McCauley, E., & Vander Stoep, A. (2011). The association between temperament and depressive symptoms in adolescence: Brooding and reflection as potential mediators. *Cognition & Emotion, 25*(8), 1460–1470. Available from https://doi.org/10.1080/02699931.2010.543642.

Miyake, A., Friedman, N. P., Emerson, M. J., Witzki, A. H., Howerter, A., & Wager, T. D. (2000). The unity and diversity of executive functions and their contributions to complex "Frontal lobe" tasks: A latent variable analysis. *Cognitive Psychology, 41*(1), 49–100. Available from https://doi.org/10.1006/cogp.1999.0734.

Mor, N., & Daches, S. (2015). Ruminative thinking. *Clinical Psychological Science, 3*(4), 574–592. Available from https://doi.org/10.1177/2167702615578130.

Murphy, F., Macpherson, K., Jeyabalasingham, T., Manly, T., & Dunn, B. (2013). Modulating mind-wandering in dysphoria. *Frontiers in Psychology, 4*, 888. Available from https://doi.org/10.3389/fpsyg.2013.00888.

Nejad, A. B., Fossati, P., & Lemogne, C. (2013). Self-referential processing, rumination, and cortical midline structures in major depression. *Frontiers in Human Neuroscience, 7*, 666. Available from https://doi.org/10.3389/fnhum.2013.00666.

Nekovarova, T., Fajnerova, I., Horacek, J., & Spaniel, F. (2014). Bridging disparate symptoms of schizophrenia: A triple network dysfunction theory. *Frontiers in Behavioral Neuroscience, 8*, 171. Available from https://doi.org/10.3389/fnbeh.2014.00171.

Nordhoff, S., Cerezo-Gálvez, S., Feurer, A., Hill, O., Matassa, V. G., Metz, G., … Edwards, P. J. (2006). The reversed binding of β-phenethylamine inhibitors of DPP-IV: X-ray structures and properties of novel fragment and elaborated inhibitors. *Bioorganic & Medicinal Chemistry Letters, 16*(6), 1744–1748.

Onie, S., & Most, S. B. (2017). Two roads diverged: Distinct mechanisms of attentional bias differentially predict negative affect and persistent negative thought. *Emotion (Washington, DC), 17*(5), 884–894. Available from https://doi.org/10.1037/emo0000280.

Ottaviani, C., Watson, D. R., Meeten, F., Makovac, E., Garfinkel, S. N., & Critchley, H. D. (2016). Neurobiological substrates of cognitive rigidity and autonomic inflexibility in generalized anxiety disorder. *Biological Psychology, 119*, 31–41. Available from https://doi.org/10.1016/j.biopsycho.2016.06.009.

Paul, N. A., Stanton, S. J., Greeson, J. M., Smoski, M. J., & Wang, L. (2013). Psychological and neural mechanisms of trait mindfulness in reducing depression vulnerability. *Social Cognitive and Affective Neuroscience, 8*(1), 56–64. Available from https://doi.org/10.1093/scan/nss070.

Paulesu, E., Sambugaro, E., Torti, T., Danelli, L., Ferri, F., Scialfa, G., … Sassaroli, S. (2010). Neural correlates of worry in generalized anxiety disorder and in normal controls: A functional MRI study. *Psychological Medicine, 40*(1), 117–124. Available from https://doi.org/10.1017/S0033291709005649.

Peters, A. T., Burkhouse, K., Feldhaus, C. C., Langenecker, S. A., & Jacobs, R. H. (2016). Aberrant resting-state functional connectivity in limbic and cognitive control networks relates to depressive rumination and mindfulness: A pilot study among adolescents with a history of depression. *Journal of Affective Disorders, 200*, 178–181. Available from https://doi.org/10.1016/j.jad.2016.03.059.

Philippot, P., & Brutoux, F. (2008). Induced rumination dampens executive processes in dysphoric young adults. *Journal of Behavior Therapy and Experimental Psychiatry*. Available from https://doi.org/10.1016/j.jbtep.2007.07.001.

Piguet, C., Cojan, Y., Sterpenich, V., Desseilles, M., Bertschy, G., & Vuilleumier, P. (2016). Alterations in neural systems mediating cognitive flexibility and inhibition in mood disorders. *Human Brain Mapping, 37*(4), 1335–1348. Available from https://doi.org/10.1002/hbm.23104.

Ray, R., Ochsner, K., Cooper, J., Robertson, E., Gabrieli, J., & Gross, J. (2005). Individual differences in trait rumination and the neural systems supporting cognitive reappraisal. *Cognitive, Affective, & Behavioral Neuroscience, 5*(2), 156–168. Available from https://doi.org/10.3758/CABN.5.2.156.

Robertson, I. H., Manly, T., Beschin, N., Daini, R., Haeske-Dewick, H., Hömberg, V., ... Weber, E. (1997). Auditory sustained attention is a marker of unilateral spatial neglect. *Neuropsychologia, 35*(12), 1527–1532.

Rochat, L., Billieux, J., & Van der Linden, M. (2012). Difficulties in disengaging attentional resources from self-generated thoughts moderate the link between dysphoria and maladaptive self-referential thinking. *Cognition & Emotion, 26*(4), 748–757. Available from https://doi.org/10.1080/02699931.2011.613917.

Rothbart, M. K. (1989). Temperament in childhood: A framework. In G. A. Kohnstamm, J. E. Bates, & M. K. Rothbart (Eds.), *Temperament in childhood* (pp. 59–73). John Wiley & Sons.

Sandrone, S., & Catani, M. (2013). Journal club: Default-mode network connectivity in cognitively unimpaired patients with parkinson disease. *Neurology, 81*(23), e172–e175. Available from https://doi.org/10.1212/01.wnl.0000436943.62904.09.

Schneider, F., Bermpohl, F., Heinzel, A., Rotte, M., Walter, M., Tempelmann, C., ... Northoff, G. (2008). The resting brain and our self: Self-relatedness modulates resting state neural activity in cortical midline structures. *Neuroscience, 157*(1), 120–131. Available from https://doi.org/10.1016/j.neuroscience.2008.08.014.

Servaas, M. N., Riese, H., Ormel, J., & Aleman, A. (2014). The neural correlates of worry in association with individual differences in neuroticism. *Human Brain Mapping, 35*(9), 4303–4315. Available from https://doi.org/10.1002/hbm.22476.

Siegle, G. J., Steinhauer, S. R., Thase, M. E., Stenger, V. A., & Carter, C. S. (2002). Can't shake that feeling: Event-related fMRI assessment of sustained amygdala activity in response to emotional information in depressed individuals. *Biological Psychiatry, 51*(9), 693–707. Available from https://doi.org/10.1016/S0006-3223(02)01314-8.

Siegle, G. J., Thase, M. E., & Carter, C. S. (2006). Use of fMRI to predict recovery from unipolar depression with cognitive behavior therapy. *American Journal of Psychiatry, 163*(4), 735–738. Available from https://doi.org/10.1176/ajp.2006.163.4.735.

Siemer, M. (2005). Mood-congruent cognitions constitute mood experience. *Emotion, 5*(3), 296.

Simmons, W. K., Avery, J. A., Barcalow, J. C., Bodurka, J., Drevets, W. C., & Bellgowan, P. (2013). Keeping the body in mind: Insula functional organization and functional connectivity integrate interoceptive, exteroceptive, and emotional awareness. *Human Brain Mapping, 34*(11), 2944–2958. Available from https://doi.org/10.1002/hbm.22113.

Smallwood, J., Tipper, C., Brown, K., Baird, B., Engen, H., Michaels, J. R., ... Schooler, J. W. (2013). Escaping the here and now: Evidence for a role of the default mode network in perceptually decoupled thought. *NeuroImage, 69*, 120–125. Available from https://doi.org/10.1016/j.neuroimage.2012.12.012.

Snyder, H. R., & Hankin, B. L. (2016). Spiraling out of control. *Clinical Psychological Science, 4*(6), 1047–1064. Available from https://doi.org/10.1177/2167702616633157.

Stroop, J. R. (1935). Studies of interference in serial verbal reactions. *Journal of Experimental Psychology, 18*, 643–662.

Thayer, J. F., Åhs, F., Fredrikson, M., Sollers, J. J., & Wager, T. D. (2012). A meta-analysis of heart rate variability and neuroimaging studies: Implications for heart rate variability as a marker of stress and health. *Neuroscience and Biobehavioral Reviews, 36*(2), 747–756. Available from https://doi.org/10.1016/j.neubiorev.2011.11.009.

Tops, M., Boksem, M. A. S., Quirin, M., Ijzerman, H., & Koole, S. L. (2014). Internally-directed cognition and mindfulness: An integrative perspective derived from predictive and reactive control systems theory. *Frontiers in Psychology*, 5. Retrieved from <https://www.narcis.nl/publication/RecordID/oai:tilburguniversity.edu:publications%2F89c09540-4e8b-437c-9f32-32deb2bfc875>.

Vanderhasselt, M., Baeken, C., Van Schuerbeek, P., Luypaert, R., De Mey, J., & De Raedt, R. (2013). How brooding minds inhibit negative material: An event-related fMRI study. *Brain and Cognition*, *81*(3), 352–359. Available from https://doi.org/10.1016/j.bandc.2013.01.007.

Vanderhasselt, M., Kühn, S., & De Raedt, R. (2011). Healthy brooders employ more attentional resources when disengaging from the negative: An event-related fMRI study. *Cognitive, Affective, & Behavioral Neuroscience*, *11*(2), 207–216. Available from https://doi.org/10.3758/s13415-011-0022-5.

Verstraeten, K., Bijttebier, P., Vasey, M. W., & Raes, F. (2011). Specificity of worry and rumination in the development of anxiety and depressive symptoms in children. *British Journal of Clinical Psychology*, *50*(4), 364–378. Available from https://doi.org/10.1348/014466510X532715.

Verstraeten, K., Vasey, M., Raes, F., & Bijttebier, P. (2009). Temperament and risk for depressive symptoms in adolescence: Mediation by rumination and moderation by effortful control. *Journal of Abnormal Child Psychology*, *37*(3), 349–361. Available from https://doi.org/10.1007/s10802-008-9293-x.

Wagner, C., Alloy, L., & Abramson, L. (2015). Trait rumination, depression, and executive functions in early adolescence. *Journal of Youth and Adolescence*, *44*(1), 18–36. Available from https://doi.org/10.1007/s10964-014-0133-8.

Watkins, E., & Brown, R. G. (2002). Rumination and executive function in depression: An experimental study. *Journal of Neurology, Neurosurgery, and Psychiatry*, *72*(3), 400–402. Available from https://doi.org/10.1136/jnnp.72.3.400.

Webb, C. A., Auerbach, R. P., Bondy, E., Stanton, C. H., Foti, D., & Pizzagalli, D. A. (2017). Abnormal neural responses to feedback in depressed adolescents. *Journal of Abnormal Psychology*, *126*(1), 19–31. Available from https://doi.org/10.1037/abn0000228.

Whiteman, R. C., & Mangels, J. A. (2016). Rumination and rebound from failure as a function of gender and time on task. *Brain Sciences*, *6*(1), 7. Available from https://doi.org/10.3390/brainsci6010007.

Whitmer, A., & Banich, M. (2012). Repetitive thought and reversal learning deficits. *Cognitive Therapy and Research*, *36*(6), 714–721. Available from https://doi.org/10.1007/s10608-011-9409-4.

Whitmer, A. J., & Banich, M. T. (2007). Inhibition versus switching deficits in different forms of rumination. *Psychological Science*, *18*(6), 546–553. Available from https://doi.org/10.1111/j.1467-9280.2007.01936.x.

Whitmer, A. J., & Banich, M. T. (2010). Trait rumination and inhibitory deficits in long-term memory. *Cognition & Emotion*, *24*(1), 168–179. Available from https://doi.org/10.1080/02699930802645762.

Whitmer, A. J., & Gotlib, I. H. (2012). Switching and backward inhibition in major depressive disorder: The role of rumination. *Journal of Abnormal Psychology*, *121*(3), 570–578. Available from https://doi.org/10.1037/a0027474.

Whitmer, A. J., & Gotlib, I. H. (2013). An attentional scope model of rumination. *Psychological Bulletin*, *139*(5), 1036–1061. Available from https://doi.org/10.1037/a0030923.

Wilkinson, P. O., & Goodyer, I. M. (2006). Attention difficulties and mood-related ruminative response style in adolescents with unipolar depression. *Journal of Child Psychology and Psychiatry*, *47*(12), 1284–1291. Available from https://doi.org/10.1111/j.1469-7610.2006.01660.x.

Zetsche, U., D'Avanzato, C., & Joormann, J. (2012). Depression and rumination: Relation to components of inhibition. *Cognition & Emotion, 26*(4), 758–767. Available from https://doi.org/10.1080/02699931.2011.613919.

Zetsche, U., & Joormann, J. (2011). Components of interference control predict depressive symptoms and rumination cross-sectionally and at six months follow-up. *Journal of Behavior Therapy and Experimental Psychiatry, 42*(1), 65–73.

Zhu, X., Wang, X., Xiao, J., Liao, J., Zhong, M., Wang, W., & Yao, S. (2012). Evidence of a dissociation pattern in resting-state default mode network connectivity in first-episode, treatment-naive major depression patients. *Biological Psychiatry, 71*(7), 611–617. Available from https://doi.org/10.1016/j.biopsych.2011.10.035.

SECTION 3

Treatments for rumination

CHAPTER

10

Cognitive behavioral therapies for rumination

Overview

In this chapter, I review the empirical efficacy of cognitive behavioral therapy (CBT) for treating rumination. After exploring evidence for traditional CBT and the lack of understanding of its mechanisms, I describe a treatment package targeting rumination specifically: rumination-focused CBT. I explain its theoretical basis, describe the therapy itself, and examine the research supporting its efficacy. Finally, I review a set of interventions involving cognitive bias modification that show promise for reducing rumination.

One potential intervention for targeting rumination is CBT. This umbrella term generally refers to treatments combining traditional cognitive therapy with various behavioral techniques. The main assumption of traditional cognitive therapy is that changing the way people think will change their feelings and behaviors (Beck, 2011). Negative and/or distorted thought patterns are identified and changed through a process called cognitive restructuring. Therapists help clients change the content of their thoughts by challenging cognitive distortions and replacing unhelpful thoughts with more adaptive responses to events. For example, a patient who is upset at his boyfriend for not calling one night might have negative thoughts such as "My boyfriend doesn't love me anymore" or "I must have done something wrong." A therapist would help the patient identify faulty logic in those thoughts (e.g., mind reading and jumping to conclusions), evaluate evidence against those thoughts (e.g., "He does tell me that he loves me a lot."), and generate more helpful reappraisals (e.g., "Maybe he fell asleep early,"

Rumination and Related Constructs
DOI: https://doi.org/10.1016/B978-0-12-812545-8.00010-3

© 2020 Elsevier Inc. All rights reserved.

"I should just ask him why he didn't call."). Over time, therapists and patients identify deeply held negative core beliefs (e.g., "I'm unlovable.") that are serving as a filter for experiencing and interpreting life events. Through similar techniques, patients learn to challenge and change these core beliefs. CBT is an empirically supported intervention for a wide range of presenting problems, especially for anxiety disorders, bulimia, anger control problems, and general stress (Hofmann, Asnaani, Vonk, Sawyer, & Fang, 2012).

Although CBT focuses on changing the *content* of thought, researchers have also examined whether it decreases the *process* of ruminative thinking. Not surprisingly, much of the research has been with depressed patients. CBT for depression typically combines cognitive therapy with behavioral activation, a technique that aims to increase patients' involvement in pleasant, rewarding activities. Studies have found that 6-8 weeks of group-based CBT contribute to significant decreases in rumination in adults high in depressive symptoms (Evans et al., 2013; Manicavasagar, Perich, & Parker, 2012). In patients with major depression, CBT plus treatment as usual (TAU) led to greater decreases in rumination than did TAU by itself (Wilkinson & Goodyer, 2008). Similarly, four sessions of behavioral activation combined with an attention training technique (see Chapter 12: Metacognitive therapy) led to decreased rumination 1 week and 1 month after treatment (Moshier & Otto, 2017).

Researchers have also examined whether CBT reduces worry in patients with generalized anxiety disorder (GAD). CBT for GAD typically replaces behavioral activation with relaxation training, problem-solving practice, and use of "worry time," in which patients are instructed to worry intensely during a predetermined window of time but not to worry the rest of the day. Patients are also often exposed to anxiety-provoking stimuli, in order to decrease their avoidance of anxious affect (Borkovec, Newman, Pincus, & Lytle, 2002; Ladouceur et al., 2000). Both individual and group-based CBT for GAD effectively reduce worry (for a metaanalysis, see Covin, Ouimet, Seeds, & Dozois, 2008). Similarly, internet-delivered CBT decreases worry (Paxling et al., 2011; Robinson et al., 2010).

What are potential mechanisms by which CBT reduces repetitive thinking? One possibility is reappraisal, or actively seeking alternative—usually positive—interpretations and understandings of upsetting events. Reappraisal has long been recognized as an adaptive coping response to negative experiences (e.g., Gross, 2001). Both rumination and reappraisal involve thoughts about an upsetting event, but the content and nature of the thoughts differ in meaningful ways that may influence subsequent emotions. In fact, some researchers theorize that rumination and reappraisal share as an underlying process the (in)ability to inhibit negative material (Cohen, Daches, Mor, & Henik, 2014). Specifically, good cognitive control prevents rumination and enables reappraisal, and vice versa. Going in the other direction, rumination impairs inhibition, whereas reappraisal enhances inhibition. This model suggests that improving people's ability to engage in positive reappraisal should contribute to decreased rumination. Unfortunately, researchers have not yet tested this hypothesis. Some experiments have compared rumination and reappraisal by asking participants to remember an angering event and then to either ruminate about it or engage in positive reappraisal (Denson, Moulds, & Grisham, 2012; Ray, Wilhelm, & Gross, 2008). As expected, reappraisal led to less anger than did rumination. These experiments, however, did not provide evidence that reappraisal actually decreases rumination.

Another possible mechanism is distraction. Behavioral activation is a common and effective intervention for depression that emphasizes engaging in short-term pleasant, reinforcing activities in order to lift people out of sad moods, anhedonia, and lethargy (Jacobson et al., 1996). The original response style theory (Nolen-Hoeksema, 1991) proposed that using pleasant or neutral distractions can divert people's attention away from their negative mood and help them focus instead on thoughts or activities that are absorbing and positively reinforcing. Common examples of distracting activities include going for a run, seeing a movie with friends, or concentrating on work (Nolen-Hoeksema, Wisco, & Lyubomirsky, 2008). As reviewed in a previous chapter (see Chapter 1, Rumination and mood disorders), experimental studies comparing induced rumination to distraction generally find that distraction decreases immediate sad mood in participants who are already depressed (Watkins, 2008). One experiment found that 8 minutes of induced distraction (e.g., think about the layout of the local shopping center) led to a decrease in state rumination in adolescents, compared to induced rumination (Hilt & Pollak, 2012). However, no other studies to date have tested whether distraction actually decreases rumination.

Moreover, theory and research suggest that distraction is not an ideal long-term response to negative events. In a reformulation of her theory, Nolen-Hoeksema suggested that chronic use of distraction can fuel avoidance and suppression, which will increase both negative mood and rumination (Nolen-Hoeksema et al., 2008). In fact, empirical evidence for the long-term benefits of distraction on depressive symptoms is not robust, especially in prospective research (Nolen-Hoeksema et al., 2008; Rood, Roelofs, Bögels, Nolen-Hoeksema, & Schouten, 2009). One reason for this is that distraction can be difficult to accomplish and maintain, and people may have trouble generating appropriate alternatives to their ruminative thoughts. In fact, people often exhibit unfocused self-distraction, or switching from one distracter to another depending on whatever is on their minds (Wenzlaff, Wegner, & Klein, 1991). This kind of flitting from one topic to another is likely not absorbing or reinforcing enough to alleviate a sad mood. People's moods also impact the kind of distracters they select. Specifically, depressed individuals are more likely to use negative distracter thoughts when attempting suppression (Wenzlaff et al., 1991; Wenzlaff, Wegner, & Roper, 1988). Not surprisingly, they experience more subsequent intrusions of negative thoughts, indicating a failure at suppression. Interestingly, depressed individuals recognize that positive distracters will be more effective than negative distracters. However, even when presented with possible positive distracters, they use more negative distracters. Thus, even against their better judgment, depressed people automatically select negative distracter thoughts. Taken together, these findings suggest that *instructed* distraction–either via experimental manipulations or therapy–may improve negative moods in the short-term because it maintains people's attention on mood-incongruent (i.e., positive) thoughts. On their own, however, individuals may select mood-congruent distracters that unfortunately lead to even more rumination and negative mood.

In sum, traditional CBT effectively reduces both depressive rumination and worry (Spinhoven et al., 2018). However, this treatment is not specifically geared toward reducing rumination, and mechanisms by which it decreases rumination have not yet been identified. In addition, CBT appears to be less effective at treating depression for patients high in rumination (Ciesla & Roberts, 2002; Schmaling, Dimidjian, Katon, & Sullivan, 2002). This could be because in addressing the content rather than the process of thinking, CBT does not effectively address a strong and constant stream of negative thoughts (Watkins, 2016). Moreover, focusing on the content of thoughts may itself trigger more repetitive thinking, especially in patients prone to rumination. Finally, many formerly depressed patients experience residual symptoms, including rumination (Roberts, Gilboa, & Gotlib, 1998). Thus, researchers from the CBT tradition have seen a need to develop treatments that specifically target rumination. In this chapter, I review one major treatment package—RFCBT—as well as a set of brief interventions involving cognitive modification.

Rumination-focused cognitive behavioral therapy

Other than Susan Nolen-Hoeksema, Edward Watkins is arguably the biggest name in the rumination field. In addition to publishing an impressive amount of basic research over a 20-year period, he has contributed several important theoretical advancements and developed rumination-focused cognitive-behavioral therapy (RFCBT; Watkins, 2016). Although this therapy was intended to target rumination as a symptom of residual depression, basic research suggests that it has the potential to decrease repetitive thinking across a range of clinical symptoms. In this section, I first review Watkins' relevant theoretical contributions. I then describe RFCBT and research supporting its efficacy.

Theory

RFCBT is based on two important propositions about rumination: (1) the negative consequences of rumination are primarily due to abstract cognitive processing and (2) excessive rumination is a mental habit. These propositions constitute important extensions of response styles theory and the control theory of rumination (see Chapter 1: Rumination and mood disorders and Chapter 7: Triggers of rumination), and they have important implications for treating people who ruminate.

In trying to understand the effect of depressive rumination, Watkins noted that it involves two separate components: (1) self-focus (e.g., attention to depressive symptoms) and (2) an abstract processing style (Watkins & Teasdale, 2004). Abstract (sometimes called analytical) processing focuses on higher order goals (e.g., happiness and success), as well as the meaning, causes, and implications of experiences. By contrast, concrete (sometimes called experiential) processing focuses on lower level goals (e.g., finish a chapter), as well as specific and sensory-related details of experiences. One processing mode focuses on *why* questions; the other on *what* and *how* questions. Watkins (2008) proposed that these different modes of processing lead to divergent outcomes.

To compare these two modes of processing, Watkins adapted Nolen-Hoeksema's classic rumination manipulation. Participants read the same 28 sentences over 8 minutes but are presented with one of two instructions (e.g., Watkins & Teasdale, 2004). In the abstract processing condition, participants are instructed to think about the *causes, meanings, and consequences* of their symptoms and feelings. In the concrete processing condition, participants are instructed to focus on the *experience* of their symptoms and feelings. Manipulation checks indicate that both manipulations increase self-focus, but only abstract processing increases analytical thinking. Compared to concrete processing, abstract processing leads to increased overgeneral memories, a more negative attributional style, and lower ratings of self-worth in depressed participants or high trait ruminators (Crane, Barnhofer, Visser, Nightingale, & Williams, 2007; Lo, Ho, & Hollon, 2010; Rimes & Watkins, 2005; Sanders & Lam, 2010). Interestingly, these studies do not find any effect of abstract versus concrete processing on self-reported mood. Instead, both manipulations increase dysphoric mood in depressed, compared to never depressed, participants (see also Watkins & Moulds, 2005).

Watkins (2008) argued that this is consistent with response styles theory, because both manipulations induce self-focused attention, which is associated with worse dysphoric mood (e.g., Mor & Winquist, 2002).

Despite the lack of a main effect on negative mood, Watkins hypothesized that processing mode increases *emotional reactivity* to a stressor. He tested this hypothesis in several experiments (Moberly & Watkins, 2006; Watkins, 2004; Watkins, Moberly, & Moulds, 2008). The basic procedure was that participants read several scenarios, but half of them were instructed to imagine the concrete details of the scene (i.e., concrete processing), and the other half were asked to evaluate the causes, meanings, and implications of each scenario (i.e., abstract processing). All participants then experienced a failure on a task that supposedly predicted career and academic success (i.e., a stressor). Healthy participants in the abstract condition showed larger increases in negative mood and decreases in positive mood after the failure than did participants in the concrete condition (Watkins et al., 2008). Two studies found this effect only in participants who were high in dispositional rumination (Moberly & Watkins, 2006; Watkins, 2004). Other research using this same procedure found that abstract processing was associated with greater indecisiveness and difficulty making decisions, particularly in individuals with depressive symptoms (Di Schiena, Luminet, Chang, & Philippot, 2013).

Watkins (2008) also proposed that abstract processing contributes to the generalization of negative events. Consider, for example, a person who has a disagreement with a colleague and then comes to believe that *everyone* is *always* mad at him and that he cannot do *anything* right (Van Lier, Vervliet, Boddez, & Raes, 2015). Because it is not focused on specific details, abstract processing may increase this kind of generalized response to negative events, which in turn likely contributes to depressive symptoms. Two experiments tested this hypothesis. In one, adolescents were trained in either abstract or concrete processing and then participated in a generalization-condition paradigm (Van Lier, Vervliet, Vanbrabant, Lenaert, & Raes, 2014). In this paradigm a stimulus (e.g., picture of a train with blue seats) was first paired with an aversive outcome (e.g., conductor yelling at you). To assess generalization, participants rated their expectations for aversive outcomes to stimuli that were more and less similar to the initial stimulus (e.g., purple or red seats). The results indicated that abstract processing led to greater negative generalization, but only for participants high in depressive symptoms. In another experiment, participants viewed images of angry faces paired with their own names and happy faces paired with another person's name (Van Lier et al., 2015). Participants were instructed to think about either the meaning and causes of the facial expressions (i.e., abstract processing) or about the sensory-perceptual features of the faces (i.e., concrete processing). As expected, participants who engaged in abstract processing showed more generalization of angry faces to the self.

In sum, these experiments show that abstract processing leads to greater negative thinking, overgeneral memory, emotional reactivity to failure, and generalization of negative events, particularly for vulnerable individuals (e.g., with depressive symptoms or ruminative tendencies). Based on these results, Watkins (2008) developed the processing mode account of rumination. Elaborating on the control theory of rumination (Martin & Tesser, 1996) and the reduced concreteness theory of worry (Stöber, 1998), Watkins proposed that abstract processing is often problematic because it is less sensitive to changes in one's environment and fails to suggest specific actions that may be helpful for coping. This kind of processing is particularly counterproductive in stressful or novel circumstances. For instance, when a child starts a new school or an adult is grieving the loss of a marriage, ruminating about an abstract goal such as happiness does not provide situation-specific guidance about how to proceed. Instead, in unfamiliar and difficult situations, concrete processing is much more constructive. Concrete processing focuses on the immediate demands of the situation, which will likely lead to more effective problem-solving. Concrete processing is also more adaptive in difficult situations because it is less likely to elicit negative overgeneralizations and emotional reactivity to negative events.[1]

Importantly, Watkins (2008) argued that sometimes the people who would most benefit from concrete processing have the most difficulty engaging in it. Self-regulation theories (e.g., Carver & Scheier, 1998) suggest that at baseline, individuals engage in abstract processing, but that they shift to more concrete processing in difficult times. This is similar to Maslow's (1943) famous hierarchy of needs: when people's basic needs (e.g., food, protection) are met, they have the luxury of focusing on higher level goals (e.g., relationships and happiness). However, when things go wrong, the ability to flexibly shift to concrete processing is adaptive. Watkins noted that this ability to flexibly shift between processing modes is impaired if people lack sufficient executive control or a stable self-worth, and if they strongly believe that it is important to make sense of feelings and problems. Of course, these tendencies

1 Watkins (2008) did propose certain conditions under which abstract processing is preferable. The pursuit of abstract goals (e.g., being happy) requires that individuals know specific behaviors that will help them attain their desired state. This is feasible when life is running smoothly and when people feel familiarity with and mastery in their current situation. In these circumstances, abstract processing can promote both consistency and flexibility, because people stay focused on long-term goals and may be able to identify several alternative ways to attain those goals.

characterize people with depression. Thus, whereas healthy people shift from abstract to concrete processing when faced with difficulties or novelty, individuals at risk for depression continue to engage in abstract processing. This impaired ability to regulate their processing mode leads to chronic abstract rumination and its negative consequences.

Research examining the degree of abstractness of rumination supports this dysregulation hypothesis. For instance, depressed individual rate their rumination about current problems as more abstract than do recover depressed and never-depressed participants (Watkins & Moulds, 2007). In an experience sampling study, undergraduates with higher depressive symptoms reported more abstract thinking on a daily basis (Takano & Tanno, 2010). Similarly, undergraduates with a history of trauma engaged in 4 minutes of depressive rumination about a past negative event and provided thought samples of the content of their rumination (Goldwin, Behar, & Sibrava, 2013). Coders rated the content of rumination as more abstract for participants with high, compared to low, posttraumatic stress symptoms. Worry is also characterized by reduced concreteness. For instance, undergraduates with higher worry tendencies generate less concrete elaborations about potential risks and consequences of specific problems (Stöber, 1998). Similarly, patients with GAD describe their worries in less concrete terms than do healthy control participants (Stöber & Borkovec, 2002). In an interesting study, healthy participants engaged in five consecutive periods of repetitive thinking about a positive, negative, or neutral potential future event (Behar et al., 2011). In general, future-oriented repetitive thinking became increasingly less concrete as periods progressed. Thus, even in healthy individuals, continued rumination becomes increasingly abstract, suggesting that the more people ruminate, the harder it becomes to intentionally shift to more productive, constructive processing.

Related to this last point, Watkins and Nolen-Hoeksema (2014) proposed that excessive rumination becomes a habitual response to particular situations (see also Hertel, 2004). Habits are automatically performed behaviors, which means that people may engage in them without awareness or conscious intent. Habits are also difficult to control and do not require extensive cognitive resources to perform. As evidence for this conceptualization of trait rumination as a habit, a majority of dysphoric ruminators report that their rumination is automatic and compulsive (Watkins & Baracaia, 2001). Furthermore, trait rumination is associated with tendencies to engage in negative self-focused thoughts that occur often, are unintended, are initiated without awareness, and are difficult to control (Verplanken, Friborg, Wang, Trafimow, & Woolf, 2007).

Watkins and Nolen-Hoeksema argued that two main characteristics of habits are important for understanding excessive rumination and its treatment. First, reflecting the principles of classical conditioning, habits develop when behaviors are performed frequently in the same contexts. Just as the sound of a bell can eventually make a dog salivate in anticipation of food, so too can a particular mood or stressful environment automatically trigger a ruminative process. Importantly, these situation-response associations are not mediated by any explicit or implicit goal. In other words, habitual rumination can be triggered without clear intention and effort. This conceptualization seemingly differs from the notion that rumination reflects conscious efforts at solving perceived discrepancies or beliefs that rumination increases insight and understanding. However, Watkins and Nolen-Hoeksema proposed that whatever the reasons people have for initially engaging in rumination, if they repeatedly ruminate in the same context (e.g., a sad mood and a chronic stressor), that context eventually becomes an automatic trigger for rumination. Moreover, whereas rumination may only initially occur in response to a personally meaningful discrepancy, habitual rumination may eventually be triggered by anything that elicits a negative mood (e.g., watching a sad movie). Of course, this association is more likely to develop if people lack a range of other coping responses or the ability to flexibly shift between processing modes. Thus, if people only respond to negative moods or perceived discrepancies with abstract rumination, rather than alternating between various coping strategies, abstract rumination is more likely to become a habitual response.

Second, habits are insensitive to changes in goals or outcomes. The traditional control theory of rumination asserted that rumination ceases when people attain a desired goal or give up an unattainable goal (Martin & Tesser, 1996). By contrast, Watkins and Nolen-Hoeksema suggest that once it is a habitual response, rumination can occur even after a goal has been reached or discarded. This may explain why depressed and anxious individuals ruminate and worry even though they recognize the negative consequences of these behaviors. Metacognitive theory (see Chapter 8: Beliefs, traits, and motivations underlying rumination and Chapter 12: Metacognitive therapy) argues that negative beliefs about rumination maintain rumination because people do not believe they can control their thinking. By contrast, this model proposes an unintentional process in which people continue ruminating despite being aware of its dangers.

Therapy

With that theoretical explanation, I now turn to a description of RFCBT itself. Designed specifically to target ruminative thoughts, RFCBT is informed by Watkins' theoretical contributions. One primary goal of the treatment is to help patients shift their processing style. Patients are coached to engage in thoughts and behaviors that are concrete, specific, active, and compassionate—rather than abstract, passive, and evaluative. Another main goal is to break the habit of using rumination in response to particular triggers. Because habits are unresponsive to new goals or outcome information, RFCBT does not aim to modify the content of thoughts through the use of cognitive restructuring. Instead, the therapy helps patients identify and then avoid or alter exposure to situations that trigger rumination. In addition, through practice and repetition, patients learn to replace abstract rumination with incompatible and more constructive responses (e.g., concrete processing, active behavior).

Watkins (2016) has provided therapists with a detailed treatment manual for RFCBT. The therapy is designed to be delivered in 12 1-hour, in-person, individual therapy sessions. Like traditional CBT, RFCBT uses a structured format, agenda setting, homework, handouts, Socratic questioning, and behavioral experiments. Initial sessions introduce the treatment rationale and explain why rumination is the primary target of therapy. Using information gleaned from the patient's experiences, therapists highlight the negative consequences of rumination. Therapists also explain that rumination is a natural way of responding to unresolved problems that unfortunately has become a habitual and automatic, learned response.

The first major component of the therapy involves conducting a functional analysis, a technique borrowed from traditional behavioral therapy that identifies the unique antecedents (i.e., triggering situations) and consequences (i.e., functions) of a target behavior (e.g., rumination) for each individual patient. This information is used to guide all subsequent intervention decisions. As part of the functional analysis, patients record episodes of rumination between therapy sessions and make note of events, emotions, and thoughts immediately before ruminating (e.g., boyfriend did not call as expected; felt sad and anxious; thought "What did I do wrong?" and "He must not love me."), as well as the effects of rumination (e.g., felt depressed). The therapist also asks questions to understand the function of rumination for that patient. RFCBT proposes that common functions of rumination include avoiding undesired feelings, seeking understanding, increasing motivation for action, preparing or planning for anticipated events, anticipating potential negative outcomes, and generating rationalizations or justifications. After analyzing several rumination episodes, the therapist develops a formulation about the functions of rumination for that particular patient and under what conditions (e.g., when, where, and with whom) it usually occurs and does *not* occur. Therapists can also use functional analysis to understand the variability of rumination, such as when rumination is brief versus long lasting and when it is helpful versus unhelpful, as well as what the patient does to stop or interrupt rumination.

Once the triggers and functions of rumination for a patient are understood, therapists select interventions that will prevent and replace unhelpful rumination. One focus of therapy is changing patients' environments in order to reduce or avoid common triggers of their rumination. When addressing environmental triggers, therapists consider what aspect of a given situation elicits rumination. For instance, patients might ruminate when they first wake up in the morning because they feel sad and lonely or because they feel overwhelmed by how much they have to do that day. Based on these varied triggers of rumination, therapists may encourage patients to do something active (e.g., exercise) first thing in the morning or to make a list of things they need to do that day. Other common triggers of rumination include being alone, feeling bored, experiencing a negative mood, being reminded of upsetting or traumatic events, and having periods of routine and/or reflection (e.g., while driving home from work, making future plans).

In addition to preventing or avoiding triggers of rumination, patients learn alternative ways of responding to triggers that they do encounter. This is particularly important when triggers are an internal state such as negative emotions, because these experiences cannot realistically be avoided. Patients are taught that if they notice a particular warning sign, they should engage in an alternative response instead of rumination. A good alternative response is a behavior that is incompatible with rumination, addresses its hypothesized function, and has a good chance of becoming a new habit. Common alternative responses include relaxation, concrete problem-solving, calling a friend, being assertive, and engaging in a pleasant activity. As with traditional behavior therapy, therapists ask patients to rehearse these alternative responses and repeatedly practice using them in response to identified triggers.

Another main focus on therapy is helping patients shift from abstract processing to a more constructive processing style. Therapists first help patients identify their abstract thinking and how it makes them feel. For instance, patients may be asked to vividly reimagine themselves in a recent upsetting situation and to ask themselves "why" questions (e.g., "Why is this happening to me?") and to notice resulting thoughts and feelings. They then repeat the exercise but this time ask "how" questions (e.g., "What details do I notice ...?" or "How do I solve this problem or learn from this?"). This exercise can help patients start to realize the downsides of abstract, evaluative thinking, and the benefits of more concrete thinking. Therapists then use several techniques to train patients to engage in more concrete processing.

Concreteness training involves therapist-guided practice in concrete processing of negative events. Using a recent or ongoing upsetting situation in patients' lives, therapists employ a visualization exercise that consists of three parts. First, patients imagine being in the situation and focus on sensory details (e.g., sights, sounds, smells, and internal sensations), as well as on what makes the situation distinct in terms of time, place, or setting. Next, therapists guide patients to notice the sequence of events that led up to the particular situation, as well as any warning signs that a difficulty was coming and any potential turning points where a different action or decision could have changed what happened. Finally, patients are asked to visualize how they would like things to be different and specific steps they can take to move forward and deal with the situation. Over several sessions, patients practice applying this concreteness exercise to several events from their lives. They are also asked to practice the exercise on a daily basis at home.

In addition to concreteness training, therapists may encourage patients to foster absorption and compassion, because they constitute mental states that Watkins argues. are incompatible with abstract rumination. Absorption emphasizes process over outcome, detailed attention to the present, direct engagement with felt experience, and lack of evaluative commentary. Compassion is another way to counter the negative self-evaluation of abstract rumination and to get people out of their own heads. Therapists may use visualization exercises such as reimagining times when patients were completely absorbed in an activity (e.g., in a state of flow) or experiencing compassion. Therapists may also encourage patients to seek out opportunities to experience absorption and compassion for self and others. This work has the potential to foster more concrete processing and to provide patients with enjoyable experiences, both of which should contribute to decreased depression.

Although RFCBT was originally designed as an individual therapy, Watkins (2016) has also developed group and internet-based adaptations. Group RFCBT is typically delivered over 6–10 sessions lasting 1–2 hours each. The groups consist of between 6 and 12 patients with one or two group therapists. The content covered is the same as with individual RFCBT, although the group format necessitates more structure, psychoeducation, and group discussion. Group RFCBT has the advantages of allowing members to normalize, provide support, and generate helpful alternatives to rumination.

Internet-based RFCBT (called MindReSolve) consists of six modules, each of which consists of 2–5 pages. Patients are encouraged to complete one module weekly or biweekly. The modules include psychoeducational text, pictures, vignettes about people with depression, and videos of actors providing patient testimonials and explaining coping strategies. The vignettes and videos are tailored to match patients' gender and age. There are also online questionnaires, rating scales, exercises, activities, and audio-recordings of the experiential exercises used in RFCBT (e.g., relaxation and concreteness exercises). Some of the questionnaires provide automatic feedback (e.g., whether negative mood increased or decreased following a particular exercise). In addition, actual therapists read patients' answers at the end of each module and provide online responses. These responses provide encouragement, support, and guidance on exercises and plans. Patients cannot progress to the next module without reading the therapist's feedback on their completed module. To make this aspect of the treatment more feasible, therapists follow templates for written feedback, although they can add their own comments and reorder the presentation of modules if this seems helpful for a particular patient.

Supporting research

Because RFCBT is a relatively new treatment, only a few published studies test its efficacy as a complete treatment package. Fortunately, other research has examined the efficacy of concreteness training as a stand-alone treatment. In addition, basic research supports the benefits of concrete processing in participants with symptoms of mood, anxiety, and eating disorders. I review all of these literatures in the following section.

A few studies have tested the efficacy of individual RFCBT for depression. In an initial trial, 14 patients with medication-resistant residual depression received up to 12 sessions of individual RFCBT (Watkins et al., 2007). Depressive rumination and symptoms were measured during each week of the baseline period, each week during therapy, and within 4 weeks after the completion of therapy. RFCBT led to significant reductions in both depressive symptoms and depressive rumination. At the end of therapy, 71% of patients met the criteria for treatment response (i.e., a decrease of at least 50% in baseline depressive symptoms), and 50% met full remission criteria. There was also a 71% reduction in comorbid diagnoses (e.g., anxiety disorders, obsessive–compulsive disorder, and bulimia) from baseline to posttreatment. Watkins et al. (2011) then conducted a randomized control trial comparing TAU to RFCBT + TAU in patients with medication-resistant residual depression. All participants had to be taking antidepressant medication, and TAU consisted of outpatient clinical and medication management. As expected, RFCBT + TAU led to a significantly greater decrease in depressive symptoms, depressive rumination, and comorbid diagnoses than TAU alone. In fact, 81% of participants receiving RFCBT + TAU achieved treatment response, compared to 26% of participants receiving TAU alone. Moreover, change in rumination mediated the association between condition and change in depressive symptoms. Another trial randomly assigned adolescents with remitted major depression to RFCBT or assessment only (Jacobs et al., 2016). Similar to previous trials, RFCBT led to decreased rumination and depressive symptoms, compared to the control condition.

Similar outcomes have been found with group and internet-based RFCBT. In one treatment trial, young adults were selected for participation because they scored high on measures of rumination and/or worry but did not have current major depression or anxiety disorders (Topper, Emmelkamp, Watkins, & Ehring, 2017). Participants were randomly assigned to internet-based RFCBT, group RFCBT, or wait-list control conditions. Both internet-based and group RFCBT led to significant reductions in worry and rumination, as well as depressive and anxious symptoms immediately after the treatment, compared to the wait-list. These effects were maintained at a 1-year follow-up. Moreover, group and internet-based RFCBT yielded significantly lower incidence rates of major depression and GAD over 1 year, compared to the wait-list. These effects were mediated by lower rumination and worry. The group and internet-based treatments did not yield any differences in outcomes. Similarly, an independent research team found that group RFCBT reduced depressive symptoms and rumination in patients with residual depression, compared to a wait-list control condition (Teismann et al., 2014). These effects were again maintained at a 1-year follow-up.

An interesting study tested the effect of RFCBT on posttraumatic stress disorder (PTSD) symptoms (Sezibera, Van Broeck, & Philippot, 2009). The sample consisted of 22 adolescent orphans who survived the 1994 Rwandan genocide, all of whom met the criteria for PTSD. The treatment occurred 13 years after the end of the genocide. In the treatment, participants engaged in narrative exposure to traumatic experiences and identified related thoughts, emotions, and efforts to cope. In addition to these common CBT procedures, they also engaged in a functional analysis of rumination and practiced more adaptive alternatives to rumination (e.g., disclosure and social sharing of emotions). Participants' PTSD symptoms significantly decreased from pre- to post-treatment. In fact, 18% of participants no longer met criteria for PTSD immediately and 2 months following the end of therapy.

Concreteness training as a stand-alone technique or adjunct to TAU also appears to be effective. For instance, Watkins et al. (2012) randomly assigned patients with diagnosed depression to TAU, TAU + concreteness training, or TAU + relaxation. Following a single 90-minute session of concreteness or relaxation training, patients were asked to engage in 15–30 minutes of daily practice at home for at least 6 weeks. After 8 weeks, patients receiving TAU + concreteness training reported significantly fewer depressive and anxious symptoms than those receiving TAU, especially if they started with less severe levels of depression. These differences were generally maintained at 3- and 6-month follow-ups. Moreover, TAU + concreteness training resulted in a greater decrease in depressive rumination, negative overgeneralization, and abstractness of problem descriptions than either TAU or TAU + relaxation. Another study randomly assigned hospice patients who reported meaningful levels of depressive or anxious symptoms to concreteness training or a wait-list condition (Galfin, Watkins, & Harlow, 2011). After a 30-minute training session, patients practiced for 10 minutes a day for 4 weeks. This time, concreteness training led to significant reductions in worry and anxious symptoms, but not in depressive symptoms. In an effort to apply this training to undergraduates, dysphoric students were randomly assigned to 1 week of daily concreteness training or a wait-list control (Mogoaşe, Brăilean, & David, 2013). This time, there was no initial training session, and participants engaged in concreteness training only with hypothetical (i.e., not autobiographical) scenarios. Participants who received concreteness training showed increases in concrete thinking, compared to the wait-list condition. However, there were no effects on depressive symptoms or depressive rumination. Thus, the efficacy of concreteness training may require an initial, in-person training session and/or practice with personally relevant scenarios.

Other studies included guided relaxation as part of concreteness training. Specifically, participants engaged in 10 minutes of guided progressive muscle relaxation before starting the concreteness training, in order to focus their attention on direct sensory experiences and improve concentration. In a sample of dysphoric participants, a single 70-minute session of concreteness training and 30 minutes of daily practice for 7 days led to a greater decrease in depressive symptoms and rumination, compared to relaxation alone (Watkins & Moberly, 2009). Another study randomly assigned dysphoric participants to concreteness training or a wait-list control group (Watkins, Baeyens, & Read, 2009). As expected, depressive rumination, depressive symptoms, self-criticism, overgeneralization, and abstractness of problem descriptions decreased more for participants who received concreteness training, compared to the wait-list condition.

Although RFCBT and concreteness training have not been tested in a wide range of clinical populations, basic research does support the benefits of concrete processing. These studies have compared manipulations of abstract self-focused versus concrete self-focused processing, as described earlier in this chapter. However, whereas the research reviewed earlier provided evidence for the detrimental effects of abstract processing, the research reviewed in this section suggests that concrete processing increases positive outcomes and decreases negative outcomes for participants with a range of mental disorders.

Concrete processing contributes to benefits in depressed participants. Specifically, concrete processing led to improved effectiveness of social problem-solving and decreased overgeneral memories, compared to abstract processing (Watkins & Moulds, 2005; Watkins & Teasdale, 2001, 2004). Moreover, in depressed and formerly depressed participants, recalling a positive autobiographical memory only improved sad mood when participants engaged in concrete processing of the memory (Werner-Seidler & Moulds, 2012). Recalling a positive memory using abstract processing maintained sad mood. These results suggest that an adaptive emotion regulation strategy (e.g., thinking about happy memories) may only work if individuals engage in concrete thinking.

Several studies have focused on PTSD symptoms and trauma-focused rumination. In survivors of motor vehicle accidents, greater concreteness of ruminative thoughts correlated with less depressive and PTSD symptom severity several months after the accident (Ehring, Frank, & Ehlers, 2008). Moreover, concreteness of rumination uniquely predicted less PTSD symptom severity, even controlling for the significant contribution of frequency of rumination. Several analog experiments have compared the effects of concrete versus abstract processing on the development of intrusive thoughts. For instance, after recalling a negative life event they had experienced in the past 5 years, participants wrote about that negative event using either abstract or concrete processing (Santa Maria, Reichert, Hummel, & Ehring, 2012). There was no effect of condition on mood. However, participants in the concrete condition showed a greater reduction of intrusive memories during and 36 hours after the experimental session than those in the abstract condition. In another study, female students read several scenarios and were instructed to either imagine the concrete details (i.e., concrete processing) or to evaluate the causes, meanings, and implications (i.e., abstract processing) of each scenario (Schaich, Watkins, & Ehring, 2013). All participants then watched a movie clip of a woman being raped and beaten. There was no effect of condition on negative mood. Concrete processing led to fewer intrusions than did abstract processing, but only for individuals high in trait rumination. Finally, healthy participants were trained to use either abstract or concrete processing while watching six traumatic film clips (White & Wild, 2016). Once again, participants who engaged in concrete processing reported fewer intrusive memories in response to the films and had lower posttraumatic symptoms 1 week later compared with participants who engaged in abstract processing.

Other researchers have focused on participants with social anxiety. In one study, college students high and low in self-reported social anxiety engaged in either abstract or concrete processing for 8 minutes (Vassilopoulos, 2008). In participants high in social anxiety, concrete processing decreased anxious mood, whereas abstract processing maintained anxious mood. Socially anxious participants in the concrete processing condition also reported more positive thoughts on a thought-listing exercise, compared to the abstract processing condition. Using the same procedure, in participants high in social anxiety, concrete processing decreased ratings of the self as worthless and incompetent, whereas abstract processing maintained these negative self-judgments (Vassilopoulos & Watkins, 2008). In this experiment, there was no effect of condition on anxious or sad mood. Across two experiments, therefore, concrete processing was more adaptive than abstract processing in individuals high in social anxiety. There was no effect of processing mode for participants low in social anxiety.

Some experiments have manipulated abstract versus concrete processing before or after speech presentations. In 12 patients with diagnosed social anxiety disorder, abstract and concrete processing were induced after giving a 3-minute speech (Nilsson, Lundh, & Viborg, 2012). Participants who engaged in concrete processing showed fewer negative thoughts. Interestingly, negative self-evaluations of speech performance were associated with more post-event rumination only for participants who engaged in abstract processing first. In other words, concrete processing appeared to weaken the association between negative self-perception of performance and post-event rumination. By contrast, another study found that for participants high in social anxiety, concrete processing both before and after a speech led to more maladaptive beliefs (e.g., "I have to get everyone's approval," "If I make mistakes, others will reject me."), compared to abstract processing (Wong & Moulds, 2012). Thus, whether concrete processing is adaptive or maladaptive before and after stressful performance tasks for people with social anxiety symptoms is unclear. Because self-focused attention in general contributes to symptoms of social anxiety (e.g., Norton & Abbott, 2016), any kind of self-focused processing before and after an anxiety-provoking situation may be problematic. Future research needs to tease apart the roles of self-focused attention and processing mode in people with social anxiety.

Finally, concrete processing shows benefits for people with eating disorder symptoms. In females with and without eating disorder symptoms, researchers induced either abstract or concrete self-focus on emotions and bodily sensations (Rawal, Williams, & Park, 2011). Participants then imagined eating food they considered extremely fattening. As with earlier studies, there was no observed difference in mood between the abstract and concrete conditions. However, in women with high symptomatology, those who engaged in abstract (vs concrete) self-focus believed they were more likely to gain weight just by thinking about eating fattening food. They also reported more attempts to avoid negative emotions triggered by the imaginal task.

These results were generally replicated in partially weight-restored female patients with anorexia. Moreover, anorexic women in the abstract condition reported a greater increase in their perceived weight following the imaginal task, suggesting that abstract processing can increase distorted body image.

In summary, the handful of studies testing the efficacy of RFCBT show that it decreases rumination, worry, and clinical symptoms of depression, anxiety, and PTSD. In addition, single in-person sessions of concreteness training plus daily practice at home generally result in decreased rumination or worry, compared to TAU, wait-list, or relaxation-only control groups. Finally, in participants with symptoms of depression, PTSD, social phobia, and disordered eating, concrete processing manipulations generally decrease symptom-specific symptoms (e.g., problem-solving problems, overgeneralized memory, intrusive thoughts, and negative self-evaluation). Interestingly, processing mode does not appear to influence negative mood. Instead, concrete processing affects the quality and content of people's thoughts.

Cognitive modification

In a departure from traditional psychotherapy interventions, cognitive psychologists have developed brief trainings that target the associations (reviewed in Chapter 9: Rumination, cognition, and the brain) between depression, rumination, and cognitive biases or deficits. Often called cognitive bias modification (CBM), these trainings generally use versions of experimental tasks originally intended to assess cognitive deficits and/or biases (for a review, see Mor & Daches, 2015). In these brief interventions, however, the tasks are modified to repeatedly direct participants to respond to certain stimuli in ways that are atypical of individuals with depression. Unlike CBT or RFCBT, which attempt to change cognitive processing from a top-down approach, CBM aims to modify cognitive processes using a bottom-up approach. Watkins and Nolen-Hoeksema (2014) argued that CBM has the potential to decrease the habitual nature of rumination, both because it involves the repeated training of desired responses and because it targets learning processes that are often outside of conscious awareness and control. Different versions of CBM address various cognitive biases and deficits.

Some trainings target the tendency for depressed individuals to attend to negative information. In one procedure, individuals are instructed to direct attention away from negative cues and toward positive or neutral cues. For instance, dysphoric undergraduates engaged in a dot-probe task in which a sad and neutral word was briefly displayed in the top or bottom of a computer screen and then were replaced by either one or two dots (Yang, Ding, Dai, Peng, & Zhang, 2014). Participants were asked to press a button indicating the location of the two dots (i.e., the target) as quickly as possible. For participants in the CBM condition, 90% of the targets appeared in the neutral word position—effectively directing attention away from the negative word. In the control condition, the targets appeared with equal probability in the sad and neutral word position. After 8 12-minute sessions of this procedure over 2 weeks, participants in the CBM condition reported a greater decrease in rumination, compared to the control condition. Moreover, rumination 4 weeks after the training mediated the effect of the change in attentional bias on depressive symptoms 8 weeks after the training. In a different study, participants saw two words and were instructed to indicate the valence of one (i.e., target) word while ignoring the other (i.e., distractor) word (Daches & Mor, 2014). In the inhibition condition the target word was neutral and the distractor word was negative 85% of the time; in the negative attention condition the target word was negative 85% of the time. Undergraduates high in trait rumination engaged in this training task four times over 2 weeks. As expected, participants in the inhibition condition reported decreased trait rumination.

Another version of CBM targets depressed individuals' tendency to interpret ambiguous information negatively. In this training, participants are presented with repeated ambiguous scenarios that are resolved in a positive or negative manner. For example, the scenario "You ask a friend to look over some work you have done. They come back with some comments, which are . . ." might end positively or negatively (Lang, Blackwell, Harmer, Davison, & Holmes, 2012). In the CBM condition, all of the scenarios end positively, presumably training a new automatic bias to positively interpret ambiguous information. Moreover, participants are instructed to vividly imagine themselves in ambiguous scenarios with positive resolutions. This use of positive mental imagery is hypothesized to be an important mechanism for overcoming negative cognitive biases in depression. In patients with major depression, 1 week of daily practice of CBM led to decreased intrusive thoughts, compared to a control condition with an equal number of positive and negative resolutions (Lang et al., 2012). Another study with depressed patients found that 1 week of daily practice of CBM decreased depressive rumination, compared to a control condition that was instructed only to listen but not to imagine themselves in each situation (Torkan et al., 2014). Even in undergraduates selected to be low ruminators, a single session imagining themselves in ambiguous scenarios with benign endings led to less state rumination than did imagining the scenarios with negative endings (Hertel, Mor, Ferrari, Hunt, & Agrawal, 2014). Given the success of this version of CBM, one research team has tested the efficacy of a week of CBM followed by 10 weeks of

CBT—both delivered via the Internet (Williams, Blackwell, Mackenzie, Holmes, & Andrews, 2013; Williams et al., 2015). In patients with major depression, this combined treatment led to greater reductions in rumination, compared to either wait-list or active control conditions.

Training in executive functioning—specifically working memory—may also decrease rumination. Specifically, researchers have used an adaptive version of the Paced Auditory Serial Attention Task (PASAT; Gronwall, 1977), a task that traditionally is used to assess deficits in working memory. In the original 20-minute task, individuals view a continuous stream of digits and have to continuously add the last two digits that they heard. Over successive trials, the speed at which digits are presented increases. Because it is a difficult task and errors are common, the original PASAT is frustrating. However, the adaptive version modifies the pace of the task based on participants' performance, such that consecutive correct responses result in the digits being presented more quickly, but consecutive incorrect responses lead to a slower pace (Siegle, Ghinassi, & Thase, 2007). This less-frustrating version of the PASAT is intended to encourage continued persistence of working memory, even in the presence of low levels of negative affect. Researchers have hypothesized that repeated practice of this task improves patients' ability to employ executive functioning under stress—an ability that should decrease rumination. In patients with major depression, 10 sessions of the adaptive PASAT over 2 weeks led to decreased depressive rumination (Vanderhasselt et al., 2015). Similarly, in patients with remitted depression, 10 online sessions of the adaptive PASAT practiced at home over 2 weeks contributed to greater decreases in depressive rumination, compared to an active control condition (Hoorelbeke & Koster, 2017). These gains were maintained 3 months later. Finally, in undergraduates with high trait rumination, 10 online sessions of the adaptive PASAT practiced over 2 weeks predicted less depressive rumination 4 weeks later (Hoorelbeke, Koster, Vanderhasselt, Callewaert, & Demeyer, 2015).

Another way researchers attempt to increase executive functioning is using the flanker task. In this procedure, participants see a line of five arrows and have to indicate whether the middle arrow is going in the same (i.e., congruent) or different (i.e., incongruent) direction as the other four arrows (Eriksen & Eriksen, 1974). Responding to incongruent trials recruits executive control because it requires inhibiting the influence of distractors. In fact, viewing an incongruent flanker stimulus before seeing negative emotional images reduces the interference typically triggered by negative emotional material (e.g., Cohen, Henik, & Moyal, 2012). One study tested whether this procedure reduced rumination and its association with negative mood (Cohen, Mor, & Henik, 2015). In the procedure, undergraduates first responded to a flanker stimulus and then saw a negative or neutral picture on the screen. In the training condition, the negative picture was preceded by an incongruent flanker trial 90% of the time; the reverse was true in the control condition. As expected, participants in the training condition exhibited less state rumination. Moreover, in the training—but not the control—condition, trait depressive rumination was not significantly correlated with state sadness. In other words, a brief exercise that recruited executive control when processing negative emotional material served to reduce rumination and eliminated the association between rumination and negative mood.

Finally, reducing the bias to retrieve negative memories may reduce rumination. Competitive memory training (COMET) targets the tendency of depressed individuals to retrieve negative material from long-term memory. This intervention is based on the theory (reviewed in Chapter 3: Rumination, anger, and aggression) that associative networks in long-term memory link together related memories, thoughts, feelings, and behavioral tendencies. Thus, a depressive network links sad mood, pessimistic thoughts, negative memories, and isolation-related behaviors. Activation of any part of an associative network—via rumination, for instance—activates other components stored in that network. COMET for depressive rumination trains individuals to let go of negative material by being less involved with and more accepting of negative thoughts and emotions so that negative association networks are less activated. Patients do this by identifying personal memories of times in which they were able to let go, either by being indifferent (e.g., some things are not worth thinking about) or by adopting an attitude of acceptance (e.g., some things are the way they are). After repeatedly reliving a memory involving indifference or acceptance, patients practice applying indifference or acceptance to a personal issue that often triggers rumination. With repeated practice, patients should become more able to let go of upsetting personal issues, rather than responding with rumination. In patients with major depression, 7–8 weeks of group-based COMET + TAU led to greater decreases in depressive rumination than did TAU (Ekkers et al., 2011; Korrelboom, Maarsingh, & Huijbrechts, 2012). Rumination continued to decrease 3 months later, and these improvements were maintained at a 6-month follow-up (Korrelboom et al., 2012).

In summary, CBM targeting depressive symptoms has trained participants to reduce attention to negative cues and negative interpretations of ambiguous information, improve working memory and executive functioning, and decrease retrieval of negative memories. All of these trainings also appear to reduce depressive rumination tendencies, and these gains are maintained several months later. The fact that even a single session of CBM reduces rumination supports the idea that the habitual process of repetitive thinking can be effectively targeted by a bottom-up approach. In fact, Watkins and Nolen-Hoeksema (2014) argue that concreteness training is another form of CBM that involves repeated practice at attending to the specific details, sequence, and context of upsetting events. Future research might examine whether decreased cognitive biases and deficits are mechanisms by which RFCBT reduces rumination and psychological symptoms.

Conclusion

In this chapter, I reviewed evidence showing that traditional CBT reduces rumination in depressed individuals and worry in patients with GAD. However, for several reasons, researchers see the need to develop treatments that target rumination specifically. RFCBT is one such treatment, based on Edward Watkins' important theoretical contributions. Specifically, RFCBT reflects the notions that the negative consequences of rumination are primarily due to abstract cognitive processing and that excessive rumination is a mental habit. Accordingly, RFCBT teaches patients to replace abstract rumination with more concrete processing and to identify the contextual triggers and maintaining functions of habitual rumination. Although it is a relatively new therapy, initial empirical evidence supports the efficacy of RFCBT—and some of its components—for reducing rumination and a range of clinical symptoms.

In addition to RFCBT, which is a traditional type of psychotherapy, brief interventions aimed at modifying cognitive biases and deficits also show promise for reducing rumination. These interventions target bottom-up processes and use procedures borrowed from cognitive psychological paradigms (e.g., the flanker task). The assumption underlying these interventions is that promoting executive functioning and retraining implicit biases in information processing and memory retrieval will counteract the habitual nature of rumination.

This presumed habitual nature of rumination implies an automatic, unintentional, uncontrollable, and often unconscious cognitive process. An alternative argument is that the initiation and persistence of rumination reflect conscious beliefs about the benefits and dangers of rumination (see Chapter 12: Metacognitive therapy). Questions about whether rumination is conscious/unconscious, intentional/unintentional, and automatic/controlled have not yet been settled by the field. Watkins and Nolen-Hoeksema (2014) suggest that rumination may start out one way (e.g., intentional and controlled) and then gradually transform into something different (e.g., unintentional and automatic). A better understanding of the nature of rumination will certainly inform existing and future treatments.

References

Beck, J. (2011). *Cognitive behavior therapy: Basics and beyond* (2nd ed.). The Guilford Press. Retrieved from <http://www.r2library.com/resource/title/9781609185046>.

Behar, E., McGowan, S. K., McLaughlin, K. A., Borkovec, T. D., Goldwin, M., & Bjorkquist, O. (2011). Concreteness of positive, negative, and neutral repetitive thinking about the future. *Behavior Therapy, 43*(2), 300–312. Available from https://doi.org/10.1016/j.beth.2011.07.002.

Borkovec, T. D., Newman, M. G., Pincus, A. L., & Lytle, R. (2002). A component analysis of cognitive-behavioral therapy for generalized anxiety disorder and the role of interpersonal problems. *Journal of Consulting and Clinical Psychology, 70*(2), 288–298. Available from https://doi.org/10.1037/0022-006X.70.2.288.

Carver, C. S., & Scheier, M. F. (1998). *On the self-regulation of behavior* (1. publ. ed.). Cambridge [u.a.]: Cambridge Univ. Press.

Ciesla, J. A., & Roberts, J. E. (2002). Self-directed thought and response to treatment for depression: A preliminary investigation. *Journal of Cognitive Psychotherapy, 16*(4), 435–453. Available from https://doi.org/10.1891/088983902780935650.

Cohen, N., Daches, S., Mor, N., & Henik, A. (2014). Inhibition of negative content-a shared process in rumination and reappraisal. *Frontiers in Psychology, 5*, 622. Available from https://doi.org/10.3389/fpsyg.2014.00622.

Cohen, N., Henik, A., & Moyal, N. (2012). Executive control attenuates emotional effects—For high reappraisers only? *Emotion (Washington, DC), 12*(5), 970–979. Available from https://doi.org/10.1037/a0026890.

Cohen, N., Mor, N., & Henik, A. (2015). Linking executive control and emotional response. *Clinical Psychological Science, 3*(1), 15–25. Available from https://doi.org/10.1177/2167702614530114.

Covin, R., Ouimet, A., Seeds, P., & Dozois, D. (2008). A meta-analysis of CBT for pathological worry among clients with GAD. *Journal of Anxiety Disorders, 22*(1), 108–116. Available from https://doi.org/10.1016/j.janxdis.2007.01.002.

Crane, C., Barnhofer, T., Visser, C., Nightingale, H., & Williams, J. M. G. (2007). The effects of analytical and experiential rumination on autobiographical memory specificity in individuals with a history of major depression. *Behaviour Research and Therapy, 45*(12), 3077–3087. Available from https://doi.org/10.1016/j.brat.2007.05.009.

Daches, S., & Mor, N. (2014). Training ruminators to inhibit negative information: A preliminary report. *Cognitive Therapy and Research, 38*(2), 160–171. Available from https://doi.org/10.1007/s10608-013-9585-5.

Denson, T., Moulds, M., & Grisham, J. (2012). The effects of analytical rumination, reappraisal, and distraction on anger experience. *Behavior Therapy, 43*(2), 355–364. Available from https://doi.org/10.1016/j.beth.2011.08.001.

Di Schiena, R., Luminet, O., Chang, B., & Philippot, P. (2013). Why are depressive individuals indecisive? different modes of rumination account for indecision in non-clinical depression. *Cognitive Therapy and Research, 37*(4), 713–724. Available from https://doi.org/10.1007/s10608-012-9517-9.

Ehring, T., Frank, S., & Ehlers, A. (2008). The role of rumination and reduced concreteness in the maintenance of posttraumatic stress disorder and depression following trauma. *Cognitive Therapy and Research, 32*(4), 488–506. Available from https://doi.org/10.1007/s10608-006-9089-7.

Ekkers, W., Korrelboom, K., Huijbrechts, I., Smits, N., Cuijpers, P., & van der Gaag, M. (2011). Competitive memory training for treating depression and rumination in depressed older adults: A randomized controlled trial. *Behaviour Research and Therapy, 49*(10), 588–596. Available from https://doi.org/10.1016/j.brat.2011.05.010.

Eriksen, B. A., & Eriksen, C. W. (1974). Effects of noise letters upon the identification of a target letter in a nonsearch task. *Perception & Psychophysics, 16*(1), 143–149.

Evans, M., Rohan, K., Sitnikov, L., Mahon, J., Nillni, Y., Tierney Lindsey, K., & Vacek, P. (2013). Cognitive change across cognitive-behavioral and light therapy treatments for seasonal affective disorder: What accounts for clinical status the next winter? *Cognitive Therapy and Research, 37*(6), 1201–1213. Available from https://doi.org/10.1007/s10608-013-9561-0.

Galfin, J., Watkins, E., & Harlow, T. (2011). Evaluation of a training programme to teach a guided self-help psychological intervention to hospice staff. *International Journal of Palliative Nursing, 17*(3), 119–124. Available from https://doi.org/10.12968/ijpn.2011.17.3.119.

Goldwin, M., Behar, E., & Sibrava, N. (2013). Concreteness of depressive rumination and trauma recall in individuals with elevated trait rumination and/or posttraumatic stress symptoms. *Cognitive Therapy and Research, 37*(4), 680–689. Available from https://doi.org/10.1007/s10608-012-9507-y.

Gronwall, D. M. A. (1977). Paced auditory serial-addition task: A measure of recovery from concussion. *Perceptual and Motor Skills, 44*(2), 367–373. Available from https://doi.org/10.2466/pms.1977.44.2.367.

Gross, J. J. (2001). Emotion regulation in adulthood: Timing is everything. *Current Directions in Psychological Science, 10*(6), 214–219. Available from https://doi.org/10.1111/1467-8721.00152.

Hertel, P. (2004). Memory for emotional and nonemotional events in depression. *Memory and Emotion*, 186–216.

Hertel, P., Mor, N., Ferrari, C., Hunt, O., & Agrawal, N. (2014). Looking on the dark side. *Clinical Psychological Science, 2*(6), 714–726. Available from https://doi.org/10.1177/2167702614529111.

Hilt, L., & Pollak, S. (2012). Getting out of rumination: Comparison of three brief interventions in a sample of youth. *Journal of Abnormal Child Psychology, 40*(7), 1157–1165. Available from https://doi.org/10.1007/s10802-012-9638-3.

Hofmann, S., Asnaani, A., Vonk, I., Sawyer, A., & Fang, A. (2012). The efficacy of cognitive behavioral therapy: A review of meta-analyses. *Cognitive Therapy and Research, 36*(5), 427–440. Available from https://doi.org/10.1007/s10608-012-9476-1.

Hoorelbeke, K., & Koster, E. H. W. (2017). Internet-delivered cognitive control training as a preventive intervention for remitted depressed patients: Evidence from a double-blind randomized controlled trial study. *Journal of Consulting and Clinical Psychology, 85*(2), 135–146. Available from https://doi.org/10.1037/ccp0000128.

Hoorelbeke, K., Koster, E. H. W., Vanderhasselt, M., Callewaert, S., & Demeyer, I. (2015). The influence of cognitive control training on stress reactivity and rumination in response to a lab stressor and naturalistic stress. *Behaviour Research and Therapy, 69*, 1–10. Available from https://doi.org/10.1016/j.brat.2015.03.010.

Jacobs, R. H., Watkins, E. R., Peters, A. T., Feldhaus, C. G., Barba, A., Carbray, J., & Langenecker, S. A. (2016). Targeting ruminative thinking in adolescents at risk for depressive relapse: Rumination-focused cognitive behavior therapy in a pilot randomized controlled trial with resting state fMRI. *PLoS One, 11*(11), e0163952. Available from https://doi.org/10.1371/journal.pone.0163952.

Jacobson, N. S., Dobson, K. S., Truax, P. A., Addis, M. E., Koerner, K., Gollan, J. K., … Prince, S. E. (1996). A component analysis of cognitive-behavioral treatment for depression. *Journal of Consulting and Clinical Psychology, 64*(2), 295–304. Available from https://doi.org/10.1037/0022-006X.64.2.295.

Korrelboom, K., Maarsingh, M., & Huijbrechts, I. (2012). Competitive memory training (COMET) for treating low self-esteem in patients with depressive disorders: A randomized clinical trial. *Depression and Anxiety, 29*(2), 102–110. Available from https://doi.org/10.1002/da.20921.

Ladouceur, R., Dugas, M. J., Freeston, M. H., Léger, E., Gagnon, F., & Thibodeau, N. (2000). Efficacy of a cognitive-behavioral treatment for generalized anxiety disorder. *Journal of Consulting and Clinical Psychology, 68*(6), 957–964. Available from https://doi.org/10.1037/0022-006X.68.6.957.

Lang, T. J., Blackwell, S. E., Harmer, C. J., Davison, P., & Holmes, E. A. (2012). Cognitive bias modification using mental imagery for depression: Developing a novel computerized intervention to change negative thinking styles. *European Journal of Personality, 26*(2), 145–157. Available from https://doi.org/10.1002/per.855.

Lo, C., Ho, S., & Hollon, S. (2010). The effects of rumination and depressive symptoms on the prediction of negative attributional style among college students. *Cognitive Therapy and Research, 34*(2), 116–123. Available from https://doi.org/10.1007/s10608-009-9233-2.

Manicavasagar, V., Perich, T., & Parker, G. (2012). Cognitive predictors of change in cognitive behaviour therapy and mindfulness-based cognitive therapy for depression. *Behavioural and Cognitive Psychotherapy, 40*(2), 227–232. Available from https://doi.org/10.1017/S1352465811000634.

Martin, L., & Tesser, A. (1996). Some ruminative thoughts. In R. S. Wyer, Jr. (Ed.), *Ruminative thoughts, advances in social cognition* (Vol. IX, pp. 1–48). Mahwah, NJ: Lawrence Erlbaum Associates.

Maslow, A. H. (1943). A theory of human motivation. *Psychological Review, 50*, 370–396. Available from https://doi.org/10.1037/h0054346.

Moberly, N. J., & Watkins, E. R. (2006). Processing mode influences the relationship between trait rumination and emotional vulnerability. *Behavior Therapy, 37*(3), 281–291. Available from https://doi.org/10.1016/j.beth.2006.02.003.

Mogoaşe, C., Brăilean, A., & David, D. (2013). Can concreteness training alone reduce depressive symptoms? A randomized pilot study using an internet-delivered protocol. *Cognitive Therapy and Research, 37*(4), 704–712. Available from https://doi.org/10.1007/s10608-012-9514-z.

Mor, N., & Daches, S. (2015). Ruminative thinking. *Clinical Psychological Science, 3*(4), 574–592. Available from https://doi.org/10.1177/2167702615578130.

Mor, N., & Winquist, J. (2002). Self-focused attention and negative affect: A meta-analysis. *Psychological Bulletin, 128*(4), 638–662. Available from https://doi.org/10.1037//0033-2909.128.4.638.

Moshier, S., & Otto, M. (2017). Behavioral activation treatment for major depression: A randomized trial of the efficacy of augmentation with cognitive control training. *Journal of Affective Disorders, 210*, 265–268. Available from https://doi.org/10.1016/j.jad.2017.01.003.

Nilsson, J., Lundh, L., & Viborg, G. (2012). Effects of analytical and experiential self-focus on rumination after a stress induction in patients with social anxiety disorder: A pilot study. *Cognitive Behaviour Therapy, 41*(4), 310–320. Available from https://doi.org/10.1080/16506073.2012.682088.

Nolen-Hoeksema, S. (1991). Responses to depression and their effects on the duration of depressive episodes. *Journal of Abnormal Psychology, 100*(4), 569–582. Available from https://doi.org/10.1037/0021-843X.100.4.569.

Nolen-Hoeksema, S., Wisco, B. E., & Lyubomirsky, S. (2008). Rethinking rumination. *Perspectives on Psychological Science, 3*(5), 400–424. Available from https://doi.org/10.1111/j.1745-6924.2008.00088.x.

Norton, A. R., & Abbott, M. J. (2016). Self-focused cognition in social anxiety: A review of the theoretical and empirical literature. *Behaviour Change, 33*(1), 44–64. Available from https://doi.org/10.1017/bec.2016.2.

Paxling, B., Almlöv, J., Dahlin, M., Carlbring, P., Breitholtz, E., Eriksson, T., & Andersson, G. (2011). Guided internet-delivered cognitive behavior therapy for generalized anxiety disorder: A randomized controlled trial. *Cognitive Behaviour Therapy, 40*(3), 159–173. Available from https://doi.org/10.1080/16506073.2011.576699.

Rawal, A., Williams, J. M. G., & Park, R. J. (2011). Effects of analytical and experiential self-focus on stress-induced cognitive reactivity in eating disorder psychopathology. *Behaviour Research and Therapy, 49*(10), 635–645. Available from https://doi.org/10.1016/j.brat.2011.06.011.

Ray, R. D., Wilhelm, F. H., & Gross, J. J. (2008). All in the mind's eye? Anger rumination and reappraisal. *Journal of Personality and Social Psychology, 94*(1), 133–145. Available from https://doi.org/10.1037/0022-3514.94.1.133.

Rimes, K. A., & Watkins, E. (2005). The effects of self-focused rumination on global negative self-judgements in depression. *Behaviour Research and Therapy, 43*(12), 1673–1681. Available from https://doi.org/10.1016/j.brat.2004.12.002.

Roberts, J., Gilboa, E., & Gotlib, I. (1998). Ruminative response style and vulnerability to episodes of dysphoria: Gender, neuroticism, and episode duration. *Cognitive Therapy and Research, 22*(4), 401–423. Available from https://doi.org/1018713313894.

Robinson, E., Titov, N., Andrews, G., McIntyre, K., Schwencke, G., & Solley, K. (2010). Internet treatment for generalized anxiety disorder: A randomized controlled trial comparing clinician vs. technician assistance. *PLoS One, 5*(6), e10942. Available from https://doi.org/10.1371/journal.pone.0010942.

Rood, L., Roelofs, J., Bögels, S. M., Nolen-Hoeksema, S., & Schouten, E. (2009). The influence of emotion-focused rumination and distraction on depressive symptoms in non-clinical youth: A meta-analytic review. *Clinical Psychology Review, 29*(7), 607–616. Available from https://doi.org/10.1016/j.cpr.2009.07.001.

Sanders, W. A., & Lam, D. H. (2010). Ruminative and mindful self-focused processing modes and their impact on problem solving in dysphoric individuals. *Behaviour Research and Therapy, 48*(8), 747–753. Available from https://doi.org/10.1016/j.brat.2010.04.007.

Santa Maria, A., Reichert, F., Hummel, S. B., & Ehring, T. (2012). Effects of rumination on intrusive memories: Does processing mode matter? *Journal of Behavior Therapy and Experimental Psychiatry, 43*(3), 901–909. Available from https://doi.org/10.1016/j.jbtep.2012.01.004.

Schaich, A., Watkins, E. R., & Ehring, T. (2013). Can concreteness training buffer against the negative effects of rumination on PTSD? An experimental analogue study. *Journal of Behavior Therapy and Experimental Psychiatry, 44*(4), 396–403. Available from https://doi.org/10.1016/j.jbtep.2013.03.006.

Schmaling, K. B., Dimidjian, S., Katon, W., & Sullivan, M. (2002). Response styles among patients with minor depression and dysthymia in primary care. *Journal of Abnormal Psychology, 111*(2), 350–356. Available from https://doi.org/10.1037/0021-843X.111.2.350.

Sezibera, V., Van Broeck, N., & Philippot, P. (2009). Intervening on persistent posttraumatic stress disorder: Rumination-focused cognitive and behavioral therapy in a population of young survivors of the 1994 genocide in Rwanda. *Journal of Cognitive Psychotherapy, 23*(2), 107–113. Available from https://doi.org/10.1891/0889-8391.23.2.107.

Siegle, G., Ghinassi, F., & Thase, M. (2007). Neurobehavioral therapies in the 21st century: Summary of an emerging field and an extended example of cognitive control training for depression. *Cognitive Therapy and Research, 31*(2), 235–262. Available from https://doi.org/10.1007/s10608-006-9118-6.

Spinhoven, P., Klein, N., Kennis, M., Cramer, A. O. J., Siegle, G., Cuijpers, P., ... Bockting, C. L. (2018). The effects of cognitive-behavior therapy for depression on repetitive negative thinking: A meta-analysis. *Behaviour Research and Therapy, 106*, 71–85. Available from https://doi.org/10.1016/j.brat.2018.04.002.

Stöber, J. (1998). The frost multidimensional perfectionism scale revisited: More perfect with four (instead of six) dimensions. *Personality and Individual Differences, 24*(4), 481–491. Available from https://doi.org/10.1016/S0191-8869(97)00207-9.

Stöber, J., & Borkovec, T. (2002). Reduced concreteness of worry in generalized anxiety disorder: Findings from a therapy study. *Cognitive Therapy and Research, 26*(1), 89–96. Available from https://doi.org/1013845821848.

Takano, K., & Tanno, Y. (2010). Concreteness of thinking and self-focus. *Consciousness and Cognition, 19*(1), 419–425. Available from https://doi.org/10.1016/j.concog.2009.11.010.

Teismann, T., von Brachel, R., Hanning, S., Grillenberger, M., Hebermehl, L., Hornstein, I., & Willutzki, U. (2014). A randomized controlled trial on the effectiveness of a rumination-focused group treatment for residual depression. *Psychotherapy Research: Journal of the Society for Psychotherapy Research, 24*(1), 80–90. Available from https://doi.org/10.1080/10503307.2013.821636.

Topper, M., Emmelkamp, P. M. G., Watkins, E., & Ehring, T. (2017). Prevention of anxiety disorders and depression by targeting excessive worry and rumination in adolescents and young adults: A randomized controlled trial. *Behaviour Research and Therapy, 90*, 123–136. Available from https://doi.org/10.1016/j.brat.2016.12.015.

Torkan, H., Blackwell, S., Holmes, E., Kalantari, M., Neshat-Doost, H., Maroufi, M., & Talebi, H. (2014). Positive imagery cognitive bias modification in treatment-seeking patients with major depression in Iran: A pilot study. *Cognitive Therapy and Research, 38*(2), 132–145. Available from https://doi.org/10.1007/s10608-014-9598-8.

Van Lier, J., Vervliet, B., Boddez, Y., & Raes, F. (2015). Why is everyone always angry with me?!": When thinking 'why' leads to generalization. *Journal of Behavior Therapy and Experimental Psychiatry, 47*, 34. Retrieved from <https://www.ncbi.nlm.nih.gov/pubmed/25479926>.

Van Lier, J., Vervliet, B., Vanbrabant, K., Lenaert, B., & Raes, F. (2014). Abstract thinking about negative events in dysphoric students leads to negative generalization. *Journal of Experimental Psychopathology, 5*(3), jep.037913. Available from https://doi.org/10.5127/jep.037913.

Vanderhasselt, M., De Raedt, R., Namur, V., Lotufo, P. A., Bensenor, I. M., Boggio, P. S., & Brunoni, A. R. (2015). Transcranial electric stimulation and neurocognitive training in clinically depressed patients: A pilot study of the effects on rumination. *Progress in Neuropsychopharmacology & Biological Psychiatry, 57*, 93–99. Available from https://doi.org/10.1016/j.pnpbp.2014.09.015.

Vassilopoulos, S. P. (2008). Social anxiety and ruminative self-focus. *Journal of Anxiety Disorders, 22*(5), 860–867. Available from https://doi.org/10.1016/j.janxdis.2007.08.012.

Vassilopoulos, S. P., & Watkins, E. R. (2008). Adaptive and maladaptive self-focus: A pilot extension study with individuals high and low in fear of negative evaluation. *Behavior Therapy, 40*(2), 181–189. Available from https://doi.org/10.1016/j.beth.2008.05.003.

Verplanken, B., Friborg, O., Wang, C. E., Trafimow, D., & Woolf, K. (2007). Mental habits. *Journal of Personality and Social Psychology, 92*(3), 526–541. Available from https://doi.org/10.1037/0022-3514.92.3.526.

Watkins, E. (2004). Appraisals and strategies associated with rumination and worry. *Personality and Individual Differences, 37*(4), 679–694. Available from https://doi.org/10.1016/j.paid.2003.10.002.

Watkins, E., & Baracaia, S. (2001). Why do people ruminate in dysphoric moods? *Personality and Individual Differences, 30*(5), 723–734. Available from https://doi.org/10.1016/S0191-8869(00)00053-2.

Watkins, E., Moberly, N. J., & Moulds, M. L. (2008). Processing mode causally influences emotional reactivity. *Emotion, 8*(3), 364–378. Available from https://doi.org/10.1037/1528-3542.8.3.364.

Watkins, E., & Moulds, M. (2005). Distinct modes of ruminative self-focus. *Emotion, 5*(3), 319–328. Available from https://doi.org/10.1037/1528-3542.5.3.319.

Watkins, E., & Moulds, M. L. (2007). Reduced concreteness of rumination in depression: A pilot study. *Personality and Individual Differences, 43*(6), 1386–1395. Available from https://doi.org/10.1016/j.paid.2007.04.007.

Watkins, E., Scott, J., Wingrove, J., Rimes, K., Bathurst, N., Steiner, H., ... Malliaris, Y. (2007). Rumination-focused cognitive behaviour therapy for residual depression: A case series. *Behaviour Research and Therapy, 45*(9), 2144–2154. Available from https://doi.org/10.1016/j.brat.2006.09.018.

Watkins, E., & Teasdale, J. D. (2001). Rumination and overgeneral memory in depression. *Journal of Abnormal Psychology, 110*(2), 353–357. Available from https://doi.org/10.1037/0021-843X.110.2.333.

Watkins, E., & Teasdale, J. D. (2004). Adaptive and maladaptive self-focus in depression. *Journal of Affective Disorders, 82*(1), 1–8. Available from https://doi.org/10.1016/j.jad.2003.10.006.

Watkins, E. R. (2008). Constructive and unconstructive repetitive thought. *Psychological Bulletin, 134*(2), 163–206. Available from https://doi.org/10.1037/0033-2909.134.2.163.

Watkins, E. R. (2016). *Rumination-focused cognitive-behavioral therapy for depression*. New York: Guilford Publications Inc. M.U.A. Retrieved from <https://ebookcentral.proquest.com/lib/[SITE_ID]/detail.action?docID = 4338852>.

Watkins, E. R., Baeyens, C. B., & Read, R. (2009). Concreteness training reduces dysphoria. *Journal of Abnormal Psychology, 118*(1), 55–64. Available from https://doi.org/10.1037/a0013642.

Watkins, E. R., & Moberly, N. J. (2009). Concreteness training reduces dysphoria: A pilot proof-of-principle study. *Behaviour Research and Therapy, 47*(1), 48–53. Available from https://doi.org/10.1016/j.brat.2008.10.014.

Watkins, E. R., Mullan, E., Wingrove, J., Rimes, K., Steiner, H., Bathurst, N., ... Scott, J. (2011). Rumination-focused cognitive-behavioural therapy for residual depression: Phase II randomised controlled trial. *The British Journal of Psychiatry: The Journal of Mental Science, 199*(4), 317–322. Available from https://doi.org/10.1192/bjp.bp.110.090282.

Watkins, E. R., & Nolen-Hoeksema, S. (2014). A habit-goal framework of depressive rumination. *Journal of Abnormal Psychology, 123*(1), 24–34. Available from https://doi.org/10.1037/a0035540.

Watkins, E. R., Taylor, R. S., Byng, R., Baeyens, C., Read, R., Pearson, K., & Watson, L. (2012). Guided self-help concreteness training as an intervention for major depression in primary care: A phase II randomized controlled trial. *Psychological Medicine, 42*(7), 1359–1371. Available from https://doi.org/10.1017/S0033291711002480.

Wenzlaff, R. M., Wegner, D. M., & Klein, S. B. (1991). The role of thought suppression in the bonding of thought and mood. *Journal of Personality and Social Psychology, 60*(4), 500–508. Available from https://doi.org/10.1037/0022-3514.60.4.500.

Wenzlaff, R. M., Wegner, D. M., & Roper, D. W. (1988). Depression and mental control. *Journal of Personality and Social Psychology, 55*(6), 882–892. Available from https://doi.org/10.1037/0022-3514.55.6.882.

Werner-Seidler, A., & Moulds, M. L. (2012). Mood repair and processing mode in depression. *Emotion (Washington, DC), 12*(3), 470–478. Available from https://doi.org/10.1037/a0025984.

White, R., & Wild, J. (2016). "Why" or "how": The effect of concrete versus abstract processing on intrusive memories following analogue trauma. *Behavior Therapy, 47*(3), 404. Retrieved from <https://www.ncbi.nlm.nih.gov/pubmed/27157033>.

Wilkinson, P. O., & Goodyer, I. M. (2008). The effects of cognitive-behavioural therapy on mood-related ruminative response style in depressed adolescents. *Child and Adolescent Psychiatry and Mental Health, 2*(1), 3. Available from https://doi.org/10.1186/1753-2000-2-3.

Williams, A. D., Blackwell, S. E., Mackenzie, A., Holmes, E. A., & Andrews, G. (2013). Combining imagination and reason in the treatment of depression: A randomized controlled trial of internet-based cognitive-bias modification and internet-CBT for depression. *Journal of Consulting and Clinical Psychology, 81*(5), 793–799. Available from https://doi.org/10.1037/a0033247.

Williams, A. D., O'Moore, K., Blackwell, S. E., Smith, J., Holmes, E. A., & Andrews, G. (2015). Positive imagery cognitive bias modification (CBM) and internet-based cognitive behavioral therapy (iCBT): A randomized controlled trial. *Journal of Affective Disorders, 178*, 131–141. Available from https://doi.org/10.1016/j.jad.2015.02.026.

Wong, Q. J. J., & Moulds, M. L. (2012). Processing mode during repetitive thinking in socially anxious individuals: Evidence for a maladaptive experiential mode. *Journal of Behavior Therapy and Experimental Psychiatry, 43*(4), 1064–1073. Available from https://doi.org/10.1016/j.jbtep.2012.05.002.

Yang, W., Ding, Z., Dai, T., Peng, F., & Zhang, J. X. (2014). Attention bias modification training in individuals with depressive symptoms: A randomized controlled trial. *Journal of Behavior Therapy and Experimental Psychiatry, 49*(Pt A), 101–111. Available from https://doi.org/10.1016/j.jbtep.2014.08.005.

CHAPTER

11

Mindfulness-based therapies for rumination

Overview

In this chapter, I review the potential of mindfulness-related therapies to treat rumination and worry. Although these treatments were originally developed without rumination explicitly in mind, their efficacy for decreasing repetitive though is robust. I begin by explaining the concepts of mindfulness and related constructs, as well as traditional ways of cultivating mindfulness. I then review the basic research—both correlational and experimental—linking mindfulness-related constructs to rumination. Finally, the chapter ends with descriptions of specific mindfulness-based treatments and evidence of their efficacy for reducing rumination and worry.

Mindfulness has its roots in Buddhism and other ancient spiritual traditions. Although it espouses a specific worldview and ethical code, as does any religion, Buddhism is at heart a psychological theory. In fact, I once heard His Holiness the Dalai Lama joke with a group of prominent Western psychologists, "You have been studying psychology for less than 100 years. We have been studying psychology for over 2000 years!" In this tradition, mindfulness is just one of a set of interconnected practices that are necessary to end human suffering, the ultimate end goal for spiritual practitioners (Keng, Smoski, & Robins, 2011). Western conceptualizations of mindfulness, however, are generally independent of any spiritual philosophy or ethical practices.

Western psychologists have offered various definitions of *mindfulness*, most of which generally involve two components: (1) intentional awareness of the present moment and (2) an orientation of acceptance,

DOI: https://doi.org/10.1016/B978-0-12-812545-8.00011-5

© 2020 Elsevier Inc. All rights reserved.

curiosity, and warmth (Bishop et al., 2004; Shapiro, Carlson, Astin, & Freedman, 2006). In other words, mindfulness encompasses a particular type of attention and a set of related attitudes toward one's experience.

Present-focused awareness describes observation and awareness of the constantly changing stream of one's sensations, thoughts, and feelings. Achieving this is no simple feat. Many people spend much of their mental lives focused on the future or the past, even if they are not worrying or ruminating. Maintaining present-focused awareness is an intentional, effortful process that requires both the ability to sustain attention on what is occurring and the ability to switch attention from one aspect of experience to another (Keng et al., 2011).

Mindfulness also includes certain qualities—or attitudes—that one intentionally brings to present-focused awareness. Specifically, the difficult task of achieving present-focused awareness is paired with acceptance, curiosity, and warmth. Rather than paying attention with an evaluative or critical attitude, people who practice mindfulness intentionally cultivate openness and curiosity for whatever is occurring. In fact, the Japanese characters for mindfulness combine the symbols for mind and heart (Shapiro et al., 2006), emphasizing the importance of kindness in bare awareness. These attitudes are particularly important when sensations, thoughts, and/or emotions in the present moment are unpleasant or unwanted.[1] Sometimes people question whether acceptance means that they need to passively resign themselves to a bad situation, or alternatively that they can engage in any destructive behavior they want. Acceptance, however, refers primarily to internal experiences, rather than external situations or behavior choices. It means a willingness to experience internal events fully, as they arise and then pass away, without become preoccupied with or avoiding them. Intentionally practicing an accepting attitude can foster the capacity to not continually strive for pleasant internal experiences (e.g., happiness and comfort) or push away aversive experiences (Shapiro et al., 2006).

Several other attitudes associated with mindfulness are worth mentioning. Shapiro et al. (2006) suggested that mindfulness leads to a shift in perspective in which people are able to observe their experiences without becoming immersed in them. This *decentering*, also called cognitive defusion, is the capacity to objectively observe emotions, thoughts, and sensations as experiences that are separate from oneself. Sometimes called the *observer self*, this skill allows people to realize that "this pain is not me" and "these thoughts are not me." In other words, people learn to

1 There is some debate in the literature about whether these attitudes are best conceptualized as components of mindfulness (e.g., Baer et al., 2008; Kabat-Zinn, 2013) or outcomes of mindfulness practice (Bishop et al., 2004; Brown & Ryan, 2003). Addressing this debate is beyond the scope of this chapter and is not relevant for understanding the potential of mindfulness to reduce rumination.

deidentify from the contents of their own minds. A Buddhist perspective on decentering proposes that mindfulness provides insight about the transience of all sensations, thoughts, and emotions (Grabovac, Lau, & Willett, 2011). This understanding of impermanence helps people realize that thoughts and emotions are just fleeting mental events, not inherent aspects of one's self. With these insights, people become less attached to pleasant mental content and less avoidant of unpleasant mental content. Just as acceptance is not resignation, decentering does not mean becoming numb to strong emotions or sensations. Instead, emotions and sensations are experienced fully for as long as they last, with the clear understanding that all experiences come and go naturally.

Although decentering involves a stepping-back in order to achieve clarity, mindfulness also fosters a warm embrace of current experience. This warmth has been operationalized as both self-compassion and gratitude (Rosenzweig, 2013; Voci, Veneziani, & Fuochi, 2018). *Self-compassion* is a way of relating to oneself when suffering. Specifically, individuals who are self-compassionate treat themselves with kindness, understand that suffering is a common human experience, and are able to hold painful thoughts and emotions in balanced awareness (Neff, 2003). The flip side of self-compassion is responding to one's suffering with self-judgment, believing that no one else suffers in the same way, and fixating on one's internal experiences. In cultivating mindfulness of all experiences, people develop the ability to relate to their own suffering with kindness and connection. *Gratitude* is the perception of having received a personal benefit that was not sought after, earned, or deserved (Emmons & Stern, 2013). It shares with self-compassion an appreciation of the interconnectedness of all people but focuses on the generosity of others or of life in general. People who practice mindfulness are less likely to wish for things they do not have and more likely to appreciate what is actually present in lives. As a friend of mine once marveled, "There is so much more happening in any one minute than we can ever notice or fully appreciate."

Cultivating mindfulness

Mindfulness as both a trait and a state can be developed with practice. However, maintaining present-focused awareness and acceptance for more than a fleeting moment requires commitment and hard work (Germer, 2013). If you do not believe me, stop reading for a minute and see how many breaths you can follow all the way through, from the beginning of the inhalation to the end of the exhalation, without your attention being pulled away by other thoughts or sensations. However many breaths you followed, that was an experience of mindfulness.

For most people, that kind of intense and intentional attention is the exception rather than the rule. Fortunately, mindfulness can be strengthened with both informal and formal practice.

Informal practice involves intentionally cultivating mindfulness in everyday activities. Many activities can be an opportunity to practice mindfulness, although the common ones used in therapy include eating, walking, doing dishes, taking a shower, or driving. These types of activities are usually so routine that people tend to perform them on autopilot, without paying full attention to the activity and instead getting lost in their own thoughts. Instead, mindfulness practice invites individuals to intentionally attend to every aspect of their experience during a single activity. When paying attention in this way while washing dishes, for instance, I may notice the sound of running water and clinking plates, the wet warmth of water on my hands, the slipperiness of soap and roughness of the sponge, an ache in my back, sensations of breathing in my throat and abdomen, and thoughts such as "is my son done with his bath yet?" Practicing this kind of mindfulness once or several times a day helps people realize that every moment is an opportunity to experience present-focused awareness. It also helps people tune in to their bodies and minds and to notice how they react to events in the external world. It does not take long for people to realize how much their minds want to frequently run away from the present, and at the same time how remaining focused on an activity almost always elicits a greater sense of calm than does preoccupation with other things.

Formal mindfulness practice involves various types of meditation. People commonly and mistakenly believe that meditation involves a blissful state of complete relaxation in which thoughts are turned off. Although some people may experience fleeting moments like this, meditation is not about reaching any particular mental or physical state. Instead, it is a focused opportunity to strengthen the skills of concentration and mindfulness, without doing any other activities of daily life. Like many types of physical exercise, it can be rather grueling. Buddhist psychology distinguishes between two types of meditation (Germer, 2013).

Concentration meditation involves focusing the mind on a single object to the exclusion of other objects. The focus of attention might be the breath, a particular word or phrase (as in transcendental meditation), a spot on the body, a candle flame, or a mental image. As soon as people notice that their mind has wandered, they gently return their awareness to the object. This kind of meditation helps develop the ability to intentionally sustain fully present attention on one thing at a time, and it may contribute to a calming of the mind.

In *mindfulness* meditation (also called insight or vipassana meditation), people allow their awareness to move from one object to another as objects come into their awareness. By objects, I mean any of the five senses, as well as thoughts and emotions. For instance, in a minute of sitting meditation, my awareness may move from the sound of the air conditioning to the sensation of cold air in my nostrils when I inhale, to the thought that I should call my mother, to pain in my left foot, to boredom. What most people notice with even a few minutes of mindfulness meditation is how much thoughts and emotions dominate their awareness. Sometimes the mind flits from topic to topic (what Buddhist practitioners call "monkey mind"), and other times people's attention become fixated on one particular thought or emotion. People may also notice how many judgments they make about their own thoughts and emotions, leading to a host of secondary thoughts and emotions. Rather than trying to change any of this, the purpose of mindfulness meditation is to examine in minute detail how the mind works and, in particular, to gain insight into the many different ways that our minds contribute to our own suffering.

In typical practice, concentration and mindfulness meditations are combined, because they complement each other so nicely. People often begin with concentration of the breath, in order to develop some basic attentional control and stability. They may then start to broaden their awareness to include other experiences (e.g., sounds, physical sensations, and thoughts). And whenever the mind gets stuck somewhere other than the present moment, people can return to concentration of their breath in order to regain stability.

With that introduction to mindfulness and related concepts, I first review basic research on the associations between mindfulness-related constructs and rumination. The remainder of the chapter focuses on mindfulness-related treatments and evidence of their efficacy for reducing rumination.

Mindfulness-related constructs and rumination

Many psychologists have noted the striking contrasts between mindfulness and rumination-related constructs. For instance, intentional attention to the present moment contrasts with the uncontrollable focus on the past (i.e., rumination) or future (i.e., worry). Mindfulness also fosters the ability to shift attention from one thing to another, whereas rumination is characterized by rigid and sustained attention to one perceived problem (Ingram, 1990). The mindful attitudes of nonjudgment and compassion are incompatible with the evaluative and negative nature of rumination. Decentering allows for detached attention to the process of thinking, whereas rumination involves immersion in the content of thoughts (Wolkin, 2015). Awareness of the fleeting nature of internal experiences runs counter to ruminative attempts to control or avoid unpleasant thoughts and emotions.

A large literature shows that trait mindfulness is in fact associated with less trait rumination. In healthy participants, for instance, greater self-reported trait mindfulness is generally associated with less depressive, angry, and general negative rumination (Brown & Ryan, 2003; Burg & Michalak, 2011; Evans & Segerstrom, 2011; Feldman, Dunn, Stemke, Bell, & Greeson, 2014; Peters, Eisenlohr-Moul, Upton, & Baer, 2013; Raes & Williams, 2010; Selby, Fehling, Panza, & Kranzler, 2016). Mindfulness is also related to less worry, both in clinical and nonclinical samples (Evans & Segerstrom, 2011; Lee & Orsillo, 2013; Roemer et al., 2009). Similarly, long-term regular meditators report less rumination and avoidance than do nonmeditators (Lykins & Baer, 2009). One study found that mindfulness was associated with extent to which rumination was experienced as uncontrollable (Raes & Williams, 2010). Trait mindfulness also appears to weaken the effect of stressors on rumination. For instance, in healthy adolescents, daily stress was less likely to predict increases in state rumination for people high in trait mindfulness (Ciesla, Reilly, Dickson, Emanuel, & Updegraff, 2012). Similarly, the association between perceived injustice in the workplace and trait rumination was weaker for individuals high in trait mindfulness (Long & Christian, 2015). In sum, trait mindfulness is associated with less rumination and worry, both in general and in response to stress.

Psychologists propose that decreased rumination is an important mechanism of the effect of mindfulness on psychological outcomes (e.g., Holas & Jankowski, 2013). In support of this, rumination mediates the association between trait mindfulness and psychological distress in healthy undergraduates (Coffey & Hartman, 2008; Coffey, Hartman, & Fredrickson, 2010). Similarly, depressive rumination mediates the associatio between trait mindfulness and depressive symptoms, both concurrently and over time, in depressed and healthy samples (Alleva, Roelofs, Voncken, Meevissen, & Alberts, 2014; Desrosiers, Vine, Klemanski, & Nolen-Hoeksema, 2013; Petrocchi & Ottaviani, 2016; but see Royuela-Colomer & Calvete, 2016). Worry and rumination also mediate the associations between trait mindfulness and less anxiety and posttraumatic stress disorder (PTSD) symptoms (Desrosiers et al., 2013; Hanley, Garland, & Tedeschi, 2017; Im & Follette, 2016; Thompson, Arnkoff, & Glass, 2011). Furthermore, rumination mediates the negative associations between mindfulness and anger and aggression (Borders, Earleywine, & Jajodia, 2010; Borders & Lu, 2017; Eisenlohr-Moul, Peters, Pond, & DeWall, 2016; Peters et al., 2015). Although correlational, these findings suggest trait mindfulness leads to less rumination, which in turn contributes to better clinical outcomes.

Trait mindfulness also weakens the association between rumination and poor psychological functioning. In one study, trait mindfulness interacted with depressive rumination, such that for individuals low in mindfulness, rumination was associated with more depressive symptoms (Brennan, Barnhofer, Crane, Duggan, & Williams, 2015). Similarly, for individuals low in trait mindfulness, greater rumination was associated with a stronger physiological stress response (Daubenmier, Hayden, Chang, & Epel, 2014). Another study found that individuals low in trait mindfulness showed a weaker relationship between state rumination and concurrent anger but a stronger relationship between rumination and subsequent anger (Borders & Lu, 2017). These results, although seemingly contradictory, may reflect the basic components of mindfulness. Mindfulness may not be able to stop the moment-by-moment interplay of rumination and negative emotions, but it may help people to be more aware of their separate thoughts and feelings. Over longer time periods (e.g., several hours), mindfulness may decrease individuals' emotional reactivity to unpleasant ruminative thoughts. Support for both mediation and moderation models is not necessarily contradictory. Taken together, the evidence suggests that trait mindfulness contributes to less rumination and at the same time uncouples the links between rumination and negative outcomes.

In addition to the many studies on trait mindfulness, researchers have tested the effects of brief mindfulness practice in the laboratory setting. Participants typically engage in 8–12 minutes of guided mindful breathing, in which they are instructed to observe the physical sensations of breathing without judgment and to keep returning their attention to their breath. The effect of this mindfulness induction on rumination is mixed. In some studies, undergraduate and adolescent participants—particularly women—who engaged in mindful breathing after a rumination induction showed decreases in state rumination, compared to various control conditions (Hilt & Pollak, 2012; Villa & Hilt, 2014). Similarly, following a post-event rumination induction, individuals with social anxiety disorder who engaged in mindful breathing reported a decrease in negative affect about the rumination, compared to control conditions (Cassin & Rector, 2011). However, when undergraduate participants did not go through a rumination manipulation first, guided mindful breathing actually increased state rumination compared to control conditions (Feldman, Greeson, & Senville, 2010). Another study provided undergraduate participants with brief mindfulness inductions several times over a single day (Huffziger et al., 2013). The induction involved reading 10 statements meant to induce mindfulness (e.g., "consciously attend to your breath for some seconds" and "take note of your thoughts and feelings without judging them"). Here again, mindfulness inductions led to increases in state rumination. Thus, although brief mindfulness practice in people who were already ruminating reduced rumination and associated negative affect, mindfulness practice by itself increased rumination.

How can we understand these mixed results? It is important to note that the majority of participants in these experiments were presumably unfamiliar with the practice or philosophy of mindfulness. For most people, being asked to step out of their normal activities and pay attention to their breath or feelings may foster self-focused attention, triggering ruminative thinking. If people are already ruminating about themselves, however, being asked to pay attention to the breath may distract them from their thoughts. This aligns with the research described earlier showing that mindfulness decreased the association between stressors and rumination. If induced rumination is perceived as a stressor, brief mindful inductions may serve as short-term distractions. Relatedly, experiments that directly compare the effects of rumination versus mindfulness versus distraction inductions have generally found that mindfulness leads to similar decreases in negative mood as does distraction (Broderick, 2005; Huffziger & Kuehner, 2009; Sauer & Baer, 2012; Singer & Dobson, 2007). Of course, mindfulness is conceptually the opposite of distraction, because it encourages attention to—rather than avoidance of—unwanted experiences. In novices, however, mindful breathing may be more akin to short-term distraction than it is to trait mindfulness. Continued research is needed to understand whether brief mindful breathing in novices actually constitutes a meaningful induction of mindfulness.

To further this point, it is worth noting that the present-focused awareness component of mindfulness encourages awareness of internal experiences, which is similar to self-focused attention (Baer, 2009). Studies that examine various components of mindfulness support this notion. Specifically, the nonjudging component of mindfulness is consistently associated with less rumination and worry, whereas present-focused awareness of internal and external experiences is often associated with greater rumination (Alleva et al., 2014; Evans & Segerstrom, 2011; Fisak & von Lehe, 2012; Peters et al., 2013; Petrocchi & Ottaviani, 2016; Royuela-Colomer & Calvete, 2016). In other words, although mindful nonjudging predicts less rumination, present-focused attention may engender more rumination—at least in novices. Interestingly, greater present-focused attention is associated with better psychological functioning in regular meditators but worse psychological functioning in nonmeditating students (Baer et al., 2008). Therefore, the effects of the present-focused awareness component of mindfulness may depend on whether people are experienced with mindfulness and meditation. The attitude component of mindfulness, however, is consistently associated with better outcomes, including less rumination. This conclusion is also supported by research on constructs related to mindfulness.

As reviewed in a previous chapter (see Chapter 8, Beliefs, traits, and motivations underlying rumination), greater experiential avoidance, or unwillingness to experience and deliberate attempts to escape from unwanted internal experiences, predicts more rumination. Stated another way, more acceptance of internal experiences is associated with less rumination. Clinical psychologists also research a construct called cognitive flexibility, which combines experiential acceptance with behaving in accordance with one's values.[2] Cognitive flexibility is associated with less rumination and worry in both clinical and nonclinical samples (Bjornsson et al., 2010; Bluett, Homan, Morrison, Levin, & Twohig, 2014; Cowdrey & Park, 2012; Cribb, Moulds, & Carter, 2006; Giorgio et al., 2010; Morina, 2011; Spinhoven, Drost, de Rooij, van Hemert, & Penninx, 2016). In one study, cognitive flexibility and rumination interacted, such that rumination only predicted depressive symptoms for people low in cognitive flexibility (Bjornsson et al., 2010). Thus, as with mindfulness, cognitive flexibility may both lead to less rumination and also decrease the negative effects of rumination.

Researchers have also studied the association between decentering and rumination. Decentering is correlated with less trait rumination, negative reactions to state rumination, and positive beliefs about rumination (Ayduk & Kross, 2010; Feldman et al., 2010; Gillanders et al., 2014; Kaiser, Andrews-Hanna, Metcalf, & Dimidjian, 2015; but see Nitzan-Assayag, Aderka, & Bernstein, 2015). One experiment compared the effects of brief training in decentering with brief training in cognitive restructuring on rumination-related distress (Yovel, Mor, & Shakarov, 2014). Healthy undergraduates were asked to remember an unpleasant event and an associated sad thought and then were induced to ruminate about the event and thought. They then read a brief rationale and completed a related exercise in either cognitive restructuring (e.g., thought record) or decentering (e.g., writing the thought in reverse, visualizing the thought from different vantage points). Compared to the control conditions, both cognitive restructuring and decentering reduced negative mood. However, only in the decentering group was improved mood associated with the metacognitive belief that thoughts are separate from oneself.

Finally, a few studies examined the associations between self-compassion, gratitude, and rumination. Greater trait self-compassion and gratitude are related with less depressive rumination, angry

2 Cognitive flexibility is measured using the Acceptance and Action Questionnaire (AAQ; Hayes et al., 2006). This measure was initially described as measuring experiential acceptance/avoidance. However, items assess not just acceptance of feelings but also whether internal experiences get in the way of valued living. Accordingly, the creators of the AAQ-II (the most psychometrically-sound version) suggest that the measure more accurately assesses cognitive flexibility (Bond et al., 2011). This change in interpreting the AAQ can lead to confusion in the literature, as various constructs are used to describe the same measure.

rumination, and worry (Fresnics & Borders, 2017; Krieger, Altenstein, Baettig, Doerig, & Holtforth, 2013; Leary, Tate, Adams, Batts Allen, & Hancock, 2007; Liang et al., 2018; Raes, 2010; White et al., 2017). These studies have generally found that rumination mediates the effects of self-compassion on clinical outcomes such as depressive symptoms, anxiety, anger, and aggression. In an experiment, students were asked to remember an event from the past 5 years that made them feel ashamed (Johnson & O'Brien, 2013). Participants in the self-compassion writing condition made a list of ways in which other people experience similar events, wrote a paragraph expressing understanding and kindness toward themselves, and described their feelings about the experience in an objective and unemotional fashion. Compared to participants who wrote about their deepest feelings about the event, participants in the self-compassion writing condition exhibited greater decreases in trait rumination 2 weeks later.

In sum, dispositional mindfulness is associated with less rumination, both in general and in response to stress. Similar results have been found with the "sisters of mindfulness" (Rosenzweig, 2013), such as acceptance, cognitive flexibility, decentering, self-compassion, and gratitude. Interestingly, rumination may function as both a mechanism and a moderator of mindfulness. In other words, in experienced meditators and people who are experiencing stress, mindfulness contributes to decreased rumination, which in turn predicts better clinical outcomes. At the same time, trait rumination appears to uncouple the associations between stress and psychological distress. Researchers are only just beginning to explore mediators of the association between mindfulness and rumination. For instance, better emotion regulation and greater nonattachment mediated the association between trait mindfulness and less rumination (Coffey & Hartman, 2008; Coffey et al., 2010). Future research should continue exploring these and other mechanisms of the effect of mindfulness on rumination. Researchers also need to better understand the divergent effects of the present-focused awareness versus attitude components of mindfulness, as well as how these components interact with prior experience with mindfulness.

Mindfulness-based therapies

The use of meditation by Western psychologists is not new. In the 1960s, many psychoanalysts became interested in Zen Buddhism and the potential of meditation to increase insight in patients. In the 1970s, researchers studied the physiological effects of transcendental meditation. However, it was not until the 1980s that mindfulness meditation was incorporated into psychological interventions for clinical problems.

Notably, Jon Kabat-Zinn started using mindfulness meditation to treat patients with refractory pain and difficult-to-treat anxiety. Since that time, mindfulness- and acceptance-based therapies have become immensely popular, spawning hundreds of empirical studies, books, CDs, and self-help workbooks. Many psychologists refer to this movement as the third wave of behavioral therapies, following the second wave of cognitive therapy (Hayes, 2004).

In the following sections, I describe Kabat-Zinn's therapy as well as other popular mindfulness-based treatments. These therapies have been effectively used with patients with mental disorders and chronic physical illnesses (for reviews, see Baer, 2003; Grossman, Niemann, Schmidt, & Walach, 2004; Hofmann, Grossman, & Hinton, 2011; Keng et al., 2011; Öst, 2008; Vøllestad, Nielsen, & Nielsen, 2012), as well as with healthy adults, adolescents, and children (for reviews and metaanalyses, see Kallapiran, Koo, Kirubakaran, & Hancock, 2015; Zoogman, Goldberg, Hoyt, & Miller, 2015). They have also been adapted for school and work settings (for reviews, see Virgili, 2015; Zenner, Herrnleben-Kurz, & Walach, 2014). Reviewing their overall efficacy and effectiveness is beyond the scope of this book. However, where research exists, I include evidence for the efficacy of these treatments at reducing repetitive thinking—primarily rumination and worry.

Mindfulness-based stress reduction

Mindfulness-based stress reduction (MBSR) is arguably the most well-known of the current Western mindfulness-based therapies and is now taught around the world to both healthy and clinical populations (Kabat-Zinn, 2013). For people who do not want to or cannot attend MBSR in person, several self-help books cover the same techniques and ideas (Forsyth & Eifert, 2007; Stahl & Goldstein, 2010). The core of MBSR involves training in both formal and informal mindfulness practices. The program generally runs for 8 weeks and consists of weekly 2.5-hour group sessions led by 1–2 therapists. In addition, there is often a 6-hour meditation retreat between sessions 6 and 7. Patients are also required to practice formal mindfulness exercises every day at home for 45 minutes.

The formal mindfulness exercises include body scan, gentle yoga, and various types of meditation. In the body scan, patients are instructed to direct their attention to various body parts, usually starting in the feet and working up to the head. They are encouraged to pay attention to whatever arises in each area without trying to change any experience. The exercise helps to develop sustained attention, flexible attention, the ability to be aware of thoughts and feelings without reacting to them, and attitudes of kindness and nonjudging. Gentle yoga is also introduced early in MBSR, with the purpose of cultivating kindness for and awareness of the body. These practices lay the foundation for starting a regular practice of meditation.

Sitting meditation is introduced first, with an explicit emphasis on paying attention to the breath. With daily practice, participants gain experience noticing the sensations of the breath, when and where their minds wander, and the intention to return to the breath. Gradually, MBSR broadens the attentional focus during meditation to bodily sensations, sounds, thoughts, feelings, and choiceless awareness (i.e., whatever arises in consciousness). Participants may also engage in walking meditation, which involves either fast or slow walking with the intention of sustaining awareness of bodily sensations while moving. Finally, loving kindness meditation purposefully cultivates feelings of kindness and compassion directed toward the self, others in one's life, and all people. In each of these formal meditation practices, the goal is not to silence the mind. Rather, participants learn to maintain their attention on whatever is happening in the present moment (e.g., thoughts, feelings, and bodily sensations) without trying to change anything. In doing so, participants experientially learn that all internal events come and go of their own accord.

In addition to formal mindfulness exercises, MBSR encourages participants to engage in informal practice throughout the day, in order to incorporate mindfulness in everyday tasks. For instance, mindfulness of eating, dressing, washing the dishes, commuting, and communicating is practiced. Brief (e.g., 3 minutes) meditation exercises are also taught that can be done anytime people find themselves with a short break or in a difficult situation. The idea of these brief mediations is to tune in to the breath and body at various points throughout the day, particularly in times that generally encourage mindlessness, worry, or rumination.

The focus of didactic material and group discussions in MBSR is on coping with stress. Because of this, some activities specifically target worry and anxiety. For instance, *worry surfing* involves imagining a worry or fear as a wave. Patients are taught to notice warning signs that a wave is approaching and then to simply watch the wave as a crests and falls. Instead of responding to the worry with any type of behavior, patients are gently encouraged to "ride the wave," simply noticing their body, emotions, and thoughts as the wave peaks and then flows away. After the wave passes, patients are congratulated on their effort to ride the wave and reminded that more waves will come again, but that they can bring the same mindful attitude and know that all worries and emotions will crest and pass, just like waves. This process of "riding the wave" applies to any emotion, thought, or craving. It often happens naturally during quiet meditation, although MBSR therapists can help patients through it using a guided meditation.

MBSR decreases rumination in patients with a variety of mental disorders and chronic physical illnesses. For instance, MBSR led to decreased depressive rumination in participants with a lifetime history of mood disorders (Ramel, Goldin, Carmona, & McQuaid, 2004) and women with a menstrual-related mood disorder (Bluth, Gaylord, Nguyen, Bunevicius, & Girdler, 2015). In patients with generalized anxiety disorder (GAD), MBSR contributed to decreases in worry, both directly (Vøllestad, Sivertsen, & Nielsen, 2011) and indirectly via increases in mindfulness (Hoge et al., 2015). In addition, rumination and worry decreased following MBSR in adults diagnosed with social anxiety (Goldin & Gross, 2010; Goldin et al., 2016; Vøllestad et al., 2011). A modified MBSR for adults recently exposed to trauma indirectly decreased rumination via decreased thought suppression (Nitzan-Assayag et al., 2017). In cancer patients, MBSR led to a greater reduction in rumination and worry than did a wait-list condition (Campbell, Labelle, Bacon, Faris, & Carlson, 2012; Labelle, Campbell, & Carlson, 2010; Labelle, Campbell, Faris, & Carlson, 2015).

Researchers have also examined the effect of MBSR on rumination and worry in nonclinical participants. In healthy adults, for instance, MBSR generally leads to greater decreases in rumination and worry than does a wait-list control, particularly for participants high in trait mindfulness (Jain et al., 2007; Robins, Keng, Ekblad, & Brantley, 2012; Shapiro, Brown, Thoresen, & Plante, 2011; Shapiro, Oman, Thoresen, Plante, & Flinders, 2008). In a type of dismantling study, healthy undergraduates were randomly assigned to receive 3 weekly training sessions in either sitting meditation, body scan, or mindful yoga (Sauer-Zavala, Walsh, Eisenlohr-Moul, & Lykins, 2013). All three types of formal mindfulness practice led to reductions in rumination. MBSR has also been adapted for school and working settings. For instance, MBSR delivered in 12 30–50-minute sessions during the school day led to decreased rumination in elementary-aged students (Sibinga et al., 2012; van de Weijer-Bergsma, Langenberg, Brandsma, Oort, & Bögels, 2014). Similarly, elementary and secondary school teachers who received MBSR tailored specifically to educators reported decreases in rumination (Crain, Schonert-Reichl, & Roeser, 2017). MBSR also contributed to reductions in rumination in therapists-in-training and healthcare professionals (Martín-Asuero & García-Banda, 2010; Shapiro, Brown, & Biegel, 2007). Finally, brief (i.e., 3–4 sessions) internet-based mindfulness programs based on MBSR decreased rumination about work-related stress (Michel, Bosch, & Rexroth, 2014; Querstret, Cropley, & Fife-Schaw, 2017).

Mindfulness-based cognitive therapy

Mindfulness-based cognitive therapy (MBCT) was originally developed to prevent depressive relapse in patients with a history of major depressive episodes (Segal, Williams, & Teasdale, 2013). It was created by cognitive therapists who studied and incorporated major aspects of MBSR. Thus, MBCT is very similar to MBSR but adds some traditional cognitive therapy components. Like MBSR, it typically involves 8 weekly 2.5-hour group sessions, a 6-hour meditation retreat, and 45 minutes of daily practice at home. Formal mindfulness exercises include body scan, sitting and walking meditation, and yoga. It does not include formal loving-kindness meditation, although it does encourage all the same kinds of informal mindfulness practice as MBSR.

Because MBCT was developed for the prevention of depressive relapse, much of the didactic material and group discussions focus on depressive thinking. For instance, patients are taught to identify how their current mood affects automatic thoughts that arise in any given situation. Unlike in traditional cognitive behavioral therapy (CBT), which might attempt cognitive restructuring by challenging negative automatic thoughts, repeated meditation experiences teach patients that thoughts are neither truth nor permanent. In addition, MBCT introduces a metaphor as the crux of its rationale for using mindfulness to prevent depressive relapse. Specifically, the MBCT model asserts that there are core patterns of brain activity—called modes of mind. These modes are analogous to the gears of a car: as the mind engages in different types of activities, different gears are recruited, each with its own functions and characteristics. Much like a car, the mind can only be in one of these modes at a time. The two modes most relevant for preventing depressive relapse are the *doing* and *being* modes.

The doing mode's purpose is to get things done and to solve perceived problems. Doing mode can be very useful for achieving goals in the external world. However, when people apply the doing mode to the internal world of thoughts and feelings, they end up ruminating or worrying constantly about how they want things to be different. There is often a frantic quality of this activity, leading the MBCT authors to refer to the problematic use of this mode as *driven-doing*. Because the focus of driven-doing is thoughts and feelings, these internal events are experienced as real. This mode also preoccupies people to such an extent that they are not tuned into the present moment. The opposite of the frantic, goal-driven doing mode is being mode. The purpose of this mode is to allow and accept whatever is occurring in the present moment, without trying to change anything or achieve goals. Internal events such as thoughts and feelings are perceived as no different than external sounds—as passing events that come into conscious awareness and then leave. People are less automatically reactive to and better able to tolerate unpleasant internal events. In other words, in the being mode, people's relationship with their thoughts and feelings is dramatically different.

Clearly, the being mode constitutes a state of mindfulness, whereas the doing-driven mode describes the experience of rumination. Both modes can function during any activity. For instance, one can wash the dishes in either a driven-doing mode or a being mode—the dishes still get washed, but the subjective experience varies dramatically. Similarly, people can meditate in either a driven-doing mode or a being mode. The purpose of this metaphor is to explain why people experience depressive relapse and to propose an antidote. The driven-doing mode may not trigger the onset of depressed moods, but it maintains and exacerbates sad moods once they are detected. Hence, driven-doing is conceptualized as the primary thought pattern that sets people up for depressive relapse. Unfortunately for people who already have a history of depressive episodes, the driven-doing mode is usually a well-known and familiar mental process. MBCT aims to prevent depressive relapse by helping patients learn to identify and decrease the tendency to respond to unpleasant internal events with the driven-doing mode. Instead, mindfulness exercises are used to cultivate the ability to achieve and stay in the being mode.

MBCT decreases repetitive thinking in currently and formerly depressed patients. In randomly controlled trials with currently or previously depressed patients, traditional MBCT led to decreased depressive rumination and worry, compared to wait-list conditions (van Aalderen, Donders, Peffer, & Speckens, 2015; Batink, Peeters, Geschwind, van Os, & Wichers, 2013; Geschwind, Peeters, kker, van Os, & Wichers, 2011; Keune, Bostanov, Hautzinger, & Kotchoubey, 2011; van den Hurk et al., 2012; van Vugt, Hitchcock, Shahar, & Britton, 2012). Subsequent analyses of 12-month follow-up data on all participants who received MBCT indicated that whereas depressive symptoms remained stable, rumination continued to decrease over the year (van Aalderen et al., 2015). When compared to more traditional cognitive-behavioral treatments, MBCT appears to be equally effective at reducing rumination (Manicavasagar, Perich, & Parker, 2012; McIndoo, File, Preddy, Clark, & Hopko, 2016). Versions of MBCT adapted for adolescents and older adults with current or remitted depression also led to decreased rumination and worry (Ames, Richardson, Payne, Smith, & Leigh, 2014; Deplus, Billieux, Scharff, & Philippot, 2016; Foulk, Ingersoll-Dayton, Kavanagh, Robinson, & Kales, 2014). Other researchers have combined MBCT with other treatment components. For instance, MBCT with additional exercises from compassion-focused therapy and loving-kindness meditation decreased rumination in patients with chronic depression (Graser, Höfling, Weßlau, Mendes, & Stangier, 2016). One research team combined MBCT with exposure-based CBT for individuals currently in a major depressive episode (Kumar, Feldman, & Hayes, 2008). In an open trial of this therapy, patients showed decreases in depressive rumination and cognitive inflexibility from pre- to posttreatment.

MBCT also decreases rumination and worry in other kinds of clinical populations. In patients with GAD, MBCT decreased worry immediately and 3 months after treatment (Craigie, Rees, Marsh, & Nathan, 2008; Evans et al., 2007; Goodman et al., 2014). Furthermore, MBCT reduced worry as much as CBT-based psychoeducation did, and worry continued to decrease in both groups over the next 6 months (Wong, Ree, & Lee, 2016). One research team adapted MBCT for patients diagnosed with bipolar disorder but not currently experiencing a manic or depressive episode (Deckersbach et al., 2012). In a small-scale open trial, patients with bipolar disorder reported decreased depressive rumination and worry immediately following and 3 months after the end of treatment. Similarly, a modified version of MBCT decreased rumination in high-functioning autistic adults with depressive symptoms immediately and 2 months after treatment (Kiep, Spek, & Hoeben, 2015; Spek, Van Ham, & Nyklicek, 2013). Finally, 6 weeks of MBCT techniques led to a greater decrease in rumination, compared to a wait list, in female breast cancer survivors (Boyle, Stanton, Ganz, Crespi, & Bower, 2017).

Some research has examined the efficacy of MBCT in healthy individuals. In one study, MBCT contributed to a greater reduction in rumination, compared to a wait-list (Heeren & Philippot, 2011). In university students with high levels of trait neuroticism, MBCT also led to greater reduction in rumination than did an online self-help group (Armstrong & Rimes, 2016). Similarly, MBCT led to reduced rumination in trainee clinical psychologists (Rimes & Wingrove, 2011).

Acceptance and commitment therapy

Although acceptance and commitment therapy (ACT) does not have roots in the mindfulness tradition, it emphasizes many of the same concepts as mindfulness-based therapies (Hayes, Strosahl, & Wilson, 1999). Unlike MBSR and MBCT, ACT is most often delivered as individual therapy. It is not aimed at any particular mental disorder and has in fact been effectively applied to many presenting problems, from mood and anxiety disorders to addictions, chronic pain, and stress in otherwise healthy individuals. Several books describe ACT, written for both therapists and patients (e.g., Harris, 2019; Hayes & Smith, 2005; Luoma, Hayes, & Walser, 2017).

With a theoretical basis in behavioral contextualism, ACT proposes that human language itself inevitably leads to suffering. Despite all of the beneficial uses of language, people also use it to compare, judge, and attempt to control. Steve Hayes, the creator of ACT, proposes that people learn to use comparative words such as "good" and "bad" to judge internal experiences (e.g., thoughts and emotions) in the same way that they use "hot" and "cold" to describe properties of external objects. The problem is that judging or comparing internal experiences makes them seem as real as external objects such as a hot iron or cold ice. This *cognitive fusion*, or believing that thoughts are real objects, contributes to suffering in many ways. It encourages people to spend a lot of time and effort focusing on their thoughts, which prevents them from noticing what is actually happening around them. The more strongly that people believe thoughts and emotions are fact, the harder they may attempt to avoid or suppress unwanted thoughts or emotions. In addition to simply not working, this experiential avoidance interferes with people behaving in ways that reflect their goals and values. In this way, unwanted thoughts and emotions end up controlling behavior. According to ACT, cognitive fusion and experiential avoidance are the two core psychological processes that cause human suffering.

The goal of ACT is to increase people's cognitive flexibility, or the ability to accept all current internal experiences and to engage in actions guided by values. Thus, therapists help patients learn to accept whatever internal experiences are present, even unpleasant ones. Patients also learn to defuse, or distance themselves from their thoughts and the idea that thoughts are real objects that can be controlled. Once patients let go of the struggle to control their internal experiences, they are available to experience the present moment and engage in committed and valued action, or behaviors that reflect what is really important to them. Thus, even though ACT as originally described did not use the term mindfulness, it clearly aims to help patients achieve a state of mindful awareness and acceptance of the present moment, along with decentering from thoughts, in order to facilitate valued living.

Although mindfulness is the main goal of ACT, it does not prescribe meditative practices. Instead, ACT therapists rely primarily on metaphors and experiential exercises to help challenge the workability of experiential avoidance and to foster cognitive defusion, experiential acceptance, and valued action. For instance, the "tug of war with the monster" metaphor asks patients to imagine being in a tug-of-war with an anxiety monster over a bottomless pit. The harder people pull the rope, the harder the monster pulls and the closer people get to the edge of the pit. Rather than pulling harder, the solution is to drop the rope; the monster remains, but the struggle is ended and people can do something more useful with their time and energy. To promote defusion, patients may be encouraged to say "I'm having the thought that ..." before a negative self-thought; to sing negative self-thoughts or hear thoughts in the voice of a cartoon character; to imagine a thought on a computer screen and then play with its font, size, and color; and to watch thoughts passing through the mind as clouds in the sky or leaves in a stream. Similarly, common acceptance techniques include approaching emotions such as a curious scientist, visualizing emotions as passengers on a bus, holding a feeling gently as if it were a crying puppy, and sending warmth and love to parts of the body where painful sensations or emotions reside. Values are clarified through exercises such as imaging desired eulogies and discussions of realistic, values-based goals. Finally, committed action is encouraged by making public commitments and identifying and addressing barriers.

Only minimal research has examined the efficacy of ACT for reducing rumination. A research team has developed a brief (i.e., 1 or 2 session) ACT protocol aimed specifically at reducing repetitive thinking (Ruiz et al., 2018; Ruiz & Odriozola-González, 2016). The therapy uses metaphors and experiential exercises to help patients recognize how repetitive thinking is counterproductive and interferes with valued living. It also helps patients to identify triggers of rumination and worry and introduces exercises to defuse from these triggers. In adults with and without symptoms of depression and/or anxiety, this brief ACT reduced rumination and worry and also increased cognitive flexibility and defusion.

Other related therapies

Based largely on ACT, acceptance-based behavioral therapy (ABBT) was originally developed to treat GAD and worry (Roemer & Orsillo, 2005). The rationale for the treatment is that people with GAD have negative reactions to unpleasant internal experiences, judgment of emotions as extreme or dangerous, and fusion with negative internal experiences (Roemer & Orsillo, 2002, 2005). These problematic reactions to internal experiences fuel active and/or automatic attempts to avoid internal experiences perceived to be threatening or negative. Worry is conceptualized as one form of experiential avoidance. Based on this theoretical model, the 16-session treatment starts by introducing patients to the idea that worry is used to avoid more distressing internal experiences, and that although experiential avoidance may be effective in short term, it ultimately prevents engagement in valued and meaningful activities. Therapists also review the important functions of emotions (e.g., preparing for action and communicating with others), in order to start challenging ideas about the danger of negative emotions. Patients are introduced to formal and informal mindfulness exercises, as well as ACT metaphors and activities, in order to increase experiential acceptance and cognitive defusion. Patients practice mindfulness at the beginning of each session and repeatedly discuss mindfulness and acceptance skills. ABBT also focuses on identifying patients' values and ways that their behavior can better reflect those values. Both open-trial and randomized control studies with GAD patients found that ABBT significantly reduced worry posttreatment and at 3- and 9-month follow-ups (Hayes-Skelton, Roemer, & Orsillo, 2013; Roemer & Orsillo, 2007; Roemer, Orsillo, & Salters-Pedneault, 2008). Similarly, internet-delivered ABBT led to greater reductions in worry at posttreatment and 6 months later than did a waitlist control (Dahlin et al., 2016).

Emotion regulation therapy (ERT) combines aspects of traditional CBT, mindfulness-based therapies, and ACT to treat GAD with comorbid depression (Fresco, Mennin, Heimberg, & Ritter, 2013; Renna, Quintero, Fresco, & Mennin, 2017). ERT is based on the theory that people with GAD and comorbid depression often experience conflicts between the motivations to seek reward versus security, and that they lack the effective emotion regulation skills to resolve these conflicts (Mennin, Heimberg, Turk, & Fresco, 2005; Renna et al., 2017). Specifically, these individuals overvalue security, which disrupts the flexible balance between approach and avoidance that typically characterizes adaptive behavioral choices. Moreover, people with GAD respond to strong emotions and the desire for security with rigid avoidance strategies such as worry or rumination, which in turn prevent them from engaging in behaviors that reflect their values and promote meaning and joy (Fresco et al., 2013). In accordance with this theoretical model, the 16-session ERT targets motivational conflicts, reactive responses such as worry and rumination, and inflexible behavioral repertoires. Patients practice breath-focused and body scan meditations in order to develop the ability to notice and accept a range of emotions and motivations without engaging in the reactive avoidance responses of worry or rumination. They are then encouraged to expand their behavioral repertoire by engaging in behaviors that are meaningful and rewarding. Open trials of ERT showed reductions in worry that were maintained at a 9-month follow-up (Mennin et al., 2005; Renna et al., 2017). Similarly, compared to an attention control treatment, ERT led to greater improvements in worry and rumination, both immediately and 9 months after treatment (Renna et al., 2017).

One research team developed mindfulness- and acceptance-based group therapy (MAGT) for social anxiety that combines abbreviated mindfulness exercises from MBCT, experiential and didactic components from ACT, and exposure exercises from traditional CBT (Kocovski, Fleming, Hawley, Huta, & Antony, 2013; Kocovski, Fleming, & Rector, 2009). Specifically, mindfulness and ACT strategies are used to promote acceptance of unwanted physical sensations (e.g., shaking and blushing) and anxious thoughts in order to reduce avoidance of feared situations. Exposure exercises are conducted not for habituation but to provide opportunities to practice acceptance while engaging in value-based behaviors. An initial open trial indicated that rumination decreased over the course of treatment and at 3-month posttreatment (Kocovski et al., 2009). Compared to a wait-list control, both MAGT and group CBT contributed to decreased rumination (Kocovski et al., 2013).

Although not based on MBSR or ACT, dialectical behavior therapy (DBT) incorporates both mindfulness and acceptance concepts (Linehan, 1993). First developed for patients with chronic suicidal and/or self-injurious behaviors, such as those with borderline personality disorder, DBT has since been adapted to other disorders. The treatment conceptualizes these kinds of dysfunctional behaviors as resulting from deficits in emotion regulation, evident in extreme emotional reactivity and an inability to modulate emotions. DBT emphasizes the need for both acceptance and behavior change in order to help patients improve their emotion regulation skills. Mindfulness is one of four central skills modules taught to DBT patients in a group setting, to accompany individual therapy. In the mindfulness module, patients are introduced to three states of mind: reasonable mind (i.e., the logical and rationale part of the mind that makes intellectual decisions), emotional mind (i.e., the reactive mind in which emotions often control behaviors), and wise mind (i.e., an integration of reason and emotion, resulting in intuitive-based decisions). Wise mind can be attained through mindfulness practice. Specific exercises used to foster mindfulness include informal practices (e.g., mindfulness while washing the dishes), brief breath-focused meditations, and experiential exercises (e.g., watching thoughts as clouds in the sky). Mindfulness skills are also used in the other three skills modules, which focus on distress tolerance, emotion regulation, and interpersonal effectiveness. Although researchers have not examined the effect of traditional DBT on rumination, a brief version of DBT combined with CBT reduced repetitive thinking in patients with acute psychopathology seeking treatment at a partial day program (Wadsworth et al., 2018).

Several other therapies targeting a specific presenting problem are modeled after MBSR, MBCT, ACT and/or DBT. For instance, mindfulness-based relapse prevention integrates MBCT exercises into traditional CBT to increase awareness of triggers, improve acceptance and distress tolerance of negative emotions (including cravings), and promote more skillful behavior choices in individuals with substance abuse histories (Bowen, Chawla, & Marlatt, 2010). Mindfulness-based eating awareness training integrates MBSR and CBT, with an emphasis on guided eating meditations, in order to address issues with body shape, weight, and appetite (Kristeller & Wolever, 2010). One team has incorporated loving kindness meditation into CBT to treat PTSD (Hinton, Hofmann, Rivera, Otto, & Pollack, 2011; Hinton, Pich,

Hofmann, & Otto, 2013). In the treatment, patients describe a recent traumatic event and then are encouraged to practice loving kindness meditation in order to bring an attitude of compassion to trauma exposure. Other researchers incorporate the keys skills of DBT into exposure treatment for PTSD (Follette, Palm, & Pearson, 2006). Researchers have not yet examined the efficacy of these therapies on reducing rumination. Given the clear role that rumination plays in substance problems, eating disorders, and PTSD, I am hopeful that relevant research will emerge.

Some therapies focus specifically on compassion. Mindful self-compassion is an 8-week group intervention for healthy individuals that includes interpersonal exercises (e.g., being a compassionate observer of someone else), guided meditations (e.g., mindfulness and loving-kindness meditations), and informal practices (e.g., placing one's hand over one's heart in moments of suffering) to enhance self-compassion in daily life (Neff & Germer, 2013). Similarly, compassion-focused therapy (Gilbert, 2010) targets clinical populations and uses imagery and experiential exercises to enhance patients' feelings of reassurance, safeness, and understanding of themselves. One study tested a three-session, self-compassion group training to help female college students deal with the challenges of university life (Smeets, Neff, Alberts, & Peters, 2014). Compared with three sessions of time management training, the self-compassion training led to greater reductions in depressive rumination and increases in mindfulness and self-compassion.

Gratitude interventions typically involve completing a brief daily journal, in which people write down 3–5 things they are grateful for that day (Emmons & McCullough, 2003). Similarly, Naikon therapy asks people to make a list of all the things they have received that day from others, as well as the things they have given to others and the trouble they have caused others. In the only study to examine rumination as an outcome of a gratitude intervention, women with cervical cancer practiced a gratitude journal plus 15 minutes of guided breath meditation every night for 4 weeks (Shao, Gao, & Cao, 2016). Compared to a treatment as usual group, the gratitude plus mindfulness intervention led to greater reductions in depressive rumination.

Finally, researchers have examined the efficacy of meditation retreats and yoga-based interventions. Intensive meditation retreats generally involve spending several hours a day in silent meditation, with or without dialog between sitting sessions. In healthy adults who participated in a 10-day, intensive mindfulness meditation retreat, depressive rumination decreased significantly compared to a no-treatment control group (Chambers, Lo, & Allen, 2008). In healthy adolescents who participated in 5-day, intensive meditation retreats, rumination decreased from pre- to postretreat, and the decrease was maintained at a 3-month follow-up (Galla, 2016). Within-person changes in mindfulness and self-compassion each uniquely contributed to decreased rumination. Yoga-based interventions also reduce rumination. For instance, 8 weeks of yoga classes reduced depressive rumination in depressed patients (Kinser, Bourguignon, Whaley, Hauenstein, & Taylor, 2013; Kinser, Elswick, & Kornstein, 2014; Uebelacker et al., 2010). Similarly, school-based yoga programs provided to elementary and high school students contributed to decreased rumination (Frank, Bose, & Schrobenhauser-Clonan, 2014; Mendelson et al., 2010).

Summary

In sum, the existing literature robustly demonstrates that mindfulness-based therapies reduce rumination and worry. These effects emerge in quasi-experimental (e.g., pre–post) studies and in experiments that compare the treatments to a wait-list or other control condition. Moreover, mindfulness-based therapies reduce rumination as much, if not more, than other empirically supported treatments such as CBT. In fact, reviews and meta-analyses suggest that changes in rumination and worry mediate the effect of MBSR and MBCT on psychological outcomes (Gu, Strauss, Bond, & Cavanagh, 2015; van der Velden et al., 2015). In other words, decreased repetitive thinking appears to be one mechanism by which mindfulness-based treatments effectively decrease clinical symptoms. Moreover, the effects of MBSR and MBCT on repetitive thinking are explained by increased mindfulness (Batink et al., 2013; Shapiro et al., 2008).

Conclusion

In this chapter, I reviewed the extensive basic research demonstrating that mindfulness and related constructs are associated with less negative repetitive thinking, as well as treatment outcome research showing that mindfulness-related treatments effectively reduce rumination and worry. The obvious contrasts between mindfulness and rumination may explain these robust effects. Whereas rumination involves rigid and critical attention to a problem in the past, mindfulness teaches people to attend to the present moment with acceptance, nonjudgment, compassion, and an open, flexible awareness.

One pertinent question for the mindfulness field is whether amount of meditation practice is associated with better outcomes. The literature yields conflicting findings on this question for clinical symptoms (e.g., Vettese, Toneatto, Stea, Nguyen, & Wang, 2009). Similarly, mixed results emerge when examining rumination as an outcome. In long-term meditators, the more years that people have been regularly meditating, the less they ruminated (Lykins & Baer, 2009). Similarly, some studies of MBSR and MBCT found that more frequent and longer meditation practice at home were associated with greater decreases in rumination (Hawley et al., 2014; Ramel et al., 2004; Rimes & Wingrove, 2011). However, other studies failed to find an association between how many minutes people spend meditating during the week and rumination (Shapiro et al., 2007, 2008). Of course, participant reporting on their home practice may be unreliable, and quantity of practice may be less important than the quality of practice. Experimental designs could more systematically examine whether the amount of meditation practice influences outcomes.

Finally, some readers might question whether rumination-focused cognitive behavioral therapy's emphasis on concrete processing (see Chapter 10: Cognitive behavioral therapies) is just another name for mindfulness. The focus on sensory and/or procedural details in concrete processing manipulations certainly seems similar to the awareness component of mindfulness. Some researchers in fact refer to the concrete processing manipulation as experiential mindfulness (e.g., Sanders & Lam, 2010). However, Watkins (2008, 2016) argues that they are not the same construct. First, concrete processing does not include the attitude components of mindfulness, such as acceptance, compassion, and decentering. Moreover, concreteness training is not necessarily present-focused; individuals are typically instructed to think concretely about events from their recent past and then to attend to the future to imagine how things might be different. Thus, the focus on sensory and procedural details might be the only overlap between mindfulness and concrete processing. Despite these apparent differences, a concrete processing pre-meal exercise (e.g., think about *how* to eat) practiced daily for 5 weeks increased mindfulness, whereas abstract processing (e.g., think about *why* to eat) decreased mindfulness (Mantzios & Wilson, 2014). Therefore, increased mindfulness may be one mechanism of concreteness training. I return to the question of similarities between second and third wave therapies at the end of the next chapter, after describing a different type of therapy that explicitly challenges patients' metacognitive processes in order to reduce negative repetitive thinking.

References

Alleva, J., Roelofs, J., Voncken, M., Meevissen, Y., & Alberts, H. (2014). On the relation between mindfulness and depressive symptoms: Rumination as a possible mediator. *Mindfulness*, *5*(1), 72–79. Available from https://doi.org/10.1007/s12671-012-0153-y.

Ames, C. S., Richardson, J., Payne, S., Smith, P., & Leigh, E. (2014). Mindfulness-based cognitive therapy for depression in adolescents. *Child and Adolescent Mental Health*, *19*(1), 74–78.

Armstrong, L., & Rimes, K. A. (2016). Mindfulness-based cognitive therapy for neuroticism (stress vulnerability): A pilot randomized study. *Behavior Therapy, 47*(3), 287–298. Available from https://doi.org/10.1016/j.beth.2015.12.005.

Ayduk, Ö., & Kross, E. (2010). From a distance. *Journal of Personality and Social Psychology, 98*(5), 809–829. Available from https://doi.org/10.1037/a0019205.

Baer, R. A. (2003). Mindfulness training as a clinical intervention: A conceptual and empirical review. *Clinical Psychology: Science and Practice, 10*(2), 125–143.

Baer, R. A. (2009). Self-focused attention and mechanisms of change in mindfulness-based treatment. *Cognitive Behaviour Therapy, 38*(sup1), 15–20. Available from https://doi.org/10.1080/16506070902980703.

Baer, R. A., Smith, G. T., Lykins, E., Button, D., Krietemeyer, J., Sauer, S., ... Williams, J. M. G. (2008). Construct validity of the five facet mindfulness questionnaire in meditating and nonmeditating samples. *Assessment, 15*(3), 329–342. Available from https://doi.org/10.1177/1073191107313003.

Batink, T., Peeters, F. P. M. L., Geschwind, N., van Os, J., & Wichers, M. (2013). How does MBCT for depression work? studying cognitive and affective mediation pathways. *PLoS One, 8*(8), e72778. Available from https://doi.org/10.1371/journal.pone.0072778.

Bishop, S. R., Lau, M., Shapiro, S., Carlson, L., Anderson, N. D., Carmody, J., ... Devins, G. (2004). Mindfulness: A proposed operational definition. *Clinical Psychology: Science and Practice, 11*(3), 230–241. Available from https://doi.org/10.1093/clipsy.bph077.

Bjornsson, A., Carey, G., Hauser, M., Karris, A., Kaufmann, V., Sheets, E., & Craighead, W. E. (2010). The effects of experiential avoidance and rumination on depression among college students. *International Journal of Cognitive Therapy, 3*(4), 389–401. Available from https://doi.org/10.1521/ijct.2010.3.4.389.

Bluett, E. J., Homan, K. J., Morrison, K. L., Levin, M. E., & Twohig, M. P. (2014). Acceptance and commitment therapy for anxiety and OCD spectrum disorders: An empirical review. *Journal of Anxiety Disorders, 28*(6), 612–624. Available from https://doi.org/10.1016/j.janxdis.2014.06.008.

Bluth, K., Gaylord, S., Nguyen, K., Bunevicius, A., & Girdler, S. (2015). Mindfulness-based stress reduction as a promising intervention for amelioration of premenstrual dysphoric disorder symptoms. *Mindfulness, 6*(6), 1292–1302.

Bond, F. W., Hayes, S. C., Baer, R. A., Carpenter, K. M., Guenole, N., Orcutt, H. K., & Zettle, R. D. (2011). Preliminary psychometric properties of the acceptance and action Questionnaire–II: A revised measure of psychological inflexibility and experiential avoidance. *Behavior Therapy, 42*(4), 676–688. Available from https://doi.org/10.1016/j.beth.2011.03.007.

Borders, A., Earleywine, M., & Jajodia, A. (2010). Could mindfulness decrease anger, hostility, and aggression by decreasing rumination? *Aggressive Behavior, 36*(1), 28–44. Available from https://doi.org/10.1002/ab.20327.

Borders, A., & Lu, S. (2017). The bidirectional associations between state anger and rumination and the role of trait mindfulness. *Aggressive Behavior, 43*(4), 342–351. Available from https://doi.org/10.1002/ab.21693.

Bowen, S., Chawla, N., & Marlatt, G. A. (2010). *Mindfulness-based relapse prevention for substance use disorders: A clinician's guide.*

Boyle, C. C., Stanton, A. L., Ganz, P. A., Crespi, C. M., & Bower, J. E. (2017). Improvements in emotion regulation following mindfulness meditation: Effects on depressive symptoms and perceived stress in younger breast cancer survivors. *Journal of Consulting and Clinical Psychology, 85*(4), 397–402. Available from https://doi.org/10.1037/ccp0000186.

Brennan, K., Barnhofer, T., Crane, C., Duggan, D., & Williams, J. M. G. (2015). Memory specificity and mindfulness jointly moderate the effect of reflective pondering on depressive symptoms in individuals with a history of recurrent depression. *Journal of Abnormal Psychology, 124*(2), 246–255. Available from https://doi.org/10.1037/abn0000027.

Broderick, P. (2005). Mindfulness and coping with dysphoric mood: Contrasts with rumination and distraction. *Cognitive Therapy and Research, 29*(5), 501–510. Available from https://doi.org/10.1007/s10608-005-3888-0.

Brown, K. W., & Ryan, R. M. (2003). The benefits of being present. *Journal of Personality and Social Psychology, 84*(4), 822–848. Available from https://doi.org/10.1037/0022-3514.84.4.822.

Burg, J., & Michalak, J. (2011). The healthy quality of mindful breathing: Associations with rumination and depression. *Cognitive Therapy and Research, 35*(2), 179–185. Available from https://doi.org/10.1007/s10608-010-9343-x.

Campbell, T., Labelle, L., Bacon, S., Faris, P., & Carlson, L. (2012). Impact of mindfulness-based stress reduction (MBSR) on attention, rumination and resting blood pressure in women with cancer: A waitlist-controlled study. *Journal of Behavioral Medicine, 35*(3), 262–271. Available from https://doi.org/10.1007/s10865-011-9357-1.

Cassin, S. E., & Rector, N. A. (2011). Mindfulness and the attenuation of post-event processing in social phobia: An experimental investigation. *Cognitive Behaviour Therapy, 40*(4), 267–278. Available from https://doi.org/10.1080/16506073.2011.614275.

Chambers, R., Lo, B. C. Y., & Allen, N. B. (2008). The impact of intensive mindfulness training on attentional control, cognitive style, and affect. *Cognitive Therapy and Research, 32*(3), 303–322.

Ciesla, J. A., Reilly, L. C., Dickson, K. S., Emanuel, A. S., & Updegraff, J. A. (2012). Dispositional mindfulness moderates the effects of stress among adolescents: Rumination as a mediator. *Journal of Clinical Child & Adolescent Psychology, 41*(6), 760–770. Available from https://doi.org/10.1080/15374416.2012.698724.

Coffey, K., Hartman, M., & Fredrickson, B. (2010). Deconstructing mindfulness and constructing mental health: Understanding mindfulness and its mechanisms of action. *Mindfulness, 1*(4), 235–253. Available from https://doi.org/10.1007/s12671-010-0033-2.

Coffey, K. A., & Hartman, M. (2008). Mechanisms of action in the inverse relationship between mindfulness and psychological distress. *Complementary Health Practice Review, 13*(2), 79–91. Available from https://doi.org/10.1177/1533210108316307.

Cowdrey, F. A., & Park, R. J. (2012). The role of experiential avoidance, rumination and mindfulness in eating disorders. *Eating Behaviors, 13*(2), 100–105. Available from https://doi.org/10.1016/j.eatbeh.2012.01.001.

Craigie, M. A., Rees, C. S., Marsh, A., & Nathan, P. (2008). Mindfulness-based cognitive therapy for generalized anxiety disorder: A preliminary evaluation. *Behavioural and Cognitive Psychotherapy, 36*(5), 553–568. Available from https://doi.org/10.1017/S135246580800458X.

Crain, T. L., Schonert-Reichl, K. A., & Roeser, R. W. (2017). Cultivating teacher mindfulness: Effects of a randomized controlled trial on work, home, and sleep outcomes. *Journal of Occupational Health Psychology, 22*(2), 138–152. Available from https://doi.org/10.1037/ocp0000043.

Cribb, G., Moulds, M. L., & Carter, S. (2006). Rumination and experiential avoidance in depression. *Behaviour Change, 23*(3), 165–176. Available from https://doi.org/10.1375/bech.23.3.165.

Dahlin, M., Andersson, G., Magnusson, K., Johansson, T., Sjögren, J., Håkansson, A., & Carlbring, P. (2016). Internet-delivered acceptance-based behaviour therapy for generalized anxiety disorder. *Behaviour Research and Therapy, 77*, 86. Retrieved from <http://urn.kb.se/resolve?urn = urn:nbn:se:umu:diva–118413>.

Daubenmier, J., Hayden, D., Chang, V., & Epel, E. (2014). It's not what you think, it's how you relate to it: Dispositional mindfulness moderates the relationship between psychological distress and the cortisol awakening response. *Psychoneuroendocrinology, 48*, 11–18.

Deckersbach, T., Hölzel, B. K., Eisner, L. R., Stange, J. P., Peckham, A. D., Dougherty, D. D., & Nierenberg, A. A. (2012). Mindfulness-Based cognitive therapy for nonremitted patients with bipolar disorder. *CNS Neuroscience & Therapeutics, 18*(2), 133–141. Available from https://doi.org/10.1111/j.1755-5949.2011.00236.x.

Deplus, S., Billieux, J., Scharff, C., & Philippot, P. (2016). A mindfulness-based group intervention for enhancing self-regulation of emotion in late childhood and adolescence: A pilot study. *International Journal of Mental Health and Addiction, 14*(5), 775–790. Available from https://doi.org/10.1007/s11469-015-9627-1.

Desrosiers, A., Vine, V., Klemanski, D. H., & Nolen-Hoeksema, S. (2013). Mindfulness and emotion regulation in depression and anxiety: Common and distinct mechanisms of action. *Depression and Anxiety, 30*(7), 654. Available from https://doi.org/10.1002/da.22124.

Eisenlohr-Moul, T., Peters, J., Pond, R., Jr, & DeWall, C. (2016). Both trait and state mindfulness predict lower aggressiveness via anger rumination: A multilevel mediation analysis. *Mindfulness, 7*(3), 713–726. Available from https://doi.org/10.1007/s12671-016-0508-x.

Emmons, R. A., & McCullough, M. E. (2003). Counting blessings versus burdens: An experimental investigation of gratitude and subjective well-being in daily life. *Journal of Personality and Social Psychology, 84*(2), 377.

Emmons, R. A., & Stern, R. (2013). Gratitude as a psychotherapeutic intervention. *Journal of Clinical Psychology, 69*(8), 846–855. Available from https://doi.org/10.1002/jclp.22020.

Evans, D., & Segerstrom, S. (2011). Why do mindful people worry less? *Cognitive Therapy and Research, 35*(6), 505–510. Available from https://doi.org/10.1007/s10608-010-9340-0.

Evans, S., Ferrando, S., Findler, M., Marianne, S., Smart, C., & Haglin, D. (2007). Mindfulness-based cognitive therapy for generalized anxiety disorder. *Journal of Anxiety Disorders, 22*(4), 716–721. Available from https://doi.org/10.1016/j.janxdis.2007.07.005.

Feldman, G., Dunn, E., Stemke, C., Bell, K., & Greeson, J. (2014). Mindfulness and rumination as predictors of persistence with a distress tolerance task. *Personality and Individual Differences, 56*, 154–158. Available from https://doi.org/10.1016/j.paid.2013.08.040.

Feldman, G., Greeson, J., & Senville, J. (2010). Differential effects of mindful breathing, progressive muscle relaxation, and loving-kindness meditation on decentering and negative reactions to repetitive thoughts. *Behaviour Research and Therapy, 48*(10), 1002–1011. Available from https://doi.org/10.1016/j.brat.2010.06.006.

Fisak, B., & von Lehe, A. (2012). The relation between the five facets of mindfulness and worry in a non-clinical sample. *Mindfulness, 3*(1), 15–21. Available from https://doi.org/10.1007/s12671-011-0075-0.

Follette, V., Palm, K., & Pearson, A. (2006). Mindfulness and trauma: Implications for treatment. *Journal of Rational-Emotive & Cognitive-Behavior Therapy, 24*(1), 45–61. Available from https://doi.org/10.1007/s10942-006-0025-2.

Forsyth, J. P., & Eifert, G. H. (2007). *The mindfulness and acceptance workbook for anxiety*. Oakland, CA: New Harbinger.

Foulk, M. A., Ingersoll-Dayton, B., Kavanagh, J., Robinson, E., & Kales, H. C. (2014). Mindfulness-based cognitive therapy with older adults: An exploratory study. *Journal of Gerontological Social Work, 57*(5), 498–520. Available from https://doi.org/10.1080/01634372.2013.869787.

Frank, J. L., Bose, B., & Schrobenhauser-Clonan, A. (2014). Effectiveness of a school-based yoga program on adolescent mental health, stress coping strategies, and attitudes toward violence: Findings from a high-risk sample. *Journal of Applied School Psychology, 30*(1), 29–49. Available from https://doi.org/10.1080/15377903.2013.863259.

Fresco, D. M., Mennin, D. S., Heimberg, R. G., & Ritter, M. (2013). Emotion regulation therapy for generalized anxiety disorder. *Cognitive and Behavioral Practice, 20*(3), 282–300. Available from https://doi.org/10.1016/j.cbpra.2013.02.001.

Fresnics, A., & Borders, A. (2017). Angry rumination mediates the unique associations between self-compassion and anger and aggression. *Mindfulness, 8*(3), 554–564. Available from https://doi.org/10.1007/s12671-016-0629-2.

Galla, B. M. (2016). Within-person changes in mindfulness and self-compassion predict enhanced emotional well-being in healthy, but stressed adolescents. *Journal of Adolescence, 49*, 204–217. Available from https://doi.org/10.1016/j.adolescence.2016.03.016.

Germer, C. K. (2013). *Mindfulness and psychotherapy* (2nd ed.). New York [u.a.]: The Guilford Press. Retrieved from <http://bvbr.bib-bvb.de:8991/F?func = service&doc_library = BVB01&local_base = BVB01&doc_number = 027280925&sequence = 000002&line_number = 0001&func_code = DB_RECORDS&service_type = MEDIA>.

Geschwind, N., Peeters, F., kker, M., van Os, J., & Wichers, M. (2011). Mindfulness training increases momentary positive emotions and reward experience in adults vulnerable to depression: A randomized controlled trial. *Journal of Consulting and Clinical Psychology, 79*(5), 618–628. Available from https://doi.org/10.1037/a0024595.

Gilbert, P. (2010). An introduction to compassion focused therapy in cognitive behavior therapy. *International Journal of Cognitive Therapy*, 3(2), 97–112.

Gillanders, D. T., Bolderston, H., Bond, F. W., Dempster, M., Flaxman, P., Campbell, L., ... Remington, B. (2014). *The development and initial validation of the cognitive fusion questionnaire*. Elsevier. Retrieved from <http://openaccess.city.ac.uk/8562/>.

Giorgio, J. M., Sanflippo, J., Kleiman, E., Reilly, D., Bender, R. E., Wagner, C. A., ... Alloy, L. B. (2010). An experiential avoidance conceptualization of depressive rumination: Three tests of the model. *Behaviour Research and Therapy, 48*(10), 1021–1031. Available from https://doi.org/10.1016/j.brat.2010.07.004.

Goldin, P. R., & Gross, J. J. (2010). Effects of mindfulness-based stress reduction (MBSR) on emotion regulation in social anxiety disorder. *Emotion, 10*(1), 83–91. Available from https://doi.org/10.1037/a0018441.

Goldin, P. R., Morrison, A., Jazaieri, H., Brozovich, F., Heimberg, R., & Gross, J. J. (2016). Group CBT versus MBSR for social anxiety disorder: A randomized controlled trial. *Journal of Consulting and Clinical Psychology, 84*(5), 427–437. Available from https://doi.org/10.1037/ccp0000092.

Goodman, J., Guarino, A., Chenausky, K., Klein, L., Prager, J., Petersen, R., ... Freeman, M. (2014). CALM pregnancy: Results of a pilot study of mindfulness-based cognitive therapy for perinatal anxiety. *Archives of Women's Mental Health, 17*(5), 373–387. Available from https://doi.org/10.1007/s00737-013-0402-7.

Grabovac, A., Lau, M., & Willett, B. (2011). Mechanisms of mindfulness: A Buddhist psychological model. *Mindfulness*, 2(3), 154–166. Available from https://doi.org/10.1007/s12671-011-0054-5.

Graser, J., Höfling, V., Weßlau, C., Mendes, A., & Stangier, U. (2016). Effects of a 12-week mindfulness, compassion, and loving kindness program on chronic depression: A pilot within-subjects wait-list controlled trial. *Journal of Cognitive Psychotherapy, 30*(1), 35–49. Available from https://doi.org/10.1891/0889-8391.30.1.35.

Grossman, P., Niemann, L., Schmidt, S., & Walach, H. (2004). Mindfulness-based stress reduction and health benefits: A meta-analysis. *Journal of Psychosomatic Research, 57*(1), 35–43.

Gu, J., Strauss, C., Bond, R., & Cavanagh, K. (2015). How do mindfulness-based cognitive therapy and mindfulness-based stress reduction improve mental health and wellbeing? A systematic review and meta-analysis of mediation studies. *Clinical Psychology Review, 37*, 1–12.

Hanley, A. W., Garland, E. L., & Tedeschi, R. G. (2017). Relating dispositional mindfulness, contemplative practice, and positive reappraisal with posttraumatic cognitive coping, stress, and growth. *Psychological Trauma: Theory, Research, Practice and Policy, 9*(5), 526–536. Available from https://doi.org/10.1037/tra0000208.

Harris, R. (2019). *ACT made simple: An easy-to-read primer on acceptance and commitment therapy (the new harbinger made simple series)* (2nd ed., revised ed.). Oakland, CA: New Harbinger Publications.

Hawley, L., Schwartz, D., Bieling, P., Irving, J., Corcoran, K., Farb, N., ... Segal, Z. (2014). Mindfulness practice, rumination and clinical outcome in mindfulness-based treatment. *Cognitive Therapy and Research, 38*(1), 1–9. Available from https://doi.org/10.1007/s10608-013-9586-4.

Hayes, S. C. (2004). Acceptance and commitment therapy, relational frame theory, and the third wave of behavioral and cognitive therapies. *Behavior Therapy, 35*(4), 639–665. Available from https://doi.org/10.1016/S0005-7894(04)80013-3.

Hayes, S. C., & Smith, S. (2005). *Get out of your mind and into your life: The new acceptance and commitment therapy*. Oakland, CA: New Harbinger Publications, Inc.

Hayes, S. C., Strosahl, K. D., & Wilson, K. G. (1999). *Acceptance and commitment therapy*. New York: Guilford Press.

Hayes-Skelton, S. A., Roemer, L., & Orsillo, S. M. (2013). A randomized clinical trial comparing an acceptance-based behavior therapy to applied relaxation for generalized anxiety disorder. *Journal of Consulting and Clinical Psychology, 81*(5), 761–773. Available from https://doi.org/10.1037/a0032871.

Heeren, A., & Philippot, P. (2011). Changes in ruminative thinking mediate the clinical benefits of mindfulness: Preliminary findings. *Mindfulness, 2*(1), 8–13. Available from https://doi.org/10.1007/s12671-010-0037-y.

Hilt, L., & Pollak, S. (2012). Getting out of rumination: Comparison of three brief interventions in a sample of youth. *Journal of Abnormal Child Psychology, 40*(7), 1157–1165. Available from https://doi.org/10.1007/s10802-012-9638-3.

Hinton, D. E., Hofmann, S. G., Rivera, E., Otto, M. W., & Pollack, M. H. (2011). Culturally adapted CBT (CA-CBT) for Latino women with treatment-resistant PTSD: A pilot study comparing CA-CBT to applied muscle relaxation. *Behaviour Research and Therapy, 49*(4), 275–280. Available from https://doi.org/10.1016/j.brat.2011.01.005.

Hinton, D. E., Pich, V., Hofmann, S. G., & Otto, M. W. (2013). Acceptance and mindfulness techniques as applied to refugee and ethnic minority populations with PTSD: Examples from "culturally adapted CBT". *Cognitive and Behavioral Practice, 20*(1), 33–46. Available from https://doi.org/10.1016/j.cbpra.2011.09.001.

Hofmann, S. G., Grossman, P., & Hinton, D. E. (2011). Loving-kindness and compassion meditation: Potential for psychological interventions. *Clinical Psychology Review, 31*(7), 1126–1132. Available from https://doi.org/10.1016/j.cpr.2011.07.003.

Hoge, E. A., Bui, E., Goetter, E., Robinaugh, D. J., Ojserkis, R. A., Fresco, D. M., & Simon, N. M. (2015). Change in decentering mediates improvement in anxiety in mindfulness-based stress reduction for generalized anxiety disorder. *Cognitive Therapy and Research, 39*(2), 228–235. Available from https://doi.org/10.1007/s10608-014-9646-4.

Holas, P., & Jankowski, T. (2013). A cognitive perspective on mindfulness. *International Journal of Psychology, 48*(3), 232–243. Available from https://doi.org/10.1080/00207594.2012.658056.

Huffziger, S., Ebner-Priemer, U., Eisenbach, C., Koudela, S., Reinhard, I., Zamoscik, V., ... Kuehner, C. (2013). Induced ruminative and mindful attention in everyday life: An experimental ambulatory assessment study. *Journal of Behavior Therapy and Experimental Psychiatry, 44*(3), 322–328. Available from https://doi.org/10.1016/j.jbtep.2013.01.007.

Huffziger, S., & Kuehner, C. (2009). Rumination, distraction, and mindful self-focus in depressed patients. *Behaviour Research and Therapy, 47*(3), 224–230. Available from https://doi.org/10.1016/j.brat.2008.12.005.

Im, S., & Follette, V. M. (2016). Rumination and mindfulness related to multiple types of trauma exposure. *Translational Issues in Psychological Science, 2*(4), 395–407. Available from https://doi.org/10.1037/tps0000090.

Ingram, R. E. (1990). Self-focused attention in clinical disorders: Review and a conceptual model. *Psychological Bulletin, 107*(2), 156–176. Available from https://doi.org/10.1037//0033-2909.107.2.156.

Jain, S., Shapiro, S. L., Swanick, S., Roesch, S. C., Mills, P. J., Bell, I., & Schwartz, G. E. (2007). A randomized controlled trial of mindfulness meditation versus relaxation training: Effects on distress, positive states of mind, rumination, and distraction. *Annals of Behavioral Medicine, 33*(1), 11–21.

Johnson, E. A., & O'Brien, K. A. (2013). Self-compassion soothes the savage EGO-threat system: Effects on negative affect, shame, rumination, and depressive symptoms. *Journal of Social and Clinical Psychology, 32*(9), 939–963. Available from https://doi.org/10.1521/jscp.2013.32.9.939.

Kabat-Zinn, J. (2013). *Full catastrophe living: Using the Wisdom of Your Body and Mind to Face Stress, Pain, and Illness* (Revised and updated edition). New York: Bantam Books.

Kaiser, R., Andrews-Hanna, J., Metcalf, C., & Dimidjian, S. (2015). Dwell or decenter? rumination and decentering predict working memory updating after interpersonal criticism. *Cognitive Therapy and Research, 39*(6), 744–753. Available from https://doi.org/10.1007/s10608-015-9697-1.

Kallapiran, K., Koo, S., Kirubakaran, R., & Hancock, K. (2015). Review: Effectiveness of mindfulness in improving mental health symptoms of children and adolescents: A meta-analysis. *Child and Adolescent Mental Health, 20*(4), 182–194. Available from https://doi.org/10.1111/camh.12113.

Keng, S., Smoski, M. J., & Robins, C. J. (2011). Effects of mindfulness on psychological health: A review of empirical studies. *Clinical Psychology Review, 31*(6), 1041–1056. Available from https://doi.org/10.1016/j.cpr.2011.04.006.

Keune, P. M., Bostanov, V., Hautzinger, M., & Kotchoubey, B. (2011). Mindfulness-based cognitive therapy (MBCT), cognitive style, and the temporal dynamics of frontal EEG alpha asymmetry in recurrently depressed patients. *Biological Psychology, 88*(2), 243–252. Available from https://doi.org/10.1016/j.biopsycho.2011.08.008.

Kiep, M., Spek, A., & Hoeben, L. (2015). Mindfulness-based therapy in adults with an autism spectrum disorder: Do treatment effects last? *Mindfulness, 6*(3), 637–644. Available from https://doi.org/10.1007/s12671-014-0299-x.

Kinser, P. A., Bourguignon, C., Whaley, D., Hauenstein, E., & Taylor, A. G. (2013). Feasibility, acceptability, and effects of gentle hatha yoga for women with major depression: Findings from a randomized controlled mixed-methods study. *Archives of Psychiatric Nursing, 27*(3), 137–147. Available from https://doi.org/10.1016/j.apnu.2013.01.003.

Kinser, P. A., Elswick, R. K., & Kornstein, S. (2014). Potential long-term effects of a Mind–Body intervention for women with major depressive disorder: Sustained mental health improvements with a pilot yoga intervention. *Archives of Psychiatric Nursing, 28*(6), 377–383. Available from https://doi.org/10.1016/j.apnu.2014.08.014.

Kocovski, N. L., Fleming, J. E., Hawley, L. L., Huta, V., & Antony, M. M. (2013). Mindfulness and acceptance-based group therapy versus traditional cognitive behavioral group therapy for social anxiety disorder: A randomized controlled trial. *Behaviour Research and Therapy, 51*(12), 889–898. Available from https://doi.org/10.1016/j.brat.2013.10.007.

Kocovski, N. L., Fleming, J. E., & Rector, N. A. (2009). Mindfulness and acceptance-based group therapy for social anxiety disorder: An open trial. *Cognitive and Behavioral Practice, 16*(3), 276–289. Available from https://doi.org/10.1016/j.cbpra.2008.12.004.

Krieger, T., Altenstein, D., Baettig, I., Doerig, N., & Holtforth, M. G. (2013). Self-compassion in depression: Associations with depressive symptoms, rumination, and avoidance in depressed outpatients. *Behavior Therapy, 44*(3), 501–513. Available from https://doi.org/10.1016/j.beth.2013.04.004.

Kristeller, J. L., & Wolever, R. Q. (2010). Mindfulness-based eating awareness training for treating binge eating disorder: The conceptual foundation. *Eating Disorders, 19*(1), 49–61. Available from https://doi.org/10.1080/10640266.2011.533605.

Kumar, S., Feldman, G., & Hayes, A. (2008). Changes in mindfulness and emotion regulation in an exposure-based cognitive therapy for depression. *Cognitive Therapy and Research, 32*(6), 734–744. Available from https://doi.org/10.1007/s10608-008-9190-1.

Labelle, L., Campbell, T., & Carlson, L. (2010). Mindfulness-based stress reduction in oncology: Evaluating mindfulness and rumination as mediators of change in depressive symptoms. *Mindfulness, 1*(1), 28–40. Available from https://doi.org/10.1007/s12671-010-0005-6.

Labelle, L. E., Campbell, T. S., Faris, P., & Carlson, L. E. (2015). Mediators of Mindfulness-Based stress reduction (MBSR): Assessing the timing and sequence of change in cancer patients. *Journal of Clinical Psychology, 71*(1), 21–40. Available from https://doi.org/10.1002/jclp.22117.

Leary, M. R., Tate, E. B., Adams, C. E., Batts Allen, A., & Hancock, J. (2007). Self-compassion and reactions to unpleasant self-relevant events: The implications of treating oneself kindly. *Journal of Personality and Social Psychology, 92*(5), 887.

Lee, J. K., & Orsillo, S. M. (2013). Investigating cognitive flexibility as a potential mechanism of mindfulness in generalized anxiety disorder. *Journal of Behavior Therapy and Experimental Psychiatry, 45*(1), 208–216. Available from https://doi.org/10.1016/j.jbtep.2013.10.008.

Liang, H., Chen, C., Li, F., Wu, S., Wang, L., Zheng, X., & Zeng, B. (2018). Mediating effects of peace of mind and rumination on the relationship between gratitude and depression among Chinese university students. *Current Psychology*, 1–8. Available from https://doi.org/10.1007/s12144-018-9847-1.

Linehan, M. M. (1993). Dialectical behavior therapy for treatment of borderline personality disorder: Implications for the treatment of substance abuse. *NIDA Research Monograph, 137*, 201.

Long, E. C., & Christian, M. S. (2015). Mindfulness buffers retaliatory responses to injustice: A regulatory approach. *The Journal of Applied Psychology, 100*(5), 1409–1422. Available from https://doi.org/10.1037/apl0000019.

Luoma, J. B., Hayes, S. C., & Walser, R. D. (2017). *Learning ACT: An acceptance and commitment therapy skills-training manual for therapists*. Oakland, CA: Context Press. Retrieved from <https://ebookcentral.proquest.com/lib/[SITE_ID]/detail.action?docID=4819719>.

Lykins, E. L. B., & Baer, R. A. (2009). Psychological functioning in a sample of long-term practitioners of mindfulness meditation. *Journal of Cognitive Psychotherapy, 23*(3), 226–241. Available from https://doi.org/10.1891/0889-8391.23.3.226.

Manicavasagar, V., Perich, T., & Parker, G. (2012). Cognitive predictors of change in cognitive behaviour therapy and mindfulness-based cognitive therapy for depression. *Behavioural and Cognitive Psychotherapy, 40*(2), 227–232. Available from https://doi.org/10.1017/S1352465811000634.

Mantzios, M., & Wilson, J. C. (2014). Making concrete construals mindful: A novel approach for developing mindfulness and self-compassion to assist weight loss. *Psychology & Health, 29*(4), 422–441. Available from https://doi.org/10.1080/08870446.2013.863883.

Martín-Asuero, A., & García-Banda, G. (2010). The mindfulness-based stress reduction program (MBSR) reduces stress-related psychological distress in healthcare professionals. *The Spanish Journal of Psychology, 13*(2), 897–905.

McIndoo, C. C., File, A. A., Preddy, T., Clark, C. G., & Hopko, D. R. (2016). Mindfulness-based therapy and behavioral activation: A randomized controlled trial with depressed college students. *Behaviour Research and Therapy, 77*, 118–128. Available from https://doi.org/10.1016/j.brat.2015.12.012.

Mendelson, T., Greenberg, M., Dariotis, J., Gould, L., Rhoades, B., & Leaf, P. (2010). Feasibility and preliminary outcomes of a school-based mindfulness intervention for urban youth. *Journal of Abnormal Child Psychology, 38*(7), 985–994. Available from https://doi.org/10.1007/s10802-010-9418-x.

Mennin, D. S., Heimberg, R. G., Turk, C. L., & Fresco, D. M. (2005). Preliminary evidence for an emotion dysregulation model of generalized anxiety disorder. *Behaviour Research and Therapy*, *43*(10), 1281–1310. Available from https://doi.org/10.1016/j.brat.2004.08.008.

Michel, A., Bosch, C., & Rexroth, M. (2014). Mindfulness as a cognitive–emotional segmentation strategy: An intervention promoting work–life balance. *Journal of Occupational and Organizational Psychology*, *87*(4), 733–754.

Morina, N. (2011). Rumination and avoidance as predictors of prolonged grief, depression, and posttraumatic stress in female widowed survivors of war. *Journal of Nervous and Mental Disease*, *199*(12), 921–927. Available from https://doi.org/10.1097/NMD.0b013e3182392aae.

Neff, K. (2003). *Self-compassion: An alternative conceptualization of a Healthy Attitude Toward oneself*.

Neff, K. D., & Germer, C. K. (2013). A pilot study and randomized controlled trial of the mindful self-compassion program. *Journal of Clinical Psychology*, *69*(1), 28–44.

Nitzan-Assayag, Y., Aderka, I. M., & Bernstein, A. (2015). Dispositional mindfulness in trauma recovery: Prospective relations and mediating mechanisms. *Journal of Anxiety Disorders*, *36*, 25–32. Available from https://doi.org/10.1016/j.janxdis.2015.07.008.

Nitzan-Assayag, Y., Yuval, K., Tanay, G., Aderka, I., Vujanovic, A., Litz, B., & Bernstein, A. (2017). Reduced reactivity to and suppression of thoughts mediate the effects of mindfulness training on recovery outcomes following exposure to potentially traumatic stress. *Mindfulness*, *8*(4), 920–932. Available from https://doi.org/10.1007/s12671-016-0666-x.

Öst, L. (2008). Efficacy of the third wave of behavioral therapies: A systematic review and meta-analysis. *Behaviour Research and Therapy*, *46*(3), 296–321. Available from https://doi.org/10.1016/j.brat.2007.12.005.

Peters, J. R., Eisenlohr-Moul, T. A., Upton, B. T., & Baer, R. A. (2013). Nonjudgment as a moderator of the relationship between present-centered awareness and borderline features: Synergistic interactions in mindfulness assessment. *Personality and Individual Differences*, *55*(1), 24–28. Available from https://doi.org/10.1016/j.paid.2013.01.021.

Peters, J. R., Smart, L. M., Eisenlohr-Moul, T. A., Geiger, P. J., Smith, G. T., & Baer, R. A. (2015). Anger rumination as a mediator of the relationship between mindfulness and aggression: The utility of a multidimensional mindfulness model. *Journal of Clinical Psychology*, *71*(9), 871–884. Available from https://doi.org/10.1002/jclp.22189.

Petrocchi, N., & Ottaviani, C. (2016). Mindfulness facets distinctively predict depressive symptoms after two years: The mediating role of rumination. *Personality and Individual Differences*, *93*, 92–96. Available from https://doi.org/10.1016/j.paid.2015.08.017.

Querstret, D., Cropley, M., & Fife-Schaw, C. (2017). Internet-based instructor-led mindfulness for work-related rumination, fatigue, and sleep: Assessing facets of mindfulness as mechanisms of change. A randomized waitlist control trial. *Journal of Occupational Health Psychology*, *22*(2), 153–169. Available from https://doi.org/10.1037/ocp0000028.

Raes, F. (2010). Rumination and worry as mediators of the relationship between self-compassion and depression and anxiety. *Personality and Individual Differences*, *48*(6), 757–761. Available from https://doi.org/10.1016/j.paid.2010.01.023.

Raes, F., & Williams, J. (2010). The relationship between mindfulness and uncontrollability of ruminative thinking. *Mindfulness*, *1*(4), 199–203. Available from https://doi.org/10.1007/s12671-010-0021-6.

Ramel, W., Goldin, P., Carmona, P., & McQuaid, J. (2004). The effects of mindfulness meditation on cognitive processes and affect in patients with past depression. *Cognitive Therapy and Research*, *28*(4), 433–455. Available from https://doi.org/COTR.0000045557.15923.96.

Renna, M. E., Quintero, J. M., Fresco, D. M., & Mennin, D. S. (2017). Emotion regulation therapy: A mechanism-targeted treatment for disorders of distress. *Frontiers in Psychology*, *8*, 98. Available from https://doi.org/10.3389/fpsyg.2017.00098.

Rimes, K. A., & Wingrove, J. (2011). Pilot study of mindfulness-based cognitive therapy for trainee clinical psychologists. *Behavioural and Cognitive Psychotherapy*, *39*(2), 235–241. Available from https://doi.org/10.1017/S1352465810000731.

Robins, C. J., Keng, S., Ekblad, A. G., & Brantley, J. G. (2012). Effects of mindfulness-based stress reduction on emotional experience and expression: A randomized controlled trial. *Journal of Clinical Psychology*, *68*(1), 117–131.

Roemer, L., Lee, J. K., Salters-Pedneault, K., Erisman, S. M., Orsillo, S. M., & Mennin, D. S. (2009). Mindfulness and emotion regulation difficulties in generalized anxiety disorder: Preliminary evidence for independent and overlapping contributions. *Behavior Therapy*, *40*(2), 142–154. Available from https://doi.org/10.1016/j.beth.2008.04.001.

Roemer, L., & Orsillo, S. M. (2002). Expanding our conceptualization of and treatment for generalized anxiety disorder: Integrating mindfulness/acceptance-based approaches with existing cognitive-behavioral models. *Clinical Psychology: Science and Practice*, *9*(1), 54–68.

Roemer, L., & Orsillo, S. M. (2005). *An acceptance-based behavior therapy for generalized anxiety disorder. Acceptance and mindfulness-based approaches to anxiety* (pp. 213–240). Springer.

Roemer, L., & Orsillo, S. M. (2007). An open trial of an acceptance-based behavior therapy for generalized anxiety disorder. *Behavior Therapy*, *38*(1), 72–85.

Roemer, L., Orsillo, S. M., & Salters-Pedneault, K. (2008). Efficacy of an acceptance-based behavior therapy for generalized anxiety disorder. *Journal of Consulting and Clinical Psychology*, *76*(6), 1083–1089. Available from https://doi.org/10.1037/a0012720.

Rosenzweig, D. (2013). The sisters of mindfulness. *Journal of Clinical Psychology*, *69*(8), 793–804. Available from https://doi.org/10.1002/jclp.22015.

Royuela-Colomer, E., & Calvete, E. (2016). Mindfulness facets and depression in adolescents: Rumination as a mediator. *Mindfulness*, *7*(5), 1092–1102. Available from https://doi.org/10.1007/s12671-016-0547-3.

Ruiz, F. J., Flórez, C. L., García-Martín, M. B., Monroy-Cifuentes, A., Barreto-Montero, K., García-Beltrán, D. M., … Gil-Luciano, B. (2018). A multiple-baseline evaluation of a brief acceptance and commitment therapy protocol focused on repetitive negative thinking for moderate emotional disorders. *Journal of Contextual Behavioral Science*, *9*, 1–14. Available from https://doi.org/10.1016/j.jcbs.2018.04.004.

Ruiz, F. J., & Odriozola-González, P. (2016). A longitudinal comparison of metacognitive therapy and acceptance and commitment therapy models of anxiety disorders. *Anales De Psicología*, *33*(1), 7. Available from https://doi.org/10.6018/analesps.32.3.227041.

Sanders, W. A., & Lam, D. H. (2010). Ruminative and mindful self-focused processing modes and their impact on problem solving in dysphoric individuals. *Behaviour Research and Therapy*, *48*(8), 747–753. Available from https://doi.org/10.1016/j.brat.2010.04.007.

Sauer, S. E., & Baer, R. A. (2012). Ruminative and mindful self-focused attention in borderline personality disorder. *Personality Disorders*, *3*(4), 433–441. Available from https://doi.org/10.1037/a0025465.

Sauer-Zavala, S., Walsh, E., Eisenlohr-Moul, T., & Lykins, E. (2013). Comparing mindfulness-based intervention strategies: Differential effects of sitting meditation, body scan, and mindful yoga. *Mindfulness*, *4*(4), 383–388. Available from https://doi.org/10.1007/s12671-012-0139-9.

Segal, Z. V., Williams, J. M. G., & Teasdale, J. D. (2013). *Mindfulness based cognitive therapy for depression* (2nd ed.). New York [u.a.]: Guilford. Retrieved from <http://bvbr.bib-bvb.de:8991/F?func = service&doc_library = BVB01&local_base = BVB01&doc_number = 025707066&sequence = 000002&line_number = 0001&func_code = DB_RECORDS&service_type = MEDIA>.

Selby, E., Fehling, K., Panza, E., & Kranzler, A. (2016). Rumination, mindfulness, and borderline personality disorder symptoms. *Mindfulness*, *7*(1), 228–235. Available from https://doi.org/10.1007/s12671-015-0432-5.

Shao, D., Gao, W., & Cao, F. (2016). Brief psychological intervention in patients with cervical cancer: A randomized controlled trial. *Health Psychology: Official Journal of the Division of Health Psychology, American Psychological Association*, *35*(12), 1383–1391. Available from https://doi.org/10.1037/hea0000407.

Shapiro, S. L., Brown, K. W., & Biegel, G. M. (2007). Teaching self-care to caregivers. *Training and Education in Professional Psychology*, *1*(2), 105–115. Available from https://doi.org/10.1037/1931-3918.1.2.105.

Shapiro, S. L., Brown, K. W., Thoresen, C., & Plante, T. G. (2011). The moderation of mindfulness-based stress reduction effects by trait mindfulness: Results from a randomized controlled trial. *Journal of Clinical Psychology*, *67*(3), 267–277. Available from https://doi.org/10.1002/jclp.20761.

Shapiro, S. L., Carlson, L. E., Astin, J. A., & Freedman, B. (2006). Mechanisms of mindfulness. *Journal of Clinical Psychology*, *62*(3), 373–386. Available from https://doi.org/10.1002/jclp.20237.

Shapiro, S. L., Oman, D., Thoresen, C. E., Plante, T. G., & Flinders, T. (2008). Cultivating mindfulness: Effects on well-being. *Journal of Clinical Psychology*, *64*(7), 840–862.

Sibinga, E., Perry-Parrish, C., Chung, S., Johnson, S., Smith, M., & Ellen, J. (2012). P02.161. A randomized, active-controlled trial of school-based mindfulness instruction for urban middle-school male youth. *BMC Complementary and Alternative Medicine*, *12*(Suppl. 1), P217. Available from https://doi.org/10.1186/1472-6882-12-S1-P217.

Singer, A. R., & Dobson, K. S. (2007). An experimental investigation of the cognitive vulnerability to depression. *Behaviour Research and Therapy*, *45*(3), 563–575. Available from https://doi.org/10.1016/j.brat.2006.05.007.

Smeets, E., Neff, K., Alberts, H., & Peters, M. (2014). Meeting suffering with kindness: Effects of a brief self-compassion intervention for female college students. *Journal of Clinical Psychology*, *70*(9), 794–807. Available from https://doi.org/10.1002/jclp.22076.

Spek, A. A., Van Ham, N. C., & Nyklicek, I. (2013). Mindfulness-based therapy in adults with an autism spectrum disorder: A randomized controlled trial. *Research in Developmental Disabilities*, *34*(1), 246–253.

Spinhoven, P., Drost, J., de Rooij, M., van Hemert, A., & Penninx, B. (2016). Is experiential avoidance a mediating, moderating, independent, overlapping, or proxy risk factor in the onset, relapse and maintenance of depressive disorders? *Cognitive Therapy and Research*, *40*(2), 150–163. Available from https://doi.org/10.1007/s10608-015-9747-8.

Stahl, B., & Goldstein, E. (2010). *A mindfulness-based stress reduction workbook*. New Harbinger Publications.

Thompson, R. W., Arnkoff, D. B., & Glass, C. R. (2011). Conceptualizing mindfulness and acceptance as components of psychological resilience to trauma. *Trauma, Violence, & Abuse*, *12*(4), 220–235. Available from https://doi.org/10.1177/1524838011416375.

Uebelacker, L. A., Tremont, G., Epstein-Lubow, G., Gaudiano, B. A., Gillette, T., Kalibatseva, Z., & Miller, I. W. (2010). Open trial of vinyasa yoga for persistently depressed individuals: Evidence of feasibility and acceptability. *Behavior Modification*, *34*(3), 247–264. Available from https://doi.org/10.1177/0145445510368845.

van Aalderen, J. R., Donders, A. R. T., Peffer, K., & Speckens, A. E. M. (2015). Long-term outcome of mindfulness-based cognitive therapy in recurrently depressed patients with and without a depressive episode at baseline. *Depression and Anxiety*, *32*(8), 563–569. Available from https://doi.org/10.1002/da.22369.

van de Weijer-Bergsma, E., Langenberg, G., Brandsma, R., Oort, F. J., & Bögels, S. M. (2014). The effectiveness of a school-based mindfulness training as a program to prevent stress in elementary school children. *Mindfulness, 5*(3), 238–248. Available from https://doi.org/10.1007/s12671-012-0171-9.

van den Hurk, P. A. M., van Aalderen, J. R., Giommi, F., Donders., Rogier, A. R. T., Barendregt, H. P., & Speckens, A. E. M. (2012). An investigation of the role of attention in mindfulness-based cognitive therapy for recurrently depressed patients. *Journal of Experimental Psychopathology, 3*(1). Available from https://doi.org/10.5127/jep.024811, jep. 024811.

van der Velden, A. M., Kuyken, W., Wattar, U., Crane, C., Pallesen, K. J., Dahlgaard, J., ... Piet, J. (2015). A systematic review of mechanisms of change in mindfulness-based cognitive therapy in the treatment of recurrent major depressive disorder. *Clinical Psychology Review, 37*, 26–39. Available from https://doi.org/10.1016/j.cpr.2015.02.001.

van Vugt, M. K., Hitchcock, P., Shahar, B., & Britton, W. (2012). The effects of mindfulness-based cognitive therapy on affective memory recall dynamics in depression: A mechanistic model of rumination. *Frontiers in Human Neuroscience, 6*, 257. Available from https://doi.org/10.3389/fnhum.2012.00257.

Vettese, L. C., Toneatto, T., Stea, J. N., Nguyen, L., & Wang, J. J. (2009). Do mindfulness meditation participants do their homework? and does it make a difference? A review of the empirical evidence. *Journal of Cognitive Psychotherapy, 23*(3), 198–225. Available from https://doi.org/10.1891/0889-8391.23.3.198.

Villa, C. D., & Hilt, L. M. (2014). Brief instruction in mindfulness and relaxation reduce rumination differently for men and women. *International Journal of Cognitive Therapy, 7* (4), 320–333.

Virgili, M. (2015). Mindfulness-based interventions reduce psychological distress in working adults: A meta-analysis of intervention studies. *Mindfulness, 6*(2), 326–337. Available from https://doi.org/10.1007/s12671-013-0264-0.

Voci, A., Veneziani, C. A., & Fuochi, G. (2018). Relating mindfulness, heartfulness, and psychological well-being: The role of self-compassion and gratitude. *Mindfulness*. Available from https://doi.org/10.1007/s12671-018-0978-0.

Vøllestad, J., Nielsen, M. B., & Nielsen, G. H. (2012). Mindfulness- and acceptance-based interventions for anxiety disorders: A systematic review and meta-analysis. *The British Journal of Clinical Psychology, 51*(3), 239. Retrieved from <https://www.ncbi.nlm.nih.gov/pubmed/22803933>.

Vøllestad, J., Sivertsen, B., & Nielsen, G. H. (2011). Mindfulness-based stress reduction for patients with anxiety disorders: Evaluation in a randomized controlled trial. *Behaviour Research and Therapy, 49*(4), 281–288. Available from https://doi.org/10.1016/j.brat.2011.01.007.

Wadsworth, L. P., Forgeard, M., Hsu, K. J., Kertz, S., Treadway, M., & Björgvinsson, T. (2018). Examining the role of repetitive negative thinking in relations between positive and negative aspects of self-compassion and symptom improvement during intensive treatment. *Cognitive Therapy and Research, 42*(3), 236–249. Available from https://doi.org/10.1007/s10608-017-9887-0.

Watkins, E. R. (2008). Constructive and unconstructive repetitive thought. *Psychological Bulletin, 134*(2), 163–206. Available from https://doi.org/10.1037/0033-2909.134.2.163.

Watkins, E. R. (2016). *Rumination-focused cognitive-behavioral therapy for depression*. New York: Guilford Publications Inc. M.U.A. Retrieved from <https://ebookcentral.proquest.com/lib/[SITE_ID]/detail.action?docID=4338852>.

White, E. J., Kraines, M. A., Tucker, R. P., Wingate, L. R., Wells, T. T., & Grant, D. M. (2017). Rumination's effect on suicide ideation through grit and gratitude: A path analysis study. *Psychiatry Research, 251*, 97–102. Available from https://doi.org/10.1016/j.psychres.2017.01.086.

Wolkin, J. R. (2015). Cultivating multiple aspects of attention through mindfulness meditation accounts for psychological well-being through decreased rumination. *Psychology Research and Behavior Management, 8,* 171–180. Available from https://doi.org/10.2147/PRBM.S31458.

Wong, M. Y., Ree, M. J., & Lee, C. W. (2016). Enhancing CBT for chronic insomnia: A randomised clinical trial of additive components of mindfulness or cognitive therapy. *Clinical Psychology & Psychotherapy, 23*(5), 377–385.

Yovel, I., Mor, N., & Shakarov, H. (2014). Examination of the core cognitive components of cognitive behavioral therapy and acceptance and commitment therapy: An analogue investigation. *Behavior Therapy, 45*(4), 482–494. Available from https://doi.org/10.1016/j.beth.2014.02.007.

Zenner, C., Herrnleben-Kurz, S., & Walach, H. (2014). Mindfulness-based interventions in schools—A systematic review and meta-analysis. *Frontiers in Psychology, 5*. Available from https://doi.org/10.3389/fpsyg.2014.00603.

Zoogman, S., Goldberg, S. B., Hoyt, W. T., & Miller, L. (2015). Mindfulness interventions with youth: A meta-analysis. *Mindfulness, 6*(2), 290–302. Available from https://doi.org/10.1007/s12671-013-0260-4.

CHAPTER

12

Metacognitive therapy for rumination

Overview

Adrian Wells and colleagues have spent over 20 years developing a model of and treatment for rumination and worry that emphasize the importance of metacognitive beliefs about repetitive thinking. This work started in the worry and generalized anxiety disorder (GAD) literature. However, metacognitive theory and therapy have been successfully applied to major depression, obsessive–compulsive disorder (OCD), posttraumatic stress disorder (PTSD), social anxiety, psychosis, and substance use. In this chapter, I first review the general metacognitive model and therapy. I then present disorder-specific models and empirical support for the efficacy of this treatment.

Metacognition refers to thinking about and controlling cognitive processes. Less formally, it involves being aware of, reflecting on, and trying to direct one's own thinking. Metacognition determines what people pay attention to, how they interpret experiences, and the strategies they use to regulate their mental processes. The concept originated in educational and developmental psychology (e.g., Flavell, 1979), where people recognized that good students think not just about specific content but also about the contexts and strategies that facilitate their own learning. More recently, psychologists such as Adrian Wells suggest that metacognition may serve as the basis for most or all psychological dysfunction. Specifically, Wells (2009) argues that people become trapped in sustained emotional suffering (e.g., depression, anxiety) when they have metacognitions that contribute to a particularly unhelpful pattern of responding to inner experiences. In other words, psychological

Rumination and Related Constructs
DOI: https://doi.org/10.1016/B978-0-12-812545-8.00012-7

© 2020 Elsevier Inc. All rights reserved.

disorders are caused not by *what* people think but by *how* they respond to their thoughts and emotions.

Wells (2009) differentiates between three forms of metacognition: knowledge, experiences, and strategies. Metacognitive *knowledge* encompasses beliefs about thoughts and how attention and memory function. It also contains information about what kinds of cognitive strategies can be used to achieve certain tasks. As with all declarative information, metacognitive knowledge is modified by experiences and specifically by monitoring one's cognition. Thus, if people notice that they have difficulty disengaging from repetitive thoughts, they may develop negative and incorrect metacognitive beliefs about their ability to control their thoughts. Metacognitive *experiences* include feelings about and appraisals of current cognitive processing. For instance, people may feel low confidence about their use of cognitive coping strategies, which may in turn influence their perceived sense of threat. Metacognitive *strategies* include techniques to regulate and control cognition. People may attempt to intensify, suppress, or change cognitive activities.

Metacognitive theory and therapy

Informed by these concepts, Wells developed the Self-Regulatory Executive Function (S-REF) model of emotional disorders (Wells, 2000; Wells & Matthews, 1996). The S-REF model identifies several metacognitive strategies that are maladaptive because they prolong emotional disturbance: (1) perseverative thinking in the form of rumination or worry; (2) excessive threat monitoring, or attention to external or internal threats (e.g., environmental stressors, unpleasant thoughts or emotions, physiological arousal); and (3) unhelpful attempts to control one's experience (e.g., avoidance, suppression). These strategies—all of which are attempts to regulate and control cognitive processes—often interact. Accordingly, Wells refers to them collectively as the *cognitive–attentional syndrome* (CAS), which is conceptualized as a maladaptive style of self-regulation. Because these metacognitive strategies increase the accessibility of negative information, they maintain and exacerbate negative emotions, thoughts, and perceived threat. Furthermore, they use up attentional resources, effectively decreasing the likelihood of engaging other metacognitive strategies or incorporating other information from the environment. Wells argued that emotional disorders are caused by chronic activation of the CAS. This should not be novel, as we have amply covered the negative outcomes of repetitive thinking.

The real contribution of this model concerns the role of metacognitive knowledge in initiating and maintaining the CAS. Specifically, the S-REF model differentiates between positive and negative metacognitive beliefs (see Fig. 12.1). People use the maladaptive metacognitive

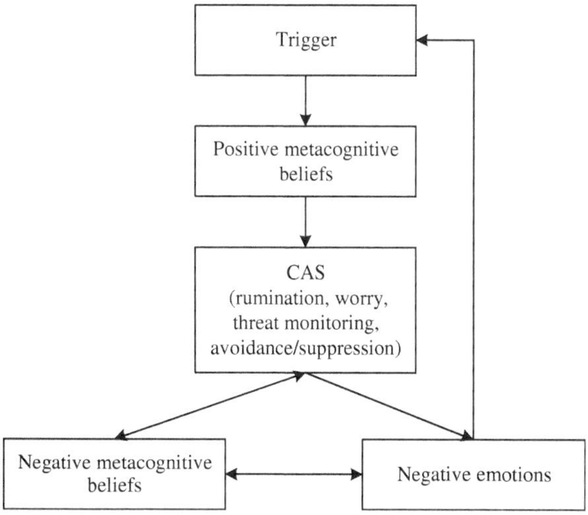

FIGURE 12.1 The general metacognitive model. Source: *Adapted from Wells, A. (2009).* Metacognitive therapy for anxiety and depression. *New York [u.a.]: Guilford Press. Retrieved from <http://bvbr.bib-bvb.de:8991/F?func = service&doc_library = BVB01&local_base = BVB01&doc_number = 017135158&sequence = 000002&line_number = 0001&func_code = DB_RECORDS&service_type = MEDIA>.*

strategies in the CAS because they have *positive* metacognitive beliefs about these behaviors. For instance, individuals believe that rumination will help them cope with difficulties, or that worrying will help them be mentally prepared, or that paying attention to signs of threat will keep them safe. Emotionally disordered or vulnerable individuals are more likely to have these kinds of positive metacognitive beliefs, which in turn drive the use of CAS. Unfortunately, the negative consequences associated with perseverative thinking, threat monitoring, and avoidance/suppression may in turn lead to the development of *negative* metacognitive beliefs about thoughts. Common negative beliefs concern the danger and uncontrollability of perseverative thought (e.g., "These thoughts will make me lose my mind." and "I cannot control my thoughts.") and the need to control thoughts (e.g., "Not being able to control my thoughts is a sign of weakness."). In addition to increasing negative affect, these negative beliefs maintain the use of CAS because people do not believe that they can effectively control their cognitive process.

In summary, metacognitive theory argues that it is people's responses (i.e., metacognitive strategies such as the CAS) to negative emotions and thoughts, rather than the negative emotions and thoughts themselves, that contribute to psychological dysfunction. Furthermore, use of these unhelpful metacognitive strategies is driven by metacognitive knowledge (i.e., positive and negative beliefs about rumination or worry). Of course, there are other types of metacognitive beliefs that do not explicitly involve the benefits and dangers of repetitive thinking. For instance, people have beliefs about the benefits and dangers of other types of coping strategies (e.g., reappraisal, avoidance), as well as their ability to engage in effective coping (e.g., efficacy beliefs). The larger point of the S-REF model is that these beliefs constitute a knowledge base that guides cognition and behaviors in response to perceived discrepancies. Emotionally disordered individuals are more likely to have a knowledge base that predisposes them to use maladaptive cognitive styles like the CAS, which in turn maintains psychological dysfunction.

Based on this theory, metacognitive therapy (MCT) aims to change how patients respond to their thoughts and emotions, rather than the content of their thoughts and emotions (Wells, 2009). Specifically, MCT targets maladaptive metacognitive knowledge (i.e., positive and negative beliefs) and strategies (i.e., the CAS). Treatment generally consists of 8–12 weekly 1-hour sessions and begins with a detailed assessment. In addition to a typical diagnostic assessment, therapists gather information about patients' metacognitive beliefs and the extent that they use the CAS. They then create a metacognitive formulation that they share with and explain to patients. Specifically, therapists help patients understand the unhelpful nature of CAS strategies and the links between metacognitive beliefs and their use of the CAS.

Specific metacognitive formulations exist for various disorders. However, the basic concept is a reformulated version of the standard A–B–C formulation of cognitive therapy. The original cognitive formulation proposes that an activating event (A) leads to activation of a core belief or schema (B), which in turn leads to emotional and behavioral consequences (C). By contrast, a metacognitive formulation proposes than an internal trigger (A) activates metacognitions (M), including both knowledge and strategies, which in turn lead to emotional consequences (C). To borrow an example from Wells (2009), imagine a depressed patient who feels alone (A), continuously thinks that things will not change (B), and subsequently feels sad and hopeless (C). A MCT formulation would replace the negative core belief (B) with metacognitive (M) beliefs such as "I need to ruminate to change things" or "If I experience the emotion, it will motivate me," as well as common CAS strategies of rumination and focusing on sad emotion.

MCT borrows some techniques from traditional CBT and uses them in the service of decreasing unhelpful metacognitive beliefs. For instance, standard cognitive restructuring questions such as "What is the evidence for and against that belief?", "Would this evidence convince someone else?", and "What is the effect of believing this?" are applied to positive or negative metacognitive beliefs about repetitive thinking. Similarly, therapists may use exposure techniques with the goal of modifying metacognitive beliefs and strengthening more adaptive beliefs and processing. For instance, a patient with GAD might be asked to read a news story about crime and then intentionally engage in intense worry as an experiential test of the belief that worry is harmful. Similarly, a patient with OCD might be encouraged to repeat a feared obsessional thought about sex while driving past a school in order to disconfirm the belief "if I have these thoughts, then I will act on them." In neither of these cases is the goal of exposure to achieve habituation. Instead, MCT uses exposure to modify metacognitive beliefs—typically negative beliefs about potential danger and uncontrollability of repetitive thinking.

In addition to using traditional CBT techniques to target positive and negative metacognitive beliefs, MCT incorporates two techniques aimed at decreasing use of the CAS, particularly repetitive thinking. First, the *attentional training technique* (ATT) aims to interrupt the CAS and increase metacognitive flexibility. If chronic repetitive thinking reflects cognitive rigidity and a lack of attentional control, then increasing control of attention should help patients prevent or halt their use of this maladaptive strategy. Doing so should also weaken negative metacognitive beliefs about the uncontrollability of repetitive thinking. ATT is a 12-minute procedure that involves listening to sounds in particular ways. The procedure is divided into three sections, each of which targets a specific type of attention. (1) The *selective attention* component instructs patients to pay intense attention to specific individual sounds among an array of competing sounds. (2) The *rapid attention switching* component asks patients to shift attention between various sounds with increasing speed (e.g., every 10 or 5 seconds). (3) The *divided attention* component instructs patients to process multiple sounds at the same time. By "sound," I do not mean beeps. Instead, therapists use or create sounds in the environment. For example, therapists might identify three sounds in the therapy room (e.g., therapist's voice, tapping of a pen on the desk, dripping of a faucet), two sounds from outside the therapy room but near-by (e.g., people walking inside the building), and another two sounds from far away (e.g., car driving by). Therapists follow a script to guide patients through the three components in a single seamless exercise. After patients learn how to do ATT in a therapy setting, they are instructed to practice at home on a daily basis. Wells makes it clear that ATT is not intended to distract patients from unpleasant thoughts or feelings. Instead, patients are instructed to let other thoughts and feelings remain while staying focused on the procedure. Although Wells did not intend for ATT to function as a stand-alone treatment, empirical evidence suggests that it is an effective treatment for several disorders (for a review, see Fergus & Bardeen, 2016).

Another important component of MCT is developing *detached mindfulness* (DM), or an awareness of thoughts as separate from one's self. With DM, a negative thought is no longer seen as having meaning for the self, so it becomes unnecessary to engage in self-regulation strategies in response to the thought. Thus, DM should help prevent or interrupt repetitive thinking. Several techniques are used to promote DM. Therapists may ask questions that promote metacognitive awareness during exposures or other experiential exercises, such as "Can you see your thought and what is going on around you in the situation at the same time?" or "Are you the thought or the person observing the thought?" Therapists also share metaphors that convey the experience of DM, such as experiencing thoughts as one would experience clouds passing by in the sky. There is no point in trying to control or stop the clouds. Instead, the only thing to do is to watch them pass by and know that they will leave in their own time. Therapists also use experiential exercises to help patients practice watching thoughts from a detached perspective. In the free association task, patients sit quietly and watch the flow of thoughts or memories that are triggered by single words the therapist says (e.g., apple, birthday, summertime). Patients are instructed to passively watch how their minds respond without trying to influence anything. In the tiger task, patients are asked to close their eyes and form an image of a tiger. Again, they simply watch how the image changes and moves over time, without doing anything to change the image. In the suppression–countersuppression task, patients are asked to spend 3 minutes trying not to think of a blue giraffe, and then 3 minutes letting their mind roam freely and noticing all thoughts—even of a blue giraffe—passively. This exercise helps patients understand that suppression makes thoughts more powerful and keeps them present, whereas DM allows thoughts to come and go on their own.

Many of the concepts and techniques in MCT are similar to those in mindfulness-based therapies (see Chapter 11: Mindfulness-based therapies). For instance, DM seems much like the concept of cognitive diffusion that is so central to ACT. ATT develops dual abilities to sustain attention and have an open awareness of multiple environmental stimuli, much like concentrative versus mindfulness meditations. In addition, like in MBCT, Wells (2009) identifies two modes, or ways, of experiencing thoughts. By default, people typically experience their thoughts in an *object* mode, as if their thoughts are accurate reflections of reality. With DM practice, however, people can come to dwell in a *metacognitive* mode, in which they consciously observe their thoughts as mental constructions rather than truths about the self or the world. Despite these similarities, Wells (2009) argues that MCT is not a mindfulness treatment. He notes that MCT does not emphasize present-focused awareness or acceptance; nor does it utilize meditation or body-focused

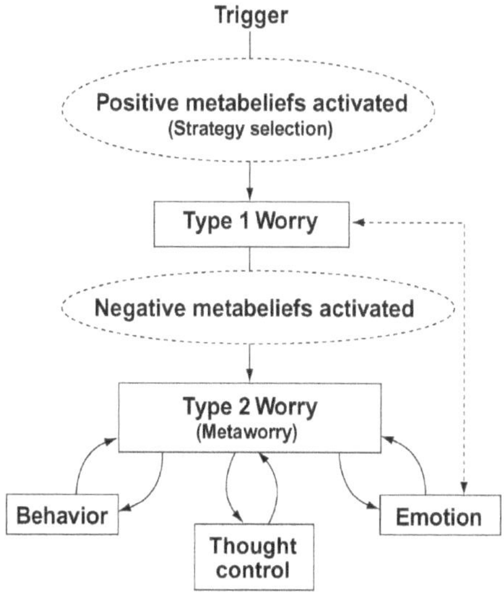

FIGURE 12.2 The metacognitive model of GAD. *GAD*, Generalized anxiety disorder. Source: *From Wells, A. (1997). Cognitive therapy of anxiety disorders: A practice manual and conceptual guide. John Wiley & Sons Inc. ©1997 by John Wiley & Sons Limited. Reprinted by permission.*

exercises. Instead, MCT explicitly targets the content of positive and negative metacognitive beliefs, using standard cognitive therapy techniques. Thus, MCT seems like a hybrid of CBT and mindfulness-based approaches that emphasizes the concept of metacognition.

In the remainder of this chapter, I present specific metacognitive models and therapies—along with supporting empirical evidence—for patients with GAD, major depression, PTSD, social anxiety, OCD, schizophrenia, and substance use disorder.

Generalized anxiety disorder

The metacognitive model of GAD (see Fig. 12.2) asserts that for most people, negative thoughts (e.g., "What if my spouse leaves me?") occur from time to time (Wells, 1999, 2010). These kinds of negative thoughts may trigger positive metacognitive beliefs about the potential of worry to anticipate, avoid, or solve problems. Strong beliefs in the benefits of worry can lead to an overreliance on or inflexibility in the use of worry as a coping strategy. Worry about oneself or external situations is called *Type 1 worry*. By itself, type 1 worry can increase anxiety but is not sufficient to cause GAD. In fact, type 1 worry typically ends when people sense that they will be able to cope with the perceived threat. The pathological worry that is characteristic of GAD emerges when negative metacognitive beliefs are activated. The most common negative beliefs center on the danger and uncontrollability of worry. These negative beliefs in turn lead to worry specifically about worry—a metacognitive experience called *Type 2 worry* (or *metaworry*). For instance, if people believe that worry will lead to heart problems, they are likely to worry about future worrying. Metaworry commonly leads to an escalation of anxiety, because people now feel threatened by their own cognitive coping process. Wells identified two other factors that maintain the problem of negative metacognitive beliefs and metaworry. First, individuals may try to control their worry by suppressing thoughts that trigger or indicate the beginning of worry. Of course, thought suppression contributes to even more repetitive, intrusive thinking. This process serves to maintain negative beliefs about the uncontrollability of worry. Second, coping behaviors such as reassurance seeking, using alcohol, or avoiding situations that trigger worry prevent people from discovering that worry is harmless and from learning that they have internal control of their thought process.

Empirical research supports much of the metacognitive model of GAD.[1] As reviewed in a previous chapter (see Chapter 8, Beliefs, traits, and motivations underlying rumination), people who endorse higher positive beliefs about worry engage in more worry, although they are not necessarily more likely to be diagnosed with GAD (Cartwright-

1 Several questionnaires assess constructs detailed in the metacognitive model for GAD. The Meta-Cognitions Questionnaire (Cartwright-Hatton & Wells, 1997) assesses positive and negative metacognitive beliefs. The original 65-item and revised 30-item (Wells & Cartwright-Hatton, 2004) versions of this measure consists of five subscales: (a) positive beliefs about worry, such as beliefs that worry solves problems and avoids unpleasant situations (e.g., "worrying helps me cope"); (b) negative beliefs about the uncontrollability and danger of worry (e.g., "when I start worrying I cannot stop," "I could make myself sick with worrying"); (c) cognitive confidence about one's attention and memory (e.g., "my memory can mislead me at times"); (d) beliefs about the need to control thoughts, including superstitious beliefs of personal responsibility and punishment for not controlling thoughts (e.g., "not being able to control my thoughts is a sign of weakness," "If a bad thing happens which I have not worried about, I feel responsible"); and (e) cognitive self-consciousness, or the tendency to monitor and focus on one's thinking process (e.g., "I pay close attention to the way my mind works"). The 22-item Anxious Thoughts Inventory (Wells, 1994) assesses social and health (i.e., type 1) worry on separate subscales and metaworry (i.e., type 2) worry on a third subscale. However, the metaworry subscale of this measure focuses on appraisals of the uncontrollability of worry, which overlap with a diagnostic criterion for GAD in the DSM-IV. Therefore, Wells (Wells, 2005) created the Meta-Worry Questionnaire, a 7-item measure that assess degree of belief in and frequency of negative appraisals of the dangerousness of worry.

Hatton & Wells, 1997; Davis & Valentiner, 2000; Esbjørn et al., 2015; Laugesen, Dugas, & Bukowski, 2003; Ruscio & Borkovec, 2004; Wells & Carter, 2001). By contrast, people who endorse more negative metacognitive beliefs are more likely to have GAD. Negative beliefs about the dangerousness of worry also predict greater frequency of Type 2 worry, which in turn predicts the presence of GAD (Wells, 2005). Moreover, when both positive and negative beliefs are included in models, only negative metacognitive beliefs uniquely predict anxiety symptoms (Cartwright-Hatton & Wells, 1997; Davis & Valentiner, 2000; Esbjørn et al., 2015; Thielsch, Andor, & Ehring, 2015). Thus, as the model proposes, positive beliefs about worry predict greater worry, but only negative beliefs robustly predict clinical symptoms, at least in part via greater Type 2 worry. In a rare experiment, GAD patients worried for 5 minutes and then were instructed to relax, during which time they received false feedback about either an increase or decrease in their physiological arousal (Andor, Gerlach, & Rist, 2008). The increased arousal feedback led to more negative metacognitive beliefs as well as greater worrying. Thus, a perceived negative outcome following worrying contributed to maintained worry and a belief about the dangers of worrying.

MCT for GAD starts by introducing patients to the metacognitive model of GAD and creating an individualized conceptualization for each patient. The major steps of therapy are to teach patients how to achieve a metacognitive mode, challenge negative beliefs about the danger and uncontrollability of worry, challenge positive beliefs about the benefits of worry, and reinforce new plans for processing worry. In addition to the DM techniques described above to promote a metacognitive mode, therapists encourage patients to practice postponing worry to a discrete worry period every day. This experiential exercise should enhance DM and begin to challenge patients' beliefs that worry is uncontrollable. Cognitive restructuring challenges negative beliefs about worry, such as when therapists ask "How long have you been worrying? Have you come to harm yet?" or "Do you know other people who worry? Have they suffered serious consequences from the worry?" These cognitive techniques are paired with behavioral experiments that allow patients to test their negative beliefs. For instance, patients might be asked to worry while jogging, or therapists might record a patient's heart rate before and after worrying, in order to test the belief that worry will damage the body.

After negative beliefs about worry have been effectively challenged, therapists target positive beliefs about worry, in order to allow patients more flexibility in responding to negative internal events. Therapists help clients question the evidence supporting their positive beliefs, like asking "Do you have any evidence that worry is helpful?", "Have you ever done something and not been able to worry? What was the outcome?", or "Do people who worry have fewer problems than people who don't worry?" In the worry-mismatch strategy, patients make a detailed description of a specific recent worry episode and then compare it with a detailed description of the event as it happened. Similarly, in worry modulation experiments, patients are asked to increase or decrease their worrying in a particular setting or about a particular event and then observe whether there was a difference in the outcome. The goal of these exercises is to illustrate how little worry is in fact tied to better outcomes. Finally, therapy focuses on helping patients create new metacognitive plans—most of which involve applying DM—for dealing with negative thoughts or worry in the future.

A few studies have tested the efficacy of MCT for GAD (for a review, see Wells, 2010). An initial uncontrolled study with 10 patients found significant decreases in type 1 and 2 worry, anxiety, and depressive symptoms, and these gains were maintained at a 12-month follow-up (Wells & King, 2006). A randomized trial showed that MCT was superior to applied relaxation in decreasing anxiety, worry, and both positive and negative metacognitive beliefs (Wells et al., 2010). Finally, a research team randomly assigned GAD patients to MCT, intolerance of uncertainty treatment, or a wait-list control (van der Heiden, Muris, & van der Molen, 2012). Both treatments reduced anxiety, worry, and both positive and negative metacognitive beliefs, compared to the control group. However, MCT was superior to intolerance of uncertainty treatment in reducing negative beliefs and pathological worry.

Depression

The metacognitive model for depression focuses on how metacognitive beliefs and rumination maintain and intensify depressive episodes. In this model, the initiating trigger is usually a negative thought about the self, world, or the future, or a depressive symptom like feeling sad, fatigued, or unmotivated. These triggers activate positive metacognitive beliefs about the benefit of engaging in rumination about the meaning and causes of the trigger. Positive beliefs in turn activate the CAS, which in depression largely involves rumination. However, other aspects of the CAS in depression may include worrying about a recurrence of depressive symptoms, threat monitoring (e.g., focusing on mood changes and other symptoms of depression), and behavioral avoidance of activities and social contact. In addition to exacerbating depressive symptoms, these metacognitive strategies and their effects on symptoms activate and reinforce negative metacognitive beliefs that rumination and depressive symptoms are uncontrollable and dangerous. These beliefs in turn contribute to continued rumination and depressive symptoms because people believe that they are no longer in control of their mind or mood.

Empirical evidence supports many aspects of this model.[2] As reviewed earlier (see Chapter 8, Beliefs, traits, and motivations underlying rumination), people who hold more positive metacognitive beliefs about rumination engage in more depressive rumination (Watkins & Baracaia, 2001; Watkins & Moulds, 2005; Wells & Papageorgiou, 2001). However, the association between positive beliefs and depressive symptoms is not robust. By contrast, negative beliefs about rumination are associated with higher levels of both rumination and depressive symptoms in depressed and nondepressed individuals (Papageorgiou & Wells, 2003; Papageorgiou & Wells, 2009; Wells & Papageorgiou, 2001; Yilmaz, Gençöz, & Wells, 2015). The metacognitive model suggests that positive beliefs may only be indirectly associated with depression, via activation of rumination. In support of this pathway, depressive rumination mediates the association between positive beliefs and depressive symptoms (Wells & Papageorgiou, 2001). The model also hypothesizes that rumination activates negative beliefs, which in turn increase depression. In support of this pathway, the association between rumination and depressive symptoms is mediated by negative metacognitive beliefs (Papageorgiou & Wells, 2003; Roelofs et al., 2007). Longitudinal studies are needed to test the temporal associations between these constructs.

MCT for depression starts with ATT in order to increase patients' metaawareness and promote control over rumination. At the same time, patients are introduced to DM as a more adaptive way to respond to triggers. The structured ATT and DM exercises also serve to decrease depressed patients' inertia. Once patients have increased their cognitive flexibility and developed some ability to enter a metacognitive mode,

2 Several questionnaires assess metacognitive beliefs about rumination. The 9-item Positive Beliefs about Rumination Scale (Papageorgiou & Wells, 2001) assesses positive metacognitive beliefs about the benefits and advantages of rumination. This scale was later adapted to remove mention of depressive symptoms, in order to prevent potential criterion contamination (Watkins & Moulds, 2005). The Negative Beliefs about Rumination Scale (Luminet, 2004) separates negative beliefs into two subscales: metacognitive beliefs about the uncontrollability and danger of rumination (8 items), and metacognitive beliefs about the interpersonal and social consequences of rumination (5 items).The 15-item Beliefs About Rumination and Acceptance Towards Negative Experiences Questionnaire (Singer & Dobson, 2007) also measures positive and negative beliefs about rumination. Its three subscales assess: 1) *positive attitude*, or the belief that rumination is a useful coping strategy, 2) *negative attitude*, or the belief that rumination is harmful and uncontrollable, resulting in attempts to voluntarily control thinking, and 3) *acceptance*, or an attitude of acceptance and openness towards negative experiences.

both of which should decrease their use of rumination, therapy targets negative metacognitive beliefs about the uncontrollability of rumination and the dangerousness of depressive symptoms. Therapists question the evidence for and against these beliefs and may ask patients to engage in behavioral experiments (e.g., ruminate intensely and then stop). Therapy next targets positive metacognitive beliefs about the benefits of rumination, again by questioning the evidence, evaluating advantages and disadvantages of rumination, and behavioral experiments to test the usefulness of rumination. Activity scheduling and planning pleasant events may also be used to decrease behavioral avoidance. Finally, therapists help patients consolidate and strengthen new metacognitive plans for responding to depressive internal triggers in the future. These plans involve identifying typical triggers of ruminative thinking, as well as common metacognitive beliefs and related thinking strategies, behaviors, and attentional focus.

Research supports the effectiveness of MCT for depression. Two small-scale nonrandomized trials found that MCT led to large decreases in depressive and anxiety symptoms in patients with depression and treatment-resistant depression (Wells et al., 2009; Wells et al., 2012). These gains were maintained at 6- and 12-month follow-ups. Treatment also led to decreases in depressive rumination and both positive and negative metacognitive beliefs about rumination. A third open trial treated patients with major depression and a comorbid anxiety disorder or avoidant personality disorder (Hjemdal et al., 2016). As expected, treatment contributed to decreases in depressive and anxiety symptoms, depressive rumination, worry, and metacognitive beliefs posttreatment and at a 6-month follow-up. Moreover, none of the 10 patients met criteria for major depression after MCT, and 7 of the 10 patients also did not meet criteria for their comorbid diagnosis. Group MCT with depressed patients also led to meaningful decreases in depressive and anxiety symptoms, depressive rumination, and both positive and negative beliefs about rumination (Dammen, Papageorgiou, & Wells, 2014). These results were replicated in a small sample of patients with treatment-resistant depression (Papageorgiou & Wells, 2015).

In addition, ATT has been empirically supported as a stand-alone treatment for depression. In a case series study, four patients with recurrent major depression received 5–8 sessions of ATT (Papageorgiou & Wells, 2000). Each patient showed decreases in both depressive and anxiety symptoms immediately after treatment, and none of the patients met criteria for major depression at a 12-month follow-up. In addition, ATT led to decreases in depressive rumination, negative metacognitive beliefs, and self-monitoring. Attention training was also incorporated into a cognitive-control training package for depressed individuals (Siegle, Ghinassi, & Thase, 2007). In a randomized control trial, six sessions of cognitive-control training added to treatment as usual led to greater decreases in depressive rumination and use of intensive outpatient services in the following year, compared to treatment as usual (Mandell, Siegle, Shutt, Feldmiller, & Thase, 2014). In a community sample of non–treatment-seeking depressed adults, just three sessions of cognitive-control training led to significant decreases in depressive symptoms (Calkins, McMorran, Siegle, & Otto, 2015).

Posttraumatic stress disorder

The metacognitive model of PTSD starts with the assumption that most individuals have a built-in *reflexive adaptation process* that helps them adapt and recover from the psychological effects of trauma. The goal of this process is to develop new plans for dealing with future traumatic incidents. Posttraumatic symptoms such as intrusive thoughts and a heightened startle reflex are part of this natural recovery process. For instance, intrusive flashbacks and attention to perceived dangers prompt people to run mental simulations of how they might deal with a future trauma. These symptoms, although unpleasant, help individuals develop a future plan, which in turn decreases their sense of perceived danger. Once this goal is accomplished, posttraumatic symptoms should dissipate on their own.

Difficulties arise, however, when individuals interpret their symptoms as threats and use unhelpful coping strategies—such as the CAS—in response to their posttraumatic stress symptoms. For instance, repetitive thinking about past traumas and future potential dangers serves to maintain a sense of threat. The verbal quality of repetitive thinking may also block the imaginal processes that would help individuals feel better prepared and subsequently less anxious. In other words, inflexible use of CAS strategies prevents adaptive emotional processing of trauma and maintains the perception of threat, which leads to a persistence of posttraumatic symptoms. This formulation proposes that individuals' positive metacognitive beliefs determine whether they will engage in maladaptive responses (i.e., CAS) to trauma symptoms. Beliefs about the benefits of worry and rumination for avoiding future threats and understanding why trauma occurred, for instance, will lead to more repetitive thinking (Wells & Sembi, 2004; Wells et al., 2008). CAS strategies maintain and exacerbate symptoms, which in turn activate and reinforce negative metacognitive beliefs about the danger and uncontrollability of posttraumatic symptoms.

Evidence linking metacognitive beliefs and strategies with PTSD symptoms is scarce. In college students, both positive and negative beliefs about worry were associated with greater PTSD symptoms in response to a recent significant stressor (Roussis & Wells, 2006). In a sample of student nurses who had experienced a distressing event during training, negative—but not positive—metacognitive beliefs were related to more severe PTSD symptoms (Bennett & Wells, 2010). Moreover, rumination mediated the associations between both positive and negative beliefs and PTSD symptoms. Much more research is needed to test the metacognitive model of PTSD.

Unlike traditional CBT, MCT for PTSD does not involve imaginal exposure to trauma. Instead, the therapy focuses on DM exercises, postponement of repetitive thinking, challenging metacognitive beliefs, and attention training. Therapists first teach patients to apply DM and worry/rumination postponement to any intrusive thoughts about the trauma. Patients are eventually encouraged to apply these responses to other symptoms (e.g., the after-effects of nightmares) and all types of negative thoughts. As in all forms of MCT, therapists decrease metacognitive beliefs via cognitive restructuring and behavioral experiments. Finally, attentional training for PTSD involves both traditional ATT to interrupt repetitive thinking and increase metacognitive flexibility and a procedure called *situational attentional refocusing*. The purpose of this refocusing training is to decrease patients' hypervigilance for threat, as excessive threat monitoring is conceptualized as another form of perseverative behavior. Therapists first challenge patients' positive beliefs about threat monitoring, through questions such as "Has focusing on threats ever actually stopped something bad from happening?" and "Does attention to threat give you an accurate or inflated impression or danger?" Patients are then asked to notice instances of threat monitoring and to shift their attention to neutral stimuli in the environment. Finally, therapists direct patients to focus on safety signals in the environment. For instance, a patient who typically scans for speeding cars when approaching an intersection would be encouraged to instead look for cars that are slowing down or stopped and for gaps in traffic.

The effectiveness of MCT for PTSD has been demonstrated in several studies. For instance, patients with PTSD showed significant decreases in PTSD symptoms, anxiety, and depressive symptoms immediately following treatment and at 3- and 6-month follow-ups (Wells & Sembi, 2004; Wells et al., 2008). In a randomized control trial, MCT led to significantly greater decreases in PTSD symptoms, anxiety, depression, and worry, compared to the wait-list control group (Wells & Colbear, 2012). These changes were maintained a 3- and 6-month follow-ups. Another randomized control trial compared MCT to prolonged exposure, a gold standard behavioral treatment for PTSD (Wells, Walton, Lovell, & Proctor, 2015). Compared to a wait-list control, both MCT and prolonged exposure decreased symptoms of PTSD, anxiety, and depression. However, MCT was superior to prolonged exposure on PTSD symptoms at posttreatment and led to greater improvements at midtreatment. Finally, two studies tested the effects of stand-alone ATT in college students who had experienced a stressful life event (Callinan, Johnson, & Wells, 2015; Nassif & Wells, 2014). Participants who received two sessions of ATT exhibited decreased negative affect and intrusive thoughts about their stressful experience, compared with participants who did filler tasks. They also showed decreased self-focused attention and increased attentional flexibility, presumed mechanisms of the ATT.

Social anxiety disorder

The metacognitive model for social anxiety is not as fully developed as the models described above. As covered in a previous chapter (see Chapter 2, Rumination and anxiety-related disorders), rumination occurs *before* (anticipatory) and *after* (post-event) a feared social encounter. *During* the social situation, individuals turn their attention inward (self-focused attention) and pay particular attention to indications of anxiety and perceived poor performance, ignoring external cues about social success. In an informal metacognitive formulation, Wells (2007b) proposed that positive metacognitive beliefs activate the CAS, specifically self-focused attention during social situations and rumination before and after social situations. Because self-focused attention and rumination increase anxiety and may actually impede performance, these strategies reinforce negative beliefs about the dangers of displaying anxiety and having a poor performance.

A few studies have examined the association between positive beliefs about rumination and social anxiety symptoms. For instance, positive beliefs about socially oriented rumination were associated with more rumination and social anxiety symptoms (Wong & Moulds, 2010). Similarly, positive beliefs about anticipatory and post-event rumination predicted greater anticipatory and post-event rumination, respectively, as well as worse social anxiety symptoms (Fisak & Hammond, 2013; Vassilopoulos, Brouzos, & Moberly, 2015). In line with the model's proposed pathways, anticipatory and post-event rumination mediated the association between their related type of positive metacognitive beliefs and social anxiety symptoms.

Wells (2007b) developed a five-session MCT protocol for social anxiety. Therapists first focus on identifying patients' positive beliefs about self-focused attention during social situations. These beliefs are challenged through cognitive restructuring questions (e.g., "What are the advantages and disadvantages of avoiding eye contract?") and behavioral experiments (e.g., performing a feared social task with internal versus external attention and comparing actual outcomes). Patients also engage in attention exercises to train themselves to sustain externally focused attention. Therapists then target positive beliefs about anticipatory and post-event rumination, again via cognitive restructuring and behavioral experiments. Finally, negative beliefs about showing anxiety or performing poorly are challenged by using brief exposures to feared social situations during which patients perform some specific test (e.g., intentionally spilling a drink at a crowded bar at watching the reactions of others). The goal of exposure is to disconfirm negative metacognitive beliefs, not to habituate to physiological arousal and anxiety.

Some evidence supports the efficacy of this treatment and its components. Brief MCT as just described contributed to decreases in anxiety symptoms, self-monitoring, and negative metacognitive beliefs in 6 patients with social anxiety disorder (Wells & Papageorgiou, 2001). In component analyses, brief exposure emphasizing a shift to external attention led to greater reductions in social anxiety symptoms and negative metacognitive beliefs than did exposure presented with a habituation rationale (Papageorgiou & Wells, 1998). Similarly, 6 weeks of attention training (including the ATT) contributed to an equivalent decrease in social anxiety symptoms as did cognitive therapy but greater reductions in self-focused attention (Donald, Abbott, & Smith, 2014). In a nonclinical sample, 12 individuals high in social anxiety engaged in 15 minutes each of DM exercises and generic cognitive restructuring before giving speeches (Gkika & Wells, 2015). Both interventions led to a decrease in anxiety about the speech. However, DM contributed to greater reductions in anticipatory rumination and externally focused attention during the speech than did cognitive restructuring.

Obsessive–compulsive disorder

The metacognitive model of OCD (see Fig. 12.3) proposes that compulsions are part of the CAS and emerge from metacognitive beliefs (Wells, 2009). In OCD, two new types of metacognition are emphasized: fusion beliefs about the power of thoughts, and beliefs or rules about rituals. Wells identified three types of fusion beliefs: (1) thought–action fusion, or the belief that a thought alone can cause a person to carry out, or is equivalent to, an action; (2) thought–event fusion, or the belief that having a thought can cause an event or means that an event has happened; and (3) thought–object fusion, or the belief that thoughts can be transferred into objects (Myers, Fisher, & Wells, 2008). Fusion beliefs lead individuals to appraise an intrusive thought (e.g., obsession) as dangerous or important. Following such an appraisal, metacognitive beliefs and rules about rituals influence people's level of distress and

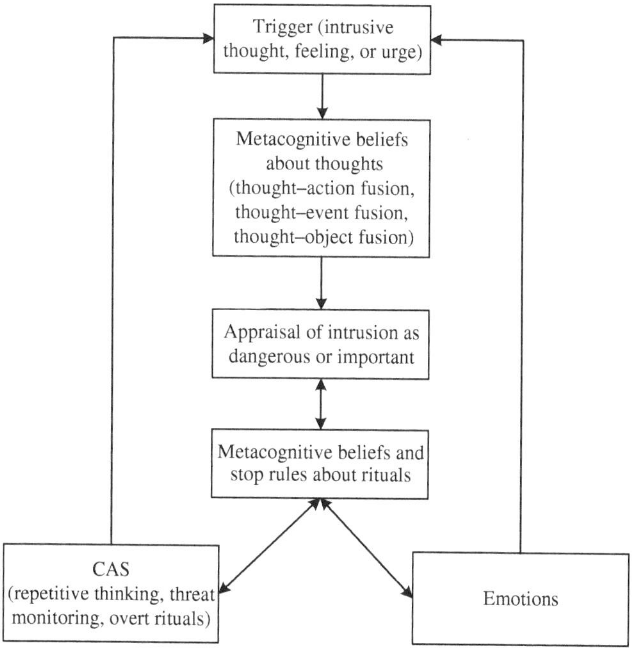

FIGURE 12.3 The metacognitive model of OCD. *OCD*, Obsessive–compulsive disorder. Source: *Adapted from Wells, A. (2009).* Metacognitive therapy for anxiety and depression. *New York [u.a.]: Guilford Press. Retrieved from <http://bvbr.bib-bvb.de:8991/F?func = service&doc_library = BVB01&local_base = BVB01&doc_number = 017135158&sequence = 000002&line_number = 0001&func_code = DB_RECORDS&service_type = MEDIA>.*

choice of metacognitive strategies. Ritual-related metacognition generally involves (1) beliefs about the need to carry out rituals in response to dangerous intrusions and (2) internal stop rules for how long rituals should be performed. For instance, people may believe "If I wash my hands, then I won't hurt my children" (i.e., belief) and "I can stop after 5 minutes" (i.e., stop rule). Maladaptive stop rules (e.g., performing rituals in the same order every time or until it is done perfectly) can exacerbate obsessive–compulsive symptoms because they are inflexible and difficult to achieve. Beliefs about rituals and stop rules trigger all aspects of the CAS. Specifically, repetitive thinking in the form of worry, rumination, and/or covert rituals reflects behavioral attempts to cope with the perceived threatening intrusive thought. People also use threat monitoring to search for external and internal signs of danger. Finally, overt rituals (e.g., checking, washing) represent maladaptive coping behaviors. In addition to increasing distress, CAS behaviors prevent metacognitive beliefs from being modified because they reinforce the belief that thoughts are important and dangerous.

Substantial research confirms that metacognitive factors predict obsessive–compulsive symptoms (for a review, see Fisher, 2009). In nonclinical and clinical samples, fusion beliefs are associated with worse obsessive–compulsive symptoms cross-sectionally and several months later (Gwilliam, Wells, & Cartwright-Hatton, 2004; Matthews, Reynolds, & Derisley, 2006; McNicol & Wells, 2012; Myers et al., 2008; Myers, Fisher, & Wells, 2009; Myers & Wells, 2005; Solem, Håland, Vogel, Hansen, & Wells, 2009; but see Hansmeier, Exner, Rief, & Glombiewski, 2016). Stronger belief in the need for rituals and endorsement of maladaptive stop rules also predict greater OCD symptoms. In a rare experimental manipulation of thought–event fusion, university students received fake EEG recordings and were informed that the EEG could sense hypothalamus activity caused by having thoughts related to thirst and drinking (Myers & Wells, 2013). Participants in the thought–event fusion condition were told that if such thoughts were detected, then they might be exposed to an aversive (e.g., loud and high-pitched) noise. Participants in the control condition were told that they might hear an aversive noise but this would be unrelated to any thoughts they had. Across all participants, the thought–event fusion manipulation led to more efforts to control intrusions than did the control condition, providing some evidence that fusion beliefs trigger the CAS.

MCT for OCD involves modifying metacognitions that give rise to the use of CAS strategies. The goals are to help patients develop alternative ways of experiencing their thoughts and to modify fusion beliefs, beliefs about rituals, and stop signals. After creating a case conceptualization and socializing patients to the MCT model, therapists first introduce patients to DM. This helps patients learn to relate to intrusive thoughts (i.e., obsessions) from a metacognitive mode. In addition to practicing the DM exercises described above, patients may be asked to postpone their typical CAS behaviors, including worry, rumination, and neutralizing rituals. Therapists also commonly ask patients to engage in *exposure and response commission*, during which they perform a ritual *while* holding a related intrusive thought in mind. This activity facilitates detachment from the thought and strengthens metacognitive experiencing. Once patients gain some ability to achieve a metacognitive mode in response to intrusive thoughts, therapists begin to target fusion beliefs. In addition to questioning the evidence for and against such beliefs, therapists use behavioral experiments. For instance, a patient might be asked to have a thought about stabbing someone while holding a pen, in order to see if this leads her to stab the therapist. Similarly, a patient may be asked to think about his partner winning in the lottery in two days in order to disconfirm the belief that thoughts cause events to happen. Therapists can also target beliefs about rituals by questioning their advantages and disadvantages and using brief exposure and response prevention in order to disconfirm the belief that rituals prevent threat.

Several small-scale studies have examined the efficacy of MCT for OCD (for a review, see Fisher, 2009). In four treatment-seeking individuals, MCT contributed to a meaningful reduction in OCD symptoms and fusion beliefs (Fisher & Wells, 2007). MCT delivered in a group format with eight patients also decreased OCD symptoms as well as positive beliefs about worry and the need to control thoughts (Rees & van Koesveld, 2008). MCT delivered via videoconferencing also effectively reduced symptoms of OCD in three patients (Fitt & Rees, 2012). In a small, randomized control study, children and adolescents with OCD received either MCT or traditional exposure and response prevention (Simons, Schneider, & Herpertz-Dahlmann, 2006). Both treatments contributed to meaningful reductions in OCD symptoms 3 months and 2 years after therapy. Finally, a self-help manual called *My Metacognitive Training for OCD* includes a combination of traditional CBT elements and MCT techniques (Moritz, Jelinek, Hauschildt, & Naber, 2010). Participants with OCD who read this manual reported greater reductions in OCD symptoms than did wait-listed participants. However, the relative contributions of MCT and CBT are not known.

Other research has examined the effectiveness of individual MCT components on OCD symptoms. In an empirical test of brief exposure and response prevention from an MCT perspective, eight patients with OCD experienced three 5-minute exposures of their feared obsessional stimulus (Fisher & Wells, 2005). Before the second and third exposures, they were provided with either a habituation-based rationale or a metacognitive-based rationale for the exposure. Although both rationales seemed credible to participants, only the metacognitive rationale led to decreases in anxiety, the urge to neutralize, and belief that their obsessional thoughts are true. The habituation rationale led to increases in all of the dependent variables. As with other disorders, ATT has been tested as a stand-along treatment for OCD. In college students with high levels of obsessive–compulsive symptoms, a single session of ATT was associated with decreased frequency and unpleasantness of a specific intrusive thought; however, ATT did not differ in effectiveness from sitting quietly (Watson & Purdon, 2008). Similarly, ATT delivered as bibliotherapy to individuals with OCD did not contribute to any meaningful changes in OCD symptoms, compared to a wait-list control condition (Moritz et al., 2010; Moritz, Wess, Treszl, & Jelinek, 2011). Thus, ATT does not appear to be an effective stand-alone treatment for individual with OCD.

Schizophrenia

Researchers have proposed various metacognitive conceptualizations of hallucinations and delusions. One early model focused on the role of general metacognitive beliefs about thoughts. As background, some researchers suggest that hallucinations reflect misattributions of internally generated thoughts to external sources (Morrison, Haddock, & Tarrier, 1995). Similarly, delusions may reflect culturally inappropriate misattributions of internal sensations, thoughts, and emotions (Morrison, 2001). Examples of delusional misinterpretations include interpreting intrusive thoughts as evidence of thought insertion or intrusive impulses as evidence of alien control. Drawing on a metacognitive model, Morrison (2001) proposed that psychosis-prone individuals likely have strong metacognitive beliefs about the benefits of controlling thoughts and the dangers of uncontrolled thoughts. When these individuals have intrusions that conflict with their metacognitive beliefs about the importance of controlling thoughts, cognitive dissonance is created. In order to reduce this dissonance and the associated emotional discomfort, individuals are motivated to misattribute intrusions to external and/or unrealistic sources, leading to the perception of hallucinations and/or delusions. In addition, these metacognitive beliefs about thoughts may also contribute to use of CAS strategies in response to intrusions.

Some research supports this conceptualization. For instance, greater endorsement of positive and negative metacognitive beliefs, particularly negative beliefs about the need to control thoughts, is associated with hallucination- and delusion-proneness in nonclinical samples (Goldstone, Farhall, Thomas, & Ong, 2013; Larøi & Van der Linden, 2005; Morrison, Wells, & Nothard, 2000). Similarly, schizophrenic patients with auditory hallucinations and patients at high risk for developing psychosis report more metacognitive beliefs than do nonpatients (Baker & Morrison, 1998; Morrison, French, & Wells, 2007; Morrison & Wells, 2003). Moreover, positive and negative metacognitive beliefs are associated with greater use of CAS coping strategies in psychotic participants (Sellers, Wells, Parker, & Morrison, 2018). Patients with psychosis use CAS coping strategies more than healthy control participants. However, several studies have found that the associations between general metacognitive beliefs and psychotic symptoms decrease or disappear when controlling for comorbid symptoms and negative affect (García-Montes, Cangas, Pérez-Álvarez, Hidalgo, & Gutiérrez Martínez, 2005; Goldstone et al., 2013; Varese & Bentall, 2011). In addition, negative metacognitive beliefs—particularly belief in the need to control thoughts—predict emotional distress in schizophrenic patients over and above the effect of psychotic symptoms (Austin et al., 2015; Sellers, Gawęda, Wells, & Morrison, 2016; van Oosterhout, Krabbendam, Smeets, & van der Gaag, 2013). Thus, general metacognitive beliefs about thoughts might be more strongly related to distress associated with psychotic experiences, rather than representing a contributing factor to the symptoms themselves.

More recent theorizing focuses on metacognitive beliefs specifically about psychotic symptoms. For instance, Wells (2007a) suggested that people may hold positive beliefs about hallucinations, such as the perceived benefits of companionship or comfort. These types of positive beliefs may make people more likely to engage with hallucinations. On the other hand, negative metacognitive beliefs involve auditory hallucinations being powerful, omnipotent, and/or malevolent and that these experiences threaten one's physical or psychological integrity. These negative beliefs may trigger emotional distress and unhelpful coping (CAS) responses, such as rumination, worry, threat monitoring, and suppression, all of which likely contribute to more intrusions. Similarly, Morrison argued that positive metacognitive beliefs about delusions (e.g., paranoid ideas may add meaning to life, provide excitement, or function as a survival strategy in response to trauma; grandiose ideas make people feel important) make people more likely to make delusional misinterpretations (Morrison, 2001; Morrison, et al., 2005). Similarly, negative metacognitive beliefs about the danger and uncontrollability of delusions may be related to distress, trigger other CAS strategies, and predict patient status. As an example of this process with paranoid delusions, a triggering situation event (e.g. seeing a young man while shopping) could activate positive metacognitive beliefs about paranoia helping to cope with the perceived threat (e.g., "It is important to be alert for danger in order to survive"), which in turn might lead to specific paranoid thoughts (e.g., "That man is going to attack me"). The experience of paranoia can activate negative metacognitive beliefs about paranoia (e.g., "My paranoia is uncontrollable"), leading to emotional distress and attempts to control or avoid paranoia (Murphy et al., 2016).

Empirical evidence supports the role of symptom-specific metacognitive beliefs. In healthy college students, positive metacognitive beliefs about hallucinations are associated with greater tendencies for auditory and visual hallucinations (Morrison et al., 2000). Similarly, both positive and negative beliefs about paranoia are associated with more paranoia, whereas only negative beliefs uniquely predict distress from delusions (Morrison et al., 2005). Patients with schizophrenia spectrum disorders report more negative metacognitive beliefs about hallucinations, as well as positive and negative beliefs about paranoia, than do healthy controls (Morrison et al., 2011; Morrison, Nothard, Bowe, & Wells, 2004; Morrison & Wells, 2003). Positive beliefs about paranoia are associated with more severe paranoia (Morrison et al., 2011), whereas negative beliefs about hallucinations and paranoia are particularly associated with distress from these symptoms (Morrison et al., 2004; Murphy et al., 2016). Unfortunately, no research has examined the association between symptom-specific metacognitive beliefs and the use of CAS strategies in psychotic patients.

A few case studies have examined the efficacy of MCT or its components in psychotic patients. For instance, ten patients with schizophrenia spectrum disorders received 12 sessions of MCT (Morrison et al., 2013). The treatment did not directly target hallucinations or delusions but instead focused on helping patients reduce their use of CAS strategies (particularly repetitive thinking), developing more adaptive coping strategies, and changing their metacognitive beliefs. Group-level analyses indicated that MCT led to significant reductions in positive symptoms posttreatment and three months later. Both positive and negative metacognitive beliefs decreased posttreatment. However, there were no significant differences in negative symptoms or general emotional distress. In another study, MCT led to large and clinically significant reductions in psychosis and metacognitive beliefs in two out of three patients with treatment-resistant schizophrenia (Hutton, Morrison, Wardle, & Wells, 2014). Similarly, eight sessions of stand-alone ATT led to reduced symptoms and metacognitive beliefs in one patient with treatment-resistant schizophrenia (Valmaggia, Bouman, & Schuurman, 2007).

Alcohol use disorder

One research team developed a metacognitive formulation of problem drinking (Spada, Caselli, & Wells, 2013). The model asserts that alcohol-related triggers, such as cravings, images, or external cues, elicit positive metacognitive beliefs about repetitive thinking, which in turn lead to desire thinking, rumination, and/or worry. For example, positive beliefs might include: "If I imagine using alcohol, I can gain control over it", "If I analyze my craving experience, I will know what is causing it", and/or "Thinking about the negative effects of alcohol will help me avoid using in the future" (p. 495). These types of positive beliefs activate the CAS, including the various types of repetitive thinking. Once activated, the CAS increases both craving and negative affect, which in turn may activate both negative beliefs about the uncontrollability of repetitive thoughts *and* positive beliefs about alcohol use (e.g., "Drinking will help me control my thoughts"). This combination of craving, negative affect, and metacognitive beliefs increases the likelihood of dysregulated alcohol use. The model further proposes that individuals engage in a form of post-event rumination following alcohol use, in which they ruminate about the causes and consequences of their dysregulated drinking. This rumination in turn increases negative affect and alcohol-related thoughts, which can serve as triggers for a repetition of the entire process.

In support of this model, metacognitive beliefs are associated with desire thinking, craving, and alcohol use. For instance, positive beliefs about the potential of desire thinking to control negative thoughts or emotions and to increase excitement and motivation predict more desire thinking (Caselli & Spada, 2013). Similarly, positive beliefs about using alcohol to reduce negative emotions or to achieve some desired state (e.g., relaxation, self-confidence) predict greater alcohol use, binge drinking, and alcohol-related problems in nonclinical and clinical samples (Clark et al., 2011; Gierski et al., 2015; Spada & Wells, 2008). In terms of negative metacognition, beliefs about the negative impacts of desire thinking on behavioral control, cognitive performance, and self-image, as well as the uncontrollability of desire thinking uniquely predict stronger craving (Caselli & Spada, 2013). Likewise, in problem drinkers and healthy participants, beliefs about the need to control thoughts predict greater alcohol use, both cross-sectionally and several months later (Spada, Caselli, & Wells, 2009; Spada & Wells, 2005). Finally, negative beliefs specifically about the uncontrollability and harm of drinking predict greater alcohol use, binge drinking, and alcohol-related problems in nonclinical and clinical samples (Clark et al., 2011; Gierski et al., 2015; Spada & Wells, 2008).

Researchers have not yet examined the efficacy of MCT for alcohol use disorder. However, one study examined the effect of brief training in DM in patients with alcohol use disorder (Caselli, Gemelli, Spada, & Wells, 2016). Participants listened to a 5-minute recording of their own alcohol-related thoughts following either exposure- or DM-based instructions. The DM condition led to decreases in distress, urge to drink, fear of alcohol-related thoughts, and negative metacognitive beliefs about alcohol. By contrast, participants in the exposure condition reported increases in all of these variables.

Conclusion

In this chapter, I described metacognitive theory and therapy—both in general and as applied to specific mental disorders—and reviewed empirical evidence supporting this model. In addition to GAD, major depression, PTSD, social anxiety, OCD, schizophrenia, and substance use disorder, researchers have also started exploring the role of metacognitive beliefs in eating disorders (Rawal, Park, & Williams, 2010) and illness anxiety disorder (Bailey & Wells, 2013). In fact, MCT and ATT by itself appear to reduce health anxiety, worry, and metacognitive beliefs in patients with illness anxiety disorder (Bailey & Wells, 2014; Papageorgiou & Wells, 1998; Weck, Neng, & Stangier, 2013).

Some research has compared the efficacy of MCT with traditional CBT. For instance, in 30 treatment-resistant patients with a range of diagnoses, although both treatments decreased depressive and anxiety symptoms, MCT led to significantly greater decreases in anxiety and metaworry than did CBT (Nordahl, 2009). A metaanalysis evaluated 16 studies—both published and unpublished—testing the efficacy of MCT for patients with depression and/or anxiety (Normann, van Emmerik, & Morina, 2014). Effect sizes for pre- to both posttreatment and follow-up comparisons were large for measures of depression, anxiety, and unhelpful metacognition. Moreover, across nine controlled trials, MCT contributed to less depression, anxiety, and worry compared to either CBT or a wait-list control. Thus, MCT may yield comparable if not better outcomes than does traditional CBT.

However, an equally interesting question is how second wave (e.g., CBT) therapies are similar to third wave (e.g., mindfulness-based and metacognitive) therapies. One suggested difference is that whereas cognitive therapy aims to change dysfunctional thoughts and reduce symptoms, third wave therapies target more metacognitive processes. However, research suggests that traditional cognitive therapy increases the extent to which patients are able to distance themselves from their thoughts (Teasdale et al., 2002). Thus, the argument could be made that both second and third wave therapies function to foster decentering, which is a metacognitive process. Future research pinpointing this or other shared mechanisms of the various therapies covered in this book could further inform our understanding of why people ruminate and how to help them stop.

References

Andor, T., Gerlach, A. L., & Rist, F. (2008). Superior perception of phasic physiological arousal and the detrimental consequences of the conviction to be aroused on worrying and metacognitions in GAD. *Journal of Abnormal Psychology, 117*(1), 193–205. Available from https://doi.org/10.1037/0021-843X.117.1.193.

Austin, S., Mors, O., Nordentoft, M., Hjorthøj, C., Secher, R., Hesse, M., ... Wells, A. (2015). Schizophrenia and metacognition: An investigation of course of illness and metacognitive beliefs within a first episode psychosis. *Cognitive Therapy and Research, 39*(1), 61–69. Available from https://doi.org/10.1007/s10608-014-9633-9.

Bailey, R., & Wells, A. (2013). Does metacognition make a unique contribution to health anxiety when controlling for neuroticism, illness cognition, and somatosensory amplification? *Journal of Cognitive Psychotherapy, 27*(4), 327–337. Available from https://doi.org/10.1891/0889-8391.27.4.327.

Bailey, R., & Wells, A. (2014). Metacognitive therapy in the treatment of hypochondriasis: A systematic case series. *Cognitive Therapy and Research, 38*(5), 541–550. Available from https://doi.org/10.1007/s10608-014-9615-y.

Baker, C. A., & Morrison, A. P. (1998). Cognitive processes in auditory hallucinations: Attributional biases and metacognition. *Psychological Medicine, 28*(5), 1199–1208. Available from https://doi.org/10.1017/S0033291798007314.

Bennett, H., & Wells, A. (2010). Metacognition, memory disorganization and rumination in posttraumatic stress symptoms. *Journal of Anxiety Disorders, 24*(3), 318–325. Available from https://doi.org/10.1016/j.janxdis.2010.01.004.

Calkins, A. W., McMorran, K. E., Siegle, G. J., & Otto, M. W. (2015). The effects of computerized cognitive control training on community adults with depressed mood. *Behavioural and Cognitive Psychotherapy, 43*(5), 578–589. Available from https://doi.org/10.1017/S1352465814000046.

Callinan, S., Johnson, D., & Wells, A. (2015). A randomised controlled study of the effects of the attention training technique on traumatic stress symptoms, emotional attention set shifting and flexibility. *Cognitive Therapy and Research, 39*(1), 4–13. Available from https://doi.org/10.1007/s10608-014-9634-8.

Cartwright-Hatton, S., & Wells, A. (1997). Beliefs about worry and intrusions: The metacognitions questionnaire and its correlates. *Journal of Anxiety Disorders, 11*(3), 279–296. Available from https://doi.org/10.1016/S0887-6185(97)00011-X.

Caselli, G., Gemelli, A., Spada, M. M., & Wells, A. (2016). Experimental modification of perspective on thoughts and metacognitive beliefs in alcohol use disorder. *Psychiatry Research*. Available from https://doi.org/10.1016/j.psychres.2016.07.029.

Caselli, G., & Spada, M. M. (2013). The metacognitions about desire thinking questionnaire: Development and psychometric properties. *Journal of Clinical Psychology, 69*(12), 1284–1298. Available from https://doi.org/10.1002/jclp.21999.

Clark, A., Tran, C., Weiss, A., Caselli, G., Nikčević, A. V., & Spada, M. M. (2011). Personality and alcohol metacognitions as predictors of weekly levels of alcohol use in binge drinking university students. *Addictive Behaviors, 37*(4), 537–540. Available from https://doi.org/10.1016/j.addbeh.2011.11.035.

Dammen, T., Papageorgiou, C., & Wells, A. (2014). An open trial of group metacognitive therapy for depression in Norway. *Nordic Journal of Psychiatry, 69*(2), 126–131. Available from https://doi.org/10.3109/08039488.2014.936502.

Davis, R. N., & Valentiner, D. P. (2000). Does meta-cognitive theory enhance our understanding of pathological worry and anxiety? *Personality and Individual Differences, 29*(3), 513–526. Available from https://doi.org/10.1016/S0191-8869(99)00211-1.

Donald, J., Abbott, M. J., & Smith, E. (2014). Comparison of attention training and cognitive therapy in the treatment of social phobia: A preliminary investigation. *Behavioural and Cognitive Psychotherapy, 42*(1), 74–91. Available from https://doi.org/10.1017/S1352465812001051.

Esbjørn, B. H., Lønfeldt, N. N., Nielsen, S. K., Reinholdt-Dunne, M. L., Sømhovd, M. J., & Cartwright-Hatton, S. (2015). Meta-worry, worry, and anxiety in children and adolescents: Relationships and interactions. *Journal of Clinical Child & Adolescent Psychology, 44*(1), 145–156. Available from https://doi.org/10.1080/15374416.2013.873980.

Fergus, T. A., & Bardeen, J. R. (2016). The attention training technique: A review of a neurobehavioral therapy for emotional disorders. *Cognitive and Behavioral Practice, 23*(4), 502–516. Available from https://doi.org/10.1016/j.cbpra.2015.11.001.

Fisak, B., & Hammond, A. N. (2013). Are positive beliefs about post-event processing related to social anxiety? *Behaviour Change, 30*(1), 36–47. Available from https://doi.org/10.1017/bec.2013.4.

Fisher, P. L. (2009). Obsessive compulsive disorder: A comparison of CBT and the metacognitive approach. *International Journal of Cognitive Therapy, 2*(2), 107–122. Available from https://doi.org/10.1521/ijct.2009.2.2.107.

Fisher, P. L., & Wells, A. (2005). Experimental modification of beliefs in obsessive–compulsive disorder: A test of the metacognitive model. *Behaviour Research and Therapy, 43*(6), 821–829. Available from https://doi.org/10.1016/j.brat.2004.09.002.

Fisher, P. L., & Wells, A. (2007). Metacognitive therapy for obsessive–compulsive disorder: A case series. *Journal of Behavior Therapy and Experimental Psychiatry, 39*(2), 117–132. Available from https://doi.org/10.1016/j.jbtep.2006.12.001.

Fitt, S., & Rees, C. (2012). Metacognitive therapy for obsessive compulsive disorder by videoconference: A preliminary study. *Behaviour Change, 29*(4), 213–229. Available from https://doi.org/10.1017/bec.2012.21.

Flavell, J. H. (1979). Metacognition and cognitive monitoring: A new area of cognitive-developmental inquiry. *American Psychologist, 34*(10), 906–911. Available from https://doi.org/10.1037/0003-066X.34.10.906.

García-Montes, J. M., Cangas, A., Pérez-Álvarez, M., Hidalgo, Á. M., & Gutiérrez Martínez, O. (2005). *Influence of metacognitive variables on paranoid ideation*. Retrieved from <http://hdl.handle.net/10481/32649>.

Gierski, F., Van der Linden, M., Naassila, M., Picard, A., Fois, E., & Spada, M. M. (2015). Positive and negative metacognitions about alcohol use among university students: Psychometric properties of the PAMS and NAMS French versions. *Drug and Alcohol Dependence, 153*, 78–85. Available from https://doi.org/10.1016/j.drugalcdep.2015.06.003.

Gkika, S., & Wells, A. (2015). How to deal with negative thoughts? A preliminary comparison of detached mindfulness and thought evaluation in socially anxious individuals. *Cognitive Therapy and Research, 39*(1), 23–30. Available from https://doi.org/10.1007/s10608-014-9637-5.

Goldstone, E., Farhall, J., Thomas, N., & Ong, B. (2013). The role of metacognitive beliefs in the proneness to hallucinations and delusions: An analysis across clinical and non-clinical populations. *The British Journal of Clinical Psychology, 52*(3), 330–346. Available from https://doi.org/10.1111/bjc.12020.

Gwilliam, P., Wells, A., & Cartwright-Hatton, S. (2004). Does meta-cognition or responsibility predict obsessive-compulsive symptoms: A test of the metacognitive model. *Clinical Psychology and Psychotherapy, 11*(2), 137. Retrieved from <https://search.proquest.com/docview/213891959>.

Hansmeier, J., Exner, C., Rief, W., & Glombiewski, J. A. (2016). A test of the metacognitive model of obsessive-compulsive disorder. *Journal of Obsessive-Compulsive and Related Disorders, 10*, 42–48. Available from https://doi.org/10.1016/j.jocrd.2016.05.002.

Hayes, S. C. (2004). Acceptance and commitment therapy, relational frame theory, and the third wave of behavioral and cognitive therapies. *Behavior Therapy, 35*(4), 639–665. Available from https://doi.org/10.1016/S0005-7894(04)80013-3.

Hjemdal, O., Hagen, R., Solem, S., Nordahl, H. M., Nordahl, H., Kennair, L. E. O., ... Wells, A. (2016). Metacognitive therapy in major depression: An open trial of comorbid cases. *Cognitive and Behavioral Practice, 24*(3), 312–318. Available from https://doi.org/10.1016/j.cbpra.2016.06.006.

Hutton, P., Morrison, A. P., Wardle, M., & Wells, A. (2014). Metacognitive therapy in treatment-resistant psychosis: A multiple-baseline study. *Behavioural and Cognitive Psychotherapy, 42*(2), 166–185. Available from https://doi.org/10.1017/S1352465812001026.

Larøi, F., & Van der Linden, M. (2005). Metacognitions in proneness towards hallucinations and delusions. *Behaviour Research and Therapy, 43*(11), 1425–1441. Available from https://doi.org/10.1016/j.brat.2004.10.008.

Laugesen, N., Dugas, M., & Bukowski, W. (2003). Understanding adolescent worry: The application of a cognitive model. *Journal of Abnormal Child Psychology, 31*(1), 55–64. Available from https://doi.org/1021721332181.

Luminet, O. (2004). *Assessment and measurement of rumination*. Chichester: Wiley. Retrieved from <http://hdl.handle.net/2078.1/137768>.

Mandell, D., Siegle, G. J., Shutt, L., Feldmiller, J., & Thase, M. E. (2014). Neural substrates of trait ruminations in depression. *Journal of Abnormal Psychology, 123*(1), 35–48. Available from https://doi.org/10.1037/a0035834.

Matthews, L., Reynolds, S., & Derisley, J. (2006). Examining cognitive models of obsessive compulsive disorder in adolescents. *Behavioural and Cognitive Psychotherapy, 35*(2), 149–163. Available from https://doi.org/10.1017/S1352465806003213.

McNicol, K., & Wells, A. (2012). Metacognition and obsessive-compulsive symptoms: The contribution of thought-fusion beliefs and beliefs about rituals. *International Journal of Cognitive Therapy, 5*(3), 330–340. Available from https://doi.org/10.1521/ijct.2012.5.3.330.

Moritz, S., Jelinek, L., Hauschildt, M., & Naber, D. (2010). How to treat the untreated: Effectiveness of a self-help metacognitive training program (myMCT) for obsessive-compulsive disorder. *Dialogues in Clinical Neuroscience, 12*(2), 209. Retrieved from <https://www.ncbi.nlm.nih.gov/pubmed/20623925>.

Moritz, S., Wess, N., Treszl, A., & Jelinek, L. (2011). The attention training technique as an attempt to decrease intrusive thoughts in obsessive–compulsive disorder (OCD): From cognitive theory to practice and back. *Journal of Contemporary Psychotherapy, 41*(3), 135–143. Available from https://doi.org/10.1007/s10879-010-9169-6.

Morrison, A. P. (2001). The interpretation of intrusions in psychosis: An integrative cognitive approach to hallucinations and delusions. *Behavioural and Cognitive Psychotherapy, 29*(3), 257–276. Available from https://doi.org/10.1017/S1352465801003010.

Morrison, A. P., French, P., & Wells, A. (2007). Metacognitive beliefs across the continuum of psychosis: Comparisons between patients with psychotic disorders, patients at ultra-high risk and non-patients. *Behaviour Research and Therapy, 45*(9), 2241–2246. Available from https://doi.org/10.1016/j.brat.2007.01.002.

Morrison, A. P., Gumley, A. I., Ashcroft, K., Manousos, I. R., White, R., Gillan, K., ... Kingdon, D. (2011). Metacognition and persecutory delusions: Tests of a metacognitive model in a clinical population and comparisons with non-patients. *British Journal of Clinical Psychology, 50*(3), 223–233. Available from https://doi.org/10.1348/014466510X511141.

Morrison, A. P., Gumley, A. I., Schwannauer, M., Campbell, M., Gleeson, A., Griffin, E., & Gillan, K. (2005). The beliefs about paranoia scale: Preliminary validation of a metacognitive approach to conceptualizing paranoia. *Behavioural and Cognitive Psychotherapy, 33* (2), 153–164. Available from https://doi.org/10.1017/S1352465804001900.

Morrison, A. P., Haddock, G., & Tarrier, N. (1995). Intrusive thoughts and auditory hallucinations: A cognitive approach. *Behavioural and Cognitive Psychotherapy, 23*(3), 265–280. Available from https://doi.org/10.1017/S1352465800015873.

Morrison, A. P., Nothard, S., Bowe, S. E., & Wells, A. (2004). Interpretations of voices in patients with hallucinations and non-patient controls: A comparison and predictors of distress in patients. *Behaviour Research and Therapy, 42*(11), 1315–1323. Available from https://doi.org/10.1016/j.brat.2003.08.009.

Morrison, A. P., Pyle, M., Chapman, N., French, P., Parker, S. K., & Wells, A. (2013). Metacognitive therapy in people with a schizophrenia spectrum diagnosis and medication resistant symptoms: A feasibility study. *Journal of Behavior Therapy and Experimental Psychiatry, 45*(2), 280–284. Available from https://doi.org/10.1016/j.jbtep.2013.11.003.

Morrison, A. P., & Wells, A. (2003). A comparison of metacognitions in patients with hallucinations, delusions, panic disorder, and non-patient controls. *Behaviour Research and Therapy, 41*(2), 251–256. Available from https://doi.org/10.1016/S0005-7967(02)00095-5.

Morrison, A. P., Wells, A., & Nothard, S. (2000). Cognitive factors in predisposition to auditory and visual hallucinations. *The British Journal of Clinical Psychology, 39*(1), 67–78. Available from https://doi.org/10.1348/014466500163112.

Murphy, E. K., Tully, S., Pyle, M., Gumley, A. I., Kingdon, D., Schwannauer, M., ... Morrison, A. P. (2016). The beliefs about paranoia scale: Confirmatory factor analysis and tests of a metacognitive model of paranoia in a clinical sample. *Psychiatry Research, 248*, 87–94. Available from https://doi.org/10.1016/j.psychres.2016.11.012.

Myers, S. G., Fisher, P. L., & Wells, A. (2008). An empirical test of the metacognitive model of obsessive-compulsive symptoms: Fusion beliefs, beliefs about rituals, and stop signals. *Journal of Anxiety Disorders, 23*(4), 436–442. Available from https://doi.org/10.1016/j.janxdis.2008.08.007.

Myers, S. G., Fisher, P. L., & Wells, A. (2009). Metacognition and cognition as predictors of obsessive-compulsive symptoms: A prospective study. *International Journal of Cognitive Therapy, 2*(2), 132–142. Available from https://doi.org/10.1521/ijct.2009.2.2.132.

Myers, S. G., & Wells, A. (2005). Obsessive-compulsive symptoms: The contribution of metacognitions and responsibility. *Journal of Anxiety Disorders, 19*(7), 806–817. Available from https://doi.org/10.1016/j.janxdis.2004.09.004.

Myers, S. G., & Wells, A. (2013). An experimental manipulation of metacognition: A test of the metacognitive model of obsessive-compulsive symptoms. *Behaviour Research and Therapy, 51*(4–5), 177–184. Available from https://doi.org/10.1016/j.brat.2013.01.007.

Nassif, Y., & Wells, A. (2014). Attention training reduces intrusive thoughts cued by a narrative of stressful life events: A controlled study. *Journal of Clinical Psychology, 70*(6), 510–517. Available from https://doi.org/10.1002/jclp.22047.

Nordahl, H. M. (2009). Effectiveness of brief metacognitive therapy versus cognitive-behavioral therapy in a general outpatient setting. *International Journal of Cognitive Therapy, 2*(2), 152–159. Available from https://doi.org/10.1521/ijct.2009.2.2.152.

Normann, N., van Emmerik, A. P., & Morina, N. (2014). The efficacy of metacognitive therapy for anxiety and depression: A meta-analytic review. *Depression and Anxiety, 31*(5), 402–411. Available from https://doi.org/10.1002/da.22273.

Papageorgiou, C., & Wells, A. (1998). Effects of attention training on hypochondriasis: A brief case series. *Psychological Medicine, 28*(1), 193–200. Available from https://doi.org/10.1017/S0033291797005825.

Papageorgiou, C., & Wells, A. (2000). Treatment of recurrent major depression with attention training. *Cognitive and Behavioral Practice, 7*(4), 407–413. Available from https://doi.org/10.1016/S1077-7229(00)80051-6.

Papageorgiou, C., & Wells, A. (2001). Positive beliefs about depressive rumination: Development and preliminary validation of a self-report scale. *Behavior Therapy, 32*(1), 13–26. Available from https://doi.org/10.1016/S0005-7894(01)80041-1.

Papageorgiou, C., & Wells, A. (2003). An empirical test of a clinical metacognitive model of rumination and depression. *Cognitive Therapy and Research, 27*(3), 261–273. Available from https://doi.org/1023962332399.

Papageorgiou, C., & Wells, A. (2009). A prospective test of the clinical metacognitive model of rumination and depression. *International Journal of Cognitive Therapy, 2*(2), 123–131. Available from https://doi.org/10.1521/ijct.2009.2.2.123.

Papageorgiou, C., & Wells, A. (2015). Group metacognitive therapy for severe antidepressant and CBT resistant depression: A baseline-controlled trial. *Cognitive Therapy and Research, 39*(1), 14–22. Available from https://doi.org/10.1007/s10608-014-9632-x.

Rawal, A., Park, R. J., & Williams, M. G. (2010). Rumination, experiential avoidance, and dysfunctional thinking in eating disorders. *Behaviour Research and Therapy, 48*(9), 851–859. Available from https://doi.org/10.1016/j.brat.2010.05.009.

Rees, C. S., & van Koesveld, K. E. (2008). An open trial of group metacognitive therapy for obsessive-compulsive disorder. *Journal of Behavior Therapy and Experimental Psychiatry, 39*(4), 451–458. Available from https://doi.org/10.1016/j.jbtep.2007.11.004.

Roelofs, J., Papageorgiou, C., Gerber, R. D., Huibers, M., Peeters, F., & Arntz, A. (2007). On the links between self-discrepancies, rumination, metacognitions, and symptoms of depression in undergraduates. *Behaviour Research and Therapy, 45*(6), 1295–1305. Available from https://doi.org/10.1016/j.brat.2006.10.005.

Roussis, P., & Wells, A. (2006). Post-traumatic stress symptoms: Tests of relationships with thought control strategies and beliefs as predicted by the metacognitive model. *Personality and Individual Differences, 40*(1), 111–122. Available from https://doi.org/10.1016/j.paid.2005.06.019.

Ruscio, A. M., & Borkovec, T. D. (2004). Experience and appraisal of worry among high worriers with and without generalized anxiety disorder. *Behaviour Research and Therapy, 42*(12), 1469–1482. Available from https://doi.org/10.1016/j.brat.2003.10.007.

Sellers, R., Gawęda, Ł., Wells, A., & Morrison, A. P. (2016). The role of unhelpful metacognitive beliefs in psychosis: Relationships with positive symptoms and negative affect. *Psychiatry Research, 246*, 401–406. Available from https://doi.org/10.1016/j.psychres.2016.10.029.

Sellers, R., Wells, A., Parker, S., & Morrison, A. P. (2018). Do people with psychosis engage in unhelpful metacognitive coping strategies? A test of the validity of the cognitive attentional syndrome (CAS) in a clinical sample. *Psychiatry Research, 259*, 243–250. Available from https://doi.org/10.1016/j.psychres.2017.10.032.

Siegle, G., Ghinassi, F., & Thase, M. (2007). Neurobehavioral therapies in the 21st century: Summary of an emerging field and an extended example of cognitive control training for depression. *Cognitive Therapy and Research, 31*(2), 235–262. Available from https://doi.org/10.1007/s10608-006-9118-6.

Simons, M., Schneider, S., & Herpertz-Dahlmann, B. (2006). Metacognitive therapy versus exposure and response prevention for pediatric obsessive-compulsive disorder. *Psychotherapy and Psychosomatics, 75*(4), 257–264. Available from https://doi.org/10.1159/000092897.

Solem, S., Håland, Å. T., Vogel, P. A., Hansen, B., & Wells, A. (2009). Change in metacognitions predicts outcome in obsessive–compulsive disorder patients undergoing treatment with exposure and response prevention. *Behaviour Research and Therapy, 47*(4), 301–307. Available from https://doi.org/10.1016/j.brat.2009.01.003.

Spada, M. M., Caselli, G., & Wells, A. (2009). Metacognitions as a predictor of drinking status and level of alcohol use following CBT in problem drinkers: A prospective study. *Behaviour Research and Therapy, 47*(10), 882–886. Available from https://doi.org/10.1016/j.brat.2009.06.010.

Spada, M. M., Caselli, G., & Wells, A. (2013). A triphasic metacognitive formulation of problem drinking. *Clinical Psychology & Psychotherapy, 20*(6), 494–500. Available from https://doi.org/10.1002/cpp.1791.

Spada, M. M., & Wells, A. (2005). Metacognitions, emotion and alcohol use. *Clinical Psychology & Psychotherapy, 12*(2), 150–155. Available from https://doi.org/10.1002/cpp.431.

Spada, M. M., & Wells, A. (2008). Metacognitive beliefs about alcohol use: Development and validation of two self-report scales. *Addictive Behaviors, 33*(4), 515–527. Available from https://doi.org/10.1016/j.addbeh.2007.10.011.

Teasdale, J. D., Moore, R. G., Hayhurst, H., Pope, M., Williams, S., & Segal, Z. V. (2002). Metacognitive awareness and prevention of relapse in depression. *Journal of Consulting and Clinical Psychology, 70*(2), 275–287. Available from https://doi.org/10.1037/0022-006X.70.2.275.

Thielsch, C., Andor, T., & Ehring, T. (2015). Do metacognitions and intolerance of uncertainty predict worry in everyday life? an ecological momentary assessment study. *Behavior Therapy, 46*(4), 532–543. Available from https://doi.org/10.1016/j.beth.2015.05.001.

Valmaggia, L. R., Bouman, T. K., & Schuurman, L. (2007). Attention training with auditory hallucinations: A case study. *Cognitive and Behavioral Practice*, *14*(2), 127–133. Available from https://doi.org/10.1016/j.cbpra.2006.01.009.

van der Heiden, C., Muris, P., & van der Molen, H. T. (2012). Randomized controlled trial on the effectiveness of metacognitive therapy and intolerance-of-uncertainty therapy for generalized anxiety disorder. *Behaviour Research and Therapy*, *50*(2), 100–109. Available from https://doi.org/10.1016/j.brat.2011.12.005.

van Oosterhout, B., Krabbendam, L., Smeets, G., & van der Gaag, M. (2013). Metacognitive beliefs, beliefs about voices and affective symptoms in patients with severe auditory verbal hallucinations. *British Journal of Clinical Psychology*, *52*(3), 235–248. Available from https://doi.org/10.1111/bjc.12011.

Varese, F., & Bentall, R. P. (2011). The metacognitive beliefs account of hallucinatory experiences: A literature review and meta-analysis. *Clinical Psychology Review*, *31*(5), 850–864. Available from https://doi.org/10.1016/j.cpr.2010.12.001.

Vassilopoulos, S. P., Brouzos, A., & Moberly, N. J. (2015). The relationships between metacognition, anticipatory processing, and social anxiety. *Behaviour Change*, *32*(2), 114–126. Available from https://doi.org/10.1017/bec.2015.4.

Watkins, E., & Baracaia, S. (2001). Why do people ruminate in dysphoric moods? *Personality and Individual Differences*, *30*(5), 723–734. Available from https://doi.org/10.1016/S0191-8869(00)00053-2.

Watkins, E., & Moulds, M. (2005). Positive beliefs about rumination in depression—a replication and extension. *Personality and Individual Differences*, *39*(1), 73–82. Available from https://doi.org/10.1016/j.paid.2004.12.006.

Watson, C., & Purdon, C. (2008). Attention training in the reduction and reappraisal of intrusive thoughts. *Behavioural and Cognitive Psychotherapy*, *36*(1), 61–70. Available from https://doi.org/10.1017/S1352465807003773.

Weck, F., Neng, J., & Stangier, U. (2013). The effects of attention training on the perception of bodily sensations in patients with hypochondriasis: A randomized controlled pilot trial. *Cognitive Therapy and Research*, *37*(3), 514–520. Available from https://doi.org/10.1007/s10608-012-9482-3.

Wells, A. (1994). A multi-dimensional measure of worry: Development and preliminary validation of the anxious thoughts inventory. *Anxiety, Stress & Coping*, *6*(4), 289–299. Available from https://doi.org/10.1080/10615809408248803.

Wells, A. (1999). A metacognitive model and therapy for generalized anxiety disorder. *Clinical Psychology & Psychotherapy*, *6*(2), 86–95. Available from https://doi.org/AID-CPP189 > 3.0.CO;2-S.

Wells, A. (2000). *Emotional disorders and metacognition: Innovative cognitive therapy*. Chichester [u.a.]: Wiley.

Wells, A. (2005). The metacognitive model of GAD: Assessment of meta-worry and relationship with DSM-IV generalized anxiety disorder. *Cognitive Therapy and Research*, *29*(1), 107–121. Available from https://doi.org/10.1007/s10608-005-1652-0.

Wells, A. (2007a). The attention training technique: Theory, effects, and a metacognitive hypothesis on auditory hallucinations. *Cognitive and Behavioral Practice*, *14*(2), 134–138. Available from https://doi.org/10.1016/j.cbpra.2006.01.010.

Wells, A. (2007b). Cognition about cognition: Metacognitive therapy and change in generalized anxiety disorder and social phobia. *Cognitive and Behavioral Practice*, *14*(1), 18–25. Available from https://doi.org/10.1016/j.cbpra.2006.01.005.

Wells, A. (2009). *Metacognitive therapy for anxiety and depression*. New York [u.a.]: Guilford Press. Retrieved from <http://bvbr.bib-bvb.de:8991/F?func = service&doc_library = BVB01&local_base = BVB01&doc_number = 017135158&sequence = 000002&line_number = 0001&func_code = DB_RECORDS&service_type = MEDIA>.

Wells, A. (2010). Metacognitive theory and therapy for worry and generalized anxiety disorder: Review and status. *Journal of Experimental Psychopathology, 1*(1). Available from https://doi.org/10.5127/jep.007910, jep. 007910.

Wells, A., & Carter, K. (2001). Further tests of a cognitive model of generalized anxiety disorder: Metacognitions and worry in GAD, panic disorder, social phobia, depression, and nonpatients. *Behavior Therapy, 32*(1), 85–102. Available from https://doi.org/10.1016/S0005-7894(01)80045-9.

Wells, A., & Cartwright-Hatton, S. (2004). A short form of the metacognitions questionnaire: Properties of the MCQ-30. *Behaviour Research and Therapy, 42*(4), 385–396. Available from https://doi.org/10.1016/S0005-7967(03)00147-5.

Wells, A., & Colbear, J. S. (2012). Treating posttraumatic stress disorder with metacognitive therapy: A preliminary controlled trial. *Journal of Clinical Psychology, 68*(4), 373–381. Available from https://doi.org/10.1002/jclp.20871.

Wells, A., Fisher, P., Myers, S., Wheatley, J., Patel, T., & Brewin, C. (2009). Metacognitive therapy in recurrent and persistent depression: A multiple-baseline study of a new treatment. *Cognitive Therapy and Research, 33*(3), 291–300. Available from https://doi.org/10.1007/s10608-007-9178-2.

Wells, A., Fisher, P., Myers, S., Wheatley, J., Patel, T., & Brewin, C. R. (2012). Metacognitive therapy in treatment-resistant depression: A platform trial. *Behaviour Research and Therapy, 50*(6), 367–373. Available from https://doi.org/10.1016/j.brat.2012.02.004.

Wells, A., & King, P. (2006). Metacognitive therapy for generalized anxiety disorder: An open trial. *Journal of Behavior Therapy and Experimental Psychiatry, 37*(3), 206–212. Available from https://doi.org/10.1016/j.jbtep.2005.07.002.

Wells, A., & Matthews, G. (1996). Modelling cognition in emotional disorder: The S-REF model. *Behaviour Research and Therapy, 34*(11), 881–888. Available from https://doi.org/10.1016/S0005-7967(96)00050-2.

Wells, A., & Papageorgiou, C. (2001). Brief cognitive therapy for social phobia: A case series. *Behaviour Research and Therapy, 39*(6), 713–720. Available from https://doi.org/10.1016/S0005-7967(00)00036-X.

Wells, A., & Sembi, S. (2004). Metacognitive therapy for PTSD: A preliminary investigation of a new brief treatment. *Journal of Behavior Therapy and Experimental Psychiatry, 35*(4), 307–318. Available from https://doi.org/10.1016/j.jbtep.2004.07.001.

Wells, A., Walton, D., Lovell, K., & Proctor, D. (2015). Metacognitive therapy versus prolonged exposure in adults with chronic post-traumatic stress disorder: A parallel randomized controlled trial. *Cognitive Therapy and Research, 39*(1), 70–80. Available from https://doi.org/10.1007/s10608-014-9636-6.

Wells, A., Welford, M., Fraser, J., King, P., Mendel, E., Wisely, J., ... Rees, D. (2008). Chronic PTSD treated with metacognitive therapy: An open trial. *Cognitive and Behavioral Practice, 15*(1), 85–92. Available from https://doi.org/10.1016/j.cbpra.2006.11.005.

Wells, A., Welford, M., King, P., Papageorgiou, C., Wisely, J., & Mendel, E. (2010). A pilot randomized trial of metacognitive therapy vs applied relaxation in the treatment of adults with generalized anxiety disorder. *Behaviour Research and Therapy, 48*(5), 429–434. Available from https://doi.org/10.1016/j.brat.2009.11.013.

Wong, Q. J., & Moulds, M. L. (2010). Do socially anxious individuals hold positive metacognitive beliefs about rumination? *Behaviour Change, 27*(2), 69–83. Available from https://doi.org/10.1375/bech.27.2.69.

Yilmaz, A. E., Gençöz, T., & Wells, A. (2015). Unique contributions of metacognition and cognition to depressive symptoms. *The Journal of General Psychology, 142*(1), 23–33. Available from https://doi.org/10.1080/00221309.2014.964658.

Afterword

This book has explored varied and numerous literatures on rumination and related constructs. Pulling them together into a single volume has been a fascinating and often challenging endeavor and one that I hope will be helpful for the field. As someone who has been researching rumination for almost 15 years, I often get asked whether I ruminate about rumination. If I were to answer this question honestly, rather than glibly, I would respond that no, I do not ruminate about rumination. I ruminate about the same things that most other people ruminate about: hurts I have caused or experienced, whether my children are happy, the meaning of particular events for me and my loved ones. Unlike most other people, however, I do spend a considerable amount of time *thinking* about rumination and what we know about it. In this final section, I reflect on two questions that I believe remain largely unanswered. Rather than providing definitive answers to these questions, I aim instead to persuade readers about their importance and suggest possible approaches that researchers might take to address them.

Are differences between the various types of rumination meaningful?

Several prominent psychologists argue that rumination is a transdiagnostic process that plays a causal role in many, often comorbid, mental disorders (Ehring & Watkins, 2008; Grierson, Hickie, Naismith, & Scott, 2016; Mennin & Fresco, 2013; Nolen-Hoeksema & Watkins, 2011). Some of the evidence supporting this assertion comes from metaanalyses or empirical studies showing that rumination, as one of many maladaptive coping strategies, is associated with symptoms of multiple mental disorders (Aldao, Nolen-Hoeksema, & Schweizer, 2010; Olatunji, Naragon-Gainey, & Wolitzky-Taylor, 2013; Watkins, 2009). Other studies have found that rumination mediates, or explains, the association between the presence or severity of different psychopathologies (Drost et al., 2014; McLaughlin, Aldao, Wisco, & Hilt, 2014; McLaughlin & Nolen-Hoeksema, 2011). Given this evidence, as well as the literatures reviewed in Chapters 1–6 on the various consequences of rumination, it seems clear that rumination constitutes a transdiagnostic risk factor.

Transdiagnostic accounts assume that the differences between various types of rumination, or negative repetitive thinking more broadly, are not as important as their common process or shared features. Some research has examined this assumption. Chapter 2, Rumination and anxiety-related disorders, reviewed the findings that items assessing depressive rumination and worry load on a single latent factor of negative repetitive thought and at the same time load onto their own measure-specific factors (e.g., McEvoy & Brans, 2013; Topper, Molenaar, Emmelkamp, & Ehring, 2014). Similar results emerge when including a broader range of measures, even those assessing more positive forms of rumination (e.g., Segerstrom, Stanton, Alden, & Shortridge, 2003). One study included 16 different measures of rumination (Siegle, Moore, & Thase, 2004). The measures demonstrated good between-scale internal consistency (Cronbach's $\alpha = 0.85$), suggesting that a mean of items from many scales yielded a reliable index of a central construct. However, the correlations between measures ranged from 0.008 to 0.80, suggesting that individuals did not score consistently high or low on all of the questionnaires. Taken together, these studies suggest that various measures of rumination generally share a common thread but also contain unique variance. Another way to interpret these findings is that although various measures all assess an underlying process of repetitive thinking, individuals may be more or less likely to engage in certain types of repetitive thought.

Thus, if we accept that rumination and the related constructs covered in this book share an underlying process of repetitive thinking, at least two important questions emerge: (1) first, how do we understand the many varied outcomes of this shared process? (2) Second, what predicts whether people will have tendencies for a certain type of repetitive thought over others? These questions were initially posed by Nolen-Hoeksema and Watkins (2011) in a seminal paper about transdiagnostic processes underlying multiple psychopathologies. They argued that any transdiagnostic model must be able to explain how a single process can lead to multiple outcomes across people (i.e., factors underlying multifinality) and different outcomes for different people (i.e., divergent trajectories).

Possible answers to the first question come from several literatures. Nolen-Hoeksema and Watkins (2011) identified specific mechanisms between rumination and varied outcomes. For instance, they suggested that mechanisms of rumination's effects on depression and anxiety disorders were similar: rumination amplifies current mood and related cognitions, impairs problem solving, and interferes with instrumental behavior. For the outcomes of substance misuse and binge eating, they drew on escape theory to argue that these behaviors provide temporary relief from the distress associated with rumination. Other possible mechanisms include increased craving (see Chapter 4: Rumination and dysregulated behaviors). Although their paper did not include aggression or borderline personality symptoms as outcomes of rumination, all of these mechanisms—as well as reduced self-control, narrowed attention, and increased physiological arousal—have been proposed by other researchers (see Chapter 3: Rumination, anger, and aggression, and Chapter 4: Rumination and dysregulated behaviors). Similarly, suggested mechanisms for the association between rumination and psychotic symptoms include narrowed attention on threat-related information and greater intrusiveness of unwanted thoughts. A proposed mechanism for rumination's association with anorexia symptoms is increased vigilance of and self-control over food cravings. At first glance, many of these mechanisms appear to function across multiple mental disorders, calling into question the idea of unique mechanisms that explain various outcomes. At the same time, mental disorders are often comorbid, making the search for unique mechanisms difficult if not unrealistic. Nevertheless, future research could examine whether specific mechanisms predict some clinical outcomes but not others.

Other researchers have focused on particular dimensions of rumination, or negative repetitive thinking more generally. For instance, based on empirical evidence about the differences between rumination and worry (see Chapter 2: Rumination and anxiety-related disorders), researchers have suggested that repetitive thinking can vary by temporal focus (e.g., Ehring & Watkins, 2008). In addition, Watkins (2008) proposed that rumination can be either abstract or concrete in nature. Chapter 10, Cognitive behavioral therapies, reviewed the extensive literature showing that abstract rumination contributes to negative outcomes, whereas concrete processing contributes to benefits across several mental disorders. Segerstrom et al. (2003) identified a purpose dimension of repetitive thought, with searching for new ideas and experiences (including measures of reflective pondering) on one end and solving problems and improving certainty (including measures of worry) on the other. Interestingly, brooding and general negative rumination scored in the middle of this dimension, suggesting that they involve both searching and solving efforts. Scores on this dimension predicted different outcomes in different populations (e.g., undergraduates, women with a high risk of breast cancer). However, no research has examined whether these three dimensions of rumination (e.g., temporal focus, level of abstractness, and purpose) predict divergent mental health outcomes.

Another possibility is that the varied effects of rumination represent inherent differences in basic negative emotions and associated thought content. Emotion researchers have discovered cognitive and motivational differences between sadness, fear, and anger (Barrett & Russell, 1999; Dickson & MacLeod, 2004; Green & Sedikides, 1999; Lerner & Keltner, 2000; Scherer, 2009). For instance, sadness is frequently associated with withdrawal, self-critical thoughts, decreased initiative, attention to detail, thoughts of past losses, and an internal self-focus (see also Bodenhausen, Sheppard, & Kramer, 1994). By contrast, fear is characterized by arousal, risk avoidance, appraisals of uncertainty and lack of control, and thoughts about how to prevent future perceived threats (see also Mathews, 1990). Finally, anger is associated with approach motivation, thoughts of revenge and self-justification, increased energy, appraisals of certainty, and an external focus of attention (see also Harmon-Jones, 2003). One possible area of future research is to examine whether these and other characteristics of specific negative emotions reliably explain the effects of rumination on various outcomes.

The second question—whether and why people have tendencies for specific types of repetitive thinking—has received much less attention in the literature. Nolen-Hoeksema and Watkins (2011) proposed some possible moderators. For instance, they suggested that rumination among people who have past experiences with loss, rejection, and/or failure might be more likely to lead to depressive symptoms, whereas rumination among people with histories of trauma, social anxiety, and/or panic attacks may lead to anxiety symptoms. They also suggested that rumination among people with greater reward sensitivity and higher exposure to alcohol use (or the thin ideal) may be more likely to lead to substance use (or disordered eating) problems. More generally, different types of triggers (e.g., types of stressors and specific negative emotions) may make people more or less likely to experience certain types of rumination and associated outcomes (see Chapter 7: Triggers of rumination). In addition, drawing on Chapter 8, Beliefs, traits, and motivations underlying rumination, perhaps people have different learning histories that lead to positive metacognitive beliefs about certain types of rumination but not others. People may also be motivated to avoid—or enhance—some emotions more than others, leading to differences in the specific types of rumination they tend to experience.

In sum, the answer to the question of whether the various types of rumination and related constructs are meaningfully different is likely yes and no. Both empirical evidence and convincing theoretical arguments suggest that many constructs covered in this book share an underlying process of repetitive thinking. This allows for rumination to be considered a transdiagnostic process. At the same time, leaders in the field have suggested that we need to better understand mediators and moderators of rumination's various clinical outcomes (Nolen-Hoeksema & Watkins, 2011). As I propose here, there are many ways we can approach this endeavor. This is an exciting challenge for future research to tackle. It is exciting in part because answering these questions requires researchers to not just focus on their primary (and familiar) clinical outcome, but to assess triggers, mechanisms, and symptoms studied in typically separate literatures. One of my main goals with this book is to assist in that process—to help researchers create bridges between areas of research that have been largely developed in isolation.

One last point I want to make is about the importance of methodology for answering these questions. In order to examine unique mechanisms and moderators of the various effects of rumination, researchers will need to think carefully about how to measure and/or manipulate rumination. Too many past studies have attempted to answer research questions about state rumination on a specific topic by using trait measures of general rumination. Fortunately, studies are increasingly employing experience sampling designs, which allow for measurement and even manipulation of state rumination. Even still, an overreliance on the gold standard measures and manipulations, most of which come from the depression literature, makes it difficult to answer questions relating to divergent outcomes and tendencies. Recent attempts to measure rumination about specific concerns or triggers (e.g., disordered eating, perceived discrimination, and relationship distress) are helpful, as are the emotion-specific rumination measures. Researchers should intentionally choose measures or manipulations that capture the rumination they want to target, as well as make efforts to include both trait and state rumination in their hypothesized models.

Why do people ruminate?

If rumination is a transdiagnostic risk factor for such a wide range of mental and physical symptoms, then why do people ruminate? This question has been asked occasionally in the field, but in my opinion not enough, and not in any systematic way. Some researchers focus on personality traits (e.g., neuroticism) or life experiences (e.g., childhood trauma) that make people more likely to develop tendencies for rumination (see Chapter 7: Triggers of rumination, and Chapter 8: Beliefs, traits, and motivations underlying rumination). The common explanation for these associations is that neurotic traits or traumatic events increase negative emotions and reactivity to stressors, which in turn provide more fodder for rumination. However, this approach does not answer the question of *why* people ruminate in response to negative emotions or stressors. This book has introduced several possible answers to this question, although the literature is not nearly as well-developed as our understanding of rumination's consequences.

Self-regulation theories imply that rumination is a maladaptive consequence of natural and adaptive efforts to cope with a stressor. These theories (see Chapter 1: Rumination and mood disorders, and Chapter 10: Cognitive behavioral therapies) suggest that rumination is one form of self-focused attention, an automatic response to a perceived discrepancy that should help in solving the problem. Although this response may be helpful for handling concrete and manageable problems, it is unhelpful for solving unsolvable and/or abstract, emotional problems (Watkins, 2008). Whereas healthy people might normally turn off self-focused attention and abstract processing when it is no longer helpful, some people (e.g., those with executive control problems, low self-efficacy, poor coping skills, neurotic tendencies, and trauma histories) have an impaired ability to downregulate their own thinking. Rumination then becomes a habitual way of responding that can be triggered without clear intention or effort. Thus rumination is a maladaptive and persistent off-shoot of what starts out as a natural and adaptive response to perceived stressors. An associated treatment (rumination-focused cognitive behavioral therapy) aims to increase people's ability to engage in more adaptive, concrete thinking (see Chapter 10: Cognitive behavioral therapies). The underlying assumption here is that maladaptive rumination is unintentional, uncontrolled repetitive thinking that has gone awry, much like malignant cells. The initial self-regulation motive may be adaptive, but any forms of rumination that have negative consequences are unwanted and should be replaced by more adaptive coping strategies.

People also likely ruminate because they think it will be helpful. Evidence in support of the metacognitive model (see Chapter 8: Beliefs, traits, and motivations underlying rumination, and Chapter 12: Metacognitive therapy) suggests that people who ruminate believe it will help them solve or prepare for problems. Similarly, one of the most well-accepted theories in the field proposes that rumination and related constructs help people avoid experiencing unpleasant emotions and/or thoughts (see Chapter 2: Rumination and anxiety-related disorders, and Chapter 8: Beliefs, traits, and motivations underlying rumination). These approaches have inspired treatments whose goals are to change people's beliefs about rumination (see Chapter 12: Metacognitive therapy) or their desire to avoid negative emotions or thoughts (see Chapter 11: Mindfulness-based therapies). However, this is much to still be fleshed out about this concept. For instance, research on metacognitive beliefs about rumination has not tackled the question of whether these beliefs are necessarily conscious, or whether they actually fuel rumination over time. In terms of avoidance, it is unclear whether rumination in fact allows people to successfully avoid unpleasant internal experiences, or what people are attempting to avoid by ruminating. The story may be more complex than we typically assume. The worry literature has a good example of this (see Chapter 2: Rumination and anxiety-related disorders): for years, researchers theorized that worry functioned to allow people to avoid internal distress and associated arousal. However, this theory contradicted findings that worry increases distress. The newer Contrast Avoidance Model suggests, with empirical support, that although worry does not allow for avoidance of negative emotions or arousal, it does successfully help people avoid negative emotional contrasts (Llera & Newman, 2014). Avoidance functions of rumination may be just as nuanced. For instance, perhaps people ruminate in ways that increase a particular emotion in order to avoid acknowledging and/or experiencing a different internal experience.

The research on contrast avoidance brings up an important question that is not asked enough in the field: does rumination actually work for people? The assumption has typically been that rumination backfires as a coping strategy, but what if this is incorrect? The work of Maya Tamir (see Chapter 8: Beliefs, traits, and motivations underlying rumination) suggests that people might ruminate in order to actually maintain or increase negative moods, to help them achieve desired goals. Specifically, people may ruminate to maintain negative emotions with the instrumental goals of increasing analytic thinking, avoiding threats, increasing helping or submissive behavior from others, fostering social belonging with individuals and groups, and verifying their views of themselves. The benefits of expression (see Chapter 6: Consequences of expressed rumination) also suggest that rumination might increase negative emotions in order to motivate people to share with others. The implication here is that rumination is not inherently maladaptive, because negative emotions can be helpful. Instead, people may intentionally ruminate in order to obtain a desired outcome, whether or not they are conscious of this intention. No research has directly examined the possibility that people ruminate to put or keep themselves in negative moods, in order to achieve some desired outcome.

Nevertheless, this book has covered various benefits of rumination, even when it is focused on negative content. As reviewed in Chapter 3, Rumination, anger, and aggression, Denson (2013) suggested that angry rumination has an evolutionary function of letting people delay retaliating in response a provocation until a later, more opportune time. Empirical evidence suggests that angry rumination in fact motivates people who have experienced injustice to engage in collective action to help their group (Borders & Wiley, 2019). In other literatures the expression of rumination to another person is associated with increased perceived closeness and connection with others (see Chapter 6: Consequences of expressed rumination). In addition, expressive writing predicts improved psychological and physical functioning, and social sharing contributes to posttraumatic growth and general well-being. In all of these cases, these types of rumination were associated with negative outcomes but also yielded some positive outcomes. Other research suggests that rumination is adaptive for some people, some of the time. For instance, repetitive thinking about health when people are not exceedingly distressed appears to contribute to better eating, greater physical activity, stronger intention to quit smoking, and more prevention behaviors (see Chapter 5: Rumination and physical functioning). Worry predicts better academic and workplace performance in people with higher reasoning skills (see Chapter 2: Rumination and anxiety-related disorders). In combat veterans without posttraumatic stress disorder, greater daily rumination predicted less negative affect the next day (Kashdan, Young, & McKnight, 2012). Thus, perhaps rumination fosters effective coping in individuals with healthy psychological and cognitive functioning. A related possibility is that some rumination is adaptive, whereas too much is detrimental. This possibility has not yet been examined empirically.

One other approach is the possibility that there are actually adaptive forms of rumination. For instance, reflective pondering is associated with less depressive symptoms in some studies and for some participants (see Chapter 1: Rumination and mood disorders). It is also associated with more creative problem-solving as well as more objective creative behavior and better musical performance (Cohen & Ferrari, 2010; Jones, Roy, & Verkuilen, 2014; Verhaeghen, Joormann, & Aikman, 2014; Verhaeghen, Joormann, & Khan, 2005). Similarly, Chapter 2, Rumination and anxiety-related disorders, reviewed evidence that deliberate rumination about trauma leads to increased posttraumatic growth. Thus, it is possible that the self-absorption and cognitive inflexibility associated with repetitive thought might have benefits in some circumstances, such as when people need to stay focused and emotionally invested in a creative endeavor or when they are ready to make sense of traumatic events. At the same time, these forms of repetitive thought are strongly associated with greater use of maladaptive forms such as brooding and intrusive trauma-focused rumination. In other words, each of these adaptive types of rumination are paired with an associated maladaptive type. Even rumination about positive emotions (see Chapter 1: Rumination and mood disorders), which is associated with less depressive symptoms and greater self-esteem and resilience, is also associated with greater manic symptoms (Feldman, Joormann, & Johnson, 2008; Hou & Ng, 2014; Werner-Seidler, Banks, Dunn, & Moulds, 2013). Therefore, all of the seemingly positive forms of rumination may be better understood as the positive side of a single coin, with negative forms and consequences on the other side.

In sum, existing literatures suggest that people ruminate because of predisposing personality traits or past experiences, inabilities to channel natural self-regulation motives into adaptive coping responses, and/or beliefs that rumination will help. What the field has not adequately explored are the possibilities that people ruminate because it helps them obtain some desired outcome, or that limited amounts of rumination in healthy people foster adaptive self-regulation. Clearly, too much uncontrolled and unwanted rumination or worry is detrimental to people's mental health. However, rumination may also have beneficial consequences, at least for some people and in some forms. In order to achieve a more nuanced understanding of why people ruminate, researchers should study novel ways that it benefits people. One important distinction the field needs to bear in mind is that negative emotions (e.g., sadness and fear) are not the same as their associated mental disorders (e.g., depression and anxiety disorders). Embracing the view that negative emotions serve instrumental motives could inspire researchers to explore new functions of rumination. At the same time, the field would benefit from assessing differences in amounts (e.g., frequency and duration) of rumination and whether these differences predict divergent outcomes. Once researchers figure out how to better assess these aspects of rumination, they might examine factors that predict healthy versus unhealthy amounts of rumination. Finally, I want to highlight the findings, in several literatures, that verbalizing and sharing ruminative thoughts lead to varied and lasting benefits. The field might be well-served by further examining what happens when private thoughts become expressed, and whether this process and its related benefits might provide further clues about reasons why so many people ruminate.

As Paul Simon expressed, there are drawbacks but also potential benefits of thinking too much. One of my goals in integrating several literatures in this book is to help researchers propose new questions that might contribute to a more complex understanding of the consequences and causes of rumination and its related constructs. In developing and delivering treatments, psychologists may want to conceptualize which aspects or forms of repetitive thought are harmful for individuals, and which aspects or forms might serve important and even helpful functions.

References

Aldao, A., Nolen-Hoeksema, S., & Schweizer, S. (2010). Emotion-regulation strategies across psychopathology: A meta-analytic review. *Clinical Psychology Review, 30*(2), 217–237. Available from https://doi.org/10.1016/j.cpr.2009.11.004.

Barrett, L. F., & Russell, J. A. (1999). The structure of current affect: Controversies and emerging consensus. *Current Directions in Psychological Science, 8*(1), 10–14. Available from https://doi.org/10.1111/1467-8721.00003.

Bodenhausen, G. V., Sheppard, L. A., & Kramer, G. P. (1994). Negative affect and social judgment: The differential impact of anger and sadness. *European Journal of Social Psychology*, *24*(1), 45–62. Available from https://doi.org/10.1002/ejsp.2420240104.

Borders, A., & Wiley, S. (2019). Rumination about discrimination mediates the unique association between anger and collective action intentions. *Group Processes & Intergroup Relations*, 136843021987521. https://doi.org/10.1177/1368430219875214.

Cohen, J. R., & Ferrari, J. R. (2010). Take some time to think this over: The relation between rumination, indecision, and creativity. *Creativity Research Journal*, *22*(1), 68–73. Available from https://doi.org/10.1080/10400410903579601.

Denson, T. F. (2013). The multiple systems model of angry rumination. *Personality and Social Psychology Review*, 17(2), 103–123. https://doi.org/10.1177/1088868312467086.

Dickson, J., & MacLeod, A. (2004). Brief report anxiety, depression and approach and avoidance goals. *Cognition & Emotion*, *18*(3), 423–430. Available from https://doi.org/10.1080/02699930341000013.

Drost, J., van der Does, W., van Hemert, A. M., Penninx., Brenda, W. J. H., & Spinhoven, P. (2014). Repetitive negative thinking as a transdiagnostic factor in depression and anxiety: A conceptual replication. *Behaviour Research and Therapy*, *63*, 177–183. Available from https://doi.org/10.1016/j.brat.2014.06.004.

Ehring, T., & Watkins, E. R. (2008). Repetitive negative thinking as a transdiagnostic process. *International Journal of Cognitive Therapy*, *1*(3), 192–205. Available from https://doi.org/10.1521/ijct.2008.1.3.192.

Feldman, G., Joormann, J., & Johnson, S. (2008). Responses to positive affect: A self-report measure of rumination and dampening. *Cognitive Therapy and Research*, 32(4), 507–525. https://doi.org/10.1007/s10608-006-9083-0.

Green, J. D., & Sedikides, C. (1999). Affect and self-focused attention revisited: The role of affect orientation. *Personality and Social Psychology Bulletin*, *25*(1), 104–119. Available from https://doi.org/10.1177/0146167299025001009.

Grierson, A. B., Hickie, I. B., Naismith, S. L., & Scott, J. (2016). *The role of rumination in illness trajectories in youth: Linking trans-diagnostic processes with clinical staging models*. England: Cambridge University Press. Available from https://doi.org/10.1017/S0033291716001392.

Harmon-Jones, E. (2003). Clarifying the emotive functions of asymmetrical frontal cortical activity. *Psychophysiology*, *40*(6), 838–848. Available from https://doi.org/10.1111/1469-8986.00121.

Hou, W. K., & Ng, S. M. (2014). Emotion-focused positive rumination and relationship satisfaction as the underlying mechanisms between resilience and psychiatric symptoms. Personality and Individual Differences, 71, 159–164. https://doi.org/10.1016/j.paid.2014.07.032.

Jones, M. E., Roy, M. M., & Verkuilen, J. (2014). The relationship between reflective rumination and musical ability. *Psychology of Aesthetics, Creativity, and the Arts*, *8*(2), 219–226. Available from https://doi.org/10.1037/a0035634.

Kashdan, T. B., Young, K. C., & McKnight, P. E. (2012). When is rumination an adaptive mood repair strategy? Day-to-day rhythms of life in combat veterans with and without posttraumatic stress disorder. *Journal of Anxiety Disorders*, *26*(7), 762–768. Available from https://doi.org/10.1016/j.janxdis.2012.07.004.

Lerner, J. S., & Keltner, D. (2000). Beyond valence: Toward a model of emotion-specific influences on judgement and choice. *Cognition & Emotion*, *14*(4), 473–493. Available from https://doi.org/10.1080/026999300402763.

Llera, S. J., & Newman, M. G. (2014). Rethinking the role of worry in generalized anxiety disorder: Evidence supporting a model of emotional contrast avoidance. *Behavior Therapy*, *45*(3), 283–299. Available from https://doi.org/10.1016/j.beth.2013.12.011.

Mathews, A. (1990). Why worry? The cognitive function of anxiety. *Behaviour Research and Therapy*, *28*(6), 455–468. Available from https://doi.org/10.1016/0005-7967(90)90132-3.

McEvoy, P., & Brans, S. (2013). Common versus unique variance across measures of worry and rumination: Predictive utility and mediational models for anxiety and depression. *Cognitive Therapy and Research*, *37*(1), 183–196. Available from https://doi.org/10.1007/s10608-012-9448-5.

McLaughlin, K. A., Aldao, A., Wisco, B. E., & Hilt, L. M. (2014). Rumination as a transdiagnostic factor underlying transitions between internalizing symptoms and aggressive behavior in early adolescents. *Journal of Abnormal Psychology*, *123*(1), 13–23. Available from https://doi.org/10.1037/a0035358.

McLaughlin, K. A., & Nolen-Hoeksema, S. (2011). Rumination as a transdiagnostic factor in depression and anxiety. *Behaviour Research and Therapy*, *49*(3), 186–193. Available from https://doi.org/10.1016/j.brat.2010.12.006.

Mennin, D. S., & Fresco, D. M. (2013). What, me worry and ruminate about DSM-5 and RDoC? The importance of targeting negative self-referential processing. *Clinical Psychology: Science and Practice*, *20*(3), 258–267. Available from https://doi.org/10.1111/cpsp.12038.

Nolen-Hoeksema, S., & Watkins, E. R. (2011). A heuristic for developing transdiagnostic models of psychopathology: Explaining multifinality and divergent trajectories. *Perspectives on Psychological Science*, *6*(6), 589–609. Available from https://doi.org/10.1177/1745691611419672.

Olatunji, B. O., Naragon-Gainey, K., & Wolitzky-Taylor, K. B. (2013). Specificity of rumination in anxiety and depression: A multimodal meta-analysis. *Clinical Psychology: Science and Practice*, *20*(3), 225–257. Available from https://doi.org/10.1111/cpsp.12037.

Scherer, K. R. (2009). The dynamic architecture of emotion: Evidence for the component process model. *Cognition & Emotion*, *23*(7), 1307–1351. Available from https://doi.org/10.1080/02699930902928969.

Segerstrom, S. C., Stanton, A. L., Alden, L. E., & Shortridge, B. E. (2003). A multidimensional structure for repetitive thought. *Journal of Personality and Social Psychology*, *85*(5), 909–921. Available from https://doi.org/10.1037/0022-3514.85.5.909.

Siegle, G., Moore, P., & Thase, M. (2004). Rumination: One construct, many features in healthy individuals, depressed individuals, and individuals with lupus. *Cognitive Therapy and Research*, *28*(5), 645–668. Available from https://doi.org/COTR.0000045570.62733.9f.

Topper, M., Molenaar, D., Emmelkamp, P., & Ehring, T. (2014). Are rumination and worry two sides of the same coin? A structural equation modelling approach. *Journal of Experimental Psychopathology*, *5*(3), 363–381. Available from https://doi.org/10.5127/jep.038813.

Verhaeghen, P., Joormann, J., & Aikman, S. N. (2014). Creativity, mood, and the examined life: Self-reflective rumination boosts creativity, brooding breeds dysphoria. *Psychology of Aesthetics, Creativity, and the Arts*, *8*(2), 211–218. Available from https://doi.org/10.1037/a0035594.

Verhaeghen, P., Joormann, J., & Khan, R. (2005). Why we sing the blues. *Emotion*, *5*(2), 226–232. Available from https://doi.org/10.1037/1528-3542.5.2.226.

Watkins, E. R. (2008). Constructive and unconstructive repetitive thought. *Psychological Bulletin*, *134*(2), 163–206. Available from https://doi.org/10.1037/0033-2909.134.2.163.

Watkins, E. R. (2009). Depressive rumination and co-morbidity: Evidence for brooding as a transdiagnostic process. *Journal of Rational-Emotive and Cognitive-Behavior Therapy: RET*, *27*(3), 160–175. Available from https://doi.org/10.1007/s10942-009-0098-9.

Werner-Seidler, A., Banks, R., Dunn, B. D., & Moulds, M. L. (2013). An investigation of the relationship between positive affect regulation and depression. *Behaviour Research and Therapy*, 51(1), 46–56. https://doi.org/10.1016/j.brat.2012.11.001

Index

Note: Page numbers followed by "*f*" refer to figures.

O

P

R

FSC
www.fsc.org
MIX
Papier | Fördert gute Waldnutzung
FSC® C083411

Kolibri 360 GmbH
Ferdinand-Jühlke-Straße 7
99095 Erfurt, Deutschland
produktsicherheit@kolibri360.de